The Nature of Culture

The Nature of Culture

By

A. L. Kroeber

E UNIVERSITY OF CHICAGO PRESS

THE UNIVERSITY OF CHICAGO PRESS, CHICAGO 37
Cambridge University Press, London, N.W. 1, England
W. J. Gage & Co., Limited, Toronto 2B, Canada

To
THEODORA

PREFACE

THIS book is an effort to put into one volume those papers and selected parts of my professional writings that might be of most general interest. Most of what I have written has consisted of contributions to factual knowledge or of organization of knowledge or of first-level generalization from it. Interest in all this factualism cannot possibly be very widespread, even if the data do now and then have a certain importance. I have therefore selected here only passages that bear on culture, and, of those, the more theoretical or general ones, or those possessing some novel element of method or approach. While this is not very representative of myself, who am by nature a worker with concrete data, the procedure does yield a kind of unity. This unity consists of a theory about the kind of thing culture is: about its properties and typical manifestations, its relation to other kinds of things, and how it is most fruitfully viewed and investigated.

This choice is appropriate enough, since my studies have prevailingly been more definitely weighted toward the discernment of cultural form and patterns than has the work of most anthropologists or sociologists. While others have been concerned about the interrelations and impingements of culture and society or culture and personality or culture and history, I have tried with cumulative consciousness to *extricate* the forms and patterns of culture from out the mixture of behavior, events, institutions, individuals, and psychic and somatic reactions which constitute the primary and raw material of the historical and social sciences.

In the presentation of this system of thinking on the nature of culture, it has seemed expedient to arrange the selections in five groups or parts. The first and largest adds up to a more or less formal sort of "theory of culture." The second part deals with kinship and with social structure. Both these topics, though easily becoming technical, also lend themselves to exemplification of cultural patterning. The third part, "On American Indians," the most concrete, illustrates some of the steps by which ethnographic data are conceptualized into cultural processes and patterns. Part IV, I call "Psychologically Slanted." The emphasis is on the slanting, for the articles contain less psychology than culture. Part V, on "History and Process of Civilization," speaks for itself as pertinent to the main theme and marks a return to outright theoretical consideration.

In each part the order of selections is chronological. This seems the most practicable. Not only has my own thinking developed over the years, but culture as an explicit concept is so recent as to be still in development. Of the fifty articles, more than half date from after 1939; sixteen from the last six years, 1946–51. Three-fourths were published between 1931 and 1951. However, nearly one-fourth are pre-1923, and two of the essays date from the first decade of our century.

Five of the fifty selections, constituting about eight per cent of the book's bulk, are here printed for the first time. Introductions, setting forth the wider significance of the articles most of which were originally written for presentation to strictly professional audiences, add up to a tenth the length of the selections themselves.

The newly written portions of this

volume of selected reassemblage thus come to a sixth of its bulk. As for the republished five-sixths, these have been touched up stylistically where they seemed to need smoothing or readier clarity. But alterations of meaning or of crucial wording have been made only as indicated in square brackets, notes, or introductions.

While the book, I hope, adds up to a consistently developed point of view and method of understanding human culture, fifty separate papers obviously cannot possess the continuity and over-all organization of a systematically planned work executed at one time. The papers were written years apart, they start from all sorts of occasions and provocations, and specifically they often shoot at quite diverse marks. I trust that the resultant variety will make up in interest for some lack of outward order in presentation. What troubles me more is that, even though the way of coming at matters is usually different, it is unavoidable that a good many points are made repeatedly. Since these restatements are in new contexts, often unexpected by the reader, I have here and there inserted, in brackets, cross-tie references between one and another of the fifty selections. Yet, because the presence in the text of very many such inserts would be cumbersome and distracting, most of them have

been reserved for a "Terminal Index of Principal Cross-References."

A full list of references to the original sources, of the amount of condensation effected, and of those persons or institutions whose permission made republication possible is given at the end. I wish to express particular thanks to the editors of the *American Anthropologist*, the *Southwestern Journal of Anthropology*, the *Journal of the Royal Anthropological Institute*, the *American Naturalist*, the *American Journal of Sociology*, the *Proceedings of the Twenty-ninth International Congress of Americanists*, and other scientific journals; to the editors of the University of California Press and its several series, of the American Museum of Natural History, of the Smithsonian Institution, of the Sociological Press, and other institutions; and to the *Scientific Monthly*, the *Journal of General Education*, *Scientific American*, *Biological Symposia*, and the Ronald Press Company, B. W. Huebsch, and Viking Press; *Character and Personality*, Thomas Y. Crowell Company; and to Harcourt, Brace and Company for permission to use copyrighted material. Of those who collaborated in the preparation of typescript, I wish to thank especially Carol Trosch, of New York, and Kathryn Gore, of Berkeley.

A. L. KROEBER

NEW YORK
November 1951

CONTENTS

[Chapters marked with an asterisk (*) have not previously been published.]

I. THEORY OF CULTURE

II. KINSHIP AND SOCIAL STRUCTURE

III. ON AMERICAN INDIANS

PART I

THEORY OF CULTURE

INTRODUCTION

THE first eighteen articles have been grouped together as all bearing cumulatively on a conception or theory of culture. In one sense, this theory was a by-product of concrete studies. I began as an ethnographer and linguist and later became somewhat of an archaeologist and culture historian, oriented primarily toward securing new information, ordering and classifying it meaningfully, and integrating it into the existing stock of knowledge as a context, which thereby would be given gradually increasing significance. I am still such a natural historian of culture. The intellectual process is one of widening generalization and understanding, not of hypotheses which are then tested out as in a laboratory. I do not mean to imply any absolute difference in method of inquiry. There are conceptual hypotheses contained in generalizing and understanding. But they tend to remain implicit longer. They get validated more by newly sought and observed facts in nature, or by a reanalysis and reclassification of knowledge, than by being put to the test of the artificially selected processes called "experiments." As regards society and culture, experiments have proved difficult and only partly successful, even in the hands of totalitarian rulers, and are as good as impossible for mere students of science. We are therefore thrown back far more on direct observation and analysis of the events and phenomena of nature (of which we should take for granted that culture is a part) than is the laboratory scientist. To apply his procedures to our material is very largely to cheat ourselves. Our equivalents of the physicist's hypotheses are not something we formulate to

begin with. They emerge gradually and pile up as we rearrange and reinterpret our facts by trial and error: they are mostly an end-product. Theorem, hypothesis, conclusion, are not sharply differentiated but develop together. There are, strictly speaking, no proofs in this method; but there is an increasingly more concordant understanding of widening areas of knowledge and therefore a sounder understanding.

I make these statements to clarify why my "theory of culture" had to be developed through eighteen separate articles not welded into a smooth continuity and each necessarily restating certain points also stated elsewhere, sometimes in different dress. The reason is that I am not a formal theoretician. My natural and first interest always has been in phenomena and their ordering: it is akin to an aesthetic proclivity, presumably congenital. From the ordering, general conclusions emerge; and, with these, eventuate certain principles as to how best to arrive at valid conclusions; in one sense theory therefore consists for me in considerable part of methodology. Perhaps the foregoing will make clear why I speak of theory as a by-product. It is not in a belittling sense. The theory just was sweated out piecemeal and slowly over fifty years.

I have written three general books concerned with theoretical problems, as it is usual to call them—"problems of a certain breadth" is the term I would prefer. These are *Anthropology*, *Cultural and Natural Areas*, and *Configurations of Culture Growth*. All three have been criticized for containing too heavy a matrix of concrete fact. Their included information has been at once

3

admired as "erudite" and deplored as a surfeit on intellectual digestion. I have a feeling that I write best, as I certainly write most easily, on concrete matters, though their appeal is less wide. It may therefore be well to outline here the principal points in the system of theory that is developed in Part I of this book.

Primary, it seems to me, is the recognition of culture as a "level" or "order" or "emergent" of natural phenomena, a level marked by a certain distinctive organization of its characteristic phenomena. The emergence of phenomena of life from previous inorganic existence is the presumably earliest and most basic segregation of an order or level. Such emergence does not mean that physical and chemical processes are abrogated but that new organizations occur on the new level: organic manifestations, which need study in their own right or biologically, as well as physicochemically, because they possess a certain, though not an absolute, autonomy. For instance, phenomena of reproduction are intelligible only on the organic level, in organic terms. Since Lloyd Morgan, many biologists have argued for this partial autonomy of the organic. A superorganic or superindividual social level was asserted, adumbrated, or implied by Spencer, Tarde, and Durkheim. Recognition of a supra-societal level of culture goes back to Spencer, who spoke of the immensely powerful accumulation of superorganic products commonly called "artificial" which constitute a secondary environment more important than the primary one; though in practice Spencer operated rather scantily on this level. Anthropologists have, on the whole, dealt more outrightly with cultural phenomena than any other group of scientists or scholars but have tended to concern themselves with its manifestations while taking it for granted. Tylor defined culture, Boas estimated very justly many of its properties and

influences, but the thesis of a distinctive cultural level interested neither of them. Indeed, it has largely been left to myself and then to Leslie White to propound it explicitly.

The risk in a high degree of consciousness of a separate order is that of going on to reify its organization and phenomena into an autonomous sort of substance with its own inner forces— life, mind, society, or culture. I have probably at times in the past skirted such lapsing and have at any rate been charged with mysticism. However, mysticism is by no means a necessary ingredient of level recognition. The value of the recognition is largely methodological. It is only by a *de facto* cultural approach to cultural phenomena that some of their most fundamental properties can be ascertained. How far such a "pure" approach can be pursued without explicit consciousness of it probably varies according to personal factors. However, if one is going to be broadly theoretical or philosophic about culture, it seems to me that its acceptance as a distinctive order of phenomena in nature cannot be evaded.

In second place I would put the related principle that it is of the nature of culture to be heavily conditioned by its own cumulative past, so that the most fruitful approach to its understanding is a historical one. I recognize the distinction of nomothetic and idiographic method, but not as an absolute dichotomy between science as investigation of nature and history as the study of man or spirit or culture. Both approaches, I hold, contrariwise, can be applied to any level of phenomena—as the simple example of historical sciences like astronomy and geology shows—and should ultimately be applied. But on the basic inorganic level it is the mathematically formulable, experimentally verifiable, analytic approach that is most immediately rewarding. On the upper levels, especially on the uppermost one of culture, it is the qualitative and the contextual associations of phenomena that are important, and isolation of specific causal factors tends to be both difficult and, so far as we can see, of less significance. After all, the history of a particular civilization has obvious meaning; the history of a particular stone on the beach, or even of a particular volcano as such, has very little meaning as history. The significance of pebbles or volcanoes is as examples of processes that form or produce them. A "physics" or "physiology" of culture would be desirable enough and may ultimately and gradually be attainable. But to transfer the method of the physicochemical sciences of the inorganic to culture would be a fallacy. By eliminating the history of a cultural situation, we cut off its largest component or dimension.

The essential quality of the historical approach as a method of science I see as its integration of phenomena into an ever widening phenomenal context, with as much preservation as possible—instead of analytic resolution—of the qualitative organization of the phenomena dealt with. The context includes the placing in space and time and therefore, when knowledge allows, in sequence. But I see narrative as incidental rather than as essential to the method of history in the wider sense. Recognition of quality and of organizing pattern seems much more important. This is unorthodox but appears to me to be cardinal.

All history, whether political or stellar, reconstructs. The reconstruction is part of the characteristic process of integration into context. Linguists, who operate with sharper intellectual tools than most of us, have always felt free to reconstruct. Organic evolutionists reconstruct and interpolate; their findings would otherwise be but sorry tatters. Similarly, the history of human culture is being reconstructed—in part by archaeological exploration, in part by recognition of cultural forms and patterns, in part by growing understanding of cultural process. Developed further, this last can grow into a nomothetic or processual analytic "science" of culture complementary to its "history" as just defined.

Patterns or configurations or Gestalts are what it seems most profitable and productive to distinguish and formulate in culture. On this point I stand with Ruth Benedict, although I differ from her in practice at several points. I agree with her that the formulation of whole-culture patterns of quality is desirable and worth while. I agree also that one kind of whole-culture characterization is in psychological terms of temperament or ethos; but this should not abrogate or displace formulations in cultural terms. I also hold that her proceeding from whole-cultural characterizations to consideration of the effects of cultures on their members as regards conformity and deviancy passes on to a separate set of problems which have returned largely to a subcultural level. Finally, I advocate going on from Benedict's essentially static and nonhistorical conception of cultures to considerations of both stylistic and whole-culture flow, as in the historic "configurations" or profiles of movement which I have tried to define for certain cultural activities. These remarks are made less in stricture of Benedict than by way of ready definition. I recognize my affinity to her.

That values constitute an essential ingredient of culture is coming to be increasingly accepted. That they are subjectively held is nothing to prevent their being objectively described, examined for their interassociations, and compared. After all, ideologies and religious beliefs are subjective too. What probably brought it about that values were shied off from so long in culture studies is their affective side. A myth or a dogma can be stated in coherent form, where a value is often a quality of suffusion of something else. Nevertheless, values are too integral in culture to be left out of consideration.

The principle of cultural relativism has long been standard anthropological doctrine. It holds that any cultural phenomenon must be understood and evaluated in terms of the culture of which it forms part. The corresponding assumption in the organic field is so obvious that biologists have scarcely troubled to formulate it. The difference is that we, the students of culture, live in our culture, are attached to its values, and have a natural human inclination to become ethnocentric over it, with the result that, if unchecked, we would perceive, describe, and evaluate other cultures by the forms, standards, and values of our own, thus preventing fruitful comparison and classification. Realization of relativism can be shocking to the tender-minded, through taking away the affective security which seeming absolutes render. Basically, of course, relativism is no more than desire for inquiry coupled with readiness to undergo unrestricted comparison.

Beyond this, there is a real and profounder problem: that of fixed, panhuman, if not absolute, values. This problem is only beginning to come to the consciousness of anthropologists, who have perhaps done most to stress the relativistic principle. It is touched only by implication in the present book. My conviction is that value-judgments as between the values of different cultures are possible, though not by any majority poll or with absolute finality, and probably with a pluralistic outcome. It is not to be expected that any one culture will differ from all other imperfect ones in having developed perfect values. The important requisite in this problem of transcending values

would seem, paradoxically, to be prolonged and increasingly deep comparison of value-systems—in other words, of cultures. The more prematurely this balancing comparison is abandoned in favor of a choice between value-systems, the shallower will such choice be, the greater the risk of a naïve return to ethnocentrism in the guise of a determination of more-than-relative values.

The recurrent insistence on comparison in the foregoing paragraphs may have been noted and may recall "the comparative method" of nineteenth-century anthropologists. The difference is that these earlier students too often disregarded and violated the natural, actual context of the phenomena they compared, in their ardor of developing logical but speculative constructs which they considered evolutionary. The comparison here advocated respects both the structural and the historical context of the cultural phenomena dealt with, in much the way that truly evolutionary biologists respect context structurally and historically in their organic phenomena.

Culture-wholes present a series of problems: as to their distinctness or continuity, for instance; as to their degree of internal consistency or integration and its nature; and as to what makes for such discontinuities and integrations as they possess. Anthropologists have acquired considerable skill in presenting culture-wholes of tribal size as discrete units—also in tracing the passage of material and forms between cultures; but they have concerned themselves little with the problems of outward segregation and inner consistency, especially of large civilizations. Interest among other students, while occasionally vivid, has been spottily rare and diverse. Some essays by myself in this field stand sufficiently apart to have been grouped for convenience in Part V; though I am convinced that this somewhat special set of problems forms part of those on the general nature of culture.

Any theory that specializes on culture must of course recognize that, in the case of man, society and culture always co-occur, so that the phenomena available necessarily have both a social and a cultural aspect. Since societies comprise individuals and especially since individuals are heavily shaped by their culture, there is also a third aspect or factor immediately involved in the phenomena, that of psychology or personality—apart from more remote considerations, such as the biological nature of people and the subhuman environment in which they operate. It is of course possible to try to study the cultural, social, and psychological aspects simultaneously and interwoven, as they occur. Such a meshed understanding is obviously the broadest and is therefore desirable in principle. However, it is also much the most difficult to attain, because more variable factors are involved. Also it is plain that the most valid and fruitful synthesis, other things being equal, must be the one which is based on the most acute preceding analysis. Such analysis is going to be more effective if directed at an isolable set of factors than at several interacting ones. Premature and short-circuiting synthesizing is thus avoided by discrimination between the aspects or levels that come associated in phenomena, and by unraveling, out of the snarl with which actuality presents us, the factors of one level at a time and seeing how far they can be traced as such, before retying them into a web of larger understanding with the other strands.

The level which I have personally chosen or become addicted to is the cultural one. This is not the only way of proceeding, but it is my way, and it seems the most consistent with an integrative-contextual or "historical" approach. It is hard to judge one's self, but I do seem more consciously and single-heartedly to separate out the purely cultural aspects of phenomena and to interrelate these among themselves, eliminating or "holding constant" the social and individual factors, than, for instance, my American colleagues Boas, Lowie, Radin, Linton, Spier, Redfield, or Murdock, and certainly more than Hallowell or Kluckhohn or Mead, or than British anthropologists such as Evans-Pritchard, Firth, Forde, or Nadel. This is a limitation, but it also results in certain gains. Thus the kind of general problems I treated in *Configurations of Culture Growth* could hardly have been even defined except in terms of assuming races and individuals to be uniform in mass effect. Thereafter, it was possible to explore more clearly the "movements" and "behavior" of the civilizational phenomena treated. The questions of how the civilizations of Asia and Europe have been interdependent in their development and to what degree the cultures of native America are derivative from those of Eurasia are particular problems of historical fact and are not in themselves general or theoretical. But they are certainly broad problems which may have import on theory. And it is plain that they can be settled only on cultural and environmental evidence, since individual psychological considerations are evidently so remote as to be practically irrelevant, and so are "social" phenomena except for their cultural facies.

It is because of this bent or warp that I came to realize [Selection No. 3] the significance of the simultaneity of many inventions and discoveries. In the historical process of cultural development, an invention is a single act or event and, within a given situation, likely to be more or less inevitable. It is only from the point of view of the several individuals involved that simultaneity and co-occurrence exist. The distinction is simple enough, once the concept of culture has been grasped. It was long in being made because of the conventional historical habit of treating general sociocultural factors and individual personal factors on the single amalgamated or undifferentiated level on which the phenomena of history are ordinarily received, perceived, and dealt with.

Similarly, the clustering of great minds, which has been recognized as a fact for two thousand years, though as a wanton one, takes on a meaning in terms of culture. Genius is seen as a product which is a function of cultural growth. This growth, in developing a style-like pattern, evokes or releases the required innate individual talents or creative abilities which presumably are always potentially present in larger quantity than utilized. As the pattern is realized, a culmination is attained; with its exhaustion, decline sets in, until a new pattern is evolved. With this culture-level approach, we have at least made a beginning of understanding how civilizations come to be and develop, instead of merely taking them for granted as miracles or accidents or deriving them from impossibly remote causes like physical environment.

The phenomena of fashion, again, seem wholly random until approached from the angle of superpersonal—impersonal, one might almost say—style patterns of culture [Nos. 42, 45]. Stimulus diffusion [No. 44] is a concept for probing certain intercultural similarities whose historic connection is tenuous or lost. One or more individuals necessarily enter each situation, but only as a cog in the mechanism of intercultural transfer, stimulus, and creativity.

It is true that, in the study of culture by deliberate suppression of individuals as individuals, the element of human behavior is also eliminated. One investigates, provisionally, the interrelation of collective and patterned products of the behavior of personalities, with these personalities and their behavior no longer taken into account. For myself, I have carried out this methodological suppression without qualms. Having begun with an interest in the forms of culture, I remained interested in the continued development of ways of analyzing the relations of these forms. The injection into anthropology of the concept of behavior, first developed as a corrective in the internal emancipation or purification of psychology, sprang from quite different motives and touched me little or belatedly. Writers of history, it is true, have always dealt with behavior in treating of individuals and events, just as they have implicitly dealt with culture in recognizing institutions. But, as has already been said, historians thrive on eating and digesting their phenomena raw. Those who want culture as such have to smelt it out of an ore.

The cultural view is not only collective, it is also almost inevitably long-range, because the dimension of time adds so much, imparting to the phenomena the quality of dynamism or flow or growth. This is why archaeology has so wide and persistent an appeal. The element of antiquity in its discoveries directly stimulates the imagination with overtones of elapsement and change; and, before long, historic problems formulate themselves. As these are prosecuted, individuals necessarily recede from sight, and even their collective behavior, no longer observable, becomes only remotely inferable. Time and decay have strained out, from what was once lived by human beings, almost everything but the cultural forms that archaeology restores. From the angle of culture, archaeological data come ready to hand as the purest there are, with language probably second. In archaeology facts are certainly less mixed, not only than in history, but than in ethnography.

With long range, the individual, even

the outstanding one, necessarily fades from view, just as, even in synchronous collocation of nations, he begins to shrink. It is only now and then that an Alexander, Jenghiz Khan, Napoleon, or Hitler stands out as a landmark in the collective submergence. With this recognition, a deterministic view tends to creep in. Before long, one finds himself a determinist, like Tolstoy. I was consciously so, for decades. I am less sure now. When one has acquired the habit of viewing the millennial sweeps and grand contours, and individuals have shrunk to insignificance, it is very easy to deny them consequential influence, even any influence—and therewith one stands in the gateway of belief in undefined immanent forces; a step more, and the forces have become mysterious. But from close by, at the moment, it is the individuals that loom as active; and no viewing them as blind controlled pawns, still less as wound-up clockworks, really helps to understand their activities. Actually, of course, the question of free or determined will is a metaphysical, theological, ethical, or practical one. It has apparently no scientific answer and is therefore not a scientific question. After all, I might have realized this long ago instead of in 1948 [No. 13]. My own theory of "deterministic" pattern realization and exhaustion contains a concealed factor of striving and will, in the individuals through whom the realization is achieved. A creative urge and spark must be accorded them, and potentialities of the same to all men, no matter how much the concept of creativity has in the past been abused and vulgarized, and may at the outset set on edge the teeth of scholar and scientist. A good modern definition of "creativity," probably in terms of cultural values relativistically and precisely conceived, and at any rate with all "spirituality" wholly excluded, is a genuine desideratum.

For that matter, my old comparison of culture to a coral reef should have warned me against too facile a determinism. To the geologist, as to the mariner, the reef is a massive, ancient accumulation of secretions, a great product and influence in its own right. But it concerns the zoölogist as a collection of living polyps, resting on reef but making more reef through their physiologies. The free will of a polyp may be minute and his individuation somewhat limited, but his activity is definite.

This brings us to the troublesome question of causes in culture. My opinions have varied on this matter; and I am still not too sure precisely where I stand. About 1917, in No. 3, and in spots in the full text of No. 42, I thought I stood at the threshold of glimpsing vague, grand forces of predestination, not so different perhaps from the "fate" that Spengler was soon to proclaim. Thirty years later, as in No. 12, I was not so sure that cause could be found, or was worth looking for, in cultural situations. On some points I seem to have had strong intuitions early, almost as a boy; such as that all search for "origins" is vain [No. 1, in 1901], and that alleged simple, specific causes for cultural and historical phenomena, whether particular or general, were almost certain to be false. I am still sure of these two things. Also I am convinced that, on the cultural level and in any "historic" approach as defined above, recognition of pattern is the suitable and fruitful aim of nearer understanding. Causation should not be denied because it is hard to determine; but to put its isolation into the forefront of endeavor, as if we were operating in old-fashioned mechanics, is naïve. Spengler, with all his dogmatism and maniac exaggeration, was not wholly wide of the mark when he rejected nineteenth-century causality for culture and its history. And his "destiny," if deflated of its absolutism and quality of tragic doom—it is already externally nonteleological—shrivels to something not too different from the larger patterning of culture-wholes.

One other thing is clear. Much more of the culture native to any given group is the product not of that living population but of its preceding generations. Likewise, the majority of the content of any culture has normally been developed by other groups and introduced and accepted. These facts do not seriously matter when attention is focused on momentary or short-term changes, on social interrelations within the group, or on personality developments, because in such considerations old and recent components of the culture tend to function and to be reacted to alike. In any diachronic approach, however, or in any broadly comparative or contextual one, age does enter into consideration, and the majority of the impinging causality is therefore somewhat like an iceberg—below the surface of the present. With ancient and recent, outside and internal, factors all at work and of an indefinitely great variety of ages and proveniences, it is easy to see why the causality of cultures, viewed historically, should be both intricate and diffuse.

Finally, while culture is essentially limited to man and is the only order of phenomena so limited, it is as much a part of nature as any other phenomenal order or level, and, in spite of its highly special properties, it must always be construed as within nature. Moreover, being distinctive of man to a greater degree than the society and mind which man shares with other animals, culture is that aspect of him which almost surely will be most significant of the determination and understanding of man's place in nature as that place and relation gradually become worked out more clearly. Anthropology is recognized and admitted as a natural science not so much because it includes

that human branch of biology called "physical" or "racial anthropology" but really rather because of its very non-biological, extra-somatic portion concerned with culture. This cultural segment of the science of man is the larger, is much the more distinctive, and is dominant, and therefore calls urgently for more avowed treatment as part of nature. As a mere animal, cultureless man was one of many, and not of the strongest; with culture, he began, and has continued increasingly, to dominate life on the planet and to control its future. Therewith the evolutionary lead has clearly passed from the organic order to the cultural order. It seems more than questionable whether any wholly genetically based new forms of life can ever overcome the competitive head-start already conferred on us by our culture. All this is part of a natural process and must increasingly be seen in the context of nature.

On the other side, much of culture, especially its history, its values, and its indispensable symbolic mechanism of speech, have long been studied, even though often anthropocentrically, by the scholars in the humanities. This body of intensive, organized knowledge is not only lying available; it is waiting to be absorbed into the naturocentric context of natural science. The obvious bridge to that absorption is acceptance of the concept of culture.

In the pages that follow, especially in the theoretical selections of Part I, I have accordingly not hesitated to stress organic precedents and parallels where they occurred to me [as in Nos. 5, 9, 10, and 14], and again to profit from the examples of historians' history and of linguistics [as in Nos. 8, 11, and 14] —this in spite of earlier insistence on autonomy for the study of culture [as in Nos. 3 and 4]. This autonomy I still hold to but consider largely achieved, and believe the time to be near when efforts for closer federation in the united sciences may well come from students of culture.

Where this leaves the relation of my profession of anthropology to the so-called "social sciences" is something I am not too clear about. For that matter, I would have difficulty defining the scope and intellectual objectives of social science. Sociology on the one hand feels itself to be a social science and on the other overlaps heavily in content with anthropology. Perhaps these two studies have remained separate just because they approach much the same content of subject matter from the two angles, respectively, of social science and of natural science plus humanities. This possibility is touched on in No. 18.

The present Part I develops a theory of culture in the sense of considering what culture is in the world. It also considers how culture can be investigated, and it therefore has considerable methodological slant. The final part, "V. History and Process of Civilization," is also theoretical but contains more concrete exemplification and less about method.

1. EXPLANATIONS OF CAUSE AND ORIGIN
1901

This stiff and somewhat didactic preachment with its old-fashioned language is from an article on "Decorative Symbolism of the Arapaho," which was, in fact, my doctoral dissertation. A portion of it is included here in spite of its obvious immaturities because it definitely foreshadows the general point of view as regards culture which I came gradually to develop—including a deep-seated distrust of origins and of allegations of specific causes that was ultimately to eventuate in a primary emphasis on cultural forms, patterns, and values.

That "it is impossible to determine the origin of any" cultural activity "whose origin we do not know" was the conclusion arrived at in 1901. The "tendencies" which are "at the root of all anthropological [cultural] phenomena . . . should be the aim of investigation." "These tendencies, being inherent in mind" and being "the tendencies of social man, . . . exist in individuals being parts of a culture" and are "determinable only from a historical study of social groups." "Specific causes or beginnings of specific phenomena are a delusion." In the "great unity" of total culture lies "the true study for the study of man. In it, as parts of it, cultures and civilizational movements, tendencies, and individual phenomena, are comprehensible. Only by understanding its totality can we really understand its . . . productions that have always a predecessor but never a beginning."

It is an awkward way of expressing the importance of the relation of all cultural facts to their context, but the point is made. And human nature is allowed for, though as something to be finally adumbrated, not as taken for granted and derived from—which was still far from universal practice at the time.

THE Arapaho, a tribe of Plains Indians belonging to the Algonquian stock, practice a form of art very similar in material, technique, and appearance to that of the other Plains tribes, of whom the Sioux are the best known. This art is in appearance almost altogether unrealistic, unpictorial, decorative. For the greater part it consists now of beadwork, which has nearly supplanted the older style of embroidery in porcupine quills, plant fibers, and perhaps beads of aboriginal manufacture. The other products of this art are objects of skin or hide which are painted with geometrical designs. On the whole, the decorative, geometric character of Arapaho art is very marked. Almost all the lines are straight. The figures in embroidery are lines, bands, rectangles, rhombi, isosceles and rectangular triangles, figures composed of combinations of these, and circles. The designs painted on hide are composed of triangles and rectangles in different forms and combinations.

On questioning the Indians, it is found that many of these decorative figures have a meaning. An equilateral triangle with the point downward may represent a heart; with its point upward, a mountain. A figure consisting of five squares or rectangles in quincunx, the four outer ones touching the central one at the corners, is a representation of a turtle. A long stripe crossed by two short ones is a dragon fly. A row of small squares at intervals represents tracks. Crosses and diamonds often signify stars. All this is in beadwork. In painted designs a flat isosceles triangle often represents a hill; an acute isosceles triangle, a tent. Many other objects are similarly represented.

This strongly marked decorative character of Arapaho art, however, is accompanied by a symbolic representational tendency of a degree of development as at first acquaintance would hardly be suspected by a civilized person. Several figures connected in meaning may be put upon one object and thus produce something approximating a picture containing composition. When as many as ten or a dozen symbols having reference to one another are combined, a story can almost be told by them. In this way the stiff embroideries on a moccasin or the geometric paintings on a bag may represent the hunting of buffalo, the acquisition of supernatural power by a shaman, a landscape or map, a dream, personal experiences, or a myth.

Arapaho art thus is at the same time representationally significant and decorative. Can the origin of this art be determined?

Since Arapaho art consists of the intimate fusion of symbolism and decoration, two theories as to its origin are possible. Either of its two elements may be the original. The Indians may have begun with realism, drawing or working lifelike forms in their art; then, however, the obstacles inherent in the material asserted themselves, or the well-established tendency toward symmetry and repetition into a pattern came out, or perhaps other causes were influential, until the early imitative representations became abbreviated into the conventional decorations that have been described. Or it is possible that the Indians began with mere ornaments. Perhaps even these were not originally ornaments but peculiarities of construction of purely useful articles, which technical peculiarities were later considered beautifying and hence devel-

oped into pure ornaments. At any rate, whatever their own origin, decorations may in the past have existed per se; later, some conventional ornament may have accidentally suggested a natural object, whereupon it was modified to resemble this object more closely; the same process occurred with other ornaments, until finally a whole system of symbolism was added to the older system of decoration. The first of these theories is that original pictures were conventionalized into decorative symbolism; the other theory is that original ornament was expanded into symbolic decoration. These are the logically possible explanations of the origin of Arapaho art because we recognize in it two factors, the realistic-symbolic and the decorative-technical.

Let us see whether either of these theories can be rendered, through the evidence of fact, actually certain or at least probable....

In moccasins the tendency to realistic symbolism and the tendency to decorative conventionalism are clearly about in equilibrium. Hence we cannot fairly say that either of these tendencies is the older and original. If one concentrates his attention on the symbolism, or happens to be temperamentally more interested in it, he is very likely to see it more abundantly than the decoration, to be more impressed by it, to consider the entire present art as merely corrupted or abbreviated symbolism, and to advance as an explanation of the origin and development of these designs the theory of conventionalized realism. But if one thinks more of the decoration as such, or if one's mind runs naturally toward the ornamental and technical, he will probably notice mostly this side, regard the significations of markings as trivial and irrelevant additions that may be ignored, and finally champion the theory of expanded decoration....

Both explanations are thus, in the case

of moccasin-designs, not only logically possible, but they are very naturally believed and advanced as the result of certain mental predispositions. But if we try to remain free from any such inclinations of mind and if we remember how strongly developed and intimately fused are both the tendencies, we must come to the conclusion that, because symbolism and decoration balance each other, the two theories of conventionalized realism and expanded ornament, though logically admissible, are actually untenable. Rather it seems likely, since the two tendencies are vigorous and combined, that they are both well established, old, and long in close union; so that formerly designs on Arapaho moccasins, though perhaps ruder than now, were of the same general character, both symbolically and decoratively, as those we know....

Some of the Arapaho say that at the beginning of the world, when the first men, their ancestors, obtained paint, they had only the skins of small animals to use for paint-bags, and that this is the origin of the animal symbolism of the present-day paint-pouches.

It is necessary not to be misled into a belief of this origin and development on the authority of the Indians. Their authority on such a point is valueless. They believe that the time when the first men obtained paint-bags was four hundred years ago, just after the formation of the world by a solitary mythic being floating on the water, and after a female whirlwind enlarged the minute earth by circling about it. Like all American savages, they are almost completely without historical sense or knowledge. Occasionally a striking event may be remembered in a distorted form for a century or two, but, on the whole, whatever of actual occurrence is retained in their tales is inextricably blended with mythic and supernatural elements. We have no right to reject the greatest part of their crea-

tion myth as so impossible that it would enter no one's mind to accept it as true, and at the same time to select here and there a point that is within the limits of possibility and proclaim it as historical and reliable. The mythic and historical elements in primitive legends are not simply mixed together so that they can be distinguished and separated, but they are both equally wonderful and equally true for the savage. No myth can be interpreted into history by mere elimination of its supernatural portions: it must be rejected *in toto*. Even though it may be founded on a basis of actuality—and this must often be the case—it is altogether myth. In law and exact science and wherever evidence is judged, an account that is in great part manifestly absurd or palpably impossible is not accepted as true after the impossibilities have been subtracted, but is disregarded as a whole. So, too, it is necessary to attach no importance to the statement of the Arapaho as to the origin of these paint-bags.

We have considered several forms of Arapaho art. In all cases we have found a well-developed symbolism and a conventional decoration. The symbolism and the decoration exist not side by side but in each other. It has been easy to manufacture explanations of the origin of this art that are plausible theories. But, as soon as we are open to recognize all possibilities, such theories are seen to arise from our opinions and methods of interpretation, and to be unsubstantiable by fact. Therefore, we can describe Arapaho art, we can characterize it, and distinguish its various coexisting tendencies. We can even, to a certain extent, enter into the spirit of the people who practice it, and understand (i.e., feel) their mental workings. We cannot in fairness lay claim to knowing the cause or origin of this art, nor can we hope to ascertain its cause and origin by studying its products.

In the art of other primitive races

conditions very much resemble those just discussed. Everywhere art is conventionalized, under the influence of a definite style. Practically everywhere also it is decorative. This is obviously true of such high arts as those of the Japanese and Chinese. It is true also of Greek sculpture and of Renaissance paintings: though in our modern civilization we are in the habit of regarding the products of these arts detachedly, and enjoy them as if they were complete in themselves, yet everyone is aware that the intent to decorate always accompanied the conception and execution of the classic and Italian masterpieces. Even so strenuously realistic an art as modern impressionism is unable to free itself totally from the reproach of being ornamental; for, whatever the purpose of the artist, the owner of such a picture has almost certainly secured it for the purpose, ostensible at least, of decorating a vacant wall. In primitive civilizations the combination of the imitative and decorative tendencies is of course much greater. With very few exceptions, such as in some Eskimo tribes, the realistic, representative impulse is thoroughly impressed and influenced by the highly conventional style; and in all cases this conventional style is decorative. Correspondingly, most primitive decoration, no matter how geometric or simple, has significance and thus is visually or ideographically representative. This is a fact that has not become known until recently, because until lately savages were rarely questioned thoroughly. Accordingly, the main characteristic of Arapaho art, its fusion (which is more truly an undifferentiation) of the realistic and decorative tendencies, is also characteristic of primitive art generally.

In Brazil we know of tribes whose painted and incised designs, which are exceedingly simple and geometrical and usually in patterns, are all significant. Diamonds whose corners are slightly filled in are rhomboidally shaped fishes; a pattern of flat isosceles triangles stood up on end is hanging bats; and so on. There are also other representations of the same animals that are slightly more realistic. The same tribes use pots of oval shape with half a dozen variously shaped projections at the rim. The whole vessel represents an animal, the projections being roughly modeled into head, tail, and limbs. Birds, bats, mammals, reptiles, and invertebrates are indicated by very slight modifications. A civilized person unacquainted with the mode of sight and thought of the Brazilian aborigines might very readily mistake a bird-pot for a mammal-pot, and so on.

In central Australia bullroarers and other objects are decorated with incised lines. These consist of concentric circles, bands of parallel lines, concentric arcs or curves, and rows of dots or small marks. The ornamentation is not symmetrical or even regular; it appears random and rude. Yet in general character these decorated bullroarers resemble one another closely. It has been found that the designs are all ideographic, though the total range of significance is apparently not very wide. Similar marks may on different objects mean things as different as trees, frogs, eggs, or intestines. It is interesting to note that, while this art is remarkably crude and unformed both as regular ornamentation and as an attempt to represent objects accurately, it contains a system of symbolic expression as well as a system of decoration, both of which are conventionalized—or, rather, the union of which is a convention. . . .

The usual method of explaining the origin of an art has been to select that one of its tendencies which was the most marked or appeared so to the investigator, to image the products of this tendency in its most isolated and pure form, and to pronounce these the original state of the art. An observer is struck by the fact that in a certain primitive art many ornamental features coincide with technical ones that are present for practical reasons. He concludes that the technical-practical tendency which he has discovered within the decoration is the original unmixed impulse that caused the art. Or he may become aware, through inquiry or study, of the fact that geometric ornament in an art has representative significance. The representation impresses him; true, it is now modified and corrupt, but that only proves that originally it was pure. Ergo, this art began with representative pictures. Such has been the method of explanation, however much the actual results in different cases differed. . . .

This method has the fundamental fault that it presupposes tendencies to have existed more unmixedly and separately at some former time than at present. In reality, they must in all cases have been in the near past very much as now and in the very remote past more mixed or mutually undifferentiated. Thus we have seen that Arapaho art must some time ago have been very much as now. What it was still earlier we know even less definitely, but we cannot doubt that its spirit must have been similar. Different objects may then have been represented, other ornamental motives employed in other materials; but even then there certainly was the combination of ideographic symbolism with crude, heavy decoration. As we go farther backward in time, we can be sure that the details of the art were more and more different from those of its present condition. Now perhaps one of its component tendencies was relatively stronger, then another. But, whatever these temporary fluctuations, it is certain that if we only go back far enough we must arrive at a stage where the tendencies were even more numerously and more intimately combined than now. But if one should believe that

Arapaho art can be explained, for instance, by the conventionalized realism theory, the realism being original and the conventionalization subsequent, he holds the view that at some time past this Arapaho art consisted of pictorial representations. This view is logically possible, but in reality it is absurd. This art could not have had so ideally simple a development that we could still trace its original condition, if it were very old. But if, therefore, it were comparatively recent in origin, there must until a certain time have been no art among the Arapaho, while at that moment it sprang up full-blown, not as a crude undifferentiated thing, but as a highly specialized pictorial art. Such an event would be extremely remarkable, not to say marvelous, and more in need of an explanation than the phenomenon it explained. By isolating any tendency that we find in any art, we are led to imagine a purely ideal condition which not only could not have been the original state of the art but is probably even more different from its original state than from its present known state.

In short, it is impossible to determine the origin of any art whose history we do not know.

Let us briefly consider the field of mythology. There have been numerous explanations of myths and several theories of the origin of all mythology. The principal of these theories are the following.

What may be called the physical or science theory accounts for myths by making them the outcome of a desire to explain natural phenomena. The shapes or colors of animals, the motion of sun and moon, the existence of the stars, strange geologic formations—such phenomena are supposed to have stimulated the wonder of primitive man so much that he made myths to explain them.

The personification theory supposes that deities and other mythic characters, together with their actions—in a word, mythology—are personifications of natural phenomena. Phoebus, Indra, Agni, are said to have originated in personifications of the sun, heaven, and fire. The solar myth theories and others of an analogous kind belong here.

The animistic theory says that there was originally a belief in soul, out of which arose the various systems of spirits and deities. It believes that myths originated from a state of the human mind to which all objects seemed equally endowed with human personality.

These three theories are at bottom the same.

What has been called the allegorical or ethical theory supposes myths to be allegorical inventions with a moral import. Miraculous stories of gods, men, and animals are thought to have been composed in order to teach ethical precepts by illustration. This view is not so much in favor now as formerly.

The historical theory makes myths the distortion of actual events. A powerful king of Crete gave rise to the mythic character of Zeus.

The etymological theory calls mythology a disease of language. Misinterpreted metaphors or false etymologies gave rise to myths. To use a familiar example, Zeus is thought to have been originally called Kronion, with the meaning "existing through all time." Later this epithet was misunderstood to mean son of Kronos, and thus gave rise to the conception of a god Kronos.

As explanations, all these theories are untrue. But the tendencies which they recognize exist.

There is undoubtedly a tendency to explain natural phenomena in myths. The Indians of British Columbia have this story: The bear and the chipmunk disputed whether there was to be darkness or light. The chipmunk triumphed, and for the first time it became light. The angry bear attacked the chipmunk and pursued it. The chipmunk escaped by tearing itself from under the claws of the bear. From this it is striped down its back. This little story, whatever its origin, clearly reflects the tendency to mythologize about such natural phenomena as day and night and the color-markings of animals. Hundreds of similar myths concerned with the spots on the moon, or the blackness of the crow, or a certain peculiar stone, or a similar fact are known from all parts of the world.

There is also a tendency to identify mythic personages with parts of nature —Thor with thunder, for instance. And the tendency toward animism is so widespread and so deep seated that it will be recognized without an example.

It must also be admitted that there is something of an ethical tendency in mythologies. Among primitive races ceremonial and ritual partly take the place of our later morality. And very frequently myths deal with ceremonial. The American Indians, the Jews, the Australians, and the Greeks have such myths.

The existence of a historical tendency in myths is demonstrated by the introduction of Attila into the Sigurd saga.

The etymological tendency, finally, is revealed in the following extract from a Dakota myth: An old couple have adopted a foundling. When he grows up, he is so successful in killing buffalo that he makes his parents very rich in dried meat. "Then the old man said: 'Old woman, I am glad we are well off. I will proclaim it abroad.' And so when the morning came he went up to the top of the house and sat, and said, 'I, I have abundance laid up. The fat of the big guts (*tashiyaka*) I chew.' And they say that was the origin of the meadowlark (*tashiyakapopo*). It has a yellow breast, and black in the middle, which is the yellow of the morning, and they say the black stripe is made by a smooth buffalo horn worn for a necklace."

From this point the myth deals with the adventures of the boy.

It is thus clear that for every one of these theories there really exists a tendency in primitive man which influences his myths.

This multiplicity of tendencies or causative forces necessarily refutes any explanation that uses and allows only one of them. Such have been all explanations of myths. Such they must be, for, when more than one tendency or cause is admitted, we can have several tentative suggestions but no longer one positive explanation. The case is analogous to that in art and does not require detailed restatement. It may be said, in short, that all explanations of myths consist of the ignoring of all the eternal and indestructible tendencies in man with the exception of one which is isolated and elevated as the sole cause of the myth. That such explanations, however clear and impressive they are, cannot be true is obvious.

Thus we come to the conclusion that all search for origins in anthropology can lead to nothing but false results. The tendencies of which we have spoken are at the root of all anthropological phenomena. Therefore, it is these general tendencies more properly than the supposed causes of detached phenomena that should be the aim of investigation. . . .

The tendencies spoken of throughout this essay must be understood to be the tendencies of social man. They are those tendencies which exist in individuals being parts of a culture, not in isolated individuals as such. There are psychological causes or mental conditions —generally considered physiological— which might also be called "tendencies." Such are the tendency to fatigue, the tendency to form habits, the tendency toward imitation by suggestion, and others. These exist nearly identically in all men, whatever their degree of civilization; they seem even to occur with little modification in animals. It is evident that these physiological tendencies are independent of cultures. Our knowledge concerning them is due to a psychological study of individual men. On the other hand, those tendencies which alone are referred to above are determinable only from a historical study of social groups. The manifestations of these tendencies are activities such as mythology, writing, ceremonials, decorative art, castes, commerce, and language.

These several tendencies, being inherent in mind, are everlasting. On the other hand, they are constantly changing and developing and varying in their differentiations and combinations. The phenomena of activity have changed as these tendencies and their relations to one another have become modified. Therefore, the products of mind (the phenomena studied by anthropologists) are, like mind itself, beginningless (for us). They have no origin. All arts and all institutions are as old as man. Every word is as old as speech. The history of every myth is at least as long as the history of mankind. Of course, no myth was ever alike from one generation to the next; no decorative style has ever remained unaltered. But no myth, no artistic convention, or any other thing human ever sprang up from nothing. It always grew from something previous that was similar. These principles are obvious, but they are ignored and implicitly denied in every search for an origin.

Every explanation of an origin in anthropology is based on three processes of thought which are unobjectionable logically but are contrary to evolutionary principles and the countless facts that support these principles. First is the assumption, implied in the word *origin*, that, before the beginning of the phenomenon explained, itself and its cause were absent; second is the belief that a suddenly arising cause singly produced the phenomenon; and the third is the idea that this cause ceased as suddenly and completely as it had before sprung up and that its product has remained, unaffected by other causes, unaltered but for wear and tear, to the present day. These three thought-processes are present in every explanation of the cause or origin of a human phenomenon, whether the explainer himself be conscious or unconscious of them. Generally, indeed, the origin is not stated unhesitatingly and clearly enough for these three steps of thought to be visible in all their baldness. Often, perhaps, the investigator advancing a theory of origin would himself deny these processes to exist in his reasoning. Nevertheless, every determination of an origin, whether "origin" means the beginning of a phenomenon or its cause, must imply the existence of, first, a previous different state, secondly, a change produced by an external (noninherent) cause, and, thirdly, the state that is being investigated.

If, then, the specific causes or beginnings of specific phenomena are a delusion in anthropology and may not be sought, what can be the subject of investigation? The tendencies that have been referred to so much? Like words and styles and myths and ideas and industrial processes and institutions, all of which are their products, tendencies are both eternally living and everlastingly changing. They flow into one an-

other; they transform themselves; they are indistinguishably combined where they coexist. So, if our view is wide enough, we cannot properly determine and separate and name and classify tendencies. They really exist only in the whole unity of living activity as parts in the endless organism. This great unity is the true study for the student of man. In it, as parts of it, cultures and civilization movements, tendencies and individual phenomena, are comprehensible. In it we know their interrelations. Only by understanding this totality can we really understand its smaller parts, those productions that have always a predecessor but never a beginning.

The fundamental error of the common anthropological method of investigating origins is that it isolates phenomena and seeks isolated specific causes for them. In reality, ethnic phenomena do not exist separately: they have their being only in a culture. Much less can the causative forces of the human mind, the activities or tendencies, be truly isolated. Every distinction of them is not only arbitrary but untrue. Both phenomena and causes can be properly apperceived only in the degree that we know their relations to the rest of the great unity that is called life. The more this is known and understood as a whole, the more do we comprehend its parts. This, the whole of life, is the only profitable subject of study for anthropology.

2. CAUSE OF THE BELIEF IN USE INHERITANCE
1916

A by-product or reflection of "The Superorganic," which follows [No. 3], the present paragraphs constitute a sort of raid into enemy territory, whereas the larger essay of the next year is a declaration of independence. There the cultural process was extricated from the merely organic; here, an early but persistent error in understanding historic organic change is interpreted as due to the false reading into the biological process of a distinctly sociocultural mechanism. So far as I am aware, no notice has been taken of the argument; but it still appears to me valid.

Nos. 3, 4, 5, and 9 return to the problem of relations with biology.

THIS note expresses an effort to view the old and recurring problem of use inheritance from the aspect of the underlying motives of thought involved instead of through a consideration of the evidence directly bearing upon it.

The heredity of acquired traits is, theoretically, biological heresy. But the interminable cropping-out of the belief even in professional circles indicates a strong psychological impulse toward the conviction. The mainspring of this impulse thus becomes a matter of some importance to the student of heredity....

While never formulated into a definite working principle until Lamarck, because of the world's lack of specific scientific interest in organic phenomena, the principle of use inheritance has nevertheless been tacitly assumed by civilized nations of all periods and is taken as self-evident even by savages. It must therefore rest on a large mass of common experience interpreted by an elementary process of thought. Such an elementary process—in fact, the only elementary process of wide scope—is analogy.

The question then becomes what may be the basis—real enough, though unscientifically employed—for the analogizing that has resulted in the conviction

that use heredity exists. There must evidently be a broad group of phenomena in human experience that bear some resemblance to the hereditary transmission of the acquired.

These phenomena are the exceedingly common ones of social inheritance or cultural transmission and growth. We do "inherit" a name, or property, or knowledge of a language, or the practice of an art, or belief in a particular form of religion. Biologically such "inheritance" is, of course, absolutely distinct from "heredity" because the mechanism of transmission is different. The source of social inheritance is not restricted to parents and actual ancestors in the line of descent but embraces a multitude of individuals, consanguineous and unrelated, dead, living, and sometimes even junior to the inheritors —in other words, the totality of the social environment, past and present, of an individual. We can and do "inherit" property from an uncle, our "mother-tongue" from a nurse, the arithmetic evolved by past ages from a schoolmaster, our dogmas and philosophy from a prophet, our political and moral beliefs from the whole circumambient public opinion.

As this social or cultural transmission concerns human beings, it is of more immediate interest to the normal unschooled mind than the transmission which gives organs, instincts, and peculiarities to animals and plants. It is therefore recognized much sooner than the processes which guide biological or organic transmission. It needs no proof that in his development man was concerned far earlier with himself than with animals or other parts of nature. It is well known, for instance, that the animism which is accepted as the basis of all religion anthropomorphizes not only its gods and the vaguer forces of nature but especially animals, plants, and objects.

It is only recently, accordingly, that the world has paid any true attention to organic heredity, whereas since the beginning of human existence there has been recognition of social inheritance. History, the science of human society, is, even in a relatively advanced form, several thousand years old and, as a rudiment, has enough interest to appeal to savages. Biology, as an organized science, has an age of only centuries.

It is significant that the first theory of organic evolution, that of Lamarck, resorted wholly to the explanation of use inheritance borrowed from social inheritance. A second stage was reached when Darwin introduced the organic factor of selection, though refusing to break with the older explanation. A last phase was inaugurated when Weismann insisted that organic phenomena must be interpreted solely by organic processes.

The priority of reasoning by analogy over reasoning by means of a specific mechanism is a world-wide historical phenomenon. The two modern views of evolution and creation are found as crude cosmic philosophies in the mythologies of the most primitive savages, as well as in the thinking of Hindus, Semites, Greeks, and Romans. But they occur, one as an analogy with the familiar phenomenon of manufacture or making of objects by hand, the other as an analogy with the equally familiar phenomena of birth and growth. What modern science has done is to adopt these age-old and crude ideas, as it has adopted the half-mythologic concepts of the atom and ether, and put them to new use. Only the uneducated think of Darwin as the originator of the doctrine of evolution. What he originated was an organic and, in his day, new mechanism, by which the old concept of evolution could be explained and therefore supported.

The distinction between the social[1] and the organic is far from a novel one. But the two groups of phenomena, and the processes involved in each, are still very frequently confounded in other domains than that of use inheritance. The whole eugenics movement, for instance, so far as it is a constructive program and not a mere matter of ordinary practical prophylactic social hygiene, rests upon the assumption that social progress can be accomplished by organic means....

In summary, the doctrine of the hereditary transmission of acquired characters is perhaps no more disprovable than it is provable by accumulation and analysis of evidence. It springs from a naïve and even primitive method of reasoning by analogy, which in this case works to a confusion of the long-distinguished and necessarily distinct concepts of the organic and the social.[1] The doctrine may however be dismissed on purely methodological grounds. It is possible that when the missing factor or element of evolution is discovered that neither Darwin nor the geneticists[2] have been able to find, this factor, leading to adaptations, will prove to be something superficially similar to use inheritance. But it will differ from the present only partly discredited factor of heredity by acquirement, in containing an organic mechanism, and will therefore be essentially different from this confused assumption.[3]

3. THE SUPERORGANIC
1917

Originally published in the "American Anthropologist," this essay was reprinted with stylistic revisions ten years later by the Sociological Press of Hanover, New Hampshire. For many years now, the article has excited little stir among anthropologists, presumably because its contentions have largely passed into their common body of assumptions. It has however continued to attract some interest among sociologists, historians, and social scientists generally, for which reason it is included here without abbreviation.

In the vista of a third of a century, the essay appears like an antireductionist proclamation of independence from the dominance of the biological explanation of sociocultural phenomena. Yet, as I look back, I cannot recall, in the two decades preceding 1917, any instances of oppression or threatened annexation by biologists. What was hanging over the study of culture, as I sense it now, was rather a diffused public opinion, a body of unaware assumptions, that left precarious the autonomous recognition of society, and still more that of culture. It was the intelligent man on the street and those who wrote for him, social philosophers like Herbert Spencer, Lester Ward, Gustave Le Bon—it was against their influence that I was protesting. The biologists, in fact, were generally ignoring society and culture. The few who did not ignore it, like Galton and Pearson, presented analyzed evidence that was handleable and might therefore be construed also in a contrary sense. Indeed, Galton has always evoked my complete respect and has been one of the largest intellectual influences on me. What the essay really protests is the blind and bland shuttling back and forth between an equivocal "race" and an equivocal "civilization"—a shuttling that is referred to at the end of one of the middle paragraphs. That confusion was certainly still prevalent at the time.

Two reservations are necessary in mid-twentieth century. First, society and culture can no longer be simply bracketed as "the social," as was customary then, in contrast to "the organic." In most contexts they are separable, and it is preferable to distinguish them. When the meaning is clearly inclusive, that fact can now be made clear by the use of "sociocultural," as is Sorokin's consistent practice. It was Bernhard Stern who pointed out in "Social Forces" in 1929 that my "social" in this essay was ambiguous. Ants and termites possess societies but no culture. Only man has both, necessarily always associated, though conceptually differentiable. Haziness today about the distinction is an intellectual fault only a little less gross than confusion of the organic and the superorganic. That my "superorganic" of 1917 referred essentially to culture is clear not only from all the concrete evidence cited but from the constant use of "civilization," "culture," "history," and their adjectival forms. Of the final twenty paragraphs, only three do not contain one or more occurrences of these interchangeably used terms. I should feel happier if I had been farsighted enough in 1917 consistently to say "cultural" or "sociocultural" wherever I did instead say "social" in a mistaken attempt to conform to prevalent usage—to pour new wine into the old bottle. Still I did not, I think, anywhere in the essay discuss or name "society," which fact shows that when I said "the social" I used it either in a wider sense to include culture or in a limiting sense to denote culture outright.

Second, I retract, as unwarranted reification, the references in the fourteenth, tenth, and sixth paragraphs from the last and in the final paragraph to organic and superorganic "substances," entities, or fabrics. While it certainly is often needful to view different kinds of phenomena as of different orders and to deal with them on separate levels of apprehension, there is no need for metaphysically construing levels of conception or orders of attribute into substantial entities or different kinds of substance. Compare in this connection No. 13 below.

The notion expressed in the seventy-third paragraph that civilization or culture "is not mental action but a body or stream of products of mental exercise" may be contested—apart from its somewhat old-fashioned wording—but is still being argued today. We seem not yet to have attained a concise, unambiguous, inclusive, and exclusive definition of culture.

I am conscious of a degree of rhetorical ponderousness in the phrasing of the essay. I trust this will be forgiven—as it has been in the past—as a by-product of the fervor of realizations that at the time seemed both new and important. The 1927 wording has been retained unaltered except for one change of a preposition.

A WAY of thought characteristic of our western civilization has been the formulation of complementary antitheses, a balancing of exclusive opposites. One of these pairs of ideas with which our world has been laboring for some two thousand years is expressed in the words *body* and *soul.* Another couplet that has served its useful purpose, but which science is now often endeavoring to rid itself of, at least in certain aspects, is the distinction of the *physical* from the *mental.* A third discrimination is that of the *vital* from the *social,* or in other phraseology, of the *organic* from the *cultural.* The implicit recognition of the difference between organic qualities and processes and social qualities and processes is of long standing. The formal distinction is however recent. In fact the full import of the significance of the antithesis may be said to be only dawning upon the world. For every occasion on which some human mind sharply separates organic and social forces, there are dozens of other times when the distinction between them is not thought of, or an actual confusion of the two ideas takes place.

One reason for this current confusion of the organic and the social is the predominance, in the present phase of the history of thought, of the idea of evolution. This idea, one of the earliest, simplest, and also vaguest ever attained by the human mind, has received its strongest ground and fortification in the domain of the organic; in other words, through biological science. At the same time, there is an evolution, or growth, or gradual development, apparent also in other realms than that of plant and animal life. We have theories of stellar or cosmic evolution; and there is obvious, even to the least learned, a growth or evolution of civilization. In the nature of things there is little danger of the carrying over of the Darwinian or post-Darwinian principles of the evolution of life into the realm of burning suns and lifeless nebulae. Human civilization or progress, on the other hand, which exists only in and through living members of the species, is outwardly so similar to the evolution of plants and animals, that it has been inevitable that there should have been sweeping applications of the principles of organic development to the facts of cultural growth. This of course is reasoning by analogy, or arguing that because two things resemble each other in one point they will also be similar in others. In the absence of knowledge, such assumptions are justifiable as assumptions.

Too often, however, their effect is to predetermine mental attitude, with the result that when the evidence begins to accumulate which could prove or disprove the assumption based on analogy, this evidence is no longer viewed impartially and judiciously, but is merely distributed and disposed of in such a way as not to interfere with the established conviction into which the original tentative guess has long since turned.

This is what has happened in the field of organic and social evolution. This distinction between them, which is so obvious that to former ages it seemed too commonplace to remark upon, except incidentally and indirectly, has been largely obscured in the last fifty years through the hold which thoughts connected with the idea of organic evolution have had on minds of the time. It even seems fair to say that this confusion has been greater and more general among those to whom study and scholarship are a daily pursuit than to the remainder of the world.

And yet many aspects of the difference between the organic and that in human life which is not organic, are so plain that a child can grasp them, and that all human beings, including the veriest savages, constantly employ the distinction. Everyone is aware that we are born with certain powers and that we acquire others. There is no need of argument to prove that we derive some things in our lives and make-up from nature through heredity, and that other things come to us through agencies with which heredity has nothing to do. No one has yet been found to assert that any human being is born with an inherent knowledge of the multiplication table; nor, on the other hand, to doubt that the children of a negro are born negroes through the operation of hereditary forces. Some qualities in every individual are however clearly debatable ground; and when the development of civilization as a whole and

the evolution of life as a whole are compared, the distinction of the processes involved has too often been allowed to lapse.

Some millions of years ago, it is currently taught, natural selection, or some other evolutionary agency, first caused birds to appear in the world. They sprang from reptiles. Conditions were such that the struggle for existence on the earth was hard; while in the air there were safety and room. Gradually, either by a series of almost imperceptible gradations through a long line of successive generations, or by more marked and sudden leaps in a shorter period, the group of birds was evolved from its reptilian ancestors. In this development, feathers were acquired and scales lost; the grasping faculty of the front legs was converted into an ability to sustain the body in the air. The advantages of resistance enjoyed by a cold-blooded organization were given up for the equivalent or greater compensation of the superior activity that goes with warm-bloodedness. The net result of this chapter of evolutionary history was that a new power, that of aerial locomotion, was added to the sum total of faculties possessed by the highest group of animals, the vertebrates. The vertebrate animals as a whole, however, were not affected. The majority of them are without the power of flight as their ancestors were millions of years ago. The birds, in turn, had lost certain faculties which they once possessed, and presumably would still possess were it not for the acquisition of their wings.

In the last few years human beings have also attained the power of aerial locomotion. But the process by which this power was attained, and its effects on the species, are as different from those which characterized the acquisition of flight by the first birds as it is possible for them to be. Our means of flying are outside of our bodies. A bird is born with a pair of wings, but we have invented the aeroplane. The bird renounced a potential pair of hands to get his wings; we, because our new faculty is not part of our congenital make-up, keep all the organs and capacities of our forefathers but add to them the new ability. The process of the development of civilization is clearly one of accumulation: the old is retained, in spite of the incoming of the new. In organic evolution, the introduction of new features is generally possible only through the loss or modification of existing organs or faculties.

In short, the growth of new species of animals takes place through, and in fact consists of, changes in their organic constitution. As regards the growth of civilization, on the other hand, the one example cited is sufficient to show that change and progress can take place through an invention without any such constitutional alteration of the human species.

There is another way of looking at this difference. It is clear that as a new species originates, it is derived wholly from the individual or individuals that first showed the particular traits distinguishing the new species. When we say that it is derived from these individuals we mean, literally, that it is descended. In other words, the species is composed only of such individuals as contain the "blood"—the germ-plasm—of particular ancestors. Heredity is thus the indispensable means of transmission. When however an invention is made, the entire human race is capable of profiting thereby. People who have not the slightest blood kinship to the first designers of aeroplanes can fly and are flying today. Many a father has used, enjoyed, and profited by the invention of his son. In the evolution of animals, the descendant can build upon the inheritance transmitted to him from his ancestors, and may rise to higher powers and more perfect development; but

the ancestor is, in the very nature of things, precluded from thus profiting from his descendant. In short, organic evolution is essentially and inevitably connected with hereditary processes; the social evolution which characterizes the progress of civilization, on the other hand, is not, or not necessarily, tied up with hereditary agencies.

The whale is not only a warm-blooded mammal, but is recognized as the remote descendant of carnivorous land animals. In some few million years, as such genealogies are usually reckoned, this animal lost his legs for running, his claws for holding and tearing, his original hair and external ears that would be useless or worse in water, and acquired fins and fluke, a cylindrical body, a layer of fat, and the power of holding his breath. There was much that the species gave up; more, on the whole, perhaps than it gained. Certainly some of its parts have degenerated. But there was one new power that it did achieve: that of roaming the ocean indefinitely.

The parallel and also contrast is in the human acquisition of the identical faculty. We do not, in gradual alteration from father to son, change our arms into flippers and grow a tail. We do not enter the water at all to navigate it. We build a boat. And what this means is that we preserve our bodies and our natal faculties intact, unaltered from those of our fathers and remotest ancestors. Our means of marine travel is outside of our natural endowment. We make it and use it: the original whale had to turn himself into a boat. It took him countless generations to attain to his present condition. All individuals that failed to conform to type left no offspring; or none that went into the blood of the whales of today.

Again, we may compare human and animal beings when groups of them reach a new and arctic environment, or when the climate of the tract where the race is established slowly becomes colder and colder. The non-human mammal species comes to have heavy hair. The polar bear is shaggy; his Sumatran relative sleek. The arctic hare is enveloped in soft fur; the jack-rabbit in comparison is shabbily thin and moth-eaten. Good furs come from the far north, and they lose in richness, in quality, and in value, in proportion as they are stripped from animals of the same species that inhabit milder regions. And this difference is racial, not individual. The jack-rabbit would quickly perish with the end of summer in Greenland; the caged polar bear suffers from temperate warmth within the massive coat which nature has fastened on him.

Now there are people who look for the same sort of inborn peculiarities in the Arctic Eskimo and Samoyed; and find them, because they look for them. That the Eskimo is furry, no one can assert: in fact, we are hairier than he. But it is asserted that he is fat-protected —like the blubber-covered seal that he lives on; and that he devours quantities of meat and oil because he needs them. The true amount of his fat, compared with that of other human beings, remains to be ascertained. He probably has more than the European; but probably no more than the normal full-blood Samoan and Hawaiian from under the tropics. And as to his diet, if this is seal and seal and seal all winter long, it is not from any congenital craving of his stomach, but because he does not know how to get himself anything else. The Alaskan miner, and the artic and antarctic explorer, do not guzzle blubber. Wheat-flour, eggs, coffee, sugar, potatoes, canned vegetables—whatever the exigencies of their vocation and the cost of transportation permit—make up their fare. The Eskimo is only too anxious to join them; and both he and they can thrive on the one diet as on the other.

In fact, what the human inhabitant of intemperate latitudes does, is not to develop a peculiar digestive system, any more than he grows hair. He changes his environment, and thereby is able to retain his original body unaltered. He builds a closed house, which keeps out the wind and retains the heat of his body. He makes a fire or lights a lamp. He skins a seal or a caribou of the furry hide with which natural selection or other processes of organic evolution have endowed these beasts; he has his wife make him a shirt and trousers, boots and gloves, or two sets of them; he puts them on; and in a few years, or days, he is provided with the protection which it took the polar bear and the arctic hare, the sable and the ptarmigan, untold periods to acquire. What is more, his baby, and his baby's baby, and his hundredth descendant are born as naked, and unarmed physically, as he and his hundredth ancestor were born.

That this difference in method of resisting a difficult environment, as followed respectively by the polar bear species and the human Eskimo race, is absolute, need not be asserted. That the difference is deep, is unquestionable. That it is as important as it is often neglected, it is the object of this essay to establish.

It has long been the custom to say that the difference is that between body and mind; that animals have their physiques adapted to their circumstances, but that man's superior intelligence enables him to rise superior to such lowly needs. But this is not the most significant point of the difference. It is true that without the much greater mental faculties of man, he could not achieve the attainments the lack of which keeps the brute chained to the limitations of his anatomy. But the greater human intelligence in itself does not cause the differences that exist. This psychic superiority is only the indispensable condition of what is peculiarly human; civilization. Directly, it is the civilization in which every Eskimo, every Alaskan miner or arctic discoverer is reared, and not any greater inborn faculty, that leads him to build houses, ignite fire, and wear clothing. The distinction between animal and man which counts is not that of the physical and mental, which is one of relative degree, but that of the organic and social which is one of kind. The beast has mentality, and we have bodies; but in civilization man has something that no animal has.

That this distinction is actually something more than that of the physical and mental, appears from an example that may be chosen from the non-bodily: speech.

On the surface, human and animal speech, in spite of the enormously greater richness and complexity of the former, are much alike. Both express emotions, possibly ideas, in sounds formed by bodily organs and understood by the hearing individual. But the difference between the so-called language of brutes and that of men is infinitely great; as a homely illustration will set forth.

A newly-born pup is brought up in a litter of kittens by a fostering cat. Familiar anecdotes and newspaper paragraphs to the contrary, the youngster will bark and growl, not purr or miaow. He will not even try to do the latter. The first time his toe is stepped on, he will whine, not squeal, just as surely as when thoroughly angered he will bite as his never-beheld mother did, and not even attempt to claw as he has seen his foster-mother do. For half his life seclusion may keep him from sight or sound or scent of another dog. But then let a bark or a snarl reach him through the restraining wall, and he will be all attention—more than at any voice ever uttered by his cat associates. Let the bark be repeated, and interest will give way to excitement, and he will answer in kind, as certainly as, put with a bitch, the sexual impulses of his

species will manifest themselves. It cannot be doubted that dog speech is ineradicably part of dog nature, as fully contained in it without training or culture, as wholly part of the dog organism, as are teeth or feet or stomach or motions or instincts. No degree of contact with cats, or deprivation of association with his own kind, can make a dog acquire cat speech, or lose his own, any more than it can cause him to switch his tail instead of wagging it, to rub his sides against his master instead of leaping against him, or to grow whiskers and carry his drooping ears erect.

Let us take a French baby, born in France of French parents, themselves descended for numerous generations from French-speaking ancestors. Let us, at once after birth, entrust the infant to a mute nurse, with instructions to let no one handle or see her charge, while she travels by the directest route to the interior heart of China. There she delivers the child to a Chinese couple, who legally adopt it, and rear it as their son. Now suppose three or ten or thirty years passed. Is it needful to discuss what the growing or grown Frenchman will speak? Not a word of French; pure Chinese, without a trace of accent and with Chinese fluency; and nothing else.

It is true that there is a common delusion, frequent even among educated people, that some hidden influence of his French-talking ancestors will survive in the adopted Chinaman: that it is only necessary to send him to France with a batch of real Chinamen, and he will acquire his mother's tongue with appreciably greater facility, fluency, correctness, and naturalness than his Mongolian companions. That a belief is common, however, is as likely to stamp it a common superstition as a common truth. And a reasonable biologist, in other words, an expert qualified to speak of heredity, will pronounce this answer to this problem in heredity, superstition. He might merely choose a politer phrase.

Now there is something deep-going here. No amount of association with Chinese would turn our young Frenchman's eyes from blue to black, or slant them, or flatten his nose, or coarsen or stiffen his wavy, oval-sectioned hair; and yet his speech is totally that of his associates, in no measure that of his blood kin. His eyes and his nose and his hair are his from heredity; his language is non-hereditary—as much so as the length to which he allows his hair to grow, or the hole which, in conformity to fashion, he may or may not bore in his ears. It is not so much that speech is mental and facial proportions are physical; the distinction that has meaning and use is that human language is non-hereditary and social, eye-color and nose-shape hereditary and organic. By the same criterion, dog speech, and all that is vaguely called the language of animals, is in a class with men's noses, the proportions of their bones, the color of their skin, and the slope of their eyes, and not in a class with any human idiom. It is inherited, and therefore organic. By a human standard, it is not really language at all, except by the sort of metaphor that speaks of the language of the flowers.

It is true that now and then a French child would be found that under the conditions of the experiment assumed, would learn Chinese more slowly, less idiomatically, and with less power of expression, than the average Chinaman. But there would also be French babies, and as many, that would acquire the Chinese language more quickly, more fluently, with richer power of revealing their emotions and defining their ideas, than the normal Chinese. These are individual differences, which it would be absurd to deny, but which do not affect the average, and are not to the point. One Englishman speaks better English, and more of it, than another, and he may also through precocity, learn it much sooner; but one talks English no more and no less truly than the other.

There is one form of animal expression in which the influence of association has sometimes been alleged to be greater than that of heredity. This is the song of birds. There is a good deal of conflicting opinion, and apparently of evidence, on this point. Many birds have a strong inherent impulse to imitate sounds. It is also a fact that the singing of one individual stimulates the other—as with dogs, wolves, cats, frogs, and most noisy animals. That in certain species of birds capable of a complex song the full development will not often be reached in individuals raised out of hearing of their kind, may probably be admitted. But it seems to be clear that every species has a song or call distinctively its own; that this minimum is attainable without association by every normal member of the singing sex, as soon as conditions of age, food, and warmth are proper, and the requisite stimulus of noise, or silence, or sex development, is present. That there has been serious conflict of opinion as to the nature of bird song, will ultimately be found to be chiefly due to the pronouncement of opinions on the matter by those who read their own mental states and activities into animals—a common fallacy that every biological student is now carefully trained against at the outset of his career. In any event, whether one bird does or does not in some degree "learn" from another, there is no fragment of evidence that bird song is a tradition, that like human speech or human music it accumulates and develops from age to age, that it is inevitably altered from generation to generation by fashion or custom, and that it is impossible for it ever to remain the same: in other words, that it is a social thing or due to a process even remotely akin to those affecting the constituents of human civilization.

It is also true that there is in human life a series of utterances that are of the type of animal cries. A man in pain moans without purpose of communication. The sound is literally pressed from him. A person in supreme fright may shriek. We know that his cry is unintended, what the physiologist calls a reflex action. The true shriek is as liable to escape the victim pinned before the approaching engineerless train, as him who is pursued by thinking and planning enemies. The woodsman crushed by a rock forty miles from the nearest human being, will moan like the run-over city dweller surrounded by a crowd waiting for the speeding ambulance. Such cries are of a class with those of animals. In fact, really to understand the "speech" of brutes, we must think ourselves into a condition in which our utterances would be totally restricted to such instinctive cries—"inarticulate" is their general though often inaccurate designation. In an exact sense, they are not language at all.

This is precisely the point. We undoubtedly have certain activities of utterance, certain faculties and habits of sound production, that are truly parallel with those of animals; and we also have something more that is quite different and without parallel among the animals. To deny that something purely animal underlies human speech, is fatuous; but it would be equally narrow to believe that because our speech springs from an animal foundation, and originated in this foundation, it therefore is nothing but animal mentality and utterances greatly magnified. A house may be built on rock; without this base it might be impossible for it to have been erected; but no one will maintain that therefore the house is nothing but improved and glorified stone.

As a matter of fact, the purely animal element in human speech is small. Apart from laughter and crying, it finds rare utterance. Our interjections are denied by philologists as true speech, or at best but half admitted. It is a fact that they differ from full words in not being voiced, generally, to convey a meaning—nor to conceal one. But even these particles are shaped and dictated by fashion, by custom, by the type of civilization to which we belong, in short by social and not by organic elements. When I drive the hammer on my thumb instead of on the head of the nail, an involuntary "damn" may escape me as readily if I am alone in the house, as if companions stand on each side. Perhaps more readily. So far, the exclamation does not serve the purpose of speech and is not speech. But the Spaniard will say "carramba" and not "damn"; and the Frenchman, the German, the Chinaman, will avail himself of still different expression. The American says "outch" when hurt. Other nationalities do not understand this syllable. Each people has its own sound; some even two—one used by men and the other by women. A Chinaman will understand a laugh, a moan, a crying child, as well as we understand it, and as well as a dog understands the snarl of another dog. But he must learn "outch," or it is meaningless. No dog, on the other hand, ever has given utterance to a new snarl, unintelligible to other dogs, as a result of having been brought up in different associations. Even this lowest element of human speech, then, this involuntary half-speech of exclamations, is therefore shaped by social influences.

Herodotus tells of an Egyptian king, who, wishing to ascertain the parent tongue of humanity, had some infants brought up in isolation from their own kind, with only goats as companions and for sustenance. When the children, grown older, were revisited, they cried the word "bekos," or, subtracting the ending which the normalizing and sensitive Greek could not endure omitting from anything that passed his lips, more probably "bek." The king then sent to all countries to learn in what land this vocable meant something. He ascertained that in the Phrygian idiom it signified bread, and, assuming that the children were crying for food, concluded that they spoke Phrygian in voicing their "natural" human speech, and that this tongue must therefore be the original one of mankind. The king's belief in an inherent and congenital language of man, which only the blind accidents of time had distorted into a multitude of idioms, may seem simple; but naïve as it is, inquiry would reveal crowds of civilized people still adhering to it.

This however is not our moral to the tale. That lies in the fact that the one and only word attributed to the children, "bek," was, if the story has any authenticity whatsoever, only a reflection or imitation—as the commentators of Herodotus long since conjectured—of the bleating of the goats that were the children's only associates and instructors. In short, if it is allowable to deduce any inference from so apocryphal an anecdote, what it proves is that there is no natural and therefore no organic human language.

Thousands of years later another sovereign, the Mogul emperor Akbar, repeated the experiment with the intent of ascertaining the "natural" religion of mankind. His band of children were shut up in a house. When, the necessary time having elapsed, the doors were opened in the presence of the expectant and enlightened ruler, his disappointment was great: the children trooped out as dumb as deaf-mutes. Faith dies hard, however; and we may suspect that it would take a third trial, under modern chosen and controlled conditions, to satisfy some natural scientists that speech, for the human individual and for the human race, is wholly an acquired and not a hereditary thing, entirely outward and not at all inward—a social product and not an organic growth.

Human and animal speech, then, though one roots in the other, are in the nature of a different order. They resemble each other only as the flight of a bird and of an aeronaut are alike. That the analogy between them has frequently deceived, proves only the guilelessness of the human mind. The operative processes are wholly unlike; and this, to him who is desirous of understanding, is far more important than the similarity of effect. The savage and the peasant who cure by cleaning the knife and leaving the wound unattended, have observed certain indisputable facts. They know that cleanness aids, dirt on the whole impedes recovery. They know the knife as the cause, the wound as the effect; and they grasp, too, the correct principle that treatment of the cause is in general more likely to be effective than treatment of the symptom. They fail only in not inquiring into the process that may be involved. Knowing nothing of the nature of sepsis, of bacteria, of the agencies of putrefaction and retardation of healing, they fall back on agencies more familiar to themselves, and use, as best they may, the process of magic intertwined with that of medicine. They carefully scrape the knife; they oil it; they keep it bright. The facts from which they work are correct; their logic is sound enough; they merely do not distinguish between two irreconcilable processes—that of magic and that of physiological chemistry—and apply one in place of another. The student of today who reads the civilizationally moulded mind of men into the mentality of a dog or ape, or who tries to explain civilization—that is, history—by organic factors, commits an error which is less antiquated and more in fashion, but of the same kind and nature.

It is only in small measure a question

of high and low as between man and animal. Many purely instinctive activities of the beasts lead to far more complex and difficult achievements than some of the analogous customs of this or that human nation. The beaver is a better architect than many a savage tribe. He fells larger trees, he drags them farther, he builds a closer house; he constructs it both below and above water; and he does what many nations never attempt to do: he makes himself a suitable topography for a habitat by erecting a dam. But the essential point is not that after all a man can do more than a beaver, or a beaver as much as a man; it is that what a beaver accomplishes he does by one means, and a man by another. The rudest savage, who builds but a shack of a wind-pierced hut, can be taught, innumerable times has been taught, to saw and nail together boards, to mortar stone on stone, to sink foundations, to rear an iron frame. All human history concerns itself primarily with just such changes. What were the ancestors of ourselves, of us steel-building Europeans and Americans, but hut-dwelling savages of a few thousand years ago—a period so short that it may barely suffice for the formation of an occasional new species of organism? And on the other side, who would be so rash as to affirm that ten thousand generations of example and instruction would convert the beaver from what he is into a carpenter or a bricklayer—or, allowing for his physical deficiency in the lack of hands, into a planning engineer?

The divergence between social and organic forces is perhaps not fully grasped until the mentality of the so-called social insects, the bees and ants, is thoroughly realized. Social the ant is, in the sense that she associates; but she is so far from being social in the sense of possessing civilization, of being influenced by non-organic forces, that she would better be known as the anti-social animal. The marvelous powers of the ant cannot be underestimated. There is no one to whom the full exploitation of their understanding will be of more service than to the historian. But he will not use this understanding by applying his knowledge of ant mentality to man. He will use it to fortify and render precise by intelligent contrast, his conception of the agencies that mould human civilization. Ant society is as little a true society, in the human sense, as a caricature is a portrait.

Take a few ant eggs of the proper sexes—unhatched eggs, freshly laid. Blot out every individual and every other egg of the species. Give the pair a little attention as regards warmth, moisture, protection, and food. The whole of ant "society," every one of the abilities, powers, accomplishments, and activities of the species, each "thought" that it has ever had, will be reproduced, and reproduced without diminution, in one generation. But place on a desert island or in a circumvallation two or three hundred human infants of the best stock from the highest class of the most civilized nation; furnish them the necessary incubation and nourishment; leave them in total isolation from their kind; and what shall we have? The civilization from which they were torn? One tenth of it? No, not any fraction; nor a fraction of the civilizational attainments of the rudest savage tribe. Only a pair or a troop of mutes, without arts, knowledge, fire, without order or religion. Civilization would be wiped out within these confines—not disintegrated, not cut to the quick, but obliterated in one sweep. Heredity saves for the ant all that she has, from generation to generation. But heredity does not maintain, and has not maintained, because it cannot maintain, one particle of the civilization which is the specifically human thing.

The mental activity of the animals is partly instinctive, partly based on individual experience; the content, at least, of our own minds comes to us through tradition, in the widest sense of the word. Instinct is what is "pricked in"; an unalterable pattern inherent in the goods; indelible and inextinguishable, because the design is nothing but the warp and the woof, coming ready-made from the loom of heredity.

But tradition, what is "given through," handed along, from one to another, is only a message. It must of course be carried; but the messenger after all is extrinsic to the news. So, a letter must be written; but as its significance is in the meaning of the words, as the value of a note is not in the fiber of the paper but in the characters inscribed on its surface, so tradition is something super-added to the organisms that bear it, imposed upon them, external to them. And as the same shred can bear any one of thousands of inscriptions, of the most diverse force and value, and can even be tolerably razed and reinscribed, so it is with the human organism and the countless contents that civilization can pour into it. The essential difference between animal and man, in this illustration, is not that the latter has finer grain or the chaster quality of material; it is that his structure and nature and texture are such that he is inscribable, and that the animal is not. Chemically and physically, there is little difference between a lump of pulp and a sheet of paper. Chemically and physically, it is of slight consequence to trouble about such minute difference. But chemically and physically there is still less difference between the treasury note stamped with "one" and that stamped with "thousand"; and yet less between the check with an honored signature and that written with the same pen, the same ink, the same strokes even, by a forger. The difference that counts between the valid and the counterfeit check, is not the broader or the narrow line, the continuous curve of a letter in place of the broken one, but the purely social one that one signer has a valid account in the bank and the other has not; which fact is surely extrinsic to the paper and even to the ink upon it.

Exactly parallel to this is the relation of the instinctive and traditional, the organic and the social. The animal, so far as social influences are concerned, is as unsuitable as a dish of porridge is for writing material; or when like the beach sand, it is inscribable, by domestication, it can retain no permanent impression, as a species. Hence it has no society, and therefore no history. Man, however, comprises two aspects: he is an organic substance, that can be viewed as a substance, and he is also a tablet that is written upon. One aspect is as valid and as justifiable as another; but it is a cardinal mistake to confuse the two views.

The mason builds in granite and roofs with slate. The child learning its letters knows nothing of the qualities of its slate, but puzzles whether to write *c* or *k*. The mineralogist gives no precedence to one of the stones over the other; each has a constitution, a structure, properties, and uses. The educator ignores the granite; but, though he uses the slate, he does not therefore rate it higher, or deny the serviceability of the other material; he takes his substance as he finds it. His problem is whether the child should begin with words or letters; at what age, for what hours, in what sequence, and under what conditions, its education toward literacy should commence. To decide these issues upon crystallogical evidence because his pupils write upon a variety of stone would be as futile as if the geologist were to employ his knowledge of rocks for inferences as to the soundest principles of pedagogy.

So, if the student of human achievement were to try to withdraw from the observation of the natural historian and the mechanical philosopher the human beings upon whom is inscribed the civilization which he himself investigates, he would be ridiculous. And when on the other hand, the biologist proposes to rewrite history, in whole or in part, through the medium of heredity, he reveals himself in little more favorable light, though he would have the sanction of some precedent.

There have been many attempts to make precise the distinction between instinct and civilization, between the organic and the social, between animal and man. Man as the clothing animal, the fire-using animal, the tool-using or tool-making animal, the speaking animal, are all summations that contain some approximation. But for the conception of the discrimination that is at once most complete and most compact, we must go back, as for the first precise expression of so many of the ideas with which we operate, to the unique mind that impelled Aristotle. "Man is a political animal." The word political has changed in import. We use instead the Latin term social. This, both philosopher and philologist tell us, is what the great Greek would have said were he speaking in English today. Man is a social animal, then; a social organism. He has organic constitution; but he has also civilization. To ignore one element is as short-sighted as to overlook the other; to convert one into the other, if each has its reality, is negation. With this basic formulation more than two thousand years old, and known to all the generations, there is something puny, as well as obtinately destructive, in the endeavor to abrogate the distinction, or to hinder its completest fruition. The attempt today to treat the social as organic, to understand civilization as hereditary, is as essentially narrow as the alleged mediaeval inclination to withdraw man from the realm of nature and from the ken of the scientist because he was believed to possess an immaterial soul.

But unfortunately the denials, and for every denial a dozen confusions, still persist. They pervade the popular mind; and thence they rise, again and again, into the thoughts of avowed and recognized science. It seems, even, that in a hundred years we have retrograded. A century and two centuries ago, with a generous impulse, the leaders of thought devoted their energies, and the leaders of men their lives, to the cause that all men are equal. With all that this idea involves, and with its correctness, we need not here concern ourselves; but it certainly implied the proposition of equality of racial capacity. Possibly our ancestors were able to maintain this liberal stand because its full practical imports did not yet face them. But, whatever the reason, we have certainly gone back, in America and in Europe and in their colonies, in our application of the assumption; and we have receded too in our theoretic analysis of the evidence. Hereditary racial differences of ability pass as approved doctrine, in many quarters. There are men of eminent learning who would be surprised to know that serious doubts were held in the matter.

And yet, it must be maintained that little really satisfactory evidence has been produced to support the assumption that the differences which one nation shows from another—let alone the superiority of one people to another—are racially inherent, that is organically founded. It does not matter how distinguished the minds are that have held such differences to be hereditary— they have in the main only taken their conviction for granted. The sociologist or anthropologist can, and occasionally does, turn the case inside out with equal justification; and he then sees every event, every inequality, the whole course of human history, confirming his thesis that the distinctions between one group of men and another, past and present, are due to social influences and not to organic causes. Real proof, to be sure, is as wanting on one side as on the other. Experiment, under conditions that would yield satisfying evidence, would be difficult, costly, and perhaps contrary to law. A repetition of Akbar's interesting trial, or some modification of it, intelligently directed and followed out, would yield results of the greatest value; but it would scarcely yet be tolerated by a civilized government.

There have been some attempts to investigate so-called racial distinctions with the apparatus of experimental psychology. The results incline superficially toward confirmation of organic differences. But too much stress may not as yet be laid on this conclusion, because what such investigations have above all revealed is that social agencies are so tremendously influential on every one of us that it is difficult to find any test which, if distinctive racial faculties were inborn, would fairly reveal the degree to which they are inborn.

It is also well to remember that the problem of whether the human races are or are not in themselves identical, has innumerable practical bearings, which relate to conditions of life and to views that have emotional relations, so that an impartially abstract predisposition is rather rarely to be encountered. It is practically futile, for instance, even to touch upon the question with most Americans from the Southern states, or those tinged by Southern influences, no matter what their education or standing in the world. The actual social cleavage which is fundamental to all life in the South, and which is conceived of mainly as a race question, is so overshadowing and inevitable, that it compels, for the individual almost as firmly as for his group, a certain line of action, an unalterable and conscious course of conduct; and it could not well be otherwise than that opinions which flagrantly clash with one's habitual activities

and with their associated ideals, should arouse hostility. It is then but natural if the Southerner frequently receives the profession of racial equality, when it can be made to carry the conviction of sincerity to him, as an affront; and that he often meets even the most abstract, impersonal, and judicial consideration of the issues involved, with resentment, or, where this is checked by courtesy, with internal dissatisfaction.

The attitude of the Englishman in India, of the continental European in his colonies, is perhaps less extremely manifested; but all accounts indicate that it is no less settled.

On the other hand, the avowed and thoroughgoing Socialist or Internationalist must take the opposite stand, however unsympathetic it may be to him personally, or renounce the aspirations that he holds dear. His inclination therefore, if generally less clearly defined, is no less predetermined and persistent.

Impartiality is thus not to be expected in this great case, except in some measure on the part of really detached and therefore uninfluential students; so that the maximum of assertion and rancor, and minimum of evidence, which prevail, are to be accepted as regrettable indeed, but as unavoidable and scarcely to be censured.

The problem, being in the present state of our knowledge unprovable, is really also not arguable. What is possible, however, is to realize that a complete and consistent explanation can be given, for so-called racial differences, on a basis of purely civilizational and non-organic causes; and to attain also to the recognition that the mere fact of the world in general assuming that such differences between one people and another are inborn and ineradicable except by breeding, is no evidence in favor of the assumption being true.

The final argument, that one can actually *see* such national peculiarities born into each generation, and that it is unnecessary to verify the assumption because its truth is obvious to every one, has the least weight of all. It is of a kind with the contention that might be made that this planet is after all the fixed central point of the cosmic system because everyone can see for himself that the sun and stars move and that our earth stands still. The champions of the Copernican doctrine had this in their favor: they dealt with phenomena to which exactitude was readily applicable, about which verifiable or disprovable predictions could be made, which an explanation either fitted or did not fit. In the domain of human history this is not possible, or has not yet been found possible; so that an equal neatness of demonstration, a definitiveness of proof, a close tallying of theory with the facts to the exclusion of all rival theories, is not to be hoped for at present. But there is almost as fundamental a shifting of mental and emotional point of view, as absolute a turning upside down of attitude involved when the current thought of today is asked to view civilization as a nonorganic affair, as when the Copernican doctrine challenged the prior conviction of the world.

Most ethnologists, at any rate, are convinced that the overwhelming mass of historical and miscalled racial facts that are now attributed to obscure organic causes, or at most are in dispute, will ultimately be viewed by everyone as social and as best intelligible in their social relations. That there may be a residuum in which hereditary influences have been operative, it would be dogmatic to deny; but even this residuum of organic agencies will perhaps be found to be operative in quite other manners than those which are customarily adduced at present.

The opinion may further be uncompromisingly maintained, that for the historian—him who wishes to understand any sort of social phenomena—it is an unavoidable necessity, today, to disregard the organic as such and to deal only with the social. For the larger number who are not professional students of civilization, insistence upon these articles would be an unreasonable demand, under our present inability to substantiate them by proof. On the other hand, the social as something distinct from the organic is an old enough concept, and is a plain enough phenomenon about us in daily life, to warrant the claim that it cannot be outright dispensed with. It is perhaps too much to expect any one wedded, deliberately or unknowingly, to organic explanations, to discard these wholly in the face of such incomplete evidence as is available to the contrary of these explanations. But it does seem justifiable to stand unhesitatingly on the proposition that civilization and heredity are two things that operate in separate ways; that therefore any outright substitution of one for the other in the explanation of human group phenomena is crass; and that the refusal to recognize at least the possibility of an explanation of human achievement totally different from the prevailing tendency toward a biological explanation, is an act of illiberality. When once such recognition, of the rationality of this attitude of mind which is diametrically opposed to the current one, shall have become general, far more progress will have been made on the road towards a useful agreement as to the truth, than by any present attempts to win converts by argument.

One of the minds endowed with as eminent power of perception and formulation as any of the last generation, Gustave Le Bon, whose name ranks high even if his regardless fearlessness has gained him but little of an avowed following, has carried the interpretation of the social as organic to its consistent consequence. His *Psychology of Peoples* is an attempt to explain civilization on the basis of race. Le Bon is really an historian of unusually keen sensitiveness and perspicacity. But his professed attempt to resolve the civilizational materials with which he deals, directly into organic factors, leads him on the one hand to renounce his skilful interpretations of history until only intermittent flashes remain; and on the other hand, to rest his professed solutions ultimately on such mystic essences as the "soul of a race." As a scientific concept or tool, a race soul is as intangible and useless as a phrase of mediaeval philosophy, and on a par with Le Bon's ready declaration that the individual is to the race as the cell is to the body. If instead of soul of the race, the distinguished Frenchman had said spirit of civilization, or tendency or character of culture, his pronouncements would have commanded less appeal, because seeming vaguer; but he would not have had to rest his thought upon a supernatural idea antagonistic to the body of science to which he was trying to attach his work; and if nonmechanistic, his efforts at explanation would at least have earned the respect of historians.

As a matter of fact, Le Bon clearly operates with social phenomena, however insistently he gives them organic names and proclaims that he has resolved them organically. That "not the 18 Brumaire but the soul of his race established Napoleon," is biologically, and under any aspect of the science that deals with mechanical causality, a meaningless statement; but it becomes excellent history as soon as for "race" we substitute "civilization," and of course take "soul" in a metaphorical sense.

When he says that "cross breeding destroys an ancient civilization" he affirms only what many a biologist would be ready to maintain. When he adds: "because it destroys the soul of the people that possess it," he gives a reason that must inspire a scientist with a shudder. But if we change "cross breeding,"

that is, the mixture of sharply differentiated organic types, into "sudden contact or conflict of ideals," that is, mixture of sharply differentiated social types, the profound effect of such an event is indisputable.

Again, Le Bon asserts that the effect of environment is great on new races, on races forming through cross breeding of peoples of contrary heredities; and that in ancient races solidly established by heredity the effect of environment is nearly nil. It is obvious that in an old and firm civilization the actively changing effect of geographical environment must be small because the civilization has long since had ample opportunity to utilize the environment for its needs; but that on the other hand when the civilization is new—whether because of its transportation, because of its proceeding fusion from several elements, or from mere internal development—the renewing of relationship between itself and the surrounding physical geography must go on at a rapid rate. Here again good history is turned into bad science by a confusion that seems almost deliberately perverse.

A people is guided far more by its dead than by its living, Le Bon says. He is trying to establish the importance of heredity on national careers. What, though unrecognized by himself, lies at the bottom of his thought, is the truth that every civilization rests in the past, that however much its ancient elements are no longer living as such, they nevertheless form its trunk and body, around which the live sap-wood of the day is only a shell and a surface. That imposed education, a formal and conscious thing, can not give the substance of a new or another civilization to a people, is a verity that Le Bon has seized with vigor. But when he deduces this maxim as an inference from the unbridgeable abyss that externally exists between races, he rests an obvious fact, which no person of discrimination has yet disputed, upon a mystical assertion.

It might nearly have been foreseen, after the above citations, that Le Bon would lay the "character" of his "races" to "accumulation by heredity." It has already been shown that if there is anything that heredity does not do, it is to accumulate. If, on the other hand, there is any one method by which civilization may be defined as operating, it is precisely that of accumulation. We add the power of flight, the understanding of the mechanism of the aeroplane, to our previous accomplishments and knowledges. The bird does not; he has given up his legs and toes for wings. It may be true that the bird is on the whole a higher organism than his reptilian ancestor, that he has traveled farther on the road of development. But his advance has been achieved by a transmutation of qualities, a conversion of organs and faculties, not by an increasing summation of them.

The whole theory of heredity by acquirement rests upon the confusion of these two so diverse processes, that of heredity and that of civilization. It has been nourished, perhaps, by unsatisfied needs of biological science, but it has never obtained the slightest unchallengeable verification from biology, and has in fact long been assailed, by a sound and vigorous instinct, as well as in consequence of the failure of observation and experiment, from within that science. It is a doctrine that is the constant blazon of the dilettante who knows something of both history and life, but has no care to understand the workings of either. Le Bon's studies being an attempt to explain one by the other, his utilization, sooner or later, of the doctrine of heredity by acquisition or accumulation, could almost have been predicted.

From a different and less aggressive temperament springs the wail that Lester Ward has voiced for a wide and aspiringly earnest element. Heredity by acquirement must take place, he argues, or there would be no hope of permanent progress for humanity. To believe that what we have gained will not be at least in part implanted in our children, removes the incentive to effort. All the labor bestowed upon the youth of the world would be in vain. Mental qualities are not subject to natural selection; hence they must be accumulated in man by acquirement and fixed by heredity. This view may be heard again and again from people who have arrived at the attitude through their own reflections, who have probably never read Ward directly or indirectly, and whose world seems to crash when its foundation of heredity is shaken. It is, if not a deep view, a common one; and for that reason Ward's formulation is, however worthless intrinsically, representative and significant. It reveals the tenacity, the insistence, with which many conscientious intellects of the day will not and can not see the social except through the glass of the organic. That this habit of mind can itself be depressing, that it forever prelimits development and eternally chains the future to the poverties and paucities of the present, does not dawn upon its devotees; is in fact probably the fixity which gives it its emotional hold.

It would seem probable that the greatest of the champions of acquired heredity, Herbert Spencer, was led to his stand by a similar motive. The precise method by which organic evolution takes place is after all essentially a biological problem, and not a philosophical one. Spencer, however, like Comte, was a sociologist as much as a philosopher. That he should have contested so stubbornly what in itself is a technical question of biology, is hardly intelligible except on the supposition that he felt the question to bear vitally on his principles; and that, in spite of his happy coinage of the term which has been prefixed as title to the present essay, he did not adequately conceive of human society as holding a specific content that is non-organic.

When R. R. Marett, in opening his *Anthropology*—one of the most stimulating books produced in this field—defines the science as "the whole history of man as fired and pervaded by the idea of evolution," and adds that "anthropology is the child of Darwin—Darwinism makes it possible," he is unfortunately depicting the recent condition of this science with some truth; but as a program or an ideal his delineation must be challenged. Anthropology may be biology; it may be history; it may be an attempt to ascertain the relations of the two; but as history, the study of the social, shot through with the idea of organic evolution, it would be a jumble of diverse methods, and therefore no science in any sense of the term.

Of all the comminglings of the cultural with the vital, that which has crystallized under the name of the eugenics movement is the most widely known and of directest appeal. As a constructive program for national progress, eugenics is a confusion of the purposes to breed better men and to give men better ideals; an organic device to attain the social; a biological short cut to a moral end. It contains the inherent impossibility of all short cuts. It is more refined but no less vain than the short cut which the savage follows, when, to avoid the trouble and danger of killing his foe in the body, he pierces, in safety and amid objurgations uttered in the convenience of his own home, a miniature image addressed by the name of the enemy. Eugenics, so far as it is more than an endeavor at social hygiene in a new field, is a fallacy; a mirage like the philosopher's stone, the elixir of life, the ring of Solomon, or the material efficacy of prayer. There is little to argue about it. If social phenomena are only or mainly organic, eugenics is

right, and there is nothing more to be said. If the social is something more than the organic, eugenics is an error of unclear thought.

Galton, the founder of the eugenics propaganda, was one of the most truly imaginative intellects produced by his country. Pearson, its distinguished living protagonist with scientific weapons, possesses one of the keenest minds of the generation. Hundreds of men of ability and eminence have professed themselves converts. It is plain that a simple fallacy must have presented itself in an envelope of enticing complications to be acceptable to them. Such men have not confounded important things that are intrinsically distinct, without a good reason. The explanation that Galton, Pearson, and the majority of the most creative of their followers were professional biologists, and therefore inclined to see the world through the lenses of the organic, is insufficient. Mere interest in one factor does not lead thinking minds practically to deny the existence of other factors. What then is the reason of the confusion into which they have precipitated themselves?

The cause seems to be a failure to distinguish between the social and the mental. All civilization in a sense exists only in the mind. Gunpowder, textile arts, machinery, laws, telephones are not themselves transmitted from man to man or from generation to generation, at least not permanently. It is the perception, the knowledge and understanding of them, their *ideas* in the Platonic sense, that are passed along. Everything social can have existence only through mentality. Of course, civilization is not mental action itself; it is carried by men, without being in them. But its relation to mind, its absolute rooting in human faculty, is obvious.

What, then, has occurred is that biology, which correlates and often identifies the "physical" and the mental, has gone one natural but as yet unjustified step further, and assumed the social as mental; whence the explanation of civilization in physiological and mechanical terms was an unavoidable consequence.

Now, the correlation by modern science of the physical and mental is certainly correct. That is, it is justifiable as a method which can be consistently employed toward a coherent explanation of phenomena, and which leads to intellectually satisfactory and practically useful results. The correlation of the two sets of phenomena is made, or admitted, by all psychologists; it clearly holds for all faculties and instincts; and it has some definite physiological and chemical corroboration, though of a more crude and less completely established kind than is sometimes imagined. At any rate, this correlation is an unchallenged axiom of those who concern themselves with science: all mental equipment and all mental activity have an organic basis. And that is sufficient for present purposes.

This inseparability of physical and mental must be true also in the field of heredity. It is well known that where instincts are definite or specialized, as in insects, they are inherited as absolutely as are organs or structure. It is a matter of common experience that our own mental traits vary as much and as frequently tally with those of ancestors, as physical features. There is no logical reason, and nothing in the observation of daily life, that operates against the belief that an irascible temper is as heritable as the red hair with which it is traditionally associated, and that certain forms of musical aptitude may be as wholly congenital as blue eyes.

Of course there is much false inference in these matters, as regards man, through the interpretation of accomplishment as evidenc of the degree of faculty. The discrimination of the two is not always easy; it frequently requires painstakingly acquired knowledge of facts, as well as careful judgment; and popular reasoning is likely to be scant of both. A powerful congenital faculty may establish the father successfully in a pursuit. This in turn may give an environmental influence, or a deliberate training, that will elevate the mediocre son, so far as his attainments are concerned, far above what his unaided natural faculties would have secured for him, and above many another individual of greater inherent capacities. The earning of a million is normally an indication of ability; but it normally requires intenser ability to earn a million after starting with nothing than to begin with a million received as a gift and increase it to three. That a musician is more frequently the son of a musician than not, at least when relative numbers are taken into account, is in itself no evidence at all that musical talent is heritable, for we know of purely social influences, such as Hindu caste, which attain similar results with far greater regularity than any one can assert heredity plus social influences to bring about among ourselves.

But it would be as unreasonable to exaggerate this caution into an outright denial of mental heredity, as to disregard it entirely.

There is then nothing in an off-hand survey of the situation to lead to a disbelief, and a large body of common experience to confirm the conviction, that characters of mind are subject to heredity much like traits of the body.

In addition, there is some proof, which, although not extensive, is hard to resist. Galton, in a fairly large series of records, has found the amount of regression—a quantitative index of the potency of heredity—to be the same for artistic faculty as for bodily stature. In another work he has investigated the blood relatives of eminent men, with the finding that eminence occurs among them with a frequency and in a degree exactly like the influence of heredity in respect to physical characters. Pearson has ascertained that the correlation—the degree of resemblance, quantitatively expressed, of phenomena available in numbers—between brothers is substantially the same for conscientiousness as for the shape of the head, for intellectual ability as for hair color, and so forth for other mental or moral and physical qualities. There is of course the possibility that in the data that underlie these results, as well as Galton's, there has been some confounding of temper with bad manners, of native intelligence with training of the intellect, of congenital artistic faculty with cultivated taste. But the attention of those who have made the records seems to have been pretty definitely directed to innate individual traits. Further, all the coefficients or figures for the inheritance of these psychic characteristics agree as closely as could be expected with the corresponding ones relating to bodily features. The case may therefore be fairly regarded as substantially proved, at least until new evidence is available.

In spite of a wide acceptance of these demonstrations, especially by those predisposed to sympathize with biological progress, they have also met with some opposition, and with more ignoring than their bearing on a question of general interest warranted. In part this negative attitude may be due to a persistence of religious beliefs, in the main already superseded but not yet defunct, that center around the old concept of the soul, and which see in every linkage of mind and body an effacement of the cherished distinction of body and soul. But this belated conservatism will not account for all the failure of the Galton-Pearson demonstrations to meet universal acceptance or arouse wide enthusiasms.

The remainder of the opposition has been caused by Galton, Pearson, and their adherents themselves, who have not confined themselves to their well-supported conclusions, but have pressed on to further inferences that rest only on assertion. That heredity operates in the domain of mind as well as that of the body, is one thing; that therefore heredity is the mainspring of civilization, is an entirely different proposition, without necessary connection and without established connection with the former conclusion. To maintain both doctrines, the second as a necessary corollary of the first, has been the habit of the biological school; and the consequence has been that those whose intellectual inclinations were otherwise, or who followed another method of research, have avowedly or tacitly rejected both propositions.

The reason why mental heredity has so little if anything to do with civilization, is that civilization is not mental action but a body or stream of products of mental exercise. Mental activity, as biologists have dealt with it, being organic, any demonstration concerning it consequently proves nothing whatever as to social events. Mentality relates to the individual. The social or cultural, on the other hand, is in its essence non-individual. Civilization, as such, begins only where the individual ends; and whoever does not in some measure perceive this fact, even though only as a brute and rootless one, can find no meaning in civilization, and history for him must be only a wearying jumble, or an opportunity for the exercise of art.

All biology necessarily has this direct reference to the individual. A social mind is as meaningless a nonentity as a social body. There can be only one kind of organicness: the organic on another plane would no longer be organic. The Darwinian doctrine relates, it is true, to the race; but the race, except as an abstraction, is only a collection of individuals; and the bases of this doctrine, heredity, variation, and competition, deal with the relation of individual to individual, from individual, and against individual. The whole key of the success of the Mendelian methods of studying heredity lies in isolating traits and isolating individuals.

But a thousand individuals do not make a society. They are the potential basis of a society; but they do not themselves cause it; and they are also the basis of a thousand other potential societies.

The findings of biology as to heredity, mental and physical alike, may then, in fact must be, accepted without reservation. But that therefore civilization can be understood by psychological analysis, or explained by observations or experiments in heredity, or, to revert to a concrete example, that the destiny of nations can be predicted from an analysis of the organic constitution of their members, assumes that society is merely a collection of individuals; that civilization is only an aggregate of psychic activities and not also an entity beyond them; in short, that the social can be wholly resolved into the mental as it is thought this resolves into the physical.

It is accordingly in this point of the tempting leap from the individually mental to the culturally social which presupposes but does not contain mentality, that the source of the distracting transferences of the organic into the social is to be sought. A more exact examination of the relation of the two is therefore desirable.

In a brilliant essay written, under Pearsonian influence, on heredity in twins, Thorndike arrives anew, and by a convincing use of statistical evidence, at the conclusion that so far as the individual is concerned heredity is everything and environment nothing; that the success of our path in life is essentially determined at birth; that the problem of whether each one of us shall outstrip his fellows or lag behind them, is settled when the parental germ cells unite, and

already long closed when the child emerges from the womb, all our careers run under the light of the sun being nothing but an unwinding, longer or shorter according to accident beyond our control, of the thread rolled on the spool before the beginning of our existence.

This finding is not only thoroughly elucidated by the author, but has the support of our common experience in life. No one can deny some measure of truth to the proverbial sow's ear that cannot be made into a silk purse. Every one numbers among his acquaintance individuals of energy, of address and skill, of what seems an uncanny prescience, or of a strength of character, that leave no doubts in our judgment that whatever their lot of birth, they would have risen above their fellows and have been marked men and women. And on the other hand, we also admit regretfully the maladroit and sluggish, the incompetent and commonplace, who, born in any station, would have been of the mediocrities or unfortunates of their time and class. That Napoleon, set in another land and era, would not have conquered a continent, is sufficiently certain. The contrary affirmation may with fairness, it seems, be said to evince an absence of understanding of history. But the belief that under other circumstances this eternal beacon flame might have remained a household lamp, that his forces would never have been called forth, that a slight change of the accidents of epoch, place, or surroundings might have left him a prosperous and contented peasant, a shopkeeper or a bureaucrat, a routine captain retired on a pension—to maintain this argues a lack or a perverted suppression of knowledge of human nature. It is important to realize that congenital differences may have but limited effect on the course of civilization. But it is equally important to realize that we may and must concede the existence of such differences and their inextinguishability.

According to a saying that is almost proverbial, and true to the degree that such commonplaces can be true, the modern schoolboy knows more than Aristotle; but this fact, if a thousand times so, does not in the least endow him with a fraction of the intellect of the great Greek. Socially—because knowledge must be a social circumstance—it is knowledge, and not the greater development of one individual or another, that counts; just as, to measure the true force of the greatness of the person, the psychologist or genetist disregards the state of general enlightenment, the varying degree of civilizational development, to make his comparisons. A hundred Aristotles among our cave-dwelling ancestors would have been Aristotles in their birthright no less; but they would have contributed far less to the advance of the science than a dozen plodding mediocrities in the twentieth century. A super-Archimedes in the ice age would have invented neither firearms nor the telegraph. Bach born in the Congo instead of Saxony could have composed not even a fragment of choral or sonata, though we can be equally confident that he would have outshone his compatriots in some manner of music. Whether or not a Bach ever had birth in Africa, is another question—one to which a negative answer cannot be given merely because no Bach has ever appeared there, a question that in fairness we must admit to be unanswered but in regard to which the student of civilization, until some demonstration has been made, can make but one reply and pursue only one course: to assume, not as an end but as a condition of method, that there have been such individuals; that genius and ability occur with substantially regular frequency, and that all races or large enough groups of men average

substantially alike and the same in qualities.

These are extreme cases, whose clearness is little likely to arouse opposition. Normally, the differences between individuals are less imposing, the types of society more similar, and the two elements involved are separable only by the exercise of some discrimination. It is then that the confusions begin. But if the factor of society and that of natal personality are distinct in the glaring examples, they are at least distinguishable in the more subtly shaded and intricate ones; provided only we wish to keep them apart.

If this is true, it follows that all so-called inventors of appliances or discoverers of thoughts of note were unusually able men, endowed from before birth with superior faculties, which the psychologist can hope to analyze and define, the physiologist to correlate with functions of organs, and the genetic biologist to investigate in their hereditary origins until he attains not only system and law but verifiable power of prediction. And, on the other hand, the content of the invention or discovery springs in no way from the make-up of the great man, or that of his ancestors, but is a product purely of the civilization into which he with millions of others is born as a meaningless and regularly recurring event. Whether he in his person becomes inventor, explorer, imitator, or user, is an affair of forces that the sciences of mechanistic causality are concerned with. Whether his invention is that of the cannon or the bow, his achievement a musical scale or a system of harmony, his formulation that of the soul or that of the categorical imperative, is not explainable by the medium of mechanistic science—at least, not by methods now at the command of biological science—but finds its meaning only in such operations with the material of civilization as history and the social sciences are occupied with.

Darwin, whose name has been cited so frequently in the preceding pages, provides a beautiful exemplification of these principles. To deny this great man genius, mental eminence, inherent superiority to the mass of the human herd, would be fatuous. In Galton's famous classification, he would probably attain, by general opinion, at least to grade G, perhaps to the still higher—the highest—grade X. That is, he was an individual born with capacities such as but fourteen, or more likely one, or still fewer, persons in every million possess. In short, he would have towered intellectually above his fellows in any society.

On the other side, no one can sanely believe that the distinction of Darwin's greatest accomplishment, the formulation of the doctrine of evolution by natural selection, would now stand to his credit had he been born fifty years sooner or later. If later, he would have been infallibly anticipated by Wallace, for one thing; by others, if an early death had cut off Wallace. That his restless mind would have evolved something noteworthy is as likely as it is away from the point: the distinction of the particular discovery which he did make, would not have been his. Put on earth by contrary supposition, a half-century earlier, his central idea would not have come to him as it failed to come to his brilliant predecessor, the evolutionist Lamarck. Or, it would have risen in his own mind, as it did in all its essentials in that of Aristotle, only to be discarded as logically possible indeed, but as unworthy of actual consideration. Or, finally, the thought might indeed have germinated and grown in him, but been ignored and forgotten by the world, a mere unfruitful accident, until European civilization was prepared, a few decades later, and hungry as well as prepared, to use it—when its rediscovery and not its barren formal discovery would have been the event of historical significance. That

this last possibility is no idle conjecture is evidenced by its actual taking place in the case of one of the greatest of Darwin's contemporaries, his then unknown brother in arms, Gregor Mendel.

It is inconceivable that the independent occurrence of the idea of selection as the motive force of organic evolution, synchronously in the minds of Darwin and Wallace, should have been an affair of pure chance. The immediate acceptance of the idea by the world, proves nothing as to the intrinsic truth of the concept; but it does establish the readiness of the world, that is of the civilization of the time, for the doctrine. And if civilization was prepared and hungry for the doctrine, the enunciation seems to have been destined to come almost precisely when it did come. Darwin carried with himself the germ of the idea of natural selection for twenty long years before he dared put forward the hypothesis which previously he had felt would be received with hostility, and which he must have thought insufficiently armed. It was only the briefer expression of the same insight by Wallace that led Darwin to publicity. Can it be imagined, if Wallace had met death at sea among the Malay islands, and Darwin, unspurred by his competitor colleague's activity, had carried his theory in hesitant privacy a few years longer and then suddenly succumbed to mortal illness, that we of the civilized world of today should have lived all our intellectual lives without a definite mechanism for evolution and therefore without any active employment of the evolutionary idea—that our biologists would be still standing where Linnaeus, Cuvier, or at most Lamarck stood? If so, the great currents of history would be absolutely conditioned by the lodgment or dislodgment of a bacillus in a particular human frame on a certain day; which conviction would certify to as much understanding as we should credit to him, who, finding in the high Andes the ultimate source of the tiny streamlet farthest removed in tortuous miles from the Atlantic ocean, should set his foot in the bubbling spring and believe that so long as he held it there the Amazon ceased to drain a continent and to pour its tide into the sea.

No. Wallace's crowding on Darwin's heels so that his too was a share, though a minor one, of the glory of the discovery, evidences that behind him trod still others, unnamed and perhaps forever themselves unconscious; and that had the leader or his second fallen by one of the innumerable accidents to which individuals are subject, the followers, one or several or many, would have pressed forward, would have been pressed forward, it would be better to say, and done their work—immediately, as history reckons time.

The failure of Mendel's revolutionizing experiments in exact heredity to achieve the least recognition during their author's life, and for years after, has already been alluded to as an instance of the inexorable fate in store for the discoverer who anticipates his time. He is fortunate indeed if he is permitted to live out his lot in obscurity; and to escape the crucifixion which seemed a meet punishment for the first circumnavigator of Africa who saw the sun on his north. It has been said that Mendel's essay, in which are contained most of the vital principles of the branch of science that now bears his name, was published in a remote and little known source, and therefore failed for a generation to come to the notice of biologists. The last assertion may be challenged as unproved and inherently improbable. It is far more likely that biologist after biologist saw the essay, that some even read it, but that, one and all, it remained meaningless to them—not because they were unusually stupid men, but because they lacked the transcendent superiority of the occasional individual to see issues that lie ahead of those with which the world of their day is wrestling. Slowly, however, time rolled on and a change of content of thought was preparing. Darwin himself had been concerned with the origin and nature of variations. When the first shock of overpowering novelty of his central discovery had begun to be assimilated by scientific conscience, this variation question trended to the front. The investigations of De Vries and Bateson, though their recognized outcome seemed only a destructive analysis of one of the pillars of Darwinism, were accumulating knowledge as to the actual operation of heredity. And then suddenly in 1900, with dramatic eclat, three students, independently and "within a few weeks of each other," discovered the discovery of Mendel, confirmed its conclusions with experience of their own, and a new science was launched on a career of splendid fulfillment.

There may be those who see in these pulsing events only a meaningless play of capricious fortuitousness; but there will be others to whom they reveal a glimpse of a great and inspiring inevitability which rises as far above the accidents of personality as the march of the heavens transcends the wavering contacts of random footprints on clouds of earth. Wipe out the perception of De Vries, Correns, and Tschermak, and it is yet clear that before another year had rolled around, the principles of Mendelian heredity would have been proclaimed to an according world, and by six rather than three discerning minds. That Mendel lived in the nineteenth century instead of the twentieth, and published in 1865, is a fact that proved of the greatest and perhaps regrettable influence on his personal fortunes. As a matter of history, his life and discovery are of no more moment, except as a foreshadowing anticipation, than the billions of woes and gratifications, of peaceful citizen lives or bloody deaths, that have been the fate of men. Mendelian heredity does not date from 1865. It was discovered in 1900 because it could have been discovered only then, and because it infallibly must have been discovered then—given the state of European civilization.

The history of inventions is a chain of parallel instances. An examination of patent office records, in any other than a commercial or anecdotic spirit, would alone reveal the inexorability that prevails in the advance of civilization. The right to the monopoly of the manufacture of the telephone was long in litigation; the ultimate decision rested on an interval of hours between the recording of concurrent descriptions by Alexander Bell and Elisha Gray. Though it is part of our vulgar thinking to dismiss such conflicts as evidences of unscrupulous cupidity and legal inadequacy or as melodramatic coincidence, it behooves the historian to see beyond such childlike plays of the intellect.

The discovery of oxygen is credited to both Priestley and Scheele; its liquefaction to Cailletet as well as to Pictet whose results were attained in the same month of 1877 and announced in one session. Kant as well as La Place can lay claim to the promulgation of the nebular hypothesis. Neptune was predicted by Adams and by Leverrier; the computation of the one, and the publication of that of the other, had precedence by a few months.

For the invention of the steamboat, glory is claimed by their countrymen or partisans for Fulton, Jouffroy, Rumsey, Stevens, Symmington, and others; of the telegraph, for Steinheil and Morse; in photography Talbot was the rival of Daguerre and Niepce. The doubly flanged rail devised by Stevens was reinvented by Vignolet. Aluminum was first practically reduced by the processes of Hall, Heroult, and Cowles. Leibnitz in 1684 as well as Newton in 1687 formulated calculus. Anaesthetics, both ether and nitrous oxide, were discovered in 1845 and 1846, by no less than four men of one nationality. So independent were their achievements, so similar even in details and so closely contemporaneous, that polemics, lawsuits, and political agitation ensued for many years, and there was not one of the four but whose career was embittered, if not ruined, by the animosities arising from the indistinguishability of the priority. Even the south pole, never before trodden by the foot of human beings, was at last reached twice in one summer.

A volume could be written, with but few years' toil, filled with endlessly repeating but ever new accumulation of such instances. When we cease to look upon invention or discovery as some mysterious inherent faculty of individual minds which are randomly dropped in space and time by fate; when we center our attention on the plainer relation of one such advancing step to the others; when, in short, interest shifts from individually biographic elements—which can be only dramatically artistic, didactically moralizing, or psychologically interpretable—and attaches whole heartedly to the social or civilizational, evidence on this point will be infinite in quantity, and the presence of majestic forces or sequences pervading civilization will be irresistibly evident.

Knowing the civilization of an age and a land, we can then substantially affirm that its distinctive discoveries, in this or that field of activity, were not directly contingent upon the personality of the actual inventors that graced the period, but would have been made without them; and that, conversely, had the great illuminating minds of other centuries and climates been born in the civilization referred to, instead of their own, its first achievements would probably have fallen to their lot. Ericsson or Galvani eight thousand years ago might have polished or bored the first stone; and in turn the hand and mind whose operation set in inception the neolithic age of human culture, would, if held in its infancy in unchanging catalepsy from that time until today, now be devising wireless telephones and nitrogen extractors.

Some reservations must be admitted to this principle. It is far from established, rather the contrary, that extraordinary ability, however equal in intensity, is identical in direction. It is highly unlikely that Beethoven put in Newton's cradle would have worked out calculus, or the latter have given the symphony its final form. We can and evidently must admit congenital faculties that are fairly specialized. Everything shows that the elementary mental faculties such as memory, interest, and abstraction, are by nature uneven in individuals of equivalent ability but distinctive bent; and this in spite of cultivation. The educator who proclaimed his ability to convert a native memory for absolute numbers or for mathematical formulas into an equally strong retention of single tones or of complex melodies, would be distrusted. But it does not essentially matter if the originating faculty is one or several in mind. If Eli Whitney could not have formulated the difference between the subjective and the objective and Kant in his place would have failed to devise a practical cotton gin, Watt or Fulton or Morse or Stephenson could in the place of the former, have accomplished his achievement, and Aristotle or Aquinas the task of the latter. It is possibly not even quite accurate to maintain that the individualities of the unknown inventor or inventors of the bow and arrow and those of firearms could have been interchanged, for the first production of the bow necessarily involved mechanical and even manual faculty, while the discovery of gunpowder and of its applicability to weapons may have required the different ability to perceive certain peculiar qualities of a more highly dynamic or chemical nature.

In short, it is a debatable point, though one of the greatest psychological interest, how far human faculty is divisible and subdivisible into distinct kinds. But the matter is not vital in the present connection, for there will hardly be any one rash enough to maintain that there exist as many distinguishable faculties as there are separate human beings; which in fact would be to assert that abilities do not differ in intensity or degree but only in direction or kind; in short, that while no two men were alike, all were equal in potential capacity. If this view is not correct, then it matters little whether the kinds of ability are several or many, because in any case they will be very few compared with the endless number of human organisms; because there will accordingly be so many individuals possessing each faculty, that every age must contain persons with low and mediocre and high measure of intensity of each; and the extraordinary men of one sort in one period will therefore still be substitutable for those of another time in the manner indicated.

If, therefore, anyone's interpretation of mentality is disturbed by some of the particular equivalences that have been suggested, he can easily find others that seem more just, without dissenting from the underlying principle that the march of history, or as it is current custom to name it, the progress of civilization, is independent of the birth of particular personalities; since these apparently averaging substantially alike, both as regards genius and normality, at all times and places, furnish the same substratum for the social.

Here, then, we have an interpretation which allows to the individual, and through him to heredity, all that the science of the organic can legitimately claim on the strength of its actual accomplishments; and which also yields the fullest scope to the social in its own distinctive field. The accomplishment of the individual measured against other individuals depends, if not wholly then mainly, on his organic constitution as compounded by his heredity. The accomplishments of a group, relative to other groups, are little or not influenced by heredity because sufficiently large groups average much alike in organic makeup.

This identity of average is incontestable for some instances of the same nations in closely successive ages—as Athens in 550 and 450, or Germany in 1800 and 1900—during which brief periods their hereditary composition could not have altered to a small fraction of the degree in which cultural achievement varied; it is certainly probable even for people of the same blood separated by long intervals of time and wide divergences of civilization; and it is, while neither proved nor disproved, likely to be nearly true, as suggested before, for the most distant races.

The difference between the accomplishments of one group of men and those of another group is therefore of another order from the difference between the faculties of one person and another. It is through this distinction that one of the essential qualities of the nature of the social is to be found.

The physiological and the mental are bonded as aspects of the same thing, one resolvable into the other; the social is, directly considered, not resolvable into the mental. That it exists only after mentality of a certain kind is in action, has led to confusion of the two, and even their identification. The error of this identification, is a fault that tends to pervade modern thinking about civilization, and which must be overcome by self-discipline before our understanding of this order of phenomena that fill and color our lives can become either clear or serviceable.

If the relation of the individual to culture here outlined is a true one, a conflicting view sometimes held and already alluded to, is unentertainable. This view is the opinion that all personalities are, while not identical, potentially equal in capacity, their varying degrees of accomplishment being due solely to different measures of accord with the social environment with which they are in touch. This view has perhaps been rarely formulated as a generic principle; but it seems to underlie, though usually vaguely and by implication only, many tendencies toward social and educational reform, and is therefore likely to find formal enunciation at some time.

This assumption, which would certainly be of extensive practical application if it could be verified, seems to rest ultimately on a dim but profound perception of the influence of civilization. More completely though this influence of civilization is upon national fortunes than upon individual careers, it nevertheless must influence these latter also. Mohammedanism—a social phenomenon—in stifling the imitative possibilities of the pictorial and plastic arts, has obviously affected the civilization of many peoples; but it must also have altered the careers of many persons born in three continents during a thousand years. Special talents which these men and women possessed for delineative representation may have been suppressed without equal compensation in other directions, in those whose endowment was unique. Of such individuals it is true that the social forces to which they were subject depressed each of them from successful attainment to more mediocre. And without question the same environment elevated many an individual to high rank above his fellows whose special abilities, in some other age and country, would have been repressed to his private disadvantage. The personality born with those qualities that lead to highly successful leadership of religious brigands, for instance, is undoubtedly assured of a more prosperous and contented career in Morocco than in Holland of today.

Even within one nationally limited sphere of civilization, similar results are necessarily bound to occur. The natural logician or administrator born into a caste of fisherman or street sweepers is not likely to achieve the satisfaction in life, and certainly not the success, that would have been his lot had his parents been Brahmins or Kshatriyas; and what is true formally of India holds substantially for Europe.

But, that a social environment may somewhat affect the fortunes and career of the individual as measured against other individuals, does not prove that the individual is wholly the product of circumstances outside of himself, any more than the opposite is true that a civilization is only the sum total of the products of a group of organically shaped minds. The concrete effect of each individual upon civilization is determined by civilization itself. Civilization appears even in some cases and in some measure to influence the effect of the individual's native activities upon himself. But to proceed from these realizations to the inference that all the degree and quality of accomplishment by the individual is the result of his moulding by the society that encompasses him, is assumption, extreme at that, and at variance with observation.

Therefore it is possible to hold the historical or civilizational interpretation of social phenomena without proceeding to occupy the position that the human beings that are the given channels through which civilization courses, are only and wholly the products of its stream. Because culture rests on the specific human faculty, it does not follow that this faculty, the thing in man that is supra-animal, is of social determination. The line between the social and the organic may not be randomly or hastily drawn. The threshold between the endowment that renders the flow and continuance of civilization possible and that which prohibits even its inception, is the demarcation—doubtful enough once, in all probability, but gaping for a longer period than our knowledge covers—between man and animal. The separation between the social itself, however, the entity that we call civilization, and the non-social, the pre-social or organic, is the diversity of quality or order which exists between animal and man conjointly on the one hand, and the products of the interactions of human beings on the other. In the previous pages the mental has already been subtracted from the social and added to the physically organic which is subject to the influence of heredity. In the same way it is necessary to eliminate the factor of individual capacity from the consideration of civilization. But this elimination means its transfer to the group of organically conceivable phenomena, not its denial. In fact nothing is further from the path of a just prosecution of the understanding of history than such a negation of differences of degree of the faculties of individual men.

In short, social science, if we may take that word as equivalent to history, does not deny individuality any more than it denies the individual. It does refuse to deal with either individuality or individual as such. And it bases this refusal solely on denial of the validity of either factor for the achievement of its proper aims.

It is true that historical events can also be viewed mechanically, and expressed ultimately in terms of physics and chemistry. Genius may prove definable in unit characters or the constitution of chromosomes, and its particular achievements in osmotic or electric reactions of nerve cells. The day may come when what took place in the tissue of Darwin's brain when he first thought the concept of natural selection, can be profitably studied, or even approximately ascertained, by the physiologist and chemist. Such an achievement, destructive as it may seem to those whom revelation appeals, would be not only defensible but of enormous interest, and possibly of utility. Only, it would not be history; nor a step toward history or social science.

To know the precise reactions in Darwin's nervous system at the moment when the thought of natural selection flashed upon him in 1838, would involve a genuine triumph of science. But it would mean nothing historically, since history is concerned with the relation of doctrines such as that of natural selection to other concepts and social phenomena, and not with the relation of Darwin himself to social phenomena or other phenomena. This is not the current view of history; but, on the other hand, the current view rests on the endlessly recurring but obviously illogical assumption that because without individuals civilization could not exist, civilization therefore is only a sum total of the psychic operations of a mass of individuals.

As, then, there are two lines of intellectual endeavor in history and in science, each with its separate aim and set of methods; and as it is only the confounding of the two that results in sterility; so also two wholly disparate evolutions must be recognized: that of the substance which we call organic and that of the phenomena called social. Social evolution is without antecedents in the beginnings of organic evolution. It commences late in the development of life—long after vertebrates, after mammals, after the primates even, are established. Its exact point of origin we do not know, and perhaps shall never know; but we can limit the range within which it falls. This origin occurred in a series of organic forms more

advanced, in general mental faculty, than the gorilla, and much less developed than the first known race that is unanimously accepted as having been human, the man of Neandertal and Le Moustier. In point of time, these first carriers of the rudiments of civilization must antedate the Neandertal race by far, but must be posterior to other extinct human ancestors of the approximate intellectual level of the modern gorilla and chimpanzee.

The beginning of social evolution, of the civilization which is the subject of history, thus coincides with that of mystery of the popular mind: the missing link. But the term "link" is misleading. It implies a continuous chain. But with the unknown bearers of the primeval and gradually manifesting beginnings of civilization, there took place a profound alteration rather than an improved passing of the existing. A new factor has arisen which was to work out its own independent consequences, slowly and of little apparent import at first, but gathering weight, and dignity, and influence; a factor that had passed beyond natural selection, that was no longer wholly dependent on any agency of organic evolution, and that, however rocked and swayed by the oscillations of the heredity that underlay it, nevertheless floated unimmersibly upon it.

The dawn of the social thus is not a link in a chain, not a step in a path, but a leap to another plane. It may be likened to the first occurrence of life in the hitherto lifeless universe, the hour when that one of infinite chemical combinations took place which put the organic into existence, and made it that from this moment on there should be two worlds in place of one. Atomic qualities and movements were not interfered with when that seemingly slight event took place; the majesty of the mechanical laws of the cosmos was not diminished; but something new was inextinguishably added to the history of this planet.

One might compare the inception of civilization to the end of the process of slowly heating water. The expansion of the liquid goes on a long time. Its alteration can be observed by the thermometer as well as in bulk, in its solvent power as well as in its internal agitation. But it remains water. Finally, however, the boiling point is attained. Steam is produced: the rate of enlargement of volume is increased a thousand fold; and in place of a glistening, percolating fluid, a volatile gas diffuses invisibly. Neither the laws of physics nor those of chemistry are violated; nature

dition of something new in kind, an initiation of that which was to run a course of its own.

We may sketch the relation which exists between the evolutions of the organic and of the social (fig. 1). A line progressing with the flow of time, rises slowly, but gatheringly. At a certain point, another line begins to diverge from it, insensibly at first, but ascending ever farther above it on its own course; until, at the moment where the curtain of the present cuts off our view, each is advancing, but far from the other, and uninfluenced by it.

In this illustration, the continuous line denotes the level inorganic; the broken

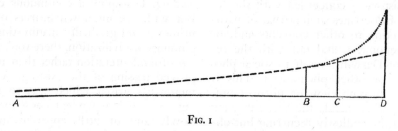

FIG. 1

is not set aside; but yet a saltation has taken place: the slow transitions that accumulated from zero to one hundred have been transcended in an instant, and a condition of substance with new properties and new possibilities of effect is in existence.

Such, in some manner, must have been the result of the appearance of this new thing, civilization. We need not consider that it abolished the course of development of life. It certainly has not in any measure done away with its own substratum of the organic. And there is no reason to believe that it was born full fledged. All these incidents and manners of the inception of the social are after all of little consequence to an understanding of its specific nature, and of the relation of that nature to the character of the organic substance that preceded in absolute time and still supports it. The point is, there was an ad-

line, the evolution of the organic; the line of dots, the development of civilization. Height above the base is degree of advancement, whether that be complexity, heterogeneity, degree of coördination, or anything else. A is the beginning of time on this earth as revealed to our understandings. B marks the point of the true missing link, of the first human precursor, the first animal that carried and accumulated tradition. C would denote the state reached by what we are accustomed to call primitive man, that Neandertal *homo* who was our forefather in culture if not in blood; and D, the present moment.

It is inevitable that if there is foundation for the contentions that have been set forth, an arguing from one of these lines to the other must be futile. To assert, because the upper line has risen rapidly just before it is cut off, that the one below it must also have ascended proportionally more in this period than in any before, is obviously uncompelling. That our institutions, our knowledge, the exercising of our minds, have advanced dizzyingly in twenty thousand years is no reason that our bodies and brains, our mental equipment and its physiological basis, have advanced in any corresponding measure as is sometimes argued by scientists and generally taken for granted by men at large. If anything, it might be an evidence that the lower, organic line has fallen off in its rate of ascent. The bodies and minds in this line have continued to carry civilization; but this civilization has met the struggle of the world in such a way that much of the stress has been directed away from these bodies and minds. We do not argue that the progress of organic evolution is *prima facie* indication that inorganic matter is more complex, more advanced in its combinations, or in any sense "higher," than it was fifty million years ago; much less that organic evolution has taken place through an inorganic evolution as cause. And no more can we infer from social development to a progress of the hereditary forms of life.

In fact, not only is the correlation of the lines of organic and social development as unjustified theoretically as it would be to argue from the compressibility or weight of water to that of steam; but all evidence directs us as to the conviction that in recent periods civilization has raced at a speed so far outstripping the pace of hereditary evolution, that the latter has, if not actually standing still, afforded all the seeming, relatively, of making no progress. There are a hundred elements of civilization where there was one in the time when the Neandertal skull enclosed a living brain; and not only the content of civilization but the complexity of its organization has increased a hundred-fold. But the body and the associated mind of that early man have not attained a point a hundred times, nor even twice, as fine, as efficient, as delicate, or as strong, as they were then; it is doubtful if they have improved by a fifth. There are, it is true, those who make the contrary assertion. Yet it seems the fair-minded must avow that such assertions rest not on objective interpretation of the facts, but on a wish to find a correlation, a desire to make the thread of evolution a single, unbranching one, to see the social only as organic.

Here, then, we have to come to our conclusion; and here we rest. The mind and the body are but facets of the same organic material or activity; the social substance—or unsubstantial fabric, if one prefers the phrase—the thing that we call civilization, transcends them for all its being rooted in life. The processes of civilizational activity are almost unknown to us. The factors that govern their workings are unresolved. The forces and principles of mechanistic science can indeed analyze our civilization; but in so doing they destroy its essence, and leave us without understanding of the very thing which we seek. The historian as yet can do little but picture. He traces and he connects what seems far removed; he balances; he integrates; but he does not really explain, nor does he transmute phenomena into something else. His method is not mechanistic; but neither can the physicist or physiologist deal with historical material and leave it civilization nor convert it into concepts of life and leave nothing else to be done. What we all are able to do is to realize this gap, to be impressed by it with humility, and to go our paths on its respective sides without self-deluding boasts that the chasm has been bridged.

4. THE POSSIBILITY OF A SOCIAL PSYCHOLOGY
1918

This is about one-third of an article published a year after "The Superorganic" (No. 3). The passages chosen are included on several accounts. One of these is the criticism of Herbert Spencer in the last four paragraphs here reproduced. Another is the little tabulation in the eighth paragraph, which foreshadows the more detailed presentation eighteen years later in "So-called Social Science" (No. 6). Third is the injection of values, though these are placed in the "depictive" versus the "processual" disciplines, rather than in the overlying fields as against the underlying (present tenth to thirteenth paragraphs). Finally, there is the attempt to extricate culture from the undifferentiated "social," leading to identification of "superpsychical" with "cultural" (twentieth paragraph). However, I was not yet out of the toils of wavering between using "social" once to denote what we today strictly mean by "social," then again for "cultural" or "sociocultural." Thus I still commend Spencer for saying insect societies are not true social aggregates but simulate them; which would be apt if, instead of "social," Spencer had said "cultural." A few sentences farther in the twentieth paragraph I affirm "the real differences between the cultural society of man and the cultureless pseudo-society of the ants." Why should it be a pseudo-society because it lacks culture? Today we might rather say that ant society is a genuine society but manifests a pseudo-culture. Apparently by 1918 the two long-undifferentiated sets of phenomena of society and culture had not yet consistently clotted out conceptually. Eleven years later Bernhard Stern was still trenchantly clarifying the meanings of the words.

Of course, my "social psychology" of the time was something very different from the social psychology of today, which psychologists and sociologists have jointly reared as a discipline that deals with out-groups, minorities, stereotypes, adjustments, attitudes, leadership, propaganda, public opinion, and other interpersonal relations within a society, without reference to cultural content or forms except so far as a cultural content may be needed to define a sociopsychological situation.

What I was dreaming of, as a distant possibility, was a true processual science causally explaining the pageant of the history of culture. I do not see in 1951 that we are appreciably nearer such a science than we were in 1918. I still think that the processes through which cultural forms can be explained causally must be largely or essentially psychological in nature. In late years I have several times discussed "cultural psychology," though as an inevitable psychological reflection or quality which all cultures must bear rather than as their basic process or cause. I do not think that in and by themselves the interpersonal or social relations of men in groups will ever explain the specific features of specific cultures—certainly not their ideologies, knowledge, skills, art, or understanding. Modern social psychologists do not even pose the problem. They are not interested in the interrelation of cultural facts; just as I, in 1918, for all my talking about social psychology, was interested in culture and very little in social interrelations. In fact, next to culture, I was then and am now much more interested in the qualities and motivations of individuals than in what human beings do to one another in groups. The present paper must have puzzled both sociologists and psychologists at the time and since. I am doubly appreciative of their forbearance.

IN A recent examination of the theoretical foundations of Wundt's folk-psychology,[1] Dr. H. K. Haeberlin has analyzed, in a manner both incisive and convincing, the basis and method of the studies made in the field of human culture by the great German psychologist. Dr. Haeberlin puts in the foreground of Wundt's thought the idea that mental phenomena possess, through their immediacy to ourselves, an actuality as great as that of physical phenomena. This actuality must be consistently distinguished from substantiality. Only on the basis of this distinction is it possible to speak of the existence of a "soul"; but in the sense of an actuality there is no denying this existence. . . .

No attempt will . . . be made here to establish the actuality of cultural phenomena. But thought about the nature of these phenomena often still is so timidly halting that it is perhaps worth while to examine some of the consequences of an application of the assumption of the reality of culture.

We begin, then, with the belief in the equal reality of four kinds of phenomena: those of matter and force as such, those of life as such, those of consciousness, and those of social life or culture. These four varieties of facts of experience may also be denominated as the inorganic, the directly organic or vital, the mentally organic or psychic, and the civilizational or superorganic or, better, superpsychic. The physicist who operates in the realm of the inorganic may cherish the conviction that all organic phenomena are in the end wholly and absolutely resolvable into inorganic factors. He does not, however, insist that the expression of organic data in organic terms is misleading. He does not even announce that it is useless. Nor does he tolerate organic science only as a secondary activity after its rooting in the inorganic has been completely traced at every possible point. If he held any such attitude,

he would have to maintain that biology is justified only after it is known exactly what life is in terms of the inorganic. Now that knowledge is to the biologist, perhaps, the ultimate goal of his work. It certainly is not his first task, else his biology would be only pure physics and chemistry. As a biologist he accepts life as something given, and he inquires into its forms and processes as such.

The attitude of the psychologist is parallel. He may share with the biologist and chemist the conviction that consciousness rests absolutely on an organic basis, and through this on an inorganic basis. But as a psychologist his business is the determination of the manifestations and processes of consciousness as consciousness. Such a task may not appeal to some. The opportunity then lies before them to interpret consciousness in organic terms. But if they exercise this choice they . . . resign claim to the pursuit of psychology in favor of the practice of physiology.

And so with those who envisage social phenomena. Their alternative is to treat them in social terms or in material, vital, and mental terms. There is no quarreling with the latter course. But neither can an a priori condemnation of the former method be tolerated. In one case the aim is a physics, biology, or psychology of social phenomena; in the other, a sociology or history of social phenomena.

Unless, then, one is ready to take an uncompromising monistic attitude and maintain that there is only one science, it is necessary to admit at least four kinds of sciences: physical and chemical, in the realm of the inorganic; biological, in the domain of the organic as such; psychological, concerned with the psychic aspects of the organic or the mental as such; and social, operating with superorganic phenomena.

There is, however, another division that runs across knowledge. Data may be viewed directly as they present themselves; or we can seek to pass through them to the processes involved. On this basis the sciences are either historical and only incidentally concerned with mechanisms, or unhistorical and wholly devoted to the determination of mechanisms. The application of this classification results in a total of eight groups of sciences, which may be arranged as in the accompanying tabulation below.

There is no idea of a sharp line between the explanational and the depicting sciences. Rather they are only extremes of method, between which lies an indefinite series of transitions....

We must therefore recognize in each of our four orders of study a sequence leading from the wholly depictive extreme of science to the thoroughly mechanistic or processual one. It is only at the latter end that the sciences of one plane begin to have direct contacts with those of the other planes.

It is also true that the more basal the dimension in which a class of science operates, the more readily is the transition from the depictive treatment to the determination of mechanisms accomplished. There may or may not be a logical reason for this circumstance. It is stated here only as an empirical fact. Conversely, as the determination of processes is more easily accomplished in these lower dimensions, the direct depiction of phenomena is more difficult, at least more difficult to achieve with significance. The astronomer attains a minimum of cosmic history with a maximum of physical and chemical mechanics as a means. Organic mechanics is far less developed, but organic history is much fuller, than cosmic or terrestrial. Human history is infinitely the

richest of all the depictive sciences, its mechanics the most backward. Even the age of the sciences points in a like direction. On the descriptive side, history, in the usual sense of the word, is the oldest—the superorganic and psychic phases were first cultivated. On the line of explanation by process, the inorganic plane was earliest productive.

It is the same situation that is alluded to when it is commonly said that historical science hangs back because its material is the most "complex." It seems very doubtful whether this is so. The phenomena of inorganic nature are probably fully as "complex" as those of human history. Its processes are, however, very much less complex, in the sense that the factors of phenomena can for some reason be far more readily isolated and determined. On the other hand, the phenomena of history, on account of their very immediacy to us, lend themselves with correspondingly greater ease to the more immediate treatment of depiction.

It may also be questioned whether the dictum is true that values inhere in psychic and superpsychic material and that occupation with this material therefore involves qualitative expression in contrast with the quantitative formulations sought by the student of the inorganic. It seems rather that qualitative values must be the ultimate aim of the depictive method, irrespective of its material, and quantitatively conceivable determinations be the goal at which all inquiry into means or mechanism is directed. According to the views of Wundt and of Rickert, for instance, it is the sciences in the upper half or quarter of the subjoined table that are concerned with values, those in the

	Formulation of Processes	Depiction of Phenomena
Superorganic phenomena	Social psychology	Culture history
Mental organic phenomena	Psychology	Biographic history
Vital organic phenomena	Physiology	Natural history
Inorganic phenomena	Physics, chemistry	Astronomy, geology

lower portion that deal with quantities. But it appears rather that it is of the essence of the depictive or historical *method* to formulate values; of the mechanistic *procedure* to seek quantitative expressible determinations. . . .

That values inhere in all the depictive sciences is clear. A person undisciplined in scientific thinking can only with difficulty be brought to entertain an interest in any formulation or law of physics. His instinctive impulse is always to avoid the scientific process itself and to center attention on the mere results of the process as manifested in practical and useful applications, or in presentations of emotional significance. On the other hand, everyone, no matter how uneducated, is always interested in the concrete determinations or suppositions of a science like astronomy—in "how things are" or "what happened"—provided only that the mechanisms involved can be omitted from the description or can be given an emotional color. Such bits of accepted or conjectural knowledge as the fact that there are stars immensely larger than our sun, that they are remote by thousands of light-years, that our earth was once part of a whirling gaseous sun, or that the moon has chilled and shrunk or that its craters were formed in a bombardment of its still plastic surface by meteors— all such facts or reputed facts have an immediate meaning to the mind and elicit an emotional reaction comparable to that produced by the story of Caesar's crossing the Rubicon or the picture called forth by the phrase "the fall of the Roman Empire.". . .

It is true that what is ordinarily called "science" as distinguished from history, that is, the kind of science which resolves into quantitatively describable factors or operates with them, has practically no achievements to its credit in the plane of the superorganic. It might therefore be doubted whether such a science is possible in the superorganic plane of culture. It is certainly of the utmost importance to realize that whatever the processual method of science may accomplish with cultural material is as yet only a hope and a possibility. Assertions that anything definitely utilizable has been attained in this respect are delusions that prevent endeavor. But, on the other hand, analogy alone is sufficient to indicate the possibility, perhaps even the probability, of an "exact" science [of process] being developed which will be able to deal with some effectiveness with civilizational phenomena. That such a science is likely always to remain outstripped by the sciences that deal with the processes of the psychic, the vital, and the inorganic, experience leads us to expect; but the very development of these in their sequence renders rash the prediction of the impossibility of a true social science.

There is no a priori reason visible, accordingly, why a science of cultural mechanics, or social psychology, or sociology is impossible; and inquiry shifts to the problem of why this possibility has heretofore been so largely or wholly unrealized. . . .

The reply appears to be that the older sociologists have not contented themselves with operating in the plane or dimension of their material but have attempted to force results by appropriating processes determined in other planes and applying these to their special phenomena. Proceeding from the data of human history, they have recognized the fact that these might be capable of generalized interpretation as well as of concrete depiction. They have therefore set up their science, but, having nothing forthwith to hand with which to fill its frame, they have reached into psychology and biology and the inorganic sciences to give substance to its emptiness. Thereby they have impeded, perhaps largely blocked, the slow and natural but alone healthy growth that might have taken place toward an understanding of the social factors that are contained in social phenomena.

This tendency has been observable from the beginning. Comte, who coined the name "sociology," had a marked sense for the social as such. It is obviously the specifically new element in his work, his definite contribution to the thought of the world. The remainder of his system is the materialistic monism of the preceding century; and his positivism is largely the symptom of the dominance of this view in his peculiar individuality. The very term "sociology" carries the fatal defect of the overshadowing of the cultural by the subcultural. . . .

If Comte founded, Spencer established, sociology. It was he who first employed the word "superorganic." Spencer certainly held the concept of culture. He speaks of a factor of social phenomena "the potency of which can scarcely be overestimated. I mean that accumulation of super-organic products which we commonly distinguish as artificial." "These various orders of super-organic products . . . ," he says, "each acting on the other orders while reacted on by them, constitute an immensely-voluminous, immensely-complicated, and immensely-powerful set of influences. . . . They gradually form what we may consider either as a non-vital part of the society itself, or else as a secondary environment, which eventually becomes more important than the primary environment."[2]

But these superorganic products, or "civilization" as we should call them, are treated by Spencer on a level with suborganic factors. His first words on the factors of social phenomena refer to the inorganic. . . .

Of the social insects, Spencer says with sound discrimination that their societies "simulate social aggregates in sundry ways; yet they are not true social aggregates." . . . The real differences

between the cultural society of man and the cultureless pseudo-society of the ants and bees fail to impress Spencer. That the social insects do not learn or acquire knowledge as groups; that they totally lack tradition; that substantially all their activities are inborn and determined by organic heredity, or depend on individual psychic experience acting upon hereditary faculty; in short, that they totally lack any body of "superorganic products" that is carried along from individual to individual and from group to group independent of the nature of these individuals and groups—all these essential characteristics of the superpsychical or cultural Spencer passes over without a word. We must indeed credit him with some foreshadowing anticipations of an understanding of the superorganic; but he certainly lacks an active conception thereof. . . .

In the main, however, Spencer is occupied with tracing a far-reaching analogy between actual organisms and "social organisms." It is true that he continually points out that the resemblance is only analogical. But he enters upon it in such detail that the general effect upon the world has been almost equivalent to a real resolution of social phenomena into organic causes. It is impossible to discuss for hundreds of pages the similarity of societies and organic beings without leaving in the minds of all but thoroughly critical and self-controlled thinkers the conviction that societies are organic, or at least that they resemble organisms so closely that the resemblance is their most noteworthy characteristic. Indeed, the very length and systemization with which Spencer deals with the analogy makes it evident that he has little else to present upon the topic of social phenomena, except now and then an isolated founding of a cultural activity in a directly psychic activity, or scattering interrelations of social phenomena with social phenomena. . . .

5. HISTORICAL RECONSTRUCTION OF CULTURE GROWTHS AND ORGANIC EVOLUTION
1931

This paper is the reflection of an interest in natural history that I have had as long as I can remember. Whether it be the shapes, structures, and functioning qualities of animals, of cultures or their parts, or of languages, they have always had an attraction for me, and one that was nearly equal. This would, I think, not hold for typical social scientists. It is clear I am not by temperament a social scientist. It took me several decades to come to a realization of the fact.

On the side, this paper opened an argument with my guru Boas—it never interfered with our personal friendship. He had disapproved of my tendency to historical reconstruction, and I was answering.

THE purpose of this essay is to discuss certain similarities of aim and method in the reconstruction, respectively, of culture growths by anthropologists and of organic history or "evolution" by biologists.

1. Cultures, especially in their cyclic aspects, have sometimes been compared to organisms. They are however obvious composites: more or less fused aggregates of elements of various origin, ancient and recent, native and foreign. They are therefore more truly similar to faunas and floras, which also are composites or aggregates of constituent animal or plant species which often are of quite diverse origin in space and time; and the aggregate wholes are representative of, or bound to, natural regions. The nearest analogues to culture areas, such as the West African or Southwest American, therefore, are faunal areas like the Holarctic or Neotropical; and cultures are comparable to biotas [No. 9, two last paragraphs].

Following this comparison further, one may compare species to culture traits or elements, and genera or families to culture trait complexes. It is plain that this analogy must not be pushed too far, especially as concerns its second half. A culture complex often is "polyphyletic"; a genus is, almost by definition, monophyletic. However, the analogy does at least refer to the fact that culture elements, like species, represent the smallest units of material which the historical anthropologist and biologist, respectively, have to deal with.

2. Corresponding to relatively stationary or persistent culture traits or complexes like flint chipping and to retarded cultures like that of Tasmania, there are long-persistent and slowly altering groups of animals, such as the sharks, and isolated, retarded faunal areas like Australia and New Zealand. Conversely, there can be recognized rapidly diffusing or expanding traits and species and cultures and faunas subject to invasion and marked by change.

3. Distributional phenomena are of equal evidential weight in the two realms. The geographical occurrence of members of the group Cactaceae with its heavy weighting in Mexico and restriction to America, for instance, allows of inferences as to the origin and areal history of the group comparable to the inferences generally made as to the origin of maize agriculture, terraced pyramid construction, and associated culture traits in the Middle American region.

In both sciences, geographical continuity greatly strengthens other evidence for relationship. But continuity of present distribution is by no means indispensable to proof of common origin; and conversely, continuity alone does not prove historic relationship, because of the possibility of phenomena of separate origin secondarily acquiring distributions that are continuous.

4. The Age and Area principle seems the same in biology and cultural anthropology. First used decisively in biology, it seems to have been hit upon independently soon after by anthropologists. In essence the principle was already clear to Ratzel, though he dulled the edge of its value as a technique by wavering between populations and cultures in making its applications.

The same limitations and strictures upon the principle hold in the two sciences. It is closely related groups of species or traits that must be compared, not distantly or unrelated ones: copper working with bronze, for instance, a simple with an elaborate complex of weaving techniques; not bronze with mudbrick-building, or a textile art with a religious cult. A botanist would hardly venture to infer respective age from the distribution of grasses and pines. A zoologist would judge age from area within a genus, family, or perhaps order, scarcely as between classes, or between orders belonging to different phyla. In anthropology this limitation has generally not been recognized explicitly, has occasionally not been observed with due caution, and unnecessary attacks upon the principle have resulted.

5. The phenomena of convergence or independent parallel origin, versus relationship by common origin or descent and spread or diffusion, have long been recognized in both groups of sciences, but their discrimination has generally made no serious difficulty in modern biology, while it has led to fundamental controversy in anthropology.

Forty years ago Ratzel pointed out that the assumption of independent origin of similar cultural phenomena generally involved a falling-back upon self-sufficient but vague forces like the "unity of the human mind," which were parallel to the "spontaneous generation" of the older biologists; and that it is historically more productive to test the facts on the assumption of a tentative working hypothesis of genetic connection. Where similarities are specific and structural and not merely superficially conceptual, this has long been the accepted method of evolutionary and systematic biology. There is no apparent reason why the same point of view should not prevail in historical anthropology. The risk that working hypotheses may now and then be stretched into systems is one that has to be accepted. As an example may be mentioned the rude pottery figurines which are found from western Mexico to Venezuela and Peru and from which as principal evidence there has been reconstructed an Archaic Middle American horizon or type of culture. If the resemblances of these figurines were demonstrated as specific at several points, no one would hesitate to accept them as evidence of the spread of a common culture, in spite of local variations. If however the resemblances are limited to the conceptual ones of use of clay, crude modeling, and human representation, the case for historic unity is obviously unproved, however valuable these resemblances may be as a suggestion or clue.

6. The fundamentally different evidential value of homologous and analogous similarities for determination of historical relationship, that is, genuine systematic or generic relationship, has long been an axiom in biological science. The distinction has been much less clearly made in anthropology, and rarely explicitly, but holds with equal force. A concept like that of caste, for instance, undoubtedly has a certain logical or psychological validity, but a very dubious historical validity. Conceptually, caste constitutes as unassailable a group of phenomena as that represented

by the category "shellfish" (mollusks, crustaceans, turtles); historically, it may be just as meaningless. On the contrary, it is difficult to see only a superficial analogy between the Aztec patolli game and the Hindu pachisi game, long ago analytically compared by Tylor. Their specific structural similarities in two-sided lot throwing, count values dependent on frequency of lot combinations, a cruciform scoring circuit, the killing of opponents' counters that are overtaken, etc., make out a strong case for a true homology and therefore a genetic unity of the two game forms, in spite of their geographical separation. Biologists would almost certainly judge so. On the other hand, the Aztec-Maya and Southeast Asiatic permutation calendars are similar essentially only in the conceptual fact of applying permutation to time counting. Their respective specific content (the name-sequences), their specific numerical structure (13×20 versus 10×12), in part their function or application in their cultures, are thoroughly different, so that, if there is any historic relation at all, it must be remote and indirect. On the other hand, if Graebner's attempt to equate the Mexican and Asiatic sequences name for name were of a character to compel conviction, a strong point of homology would be established, and therewith a prima facie case for historic connection.

In such situations consideration must be given the factor of limited possibilities. There are, for instance, only a few possible types of arrow-release. Recurrences of these in different regions do not accordingly have the same weight as evidence in favor of historical connection, as recurrences in some trait where the possible variations are many. The totality of distributions and especially of associated traits must therefore be scrutinized much more closely before decisions are arrived at. Similarly with standard or regularly used "sacred" numbers. These must almost of necessity

be chosen from the numbers between three and twelve. The biological parallel is not exact, but a somewhat similar situation is presented by the limited number of choices which nature has between exo-skeleton, endo-skeleton, and no skeleton.

7. It is the totality of structure which decides relationships between groups of organisms or between culture trait complexes. That some butterflies have only four legs instead of the basic insect pattern of six is of no significance for fundamental relationship, because of the overwhelming identity of structure of these and other butterflies in other respects. The lower number is evidently a secondary phenomenon of reduction and is significant only for subclassification within the more immediate sphere of relationship. So with a cultural complex which is on the whole a fairly uniform system, like our week, variations are of only secondary moment as long as the essential features of the system recur: a series of seven days named after heavenly bodies or their god-equivalents in a certain sequence. Wherever this set of traits occurs, one cannot doubt direct derivation from a single common source. On the other hand, a market or ritual day recurring every seventh day is by no means necessarily derived from the same source as our week, because the resemblance extends to only part of the features.

There are cases in which it is not a simple matter to decide whether the totality of traits points to a true relationship or to secondary convergence. The ratite birds are an instance in point. It has been held that the ostrich, rhea, emu, etc., form a true group, and again that they represent merely secondary assimilations of originally diverse ancestors. Similarly, the pinnipeds are of doubtful phylogenetic unity. They may be derived from several families of carnivores. Yet few biologists would doubt that sufficiently intensive analysis of structure will ultimately solve such problems of descent as these. There seems no reason why on the whole the same cautious optimism should not prevail in the field of culture; why homologies should not be positively distinguishable from analogies, when analysis of the whole of the phenomena in question has become truly intensive. That such analysis has often been lacking, but judgments have nevertheless been rendered, does not invalidate the positive reliability of the method. Masks, secret religious societies, couvade customs, matrilinear institutions, the kingship, are a few among many culture-complexes whose history should ultimately be ascertainable with reasonable positiveness, at least in outline. Rivet, Jijón, and Nordenskiöld have definitely shown the extremely high probability of the independent American origin of bronze by taking into consideration all possible associated phenomena, such as the shapes of objects. Without these associated data, the problem would have remained insoluble, other than by mere opinionating.

These remarks do not refute what has been said above in favor of Ratzel's recommendation to consider connection as a possibility in spite of geographic gaps—so long as resemblances are more than conceptual and so long as any hypothesis remains genuinely tentative and an instrument for further inquiry.

8. Similarly, it must be the totality of constituents which decides relationships between faunas or floras or cultures. These are necessarily always complex, though in varying degree. It may be proved that the Aztecs played a game of Hindu origin and the Mayas sculptured elephants, and yet the bulk of Middle American civilization be a purely native growth. Biologists no longer expect any fauna to have originated wholly in any one remote other region. Neither should anthropologists in regard to a culture. And yet there may be a decisive preponderance. This obviously is expressible only in terms of the totality of species or traits involved.

9. In this connection absences and paucities become important evidence: the virtual absence of placental mammals from Australia, for instance, especially as coupled with the rarity of marsupials elsewhere. Similarly, the absence from native America of iron, wheels, plows, the usual grains and domestic animals, stringed instruments, ordeals, and proverbs, as pointed out by Boas, indicates strongly that culture in America must have had a history very considerably or prevalently separate from the rest of the world; although such a conclusion leaves some, probably lesser, introductions into America entirely possible, even expectable.

10. Degeneration or simplification is a factor in cultural as well as natural history. Not only can areas become impoverished biotically or culturally, but a system such as a manufacturing technique or sculpture, an alphabet or cult, can degenerate much like an organic group: for instance, the ascidians, whose simple, regressive structure caused them long to be excluded from their place among the chordates. Even the suppression of parts due to parasitism has its cultural parallels: quite probably among the Negritos and among pastoral nomads in contact with farming and town populations. Rivers' work on the disappearance of useful arts is important in this connection; and Perry and Smith have made out some cases for deterioration which are not the less valuable in themselves because they are used also as arguments for a larger and generally unaccepted scheme.

In the light of the foregoing parallels of biological and cultural method, several former and current anthropological theories or points of view appear inadequate when judged by comparable standards in biological science. All explanations of specific culture manifestations as due essentially to the common psychic structure of mankind are about as offhand and antiquated a dismissal of real problems as would be the assumption that organic forms originate spontaneously and independently. Universal schemes of unilinear typological development seem in principle to deserve little, if any, more consideration than general schemes of unilinear evolution would receive in biology. The Smith-Perry view that substantially all higher civilization is due to the spread from an origin in Egypt about five thousand years ago is about as likely to be right as a thesis that the principal mammalian orders originated at one specified period in one named area under one set of circumstances, and then spread out over the earth with not much more change than the loss of some species, genera, and families and the modification of others. The Kulturkreis theory, or as it is sometimes renamed, the Kulturgeschichtliche Methode, is not quite so simplistic. But the six or eight blocks of culture trait associations which it posits as primary are comparable to six or eight associations of species which might be asserted as having produced all the faunas of the world. If any modern zoölogist were to advance such a view, he would at least indicate the approximate time and place and peculiar circumstances of origin of his primary blocks or associations. This the Kulturkreisler have hardly, or only secondarily, begun to do. After all, pointing out that this and that recent culture here or there consists largely of constituents found also in such and such primary blocks is not the equivalent of defining the circumstances of the origin of the blocks. Father Schmidt's valiant and brilliant remodeling has done much to deprive the original Graebner scheme of its stark baldness and mechanical rigor. But the value of his modifications lies in themselves, not in rendering the scheme more demonstrated. They would prob-

ably be having more influence if they had been made independently of the scheme. And finally, the claim to the names "diffusionist" and "culture-historical" is about as unfortunate as if the adherents to a particular set of palaeontological or systematic interpretations were to proclaim these as "the evolutionistic view." All modern ethnologists recognize diffusion and all deal with culture history.

Anthropology is younger than biology and controls a smaller and less intensively organized and classified body of accurate fact. It is natural, therefore, that critical standards have generally been less exact; that there has been much formulation of broad, conceptually simple schemes subsequently fortified by selected evidence; that too often the necessity has not been felt for purely empirical procedure and strictly inductive interpretation. The foregoing pages have attempted to show that, in spite of the difference between organic and superorganic or cultural phenomena, and the widely diverse mechanisms inherent in them, the historic course of the two sets of phenomena, the problems which they present, and especially the methods by which these problems can be approached and valid solutions given, are strikingly similar at many points.

In anthropology as in biology, interest can center primarily in process or in event—in "physiology" or in "natural history." Many physiologists, having only a weak interest in phenomena, are little impressed even by the soundest, empirically founded, careful reconstructions of events, but are correspondingly sensitive to errors and excesses in such reconstructions. They therefore generically distrust the findings of historical—unfortunately miscalled "evolutionary"—biology and would restrict natural history to a relatively sterile, static, descriptive "systematics," admitting sequences only so far as they are established by the palaeontological record, which will necessarily always be extremely incomplete.

In the same way in anthropology a preponderant addiction to the so-called "dynamic" or processual aspects can lead to a generic suspicion or dislike of all historical reconstruction, whether critical or fantastic, with ethnography relegated to an essentially descriptive role, and only archaeological evidence admitted as historically sound—though, even then, relatively unimportant because processes can never be traced with the same fulness in excavated as in historic or living cultures.

If "physiology" were the only valid aim of the sciences of life and culture, these attitudes would be justified. But, since there are no events without processes and no processes without events, and neither can be wholly grasped without knowledge of the other, what is actually involved is a different centering or weighting of interest; and this reflects temperament or personality as much as anything else. There are those who prefer to deal directly with phenomena, treating process chiefly as it is inherent or implicit in them. There are others whose bent it is to abstract processes, to render them explicit; and to such minds events have little meaning except as stepping stones or illustrations. Each procedure achieves results peculiar to itself; each supplements the other. Carried to extremes in isolation, the one method would lead to an unorganized phenomenalism; the other, to a barren, arid conceptualism. A healthy and complete science must rest on both approaches, on a reintegration of the two. Fundamental misprizal of either approach is unwarranted. A generation or two ago biology entered upon a phase in which some saw virtue and profit only in the laboratory table and experiment. Natural history was decried as merely factual, as antiquarian and descriptive, as productive of the materials of science but not scientific in itself; as uninterpretative when sound, and subjective when interpretative. But natural history has survived and flourishes. Anthropology, having only lately consciously discovered process in culture, is now showing signs of entering the same phase of development. According to some, culture history is to remain a descriptive prolegomena; culture reconstruction, however undertaken, is felt as a waste of effort or dangerous delusion. Except for biology's being farther developed, the situation is much the same: within each discipline, tolerance of both the possible approaches is called for. In anthropology, as in biology, good science consists primarily not in seeing event through process or process through event, but in tempering imagination with criticism and in ballasting judgment with evidence.

6. HISTORY AND SCIENCE IN ANTHROPOLOGY
1935

This continued and enlarged my argument with Boas in No. 5, but I have no wish to preserve the argument. I have therefore extracted from this paper only one passage, constituting about one-seventh of the total, that deals with general principles.

I SUGGEST as the distinctive feature of the historical approach, in any field, not the dealing with time sequences—though that almost inevitably crops out where historical impulses are genuine and strong—but an endeavor at descriptive integration. By "descriptive" I mean that the phenomena are preserved intact as phenomena, so far as that is possible; in distinction from the approach of the nonhistorical sciences, which set out to decompose phenomena in order to determine processes as such. History of course does not ignore process, but it does refuse to set it as its first objective. Process in history is a nexus among phenomena treated as phenomena, not a thing to be sought out and extracted from phenomena. Historical activity is essentially a procedure of integrating phenomena as such; scientific activity, whatever its ultimate resyntheses, is essentailly a procedure of analyses, of dissolving phenomena in order to convert them into process formulations.

These two approaches are applicable to all fields of knowledge, but with varying degree of fruitfulness. It is in the nature of things—I do not pretend to explain why—that in the inorganic realm the processual approach of science has yielded most results, but, as we pass successively into the realms of the organic, psychic, and social-cultural-"historical," this approach encounters more and more difficulties and its harvest diminishes. It is customary to say that the phenomena are more "complex" on the organic and superorganic levels. I incline to doubt this and to believe rather that the difficulties lie in their being epiphenomena—from the point of view of the analytic, processual science approach. Hence the constant tendency to resolve organic phenomena into physicochemical explanations, psychological phenomena into biological ones (the reflex arc), social-cultural phenomena into psychic ones. From the angle of science this procedure is perfectly correct, because, so far as it can be applied, it yields coherent and verifiable results.

The historical approach, on the other hand, was first applied and proved most readily productive in the field of human societies; and it encounters increasing difficulties as the inorganic is approached. In the organic field it is still fairly successful; in geology and astronomy it leans so heavily on processual science that the nature of these disciplines, which by their objectives are clearly historical, is generally understood as being completely "scientific." As regards biology, I recently pointed out, in an essay on that subject [see No. 5], that a whole series of phenomenally formulable "processes" familiar in anthropology—convergence, degeneration, areal grouping, etc.—were equally important in those biological activities covered by the old term "natural history"; and that the problems of natural history run closely parallel, at many points, to the problems of human or cultural history. I do not believe in the slightest degree that these resemblances are "mere" analogies and empty and misleading. That may be true from the point of view of processual, experimental science. From the point of view of historical science, however, or history, or the historical approach to the world, they are obviously of methodological significance, because corresponding objectives involve corresponding methods.

I am not trying to assert that these two approaches—the historical and the processual—can never meet, still less that they are in any sense in conflict. Ultimately, and so far as possible at all times, they should supplement each other. The degree to which astronomy has profited by leaning on and borrowing from experimental science is a case in point. But, precisely if they are to co-operate, it seems that they should recognize and tolerate each other's individuality. It is hard to see good coming out of a mixture of approaches whose aims are different.

As to the element of time sequence: if I am correct that the essential quality of the historical approach is an integration of phenomena, and therefore ultimately an integration in terms of the totality of phenomena, it is obvious that the time relations of phenomena enter into the task. I am not belittling the time factor; I am only taking the stand that it is not the most essential criterion of the historic approach. Space relations can and sometimes must take its place.

If this is correct, the point often made, not only by Boas and his followers but by sociologists and functionalists, that history is legitimate and proper, but historical reconstruction unsound and sterile, loses much if not all validity. I would maintain, on the contrary, that history and historical reconstruction have the identical aims and approach and make use of the same mental faculties. (In technical language, they pos-

sess the same basic objective and method; but it seems best to avoid the latter word because it is likely to be ambiguous in the present connection.) It is true that history has the time relations largely given it in its data, whereas historical reconstruction largely seeks to ascertain them. But this makes the latter only a special and somewhat more difficult case of the former, taken in its widest sense.

A little reflection will show that all historical procedure is in the nature of a reconstruction and that no historical determination is sure in the sense that determinations in physical science are sure, that is, objectively verifiable. Historical determinations are in their essence subjective findings, and at best they only approximate truth or certainty. They differ from one another in seeming more or less probably true, the criterion being the degree of completeness with which a historical interpretation fits into the totality of phenomena, or, if one like, into the totality of historical interpretations of phenomena.

History is supposed to tell "what really happened." But obviously this is impossible: the "real" retelling would take as long as the happenings and be quite useless for any conceivable general human purpose. The famous principle is evidently to be understood obversely: history is not to tell what did not happen; that is, it is not to be fictive art. More useful is the definition of a historian as one who "knows how to fill the lacunae." But even this is too narrow. The professional historian is no doubt most conscious of the occasions when he encounters frank gaps in his data; but he is all the time, habitually and largely unconsciously, reading between the lines of his data on the one hand and omitting less significant data on the other. If he did not, he would never reach an interpretation. Whether this procedure is avowed or not, or, if avowed, whether or not scientists know it, does not much matter: it has been and is the procedure of all historians [see No. 8]. If some of us ethnologists attempt to do time history for the poor dateless primitives, we have an additional unknown to deal with, and our results are undoubtedly more approximative therefor. But if we frankly admit that fact, there seems no valid reason why we should be condemned as inherently unsound for doing under greater difficulties the same type of thing which historians are respected for doing. That historians pay little attention to us, their poor relations, is expectable enough: who are we to enter the houses of the substantial when we do not possess even one document written before our day?

Many scientists do not know what history is, or merely assume that it is not science. But it is old and reputable and is accepted as long as it sticks to documents. In counterpart, scientists make scarcely any effort to apply their methods to documentary materials. If the aim of anthropology is to ascertain the processes of change or dynamics in human societies and cultures, why this timorous sticking to the primitives whom we can observe only an instant, while rich data on change for centuries back are available on our own and other lettered civilizations? The usual answer is "complexity." But is this a serious obstacle as against the advantage of operating with timed data in studies of change?

Well, the result is that historical reconstruction on the basis of datable documents is not seen as reconstruction and is held up as laudable or permissible even though not scientific; but once the reconstruction is patent, because the dated pieces of paper are not there, it is considered wasted effort or unsound. . . .

7. SO-CALLED SOCIAL SCIENCE
1936

This paper carries on the theme of Nos. 4, 5, and 6. Being addressed to an audience wider than anthropologists, it is pitched in a more general key.

Society and culture are now wholly distinguished, and "sociocultural" appears for the first time in my writing.

THIS is an attempt to understand more clearly the nature of what it has become customary to call the "social" sciences. This task of course involves the question of their relation to the remainder of science or organized knowledge.

The problem involves two main considerations: the material of the various sciences, and their objectives. Methods are in part dependent on material, still more so on objective. The history of the sciences as a whole shows some sort of connection or partial correlation to exist between material and objective: methods leading to successful attainment of certain objectives are more easily evolved for certain materials than for others. This fact I do not examine epistemologically but posit as given by the sum of experience. The part-correlation has led to an assumption that certain purposes and methods of understanding pertain inherently to certain materials and not to others. It is certainly borne out by the majority of evidence which we possess on the history of science in the past. But there is a definite minority of experience in the total record of science which is to the contrary. This minority of evidence invalidates the assumption, unless it can be explained away. Instead of explaining it away, we can more profitably grant as true the fairly numerous evidences contrary to the assumption, and start from the opposite premise that any objective of understanding, with the methods flowing from it, can be pursued in any body of phenomenal material, although with relatively different degree of ease, profit, and success. Why there are these differences is a separate problem for which I have no answer. It is perhaps a problem for the philosopher rather than the scientist.

I

The subjects or materials of science—the phenomena of the world—fall into four main classes or levels: the inorganic, organic, psychic, and sociocultural or superpsychic, as it is less ambiguous to call it than "superorganic." Again I am speaking empirically without knowing what there is in the nature of things or the human mind that produces the substantial segregation of phenomena into these four classes or levels. They can legitimately be called "levels" because all experience to date in the field of science in the narrower or stricter sense—as it will be defined shortly— is to the effect that there is a hierarchy between the classes. This hierarchy rests on the fact that phenomena of one class can at times—not as yet always, but frequently enough—be scientifically understood by conversion of their processes into terms of another class, but never in the reverse direction. Some fraction of organic phenomena are already intelligible, or coherently expressible, in terms of physicochemical processes. But it is a truism that we have no cases of a physicochemical phenomenon being explained by an organic process. Similarly as between the pyschic and the organic: such convertibility as there is, is always one-way. This fact justifies the designation of the classes of phenomena as levels. The phenomena of an upper level are epiphenomena from the point of view of a lower [see No. 6, paragraph 2].

There is no intention to assert that the levels are absolutely separate, or separable by unassailable definitions. They are substantially distinct in the experience of the totality of science, and that is enough. To indicate that I am not asserting more, or dealing with metaphysical entities, I have, in the accompanying diagram, deliberately set biochemistry on the line between the organic and inorganic levels, between physiology and chemistry. If that is incorrect in the eyes of biochemists, let them correct me: my judgment of the case is by way of an example.

In the year of our Lord 1936 it appears that this distinction of the four levels should be, and in the main is, a commonplace needing no substantiation, though no doubt there are some scientists of the inorganic so absorbed in their own levels—and it is the most self-sufficient one—as to remain a bit hazy as to the difference between the two upper levels. Most of the doubt or dissent still remaining comes from workers in the upper levels and seems due to two factors.

One is that some men formally operating in one level are really interested in the next below, and therefore resent boundaries: the nominal psychologist who is substantially or by desire a physiologist, the historian or anthropologist who would actually rather psychologize than make findings in his own field. Such hyphenates or internationalists have their place and value, but their claims that *de facto* boundaries, grown out of long common experience, are illusory or insignificant are likely to be colored.

The other resistance to acceptance of the levels springs from a confusion: the

Levels   *Approaches*

	LOGISTIC	HISTORICAL	SCIENTIFIC	PRACTICAL
SOCIOCULTURAL	Sociology Economic Theory	History Economic History	Sociology Economics	
PSYCHIC	(Pre-experimental Psychology)	Personality Psychology?	Psychology	Educational Psychology
ORGANIC	(Superseded)	Natural History Palaeontology	Genetics Physiology —Biochemistry—	Medicine
INORGANIC	(Superseded)	Geology Astronomy	Chemistry Physics	Engineering

Mathematics

inference that, because some psychic phenomena have been converted or explained, under the special treatment of science, into organic process formulations, and the remainder presumably can ultimately be so converted, psychic phenomena therefore do not exist, and there is only one level, not two. Similarly of course as between superpsychic and psychic. At bottom this confusion appears to rest upon simplistic impulses. There are those who are better satisfied with a system, provided that it is simple and closed, than with facing the rich and largely inexplicable diversity of phenomena which the world presents.

It need hardly be pointed out that this attitude, if really and generally acted out, would produce an immediate short-circuiting of science. It would divert all the multiple activities of science into the promulgation of a mechanistic system of philosophy. Phenomena are and remain organic, psychic, and sociocultural as well as organic, even though the processes in them may ultimately all be expressible, through the mechanism of true scientific method, in physicochemical terms as well as in terms of their own levels.

The number of levels could also be increased from four by subdivision. Physics and chemistry examine different aspects of inorganic phenomena. Of these, the physical are usually considered more basic: chemical findings convert more often into physical ones than the reverse; and the discoveries of the next upper or organic level usually are chemically rather than physically expressible. Somewhat similarly between society and culture. Society carries culture; and it is composed of persons with individual psyches. Within the uppermost level, culture can therefore be construed as the top, society as the bottom, stratum. Perhaps the organic level could be properly subdivided into sublevels concerned, respectively, with plants and animals, the latter alone carrying a nervous system, which in turn is the basis for the psyche of the next level. We do have the fairly segregated sciences of botany and zoölogy corresponding to this subdivision.

In short, an argument could be made for six or seven or possibly more levels instead of the four with which I content myself. I do not deny the greater number or go into the essentially philosophical problem of what the levels of phenomena rest on. I merely hold that there are at least four readily discernible ones and that they are differentiable on the basis of empirical experience acquired in the development of science or understanding as a whole.

Similarly, arguments can be and have been put forth for reducing the number of primary levels from four to three, by construing either the organic-psychic plane of cleavage, or the psychic-superpsychic, as less clear and decisive than the two others. Subjectively, some would be disposed to agree with one of these reductions, some with the other. Still others, on the contrary, under the influence of the *Naturwissenschaft-Geisteswissenschaft* dichotomy, might see the organic-psychic cleavage as transcending both others in importance. Again, these are epistemological problems, proper in their place, but into which it would be unprofitable to enter in the present connection, even if I were competent.

I do not know what to do with mathematics. It does not deal with a level of the same sort as the others because it is nonphenomenological. I have therefore set it outside the frame of the diagram, underlying all the levels of the proper scientific and utilitarian approaches.

II

Objectives, being human and therefore frequently of mixed motivation, are harder to disentangle than phenomena, which mainly lie outside us. The segregation which follows, of organized knowledge or science as a whole into four approaches, may therefore encounter more resistance than that which has been made into levels. We can call the four approaches the scientific proper, the practical or applied, the historical, and the logistic. There is much intergradation between them—motives have a way of coming mixed. Nevertheless, there are four separate basic purposes at work and, flowing out of these or at least corresponding to them, four fundamental methods. Hence the use of the term "approach."

The *scientific* method proper is of course exemplified by physics, chemistry, physiology, experimental psychology. The objective of this approach is understanding of the world by the conversion of sensible phenomena into nonqualitative concepts. Hence the quantification of science proper. Hence, too, Windelband's designation of science as nomothetic. Experiment is a valuable tool of this objective, but not its fundamental characteristic. In fact, experiment is merely a special form of observation, a controlled and directed kind. It has been important in science for less than two hundred years. Until 1750 enormous accomplishments were made in pure science with only the meagerest experimentation. The essential qualities of the genuine scientific approach are, first, that it seeks understanding as an end in itself; second, that in seeking this understanding it insists on starting from and with phenomena; and, third, that as it achieves success it destroys the phenomena as phenomena by transmuting them into abstract concepts—laws, constants, mathematical relations, and the like. Hence the saying that science converts qualities into quantities. All this is commonplace enough, but needs to be stated with reference to the distinctions that follow.

Applied science is practical. It does not aim at understanding for its own sake, but at tangible effects which are acceptable as profitable and desirable—curing the sick or building bridges. Hence the characterization of medicine and engineering as "arts"—useful arts as distinct from the fine arts, whose purpose is aesthetic inward satisfaction. Engineers, leaning heavily on physical science, may sometimes have come to feel that their profession is science rather than an art; but it must be the purpose and end-product of an activity that is determinative in a classification such as this. The applied sciences use the pure sciences, as they were wont to be called before linguistic fashion renamed them the "fundamental sciences," for practical ends and hence are in one aspect thoroughly distinct from the pure sciences, whose objective of mere understanding is per se free from practical considerations. That many scientists are quick to see the practical applicabilities of their discoveries, and many physicians and engineers are eagerly combing the results of science for findings which they can use, proves only the intimate and fruitful interrelations of two activities whose goals—and therefore basic methods—are distinct. Here again we have nothing new; but the differentiation acquires significance when we come to consider the social science field.

The third or *historical* approach makes the most difficulty. It includes intellectual activities so distinct as history in the conventional sense—a recognized profession or discipline concerned with the narration of human events—and geology and astronomy. Between these two extremes lies the realm of what used to be called by the appropriate phrase "natural history," which has been almost superseded, in academic usage, by such terms as "systematic," "taxonomic," and "evolutionary" biology. These are somewhat unfortunate because in part they carry a suggestion of odium and because they refer to specializations of technique rather than to basic method; or, in the case of "evolutionary," because the reference is too often to an implication of progress. That astronomy and geology are historical sciences I shall not attempt to prove, because it is admitted by most good astronomers and geologists. Where the fact is overlooked, it is because both sciences utilize so much physics and chemistry, though for their own ends, that they may superficially seem as properly scientific as these. The error however is as great as if engineering were construed as a basic or pure science. Again it is the objective and the fundamental method arising out of objective that really define the kind of approach.

We have, then, a series of intellectual activities ranging all the way from human history, which operates at least largely on the sociocultural level, to astronomy on the inorganic, whose historic quality of some sort is conceded. What is the common factor?

The dealing with time sequences is likely to be the first answer. But this trait seems only an incident. The essential characteristic of the historic approach appears to be the endeavor to achieve a conceptual integration of phenomena while preserving the quality of the phenomena. This quality the strictly scientific approach does not attempt to preserve. On the contrary, it destroys phenomena as phenomena in utilizing them for its own conceptualizations of a different order. Time and space certainly enter into the considerations and results of science proper; but its findings or end-results are timeless and spaceless formulations, in the sense that they are independent of specific or particular time and place. The findings of the historical approach on the other hand are necessarily always given in terms of specified time and space—phenomenal time and space, we might say, in contrast to the abstract measure of time and space in science. A dateless and placeless finding in human history, natural his-

tory, palaeontology, geology, or astronomy would make no sense. If a dateless and placeless block of phenomena is discovered, the first problem of any historical discipline is recognized to be the finding of its date and place. Conversely, where a phenomenal lacuna appears in the date-place frame, the filling of this lacuna with the relevant phenomena is felt to be a need and problem. The historical approach is therefore always reconstructive in its nature—reconstructive as to the phenomena themselves and as to their dates and places.

Now what is the nature of this conceptually reconstructive or integrative process which characterizes the historical approach? It does not seem to have been defined except for the fact that on the one hand it is conceptual and integrative and on the other phenomenological, whereas science proper is also conceptual, also integrative but in a different manner, and abstracting instead of phenomenological. This balancing distinction may not hold much meaning for the routine physicist who sees in astronomy only special applications of physics and in human history only an entertaining or boring aesthetic narration; or for the would-be social scientist who disposes of history as antiquarianism; but whoever has competently used the historical approach will be aware of the antithesis, whether or not he agree wholly with the above attempt to define it.

Rickert has given a valuable formulation of the problem when he has science and history agreeing in destroying immediate apperceptions in the endeavor to construct concepts, but differing in that science also destroys individuality whereas history preserves it. Art—that is, pure art—he goes on to say, does not aim at concepts, and further differs from history in that it preserves immediate apperceptions but destroys individuality—presumably by converting it into nonconceptual generalizations of the type which we call aesthetic. History, he concludes, is therefore truly the science of reality; and its essence lies in its way of transmuting apperceptions into concepts. There might be much discussion of what is meant by "individuality"; but it is evidently not far from what I have just called "phenomenological quality." Windelband's designation of history as idiographic also aims at something very similar.

Phenomena or events, then, with their adhering dates and places, are the material—not merely the starting point, but the perpetual material—of the historical approach. It cannot free itself from them, else itself is dissolved. While it conceptualizes, it does not wholly abstract. Thorough abstraction in any field of history becomes deadening generalization, formula, scheme, which able historians, whatever their material, have always felt to be fatal to their objectives. The essence of their pursuit is the building-up of selected and reconstructed phenomena—not the reproduction of phenomena, which would be at once useless and impossible—into significant conceptual relations or groupings. The ultimate validation of findings by the historical approach seems to lie in the degree of their fit or integration into the totality of conceptual findings made by the method.

The establishment of time sequences is a normal, but not the fundamental, feature of the historic approach. Sequence of events is a definitely minor element in astronomy, except in its more speculative aspects. The bulk of its results are descriptive. This characterization is not a paradox. Rather is there a superficial confusion involved: because astronomy has had to concern itself so heavily with the measurement of time, the means has been taken as the end. Much of history proper is also statically descriptive rather than narrative: whenever, for instance, a historic moment or period in a given area is held fast for

analysis of its phenomena and their reintegration into the formulations which characterize the period or culture. Whole fields obviously adjacent to history—ethnography, for instance—are primarily descriptive: this discipline ordinarily can narrate only in proportion as its reconstructions or formulations assume a speculative tinge. On the natural history level, systematic biology is immediately descriptive, although its work is done with an eye to the tracing of developments in time.

A corollary of the historical approach being bound to phenomena is the fact that process remains secondary or implicit. The scientific approach destroys phenomena by systematic analysis in order to extract processes, and therefore ends, per se, in abstractions. The historic approach preserves phenomena in order to integrate them as concepts to which concreteness still adheres. In a former publication [No. 4] I tried to express this distinction by using the somewhat inadequate terms "depictive" and "explanational" (or "processual"). In principle it is clear that the same phenomena, whether they be planets, animals, human beings, or sociocultural products, can be attacked by both methods, though not necessarily with the same readiness or success. Hence the possibility and ultimate need of fruitful relations between the two approaches on all levels.

The fourth approach is the *logistic*, or distinctively logical. It is more or less scientific, in that it is not purely formal but deals with bodies of phenomena. The phenomena however are primarily those of common observation or experience, as distinguished from dissected, weighed, or tested experience; and the procedure in operating from these is one of logical constructs. As these constructs develop, they are frequently brought into new relation with phenomena, after which the logical process is resumed, and so on, sometimes to great heights.

It will be obvious that at bottom the logistic approach is only quasi-scientific and characteristic of the immaturity of science on a given level. On the plane of the inorganic, it has long since been crowded out by the progress made by astronomy, physics, and engineering. However, it still looms large on the sociocultural level, holding a considerable place in economics and sociology.

Of course, these four approaches intergrade: much scientific activity is composed of work done by two or more approaches. Also, the diagram does not properly provide for all the relations and intergradations, because it is two-dimensional. A more adequate representation might be by means of an erect cylinder with four longitudinal sections, each in more or less contact with the other three, for the approaches; and cut by three transverse planes to indicate the four levels.

III

Turning now to the so-called "social" sciences, we find all four approaches represented on the uppermost level, but very unevenly, and with far the least development in the scientific approach proper, where I have left a deliberate blank....

History is of course the mother of the whole brood of social sciences. In a sense they must be her illegitimate or spurious children because they claim a scientific name and therefore paternity, whereas history has never admitted to being the bride of science but has maintained her virginal integrity in her proverbial tower of ivory. History also has rarely asserted her utility: most such assertions, like most attempts at applying history, have come from nonhistorians. Similarly, the logistic element has never been obtrusive: whenever it became obtrusive, it has been gently but decisively pushed aside as *Geschichts-*

philosophie. It is plain that historians have felt that they knew what the business of history is and have stuck to it with consistency. Their tradition has been strong, even if their explicit definitions of their work often are brief or wavering.

As a developed activity, history is as old as physics. Thucydides is equidistant between Pythagoras and Archimedes and is recognized as of comparable greatness and significance. Until very recently there has been no sense of conflict between the two, and little need for delimitation of frontier. History has gone on being particularistic about human events, science has dealt with the repetitive generalities of subhuman phenomena. Now however that science has been put on a pedestal of primacy and has *de facto* become the god of innumerable laymen, a totalitarian realm is claimed for it. History, merely trying to continue on its autonomous way, is challenged and put on the defensive. In contrast with the social sciences, it is said, history will be neither utilitarian nor scientific, and its right to exist, except as a harmless amusement, is being questioned.

While this attitude is the product of the rapid extension of science since about 1750, it is not its logically necessary outcome. In part the attitude rests upon the fact that the earlier history was confined to the two upper or human levels, the earlier science to the subhuman levels. The attitude also fails to recognize the fact that certain admitted sciences are historical in objective. Hence the dichotomy that history concerned itself with human events and values in its individualizing way and was *Geisteswissenschaft*, but that science concerned itself with subhuman phenomena in a generalizing way and was *Naturwissenschaft*. Even Rickert is not free from this antithesis, though he has taken the long step of substituting culture for *Geist* as the material or field of history. As soon however as we recognize a historical approach as not only possible but existent on the organic and inorganic level, the converse possibility of a genuinely scientific attack on psychic and cultural material is forced upon us. Psychology, since it became experimental, has actually realized the beginnings of a true science on its own level. History, however, has tended to insulate itself against such extensions and has proposed none of its own. It has failed, on the whole, to distinguish between historical approach or essential method and historical field or material, but has continued to treat the two as facets of the same thing. Thus history remained self-contained while science tried to progress, and to considerable extent did actually progress, from level to level. The result is that history does not know what to do with the flock of social sciences milling around her knees. She wavers between claiming them as offspring because they deal with her material, and repudiating them because they do not treat it historically. It is an attitude at once somewhat annoyed and disdainful.

In brief, as soon as we see history and science as differing not primarily in their field but in their basic approach, and each approach as capable in principle of being carried through all levels of phenomena, conflict or even collision is eliminated and co-operation is in order. It is true that there is something in the nature of phenomena (or of our minds) which invites the historical approach as most easily fruitful in the uppermost level, and the scientific in the lowest; but this may not, and must not, be construed as meaning that there is an inherent absolute delimitation of spheres.

The two great principles recognized by modern historians as constituting the basis of their methodology are the continuity of history and the uniqueness—nonrepetitiveness—of historical phenomena. The former implies that history is

an integrating activity; the latter, that it is individualizing. To be at once integrative and particularizing is of course meaningless from the point of view of science, whose procedure is analytic and generalizing. This difference alone should be sufficient to show that the two approaches are parallel and not merely different by position on one line. But the difference in preoccupation according to level is one of emphasis or weighting, not of inherent nature.

In this connection two problems discussed by Rickert may be referred to: how far history deals properly with values, and whether it is teleological or causal. It must be kept in mind that to Rickert history is still limited to culture, as distinct from nature which is the domain of science; while I hold that anything essentially characteristic of the method of human history ought also to be characteristic of the historic approach in any field. As to values, Rickert concludes that, while history is not concerned with passing judgments of praise or blame, it does deal with values, and that is its business: the values existing in culture are the subject matter of history. On the second point his answer is that history need not be teleological—in fact, should not contravene the causality of reality, which presumably is that determined by science; but he implies, if I understand correctly, that history accepts the causality of science, and conforms to it, rather than seeking to establish a causality of its own. The nexuses or relations with which it is concerned are of a different order from the mechanical-mathematical nexuses of science. When soundly discerned, they do not clash with mechanical causality, but neither do they reduce to it; they form a gradually integrating system of their own, whose degree of integration is the ultimate measure of their validity. I accept his finding that history is the true study of reality. . . .

We may conclude that historians possess a consistent methodology which satisfies them, which has long proved satisfactory to the world, and which they rightly feel to be distinct from and independent of the method of science proper. This is a showing of great definiteness in comparison with economics and government, which combine or mix three or four methods or approaches. It remains to ask what the limitations or deficiencies of history are as practiced.

Mainly the difficulties of the profession of history during the past generation or two are due to its not recognizing the import of the changes in civilization which have brought it about that science is no longer ruler merely of the remote realm of subhuman nature but is actively attempting to extend its particular type of control over all levels of phenomena. Theoretically, a true science of society and culture is not only possible but is as desirable as it may be difficult, and ought to prove immensely stimulating and enriching to history. Actually, historians, too often delimiting their subject in terms of its material instead of its characteristic method of approach, have failed to recognize the opportunities of mutually fruitful interaction between two parallel autonomous sets of activities concerned with the same material, and have remained indifferent, deliberately aloof, suspicious, or defensive. The situation was not made easier for them by the fact that, for every inch of the sociocultural field conquered by true science, there has been a foot of claim made by practical and logistic approaches in the name of science. One result is that most historians have become doubly resistive toward all generalization, many of them even to proper historic generalization. There has been an inclination to cling to narrative as being least easily convertible into generalization; to hug events rather than engage with their patterns; to resign the economic aspects of history to economists rather than include them; to ignore the results of ethnography on the external ground that they were dateless and therefore nonhistorical; to allow the history of the great East Asiatic civilizations to settle behind watertight bulkheads; to view any larger culture history askance; to emphasize the mechanics of documentation as evidence that history, too, was objective and scientific. These have been the shortcomings of the mass, it is true, not of the leaders, as is shown by the fact that the greatest historian of the last generation did not hesitate to take as his subject five thousand years of nearly all aspects of culture—only the economic is somewhat slighted—in the whole Mediterranean world as far east as Mesopotamia and Iran. Still it is unfortunate that the body have not more willingly followed the leaders in spirit and purpose, even though their execution might remain humbler.

Anthropology shares with history the feature of never having seriously held the opinion that it is of practical utility, but of assuming that its end of understanding is sufficient justification in itself. It is also relatively free from logical systematizing. It experienced its share of this in its earlier days; but by about 1900 the turn was made, and logistic interest is now randomly represented [see No. 17]. For more than a generation past, anthropological activity has been rather fairly in balance between the historical and the scientific approach. The working-out of the specific interrelations of these approaches within anthropology, and with particular reference to the important influence of Boas, I have discussed in some detail in a recent article [No. 6].

The prehistoric and archaeological parts of anthropology are of course patently historical in their nature, even when they still lack absolute dating. Much descriptive ethnography is also historic material, whether it is so recognized or not. Comparative ethnography inevitably obtrudes historic problems. These are often difficult or insoluble with present data, and a number of Gordian attempts have been made with the sword of a scheme or formula; but more patient work has gone on undeterred. Frequently lacking any time element in their data, anthropologists have developed the technique of inferring this from the distribution of cultural phenomena in space—sometimes with skill, sometimes crudely. The attempt has been made to distinguish these indirect reconstructions as different in kind from the document-based constructs of history. But the difference, while real, is superficial, because all historic approach produces reconstructions if it produces anything [No. 8, Sec. III]. The most important difference between history and anthropology lies not in the matter of dates but in the fact that anthropologists usually have few or no events—as distinct from patterns—given them in their data, whereas events are the accustomed primary material of historians. The abler historians weld the events into patterns or conceptual formulations; the less able cling to events and may end by believing that anything which does not deal with events happening to individuals at specifiable times cannot be historical. The rarity of recorded events in primitive life has helped to force anthropologists into recognition of the forms or patterns of culture, and from this into the clear recognition of culture as such. In short, more perhaps than any one other group, they discovered culture. To be sure, this was long after intelligent historians had known the fact; but these took it for granted and tended to deal with culture indirectly or implicitly, whereas anthropologists became explicit and culture-conscious.

At any rate, the difference is quite marked between anthropology on the one hand and sociology, government, and economics on the other. [See correction as of 1951 in No. 18.] These three still operate largely not indeed with a denial of culture or in ignorance of its existence but as if they could proceed without understanding its nature as such and in detail. They are evidently strengthened in this attitude by the conviction of their utility. When immediately practical needs are to be satisfied, there is little time available for slow researches into the basic nature of things: a deductive formulation is much more ready to hand. In their relative freedom from both the logistic and the utilitarian approach, in historic-mindedness, and in their *de facto* awareness of culture, history and anthropology accordingly group together among the sociocultural disciplines.

The genuinely scientific component in anthropology is in part the result of historical accident. As the subject began to constellate itself, it found its unpreempted materials consisting of several specialties or leavings: the dateless primitives, the dateless prehistoric portion of archaeology, the unwritten languages, the racial history of man. The latter of course is pure biology. Even though the attack on race data proved necessarily to be more largely through the historical than the proper scientific approach, here was a rooting in the subhuman level; and through this root there flowed a stream of natural science views and tradition such as the other social disciplines did not experience. Then the more remote data of prehistory were found to be inextricably associated with the biological data on fossil man, and through these with palaeontology. Nearly all this natural science influence was really much more of the historical than of the strictly scientific or nomothetic order; but, the two orders or approaches being well associated in successful interaction on the organic level, some pure science attitude came to be carried up into anthropology.

It is a curious fact that this stream of

influence long went entirely past the intervening psychic level. Psychology and anthropology have had few intrinsic relations, in spite of their frequent and theoretically quite sound bracketing together. Wundt broached large problems concerning the psychology of culture in a large way but has had no appreciable influence on the current of anthropological thought. It is really only in the most recent years, when some anthropologists began looking beyond cultures at the personalities which carried these with inevitable interactions, and some psychologists began leaving experiments and tests for glimpses and then analyses of total functioning personalities, that the first active rapports were established.

Another factor which led to the strengthening of the scientific approach in anthropology was the primitives themselves. The most outstanding fact about any group of primitives is their culture—its striking difference from our own. The first interest in this culture was very often precisely its exotic qualities. But, as time went on, these small, apparently insignificant, easily mastered cultures were found through their very remoteness to be much more readily treatable objectively than any others: they came to be accurately and dispassionately analyzed much as a biologist dissects a worm or a crayfish. This habit in turn contributed enormously to the discovery or consciousness of culture, which has already been cited as the distinctive achievement of anthropology. All anthropologists would probably agree that their central problem is what culture is—that is, how it can be accurately described—and how it functions, or, historically, how in its total range it has functioned. In its first form this problem is a strictly scientific one, and, it seems to me, a more fundamental one than the other social disciplines pose for themselves, in so far as their prime concern is with societal, economic, or political parts of the sociocultural whole. On the other hand the problem is as nonpractical as it is a sound intellectual one.

The words with which Eduard Meyer opens his final edition of his *Geschichte des Altertums* illustrate what the greatest historian of his day thought of the scientific element in anthropology. He speaks of "anthropology, the study of the general" (or universal, *allgemeinen*) "forms of human life and human development—often miscalled philosophy of history."

Sociology ought in principle to be rather difficult to distinguish from anthropology, since the two studies share so much of their subject matter. Yet, in fact, sociology and anthropology are temperamentally almost antithetical in their motivations. Sociology definitely had a logistic beginning with Comte. It definitely aims to be useful. And, in America at least, it has been overwhelmingly nonhistorical in its interests. . . .

IV

If the fundamental thesis here advanced as to approaches and levels is correct, we are now, after review of what the social disciplines are actually doing, in position to cast up a balance. We find the so-called "sciences" very unevenly distributed in the four compartments of their proper level. Three of them—economics, government, and sociology—operate heavily through the logistic and utilitarian approaches; the two others—anthropology and history—little or not at all. The historical approach is used exclusively and consciously by history; considerably but hesitatingly and often without clear recognition by anthropology; as a recognized minor subactivity by economics and government; not at all by sociology. The great vacancy comes in the properly scientific compartment. This, sociology has proclaimed as its own for a century, but has done little to develop.

Anthropology has made the beginning of a contribution, but this is bound to remain unimpressive as long as anthropological concern remains timidly attached to primitives alone. History deliberately refrains from entering a field which calls for scientific approach. Government and economics are more or less aware of the existence of the field but have so far been prevented by their historic antecedents from prosecuting systematic activity within it. After all, economics and politics are only single facets of society and culture, and no one primarily interested in the more general and fundamental problem of what culture is and how it operates would be likely to want to limit his operations to these particular facets.

In short, we have to date, in the intellectual attack on sociocultural material, the logistic, historical, and practical approaches well represented, though irregularly distributed, but the proper or strict scientific approach as yet very meagerly developed. It is therefore as the depiction of a condition that I have used the term "So-called Social Science" as a title for this essay.

It is illuminating to compare the condition which obtains at the opposite end of the series of levels, the inorganic one of astronomy, geology, physics, chemistry, and engineering. Here it is the logistic approach which has been discarded; but the three other approaches not only are well developed but are intimately co-ordinated and interrelated. The three approaches group, with little doubt, around basic physics-chemistry as their joint pivot. But there are interacting co-operation, mutual stimulation, and genuine support from one to the other. There can hardly be any real question, in the light of this history of success, that strength of the logistic approach is an index of immaturity of the *Wissenschaften* on a given level. . . .

Why have we to date accomplished so little in the way of a physics and chemistry of society and culture? There are quite likely to be several answers; but the chief one seems to be that society and culture are inherently difficult to treat by strict scientific method. Their data, like those of psychology, but by even one degree more, are a sort of epiphenomena to those of the lower levels. [Not that sociocultural data lack actuality or even a causality of their own; but their specific causality must conform to the more general causality of the lower levels of phenomena.— 1951.] There is thus no great ground for hoping that anything as simple and basic as, say, the gravitational and periodic laws will ever be discovered in the psychic and superpsychic fields.

However, one must not go too far. Only forty years ago there seemed little prospect that any discovery of something so regularly repetitive and fundamental as the Mendelian laws would be made on the organic level. The analogy incidentally carries a still further implication in the fact that in 1895 the basic laws of genetics, while not yet discovered by science, had actually been formulated for thirty years. It is just conceivable that enough hard preliminary work has been done in sociocultural science proper that, when somewhat greater insight comes along, a decisive organizing step may be taken rather easily.

From what existing activity, recognized or unrecognized, the fuller development of sociocultural true science will mainly stem is impossible to predict. . . . There is a possibility that this science of the future may turn out to be something psychological—perhaps a "social" or cultural psychology. In a former article [No. 4, 1918], I ventured this very suggestion.

It does look as if the future science would probably be more concerned with culture than with society. Apart from the greater variety and richness of cultural phenomena and the indication that society is more easily construed as a part of culture than the reverse [No. 18, Sec. V], there is this fact: Psychology and human biology apparently find more material which they can bring into some sort of relation with their own, in culture than in society. The influences which bear on personality, for instance, are either other individual personalities or the content and form of the ambient culture, far more than the structure or organization of society as such.

The question however is one on which no one is yet qualified to speak with much positiveness.

*8. HISTORICAL CONTEXT, RECONSTRUCTION, AND INTERPRETATION
1938

The following passages have not been published until now. They are extracts from a series of four lectures on "The Study of Culture," delivered at the University of Chicago, April 7–28, 1938, under the titles: I, "Society and Culture"; II, "Historicity"; III, "Interpolation and Extrapolation"; IV, "Constants."

I

AS REGARDS historicity, or the historical approach, I wish to submit the proposition that there exist no full proofs for the interpretations which history makes. This statement means that the findings of history can never be substantiated by proofs like the proofs of natural science.

There is, first of all, no testing of historical data or interpretations by experiment. This obvious fact needs no elaboration, but is of basic importance.

Here a distinction needs to be observed between so-called historical "facts" and historical "findings" or interpretations. Historical facts are often established by eyewitnesses, contemporary written records, mass testimony, and the like. No one doubts that American independence was declared in Philadelphia by Jefferson and certain others on July 4, 1776. Such data are however merely the brute facts or raw materials of history. As an intellectual pursuit, as an attempt at understanding, history begins only when it commences to operate on such facts in order to make findings or interpretations. It is true that historical narrative as such must stick to phenomenal facts. It cannot divest itself from them, or abstract far from them; it necessarily remains attached to them, however much it may both summate and interpret them. Historical interpre-

tation may be compared to a cement which binds the isolated and per se meaningless facts or events of human history into a meaningful pattern or design. . . .

What is it that the historian really does if he does not "prove"? He infers. He infers greater or lesser probabilities—probabilities of fact, of relation, of significance. His whole business, beyond the assemblage of materials, is a judicial weighing of possibilities and a selection and combination of these into the most coherent whole or pattern. The process is one of progressive reconstruction, until the total fabric, with all its ramifications and complications, attains the most harmonious fit possible of all its parts—and, it may be added, the most harmonious fit to all the remainder of reconstructed history . . . [compare "context" in No. 14].

All genuinely historical work is complex, because it aims to preserve as much as possible of the complexity of individual events, which vary endlessly, while also constructing them into a design which possesses a certain coherence of meaning. If the resultant pattern or design seems inherently improbable, on the basis of all other historic designs, or because it obviously neglects to accommodate large masses of data which fall within the framework of its period and area, the historic construct fails. If, on the contrary, the design is convincing, it is because of its success in revealing

* Not published previously.

the harmonious interconnection, direct or indirect, of as many data as possible....

Santayana, in a passage cited in an essay read here in Chicago in 1936 by Radcliffe-Brown, says that "inferred past facts are more deceptive than facts prophesied." The predictor may in time be proved right or wrong by the event. Whereas, Santayana says, "the historian, while really as speculative as the prophet, can never be found out."[1]

I accept this judgment, so far as it refers to inferred facts of the past being merely such and never absolutely corroborable. I do not accept Santayana's statement that, while there is risk of error in the inference, there is no possibility of discovering the error. The errors are constantly being discovered. Historians are forever finding one another out. That again is part of their business. And that is why history is still being written and rewritten.

It may be added that Santayana was speaking of "a natural science dealing with the past." That would include with human history also natural or biological history, palaeontology and geology, and astronomy. I have elaborated elsewhere [see No. 7, above] that however great the disguise due to special techniques and aids from co-ordinate laboratory science, nevertheless the fundamental aims, manners of handling evidence, and limitations of these so-called "natural" sciences and of human or cultural history are the same. If the contention is not more generally admitted, it is because we live in a time which is under the sign of the fetish of science and because the scientific apparatus fruitfully borrowed by historical biology, geology, and astronomy has disguised, to hasty eyes, the essentially historical character and purpose of these disciplines. Most scientists who have thought about what science is recognize "systematic" biology, geology, and astronomy as being historical in nature. So,

if the human historian could not be found out, neither could the phylogenetic historian and geologist be found out, or the astronomer who holds opinions on the history of the solar system.

One general point more. The true historical approach never eventuates in a scheme or formula. Formulas are the legitimate product of good scientific method. In historical study they are the sign of naïveté—or occasionally of a misguided scientist trying to apply his method to problems which it will not solve. More need not be said in explanation of this seemingly dogmatic statement, because all historians of recognized standing will indorse it.

With the formula, there also falls the origin. In sound history there is no definitive or ultimate "origin" of anything [No. 1]. There are origins, in the sense of incipient stages, and, beyond these, remoter influences. "The origin" of any movement or institution, in the strict sense of the word, is simply not a historically valid conception. A good historian does not really pose the question. It would violate his two fundamental axioms of the uniqueness of all historical phenomena and of the continuity or unity of history. To seek "the origin" of Christianity, or of the Hindu caste system, or of the unilateral clan is in itself unsound procedure. It is simplistic and emotional. The word "origin" is, historically, permissible only as a shorthand abbreviation, a colloquial reference to a set of processes or events understood to be complex and nonunitary.

If there is any set of institutions which should have a precise, particular, definable, unitary origin, it is the great cosmopolitan religions with personal founders: Buddhism, Christianity, Mohammedanism. If Christianity has "an origin," it should be the personality of Jesus. So indeed the layman would answer, and perhaps such scientists as quickly become laymen beyond the confines of their own science. But to the historian the problem is only opened, not settled, by any such answer. What were the influences to which Jesus was subjected? And his contemporaries? What partial parallels to his beliefs and acts appear in the immediately preceding generations in Syria, Egypt, Persia? And in more remote centuries? What was added to the personal contribution of Jesus in the first century of the new religion, in the second, third, and following ones? I need not elaborate. The supposed "origin" is only the starting point for a vast series of inquiries, with highly intricate answers, which will never be given in final form. . . .

II

By contrast with sound history, I should like to cite an instance of bad history.

Some years ago, a student of languages, wandering into the field of native names for tobacco, committed himself to the opinion that some of the American Indian names for tobacco resembled some of the African and Arabic ones, and that the latter were prior. From this he went on to the assertion that tobacco and smoking were introduced into America from Africa; and finally he came to the conclusion that many of the remains of American culture generally considered prehistoric—such as Teotihuacan pottery figurines and the Mississippi Valley mounds—were not only African-derived but post-Columbian. On this thesis he wrote some volumes of argument full of citations of evidence. No one else now shares his view. I do not know of a single anthropologist who would consider it even possibly true in the bulk of its findings. As regards soundness, there is no profit in considering the work. But it is worth inquiring, as an example, in what its unsoundness lies.

The author deals with the customary kind of evidence: linguistic, documentary, archaeological, and so on. He has

hundreds of pages of such evidence; it comes from an enormous range of sources and therefore reveals learnedness; and to a non-Americanist it might seem as impressive as the evidence for, say, a reconstructed pre-Columbian history of maize or of metallurgy. But it runs directly counter to some stubborn bodies of fact: such as the presence of smoking pipes in hundreds of American prehistoric sites free from any admixture of Old World artifacts. Such bodies of fact are either ignored or explained away by the author; but the explanations require increasing ingenuity. This is not the case with the inferential history of maize-growing or metal-working. Secondly, the proponent of the African-origin theory is driven in his explanations to set up numerous ancillary theories: for instance, that the early sixteenth-century Indians on the St. Lawrence maintained active and systematic trade in tropical fruits and the like with Europeans on the Gulf of Mexico; which again runs counter to the trend of all knowledge accepted by historians and anthropologists.

In short, the author of a thesis like this uses the same kind of evidence as does a sound historian, but he misuses it. He selects a position and then manipulates the evidence to support it, usually leaving out masses of it which cannot be manipulated. Phenomena are thus mostly taken out of their context of phenomenal occurrence. The sound historian, on the contrary, basically respects the context of phenomenal occurrence. He does not start out with a specific thesis; therefore, he can let the facts, or the preponderance of their drift, carry him to his conclusions. If the drift of the facts is unclear or fluctuating, he can afford to say so, because he is not determined to reach a particular goal. Throughout, he does not force the facts; rather do the facts force his conclusions.

There is indeed a reasonable degree

of analogy between grossly unsound historical work and a paranoidal delusion system. In both, there is the start—and finish—with a specific idea, whose source seems random or obscure. In both, we see such an idea obtain an increasing hold on the thinking process and push itself obsessively over larger and larger areas. The reasoning, at any given point, is acute and may seem plausible. Its monomanic character becomes evident through the fact that all phenomena dealt with become absorbed into the system. In nature, in the world of reality, this does not happen. Nature is far too complex, conflicting, uncertain, and irrational. The sane man remains more or less open to all experience, potentially at least. In the last analysis, he tries to judge reality, at a given point, by the sum total of his experience. He measures his problematic area for its fit with this totality. To the paranoiac or delusionist the problem has become converted into a fixed attitude which is accorded priority, and the rest of experience is fitted, as best it may be, around this, or is ignored.

Something like this difference between the normal man and the paranoidally inclined is the difference between the good and the bad historian. The unsound one has a thesis, something to prove, a particular proposition to advocate. Sound work shows not only that possibilities have been balanced but that they are not necessarily wholly exclusive. There is, except sometimes in correction of previous imbalance, no specific point established, but a large mass of phenomena is ordered into a pattern which impresses us as balanced, precisely because it is not too simple, but nevertheless possesses internal coherence alongside of significance.

The history of Thucydides has value —that is, it is full of insight and meaning—precisely because it cannot be formulated into a proposition. Conversely, the *History of Melanesian Society* by Rivers, an unusually able scientist, is nearly valueless and essentially fantastic as a piece of history, because it can be reduced to a formula or proposition. . . .

III

It remains to consider the matter of historical lacunae or gaps in knowledge. It is well known that among professional historians skill is measured to a considerable degree not only by ability to perceive relations but by ability to fill lacunae, to build convincing bridges across the gaps, the stretches where data are lacking. Now it might be argued—in fact, has been argued—that this is indeed part of the historian's task, but that in the main he is confronted by more facts than gaps in his fact; whereas the anthropologist, who is generally without archives, faces far more gaps than facts when he attempts to develop a historical interpretation. Metaphorically, according to this view, the historian would be a sort of engineer who in building a road had now and then to construct a bridge across a river; but the ethnologist would be a fantast, dreaming of imaginary bridges between sporadic islands in a great sea. Or, in more technical and less metaphoric language, the archival historian might be construed as occasionally finding it necessary to interpolate, the ethnologist as dealing largely in extrapolation.

While I grant at the outset that there is considerable relative or quantitative difference in fulness of data, it would need to be shown that this difference is significant as regards method or approach, before the above contention would have force. There are several considerations against such a significant difference, of which I shall develop one.

The extent of the lacunae in orthodox history is greatly underestimated by outsiders. Like everyone else, historians are more occupied with telling what they know or think they have found out than in what they do not know. Their normal business is to tell a story, not to interrupt it by deploring their ignorance or lengthily weighing alternative possibilities. Their train therefore rolls smoothly on without the lay passenger's being more than dimly aware of whether he is on cut or fill or bridge. . . .

To illustrate this position, I should like to analyze briefly a specific problem in documentary history.

The instance concerns the origin of the mediaeval town, as outlined by Carl Stephenson in the casebook edited by Rice in 1931 under the title *Methods in Social Science*.

In the earlier nineteenth century, historians asserted that mediaeval towns were persistences of Roman municipalities. In 1831 Wilda derived them from guilds. In 1854 Arnold advanced the view that the mediaeval cities grew out of groupings of free men around a bishop, in whose privileges of immunity they participated. Five years later Nitzsch advocated the contrary opinion of origin from a servile community under the manorial jurisdiction of a great landholder. In 1869 Maurer added a new interpretation: the town was a special variant of the march or mark, the self-governing village which was the primeval unit of Teutonic society. Soon after, Sohm emphasized the mercantile character of the towns, deriving them from markets. Beginning in 1887, Von Below, while accepting the march or *Landgemeinde* interpretation as to origins, traced the actual development of towns to four factors: markets, walling, jurisdictional entity, and dispensation from certain political responsibilities, such as taxation and military service. These four features, he held, were economically determined and then legally validated.

From 1893–95 on, Pirenne developed the view that the nucleus of the mediaeval town was a settlement of traders, usually a stockaded quarter adjacent to a castle or abbey situated favorably for

commerce as this began to revive. Independently and at about the same time, from 1894 to 1897, Rietschel developed much the same interpretation for German towns as Pirenne had for Belgian ones. Contemporaneously, in 1894, Keutgen took an opposite view: in origin a rural commune, the town became a town when it received royal bann of peace; its identity was established by legal recognition of a military, not a commercial, privilege. In 1915, Von Below accepted the Rietschel interpretation for the later stages of town origins, while retaining the march concept as fundamental for the incipient stages.

In England, the Maurer–Von Below view of march or village or township origin was adopted by Stubbs, up to 1903, and Vinogradoff in 1905; but Maitland in 1897 held to a fortress explanation similar to Keutgen's. In France, Luchaire in 1890 characterized the commune or town as a *seigneurie collective* of unknown origin. Giry and Reville in 1893 emphasized economic factors, without arriving at the specific interpretations of Pirenne. However, Bourguin in 1903 leaned toward the Maurer–Von Below doctrine of the fundamental importance of the march. Halphen in 1911 and Coville in 1928, on the contrary, indorse the Pirenne view.

So much for the summary of Stephenson's analytic review, written as a historian's contribution on historical method as applied in a concrete case. Let us examine the implications.

In the first place, we have here the results reached by professional and recognizedly eminent historians, working on documentary materials dealing with aspects of our culture within the last thousand years. If this is not history in the straitest sense, there is no history. Next, there is here, except now and then incidentally, no annalistic story-telling, no mere stringing of items or events, no primary preoccupation

with dates as dates. All the bogey characteristics with which those ignorant
of history, or unable to comprehend it,
invest history are lacking. We have
instead, as the end-product, a series of
pattern formulations or interpretations
as to the nature and growth of an institution. And these interpretations are
nothing but reconstructions—I under-
score the word: reconstructions. There
are five or six of them on this one body
of material, plus a dozen variants and
combinations. Not one is final; not one
can be proved, in the sense of what
constitutes proof in mathematics or experimental science [No. 5, §§ 3–6; No. 6,
paragraphs 5–9].

Now how does this situation differ,
except in detail, from a typical problem
in ethnology, say as to the history of
clans in native North America? I believe we must admit that it does not
differ in aim or principle or method.
One ethnologist believes it most likely
that clans originated once in the continent, another that it was twice, still another that it happened four or five separate times. One finds it difficult to believe that a mother-clan could change
to a father-clan or vice versa; a second
sees both as only co-ordinate subsidiary aspects of unilateral descent; a third
seeks indirect evidence for change of
one to another. The views are no more
in absolute conflict than those about
the mediaeval town, where authorities
differ as to whether the founders were
servile or free; whether clergy or aristocracy served as chief rallying points;
whether economic or politicojuridi-
cal factors were more determinative;
whether the origin lies rather in agrar-
ian communal life or in royal policy,
in open rural markets or in stockaded
groups of merchants.

The earlier reconstructions of the mediaeval town and its history tended to
be simplistic and to solve the problem
conveniently but somewhat off-hand-
edly by explaining what was partially
known in terms of something antecedent but sometimes even less known.
The later reconstructions generally
avoid this pitfall and are on the whole
more complex: they balance more factors. The same change is perceptible
in the progress of ethnology. Finally,
in each case the reconstructions are in
the nature of patterns: what the essential pattern of an institution-complex
was at given moments and how such
successive patterns changed from one
to another. Underlying these pattern
determinations is a typology of pattern
elements: how the march, guild, market,
burg, should be conceived in the one
case; the clan, moiety, totem, calpulli,
in the other.

As against these parallels, the differences in technique are external. The
geographical distribution of a clan phenomenon and a twelfth-century parch-
ment reference to a municipality are
both only pieces of evidence. Belief in
the greater factual validity or truth of a
piece of evidence because it comes out
of an archive is pure fetishism. Mainly,
too, it is laymen's, not historians', fetishism.

The objectives, the procedures, and
the type of results in these two cases,
and in most cases in history and ethnology, are, I submit, essentially alike
and closely alike.

9. STRUCTURE, FUNCTION, AND PATTERN IN BIOLOGY AND ANTHROPOLOGY
1943

This essay returns to the biological comparison begun in Nos. 2 and 5, but carries the argument further. Building on distributions, convergences, reconstructions, and relationship based on total structure as already discussed in Nos. 5 and 8, it specially emphasizes pattern. This is a concept that has grown in strength in recent studies of culture; but it has been used much longer in biology.

Nos. 26 and 27 of Part II return to the problem of fundamental versus superficial patterns, with reference to the structure of kinship and social forms.

THE concepts of the aspects of structure and function are familiar in biology. It is proposed to examine here how far the two concepts can and cannot be applied properly in anthropology.

The terms structure and function are considerably used in anthropology, but with variable meaning. Function especially has been employed in so many and ambiguous senses that some cultural anthropologists, such as Milke, advocate its discontinuance. On the contrary, Linton has attempted to distinguish the form, meaning, use, and function of cultural phenomena. Structure sometimes has its common-sense meaning, as when we speak of the structure of a canoe. Sometimes it emphasizes form; sometimes organization, as in the term "social structure," which is tending to replace "social organization."

At bottom, it would seem in biology, when the structures of organisms have been sufficiently analyzed they fall into certain patterns. These patterns group or classify the organisms; and those showing the same pattern are considered not only similar, but related—that is, connected in descent. In short, one significance of structure is that it yields classification by pattern, which in turn has genetic or "evolutionary" significance—in other words, historical significance. This is of course not the only significance with which biology is concerned: physiological biology is occupied with process—with the direct interrelation of specific structures with specific functions as they exist, without inquiry into how they came to be. However, in historical biology—comparative morphology, systematics, palaeontology, partly in genetics—operations are explicitly or implicitly in terms of basic patterns that have historical depth.

Thus the placental mammalian pattern of dentition is 44 teeth: 3 incisors, 1 canine, 4 premolars, 3 molars on each side of each jaw; and this pattern—though it may be reduced and greatly modified by specialization of shape—is not violated except in the case of a few ancient lines of organisms, like the whales and edentates, whose total structure, as well as total functioning, is highly modified. The vertebrate pattern, at any rate above the fishes, provides for a pair of limbs at each end of the trunk.

Again, when an altered function is achieved, like flying, it is by conversion of a pair of legs into wings. In the bats and certain ancient reptiles the flying surface of the wing is supported by a specialization of digital structure. In the birds and certain other extinct Reptilia the wing is supported on the proximal heavy bones of the limb, with loss of its digital portions. But in no case has a vertebrate achieved flight except by functional—and structural—conversion of one of the pairs of limbs generally and originally serving terrestrial or water locomotion. This is in contrast to the insects, whose basic pattern includes three thoracic segments, each provided with a pair of jointed legs and two of them with wings also. An insect accordingly flies without giving up any of its legs by conversion.

Deep-seated as this insect pattern is—and it has geological antiquity—it is not absolutely basic. The other arthropods are wingless but possess more than six legs in their patterns: spiders eight, crabs ten, other crustaceans, scorpions, and centipedes more yet; but always with one pair only per segment. The insect pattern, therefore, represents an important modification of a still more ancestral pattern.

The idea of basic pattern has not been wanting in anthropology. Sapir articulated it most clearly. Language is the part of culture which particularly lends itself to pattern recognition, because its precision of form facilitates analysis. However, as a concept or tool, basic pattern has been used much less, and has been formulated less clearly, in anthropology than in biology. One reason is that in culture the tremendously conservative force of organic heredity is not operative; at any rate, it is obviously not the direct or immediately operative factor. Cultural patterns therefore tend to be relatively short-lived: we may trace them for a few thousand years, but not for many millions. Moreover, widely divergent cultures can and do hybridize; organisms, only within very narrow limits of relationship and descent. There is nothing in the biologic realm comparable to the fusion of Helleno-Roman and Asiatic civilizations to produce Christian civilizations; or of Sino-Japanese and Occidental culture in Japan since 1868. The tree of life is eternally branching, and never doing anything fundamental but branching, except for the dying-away of branches. The tree of human history, on the contrary, is constantly branching and at the same time having its branches grow together again. Its plan is therefore much more complex and difficult to trace. Even its basic patterns can in some degree blend, which is contrary to all experience in the merely organic realm, where patterns are virtually irreversible in proportion as they are fundamental.

However, granted the relative mutability, plasticity, and ultimate fusibility of all patterns in human history, there remains no doubt that there are cultural patterns which are more basic or primary and on the whole older, and others which are more superficial, secondary, and transitory. Obviously, if we wish to trace the history of human civilization—especially in its preliterate and therefore prehistoric phases—it is of the utmost importance to recognize the basic patterns and distinguish them from their secondary modifications. The older anthropology, it seems to me—Tylor for instance—made a deliberate attempt to do this. It failed, to a large extent at least, because of several related deficiencies. Sometimes it substituted common denominator for true pattern. Again, it synthesized prematurely into formulations like animism and magic and totem, which are part basic pattern indeed, but in part only denominator. And, finally, it forgot that all recorded history was a series of objectively unique events whose major significance lies in their organization into distinctive patterns and not in ill-defined formulas or generalized denominators—and that very probably the same held of the prehistoric and primitive part of the human story. True, we also use the word "formula" for mammalian dentition. But the mammalian dentition formula is quantitative; it is entirely precise; it is highly distinctive—in fact, unique; and it has, so far as the totality of our knowledge allows us to judge, authentic historical depth and significance. In contrast, a formulation like animism or totem has none of these qualities, except historical depth, and this may prove to be an accidental denominator; even the historical significance is none too sure, especially for the totem. Whereas the relatively mutable patterns of culture are more difficult to extricate than the relatively stable ones of life, the earlier anthropology, even though headed in a sound direction, made a premature, superficial synthesis—perhaps precisely because of its immaturity as a branch of study.

The need of more exact and deeper analysis was recognized in the next stage of our science; but, with it, the synthetic impulses faded. A healthy distrust grew up for the hazy formulations of the earlier generation. If we now used them, it was of necessity; they were crutches, no longer goals. We reveled in discovering the rich diversity of forms which culture assumed. We analyzed as carefully as any historian; but we refrained, for a time, from doing any history, from probing for time depth and relative sequences. We had become shy of the sort of findings which our predecessors considered historical, or an equivalent of historical findings; but we had not yet attained to the concept of the basic pattern as a tool which inevitably carries at least historical implication, if not outright significance.

In the present stage of anthropology, two currents are flowing in opposite directions. First, there is a resumption of historic interest: analysis is continued from the preceding stage, but it is being used more courageously for constructive historical objectives, with increasing recognition of the value of the basic pattern method. It is important to remember that this approach is not wholly phenomenological and undynamic. After all, as a pattern is basic, it is determinative of its modifications: it sets the frame

within which change can take place; it is one of the factors which jointly produce what happens. The charge sometimes leveled that history is only a series of facts, unorganized but for their time order and meaningless except in themselves, proves only one thing: that those who so hold have, through overpreoccupation with other interests, a blind spot for the historic approach, whether in biology or in human affairs, and fail to recognize the significances which inevitably attach to pattern organizations.

The other current in contemporary anthropology aims at a sort of physiology of culture and society. It is concerned with extricating process, with uncovering dynamics. It comprises those who accept the name of functionalist, and the like-minded who insist on working with present-day phenomena and have little concern with the past. They hope to move from the contemporary directly into generalization, perhaps into universals. It is true that knowledge of living phenomena is inevitably capable of being fuller than knowledge of former ones. A "physiology" of cultural and social phenomena is presumably possible and would certainly be extremely important. The danger is in confusing a goal with an attainment. The public at large is unaware of the fact that in biologic physiology selective experiment with control is the essence of method, but that in social physiology it is selection alone that is chiefly possible, both experiment and control being as yet scarcely devised, if devisable at all. Also, with focusing on the contemporary, time perspective goes out and with this the best opportunity of recognizing the fundamental patterns involved. In fact, it would appear that the area of which there is immediate consciousness in studies of contemporary cultural and social change is the special modifications which are taking place at the moment, while consciousness of the more enduring and basic structural features tends to be lost sight of—both by those desiring to bring about change and those interested in studying it. It is accordingly no accident that Malinowski avowed an antihistorical bias; that Radcliffe-Brown admits the historical approach but confines it to documented data and cites as his exemplars of historical anthropology chiefly the precursors of Tylor; and that Warner avoids a quarrel but actually considers only recent antecedents, and those mainly in order to heighten background contrast.

All the functionalists put unusual emphasis on integration. Either this amounts to making explicit what has always been taken for granted, or, when most rabid, it comes to elevating integration into a final principle—which thereby chokes off further inquiry. It is very much as if physiologists were to proclaim as their ultimate finding: See how the human body hangs together! See how harmoniously it works!

There is of course no valid quarrel with a primary interest in function in the sociocultural field, provided that such interest is not stretched into a superiority dogma or panacea. It is as one-sided, and ultimately sterile, to be exclusively preoccupied with structure as with function. This has long since been learned in biology and will have to be learned in anthropology.

One concept shared by biology and anthropology is that of convergence—for instance, the pseudo-vertebrate eye, beak, and backbone of the molluscan squid. Trees, and again vines, have over and over originated independently in separate families of plants; so has the habit of male and female sex organs being borne separately—alternatively—by different plant individuals. Snakes move like worms, and whales swim like fishes. Flight has been attained separately by insects, reptiles, birds, and the mammalian bats, not to mention man if we transcend the organic level. Almost exactly parallel socialization has been attained by the termites, who are descended from the roach stem, and by the ants, who are Hymenoptera. There are thousands of instances, some of them highly special, like the horny forehead shields with which access to the burrow is blocked both by some toads and by some termite warrior castes.

Now what is characteristic of all organic true convergences is that they are analogues, not homologues. There is a similarity of function, but a dissimilarity of structure. The dissimilarity is usual even in the converged organ or organs, invariably present in the total structure of the organisms. In short, it is because the basic patterns differ that the similarity is convergent. The histories are unlike, the secondary results are like, especially as regards function, use, and behavior, though the like results need not be superficial or trivial—in fact may be accompanied by pervasive modifications of the organism.

While we have long recognized convergence in anthropology, we have tended to deal chiefly with limited, specific cases in which reasonable proof was not too difficult to bring. Probably we have been too unsure of fundamental pattern structure in the protean field of human history to venture to class larger phenomena, corresponding to arboreal habitus, flying, crawling, socialization, either as convergences or as historic pattern persistences. This is certainly a matter in which anthropology is backward. But it is clear that progress can ensue only in the degree that we learn to dissociate patterns into basic and derivative or modificatory ones. This is obviously going to be harder in the field of culture than it has been in biology; but precedent should at least encourage the attempt.

One fact may help. Organic convergences not only always involve function strongly, but their similarities are easily recognized; lay observation and common-sense observation suffice to recognize trees, flight, socialization, and the like. This suggests that long-recognized, frequently recurring phenomena of culture are likely to be the ones among which our broad convergences are to be found. As examples might be mentioned the clan, totem, cross-cousin marriage, the mother-in-law taboo, potlatch, feudalism. As regards several of these, multiple causations and origins have for some time been advocated on specific associational grounds. Other possible examples are taboo, sacrifice, kingship, urbanization, writing, navigation, secret societies.

As a boy I got hold of a popular natural history, probably reprinted from an original that was several generations old, which classified animals into Schalthiere, such as clams, lobsters, turtles, and armadillos, that had shells; Kriechthiere, which included worms and snakes, which crawled; and so on. The wonder is that such a work was still in circulation to come into the home and hands of anyone born in the last quarter of the nineteenth century. The classification is logical, naïve, and essentially functional. Shells, it is true, are nominally structural, but their real likeness is confined to their protective and defensive function. Function, apparently, is what the prescientific mind first takes hold of. Analysis into structure comes later, because its implications, its resultant significances, are not readily visible: inquiry into it tends at first to pass as aimless antiquarian idling.

Now we have done enough analysis in anthropology to have good reason to believe that the recurrent phenomena which we loosely call feudalism, clans, cross-cousin marriage, etc., have polygenetic origins; and therewith the inference is near that they are merely derivative and not basic patterns. It seems that we might do well to avow this inference more explicitly and, at the same time, search more rigorously for patterns that are basic. This is not so easy as in biol-

ogy, where we can at least begin by laying a specimen on the table and cutting into it with a knife, and then bringing up the microscope and reagents when needed. If our search were as simple as that, anthropologists would have got farther than they have. But, granted the difficulties, have we nevertheless tried as wholeheartedly as we might?

Two endeavors are indispensable in such search for basic patterns: analysis and comparison. Analyses we do sufficiently well. For some forty or fifty years there has been produced an increasing number of monographic, analytic studies of tribal cultures, sufficiently detailed in many cases, not always inspirational, but mostly competent and useful. It is in comparison that we hang back, perhaps in undue fear that all broadly comparative work will suffer the stigma of the old comparisons which were designed forthrightly to discover universals. When modern anthropologists make comparative studies over a wide range, these tend to be limited to items, such as the spear-thrower or oil lamps, rather than to whole cultures or systems. In all this, there is manifest a lack of courage about attacking problems that could be labeled constructively historical. But are we going to be deterred forever because there have once been simplistic speculators who constructed pseudo-histories?

One criterion will help. With a valid basic pattern, its various manifestations show a point-for-point correspondence. Not that every placental mammal must have 44 teeth of four shapes; but such teeth as it has must correspond to particular ones of the 44; and, once they do, the greater their modification from the general or original shape—like the elephant's incisor tusks and successive molars—the more interesting are their fit, adaptation, and history. In comparative linguistics, indeed, which is historical linguistics, such as Indo-European, Semitic, Bantu, this insistence on point-for-point correspondence has successfully become a cardinal principle of method. Culture history is no doubt more difficult; but there is every reason to believe that the principle applies.

Perhaps it is time that I cite some examples of basic patterns in culture. They are of course surest where cultures have been documented for a considerable period. Hebrew-Christian-Mohammedan monotheism seems a good illustration—and a rich one, if we remember all its diversifications into religions, churches, and sects. We know that the three "religions" are historically connected: they are outgrowths of one another. We can also define the pattern: a single deity of illimitable power, excluding all others except avowed derivatives, and proclaimed by a particular human vessel inspired by the deity. If we contrast with this the supreme deities of other religions, philosophical and primitive, we find them invariably lacking one or more of the characterizing features—usually all three. These other supreme deities, accordingly, are analogous convergences only.

Another example is the alphabet, as set off from other methods of writing. All alphabetic writing—that is, graphic symbols denoting the smallest acoustic elements of speech, but no symbols of other kind—has spread from a single origin in western Asia about three thousand years old. And there is point-for-point correspondence in all the manifold varieties of alphabets. Aleph, beth, gimel, daleth, correspond to alpha, beta, gamma, delta, and to A, B, C, D. Where there are changes of shape of letter, or of its sound value, or its position, these can be accounted for, at least in the overwhelming majority of cases, and lead us back to the original pattern. For instance, we know why, how, and when C came to replace G as the third letter in our own form of alphabet, and when W was added.

Such a pattern, or our monotheistic one, is really a system which extends across cultures, and is not coterminous with any one culture. It is possible that the same will hold true generally for all associations or complexes of cultural phenomena which fall into basic patterns. They represent pure inventions, or a series of inventions, corresponding more or less to mutations or series of mutations in organic nature. The word "mutation" is here used not in any specific sense which it may have in genetics with reference to a particular mechanism but as a generic label to indicate any radical, drastic, or significant change in hereditary type.

By contrast, systems of writing like the Egyptian, Cuneiform, or Chinese do not share any point-for-point correspondence either with the alphabet or with one another: neither in the shape, value, nor order of their characters. So far as they are similar—in being pictographic and ideographic and syllabic—they are alike only in general function, not in specific structure; and they represent analogical convergences. What they have in common, such as the tendency to represent the sounds of speech by a sort of punning—the rebus method—and the tendency to deal with syllables rather than elemental sounds, is due presumably to psychological factors of the human inherited constitution, and therefore is really outside the level of culture as such. Just so, certain generic features common to organisms which share, say, an arboreal habitus or a swimming or flying one, are conditioned by mechanical factors to which the organisms adapt themselves.

When it comes to the material or technological aspects of culture, physicochemical factors similarly impinge on culture. That bronze is composed of copper and tin and that it is harder and casts better than either metal alone are physicochemical facts. Consequently, the mere fact that ancient Mesopotamia, China, and Peru made bronze is of no relevance to the problem of whether their bronze arts belong to the same or different patterns—that is, whether they are genetically connected or separated. That must be determined from specific cultural features, such as noncompulsory techniques in the metallurgical process, the forms cast, and the like. With these features considered, it becomes probable that Mesopotamian bronze and Chinese bronze are stylistically variant manifestations of one pattern, but that ancient Peruvian bronze represents a separate pattern and origin. For instance, Mesopotamia and China used bronze for swords and for ritual vases or other vessels; Peru did not.

Plow agriculture constitutes another example of a basic pattern. This pattern comprises at least three essential features; the plow itself; animals to draw it, which of course must be domesticated; and food plants of such a nature, like barley, wheat, millet, that they can be profitably grown by broadcast sowing, which in turn involves fields of at least fair size, as compared with gardens. Still other features have become associated, such as the use of the dung of the animals as fertilizer. The plow is generally considered to have been an unrepeated invention, whose precise time, place, and circumstances we do not know, though it took place in the last Stone Age and probably in or near southwestern Asia, and spread along with cattle, with barley and associated plants, and usually with manuring, to all those parts of Europe, Asia, and Africa in which it was used in 1500. Native America also evolved a highly developed system of agriculture on which we of today have drawn for important loans. But native American agriculture belonged to a radically different pattern. It did not know the plow. It did not use draft animals, though it had domesticated ones like the llama. It did not sow broadcast but planted by hand and cultivated in hillocks. It totally lacked wheat, barley, and their associ-

ates, substituting for them a series of others, of which maize was the most widespread and principal. And it either did not fertilize at all or it used fish. It has therefore long been the conclusion of conservative, nonspeculative students that New World agriculture had an origin and a history entirely separate from Old World plow agriculture. In short, we have two patterns and two histories.

Agriculture as such I would not call a pattern, but rather a common denominator. Numerous primitive peoples in Africa, Asia, and Oceania farmed, planting with hoes or digging-sticks, without using associated animals, and raising root crops, fruits, and even some cereals like rice or sorghum. We are not able to affirm whether all this farming or gardening had a single origin or several. It is possible that plow agriculture represents an "invention-mutation" added to some phase or other of this more primitive gardening. But we cannot say at present to which phase, any more than we know whether the phases were historically connected or independent developments. In brief, plow agriculture is a specific pattern phenomenon, or set of associated phenomena, like mammalian dentition; whereas agriculture is rather a generalization, or concept, logically definable indeed, but rather too vague, variable, or amorphous to serve as a solid foundation for a scientific structure; just as concepts like shellfish or arboreal habitus or aerial locomotion have proved unserviceable for primary scientific classification.

A given trait may form a critical part of a pattern in one situation but have low pattern value in others. Teeth, for instance, have less diagnostic and classificatory significance in the lower vertebrates and invertebrates than in the mammals. The same holds in the field of culture—for instance, as regards "dichotomized" social structure or moiety organization. In native Australia moieties are almost universal, and in New Guinea and Melanesia they are frequent. They basically determine marriage and descent —whom one may not marry, whom one must marry. In Australia there is re-dichotomization into four sections, and even re-redichotomization into eight subsections [No. 26, Sec. II; No. 27]. Related to this plan is the fact that all human beings with whom one has dealings are considered kin—are made into kin, if necessary—and put into one or the other moiety. This whole organization, often very elaborate, is superimposed on one of another type: the small local horde, autonomous and owning a territory, all its members interrelated through male descent, and therefore unable to marry horde members. The two plans of organization do not conflict but supplement each other. The moiety is inter-national, as the native sees it, and there-fore makes for successful amities and bonds outside, while not interfering with the subsistential and familial solidarity of the horde. This Australian scheme is very distinctive—infinitely varied in minor detail, but remarkably constant in underlying pattern.

Now moieties occur also in all other continents, but sporadically, by contrast. They occur often among peoples who are not living in hordes and who do not insist on classifying everyone as a kins-man. Sometimes they are exogamous, occasionally endogamous, sometimes not connected with marriage or descent at all, but with ritual or games or govern-ment [No. 27]. All these other social dichotomizations in Asia, Africa, and the Americas do not reduce to a consistent pattern; and their geographical distri-bution is tantalizingly spotty, instead of continuous. They are therefore justly regarded as probably having had a num-ber of origins, separate in circumstances as well as in time and place, and with separate and different growths. Such similarities as they present, to one an-other and to Australian moieties, are therefore superficial and of the order of convergences.

There may well be in the nature of the human mind a deeply implanted tend-ency to construe and organize its world in terms of duality, bipolarity, and di-chotomization, and this inclination may lie at the root of all moieties, in Australia and elsewhere. But if there exists such a tendency, it is a psychological fact. It is a condition of culture, not a phenome-non of it. On the cultural level, there remains the difference that in the Aus-tralian area the psychological trend to-ward dichotomization has been chan-neled into consistent, widespread, influ-ential, and probably ancient expression in a pattern of social structure, but else-where the same trend has entered only into local, intermittent, and secondary patterns.

These examples from the religious, in-tellectual, technological, economic, and social fields may suffice to illustrate what is meant by "fundamental patterns of culture." It is clear that they are some-thing different from Benedict's "Pat-terns of Culture." These latter are psy-chological orientations of societies com-parable to personality orientations or attitudes, such as paranoid, megalomanic, Apollonian, etc. When strongly devel-oped, they are also influential, but selec-tively so, and on the slant of a given culture, whereas the basic patterns here discussed operate constructively and often cross-culturally. In the Benedict approach a pattern is a psychic constel-lation molding the typical personality of a society by imparting a certain warp to that society's culture. The basic pat-terns referred to in the present essay are the more pervasive and permanent forms assumed by a specific mass of cul-tural content, and they tend to spread from one society and culture to others. In short, basic patterns are nexuses of culture traits which have assumed a defi-nite and coherent structure, which func-tion successfully, and which acquire major historic weight and persistence.

Returning to the biological analogy, we must distinguish where the pattern parallel holds and where it does not hold. A particular culture is not comparable to a species, even though the members of any one society are given, by their common culture, a certain likeness of behavior somewhat comparable outwardly to the likeness of the members of one species. (The mechanisms which produce the likeness are of course quite different.) A culture is always, so far as we can judge, highly composite in the origin of its constituent materials. As I have just said, the branches of the tree of human culture are always growing together again. It is a commonplace that in our American civilization we speak a Germanic language shaped in England with the absorption of a larger Latin content; have a Palestinian religion; eat bread and meat of plants and animals probably first domesticated in or near western Asia, with additions from tropical America; drink coffee from Abyssinia and tea from China; write and read these words with letters originating in Phoenicia, added to in Greece, given their present shape in Rome, and first printed in Germany; and so on. There is no reason to believe that any living culture is less intricately hybrid. Therewith the analogy between cultures and species breaks down. Rather, it is ecological aggregates to which cultures can be compared: local associations of species of diverse origin. Certainly the larger faunal and floral regions, like the Palaearctic, Neotropical, Indo-Oriental, Ethiopian, Australo-Papuan, correspond strikingly, even in part to geographic coincidence, with the generally accepted major cultural regions [No. 5, § 1]; and there are parallels in retardation, specialization, and expansive productivity of new forms.

All this suggests that the nearest counterpart of the organic species in the field of culture is perhaps the culture trait or trait cluster but not the culture entity or whole culture. It is the species that is repetitive in its individuals; the trait that is repetitive in its exemplars —in the thousands of automobiles or stone axes manufactured according to one model or form; in the word or grammatical construction that is uttered over and over again. It is related species or genera or families or orders that have persistent structural patterns in common; and it is among the traits that belong to one field of culture—such as writing, belief in deities, agriculture— that the persistent systematized patterns of culture grow up. It would be easy to stretch the analogy too far; but within due limits it would seem to have utility in stimulating reflective inquiry, especially as regards the historical aspects of organic and superorganic phenomena.

Postscript, 1951.—The parallel of organic and cultural pattern seems to me to remain valid as an analogy. It serves at any rate to focus more sharply what is basic and what is incidental in cultural patterning.

In *Anthropology* (1948) I named the patterns here instanced "systemic patterns." However, as a result of discussing the subject with several classes since then, I am less inclined than in 1948 to limit the category "systemic patterns" to grand aggregations of culture. Christianity, for instance, is a system as truly as is the larger group of exclusively monotheistic religions. There is, after all, a great deal of common pattern recurrent in all Christian sects and denominations. Even religions with less sharply formulated dogma, such as Shinto, Brahmanism, or the Hellenic cults, contain much system pattern. Again, the well-set-off group of Indian writings and their derivatives form a clear subdivision within the system of the alphabet; in fact, they are marked by a considerable recasting of the system—resyllabification, a new order of letters—which then became the pattern system basic to their historic group. In short, the characteristic qualities of systematized patterning can be found in cultural growths roughly corresponding in scope to smaller biological developments, such as families or orders, as well as to the larger classes or phyla.

It is also clear that any group of historically related languages such as the Indo-European ones or the Semito-Hamitic, share a pervasive pattern of structure. This may be considered a grand system, to which the smaller correspondent would be any particular language with its tendency to maintain much of its particular plan of structure through successive periods of alteration.

The great difference between organic and cultural phylogeny remains of course in the mechanism of perpetuation or transmission, which brings it about that when two organic forms have diverged to a relatively small degree from their common source, they can no longer reintegrate or merge. Cultural growths, both partial or total, can and do interpenetrate and merge one with the other even when they have become very different. Now it may prove that evenly balanced fusion of half and half is rare and difficult even in culture—that one pattern or one culture normally preponderates in the formation of any new system. But, even if so, there is admittedly an enormous amount of compounding and melting together of cultural content, whereas beyond a quite narrow range organic forms cannot "recompound." The consequence is that, even with the utmost degree of segregation and shelter, the pattern systems of culture must be enormously brief in their expectation of duration as compared with patterned organic developments.

10. HISTORY AND EVOLUTION
1946

The argument carries forward that of Nos. 4–8, with added attention to evolution.

I

LESLIE A. WHITE'S recent stimulating paper on "History, Evolutionism, and Functionalism,"[1] adds "evolutionism" as a third method to the well-recognized ones of "history" and "science." Some of what White describes as evolutionistic approach seems to the present writer plainly historical, as will be set forth. The residuum after subtraction of this element is less easily characterized, and will then be examined.

White recognizes three "processes"[2] in culture, to which correspond three "interpretations." These are: Temporal, concerned with chronological sequence of unique events, yielding history; Formal, nontemporal but structural-functional, leading to science; Temporal-formal, temporal sequence of forms, "the interpretation of which is evolutionism." This is, on the face of it, reasonable enough; but definition of historical treatment as being merely concerned with unique events in their chronological sequence is too narrow. It suggests an annalistic conception of history, such as not even political historians, let alone historical biologists, would accept as a frame. The setting of White's remarks about uniqueness, and his exemplifications, suggest that for him that quality carries also an implication of isolability —in fact, of isolation—of the facts dealt with. Thus he speaks of a "chronological sequence of events, each of which is regarded as unique," where "unique" seems to include also "discrete." Certainly most of his examples suggest that he regards the facts of what he calls "history" as essentially discrete and per-

haps unrelated. The biologist interested in the history of man "wants to know where and when certain physical types —Bushmen, Pygmies, Ainu, Nordics— appeared, where they migrated and when, with whom they intermarried, and so on." Customs have a history because each "originated at a certain time and place and diffused subsequently to certain places at definite times." This is contrasted with the temporal-formal or evolutionistic approach, "in which an organization of functionally interrelated elements is temporarily transformed, in which one form grows out of an antecedent form and into a subsequent form."

Most scholars would call this last, history: pure history. What else would any history of the French Revolution be than just this, the recording of how "one form grows out of an antecedent form"? All history—whatever the field—which is worth its salt does deal with relations, with functions, with meanings. It certainly is not a tracing of the wanderings of detached and unrelated items through time and space, nor a precise but arid roster of names, dates, and places. In biology, again, White contrasts the "history of species, varieties, etc.," with the "evolution of life, of species." This suggests that the story of how life diverged into phyla and orders, how genera and species originated, and how they are related to one another is the concern of the "evolutionist"; but the historian begins with a species as already given, as something isolated and distinct, whose wanderings and breaking up into subspecies he then traces with the absorp-

95

tion of an antiquarian uninterested in major relevances.

White thus does "history" the signal but dubious honor of appropriating all that is most vital and significant in it and assigning it to evolutionism. The motivation of the imbalance is obvious: the foster-child needs *Lebensraum*. If he claimed the whole of the historical domain for "evolutionism," I should not particularly quarrel: the change would be nominal, like that of a color on a map. But it will not do to gut history and leave its empty shell standing around; there might be the embarrassment of no one's claiming it.

The attitude is strangely reminiscent of that of Radcliffe-Brown, who however differs in wanting to develop a physics or physiology, that is, a generalizing science, for society—though not, except perhaps grudgingly, for culture, which seems to be only a sort of set of rules that somehow got attached, without too much significance but rather distractingly, to society. Radcliffe-Brown is fully aware of the dichotomy of science and history and in principle allows the latter its place in the sun. But history to him is of two kinds. One is unverifiable speculation as to ultimate origins, which he charges with being an "Illusion of Historical Explanation." Presumably everyone nowadays would agree with this verdict; though one might strengthen it by rewording the error as "the illusion of explanation by pseudo-history." Radcliffe-Brown's "other kind of history is that of the historians, who examine actual records of past events" in order to "determine with fair probability the real order of events." This seems to mean that when history is not illusory it is restricted to using documents to ascertain chronology. Radcliffe-Brown seems as innocent as White of realizing that history is always interpretative, in its own way; is therefore concerned with functional relations; is in its very nature reconstructive; and can never long dispense with interpretations. This is as true of the "history of historians" as of culture historians, archaeologists, palaeontologists, other historical biologists, and geologists. I do not know the motivation for Radcliffe-Brown's depreciation of the historical approach, unless that, as the ardent apostle of a genuine new science of society, he has perhaps failed to concern himself enough with history to learn its nature.

Malinowski was a conscious, petulant, and versatile aggressor. In his famous article on "Culture" in the *Encyclopaedia of the Social Sciences* he tried to provide anthropology with a foundation of his making, an aprioristic closed system of theory, analogous to classical economic theory in economics. Anything as empirical and fluid as history, of course, would not fit at all into such a system; so he proceeded to belittle history away—at least the history of nonliterate cultures; there was more to be gained by ignoring than by attacking the history of the historians. The way of belittling was to charge the historical approach with operating through irrelevances, fortuities, and absences of knowledge; and deliberately to bracket the names of the most critical and least critical followers of the historical method in anthropology, Boas with Elliot Smith, Wissler with Graebner. Malinowski was agile and presumably knew what he was doing. But there remains his astounding implication that history deals with events of no significance and of no relation (except, perhaps, the external one of time)—whereas in fact all real history is nothing but an interpretation by means of description in terms of context.

It seems fit to consider how eminent scholars can solemnly and premeditatedly maintain such a remarkable view.

First, presumably, they have not really read much of either ordinary history, or culture history, or biological history, and therefore know little or nothing about them by personal experience and have been uninterested in appraising the nature of what they have read.

Next, so far as they are Americans, they belong to a nation which in virtue of recent migration has an unusually brief history of its own, prides itself on the fact, and mostly assumes that the way to surpass other nations in civilization is to develop more present energy through having shallower historic roots. Some absorptions such as this from circumambient folk attitudes are likely—even for anthropologists—unless one is awarely on his guard.

Probably most important, however, is the current high prestige of science, which has attained fetishistic proportions in contemporary civilization, with a corresponding depression of history. The callower our graduate students, the more concerned are they about getting their anthropology "scientific." White at least is free from this influence.

II

So far, I have maintained that much of what White calls "evolutionism" is history, his claim of it for evolutionism resting on so narrow a construal of history as to leave history nothing but an exoskeleton or perhaps scaffold. Assuming that the controversial territory is reawarded to history, the question arises: Does there remain a legitimate, evolutionistic homeland? And of what does it consist? Here the reply becomes less confident.

White's examples suggest that he regards the historic "process" as being operative when the phenomena are so specific that we cannot but label them unique; but he sees the evolutionistic process at work in phenomena that fall into classes, within which there are more or less recurrent repetitions. Thus "firearms, porcelain, the potter's wheel, the calculus, painting, the rite of cir-cumcision, the ritual of shaking hands, Buddhism," have a history; but "the development of the ax, the loom, the clan, money, writing, occupational groups, stratified classes, mathematics, monarchy, physics," provide examples of the temporal-formal or evolutionistic process.

Now it is generally accepted that we cannot write a genuine history of monarchy but that we can have either histories of monarchies or a "sociology" of monarchy in general. The very idea of a history of a *class* of phenomena is certainly calculated to set on edge the teeth of any historian, even of a broad-minded institutional historian. One can write a history of chess, which is a specific game (though a much more variable and plastic one in its form and function than is generally assumed); but one can hardly write a real history of human games. Yet the question remains: Is there a difference in principle between an inquiry into subjects like games or monarchy by the method of general science which White calls "functional," and his "evolutionistic" method? By his definition the former is concerned with form and function, the latter with form and function plus time. Does this addition of the time factor legitimately constitute a new and separate approach or manner of understanding, or does it perhaps contain a logical contradiction? The question is fair because a number of philosophers[3] have agreed in recognizing a theoretic-scientific method and a historical method, as have a long series of anthropologists and sociologists whom White enumerates.[4] Either, therefore, White's evolutionism will turn out to be a somewhat disguised or special form of one of the two generally recognized fundamental methods; or, if it proves to be a genuinely distinct method, its recognition will be extraordinarily important.

III

Before grappling with the alternative directly, I should however like to clear the ground by examining another of White's exemplifications.

He says that both Tylor and I in discussing writing begin evolutionistically with stages but end historically with a narrative of the alphabet. He points out that in a chapter called "Spread of the Alphabet" I begin with consideration of writing in general, writing as a means of communication, and mention "three stages logically distinguishable in the development of writing"—pictures (including ideograms), rebus or transitional, and wholly phonetic writing. Therewith I have presented a formula descriptive of "a temporal-formal process," "applicable to all systems of writing in all time and in all places." After "disposing of the evolution of systems of writing," he says I turn to history, reciting the time and place of the origin of the alphabet, the subsequent diffusion to other lands and peoples, "and so on."

As a matter of fact, the "and so on" is a basic ingredient of my story of the alphabet. My chapter title mentions "Spread," and there is a map on which centuries are entered. However, the main concern is not to trace the space-time wanderings of a fixedly invariable unit called the alphabet, but to trace the changes of this unit or system in form and function, its derivatives, losses, and increments, invention of vowels and resyllabification, growths of systematization and of simplification, nonacceptances, prestige associations, stylistic modifications, petrifactions, and revolutionary changes. In short, the alphabet neatly illustrates somewhere in its history most of the processes operative in culture: it is a convenient microcosm of cultural process, with the added advantage that, being a single historic growth, its phenomena possess not only space-time continuity but a continuity or co-herence of form and of function or relation. And, for purposes of exemplification, it then seemed to me, and still seems to me, that a coherent nexus of closely related phenomena possesses certain advantages over a scattering selection of disparate and unrelated phenomena, from the angle of illustrating change and dynamics. So much for the main historical portion of the chapter in question: White and I are agreed that it is such, and we differ only in that I think once more that, like all significant history, my account deals with far more than tracing the movements of a cultural atom through time.

And now about the introductory passage on stages, in which I appear to have turned evolutionist. First of all, the stages are mentioned as *logically* distinguishable,[5] which is not the same as asserting that they normally or necessarily succeed each other. It is true that when I said "first stage" I probably did mean to refer to first in order of development as well as to the first named. But there is also mention of how this stage "fails to flow spontaneously out of the human mind." And there is explicit statement that, of many nations which had more or less entered the stage of pictography, only five or six at most, possibly only two, had proceeded on their own initiative to the transitional or part-phonetic stage; and that completely phonetic writing had been originated but once, namely, in the alphabet. Moreover, the possibility is at least considered of all full occurrences of the first or pictographic stage being "the result of a single diffusing development." And the parallelism of syllabification in the Hindu, Japanese, Cherokee, and Vei contributions to writing is expressly explained as determined by a psychological fact—the tendency to apperception of syllabic units in slow speech. It may well be that my thinking in the paragraphs in question contained some remnants of influences from Tylorian days. But in the main the argument seems to me to have been historically motivated, though the total prealphabetic data were and still are so incomplete that the story was largely reconstructive to the point of being implicitly somewhat speculative; and the speculations were at least limited by avowedly psychological findings.

Even the succession of three stages can be given such a construal. Not only do the historical facts show that the succession of styles has been pictograph-ideogram-rebus-phonogram in the known instances, but an argument could well be adduced that that order is psychologically irreversible in a free internal development uninfluenced by alien inventions. There is every reason to believe that a visible mark, sign, or figure would first evolve an association of a visible form, and might readily become construed or accepted socially as a symbol of a visible object or visible act. But there is no known or conceivable psychological mechanism by which such a figure would spontaneously evoke a consistent auditory association and directly become a symbol for a sound-cluster. Psychologically the chain *must* be: made visible figure or picture, symbolic pictogram (or ideogram), spoken word for the object or idea, transfer of reference to a similar-sounding word happening already to function as audible symbol of another object or idea, further transfer of reference to any similar sound-group irrespective of semantic meaning. Such a step-by-step transference is wholly conceivable psychologically, whereas the direct or immediate use of a visual figure as symbol for a sound-cluster makes no psychological sense. It is in this way that we may legitimately speak of the developmental process implied in the three[6] stages as being irreversible: the one-wayness is on the psychological, not on the cultural, level.

The distinguishing of logically or psychologically possible stages is perhaps related to what Milke has called a "typology of possible developments whose causal conditions remain largely unknown" and has attributed specially to Spier and Boas.[7] In an article cited by Milke, Spier repudiates historical reconstruction, including his own, in favor of study of process of change. Boas' work also is now recognized as mainly lacking specific historic content or result, that is to say, determinations which include larger contiguities of space and time. Boas was not interested in such, but in processes; and, in the analytic search for processes, he took into consideration, in each case, only the unavoidable minimum of space-time context. But he did consistently try to outline the total range of possible processes and of possible kinds of results of these processes. That is, he was interested in determining the variety and extent of the forces that can shape culture. In this interest he either was akin to Wundt or was influenced by him. At any rate, Wundt's *Völkerpsychologie* seems to have had precisely this objective.

This discussion has become somewhat ramifying; but much anthropological work, both past and present, defies assignment to any simple categories of history and science or history and functionalism. These are ideal manners: the actual course of work is most often mixed, both as to method and as to level. The question still remains whether White's evolutionism may not really represent special cases of such mixed or impure methods.

IV

In White's tabulation,[8] he cites as examples of evolutionistic process the disintegration of radioactive substances and the growth of organic individuals. Radium breaks down into lead and helium at a fixed rate. This change is temporal as well as formal; therefore its process is evolutionary. This exemplification sug-

gests that what White means by "evolution" is a fixed, necessary, inherent, and
predetermined process. The other example just referred to—growth of organisms—implies the same, in spite of the
brevity of such developmental duration.[9] Organisms may be checked or
mutilated in growth, but their maturity
is a predetermined end according to
each species.

This quality of predetermination, of
spontaneous metamorphosis, of a teleological course, seems to be what is specifically characteristic of White's evolutionistic process. Like radium and the
caterpillar, so galaxies, molecules, life,
and culture also have a set course to run.
White does not say this; but those of his
illustrations which are unequivocal suggest it as holding also for the less defined
examples. And the stages of writing fit
in: they too are evidently conceived as a
necessary sequence. White's evolution
thus seems to be an unfolding of immanences. If not, it is for him to tell what
rather it is. This is said not in stricture
but in an attempt to clarify his position.

In fact, there is no inherent reason
why one should be afraid or ashamed of
belief in immanence or what is perceived
as such. What counts is understanding
of the involvements. The irreversibility
of the pictographic-phonetic succession
in writing is an apparent immanence on
the level of perceptual consideration of
culture, whereas we have seen that it
finds a simple causal explanation in terms
of psychological association. Similarly,
every growth from egg to mature organism is on the face of it a piece of predetermination and immanence; the question remains whether it is limited to remaining that or whether it resolves also
into causal explanations of generalizing
science (White's "functionalism"). Certainly neither the anatomical nor the
physiological processes, which in his
table he assigns to "science," cease being operative during organic growth,
though whether all features of growth,

including its apparent predetermination,
can be accounted for by these physiological processes, or only by still more
underlying ones, I am not biologist
enough to affirm with certainty.[10]

V

This brings us to White's basic philosophy as developed in "Science Is
Sciencing" and resummarized in his present article. Events occur, he says, in a
four-dimensional continuum of three
space co-ordinates and of time. From
this we select certain aspects according
to our approach. The historian interprets
events in terms of time, "disregarding
their formal aspects." (The context allows of no other interpretation than that
formal and *spatial* are equated here!)
Scientists (in the ordinary strict sense of
the term; viz., the students who use
experiment, quantification, and prediction) "exclude the temporal factor and
deal only with the formal-functional
aspect of events." (This appears to be
another slide-over of meaning from spatial to formal-functional. At any rate,
the space factor disappears, and the
structure and function suddenly appear.[11]) Finally, the evolutionist interprets phenomena "in terms of space-
time." (Here space is again the equivalent of form and function, since elsewhere the evolutionistic "process" is
characterized as "temporal-formal" and
as "a temporal sequence of forms, time
and form being simultaneously and inseparably significant.")

To most readers, this seemingly immediate derivation of form and function
from space will presumably appeal as
something in need of justification; or, if
the derivation is not immediate, the steps
which lead to the equating need to be
cited. Perhaps White is in position to do
this, or possibly has already done so elsewhere. Apart from this one major point,
however, his scheme is a logically possible one and deserves consideration because his case for evolutionism as a meth-

od of inquiry seems to rest wholly upon this scheme.

VI

Nevertheless, I wish to outline a different scheme of knowledge[12] derived from consideration of how the several sciences actually operate, and perhaps also more in accord with prevalent epistemology.

This view, basing on Rickert but going beyond him, holds that the method of history is to examine phenomena or events in their space and time contiguity. This contiguity may not be violated if the inquiry is to remain historical in its character. Hence the basic importance of context. Historical validation per se is achieved in terms of accord or fit with increasingly larger context. The attachment to contiguity in space and time, to continuity of the spatiotemporal relations of the phenomena, coupled with attachment to the phenomena themselves, is what gives the historical aspects of phenomena their semblance of immediate reality. It is also the factor which prevents the historical approach as such from attaining to "laws," to general theory, to exactness of measurable findings, and to genuine verifiability, as by experiment. It is also what gives historical findings their quality of uniqueness, their individuation, their physiognomic property. Also, the attachment to the forms and successions of the phenomena themselves, in their actual concatenation or contiguities, yields a recognition of patterns which is akin to stylistic formulation.

Science,[13] on the contrary, abandons most of what history holds onto: position in the space-time continuum, singularity of quality, physiognomy, style. It attains to quantitative instead of qualitative precision. By systematic analytic dissolution of the concretenesses of phenomena, it achieves generalization, repetitive constants, verification. The essence of the method is abstraction: the resolution of phenomena into metaphenomenal formulations. The validation of the system of science is not achieved—at least not directly—through an increasing context, since, intellectually, strictly scientific operation *destroys* phenomenal context (as it does phenomena) except for the minimum preserved as internally relevant to a special situation; the validation is in prediction or experimental correction and verification.

In principle these two approaches are applicable to any kind of phenomena. In actual inquiry, however, experience to date has been that scientific method wins its greatest successes on the inorganic levels[14] of phenomena, and decreasingly in the successively superposed ones. Pure historical method, on the contrary, was applied first, and still is applied with most result, to human events on the psychosociocultural level. The more basic the level, the greater the dependence of the historic interest and approach on the corresponding scientific approach: as of astronomy on physics.

The use of space and time factors under this dichotomy requires further specification. Science of course does not shut out considerations of space and time. They enter into its most elementary findings[15] and into the problems on the most advanced firing line. But it is abstracted or relative time and space that are dealt with: such time and space only as are pertinent as measures to the problem of a given situation. Once a strictly scientific finding has been made, the results float completely free in the infinite continuum of total time and space.

A datum that floats as detachedly as this is not a datum of history on any level. Completed historical findings are placed in the continuum of total space and time, so far as possible, by reference to other points taken as fixed. This is one reason for the inescapable significance of context. But the primary concern of historical study, after all, is with qualities of phenomena as such. Of these qualities or properties of phenomena, their placement is part—but only a part; the physiognomy of events, or whatever we wish to call it, is after all the most significant, although the significance becomes complete only upon placement being included.

A consequence is that the time element is not the most distinctive factor in history, as is still so often, but superficially, assumed and asserted. Space determination is equally important with time determination in history. It happens to be more often given or assumed in the field of inquiry: geology of this planet, evolution of land animals, history of France, archaeology of Egypt. In such cases the time element tends often to be one of the unknowns which are sought; though the fundamental objective is always a qualitative configuration, a style or physiognomy, to which the spatiotemporal placement adheres as a property. Particular histories can suppress, or hold constant, either time or space: as the history of one city, or on the other hand a descriptive cross-section or characterized moment in the history of an empire, or of human culture, a work of, say, the order of Burckhardt's *Renaissance* or Tacitus' *Germania*. In that case the product of inquiry is not a narration but an analytic-synthetic, characterizing description. To the same class belong ethnographic descriptions. To be sure, these are potential raw materials for a science of culture which is slated to be erected sometime. But they are also potential materials for a history of human culture which is to be written. Yet the prime significance of any inquiry is that which it has at the time, not that to which it may contribute later; and as what else can an ethnography be primarily designated, in its essential contemporary nature, than as an account of a particular cultural style, a timeless piece of history? I realize that this concept of synchronic historical

treatment is so contrary to habitual thinking that it is likely to seem unintelligible, as it did to Boas in 1936. On the contrary, I am convinced that the essence of the process of historical thought will continue to fail of being grasped as long as time is considered most important in that essence. This essence is the characterizing delineation of groups of phenomena in context, into which both time and space factors enter; but, with spatiotemporal place once established, either of these two considerations can be temporarily suppressed by being held constant by the historian, if circumstances or his objective warrant.

On reflection, why should concern with time be a main diagnostic criterion of the historical method in distinction from the abstracting procedure of scientific method? Time is not the complement of abstraction. Moreover, if it is time that distinguishes history, what is the branch of inquiry which is correspondingly dedicated to primary concern with space?—unless we are ready to accept White's answer that it is science. Or if there is none such, why not?

VII

If this dichotomous view is sound, there is no apparent room left for White's evolutionism as concerned with form-plus-sequence. The nonrepetitive parts of what he so designates, like the evolution of our universe, organic life, and human culture, are merely large histories. Other subjects in evolutionism, such as the growth of organic individuals or radioactive deterioration, are repetitive and therefore are parts of the findings of science, in situations in which sequence and duration happen to be unusually conspicuous. Certainly organic growth is intimately allied to heredity, if indeed it is not merely an aspect of it. But the normal functioning of heredity is in fixed recurrence, which is certainly far from any evolution.

I do not wish to press this view intransigently. White may yet redefine evolution in a more generally acceptable way; evidently a great deal of anthropological and other study is mixed in character; and certainly there are studies which are difficult to classify. Thus, like my own "formula" on the three stages of writing, Lowie's remarks on the occurrence of clans look on the surface as if they recognized universal stages of culture and hence were a slip into evolutionism. They may be nothing more than summarized culture history; I am not certain; and it would be best for Lowie himself to characterize them. But there is much scholarly product whose precise nature still is hard to define; progress in clarification is slow; and it will no doubt be better speeded by cooperative attempts than by wrangling. If the evolutionistic method has something of its own which is more than a reduction of historical findings to the generalization of formula, the rest of us surely want to know about it. Perhaps White can come nearer to showing us on another try or, better yet, by precise and full exemplification.

SUMMARY

White's recent distinction of the historical, evolutionary, and "functional" (scientific) methods on all levels of phenomena is inadequate in that it virtually limits historical study to tracing the movements of discrete culture items (treated as if essentially invariable) in the continuum of time. Position in space is equally important; and, far from the phenomena being viewed atomically, the aim of the historical approach is to see them in individuated configurations or nexuses which constitute unique patterns or styles. Some of what White calls "evolutionism" seems actually to be history; some of it, science; the nature of the remainder, or whether there is a remainder, is not clear. Possibly the core of what he calls "evolutionistic study" is the recognition of predeterminations or immanences; or it may be only a sort of generalized history with the detail suppressed. White's statement as to the respective parts played by time, space, form, and function in the three approaches seems to contain an inconsistency, the equating of space with form; and this in any event needs clarification.

*11. CULTURE, EVENTS, AND INDIVIDUALS
1946

This is the slightly revised version of the mimeographed abstract of a talk given at a meeting of the Viking Fund on October 25, 1946, and is published here for the first time.

CULTURES, societies, individuals, and events, respectively, represent roughly the characteristic subject matters of anthropology, sociology, psychology, and history as actually practiced. Without claiming either substantiality or complete self-sufficiency for culture, and admitting it as an "attribute of human behavior," the anthropologist nevertheless, if he wishes to remain such, has necessarily to concern himself first of all with that aspect and product of human behavior—and reinfluence upon it—which is usually called "culture."

Qualities of culture are: (1) It is transmitted and continued not by the genetic mechanism of heredity but by interconditioning of zygotes. (2) Whatever its origins in or through individuals, culture quickly tends to become supra-personal and anonymous. (3) It falls into patterns, or regularities of form and style and significance. (4) It embodies values, which may be formulated (overtly, as mores) or felt (implicitly, as in folkways) by the society carrying the culture, and which it is part of the business of the anthropologist to characterize and define.

As to points 2 and 3, superpersonal anonymity and patterns, these qualities are overwhelmingly evident in linguistics and about equally so in archaeology; they used to be generally accepted for ethnology and in principle still apply to its material. If so, why the recent emphasis, in certain sectors of anthropology, on individual psychiatric

* Not published previously.

approach, persons in culture, autobiographies, personality determinants, etc.? These approaches furnish vividness of exemplification and add stereoscopic relief to description. But it is not clear that they contribute anything essential to the comprehension of culture—either of its patterns or of its values, or perhaps even of its processes.

In the division of scientific labor, to paraphrase Bloomfield, the anthropologist deals with the interrelations of cultural phenomena; he is not competent, as such, to deal with problems of psychology or physiology, and his findings may ultimately be all the more valuable for the psychologist if they are not distorted by prepossessions about psychology.

Applications of Rorschach tests, for instance, are psychology. They will tell nothing about culture as such that probably cannot be got more directly and fully by anthropological techniques. An interculturally comparative psychology (in addition to animal or intergenetic psychology) is a desideratum. Such an intercultural psychology can be conceived as taking two forms. It can be empathic, describing the varying psychic values characteristic of different cultures—their typical personalities, so to speak. This approach will almost certainly be left by psychologists to anthropologists or historians. As an objective study, intercultural psychology could consist of tests given with a view to analyzing not the individuals tested but the psychic factors or qualities respectively more or less developed or

104

retarded by various cultures. To be systematic, such a psychology should probably in principle be developed by psychologists, whenever these become ready to handle situations involving cultural components.

Geniuses are individuals psychologically differentiated from the average and studiable as such. But, if their individuated personalities are deliberately ignored in favor of using the occurrence and degree of genius as a measure or index of the developmental profiles of patterns of growth of supra-individual products, geniuses become material for the analyst of anonymous cultural process. Like almost all human data, geniuses are capable of multiple significances on different levels of approach.

History, in its origins, deals with particular persons and particular events; but Greek and Roman and Chinese historians already generalized beyond itemization. Today institutional, economic, and cultural history far transcends personalities and individuated events in their significance, though remaining attached to them. An interpretation like Toynbee's uses events and persons chiefly as indexes or markers of the growth of cultures—often called "societies" by Toynbee—and of psychological or moral processes seen by him as operative in organized civilization generically. A history, say, of nineteenth-century Europe with no naming whatever of persons or of discrete events may not yet be quite feasible; but it is conceivable, at least as the limit of an approach. It would involve a selection of data on the basis of moving pattern. Yet such a selection would certainly be more sophisticated than personalized history. Events, persons, and patterns are of course interassociated in the world of phenomena; whatever we do with them, we select according to interest and purpose.

Values inhere in culture. Cultural items may be neutral or indifferent in value; but patterns seem normally to imply values. Part of the business of the anthropologist in his characterization of cultures is the recognition of their values. This recognition must be in terms of the values themselves or of their total cultures of course, not in terms of a supposedly absolute but really ethnocentric standard. The recognition must be descriptive or physiognomic, not normative. History is also concerned with values. It is usually considered successful in proportion as it extricates itself from the limitations of particular national or partisan systems and recognizes comparative values. The historian, like the anthropologist, makes unabashed use of his faculty of empathy, without abatement of knowledge, analysis, and organization as requisites.

The formal psychologist, being only recently reformed from introspection to one or another form of behaviorism, is at the moment a puritan; he shuns empathy because he must at all costs show himself scientific. This is perhaps why there has been so little relation of orthodox psychology toward anthropology. But the psychoanalyst, the psychiatrist, and the clinical and personality psychologist use empathic recognitions; hence their marginal orthodoxy. Also, as they deal with personality-wholes, cultural influencings are thrust into their cognizance; whereas the orthodox psychologist operates with abstracted problems, from which he tries first to eliminate cultural factors.

There is now a pretty well-standardized field called "social psychology." This, though largely stimulated in its beginnings by sociologists, has become an extension of individual response-psychology into the area of average interrelations of individuals seen as groups or masses in societies, as these can be statistically defined, but without particular reference to the varying personality-wholes of the individuals. The concern is with learning, socialization, prestige, propaganda, etc. Social psychology deals with the mechanisms at work in societies considered as societies, without direct regard to the cultures attached to these societies. Thus it investigates the mechanism of influencing opinion, not the opinions; the process of socialization or "culturalization," with only incidental reference to the content of the result attained.

Cultural psychology—the intercultural comparative psychology referred to above—is as yet an unorganized field of study. Most of the empirical efforts to develop the field have come from anthropologists. Psychoanalysts are equally interested; but, since they enter with systems of ready-made hypotheses of mechanisms, their findings seem to most anthropologists predetermined rather than empirically derived.

*12. CAUSES IN CULTURE
1947

This was also a Viking Fund supper-meeting talk, December 12, 1947. The mimeographed outline used has not been published and is here extended to about double its original length.

WHAT the causes are which operate in culture obviously depends on what culture is. Everyone is agreed that culture at least contains channeled or selected forms, norms, and values—a stream of related ideas and expressible patterns. Some would stop there; but most anthropologists would include in culture also human behavior—at any rate such human behavior as is influenced or conditioned by ideas or forms and in turn is engaged in producing, maintaining, or modifying them. The locus or residence of culture, according to either definition, is obviously in human beings, from whose behavior (which also contains noncultural elements) it is inferred and construed, that is, is formulated by abstraction. The narrower or "purer" definition evidently represents a farther degree of abstraction than the more inclusive, "mixed," or behavioral definition. Each has its value for certain purposes.

Now there are actual, established fields of organized study which deal almost exclusively with quasi-cultural forms, and which therefore serve as useful touchstones for the qualities that may be expected to distinguish sciences of the narrow as compared with the broad construction of culture. Of such studies, linguistics is the best known, most reputable, and neatest and most advanced in method. Relatively to other studies of man, linguistics is characterized by several traits: (1) Its data and findings are essentially impersonal, anonymous. (2) Its orientation is spon-

taneously historical, and potentially historical even for languages whose past has been lost. (3) The emphasis is on pattern, or structural interrelation, and away from so-called "functional" interpretation involving need satisfaction, drives, stimulus-response, and other explanations which "decompose" the phenomena dealt with into something ulterior. (4) Explanation is not in terms of genuine scientific cause, that is, efficient causes in the Aristotelian sense, but of "formal causes," that is, of other forms as being antecedent, similar, contrasting, or related. (5) Indeed, "explanation" in terms of producing cause is largely replaced by "understanding" in terms of historic contexts, relevance, and value significance.

On transposition of these criteria—impersonality, historic orientation, pattern emphasis, absence of causality, value significance—to studies of culture other than language, it is evident that standard ethnography, archaeology, and both kinds of culture history—that of disparate traits and that devoted to culture-wholes—pursue mainly the method of linguistics. In contrast, consciously functional anthropology, social anthropology, and sociology tend to be nonhistorical, reductionist, and interested in cause.

The difference is one of goal and interest, not of intrinsic superiority of either procedure over the other. The functional-social approach is more concerned with timeless process than with historic relation; more with cause than with pattern; with the behavior of hu-

* Not published previously.

man agents rather than their products; with society rather than with culture; with personality factors as motive forces more than with the attitudes or psychological qualities inherent in cultural manifestations; more readily with application to action, as contrasted with remote understanding. The functional-social approach is microscopic, immediate, analytic, focused on individuals, concerned with cause and effect and with the practical. The complementary historical-cultural approach is macroscopic or telescopic and is oriented toward the interrelations and significances of superpersonal products.

The above are polar positions. Actual scholarly activity is often transitional, less extremely characterized.

There are some considerations special to anthropology. One is the dilemma of ethnology, as it used to be called, which in England seems largely to be reconstituting itself as "social anthropology." What is "social" distinctive of in this title, what does it contrast with? Why the adjective at all? Perhaps it is the influence of a more belated explicit recognition in Britain of "social science," of an approach that is somehow of bearing on current issues. The ethnology done under this new banner is good enough ethnology. It deals wholeheartedly with culture and with aspects of culture, such as religion, economy, technology, environmental relations, that extend far beyond the structure and functioning of society *sensu stricto.* To some extent there would seem to be involved a reaction to the long underdevelopment in Britain of a nonphilosophizing, empirical discipline of sociology, in comparison with its luxuriance in the United States. It is rather interesting in this connection that culture-and-personality as a field has had a quite cool reception in England, as had our previous American vogue of acculturation.

Culture-and-personality may be construed essentially as an attempted use of culture to understand personality better. It is interested in people and their behavior, less in forms of culture. It is legitimate as a shift of focus and problem, not as a new attack on old problems. Culture consideration enters into its purview only peripherally, as a means. If culture remains the distinctive core subject matter of anthropology, culture-and-personality must be regarded as a marginal province thereof.

A contradiction remains unresolved between the body of Sapir's actual culturo-linguistic work and the several programmatic papers of his later years in which he seemed to assert that culture is fully meaningful only in terms of individual psychiatric personality. This view can possibly be explained as a personal reaction to a sense of ego frustration finally induced in him by years of preoccupation with cultural and linguistic forms; though he also continued to find internal satisfaction with such activity, which he continued as long as he lived [see also No. 17].

Malinowski was far less troubled by his inconsistency of exalting culture as *sui generis* and a completely interrelated system, and at the same time as derivable from and reducible to the needs and derived imperatives of physiology and psychology. It would seem that Malinowski's inconsistency was intellectual and nondisturbing; Sapir's, emotional and near-tragic.

The relation of the anthropological study of culture respectively to natural science, natural history, social science, and the humanities presents some points of interest. The subject matter of both the first is subcultural; but historical biology, geology, and astronomy are obviously linked to the historical study of cultural forms by a bond of common approach. As against this parallelism, there exist to date some hopes indeed, but scarcely any notable achievements, in the formulation and manipulation of process constants in culture corresponding to those attained in the nonhistorical activities of physics, chemistry, biochemistry, and physiology.

Among the recognized social sciences there is none, besides anthropology, that commits itself squarely and directly to recognizing culture as the distinctive and pervading aspect of their content. Sociology, economics, government, remain *de facto* "social" in their view, as well as in name, where anthropology has long since gone on to be primarily and explicitly cultural. This situation will presumably provoke some problems not now generally foreseen in the internal adjustments of the republic of the sciences—particularly, perhaps, in connection with the frequent absorption in university organization of anthropologists into larger sociological departments or nominally joint ones.

As to the humanities, their status is special, in that they are committed to cultural material, with consideration of forms, styles, and values, but often also with habits of addiction to propaganda or apology for particular sets of values. On the whole, also, the humanities lack an explicit, systematic, general theory of culture. Linguists are in excellent accord as to what language is, but they seem more concerned in preserving its autonomy than in relating it to the nonlinguistic remainder of culture.

The position of history as done by the historians is typified by Eduard Meyer, who recognizes the constant interaction of "general" superpersonal influences and of individual personalities, of causally produced "accident," and of purposive wills.

In the light of the foregoing it is also of interest to appraise the causality used in histories of total human culture, or interpretations of the process of culture viewed as history: Danilevsky, Spengler, Toynbee, Sorokin, Northrop, etc. Formal, efficient, moral, and immanent causalities have all been applied in this field, which remains diverse in motivation and approach.

13. WHITE'S VIEW OF CULTURE
1948

Two years later than No. 10, this analysis returns to Leslie White, who is always provocative and worth while. I recognize that his philosophy and mine are kindred, though he seems to me to push his too intransigently.

IN A recent paper, "The Expansion of the Scope of Science" in the *Journal of the Washington Academy of Sciences* for 1947, Leslie A. White maintains a series of propositions with which the present writer finds himself mainly and enthusiastically in accord, but which, precisely because of their importance, seem in need of certain limitations and clarifications.

The procedure will be followed of restating White's principal propositions, reworded by myself, and of then commenting upon them.

1. *Phenomena can be viewed, studied, and construed on a series of levels—such as the organic, psychic, social, and cultural levels or "dimensions"—whose recognition in the history of knowledge comes successively, gradually, and empirically.*

This is by now a widespread opinion. It has grown without self-consciousness, has no one outstanding name attached to it, and its full implications are as yet hardly recognized among many who essentially accept the view. Its recognition has come from students of science, as a by-product of their work. There appears to be no system of philosophy as such that makes serious use of the point of view. Comte's and Spencer's approximations to it are imperfect, are a century old, and their potentialities seem not to have been further developed and explored by philosophers. Personally, I know of no adequate attempt to examine systematically what the levels constitute or mean in terms of a theory of knowledge.

2. *Regularly, some of the phenomena of one level are explainable in terms of factors of the level or levels below.*

This is the familiar process of *reductionism*. Phenomena of one level, or certain of their properties, are made intelligible also in terms of factors, forces, or conceptual elements of a lower level. At least, they seem to be "more" intelligible when they also fit into a system of greater depth. Thus the properties of chemical elements correspond with a degree of regularity and predictability to the physical structure of the atom, the number, spatial relation, mass, and energy-charge of its constituents. Psychological emotions like anger and fear are called into activity by the physiological release of adrenalin into the blood stream and the consequent discharge of sugar from the liver. Biochemistry is actually the conversion of descriptively or functionally conceived processes of physiology into chemically conceived ones.

The over-all tendency of reductionism is obviously monistic. Phenomena of one level are explained away as such —in one sense—in being resolved into factors of another level or order.

3. *With equal regularity, however, certain phenomena of each level stubbornly resist reduction. These remain inexplicable and meaningless in terms of the lower level, whereas on their own level they may fit into intelligible relations.*

Anger and fear *both* reduce to adrenalin and glucose discharge, indistinguishably. Which one is felt and behaviored is not a matter of chemistry within the organism but depends on a relation between the total organism and the surroundings outside it. Jealousy is a very definite though variable thing psychologically, but a very obscure one physiologically, as White says. An affect of hostility may be directed toward the rival, the love-object, both, or neither. It is the total previous history of the person that determines the choice between such possible outcomes. So far as a hormone may be involved, it could only be as a cause giving a consistent effect. The business of the psychologist is precisely to tell in terms of the complete situation—which means the individual's whole experience, including his interpersonal and cultural exposure—why he has the impulse to punish once his girl and another time his rival or perhaps himself instead. Obviously, physiology as such cannot touch this problem.

In general, approach from an underlying level may hope to explain the uniformities in phenomena of an upper level, but does not even attack the problem of their diversities. Granted that we knew the full biochemistry of the sex drive, we would still know nothing of why a thousand human populations are likely to practice five hundred distinguishable kinds of marriage besides innumerable varieties of extramarital sex behavior. White is explicit and emphatic on this point. Presumably most cultural anthropologists would agree. It is certain that all historically minded ones would.

4. *It may accordingly be concluded that reductionism is valid and fruitful so far as it can be established, but that complete reduction of the phenomena of the cosmos to factors of a single, unified order or level is an unattainable limit.*

No one can foretell the future, but our experience to date makes it likely that there will always be irreducible residues which do make sense and do have meaning in terms of relations within their own level. It is in fact conceivable that as the body of reduced or trans-level understandings grows, our corpus of unreduced intra-level understandings will also continue to grow. Its simplicity is what renders reductionism attractive as a conceptual system. To believe that essential reduction has been accomplished is an illusion; that it is about to be, is a wish fulfilment. Our fullest understanding of the world may well continue to be in pluralistic terms.

How far, or in what sense, the intelligible relations determinable within one level are causal, will be examined below, under 8.

5. *The levels relate to separate aspects of phenomena, but this does not have to be taken to mean that there exist separate actualities or autonomous entities for each level.*

The realization of the pragmatic utility and necessity of recognition of distinctive levels runs a risk of being pushed to a point of excess. In that event the aspects or properties characteristic of each level are exaggerated and transcendentalized into entities or kinds of realities in their own right: life, mind, society, culture. Sometimes the motivation of such hypostasizing or reification is the ardor of a new attitude. Sometimes it is a hangover from old prescientific concepts, like soul. The result is that radical innovators and diehard reactionaries of the intellect may find themselves fellow-partisans against an orthodox bourgeoisie of reductionists, and that the latter do not discriminate between their opponents.

From a mere insistence on the importance of recognizing culture as a distinct domain of phenomena, there has been considerable spilling-over to the further but hasty and usually hazy attitude which sees culture as a special kind of entity or substance. Malinowski thought he could eat his cake and have it too. In the same essay he credited culture with being "a reality *sui generis*" and yet saved his monism by deriving the manifestations of this same culture from physiological needs and psychological imperatives.

I have been under fire, long ago from Boas and Benedict for mysticism, and subsequently from Bidney for idealism, in reifying culture. White has cited several such criticisms.[1] I take this opportunity of formally and publicly recanting any extravagances and overstatements of which I may have been guilty through overardor of conviction, in my "Superorganic" [No. 3] and since. As of 1948, it seems to me both unnecessary and productive of new difficulties, if, in order to account for the phenomena of culture, one assumes any entity, substance, kind of being, or set of separate, autonomous, and wholly self-sufficient forces. I do not find that I have ever explicitly declared my belief in such. But I do find that I have been ambiguous, and that I have written a number of passages which might be so construed and which quite probably do contain implications in this direction. I am grateful to my critics in proportion as they have been specific in indicating such implications. My present conception—free from ambiguity or unsoundness, I hope—of the nature of the forces or causes that make culture is discussed under 8 below.

It is easy to say more than one means, or to mean more than one is aware of, in this field. Nobody would accuse Lowie of mysticism or of lack of clarity. Yet White quotes Lowie's own words to the effect that culture represents "a distinct domain," is "a thing *sui generis*," "can be explained only in terms of itself," and "appears as a closed system."[2] A thing *sui generis* which is also a domain is not quite the same as a reality *sui generis*, but it is far along on

the way. Lowie's habitual precision and sanity, and above all the total context of his work, free him beyond doubt of any attainder of "mystically" regarding culture as a sort of autonomous substance. Presumably it is my past claim of autonomous *forces* that has given alarm and has earned me the label. As a matter of fact, I would not at present go as far as Lowie once did. I would now say that culture was *primarily* intelligible in terms of itself, not *only* in terms of itself.

6. *There is general agreement that the basic level or levels are the physical and the chemical (jointly the inorganic), and, next above, the organic one. Whether the organic is stretched upward to include the psychological is a function of how strait a reductionist one is. There does seem to be general agreement that the last four levels are the physiological, psychological, social, and cultural.*

The number of levels is not absolute. It varies according to reference and goal of consideration. For some purposes it is convenient to treat all suborganic phenomena as a unit. On the contrary, it is now and then useful to separate organic phenomena into those of plants and animals,[3] the latter alone showing evidences of a superimposed psychic level of phenomena. A single psychosomatic level is fashionable at the movement. The social and cultural are often still not distinguished, as White points out, when it is useful to do so. Yet there are situations in which reference to undifferentiated sociocultural phenomena is also convenient.

In short, it is the position order of the levels that is important. The degree to which it is useful to separate or merge adjacent levels varies with the objective of discussion.

7. *White holds that the scientific recognition of levels occurs historically in the order of ease of coherent explanation in terms other than of the autono-*

mous self or soul or free human will.

In other words, according to White, animism is least insisted on by an undisciplined intellect on the inorganic level, and most easily displaced there by a system of scientific interpretation; and the last citadel of animism lies in the domain of culture.[4]

This is largely true; but, historically, White has oversimplified the process. Chemistry should, according to his formula, have been developed before anatomy and everything above anatomy, whereas chemistry notoriously was a late science to crystallize out. This was for reasons such as historic lateness of systematic experimentation, which have nothing to do with level. It is however a fact that recognition of specifically social aspects of phenomena did come late, and of cultural ones still later—as witness the formal nondifferentiation of the two by Comte and Durkheim.

8. *Laws, forces, and perhaps complete causalities lying within the cultural level are determinable, according to White.*

This proposition can be seen in two ways, as is evident from White's citations from Simmel. While culture is a "structure of independent reality [*sic*], which leads its life after peculiar laws and by virtue of peculiar forces, independent of all its individual components," nevertheless "in the last analysis only individuals exist," according to Simmel, and the "spiritual structures" of which culture apart from artifacts consists "have their existence only in personal minds," so that "to think of them outside of persons is a mysticism."

With a philosopher of the stature of Simmel arriving at this sort of seeming impasse, it is evident that this part of the problem is not easy.[5] Culture is credited with having a reality with laws and forces of its own, but also with existing only in persons. It is no wonder that nonphilosophers have floundered a bit in this area.

For my part, I am ready to concede that culture exists only in persons in the sense that it resides, has its locus, only in them. Incidentally, culture also exists then in physiological reactions, in biochemical ones, and beyond, in physicochemical ones. And therewith is evident the absurdity of reductionism as a practical method of exploratory scientific operation. In fact, reductionism is not an investigatory tool at all. It is not a method of extending understanding over new domains, but a procedure for integrating understandings that have been attained. It consolidates territory already overrun.

To the investigator of culture, as long as he remains merely such, it seems irrelevant for the time being where culture resides, or whether it exists autonomously or not, as long as he has genuinely cultural data to operate with and is free to operate upon them with the methods he finds most productive. The locus and reality of culture are irrelevant in the sense that they do not affect his specific cultural problem nor his specific method of dealing therewith. There are two courses open to students of culture. They can either try to resolve it into something else, in which case they will obviously not learn very much about culture; or they can try to learn about its manifestations in the world of nature. If to do this necessitates the provisional freezing of cultural phenomena as such on the cultural level, and acting as if culture were an autonomous realm, well and good: for, except by so doing, we shall never find out how much autonomy cultural phenomena have or have not, nor what kind of autonomy. The *as if* attitude gives us a perfectly adequate way to proceed; and White's acceptance of this attitude seems much more fruitful than his denunciation of Simmel as stubborn, mired, and blinded by an obsolete metaphysics. White's two positions on this point are of course not wholly consistent: if Simmel is just perversely wrong, then culture does really "exist" as an entity on its own level, and we do not have to fall back on any "as if" attitude.

As for those who contend that cultures do not enamel their fingernails, we who are interested in culture phenomena can cheerfully concede this and keep on our way. Lynd is not a pettifogging literalist. He is interested in subcultural phenomena of social relations, whose focus tends to be somewhat disturbed by the impact of the cultural approach, to paraphrase slightly White's appropriate citation from MacIver. A few neighborly comments like this across the back-yard fence of sociology and anthropology should not be taken too earnestly. They pass just because we are neighbors in area and endeavor.

If we waive a separate substance or locus of residence for culture, what then about its autonomous laws, order, and forces? Is there anything of that sort left, or do we have to go completely reductionist?

The partial solution which I propose I owe to Bidney[6] and his bringing the four Aristotelian kinds of "causes"[7] to bear on the problem. The efficient causes of cultural phenomena unquestionably are men: individual personalities who are in interpersonal and social relations. It seems to me that this cannot be denied and that there is neither use nor honesty in trying to whittle any of it away. But the manifestations of culture come characteristically in certain forms, patterns, or configurations, many of which are large, ramifying, and enduring. Now while persons undoubtedly make and produce these cultural forms, our knowledge of persons—and very largely also our knowledge of societies of persons—has failed conspicuously to explain the cultural *forms*: it has failed to derive specific cultural effects from specific psychic or social causes. In fact, psychological and social

concepts or mechanisms are not even much good at *describing* cultural forms.[8] Such descriptions or characterizations begin to mean something only when they are made on the cultural level—in terms of intercultural relations and of cultural values.

Every anthropologist or historian concerned with culture realizes that cultural situations make more sense, reveal more meaning, in proportion as we know more of their cultural antecedents, or, generically, more total cultural context. In other words, cultural forms or patterns gain in intelligibility as they are set in relation to other cultural patterns. This interrelating of forms is evidently like the consideration of Aristotelian "formal causes."[9] Of course, they are not "causes" at all in the sense of modern mechanistic science, whose concern is with efficient causes (if with any). And if Aristotelian terminology be objected to in 1948, I shall be happy to adopt whatever more appropriate new term may be coined or proposed.

I am convinced that this primacy of patterns[10] and pattern relation must be accepted in our intellectual operations with cultural data, possibly not forever, but at any rate in the present development of our learning and science.[11] It is easy to cry for dynamic mechanisms, but they have been very hard to find. What the mechanisms or efficient causes residing in persons have explained in culture is perhaps some of its vague recurrences, its hazily defined common denominators. All the characterized qualities of culture, all its variations and specificities, remain essentially unexplained by dynamic psychic mechanisms. Historians, though their material consists of a mixture of culture, persons, and events, increasingly realize the inadequacy of specific causal explanations, and more and more are content to present sequences of significant forms.

The clearest case is furnished by linguistics, easily that one of all social and humanistic studies which follows the most rigorous and exact method. Speech is a wholly human and wholly social phenomenon, but linguistics thrives by being completely anonymous and impersonal, with a minimum of reference to its carriers and their psychology, and by dealing with the relations of specific forms without serious concern for their specific productive causes. The relation of *d, t, ts* in *deux, two, zwei* is a "law" in the sense of being a regularity of form, of consistent relation of pattern. But the linguist does not generally ask what made English have *t* where French has *d*. He could not give the answer, and he knows that he could not; and—if he has ever thought about it—he probably suspects that no reductionist could give it either. The linguist may also be quite ready to concede that in his way the physicist is right if he claims that actually language *is* only air vibrations made by the larynges and mouths of individuals of *Homo sapiens*. On the physicist's level language is that and remains that. The linguist gets something more significant than air waves out of his material because he does not try to explain it through efficient causes residing in persons, but takes such causality for granted and concerns himself with the *interrelations* of linguistic *forms* in his linguistic phenomena.

Culture as a whole is more manifold and less channeled than its part, language. That perhaps is why students of culture have been less courageous or decisive in realizing that their most fertile procedure is essentially the same. Like language, culture exists only in and through human individuals and their psychosomatic properties; and, like language, it acquires a certain larger intelligibility and systematic significance in the degree that it takes these persons for granted and proceeds to investigate the interrelations of superpersonal forms of culture.

In these statements I do not feel that I am, as White thinks, failing to "hold consistently to the culturological point of view"; I am only delimiting and trying to clarify it. That a historical approach happens to be more fruitful with reference to culture, and a mechanical-scientific one more fruitful in regard to matter and energy, is the concession of a difference, not of an inferiority. And culture may well yet reveal "laws" similar to the "laws" which the linguist calls sound shifts; only they will presumably be, like these, primarily relations of forms (synchronic or sequential), not laws of efficient causality. So far as the latter are determinable for culture, the prospect seems to me to be that they will continue to reside in the psychic or psychosomatic level. And why not? Who are we that we should claim utter self-sufficiency for our domain?

9. *Determinism—as opposed to free will or animism—being resisted vigorously by scientifically undisciplined personalities, the apperception or recognition of cultural phenomena as such is still being fought, according to White; in fact, is being fought with increasing success since about 1930, he says.*

This seems to be a half-truth. I have myself made a similar charge, in a specific case where I felt that chaos in phenomena was more congenial to my opponent than any determinate order that limited the freedom of the human person. But I hesitate o generalize the accusation. I am myself a determinist by inclination. But I do not see any one-to-one correspondence between determinism and enlightenment, nor between intellectual reactionism and free will. If Bidney can leave room for God and prayer in his interpretation of culture, or Toynbee for God and free will in his history—well, I do not operate that way, but do not see why I should be concerned over their doing so, at least not until it is evident that their attitude affects the results of their studies. After all, there have been and are determinists and Calvinist predestinarians in religious dogma as well as free-willists. And further I am aware that in living my practical life I must necessarily, if I am to act at all, do so *as if* I enjoyed freedom of will, even though intellectually and impersonally I choose to remain a determinist. This is the reverse and complement of what the humanist historian would do in pursuing his profession if he happened to be a personal determinist; and there perhaps are such.

In short, the correlation seems to me considerably less simple than to White, even though we both are determinists, at least of a sort.

I also doubt that there has been a recession since around 1930. In the conviction of a cause, it is easy to be pessimistic about its progress. Looking back thirty years on my essay called "The Superorganic" [No. 3], I am struck by the sense that pervades it of a great need for freeing cultural phenomena[12] from the oppression of biological thinking. I do not think now that the yoke of the organic really lay heavy on our "culturological" necks in 1917. If there was such a yoke, the biologists of the time were probably hardly aware of imposing it. It has certainly lifted completely by now, at least in intellectual circles, and that spontaneously, without the pomp of a formal revolution.

It is well also to remember that American students come to a university, and mostly leave it, with astonishingly little experience in historical attitude of any sort, and hence with considerable difficulty in apprehending at first hand what cultural phenomena actually are like when viewed historically. On the other hand, personality is the slogan of the moment; and so they clamor by the dozens and hundreds to be told the latest final insight into culture and personality, without being very clear as to what either is. Add that as a nation we love gadgets, that devices like "ink-blot tests" have some of the outward qualities of a gadget—and the prospect may look dim to those who are interested in culture as such. But with experience one learns that these waves go much as they come. In a decade or two Rorschachs may be conventional routine or may have been displaced as stimuli of fashion response by their successor of the day. As late as 1915 the very word "personality" still carried overtones chiefly of piquancy, unpredictability, intellectual daring: a man's "personality" was much like a woman's "it." And who spills any feeling now about acculturation, since the word has lost its emotional charge and has been seen to denote part of one of the ever present, regular, humdrum processes of human history?

I am not sanguine as to progress of interest in culture being rapid, but I see no recession.

10. *The supposed recent regression from an autonomous science of culture White construes as due to the obsoleteness of our social system of capitalism and imperialism, its dedication to the status quo, and our unwillingness to recognize both evolution and culture; but the halt will be only temporary.*

These points in the two final paragraphs of the body of White's essay are largely a *non sequitur*. They are mentioned here only in the endeavor to keep them out of the discussion which the remainder of White's challenging paper will expectably provoke.

It may be doubted that our social system is obsolete—this because of the fair rapidity with which it is adapting to change. We do alter our status quo, even though it is favorable enough to make us want to keep much of it. We can cheerfully admit our capitalist "system" as a gradual historic growth, while laughing off the implication of its being a plotted conspiracy. And so on. Yet, even if our social and political direction as a nation were belated and benighted, it is hard to see what that has to do with the more or less explicit theoretical recognition or nonrecognition of culture by some hundreds of professional anthropologists and sociologists. Can it really be that soon the final judgment day is coming when *all* the truths in the world will segregate themselves on the one side, *all* the symbols of error and powers of evil on the other? Unless that be so, these final sweeping dicta by White are irrelevant to his main intellectual thesis, and their injection tends to detract from the consideration which most of his trenchant essay deserves.

14. THE CONCEPT OF CULTURE IN SCIENCE
1949

This address was delivered on November 1, 1948, at the University of Chicago, in a symposium on "The Landmarks of Scientific Integration." It was published in the "Journal of General Education." This is perhaps the most mature and rounded of my general statements on culture.

I PROPOSE to discuss the concept of culture—its origin and validity, its use and limitations. Like every concept, this one is a tool; and as a tool the concept of culture is two-edged. It ties some phenomena and interpretations together; it dissimilates and distinguishes others—about which more later.

Like all important ideas, that of culture was the realization of many minds, and it developed gradually. There are still great civilized nations—the French, for instance—who refuse to admit the word "culture" into their intellectual vocabulary. On the other hand, the ancients knew, and modern primitives are aware of, some of the phenomena of culture—as, for instance, distinctive customs. "We don't do that way, we do like this"—such a statement, which every human being is likely to make at some time, is a recognition of a cultural phenomenon.

Phenomena have a way of occurring composite in nature, intricately blended. Their qualities, still more their conceptualized general aspects, can be extricated only gradually from the welter of appearances. Until well into the nineteenth century and in certain situations and contexts until today, the concept of culture has remained unextricated from that of society. When Comte founded sociology and coined its name more than a century ago, he stamped on it the impress of the social. But his famous three stages of mythology, metaphysics, and positivism are stages primarily of ideology, and therefore of culture. Only incidentally are they stages of specifically social or interpersonal relations. Still more does this essential reference to culture instead of society hold of Comte's differentiating characterizations of Catholicism and Protestantism and hundreds of other special dicta.

When so original and penetrating a thinker as Durkheim hypostasized society as that by which early groups were impressed, which they worshiped, and thus originated religion, he put forth a view which has generally seemed far-fetched and, to many, mystical. But as soon as we substitute for his nondifferentium of "society" the customs and beliefs which hold together primitive societies and seem to help them to survive—in another word, their "culture"—then the Durkheim interpretation begins to assume reasonableness. It seems fair to assume that that is what Durkheim "meant," what he would say today.

That nondifferentiation of the two aspects should continue up to a certain point is expectable, since culture by definition includes, or at least presupposes, society. As something shared and supraindividual, culture can exist only when a society exists; and conversely every human society is accompanied by a culture. This converse, to be sure, is not complete: it applies only to *human* societies. In principle, however, the limitation is extremely important. The existence of cultureless or essentially cultureless subhuman societies, especially the highly elaborate ones of the social insects, serves as an irrefutable touchstone for the significant discrimination of the concepts of the social and the cultural: they *can* exist separately. At any rate, one of them does exist separately.

The word "social" is itself a relatively late appellation. The Roman term was *civilis, civitas,* from *civis,* a "citizen," corresponding to Aristotle's definition of man as a *zoon politicon* or "political animal"—a civil animal to the Romans, a social animal to us. Of course, institutions were implied in the term "political animal," and therewith culture was implied, but not as a segregated, coagulated concept. These ancient Mediterranean terms are illuminative of how abstract ideas originate in a matrix of the concrete. When Aristotle wanted to talk generically of what we call "society" and "culture," he used the word *polis,* which still carried full implication and imagery of citadel and city wall, of free citizens entitled to vote and to fight.

The word "culture" in its modern scientific sense, as, for instance, any anthropologist would use it with assurance that every other anthropologist would know what he meant, and not something else—this modern meaning of "culture" is still more recent. The first definition of "culture" in this broad but definite sense of its current social science usage—as distinct from cultivation and refinement, from nurture, from agriculture and pearl culture and test-tube cultures—the first definition I have found in an English dictionary dates from the late twenties. The first deliberate usage in a book was by Tylor when in 1871 he published *Primitive Culture* and formulated that most-quoted of definitions of culture which begins: "that complex whole which includes...." It is clear that Tylor was conscious of establishing the term, just as he was aware of using "culture" and "civilization" as synonyms in his discourse. To be exact, he already had

used the word "culture" a few times as a hesitant alternative for "civilization," and in the same sense but without definition, six years earlier in his *Researches,* as if trying it out on the British public. He may have got it from the German ethnographer, Klemm, whom he read and cited. Klemm spells the word with a C—*Cultur*—in his 1843 as well as his 1854 book. The word appears to have been in general German usage at that period with its modern meaning, and was in no sense handled then like a new coinage. I do not know precisely how far back the German word *Cultur* goes with its modern scientific meaning. Kant uses it repeatedly in his *Anthropologie,* but it is mostly difficult to say whether he is thinking of culture in our sense or of "becoming more cultured." Arciniegas quotes Paul Hazard as saying that the word first appears in the German dictionary of 1793.

Let us take a long step back from both culture and its undifferentiated immediate matrix, which we would today call "sociocultural"—a step back to the psychosomatic. Just as culture presupposes society, so society presupposes persons. It is an assemblage of individuals—plus something additional—that something which we and termite societies share. Well, here, then, are three elements or sets of factors: culture, society, persons, each resting upon, or preconditioned by, the next. In fact, we can immediately go one step further and separate persons into bodies and minds as two aspects which in some situations at least it is profitable to deal with separately—in all strictly psychological situations, for instance. That the separation is warranted, when it is useful, is clear not only from the current distinction of biological science from psychology but also from the fact that plants, though possessing somas, are generally conceded as showing no evidence of having psyches.

So now we are already facing four

superposed aspects—four "levels," let us call them: body, psyche, society, culture. By now it is obvious where the line of thought is leading us; the next step prefaces the inorganic as underlying the somatic, the psychic, the social, and the cultural.

De facto, phenomena of the inorganic level can also be split up, when, as, and if useful—and in many situations, perhaps most, it is useful—into physical and chemical. Indeed, we can split finer and laminate off a subatomic level and perhaps another for supermolecular virus phenomena or for crystal manifestations. All these segregations, however, fall within the larger inorganic or suborganic end of the scale; and, as our particular concern here is with the ultraorganic, with the most superorganic at the opposite end, it would be digressive and distracting to enter here into these finer distinctions at the bottom of the hierarchy.

It has become customary of late to designate these hierarchical planes as "levels of organization" and, alternatively, as "dimensions." The latter term is appropriate in certain contexts, as when it is said that every human situation has environmental, organic, social, and cultural dimensions. The word "dimension" here is equivalent to "aspects" or to "class of impinging factors." It definitely avoids even implication of hierarchy. Dimensions cross-cut one another, levels imply parallelism. In a so-called "field approach" to a limited phenomenal area, such as a personality, where emphasis is on the interaction of factors converging at a single point, it is natural to see cultural, social, organic, and physical factors as so many dimensions "radiating" out from the point under observation. By contrast, as the approach is macroscopic, or even telescopic, as in the tracing of large historic patterns or their interrelations, the dimensions automatically segregate themselves into parallel and superposed layers, and the term "levels" is more appropriate.

However, it is necessary not to confound "levels of organization" with "levels of abstraction." It is true that, while we are focusing on cultural aspects, we are in a technical sense "abstracting" from the organic and physical aspects pertaining to the same phenomena. "Abstracting" here means removing our consideration from, ignoring; it is temporary, shifting, reversible. But cultural phenomena are *not* more abstract than physical or organic phenomena in the sense of being more abstruse, rarefied, unconcrete, or conceptualized. The surge of anger is as concrete a phenomenon as is a contracted eyebrow or a constricted blood vessel. The custom of headhunting or of catching the bride's bouquet is certainly thoroughly concrete. It is only culture as a generalized concept that is abstract; but so are society, psyche, body, matter, and energy abstract. What is much more significant than abstractness is that cultural phenomena occur organized on different principles from social phenomena, social phenomena from psychic, and so on down the series.

What is clearest about the levels is that certain properties or qualities of the phenomena of each are peculiar to it. Presumably this is due to a difference in arrangement or organization. That which is specifically characteristic and distinctively significant of phenomena of a level is intelligible only in terms of the other phenomena, qualities, or regularities of that same level. The most characteristic qualities or phenomena are never explained by what we know of another level: they are not really reached by other-level knowledge, especially when the levels are well separated. The findings of a study of lower-level phenomena do indeed *apply* to those of higher level, but they apply with decreasing significance.

Thus gravitation, electrical conductivity, and element valence apply to organic bodies as well as to inorganic ones. But principles or laws such as these are the only ones which apply to inorganic bodies; and yet they do not to any serious degree explain the specific organic phenomena of hereditary repetition, of conception and death, of adaptability. These specifically organic processes *conform* to established physicochemical processes; they cannot be *derived* from them. Laws of a lower level set the frame within which phenomena of a higher level operate; they do not per se produce those phenomena. The lower-level laws will explain the constants, universals, and uniformities of phenomena on an upper level. They will explain or describe those qualities or properties which an upper level shares with a lower—that an organic body has mass or conductivity, for instance. They fail to explain or even describe those properties that are specific of a level, distinctive of it—as how an organic body repeats itself in its offspring.

In short, it appears that the total work of science must be done on a series of levels which the experience of science gradually discovers. To reduce everything in the universe to a monistic set of principles, mechanical or otherwise, may be a legitimate philosophy—or may not be; it is certainly not an adequate operational method of science. It involves using the hard-won earnings of physics for verbal extensions into biology or sociology, and thereby short-circuiting genuine problem solution in those very domains. Apparently, true progress is made when every science is autonomous in its procedures, while also realizing its relation of dependence on the subjacent ones and of support to the independent overlying ones. It is investigation on autonomous levels that is a precondition of most extensions of our understanding of the world. After enough such extensions have been made,

it is valid reductionism that gradually integrates and consolidates them. Premature reductionism is just verbal forcing.

This does not mean that a new entity is hypostasized as the unique substance of each level. Life, mind, society, and culture are not outside matter and energy, not outside space and time and free of them. They are in and of nature with matter and energy. They are different organizations of matter and energy, if one will, which physicists and chemists cannot, in virtue of their physical and chemical methods, deal with fruitfully; and similarly all the way up the scale.

This is where the modern level-approach differs from the older segregation of spirit from matter, of soul from body. In this the higher substance was reserved from the operations of nature, was excluded from its sphere. The body perished, but the soul went on; matter was subject to mechanical laws, but the spirit was free of them—it stood outside nature. On the contrary, the scientific point of view is that every phenomenon is in nature and part of it. The levels represent empirically found segmentations of the total field of nature, in each of which somewhat distinctive intellectual procedures or operations seem to be most productive. The whole recognition of levels is, in one sense, an affair of scientific methodology, is wholly internal to science. It does not portend the reintroduction of vitalism, mentalism, spirit, or *Geisteswissenschaften*.

Philosophically, cognizance of a system of levels seems to have been recent and rather perfunctory. Bergson has been reckoned a proponent of the view of emergence of the new; but, so far as his *élan vital* is extra-natural, his emergents would be something more than levels. Alexander's *Space, Time, and Deity* (1920) is often credited with being the fullest exposition in English of the point of view by a professional philosopher. Alexander works from space and time successively through matter, life, and mind toward God. This view may stem partly from scientific experience but is used to transcend science and nature. C. Lloyd Morgan's *Emergent Evolution*, three years later, is perhaps the most-cited work on the subject. "There is more in the events that occur in the living organism," he says (p. 20), "than can adequately be interpreted in terms of physics and chemistry, though physico-chemical events are always involved." Vital relatedness—organization on the organic level—is effective because changes occur under it "the like of which do not occur when life is absent." Morgan credits Lewes with the word "emergent," and Wundt with the term "principle of creative resultants," namely, that psychical products are more than a mere summation of elements and represent a new formation. J. Needham and William Morton Wheeler have expressed similar views, which Koestler's second *Yogi and Commissar* essay also sets forth with charm and originality.

Two things hold about most of these formulations. First, they concentrate on biological and psychological autonomy from the physicochemical and fail to pursue the principle onto the social and cultural level, at any rate explicitly so. (Wheeler does go on up to the social level but not to the cultural. Warden in 1936 did explicitly recognize culture as an emergent.) Second, the stress is on an evolving universe and on emergences in the course of this. Evolution is therefore a primary postulate, and emphasis is on emergences within this—in other words, on innovating changes. Logically, however, a hierarchical series of levels of phenomena could exist in a static world. How they successively emerged to become graded as they are is a separate problem, which logically need not obtrude. My point is not to combat or deny that there may have been cosmic evolution but to assert that the concept

of evolution and the concept of levels are not necessarily involved or implied with each other. Emergence is no longer contained in the idea of levels as soon as levels are separated from evolution. New levels leap into appearance only if one has already assumed an evolutionary and progressive process. I would contend that the whole linkage with evolution has happened because our generation silently takes evolution for granted, as most former generations assumed deity: evolution is a compulsion culturally and emotionally difficult for us to escape from. A scientific methodology based as purely as possible on scientific experience is perhaps really better off without emergence, because unencumbered.

More fruitful is Koestler's metaphor and diagram of a staircase. Viewed from above, from the angle of strictly scientific exploration, this staircase looks like a plane surface, like a flat continuum to which everything is already reduced and in which everything therefore appears explainable. Viewed from the front, however, by phenomenal contemplation, it is the rise of the series of steps, and the nonpredictabilities between them, that are impressive. In short, primary organizing relations are operative within levels rather than trans-level.

There is another aspect of the levels which scientists have generally not noted and philosophers have fumbled when they did note. This is a fact which is not yet fully explained, but nevertheless it is indubitable on the basis of the overwhelming run of empirical experience to date. This fact is that the more basic a level is in the hierarchy, the more successfully do its phenomena lend themselves to manipulation by the methods of science in the strict sense—methods resulting in uniformities, repetitive regularities, and therefore predictability. But, on the contrary, the higher the level, the more recalcitrant are its phenomena to treatment by methods homologous or perhaps even analogous to those of physics and chemistry; whereas they yield readily—and with significance, though of a somewhat different kind—to intellectual treatment similar in principle to that which historians follow. The neo-Kantian philosophers have long since pointed out that, while a strictly scientific approach is generalizing and nomothetic, a historical approach is idiographic, in that it remains much more attached to the particular phenomena per se. Instead of dissolving them away into laws or generalizations, the historical approach preserves its phenomena, on whatever level it happens to be operating, and finds its intellectual satisfaction in putting each preserved phenomenon into a relation of ever widening context with the phenomenal cosmos.

From here, however, the neo-Kantians have not gone on to take the next steps which would seem compelled by a judicial inspection of the actual practices obtaining in the entire study of nature. These further steps are two. First, the contextual relations which a historical approach determines involve relations of absolute space equally with absolute time—not of time alone or primarily, as is so often asserted for history. Also, context involves relations of form, including function but perhaps excluding cause; and therewith it involves relations of value. The question of cause has its complexities, in part because scientists proper are also beginning to challenge and repudiate causality, especially in prestige-laden ultraphysics. However, it is notorious that, in the three uppermost levels of mind, society, and culture, specific causality is extremely difficult to determine. Presumably, this is because the phenomena of these levels are at least in part epiphenomena to phenomena of lower levels. It is therefore probably by trans-level reductionism that the complex

causes of upper-level phenomena will be found, if at all. However, relations of absolute space and time, of form, structure, and function, and of value do remain characteristic of the historical approach.

Second, while it is obvious that the great triumphs of strictly scientific method have been won on the lower levels and the ready development of the historical approach has taken place on the levels of man's mind, society, and culture, nevertheless it does not follow that a dichotomy of levels corresponds in a one-to-one manner to the dichotomy of intellectual procedures. Rather should it be assumed, on trial at least, that the correspondence is only partial and that the historical approach is applicable also on the basal levels—though with certain considerable difficulties—and the strictly scientific approach on the upper levels—again with difficulties. Such a view is not strange, nor is it paradoxical, when one remembers that astronomers admit astronomy to be a historical science; that much of geology is on its very face avowedly historical; and that evolutionary biology, from palaeontology through comparative morphology to systematics, professes to be the grand history of life on earth. Until this situation has been met by explicit and straightforward counterargument—which it has not been, so far as my knowledge goes—we must then assume that both the fundamental methods of intellectual understanding—the scientific and the historical—are applicable to all levels of phenomena, though with a sliding degree of fruitfulness.

After brilliantly showing that the *Geisteswissenschaften*, as so called in nineteenth-century Germany, were really disciplines dealing not with spirit or soul as such but with culture and that their *de facto* approach was essentially historical, the neo-Kantian Rickert blocked his farther progress with a simplistic dichotomy, to wit: Culture, historically intelligible, versus Nature, scientifically intelligible. Here the antithesis, culture : nature, is a relic of the older idealistic antithesis, spirit : nature, as this in its turn had been a softening modernization of theological soul : body opposition. And it is the same sharp antithesis which led Rickert to misappraise thoroughly the genuinely historical component in the sciences of astronomy, geology, and biology.

In any event, it is cultural phenomena —or, let us say, phenomena organizable in cultural terms and relations—that constitute the very top level of our hierarchy. If it seem rash to affirm this when the concept of culture is of as recent emergence into consciousness as we have seen it to be, we can modify the statement to say: culture is the top level recognized to date. Personally, I would not have the glimmering of a suspicion as to what a level of organization higher than that of culture might be like. Yet a future generation may see more clearly. For the present, however, let us examine the consequences of this top-level position of our subject matter.

First of all, while culture is underlain and preconditioned by social and psychosomatic factors, the enormous influence of culture on the behavior and activity of individual men and of men in groups has become fully recognized. So heavy is this overlay that "human nature," as that which is biologically given before culture begins to operate, has receded into a remote background in the social sciences and is maintained by biologists as a citadel of principle rather than with specific effectiveness. Now, in general, it is the lower levels that condition the upper: life conforms to physicochemical laws, not the reverse, and so on. There is, accordingly, something anomalous to the general scheme of things in the degree to which the human hereditary organism, individually and in groups, conforms to the sway of the culture to which it happens

to be exposed. It is doubtful whether there is another instance of factors on a higher level influencing events on a lower to so great a degree as this. Even the physical world is not immune from the agency of the restless human beavers operating with their cultural activities and artifacts: canals, dams, bridges; river diversions and soil erosion; deforestation and reforestation; pilfering of coal, gas, and other resources of the earth's crust; even attempts at artificial weather.

However, it is only the degree of the influencing and its special manipulative quality that are new as regards culture. There is at best only a trend in nature, not a rigorous law, making lower-level factors the prevailingly influencing ones on upper. A moment's reflection reveals that purely organic agents also have perceptibly modified the surface and outer shell of this physical planet: coral reefs, limestones, coal beds, domes of hydrocarbon oil and gas are among their residues.

Second, it is reasonable to assume that the findings of the top level will differ considerably in kind from those of the bottom levels. All our experience to date corroborates this. The revolutionary extension of physicochemical science by speculation and devised trial during the last fifty years centers around subatomic particles. In the same half-century we have also become much more aware and informed of the domain of culture. But this better understanding of culture has given no sign, until now, of including anything corresponding to the subatomic particles or the geneticists' genes. There is nothing in sight which suggests that we shall discover in culture any invariable elemental units, or even definite relations of integral number or fixed association.

Reflection confirms this negative appraisal. Context, significant of the historical approach which is dominant in the apprehension of culture, concerns external relations viewed as widely as possible—ultimately, in total relations. By contrast, the primary problem of physics, as of genetics and physiology, is to isolate or extricate valid simplicities, recurrent regularities, from the amorphous confusion of nature's phenomena. We may be reasonably confident that nothing corresponding to allelomorphic unit-characters or genes, to protons or neutrons, even to atoms or molecules, is likely to be discovered on the level of culture. Whatever such elemental units may be operative on culture—if any—we may expect to be elements of a lower level.

Indeed, such more or less recurrent near-regularities of form or process as have to date been formulated for culture are actually mainly subcultural in nature. They are limits set to culture by physical or organic factors. The so-called "cultural constants" of family, religion, war, communications, and the like appear to be biopsychological frames variably filled with cultural content, so far as they are more than categories reflecting the compartmenting of our own Occidental logicoverbal culture. Of processes, diffusion and socialization are both only psychological learning, imitation, and suggestion under special conditions. Custom is psychobiological habit on a social scale and carrying cultural values. And so on.

What evidently takes the place of the formulation of law, in intellectual operations on the cultural level, is the recognition of significances, including values. At any rate this holds in the degree that the approach to consideration of the phenomena is historical in kind, in the sense in which a historical approach has already been referred to as distinct from (though complementary to) the more narrowly scientific or nomothetic one. This becomes clear on consideration of history in its specific sense, the history studied by historians. This is indeed mixed as to its content: a jumble of pieces of individual biographies, more or less dramatic events, social contacts and clashes, definition of or implicit reference to institutions, that is, cultural forms and their succession, with perhaps occasional recognition of dashes of influence from inanimate nature or organic race. Now the recognized failure of history to discover laws may perhaps be due partly to the fact that it operates with its materials nearly as mixed as they come to hand, without consistently selecting them according to one or another aspect or principle. But the notorious weakness of historians in successfully assigning causes—they can ordinarily deal best with minute and immediate ones: why the Bastille fell on July 14 and not 15, as against the causes of the French Revolution—this failure of the historians is compensated for by their ability to express significances. And both the failure and the ability seem to be due to the considerable upper-level, sociocultural component in the materials of intellectual history which attempts more than representational dramatization.

That this is so becomes more evident as soon as consideration is given to bodies of sociocultural and especially cultural materials least contaminated by admixture with individual personalities and particular events. In the study of English as a language it does not matter whether "Give me Liberty" was uttered by Patrick Henry or by any other Anglo-Saxon speaker; whether in the eighteenth, nineteenth, or twentieth century; or whether the occasion was historically momentous or not. (Note the term "historically momentous": that is, historically effective or significant—significant to a larger pattern of events, to a context of currents of events and of institutional forms.) To the linguist all this is irrelevant. What he sees in the phrase "Give me Liberty" is data bearing on the form, structure, and relations of certain sounds and meanings. And these sounds and meanings, as well as their form and structure, are constant and repetitive, thoroughly social, and yet anonymous—are therefore anonymous, we might say. The phrase is always uttered by an individual; but by which individual and from what motivation and with what consequences in which circumstances are irrelevant to the linguist.

We have here a clear-cut instance of the selective extrication of upper-level phenomena—in this case linguistic phenomena—from the welter of events in which they occur, and of their intellectual treatment purely as phenomena of that level. What eventuates in such a case is, in popular phraseology, an English grammar. Such a grammar is an organized analysis and resynthesized description of the phenomenal appearance, the structure, and the internal relations and functioning of a language. Such a synthesized description makes sense precisely because it is self-contained and self-sufficient. It deals with superindividual forms and relations; and therefore, while it does not deny the necessary participation of individuals in the phenomena, linguistic science normally and basically suppresses the individual, "holds him constant," "abstracts from him." Why this is so needs no elaborate proof.

It is clear that to operate successfully as a linguist one does not have either to personify or reify languages or to endow them with a substance of their own. One analyzes and synthesizes, so long as results are forthcoming, *as if* one's data constituted a self-contained system. That ultimately they are not wholly self-contained is obvious. But it is a truism that the scientist's concern as scientist is not with ultimates—certainly not to begin with.

It is also clear that linguistic science is consistently backward and weak in ascertaining causality but that its particular selective concentration is what enables it to determine significant relations of form and structure—patterns and their interrelations. The causes of linguistic phenomena such as changes of form or meaning of words—the causes of these in the ordinary sense of "efficient" causes—evidently lie below the linguistic-cultural level itself and presumably are numerous, obscure, conflicting, and determined by still more remote causes. But it will be noted that the linguistic phenomena which result from these sublinguistic causes come highly regularized, formalized, patterned, and definitely interrelated, as soon as we look for the forms contained in them. The phenomena even contain a great deal of predictability, which we are ordinarily neglectful of because it is so commonplace in experience. For instance, the next Anglo-Saxon uttering Henry's sentiment would also say "Give me Liberty" and not "Gave mine liberting." In short, intellectual order and intellectual significance are most readily and successfully attained on the linguistic level by directing attention to form-patterns and form-relations and not toward causal relations.

Finally, as regards approach being "historic" in the larger sense in which the word has been used here, the linguist can operate synchronically and descriptively, or again he can operate diachronically and historically in the narrower, conventional sense. This, however, is a detail and an incident. In both cases the linguist deals with forms and form-relations which have significance to him; and he deals with them to an equal degree in the two cases. In both instances his material remains essentially superindividual, anonymous, patterned, predictive as to its repetitiveness, and almost unconcerned with cause. What this likeness of method of synchronic descriptive linguistics and of diachronic linguistics imports is this: The differentiation into synchronic and diachronic treatment being secondary, the approach which I call the "historic" one, in contrast with the nomothetic approach, is thereby shown to be characterized primarily not by accentuation of the time element and succession in time, as is still so often supposed, but is characterized rather by its other properties that have been enumerated. It is these other properties—superindividuality, patterning, relative nonconcern with cause —that are fundamental to the generic historic approach.

Language has been chosen here as illustration because it is somewhat narrower, somewhat more set off and self-contained, than the rest of culture and therefore somewhat more clear cut. But the difference is only of degree. To understand cultural manifestations, we must also seek for idiosyncratic and physiognomic forms and seek for their significances first within a coherent, largely self-sufficient system of forms such as a particular civilization; and beyond that in a great context of total forms achieved in human history. We must also expect to discover in our material little of causality in the sense of the physicist's causality. We must be ready, where we get further by it, to ignore and suppress the individual, who from the angle of the understanding of culture is perhaps more often irrelevant and distracting than helpful. The ordering or relating which yields understanding in the study of culture is basically best defined, perhaps, as a process of perceiving significant interrelations of forms as forms.

It is evident that the ultimate relating of cultural forms to their largest possible context, in order to bring out their fullest significance, carries in it an element of weighting of the large relation, of the long-range view. And this, in turn, is akin to diachronic interest, to unwillingness to remain restricted to the moment. The moment is sufficient in interest when it is typical of repetitive totality, when it contains totality, as it were, as it does in physics. When the

moment or spot is not containing or representative of a larger whole, as when it is uniquely idiosyncratic, then intellectual interest pushes on from it to the whole. Therewith the view tends to become diachronic, and the approach is characterizable as historic in nature, whether or not it succeeds in becoming actually chronological.

In the entire realm of style the superpersonal flow of form is obviously strong. The word itself—*stylus*, the "pencil"—originally had anthropomorphic reference to the particular quality or manner of writing of an individual. The word "style" tends nowadays to be used for a group similarity, for what is the manner common to a school or series of writers or artists, for a superindividual quality. We can still speak of Shakespeare's "style": we more often speak of "Elizabethan style." And we successfully trace and analyze styles which we cannot, for lack of knowledge, segregate into the contributions of individuals. This holds, for instance, of much of Greek vase painting and of much of Romanesque and Gothic architecture, not to mention the beginnings of most arts and all primitive ones.

Allied to styles are the courses of dress fashion or mode—that which to the unsophisticated the word "style" is in fact most likely to denote. Names of individuals—Prince Albert, Empress Eugénie—are now and then applied to such fashions, but secondarily and arbitrarily, as picturesque handles. Actually, dress fashions arise obscurely, are due to undetermined causes, and are almost wholly shaped and executed, as well as accepted and used anonymously, by the great nameless throng—superindividually, in short.

Even in the fine arts it is only when these become a self-conscious cult that real interest in the individual artist arises and that he is sought after and his work prized as peculiarly his, as Chambers has set forth in *Cycles of Taste*. In most of human history, and to most men, it is objects and styles that are meaningful; the artist is only a personal exemplification and a passing incident.

It is much the same with inventions. Today we think in terms of inventors. But the discoveries and inventions of other lands, of the past, of our own Middle Ages, are anonymous. Metalworking, blacksmithing; plows, screws, shears; stirrups, horseshoes, harness, wheels, axles; clocks, levels, lamps, candles; glass and pots; fertilizing, irrigating, castrating, riding—the whole basis of mechanical civilization has no personally known authors. They were never recorded or have been long forgotten, because they did not matter.

When finally this condition changes and legend or history gives us, first, imagined inventors and then documentarily authenticated ones, a strange persistence of the ancient condition nevertheless continues. The inventors now come in contemporary pairs or triplets or teams of competitors. Wallace synchronizes with Darwin, Leverrier with Adams, DeVries with Correns and Tschermak; Langley's flight with Wright's; Bell anticipated Gray by a day; Fulton contests with Symington, Fitch, Rumsey, and Stevens. That the making of inventions is normally multiple and simultaneous is by now a fairly well-established fact. From the angle of the individual, the inventors operate independently. From that of the culture, it is the trend, the antecedents, the moment, that unite to force the invention; within its setting it has become, as it were, inevitable; which person is the vehicle of discovery matters little to the society and to the growth of the culture.

Another long-noted phenomenon points the same way, if one will see it so. This is the clustering of great men in certain epochs of certain civilizations and their rarity elsewhere. Nothing now known in biological heredity, nothing in

the laws of chance, can account for these tremendous variations in the frequency and intensity of genius. The only explanation yet advanced which is not wholly speculative or arbitrary sees a correlation between realized genius and opportunity given by stage of a civilization's development—the stage where its productive cultural patterns are defined and mature but where their inherent potentialities have not yet begun to be exhausted. By this view, it is the phase of developing culture patterns that is primarily determinative of greatness and fineness of human achievement; geniuses are the index of such development of pattern. What we are wont to call "great men" are those among many more individuals of above-average ability who happen to get born in a time and place and society the patterns of whose culture have formed with sufficient potential value and have developed to sufficient ripeness to allow the full capacities of these individuals to be realized and expressed. This is not really a revolutionary view. It should not even be disturbing to anyone who has apprehended the strength and fulness with which culture holds us all. It ought certainly not upset him who has read and absorbed Sumner's *Folkways* of more than forty years ago and has made the inevitable short extrapolation from the folk to the sophisticates and has realized that we are all in the grip of our ways and our mores—in the grip of our culture.

I have just spoken of greatness and fineness, of potential and realized achievements. Therewith we are plumb in the field of that which the scientist has long said is not for him to touch: values—human values which are cultural values, whether moral, aesthetic, sensory, intellectual, or what not.

One must grant that human cultural values have nothing to do with physics, have no place in it or in any science that models itself on the plan and rules of physics. But how is it possible, without the most sterile stultification, to make intellectual study of social man who is cultural man, and yet permanently to leave out of consideration his product, culture, and that essence of culture, its forms and its values?

This is not to affirm that all study which has man for its subject need take cognizance of values. It is possible to investigate responses or learning or the mechanism of propagandizing or the structure and size of social groupings and never tread on a value. But that it is possible to skirt values and yet not touch them is not per se a moral mandate to do only that. It is evident that we shall have to admit two nonconcurrent plans or ways of investigation into what are called "social phenomena." One approach tries to follow as best it may the methods of the physicist or to find near-surrogates for them, to measure and experiment, and to dispense with consideration of values. The second approach accepts values as inherent in culture and characteristic of it, as thus being part of nature and therefore susceptible of study like any other set of phenomena in nature, and of study by methods analogous to those used in the study of the other parts of nature, though not necessarily identical with those of physics. Values, along with the culture forms to which they attach, can obviously be described; their differential qualities as well as common characteristics can be compared; their developmental phases, sequential relations, and connections can be investigated. This has, in fact, been done in every study of the history of an art, in every attempt to present a religion, in all ethnographic accounts that rise above mechanical itemization, in all writings on culture history that are more than atomistic.

It is true that it is customary to relegate many such studies to what are named the "humanities" and therewith to read them out of the so-called "social sciences." But what of that—provided that the phenomena considered and the forces in them are regarded as natural, as part of the rest of nature and in no sense supernatural? And provided also that they are subjected to dissection, re-combination, and inference according to the basic rules of evidence followed in the investigation of other parts or realms of nature, without admittance of bias, personal advantage, self-superiority or ethnocentricity.

In the past the trouble has been that values were claimed and regarded as direct products of deity, which stood outside nature and above it, or as emanating from the soul, whose spirituality, first protected by separation from the body, was further preserved by exclusion from the domain of nature and nature's matter and energy. But surely those days are over. It is difficult to imagine a ground on which contemporary natural scientists would deny validity to any endeavor to understand any set of manifestations occuring in nature, provided that the endeavor is free of reservations, overt or concealed, as to exclusions from nature.

Cultural values, along with cultural forms and cultural content, surely exist only through men and reside in men. As the products of human bodies and minds and their functionings and as a specialized extension of them, cultural values thus form a wholly "natural" part of nature. Here the concept of the hierarchy of levels helps. Not only are the levels separated into steps; their superposition one on the other also ties them together, though not into an undifferentiated unity.

Values, like all sociocultural manifestations, are largely superpersonal. That is, far more of any individual's values are instilled into him from outside, directly or indirectly from his society, than he produces within and by himself. Hence values participate in what used to be called the "collective" or "mass" origin—what I prefer to call the "essential anonymity" of origin—of phenomena like customs, morals, ideologies, fashions, and speech. Sumner's "folkways" excellently conveys this same quality except for its false implication that there also exists a social intelligentsia exempt from being folk. It is possible to exalt collectivity into something self-containedly mystical, as shown by the example of Jung and perhaps of Durkheim. But it is not necessary to be mystical in dealing with collectivity, and we shall therefore assume that we are concerned with the collective only as something completely in relation with the remainder of nature.

Now the collective or anonymous, being everybody's, is also nobody's: there is a quality of the impersonal about it. The things that are everyone's enter individuality more diffusely than those which a person has sweated out for or by himself. These latter he is likely to prize, almost certain to be well aware of, and to have a conscious history and highlighted reasons for, whether these reasons be true or false. But what he shares with the collectivity is more massive and extensive, often more firmly rooted, and also more obscure; it tends to be less in the focus of consciousness. Hence what has been called the "covertness" of many patterns of culture; they have been set aside from the overt patterns as "configurations" by Kluckhohn. "Covertness" here does not imply intent of concealment, as it does so often in interpersonal motivations, rather only lack of awareness. It is probably a case of cultural forms being relatively more and less in focus of awareness along a sliding scale partly of occasion and partly of generic situation. Thus rules of conduct, which serve as protections to personality, are likely to be formulated with awareness and explicitness, though also subject to attempted warpings by self-interest. At the other end

of the scale, rules of grammar in speech, which normally serves to connect personalities when they feel relaxed and in least need of protection, are unformulated, except as a result of the highly sophisticated curiosity of linguists, and can properly be described as having grown up both anonymously and unconsciously. Breaches of grammatical rule, though instantly observed, are ordinarily not resented, because they invade nothing particular to the individual, but are accepted with tolerance, amusement, or contempt.

Allied to this unawareness or unconsciousness of cultural form and organization is the irrationality of much of the collective in culture. "Irrationality" is what it is sometimes called. I have used the term myself. It covers a variety of happenings in culture which have in common a factor of inconsistency. The totality of a situation or way of doing comes out less regular and less coherent than it might have been under rational planning. Daylight saving; the letter *Double-U* after *U* and *V*; mannered mediaeval instead of classic Roman script; ideographs when an alphabet is available; the spellings "ought" and "eight"; the plural "oxen" instead of "oxes," will serve as examples. The point, of course, is that such irregularities and inefficiencies *were* not thought out but are the result of long and complex histories, with quite different factors often impinging successively. Established individual habits, prestige values, change in one part of a system with lag in another, actual economic cost, mere inertia or nostalgia—all sorts of reasons, mostly rational enough in the concrete situation, have been at work; and the resulting system shows the effect of compromises and patches. Any fool could devise a more consistent system than exists, but even a despot rarely can institute one. In one sense the outcome is "irrational" indeed, in that the institution lacks the full reasonableness which its defenders claim for it. Actually, it rather is nonrational, and only partly that. Most strictly, it is that the institutional pattern is irregular, not wholly consistent.

These considerations rather foreshadow what might be said of the integratedness of the cultures of particular societies. Cultures tend toward integration and, in the main, largely achieve some degree of it, though never total integration. This latter is an ideal condition invented by a few anthropologists not well versed in history. It is hard to imagine any historian—other than a propagandist—bringing himself to advance such a claim as the complete integration of any culture, in the face of his professional experience.

That values constitute an essential element of cultures leads to another consideration. A first account of a new culture, having necessarily to seize and portray the values which help to give it organization and orientation, is likely to emerge as a somewhat idealized account, since the values of the culture are reflected in the society's ideals. Of course, no society is ideal in its behavior. The society aims to conform to the value standards; but we are all more or less lazy, mean, self-centered, cowardly, spiteful, motivated by personal interest. There is thus an unavoidable gap between the ideal or "pure" picture of the culture and the actuality of how this ideal is lived out by the average adherent of the culture. The psychologically minded analyst of behavior, the student of personality and culture, for whom culture is less an end than a take-off of interest, will accentuate the actuality; and between personality stresses and strains, traumas and frustrations, the ideal values of conduct which the "culturologist" has built up into such gleaming, streamlined patterns will emerge tarnished and battered or even cracked. This is a difference to be aware of without worrying too much over it. He

who is really interested in the phenomena of culture knows that their ideal values always suffer in actual human living of them. But, at the same time, he knows that in apprehending cultures the most essential thing to apprehend is their values, because without these he will not know either toward what the cultures are slanted or around what they are organized.

Incidentally, it seems to be with reference to this value-ideal content that the full study of culture has sometimes been called "normative" and "humanistic." Not that we should study cultures merely in order to learn proper conduct in life but that, without cognizance of their norms, we are studying only their shells.

Its extraordinary variability or plasticity is one of the most marked properties of culture. Living organisms are also adaptable and modifiable but do repeat their basic plan of structure closely in successive generations of individuals. There is almost nothing in culture to correspond to this organic repetitiveness. Allegations of regular recurrences in culture refer to shadowy, large resemblances which are only dubiously substantiable because they are not precisely definable. Itemized bits of culture content may persist with tenacity for long periods. Functioning organizations of cultural material apparently always change, even if they persist, until it is often difficult to say whether we are still within the original complex, form, or pattern or have slid into a new one. This inherent plasticity is evident as soon as one is in position to follow any one institution in detail through the centuries; or, equally, to follow an institution or custom through its provincial or regional variants, or through its appearances among a series of nonliterate tribes that are geographically contiguous.

The reason for this strong propensity of culture to vary seems to lie in the following fact: All cultural phenomena are invariably related to certain other cultural phenomena to which they are similar and which precede or succeed them or occur near them contemporaneously; and their fullest understanding can be attained only through cognizance of these relations. While these relations are indisputable, they are relations of form, value, and significance. They are not, directly, relations of cause in the ordinary sense of efficient cause. The efficient causes of cultural phenomena are the actions or behavior of men—of psychosomatic individual human beings. A denial of this proposition seems to leave no alternative but admission of a set of insulated, self-contained cultural forces operating in and on a self-sufficient cultural substance. This would be a large assumption and would immediately incur the charge, from scientists, of being a mystical tenet aiming to exclude a particular domain of phenomena from the sway of the remainder of the cosmos as studied by total science.

Now, as soon as the efficient causality of culture is admitted to lie essentially on the psychobiological level, it is evident that cultural phenomena are, in the strict sense, only by-products of organic activities, epiphenomena of primary organic phenomena. This conclusion, in turn, would seem to explain the irregularity, unpredictability, variability, and "plasticity" of cultural phenomena. They may once be the large cultural products of inconsequential subcultural forces or, again, the relatively insignificant side-effects of organic causes whose primary expression is in organic consequences. It cannot be doubted that single individuals occasionally affect the stream of culture perceptibly: Napoleon with his Code, Caesar on the Calendar, Shi Hwang-ti with the Burning of the Books, Copernicus with his revolution—not to mention religious leaders. Even suborganic influ-

ence on culture must be admitted: catastrophes that wipe out one society, obliterating its culture, but spare another, leaving its culture intact; changes in climate favorable to prosperity and increase of particular populations, with consequent dominance of their cultures over those of disadvantaged peoples. It is evident that the greater the number and variety of these subcultural causes, the greater the variability or "plasticity" of cultural phenomena is likely to be.

Of course, the total outcome is not utter cultural randomness but only a high degree of what may properly be called plasticity; and this for the following reason.

Predominantly it will be the psychosomatic actions of human beings that contain the immediate causality of cultural phenomena. But human beings, with their extraordinarily high symbolizing faculties, which means cultural faculties, are always culturalized. That is, they are culturally determined—and heavily determined—by the time they reach the age at which they become potential causes of culture. What is therefore operative is a powerful system of circular causality. The human beings who influence culture and make new culture are themselves molded; and they are molded through the intervention of other men who are culturalized and thus products of previous culture. So it is clear that, while human beings are always the *immediate* causes of cultural events, these human causes are themselves the result of antecedent culture situations, having been fitted to the existing cultural forms which they encounter. There is thus a continuity of indirect causation from culture event to culture event through the medium of human intermediaries. These intermediaries are concerned, first of all, with relieving their own tensions and achieving their personal gratification; but in so doing they also transmit, and to some degree modify, the culture which they carry because they have been conditioned to it. In a sense, accordingly, a kind of cultural causality is also operative. However, compared with the immediate efficient causality of men on culture, the causation of culture on culture is indirect, remote, and largely a functional relation of form to form. At any rate, as long as one's interest is in what happens in culture, it is the cultural antecedents that become significant. The human transmitters and carriers and modifiers are likely to average pretty much alike. As causes they tend to average uniform and constant, except so far as cultural exposure has differentiated them.

The inquirer, if his interest is really in culture, tends therefore to omit the human agents. He operates *as if* individual personalities did not have a hand in cultural events. In the main he is justified in this procedure. He is certainly justified in proportion as his view is long-range. On telescopic inspection of the greater cultural currents, even the greatest and most influential personalities shrink to minuteness.

As the range contracts and the segment of culture examined begins to be minute, the role of individuals, under the microscopic dissection being carried on, looms correspondingly larger. Here is an equally legitimate method of study; but, of course, it yields results of a quite different order. It gives insight into the interaction of persons and culture: on how individuals get caught in the net of their culture; of how some kinds of them stretch the net or tear rents in it; how others, meanwhile, are weaving new ranges of mesh. The value of such studies is as examples of the close-up mechanism of the change which culture is always tending to undergo. An additional value is in the illumination thrown on the reactions of human beings, viewed as integral personalities, to their enveloping culture. These are certainly important fields of knowledge. But they are obviously different from straight culture history or from the analytic comparison of cultural forms and values as such.

What "culture and personality" as a field of study seems to be, in its purest form, is what has just been described as the interaction of persons and their enveloping culture. Really to pursue this study, it is obviously first necessary to understand pretty well what the culture is and what the persons are like. It would be vain to hope that worth-while results will eventuate from operating with an indeterminately variable X matched against an indeterminately variable Y. Kluckhohn, prominently identified with the "culture-and-personality" movement, has recently proposed shifting its focus from the mutual interaction of the two factors, as just described, to a focus within personality, as this is affected by hereditary constitution, by social environment, by society, and by culture. This would make personality the real subject of investigation, and culture only one of several factors impinging on it. This is less, and rather more one-sided, than a true culture-and-personality field as it has just been envisaged. But such an evenly balanced field is an especially difficult one to investigate until both the contributing fields or levels, whose relation is being investigated, are fairly thoroughly understood. And that can as yet hardly be affirmed of either culture or personality. The danger is therefore of a Scylla of inconclusiveness faced by a Charybdis of forced verbalistic conclusions. Nevertheless, whichever approach is used, the entire legitimacy of the translevel subject of culture-personality interaction is unquestionable.

Of course, some personality study and attempted culture-and-personality study is motivated primarily by a lack of interest in culture or understanding of it—in short, by a desire to escape from dealing with it. There is no valid quarrel with this attitude, only with the non-avowal of its motivation.

Allied are productions like Chapple and Coon's *Principles of Anthropology*, from which even the word "culture" has been expunged except for a few oversights. This is a seemingly conscious attempt, at any rate a *de facto* one, to explain culture away into phenomena and factors of lower level. In short, the purpose is outright reductionist.

The problem remains unresolved of how far general forms, therefore recurrent forms, can be demonstrated in culture. The difficulty has been that the recurrent forms are lax and ill defined. With strict analysis, the stable content of concepts like feudalism, clan, mana, soul, and taboo shrinks increasingly. This seems to be because the actual cultural content of such general concepts has been acquired by them during their historical development, which is always complex and always tending toward the unique, as historians have long ago learned to take for granted. The general or recurrent remnant in these seemingly recurrent phenomena is usually not cultural but of lower level, especially psychological. What is common to clans is that they function as associations of people felt to be kindred, toward whom one has or develops kinsman attitudes. This is essentially a finding in social psychology. More specific recurrences show this even more clearly. The tendency of writing systems to devise or revert to symbols for syllables is quite evidently the result of a psychosomatic inclination to syllabify when speech is being rendered very distinctly or analytically. Psychologists are generally not concerned with any finding so concrete and specific as this one, so they have not announced it. But, so far as it is a little "law," it is a psychosomatic one explanative of cultural phenomena.

Another feature of these partial recurrences or resemblances is that they cut across resemblances due to historical connection and are therefore left without benefit of explanation of similarity as due to community of origin. If, then, the recurrence is due to some deeper-seated, generic factor, the question arises why the results of this are not universal, as they almost always fail to be. The situation is like one familiar in botany. Trees have quite evidently been independently developed in a whole series of families, even orders, of plants. Likewise vines; likewise herbs; and so on. The botanist does not therefore put all trees into one order, all vines into another. Neither does he discard the common-knowledge concepts or categories of tree, vine, bush, herb, altogether; he uses them as a more or less useful adjunct or supplement in description. It would seem that this would turn out to be about the proper function of the corresponding categories of recurrences in culture, such as feudalism, caste, shaman, taboo, totem.

There is also no agreement as yet as to the most general forms among which the totality of culture could be distributed, so far as recurrences or regularities do hold water. The earliest such attempts took the shape of stages and suffered from intellectual naïveté. There was the hunting-herding-farming stage sequence; the mythologic-religious-positive one; even the chipped stone–polished stone-bronze-iron classification.

Of more promise is the concept of recurrent functional nexuses of internal relations: say, of feudalism, piety, and mediaevalistic economy. This Weberian approach is still rather inadequately explored.

Finally, there is the question of how far the maximum nexuses or totalities which we call "civilizations" show recurrences in their developmental phases --in other words, show a recurrent pattern of growth. If they do, empirically, show such a recurrent pattern, civilizations would provide an actual and natural segmentation which would help us to organize intellectually the otherwise variably tossing and endlessly stretching sea of the variable continuum of culture as a whole. There is a growing recognition of the probable reality of such segmentation, as well as of its specific limits and inclusions—in other words, of what each civilization takes in.

As to what is at work in the formation of these great units, however, there is wide divergence. Spengler sees immanent predestination, Toynbee moral free will, Sorokin a pendulum beat between sensate and ideational proclivities. This area of inquiry will unquestionably undergo considerable further cultivation, if for no other reason than that our thinking of history has until recently been too ethnocentrically weighted, too "auto-culturo-centric," for the large problems in this area to be effectively conceived or framed.

The question remains whether the concept of culture will serve as a mechanism for integrating more closely the several social sciences. The answer is both Yes and No. There is no doubt that cultural aspects can be recognized and followed through all human areas commonly recognized as social. Economics and government *are* only segments of culture. The data of formal sociology are so intertwined with cultural ones that subjects like family, kinship, associations, the state, are claimed and treated equally by sociologists and by cultural anthropologists. Formal history, even at its most biographical, cannot wholly avoid institutional implications; and, at the opposite end of its range, history is institutional, and thus *de facto* cultural. Psychology can pretty much eliminate cultural factors by narrowing its analysis and by holding the cultural factors constant in selective experiment. Yet, as soon as it rewidens its activity to take in total personalities, a flood of cultural considerations inevitably pours in on it.

However, what all this means is that, if one is interested in cultural manifestations, one can recognize them and deal with them selectively in every scientific study that has man for its subject. And such a selective pursuit will yield certain understandings unattainable by any other and less differentiated method. But it *is* selective; that is a fact that must not be forgotten. There are other bases of selection, and each has its own kind of fruitfulness. Economic theory, though validated by empirical techniques rather than derived from them, seems reasonably to satisfy economists and is not likely to be given up by them for any more generalized theory of culture. Historians presumably will continue to prefer their accustomed mixed diet of events, persons, and institutional forms, with its maximum of adherence to raw phenomena, opportunities for stirring dramatic representation in narrative, and minimum necessity of generalization—and then generalization merely as incidental commentary. We have already considered the translevel or interlevel studies of fields like personality in culture, which, though still groping and unsure of method and occasionally confusing hope with fulfilment, are certainly legitimate and to be counted on to grow.

In summary, it is evident that the cultural approach, now that it is well isolated and developed, will continue to be used because it yields distinctive results. Yet it is equally clear that the cultural approach is not exclusively valid within the area of superorganic phenomena; nor, of course, is it a panacea. It is a selective approach, fruitful because of its selectiveness, but, for the same reason, not unlimited in its scope.

15. VALUES AS A SUBJECT OF NATURAL SCIENCE INQUIRY
1949

These are few pages in which to develop a subject as large as this, but National Academy papers are limited to fifteen minutes.

This statement has finally broken with Rickert. Culture, including its values, is explicitly viewed as part of nature; and values do not reside exclusively in culture.

My first attack on what to do with values was made in No. 4 in 1918, and they are discussed again in Nos. 11, 12, and 14.

THIS essay maintains the proposition that the study of values is a proper and necessary part of the study of culture, viewed as an existing part of nature. This is said not merely as proposal or program, but as a descriptive fact holding for much of actually existing practice in anthropology and the study of culture.

Whenever a cultural fact has significance or historical reference, it also contains a value. Significance must be distinguished from cause—from that which made a cultural phenomenon happen or come to be. Significance must also be distinguished from the end or purpose served; and from organic needs, which in their turn can be resolved either into causes or into ends of culture phenomena.

That needs—also called drives, press, imperatives, and such—exist, and that they underlie and precondition culture, is indubitable. It is also obvious that culture canot be explained or derived from needs except very partially. Hunger has to be satisfied; but *how* it is satisfied by human beings can never be derived from their being hungry, nor from their specific bodily construction. Overwhelmingly the *how* can be understood only with reference to the remainder of the culture adhered to, present and past; modified somewhat—or preconditioned —by interaction with the opportunities afforded by natural environment. Moreover, large segments of culture begin to operate, to come into being, only after the primal needs have been satisfied, have had their tensions reduced or alleviated. Such are art, religion, science. Hence these segments cannot be explained at all from physiological needs.

The essential characteristic things about a culture are its forms and patterns, the interrelations of these into an organization, and the way these parts, and the whole, work or function as a group of human beings lives under them. A culture is a way of habitual acting, feeling, and thinking channeled by a society out of an infinite number and variety of potential ways of living. The particular channeling adopted is heavily preconditioned by antecedent ways and organizations or systems of culture; though it is not predetermined thereby except within certain limits. Every such system of channeling is accompanied by or contains a system of affects, which vary from place to place of their appearance, and from time to time, but some of which are usually powerful and persistent. Interconnected with these affects is a system of ideas and ideals, explicit and implicit. The combined affect-idea system of a culture at once reflects the habitual ways of action of members of the society, validates these ways to themselves, and to an extent controls and modifies the ways. It is in this affect-laden idea system that, in a certain sense, the core of a culture is usually considered to reside: in it lodge its values, norms, and standards—its ethos and its eidos.

When we speak of the significance of a cultural trait or item or complex of traits, what is meant is the degree to which the trait is meshed, affectively as well as structurally and functionally, into the remainder of the total system or organization that constitutes the culture. Low degree of integration normally indicates that the trait has relatively low significance for the culture as a functional unit—though it may still have considerable significance as an index of historical relationship with other cultures.

It follows that if we refuse to deal with values, we are refusing to deal with what has most meaning in particular cultures as well as in human culture seen as a whole.

What we have left on elimination of values is an arid roster of cultural traits or cultural events which we are constantly tempted to animate by reintroducing the values we have banned, or else by backhandedly introducing values from our own culture. Or it is possible to attempt to explain the value-rid phenomena of the culture and their changes in terms of some causality—or possibly by a teleology.

As a matter of fact, it is and long has been prevailing practice in the description of cultures by anthropologists, or of civilizational phases by historians, to formulate the values of these cultures. Thereby the description becomes a physiognomic characterization of the culture. Such a characterization has internal import as regards both its own coherence and consistency, and its external import through implicit or explicit comparison with other characterized cultures. This type of presentation, with clear-cut value designations, comprises all the most successful characterizations or resynthesized analyses of cultures, both by anthropologists such as Malinowski, Firth, Evans-Pritchard, and by nonprofessionals like Codrington on the Melanesians, Doughty in Arabia Deserta, Fustel de Coulanges's Ancient City, Albiruni on India a thousand years ago, and as far back as the Germania of Tacitus.

Reference in this matter is to values as they exist in human societies at given times and places; to values as they make their appearance in the history of our species; in short, to values as natural phenomena occurring in nature—much like the characteristic forms, qualities, and abilities of animals as defined in comparative zoölogy. There is no reference to any absolute standard or scale of values, nor to judgments of values as better or worse—which would imply such a standard.

An absolute standard involves two qualities. First, it must be extra-natural, or supernatural, to be an a priori absolute. And second, ethnocentricity is implied in the elevation of any one actual standard as absolute. By contrary, standards or value-systems conceived as parts of nature are necessarily temporal and spatial, phenomenal, relative, and comparative. That the first condition to the scientific study of culture is the barring of ethnocentrism has been a basic canon of anthropology for three-quarters of a century.

The forms of any culture must be described—can be appraised, one might say—only in terms of their relation to the total pattern-system of that culture. The pattern-system in its turn needs portrayal in terms of its total functioning and products. And so far as the pattern-system is appraisable, it is in terms of comparison with the functions and results achieved by other total cultures with their respective master-patterns. This is like the comparison of the total functioning and capacities of, say, an earthworm with the functioning and capacities of other organisms.

In a sense, recognition of the functioning and capacities of an organic species is a sort of formulation of the values genetically inherent in that species. At any rate, it *can* be that, even if biologists usually are not aware of the fact and might resent the imputation of any concern with values. Further, the comparison of such values, in order to ascertain their common elements, their particularities, their apparent total range of variability, their effectivenesses and long-range permanences—such a comparison of biological values would still be within the scope of examination of natural phenomena by natural science methods.

It is as something analogous to this kind of biology or potential biology that the study of cultural forms, structures, and values must be conceived. Or rather, we should say that such study has actualy been made, time and again, often without explicit awareness of values being involved, and perhaps as often without awareness that the study had natural scientific significance.

It is true that values can also be viewed extra-scientifically or supernaturally. Mostly they have been so construed, with ascription to deity, soul, spirituality, or a self-sufficient system of eternal, unmodifiable values lying outside the domain of science over nature. But the present paper has no concern with such a view. Contrarily, it claims values, along with all other manifestations of culture, as being part of nature and therefore in the field of science.

A few specifications seem desirable.

There is always a gap between values and behavior, between ideals and performance. Even though values always influence the behavior of cultural organisms, that is, of men, they never control it exclusively. Hence the student of culture needs to distinguish, but also to compare, ideal values and achieved behavior, as complementary to each other. The one alone falls short in substantiality, the other in significant motivation and organization of the data.

Next, values being sociocultural, they inevitably also posess psychological aspects. But as a specific quality of culture —as, indeed, a product of culture—their reduction to explanations in psychological terms, and of these to physiological and biochemical explanations, necessarily loses or destroys the essential specific properties of the values. These are retainable in full only as long as the phenomena of value continue to be inspected on the cultural level.

Finally, since cultural phenomena are determined in several ways—inorganically by environment, organically, psychologically, and socially, as well as by existent culture—it is evident that the causality of cultural phenomena is likely to be unusually complex. Moreover, they lend themselves with very great difficulty to the isolation and simplification of experiment. Within culture itself, these considerations seem to apply with even more strength to values than to, say, artifact production or subsistence economy. Other things being equal, a descriptive or historical approach would accordingly seem more readily fruitful, in scientific inquiry into values, than any searching for causes —even immediate causes. This statement is not to be construed as a methodological ban against the study of causality in values, but as an intimation that the causal approach is inherently difficult and that valid, nonspeculative results bid fair to be thin and slow. While a formal approach is thus indicated as more fruitful, this need by no means be limited to enumerative description, nor to enumeration of sequences. Beyond these, the comparison of organization, functioning, and interrelations of cultural values, and value-systems invite methodical scientific research.

16. A HALF-CENTURY OF ANTHROPOLOGY
1950

This appraisal is one of ten made for their several sciences by as many authors and published in "Scientific American," September, 1950. It was there headed simply "Anthropology" and is reissued here by permission.

THE most significant accomplishment of anthropology in the first half of the twentieth century has been the extension and clarification of the concept of culture. The idea that culture—a society's customs, traditions, tools, and ways of thinking—plays the dominant part in shaping the development of human beings, and therefore ought to be the central concern of anthropology, did not originate in our century; its importance had been recognized by the great English anthropologist Edward B. Tylor in 1871. But during the last fifty years the concept has been given a wide and consistent application which has immensely advanced the growth of anthropological science.

The outstanding consequence of this conceptual extension has been the toppling of the doctrine of racism—that bland assumption of race superiority which is so satisfying emotionally to most people and so unwarranted. We have learned that social achievements and superiorities rest overwhelmingly on cultural conditioning. Racial heredity has not been totally ruled out as a factor in social accomplishment, but clearly it is a tiny factor in comparison with cultural influences. The racist illusion rests on a naïve failure to distinguish fixed biological processes from essentially variable cultural processes. Once the nature of the cultural process is clearly grasped, the racist illusion is bound to melt away rapidly. Hitlerism represented its last, die-hard, desperate lashing-out as an organized national creed, just as the Dayton trial proved to be the final stand of antibiological literalism in American Protestant theology.

The comparative study of culture has similarly helped to diminish ethnocentrism—the parochial conviction of the superiority of one's own culture—from which so much intolerance springs. The widespread social and emotional drift in this more liberal direction has certainly been given intellectual support by the anthropological analysis and comparison of various cultures. Anthropologists now agree that each culture must be examined in terms of its own structure and values, instead of being rated by the standards of some other civilization exalted as absolute—which in practice of course is always our own civilization. This anthropological principle leads, it is true, to a relativistic or pluralistic philosophy—a belief in many values rather than a single value-system. But why not, if the facts so demand? The domain of life is certainly pluralistic, what with a million species on our own small planet. I have not heard of biologists bewailing the diversity of species. Rather, they try to find some kind of order in it. Quite correspondingly, anthropologists try to treat all cultures, including our own civilization, as parts of nature—without preferential and partisan priorities. This may be distasteful to partisans, but it is certainly the only way of science.

The staunch adherence of modern anthropologists to this principle has brought about a growing conviction that anthropology holds promises of importance for the world's future. Yet anthropology offers no pat answers to our problems: I do not believe it has even one specific categorical remedy to contribute to the world—let alone a panacea. Its contribution is an attitude of mind. This attitude holds that cultures—each of which contains a value-system—need not be viewed as rallying points for rival emotional loyalties but can be studied as natural phenomena by methods of natural science.

The growing recognition of culture as a force has had repercussions in other fields of science, especially in personality psychology and psychiatry. Freud attempted to annex the whole of culture at one blow, contending that it was all derived from the Oedipus complex. Some later psychoanalytic theorists have tried to maintain this claim in a different form; they have proposed less simplistic mechanisms, such as "basic personality structure," as the foundation of culture. But as these mechanisms are admittedly dependent on the culture, the culture cannot really at the same time be derived from the personality. On the whole, in this field of culture-personality relations it is culture that has so far proved to be the active and molding force, and personality the molded element.

Fifty years ago anthropologists still were remarkably ready to look for simple, fundamental causes of behavior and to come up with them—but often each man came up with a different pearl of speculation. The commonest theory then was that primitive culture and high civilizations alike emanated spontaneously from "human nature" or the "unity of the human mind." Sir James Frazer took that point of view in *The Golden Bough*. He influenced more of his contemporaries than any other anthropologist. By the sheer weight of his comparative examples he helped to liberate their minds from ethnocentrism. But he was innocent of what constituted a solu-

ble scientific problem; he simply made whatever assumptions were necessary. By now we have become more humble. Human nature certainly exists, but we recognize it as a heaving jumble of gene effects tremendously elaborated and distorted by cultural pressures. And we no longer venture to define what human nature is, except that we may sometimes indicate certain sketchy limits within which, common-sense experience tells us, this nature generally manifests itself.

Somewhat later came the pseudo-historical explanations. Thus Elliott Smith suggested that everything in higher civilization could be traced to an origin in ancient Egypt, from where it was spread over the world by Phoenician treasure-seekers. No, objected F. Graebner, there were six origins: the boomerang culture, the totemistic, the matrilineal, and so on; spreading from their respective birthplaces in various parts of the world, they eventually were more or less mixed together. We had only to learn how to unscramble the world's cultures to reduce them to the six original blocks.

The answers are more limited and hesitant nowadays, since we realize that answers are the end-product of investigation, not what one starts with and then fights for. In the investigations of the past half-century many things have come out in the wash quite unexpectedly. In 1912 Charles Hose and W. MacDougall published a book on the pagan tribes of Borneo. They had found that the Borneans made blood sacrifices of domesticated animals to their gods, consumed the victims at worshiping festivals, and divined the future by signs in the liver or gall of the sacrificed animals. A reviewer pointed out how much some of the Bornean customs smacked, in a primitive way, of the social and religious practices of the Greeks and Romans. Could there be an actual connection? Or was it a case of the same old X, human nature, spouting forth the same old similarity spontaneously—somewhat as life used to generate spontaneously in the naïve days of biology? We know now that there was indubitably a historical connection between these similar customs, with Mesopotamians and Hindus and Chinese as connecting links between the Indonesians and the Greeks and Romans. Wherever Christianity, Islam, or Buddhism became established, this set of customs was forced out of use as pagan; but at the remote edges in the interior of Borneo and of the Philippines it survived, as in Africa and in spots in India. It never penetrated to Australia nor to America. These conclusions, which would have seemed revolutionary fifty years ago, were arrived at by induction—a piece of inferred, instead of documentary history. But they are supported by consistent, unselected bodies of distributional fact, both positive and negative, and by the parallel of dozens of other disseminations that are documentarily proved—such as, to name just one example, the diffusion of the art of papermaking from China to Europe.

Even greater has been the increase of knowledge due to archaeological exploration and discovery. Before the twentieth century, archaeology, apart from concern with the Stone Age in western Europe, dealt largely with early civilizations rather than with prehistoric times. In Egypt, in Mesopotamia, in China, in the Mexican and Mayan area, archaeologists looked for antiquities that bore inscriptions and dates and thus supplemented and extended the written records that had been transmitted to us in documentary history. No profound skill was involved in dating the inscription of an eighteenth-dynasty Egyptian king as later than that of a fourth-dynasty ruler. But to put the antiquities that *predate* writing into a reliable time sequence, and to bridge their gaps by new explorations—this was an adventure that called for real ingenuity and refine-

ment of techniques. It is during the last forty or fifty years that the overwhelming bulk of knowledge of this sort, for all the world except western Europe, has been accumulated and interpreted. This new knowledge includes a huge amount of material on the prefarming stage and Stone Ages in Egypt and Mesopotamia, in Turkey, Syria, Iran, North Africa, India, China, and other Far Eastern regions. In the Americas the search for remains of the older cultures that predated writing commenced around 1920. The archaeologists' satisfaction in dealing with things that were old began to give way to a new interest in *how* old the remains were—and this of course included the question of which were the more or the less old. In the eastern United States, in the Southwest, in California, in the Caribbean, dependable sequences were worked out and filled in. For Mexico and the Maya, the chronologies suggested by the early investigators are being worked out anew on a sounder basis. For Peru, collaborating investigators determined a succession of culture stages extending back about 2,000 years before the Incas whom Pizarro found in control; then in 1946 this span was perhaps doubled by discovery of remains of a society that was premetallurgical, preceramic, premaize-growing, but already cultivating the soil.

Most of the known biological history of man and his immediate fossil ancestors also has been discovered since 1900. Four principal findings sum up much of this exciting quest. First, we now have solid information on Pithecanthropus and his close twin Sinanthropus. They were low-grade men, but they definitely were men, and they lived at least as early as the middle of the Pleistocene, the last geological period. The second major finding is the South African Australopithecines, including Plesianthropus and Paranthropus, which essentially had the teeth, jaws, hips, and posture of men, along with brains the size of gorillas and big chimpanzees. We do not yet know when they lived. Third, there is the famous Neandertal man, the slightly brutalized sideline outcome of an experiment conducted by nature in what we call the course of human evolution; but we now recognize that he was neither very primitive, very early, nor very brutal. Finally, there is fairly strong evidence, still strengthening, that true human beings—actual members of our living species *Homo sapiens*—were already in existence well back in the Pleistocene, and that long before them their ancestors must have been pretty thoroughly set off from all other forms, living or extinct. That great mysterious X of a generation ago, the famous "missing link," has become quite outmoded. The story leaves him stranded and forgotten, and its path is all the more intricate and dramatic for it.

The study of living human races has unfortunately been unable to profit much from the half-century's greatest biological development: genetics, the quantitative study of heredity. This is so for various reasons: because human chromosomes and probably their genes are numerous, and our heredity is therefore complex; because human lives are long and generations grow up and pass slowly; and because we cannot experiment with large-scale controlled breeding of men as we can with fruit flies or pollinated plants. The relatively few human traits as yet proved to work out according to calculable rules of heredity are either abnormalities or relate chiefly to laboratory-revealed blood factors which are seemingly without influence on man's general functioning or capacity.

At present all except the most obvious groupings in race classification still depend essentially on subjective judgments. For instance, the Hottentots and Bushmen, who undoubtedly have some relationship with Negroes (frizzy hair,

wide noses) and possess some distinctive features peculiar to themselves (hollow backs, fat buttocks, flat ears, wrinkly skin), also tend to have an eye fold like that of the Mongolian race. Is the Mongolian-like eye fold of the Bushmen due to their having at some time in the past experienced contact and admixture with Mongoloids? Or is it just a specialty they happened to develop as an independent genetic variation in their isolation? In short, have we here a case of inherited contamination or of an inherited mutation?

Even authorities can give only personal judgments in situations of this sort. But if we can accumulate race data on enough blood-type and similar genotypic factors—not only the known blood types O-A-B-AB, A_1-A_2, Rh, and M-N but a lot of new factors in addition—it will be possible to determine from the percentages of these inheritances whether the Bushmen ever really experienced a significant Mongoloid admixture. If hereditary links do not appear in these factors, the eye fold will be pretty well demonstrated as an independent local development. Similarly, enough knowledge of demonstrably genotypic factors might reveal whether the Bushmen were a deviant derived from the Negro stock or the remnant of an old, co-ordinate, primary race. These minute, simple-unit traits of heredity are a bit like fingerprints—rather insignificant in man from the standpoint of the total organism's functioning, but sometimes quite telltale as to who contacted whom in the past.

Finally there is the important contribution that the comparative study of languages can make to anthropology. Most linguists are also philologists, and thus accept their customarily assigned place in the humanities. However, the philologists and the anthropological linguists now agree that the structure of every language needs description and understanding, first of all, in terms of its own phenomena and plan—not by any absolute standard. This is of course the anthropologist's basic principle of relativism all over again, merely accentuated a bit more for that part of culture—speech—which is the most outrightly symbolic, the most nearly autonomous, and the most rigorous patterned.

Linguistic anthropologists have differed from other linguists only in the accident that they have dealt mainly with wholly unwritten languages that consequently had no known history or preserved ancient forms. Thus linguistic anthropologists have had to operate comparatively rather than by directly historical methods; they have had to frame their alphabets and grammars while making their investigations, instead of proceeding from given languages. Under the leadership of Franz Boas and Edward Sapir, special techniques for this were developed. When World War II came and it was important to teach exotic foreign languages rapidly, these techniques proved their practical value as an educational device for attaining quick spoken control of Chinese, Japanese, Russian, Arabic and other languages in which a totally foreign and often elaborate script—or a badly formulated conventional grammar—makes acquisition by the old book methods usually a matter of years.

What the past half-century has accomplished above all for anthropology is to transform a loose collocation of separate physical, social, cultural, and linguistic interests, ancient and modern, primitive and civilized, into an integrated attack on the bological, the sociocultural, and the linguistic phenomena presented by man—an attack held together by a common attitude. This attitude is expressed by the principle of the relativistic approach. It might equally be called "the naturalistic" approach. It insists on treating the customs and histories, the ideals and values, the societies and languages of man as being phenomena of nature to exactly the same degree as the biology of men, or for that matter of animals and men.

This may seem a simple and trite program. Perhaps it is simple conceptually, but operationally it has been difficult and hard-won. How far are men and their activities actually treated as a part of nature in most economic and sociological study, in most history and philology? Hardly at all; in these fields human activities are consistently set apart from nature, and primary emphasis is given to what is within one's own culture, rather than to the broad and varying panorama of total human behavior through time and space. That is why in the organization of universities and of the great research councils of national scope these fields of study are assigned to the social sciences or to the humanities. Anthropology, on the other hand, is represented not only in the social sciences and the humanities but also in the natural sciences. This is not so much because in its so-called "physical" branch anthropology includes a concern with human biology. Rather it is because in everything that anthropology touches —cultures, societies, and languages as well as physiques—it aims to proceed wholly with the broad attitudes of natural science, plus such special methods and techniques of its own as may be called for in each situation confronted.

*17. THE HISTORY AND PRESENT ORIENTATION OF CULTURAL ANTHROPOLOGY

1950

This paper was prepared for the meeting of the American Anthropological Association at Berkeley on December 28–30, 1950, to commemorate the formal establishment of anthropology at the University of California during the fiftieth year preceding. Some introductory paragraphs of local reference are omitted here. In contrast with the preceding selection, this review was intended for a specifically anthropological audience rather than for readers of general scientific interest.

THE last fifty years of anthropology find their perspective in the past that preceded them. This past could be stretched legitimately, if one would, to Herodotus. It is, however, possible and profitable to divide the history of anthropology into an unorganized and an organized portion, separated, with more sharpness than might seem expectable, at the year 1860. Before that date there were some keen interests that we would now call genuinely anthropological, but they were random. They came from different stimuli and inspirations, they moved in unrelated directions, they did not cohere. There were some great names— Kant, Herder, Comte, Blumenbach, Humboldt, Gobineau, Prichard; yet their efforts did not add up to a consistent system of thought. Ethnological societies were formed in the forties in Paris, London, New York, but they soon withered away again: only the American Ethnological Society remains alive from those days, and even it barely revived from one long period of inanition such as were wont to befall these early groupings. There were, before 1860, cabinets but no museums; lectures but no chairs or courses; there was no provision for research in the field, and no regular avenue for publication.

Now these aids and equipment did not of course all come into existence at our critical date of 1860. In the main they lagged a generation behind, and even then appeared gradually and modestly. The establishment of anthropology at California in 1901 was preceded by only a few years by the beginnings at Harvard, Clark, Pennsylvania, and Columbia, and in turn antedated the formal recognitions at Chicago and Yale. Before there could hope to be chairs and departments and journals in anthropology, there had to be an organized body of theoretical thought, a systematic ideology characterizing a field of knowledge. It was this that was born about 1860; and the chairs and the rest followed in due course and consequence.

In 1860 appeared Bastian's first book; in 1861 Maine's *Ancient Law* and Bachofen's *Mutterrecht*. The burst in the first dozen years was phenomenal: Jacob Burckhardt, 1860; Fustel de Coulanges's *Ancient City*, 1864; McLennan's *Primitive Marriage*, 1865; Tylor's *Researches*, 1865; Lubbock's *Origin of Civilization*, 1870; Morgan's *Systems of Consanguinity*, 1871; Tylor's *Primitive Culture*, 1871. It is undoubtedly no mere coincidence that these

* Not published previously.

twelve years also spanned Darwin's *Origin of Species*, 1859, and his *Descent of Man*, 1871. In 1923 I contested Marett's characterization of anthropology as "the child of Darwin." The historical anthropology of culture which I knew and aimed at was certainly not derived from Darwin's organic mechanism or dependent on it. But the classic speculative anthropology that flourished during Darwin's lifetime was obviously evoked and enormously stimulated by the overdue evolutionism which Darwin had finally validated.

Here, then, was the intellectual kernel of a new science. How far the views then held were right or wrong is of less concern: most beginnings are bound to be inadequate. What did matter was that there was a direction, an attitude, a notion of method; above all, a set of problems.

It is also well to remember that this happened not so very long ago. It is fifty years back to the occasion we are commemorating; only forty beyond that to 1860. Thus the half-century of progress which I am to review takes in more than half the history of organized anthropology.

These early works of the classical school were pseudo-historical, evolutionistic, comparative; they were documented, but by heavily selected evidence. They tended to give total answers. They were confident in assigning causality; but they sought immediate causes less than ultimate origins—a sure index of the naïveté that accompanied their intellectual vigor. Yet, above all, the classical evolutionistic books had asked important and definite questions, even if they had not asked them in quite the present-day way. Their famous "comparative method" failed, we can see today, because it violated context. It compared loosely when it should have compared closely and systematically. But it had the supreme merit of not being ethnocentric, the

merit of aiming at something outside, and therefore of containing, at least implicitly, the idea of culture and the relativistic approach to it. In fact, Tylor, the wisest and best balanced of the group, established as early as 1871 not only the name and definition of culture but the characteristic anthropological attitude toward it.

Of course the movement was not limited to one decade. McLennan's *Ancient History* followed in 1876, Morgan's *Ancient Society* in 1877, Howitt's *Kamilaroi* in 1880, Tylor's *Anthropology* in 1881. In 1884 Andrew Lang began to publish anthropologically; in 1887 Frazer, whose first *Golden Bough* version appeared in 1890, though the expanded versions were not completed until 1915. Westermarck began in 1901, Hobhouse in 1906; Hartland's *Primitive Paternity* was as of 1909, his *Primitive Law* as of 1924. It is observable that, with time, the participation in classic evolutionism became overwhelmingly British, ending as it were in almost an old-school-tie mannerism. There is also a falling-off in hardness of intellectual core: as compared with Tylor, Frazer—twenty-two years his junior—represents a definite methodological recession. Perhaps that is why Frazer has been the more popular and the more influential outside anthropology, among psychoanalysts, laymen, and littérateurs.

In France, in Germany, in the United States, other currents began to be manifest by about 1890. These new movements of anthropological thought are exemplified by two men born in the same year—1858—which was also the birth-year of Freud. They are Durkheim, in France, and Boas, who was born and trained in Germany but lived for fifty-five years in America.

French physical anthropology and prehistory, with their heavy factual content, had flourished in the same decades from 1860 to 1890 as had British classical evolutionistic anthropology. This is a significant fact; but, ideologically speaking, the French had participated relatively little in the evolutionistic development. They were inclined to look less for "origins" than for "laws." Durkheim was born sixty years later than Comte; yet though that interval was far from being intellectually arid in France, it was arid as regards anthropological or sociological theory: Gabriel Tarde's work, for instance, aimed at being psychology. Durkheim, to sum him up, may be rated a positivist; an empiricist in principle, but with only mild urge toward the use of wide context; like most of his countrymen, more interested in sharp principles than in variety of comparative data; not ethnocentric but yet little given to relativistic and pluralistic recognitions; and continuing to the end to believe that cultural phenomena can be adequately subsumed under purely social concepts. Durkheim left a school, but his actual constructive influence outside France has been slight, except on and through Radcliffe-Brown.

Boas came to anthropology via physical geography from a grounding in physics and mathematics. Though never interested in laboratory or experiment, he was trained to distinguish rigorous proof from speculative schemes buttressed by selected facts. His unsparing mind exacted proof even in the complex and difficult situations which prevail in culture, and he refused to deal with problems in which strict proof seemed impossible. He was skeptical of laws or universals in anthropology, and was tireless in pointing out that contradictory "origins" of culture phenomena might both be true at different times, or that conflicting processes of alleged constancy might all be effective, and that therefore no origin and no process could be a true constant or unqualified universal. His interest in phenomena lay in the processes they

revealed, but these processes he saw as multitudinous, variable, and complexly meshed—as they undoubtedly are in the main. He became the great destroyer of intellectual illusions. Tirelessly he pulled down the various schemes of origins and "evolutionistic" stages, of quasi-spontaneous generatings out of the "nature" of the mind of man; he pulled down racism as an explanation of cultural differences; he denied environmental determinism; unitary as well as Kulturkreis determinism by diffusion—in short, all simpliste determinations. He found anthropology a playfield and jousting ground of opinion; he left it a science, pluralistic but critical.

Boas was negativistic in his concern about premature or oversimplified explanations. Even his pointing out the importance of unconscious factors in linguistic and cultural manifestations contained the negative element of exposing the illusoriness of the generally supposed rational motivation of language and culture. But Boas was a constructive positivist as regards data, and he tirelessly collected data from unknown cultures and languages in his search for a better understanding of processes. For this understanding he insisted, as against his more speculative predecessors, on the need of context for each fact used; it must not be torn out of the matrix. However, beyond that respect for the immediate setting in the situation, Boas did not go. He did not seek context beyond context in a progressive enlargement of horizon as an end in itself; and therewith he cut himself off from productive historical interpretation, even though he himself construed his method as being historical because he respected nearer context as the speculative evolutionists often had not respected it. Boas did not deal with patterns beyond those of the first level as given in the more manifest structure of sociocultural phenomena—as, for instance, in a grammar. Patterns within patterns, or embracing patterns, as Benedict formulated them for cultures and Sapir for languages, Boas distrusted because they were attained by empathy and were validable only subjectively. He maintained that cultural phenomena rested on the psychic activity of individual men; but he saw this same activity as so heavily molded by culture that specifically he resisted almost all psychological findings. Psychological experimentation, behaviorism in psychology, stimulus-response, Gestalt—all elicited little reaction; psychoanalysis he just flatly disbelieved. If he left anthropology a science, he also left it somewhat bewildered and isolated.

The pulses of anthropological thought overlap. Just as the classical evolutionistic or speculative movement began well back in the 1860's but Frazer's widest influence was around 1910 and the school continued active until 1925, so Boas, beginning about 1885 and developing the essentials of his position by 1900, had his work exerting its full effects on the world only around 1925 and continuing until today. For instance, the theoretical position and methods of Lowie, Spier, and Herskovits remain fairly close to those of Boas. In one sense, accordingly, much of our half-century is also the period of dominance of the Boasian approach. Nevertheless, from about 1925 on, a series of new interests and activities arose, of which some will no doubt flourish, some wither, others transform, but which bid fair to hold much of the spotlight in the next quarter-century. None of these newer currents are very consciously anti-Boasian. A number of them emanate from students of Boas but attempt to carry his point of view further. Others have their sources in wholly alien interests and ignore his position. I shall now touch on the principal of these varied newer currents.

On the one hand is the tendency, represented for instance by myself, increasingly and deliberately to abstract culture, or extract it, as I should prefer to say, from the societies and the individuals and the needs and psychologies of human beings, and to try to hold these constant, in order to investigate with better control, and set into clearer focus, the interrelation of purely cultural forms and events. For instance, I have used genius, which is certainly individual, as an index for defining—measuring, as it were—cultural configuration—that is, pattern and change in culture. There is plenty of precedent in principle for such a procedure, and it certainly ought not to shock anthropologists, since it is anthropologists who were the first group to be conscious of culture. How much new understanding can be attained by the method can be ascertained only by applying it further —by pushing it to its effective limit. There are two risks in the approach. One is that of a reification or substantification of culture—yet this is unnecessary and distractive. The second is the risk of using abstract culture as a springboard for the pursuit of neo-evolutionistic schemata. Neither danger is insuperable.

In his last years, Edward Sapir sometimes preached but did not himself seriously practice an almost anticultural attitude. He proclaimed that society and culture as such are barren abstractions, and that cause and effect in human history will ultimately be read by a psychiatry which shall have freed itself from the influence of anthropology and anthropological analysis of culture and shall also have evolved an adequate theory of personality. This seems somehow almost as if it were a personal disappointment reaction in Sapir. It is certainly an aspiration rather than a present or realizable program. As a program it is oriented in reverse from Sapir's own lifework with languages, in which, in common with all linguists, he dealt with relations of forms and essentially eschewed both personalities and specific causality [cf. No. 12]. Now there is little doubt that the active causes of history must reside chiefly in persons. There is also no doubt that the causality must therefore be infinitely manifold. But how any psychiatry or psychology could really evolve "a theory of personality" that would reduce these myriad times myriad causes into a system or organization—with or especially without the aid of cultural analysis—seems a complete mystery. The idea sounds like a wish-fulfilment expression set against the backdrop of a partly regretted career. Its historic significance is presumably connected with the personality-and-culture movement to be discussed in a moment.

Almost wholly a matter of the last twenty years is the preoccupation with patterns as the structuring property of culture. This is a balance to the atomizing historical approach, which is indeed necessary and fruitful in many special situations but which, as a sole method, ends by cumulatively losing instead of achieving significances after a certain point has been reached. Patterns have largely replaced integration as the principle with which Malinowski sought to subsume and vivify culture. He failed: both because his approach was less substantive than programmatic, and because integration is never complete and often is secondary. Patterns do integrate, but more like mutually adaptive organs, or like coexisting species in an ecologic setting, than in any total or summary fashion. Also, patterns can be dealt with empirically and independently of the physiologico-psychological needs that seem to be so conveniently ready to serve as simple causal explanations of culture, but that fail so conspicuously in this task in face of the infinite diversity of culture. By contrast, the pattern approach is definitely oriented in the direction of style and of values, which have heretofore been left

largely to humanists to judge and to propagandize for. Values and style lie open to anthropologists as a new field of research by natural science methods, somewhat comparable to what linguists have begun to do with language. Benedict, who did most to formulate the pattern approach, however also coupled with it a psychiatric dress and a strong interest in effacing distinction between normal and deviant personality. These biases of hers have tended to blur the conceptual clarity of the pattern approach for culture and have sometimes attracted factitious interests.

One of the current vogues in anthropology is "personality and culture." The real roots of this go back much farther than most participants in the movement are aware of: one need only mention Tarde. Psychologizing, though of wholly naïve kind, underlay such theoretical framework as the turn-of-the-century productions of Frazer and Brinton. Then came Freud with *Totem and Taboo*, at one swoop annexing and answering the cardinal problem of culture by finding its origin—leaving us anthropologists to fill in the details if we would. Subsequent psychoanalysts down to Roheim and Kardiner have been less simplistic, but they still maintain complete and positive answers to the problem of culture which anthropologists first defined. Then there have been the waves of vogue of concepts like co-operation, frustration-and-aggression, and security, many advanced by psychologists sufficiently aware of culture to want to explain and resolve it into psychology. And they were accepted largely by younger students who had not yet really made the hard discovery of culture and thought that now they would not have to find out much about it because it all resolved into something much more familiar.

The relation of culture and the psyche of course remains a basic problem. It is a difficult problem that should be approached with humility. Two things are clear in this connection as regards the modern science of psychology. One is its recognition of culture as an element constantly intruding into the behavior of the psyche and therefore necessarily to be accounted for or eliminated if the psyche as such and its processes are to be defined. The other is the refound courage of the psychologists to face the psyche as a whole, now renamed "personality." But, alas, the personality is also a very easy thing for the amateur to talk about. On the side of anthropology, there is no doubt that the immediate efficient causes of social and cultural phenomena are persons, and that in principle the explanation—or at any rate one explanation—of culture must ultimately be made on a psychological level. This has however so far proved extremely difficult to do, and no doubt will continue to be difficult. Apart from the troublesome multiplicity of the personal causation, human beings are always so conditioned by existing culture, as well as by their own psychological and social events, that we are here caught in an immense vicious circle. Moreover, every existing culture is always heavily determined by previous culture, and often its relation to the previous culture is through historical "accidents" in which individual personality factors may be rather small. The contention that personality will really give a new understanding of culture seems doubtful. It undoubtedly does give a more saturated understanding—a feel of texture, as it were. There can be no doubt of an important interrelationship between culture and personality; but, to date, culture has done more to make personality increasingly intelligible to psychologists than the reverse. Indeed, it may be suspected that culture-and-personality studies actually deal largely with interpersonal relations, or the relations of individuals to *society*, for which "cul-

ture" has been substituted as a newer, more connotive and modish term.

In fact, it is clear that there are whole sets of problems in which answers become more adequate and specific when psychological considerations are excluded. In problems of culture history, for instance, the injection of personality factors is more likely to clog than to facilitate understanding. This is because cultural processes, while not wholly independent, possess a considerable degree of autonomy, and are therefore most readily and effectively discovered, isolated, and defined on the strictly cultural level—though this of course does not mark the total end of inquiry. The example of linguistics is significant here, since while language is a more autonomous system than culture the difference is obviously one of degree only. Now, as linguistics has become a more efficient and advanced science, it has progressively declined to admit causal psychological factors into consideration of its patterns. Under Bloomfield it formally expelled them as pernicious "mentalism."

Some of the culture-and-personality enthusiasts hardly know any culture history—in fact, have perhaps never viewed a cultural situation in really cultural terms and might be at a loss to do so. They enjoy the savor of personality, which, being immediately present in our daily life, can be readily discussed in a common-sense way without the broad knowledge and prolonged intellectual discipline required to deal intelligibly with culture—required, for one thing, just because culture is always in part a superpersonal and historical product. An unhistorical or even antihistorical orientation is still widely prevalent in our country. We tend to believe we are effective as a nation because our history is short. This orientation has almost certainly contributed to the furore about understanding culture through personality. The attitude, in-

cidentally, has had almost no counterpart in any European country, where
the value of historical knowledge is
taken for granted.

One of the things that anthropology
has definitely begun to do in the past
twenty-five years is to escape its almost
exclusive addiction to the primitive—
the nonliterate, exotic, distant, or remote in time. This attachment had to
be overcome if anthropology was not
to remain a marginal, perhaps antiquarian science. The larger civilizations are
approachable from the side of transcul-
tural interrelations, or of whole-culture
inquiry into their patterns, profile
courses, or ethos or value structure.
More or less, such studies are supposed
to fall into the domain of the historians.
But historians seem hesitant of them
other than as by-products; and historians are not trained in systematic comparison as anthropologists are; besides
being wont to see larger patterns chiefly as they are implicit in masses of
events which often are largely extraneous to the culture patterns. With reasonable courage and enterprise combined
with modesty, it seems that anthropologists could enter this field and effect
fruitful co-operation with historians.

Some twenty or so years ago, acculturation was being given a whirl of
fashion much as personality-and-culture
is having it today. Concern then was
with the absorption of small societies
and primitive cultures into a large civilization. This is a legitimate aspect of
the process of cultural change, and the
studies were empirical and painstaking.
Yet, since the end-product of the process was assimilation to our own civilization, the movement involved a partial
recession to ethnocentric interest. Before long it became evident that in
principle the acculturation process being studied was but a special exemplification of an everlasting and world-wide
process of intersocietal and intercultural
influencing, which had been not only

recognized but analyzed and named
"acculturation" by McGee as far back
as the 1890's. Later on, assimilation-
acculturation studies tended rather to
merge into studies of the adaptation of
ethnic minorities and the like.

Another development has been that
of "community studies" in our own or
Latin-American or Far Eastern civilizations. These studies involved societies
of about the size of a tribe, and they
could be carried on by the technique of
face-to-face individual informant-ques-
tioning and observation in which anthropologists are experienced, and
which remains the cornerstone of anthropological research technique. An
early hope that the communities would
serve as cross-sections or convenient
microcosms of national societies or
whole large cultures was not borne out,
as Steward has shown: the community
represents only one intermediate level
of several on which the total culture is
organized. An approach manageable by
anthropologists which will yield an
adequate functional interpretation or
even formulation of a living large civilization as a totality still remains to be
worked out.

Applied anthropology as an organized subscience, with an association of
its own, is now about a dozen years old
in the United States. It envisages a vast
field, within which it has occupied and
begun to work only a few areas, such
as certain aspects of industrial relations,
personality, and administration. As one
who has spent his life following anthropology as a purely intellectual pursuit
and has conscientiously avoided active
practical decisions based on professional
equipment—"action research"—I am
evidently not qualified to be either a
judge or a historian of this movement.
Its journal impresses one as dealing
somewhat narrowly with certain select,
limited problems—such as governmental
administration and industrial relations—
some of which are almost wholly out-

side the customary concerns of anthropologists generally. At applied anthropology meetings, on the other hand, papers and discussions have the familiar tenor and attitude in ·spite of the changed topics, and make one feel at home at once.

One observation of historical or perhaps nationalistic relevance deserves to be made in regard to that steadiest of anthropological approaches, archaeology. This observation is likely to surprise our younger archaeologists, because now it no longer holds true and they will have difficulty imagining how late the change came. It is a remarkable fact that only in the last thirty-five years did American archaeologists operating on American data venture, or know how, to attack chronological problems—even of relative chronology—by properly archaeological, nondocumentary methods. Even explorers as experienced as Holmes and Fewkes saw their archaeological pasts almost completely flat. This in spite of the fact that for European and Near Eastern prehistory the value of levels of superposition, of stratifications, had been worked out soon after the 1860's, and that, in Peru, Max Uhle single-handed had, by 1910, correctly roughed out many of the main successions of styles and periods. Our lateness may be another result of the American unhistorical-mindedness already spoken of: the past is felt not as a receding stereoscopic continuum but as a uniform nonpresent. At any rate, incredible as it may now seem, by 1915–25 so little time perspective had been achieved in archaeology that Wissler and I, in trying to reconstruct the native American past, could then actually infer more from the distributions and typology of ethnographic data than from the archaeologists' determinations. Our inferences were not too exact, but they were broader than those from excavations. By contrast, it is evident that during the past generation the progress of American archaeology has spurted enormously.

And that note of optimism is perhaps a fitting one on which to close.

*18. REALITY CULTURE AND VALUE CULTURE
1950/1951

The core of this essay was written for the meeting of the National Academy of Sciences in April, 1950. As the Academy rules limit oral presentations to fifteen minutes, a 1,800-word skeleton had to be extracted for its session; after which, I added to the paper, and rewrote portions of it in the interest of clarity, until it was more than twice as long as before.

Holding cultural phenomena to be part of nature and therefore a proper subject of investigation by natural science, of which the Academy is the exponent, I nevertheless am aware of one curious angle in this paper. The three men whose work stimulated my approach—Weber, Merton, MacIver—are all sociologists, and therefore currently classed as social but not as natural scientists. Moreover, sociologists are, by usage and almost by definition, committed to a primary concern with society, anthropologists rather with culture. Yet these three sociologists had occupied themselves with distinguishing ingredients and properties within culture as no anthropologists have done, to my knowledge. Like others, I had recognized an accumulative tendency in the history of culture that is lacking in the organic process, discussing it, for instance, in chapter vii of my 1948 Anthropology.[1] But I had failed to make explicit what is quite patent on analysis, namely, that the property of accumulativeness is characteristic not of the whole of culture but chiefly of its scientific-technological component. But with this recognition the foundation is laid for an instrumentally productive internal classification of culture—which I feel now it was the business of culture specialists, such as anthropologists, to have made first, or at any rate to have made for themselves. Evidently we were not in the habit of thinking systematically along the lines of this type of generalization—at least not systematically enough for fruitful results.[2] Thus, as far back as 1927, while discussing certain forms of instability unexpectedly manifest in burial practices, I somewhat casually divided culture into "subsistence," "institutional," and "fashion" (stylistic) ingredients[3]—only to modify the scheme again in 1938, as per No. 27 of this volume.

Instead of touching on such classifying ideas and dropping them again, the sociologists mentioned stayed with them and developed them systematically into points of view of importance. It is a pleasure to offer this acknowledgment, which may also serve as a spur to anthropologists.

However, the problems we face between us in the two approaches are not yet all solved. In the second half of the present paper I have brought up one of the more obscure or confused questions: how social structure can be equally "social" and "cultural," while no one would make such a claim for religion or art.

I

THE idea of "human progress" is essentially one of advancement in "social conditions," in civilization. It has long been generally accepted that social changes for better or for worse take

place within that artificial environment of ways and rules which man constantly creates for himself, in the customs that he cakes himself over with, to a far greater degree than change occurs in his intrinsic human nature. Racist theories of inborn superiorities for a time

* Not published previously.

152

impeded or partly delayed approval of this view; but it is now universally accepted by biologists, psychologists, and anthropologists that sociocultural changes are at least overwhelmingly due not to stably hereditary organic, genetic factors but to a much more complex and shifting causality which includes impingements of natural environment and individual persons but which appears to be composed largely, and most immediately, of factors that are themselves sociocultural.

The idea of progress arose in eighteenth-century western Europe, as part of the ideology or attitude of Enlightenment and faith in the triumph of reason. Viewed comparatively, the idea that civilization has progressed, and will continue to progress, is far from having been assumed by peoples of the world in general. In fact, the notion is exceptional in history. Far more frequently wisdom, excellence, innocence, and virtue are attributed to the sages and heroes of the past. At the beginning was the Age of Gold; we of today live in the degenerate and contentious Age of Iron.

In reversing this age-old postulate, eighteenth-century Enlightenment really devised a novel and original idea, though progress was equally aprioristic. How and why it originated then we need not go into here: a partial answer is given in Carl Becker's stimulating *The Heavenly City of the Eighteenth-Century Philosophers.*

In any event, the nineteenth century received, carried on, and fortified the postulate of progressive development, which is still widely accepted in mid-twentieth century in nonscientific circles. Among others in the nineteenth century, the anthropologists accepted the assumption; and most of the theoretical structure of early anthropology was reared on this a priori, usually under the name of "evolution."

Toward the end of the century,

doubts began to arise among anthropologists as to the postulate of continuous progress and unilinear evolution of culture. These doubts hardened into a denial, especially under the consistent criticism of Boas, and along with development of the concepts of diversity of cultural forms and relativity of cultural values. By about 1925 progress "evolutionism" had pretty well died out in anthropology, except in the Marxist version. The "relativity" principle, which took its place, held that appraisals of cultures or their parts in terms of any absolute canon were ethnocentric and biased, and that scientific comparison required the recognition and description of cultural traits in terms, first of all, of the total pattern or value-system of the culture of which they formed part—much as biologists had long since done with organs and organisms.

The anthropologists began their work with attention directed chiefly toward the minor cultures of little or "primitive" societies. They ventured only gradually to try to include also the greater and richer civilizations known through their history. They made the attempt because the basic anthropological concept of culture and the basic method of investigating this relativistically—that is, comparatively—left no room for any fundamental division between the more retarded and the more advanced cultures.

Concurrently, though mainly by non-anthropologists, a comparative morphology of cultures began to be attempted, directed at the principal major civilizations, such as the Chinese, Indian, Near Eastern, Egyptian, Graeco-Roman, and Western. Initiated by the Russian botanist Danilevsky, and carried on by the Egyptologist Flinders Petrie, the thinking in this field reached its most extreme and exaggerated form under Spengler, and has Toynbee as its best-known contemporary representative, while Sorokin and the present speaker have also grappled with its problems. All this group except Spengler start from three empirical premises. The first of these is that there have been enormous transmissions or diffusion of cultural material between civilizations, as of papermaking from China to the West, of metallurgical arts from the West to China. Second, the essential historical distinctness of the major civilizations is nevertheless clear, a distinctness as cultural bodies as well as societies. Third, this cultural distinctness, which constitutes a civilization, rests upon an objectively expressed system of subjective values, which has been called "ethos," "genius," "ideology," "master-pattern," or "superstyle"; and such a system is gradually developed by certain societies, usually of supernational scope, partly out of creative originations of their own and partly out of culture material imparted to them from other societies. Spengler differs from the other inquirers of the group chiefly in that he is so extravagantly impressed by the third factor—the master-pattern or superstyle—that he construes it as totally unique and unrelated in each culture, and hence refuses to allow any significance to the first factor—the interflow of cultural material between civilizations—a refusal which is invalidated by the whole upshot of dispassionate culture history.

In this trend of thought, as well as in modern anthropology, the terms "culture" and "civilization" usually are essential synonyms, referring to the same conceptual cluster of phenomena, with at most a nuance of connotational divergence. If there is a difference, it is that the term "civilization" includes only the major cultures, but that all human societies equally possess cultures, whether major or minor, advanced or retarded.

II

Now, however, I wish to discuss a view which contrasts civilization with culture as differentiable constituents of what so far I have called civilization *or* culture. Reference is not to Spengler, who used the term "civilization" to denote the final stage of ossification and senility which sooner or later, he said, overtook every culture, be it Chinese, Egyptian, Graeco-Roman, or our own. This personal meaning of the term "civilization" by Spengler had some spread in German, but not in English. The distinction between "civilization" and "culture" here referred to seems to have originated with Alfred Weber,[4] brother of the better-known Max Weber of Protestant-capitalist-ethic fame. It has been set forth in simplified form in English by Merton.[5] A similar distinction has also been made by MacIver, though with a somewhat different emphasis on means and ends.[6]

The Alfred Weber view is really a trichotomy of sociocultural phenomena into society, culture, and civilization. In society he includes not only social but economic and political phenomena and processes. This aggregation has at least the pragmatic validation that sociology, economics, and political science constitute the core of the social sciences as usually practiced; although no anthropologist would concede for a moment that social, economic, or political structure and functioning were something outside the totality of what he considers culture. However, let us provisionally disregard this sociopolitical-economic field over which the social scientists and the anthropologists are contesting as to whether it is outside or in culture as a whole. That leaves us specific "culture" and specific "civilization," and the problem: Are they two or one; and why?

The Weber view makes civilization correspond with science and technology; culture with philosophy, religion, and art. Science and technology discover (or utilize) something pre-existent. They reveal things independent of culture, like the revolution of the earth,

X-rays, "laws of nature," pistons drivable in cylinders by steam. These scientific and technological discoveries tend to be transmitted rapidly from society to society and thus to become universal, says Weber. They are also transmitted through time with little deterioration. Temporary or local losses or impairments may occur, but are slight. On the whole, therefore, the scientific-technological process is an accumulative one. Each generation or new society can begin where others left off. The accumulative tendency which anthropologists have long noted as one quality of the total cultural process as distinct from the organic process as such is evidently due essentially to this scientific-technological ingredient, which Weber calls "civilizational."

By contrast, culture proper in the Weberian sense—the most specifically cultural part of what anthropologists call culture—namely religion, philosophy, and all the arts, tends much more to be nonaccumulative, because it diffuses with more difficulty from one society to another, especially to those societies of separate historical experience and antecedents. It is indeed a truism that while science can more or less go on from where it stopped, the arts have always to begin all over again. They progress independently, in different directions; whereas science and the mechanical arts progress on the whole in a direction determined by nature as it exists prior to man. Religions, and even philosophies, share with the arts the quality of a relatively high degree of impermanence. They tend to replace each other instead of building up cumulatively. The difference may not be complete, but it certainly exists.

It is also evident that it is mainly in this "cultural portion of culture," which has religion, philosophy, and art as its core, that the values reside which anthropologists are coming increasingly to face. I discussed here last year [No.

15] the legitimacy and need for naturalistic recognition, description, and comparison of cultural values as one of the tasks of contemporary anthropology. This natural science treatment of values must of course be sharply distinguished from the introduction of value-judgments into scientific operations. While values accordingly inhere in the "cultural" part of culture and are characteristic of it, it is equally clear that they are of much less strength and consequence in the "civilizational" part that comprises science and technology. That a steel ax bites deeper than a stone ax, that one machine works and another does not, are veritable isolated facts, not part of a value-system.

Merton distinguishes civilizational culture as being objective, from cultural culture which is subjective. This is true enough up to a certain point, but it is likely to be misleading because it seems not to be the core of the distinction. Perhaps that is why Weber does not deal with the objective-subjective aspect except sidelong and incidentally. All culture of course has a subjective aspect. Thus the most objectively practiced science or engineering has different value according to its context and association in one or another culture. Conversely, religion and art necessarily have their objective aspects. Above all, the objective-subjective antithesis has been developed in so many contexts, and is so invested with a Kantian and neo-Kantian aura of nature versus spirit, that it seems more profitable to de-emphasize the consideration if a fresher and more specific replacement can be found for it, as I hope in a moment to suggest.

MacIver began, soon after Weber and before Merton, by also distinguishing civilization from culture, largely as being respectively social means and social ends in themselves. His final formulation of 1942, in *Social Causation*,[7] restates his case somewhat, both in emphasis and in terminology. He now recognizes three primary "realms" of being, Physical, Organic, and Conscious. These obviously correspond to the levels of phenomenal attributes, sometimes designated "emergent," and recognized by many other thinkers in the last thirty years. His Conscious realm is implicitly equivalent to the psychic plus social plus cultural levels of others. Within the realm of Conscious Being, he distinguishes three "orders": the cultural, technological, and social. The social order he sees in a straiter frame than Weber and as consisting of modes of relationship between "social beings" as expressed in group formations and conditions of association. He omits economics and politics from this narrowed social order.

The technological order of MacIver is the "civilization" of his earlier writing, and of Weber and Merton, and corresponds to what I am proposing below to call "reality culture." It comprises devices, instruments, and skills directed to the achievement of goals, and is expressed not only through technology in the widest sense but also through economic systems of both production and distribution and through political systems, whether operating through manipulation, control, or military execution. Here is a definite difference from Weber, who includes economics and politics in his social process. MacIver does admit that whereas technology controls *things*, economic-political activity controls the relations of *people* to things and is therefore more open to change due to shifts in "social valuations."[8] Economics and political activity could accordingly be viewed also as an aspect of the social order, he admits. But, since it *regulates* the social order rather than *constituting* it in the sense in which the fundamental human relationships constitute it, the two are best kept apart, to his thinking.

MacIver does not include science in his technological order. In fact, he seems to omit, in his later work, assigning science to any of his three orders. This noncommitment may be due to his sensing a point I shall develop in a moment, namely that the historic behavior of scientific activity resembles much more nearly the historic behavior of philosophy and the arts than that of technological activity. More likely, however, MacIver recognizes that when science is pursued as such, without reference to its *useful* applications, it is a goal in itself and no longer, like technology, an instrument.

MacIver's cultural order deals with "operative valuations" and with goals. Besides the arts and philosophy, it comprises "faiths," that is, religions, also traditions, codes and customs ("mores, folkways"), as well as play-activities; plus—somewhat vaguely and generally—"modes of living."[9] Subsequently MacIver says that the cultural order is "the system of primary human interests," in distinction from the technological "apparatus" used in pursuit of these same interests.[10] Here we approach the criticism which Merton[11] has leveled at MacIver's earlier dichotomy of civilization as a set of means and culture as a set of ends; namely, that the distinction is one of motivation, whereas motives can be different for the same activity. MacIver's reply in *Social Causation* is that what is relevant is the motivation of patterns of social activity, not the motivation of individuals or occasions. In illustration he cites the bank and the factory as purely instrumental in their nature, but the church, the theater, the club as "foci of final consumption."[12] He dismisses Ogburn's doctrine of cultural lag as one-sided in seeing technology as creative, culture as merely responsive, whereas in fact the controlling principle of adjusting specific means [technology] to broad value-systems "must always reside" in the cultural order.[13] While the cultural order and its parts are probably less well integrated than the technological, they are in no sense derivative from it as the Marxians claim. The cultural order results for every society in a characteristic "whole style of living," which is influentially pervasive and real, though it may be hard to describe. Thus MacIver on the autonomy of his cultural order.

III

Let us accept all three of these overlapping formulations by Weber, Merton, and MacIver as containing points of validity and significance, and see whether we can carry the argument farther.

First, to clarify terminology, MacIver's "technology" would best be replaced. It is not properly complementary to society and culture. Also, to include economic and political activity under technology is a stretch of the ordinary meanings of all three words.

It is also plain that we cannot permanently go on talking about "civilizational culture" and "cultural culture." Nor will Weber's terms "civilization" and "culture" (sometimes varied to "civilizational process" and "cultural movement") be other than confusing, especially in English. Both terms have too similar a denotation in general English and too many strongly intrenched connotations—for instance, "cultured person," "uncivilized peoples," "attain to civilization," "minority cultures." The two words overlap too largely—not to mention special confusing significances, such as Spengler's.

I propose therefore to retain "culture" with the well-understood broad denotation which it has for all anthropologists and many sociologists and psychologists at least in the United States, as well as in Germany and largely in Britain and Latin America—namely, culture as the historically differentiated and variable mass of customary

ways of functioning of human societies. After that I would distinguish the two ingredients under discussion, namely, Weber's "civilization" and "culture," as "reality culture" and "value culture," reality and values being what the two ingredients are most characteristically directed toward.

This terminology has the further advantage that it allows social and political and perhaps economic structure and behavior to be designated correspondingly as "social culture."

IV

Now for certain strictures and limitations.

First of all, though science and technology are directed toward reality and are obviously related, they differ in that one is directed toward the understanding, the other toward the control and use of nature. Science is an intellectual activity, technology a practical one. Yet when the achievements of science are examined in their total historical profile, it is evident that they are manifested overwhelmingly in spurts or bursts, quite like those in the arts and philosophy. This I have demonstrated for science in my *Configurations of Culture Growth* of 1944.[14] While this book has been criticized as being insufficiently conclusive, it has generally been judged as more genuinely empirical than most of its predecessors. Until there is a re-examination of the summary there given of the history of science in its principal manifestations on this earth, we may thus conclude that however much science is dedicated to the uncovering or discovery of reality, as a cultural process or activity it is largely subject to the influence of factors of the same kind as those at work in producing value-culture activities. For instance, the role of creativity, of genius, and its clustering are parallel in the sciences and the arts. What is achieved by science and by the arts of course differs radically; but the relation of achievement to the flow of the stream of the total regional or secular culture, to the flow of the particular "civilization" in which science is being manifested, the dependence on this flow, is substantially identical in science and the fine arts.

In line with this determination is the fact of qualitative differences between the sciences that have grown up in diverse cultures. Such are Greek mathematics, with its geometric foundation and orientation, as against modern Western functionally oriented mathematics. Or again there is the difference that the Greeks were able to make a fair beginning of physics but none whatever in chemistry. It is true that Spengler, in calling attention to these differences, exaggerated them, as was his nature, into total and irreconcilable distinctions. Weber, whose essay clearly was stimulated by Spengler—one might describe it as the reaction of his systematic thinking to Spenglerian influences which he largely rejects but partly accepts—freely admits these partial qualitative differences, as I believe every discerning historian of culture must admit them. The position I am expounding is of course a somewhat delicate one to present to an audience of eminent scientists. The claim is not that the validity of the results of science is plural, relative, and fluctuating, but that the fact and kind of scientific activity prosecuted at different times are a function of the culture of which the scientific activity is a part; and that therefore the scientific activity will vary qualitatively according to period and society. Especially illuminating on this point is the peculiar mathematics developed in China around 1300 and carried further in Japan about 1700, which was without geometric foundation, which seems to have been mainly of native derivation but with probably a dash of algebraic fertilization from the

West, and which developed an orientation, methods, and techniques that were largely unique—in short, a distinctive mathematical style.

Or again, consider this startling constellation in the history of science. Since at least Aristotle, biology has always recognized both the constancy of the genus or kind and the variability of individuals within it. In fact, it was mainly biology that contributed this polar concept to Greek, Arab, Mediaeval, and Modern logicophilosophical thought. Nineteenth-century biology sensed increasingly that the distinction was concerned with the problem of organic change, and in its Darwinian culmination and reorientation—whose fundamental book was titled *The Origin of Species*—biology was almost obsessively preoccupied with heredity, variation, and adaptation. Darwin's specific new contribution was the correlation with these three of his new factor of automatic selection. Yet it was not until 1900 that the first regularities in variability within heredity were recognized and the science of genetics was born—forty-one years after Darwin's revolution. In retrospect, we can see why this origin of genetics came so late. The whole nineteenth-century climate of scientific opinion was still wholly insensitive to experiment with heredity. Laboratories were well developed, but they were laboratories of the shop or work table, not of the garden; experiments were directed at parts, components, or properties of objects or organisms, not at the relations of whole organisms across generations. Hence Mendel's simple, beautiful, and significant experiments of controlling variability within a stream of heredity went unheeded even by his acutest fellow-biologists, and died stillborn. If Darwinians saw no meaning in these experiments, it is plain that pre-Darwinians could not have seen any. In short, scientific discoveries can be made only when "the time is ripe" for them, when certain antecedents have been developed, when the pattern of scientific flow has reached a particular stage. All this is very similar to the fact that, in painting, romanticism, impressionism, and abstractionism develop only at certain times and in particular sequences, and not at all in random order or contemporaneously.

In this connection it is also significant that philosophy is customarily reckoned as primarily an intellectual activity, and that it certainly is directed at reality and not at avowed figments thereof; and yet it is ordinarily classed in what I am now calling "value culture." Since science and philosophy agree in being intellectual and nonutilitarian, it is clear that science cannot well be ruled wholly out of value culture and philosophy left in.

Can this conclusion mean that pure science is to be moved out of reality culture and only applied science or technology left in its domain? So indeed MacIver tacitly proposes. But no; this would be going too far. Science not only professes to seek reality but subordinates itself to reality by submitting to the tests of experiment and prediction. Also, in the modern phase of our own culture, the relations of science and technology are extraordinarily close. It is our science that has made our technological advances possible. And in return many of the gains of science are made possible by what technology equips it with. In fact, Western technology had definitely begun to move into an ascendant, expanding phase well back in the Middle Ages, at least three to four centuries before creative theoretical science began to move productively in Europe with Copernicus.

It is true that history makes it clear that there does not exist any one-to-one or even constant correlation between science and technology. Greek science

outstripped Greek technology—sufficiently so to be in the end hampered by the lack of reinforcement from technology. In China the reverse held; and here it was technology that ultimately was restricted by enormous prestige-weighting of the verbal over the manual—a weighting that tended to suppress scientific training of the intellect and to leave technology in the unassisted hands of the artisan. Even the burst of Chinese mathematics already mentioned was nonscholarly, popular, and not accepted into classical, rewarded learning.

In fact, the true relations of creative activity are better viewed as extending along a scale than as distributed between wholly disparate steps of concern with reality as against values. I would envisage a continuum from technology to science to philosophy to religion to art. Science begins with reality and remains unqualifiedly committed to it; but it does express reality in patterns *of its own making* instead of the utilities of technology. Philosophy operates on patterns of thought which it aims indeed to conform to reality but often not immediately so, as in idealistic and mystic systems; and the conformity is probably never really testable. Religion still professes to cover and include the phenomena of the actual world, but as partially or wholly subordinate to something that is supernatural, outside or above ordinary reality—"surrealistic," I am increasingly driven to name it as I keep thinking about it [cf. No. 39]. From the standpoint of strict reality alone, the findings of religion already are pure figments, whatever their claims. Art, finally, does not even pretend to be anything but figments, though often placating reality by professing to keep in step with it—or not too much out of step. And beyond— though this is of secondary moment from the angle of values—the arts have some dependence on their materials, pigments, and instruments, which, being technological, bring us back in a near-circle close to our starting point.

There are further connections and transitions. Myth, for instance, may fairly be definable as religious philosophy aesthetically expressed—a nondifferentium of the three activities. Mathematics, again, alone of the sciences, has no empirical content and therefore no intrinsic relevance to reality. True, it has proved increasingly useful or necessary to science, as philosophy has been felt less useful of late. Still, pattern systems of mathematics have their validity in themselves rather than in any conformity to sensory reality, so that mathematics might reasonably be classifiable with logic, or even with the arts when these become sufficiently abstract.

I think it sufficiently clear that useful as the distinction is between the reality and value ingredients in culture, it must not be treated as an absolute one. Rather should it be viewed as a conceptual axis with well-separated poles, or as two foci of influence within one area.

V

As against reality culture and value culture, we have so far not discussed social culture—Weber's "social process" and MacIver's "social order within the realm of conscious being." Weber includes economic and political activities in this social segment, MacIver attaches them to his technological order. I do not wish to take sides in the matter of this difference, but rather to discuss a consideration that seems more fundamental.

This is the fact that it would not occur to any modern anthropologist to separate off the family, kinship, communities, or any social groupings in order to contrast them with culture and therewith to omit them from culture. To him these social structures and their activities constitute one part or segment of culture, namely, social culture, which he assumes to be wholly co-

ordinate with, say, religious culture, or with economic or technological ("material") or aesthetic or intellectual culture. True, each of these segments of culture has its own characteristics and special relations with other segments. But we cannot see culture as the totality which it is, anthropologists say, while excluding any one of these segments on the ground that it possesses certain peculiarities; for all segments of culture show some particular properties.

The sociological position is really less consistent. It will however be expedient for clarity to defer exposition of this sociological inconsistency for a moment, in order to point out what it seems to be due to. I believe it is due to a resistance or reluctance on the part of sociologists (though in quite varying degrees) to accept a broad concept of culture, or at least to deal with culture as such. Anthropologists, contrariwise, have not only accepted the theoretic concept since Tylor eighty years ago, but they have assumed that culture was, either by itself or along with language, race, and perhaps personality, that which it was their business to deal with. They have seen culture as a highly diversified, intricately intra-related realm or order of phenomena, produced, it is true, by human beings in societies but at the same time influencing human beings enormously, from individual personalities up to the total human species. The totality and the basic coherence of this cultural order of phenomena have impressed them so strongly that problems of differences between its parts or segments have appeared of only secondary consequence and have therefore not been much pursued—perhaps, indeed, unduly neglected. After all, so far as I can recall, the present essay is the first by an anthropologist to consider, explicitly and systematically, what the nature of the grand divisions of culture may be; and it is equally significant that this essay begins with the findings of three sociologists!

Anthropologists, temperamentally attracted by the different, the remote, the exotic, began their work with the "primitive" cultures of little societies, of tribes. They were able without too much difficulty to see these cultures as wholes, or at least to treat aspects of them as parts of wholes. Also it was relatively easy to pass from the integral analysis of such little wholes to comparison of them. Therewith the relativistic attitude was born, which in turn was in its very nature bound to re-emphasize the idea of culture; for it is obvious that it is men's cultures that vary more widely than races or societies of men vary—perhaps even more than individuals within societies vary.

A selection, complementary to the one that recruited anthropologists from among those who were centrifugally inclined in their intellectual tastes, seems to have drawn sociologists mainly from the centripetally minded. In this camp, the strange and long distant, the little societies so different from our own, all seemed small and unimportant. There is no doubt that sociology began with primary interest in our own Western society and its social institutions and that the core of its concern still is attached there. Race, fossil men, prehistory, language, are still marginal in sociological attention. They serve perhaps to frame the field but are scarcely of it; the active problems of sociology are pursued with no real reference to these phenomenally wider considerations.

Human social phenomena (in the older sense of the phrase) being thus viewed with a contractile slant, these same social phenomena tended to remain construed as *societal* by sociologists, while anthropologists in their expansive ardor largely went on without a quaver from social to cultural phenomena; until before long they saw a larger significance in culture and were treating society as merely a part or segment of culture, which they were trying to see as a whole.

In an eloquent passage in *Social Causation* MacIver points out that in the "simpler societies," technology and culture (in his technical sense of these words) are undifferentiated.[15] There is no relatively detached utilitarian system: artifacts are "culturally expressive" as well as "functional." The cultural and the utilitarian are interfused. Ritual is as important as craftsmanship; prayers, as arms of war. "Culture, technique, authority, people, and land are subjectively unified." Values and instruments are "socially wedded." Thus it is that "anthropologists can conveniently use the single term 'culture' to signify a totality of artifacts and folkways."

That there is a distinction of non-literate peoples from ourselves is indubitable, though it is certainly one of degree only. It is also indubitable that the lesser differentiation in the smaller societies has affected anthropologists in the direction of seeing culture as an integral whole rather than as only a part of something larger. But the point that MacIver makes about the nondifferentiation of reality culture and value culture ("utilitarian-technological" and "cultural" in his terminology) can obviously be made also about the relation of both to social culture (his "society"). And anthropologists have recognized this additional relation, and have wanted to deal with the larger totality that included it, and therewith with all three aspects or orders. It so happened that they came to call the larger totality "culture," following Tylor, who in turn seems to have derived the term from German usage. Sociologists, on the contrary, tended less to deal with the larger concept and concentrated their attention on *specifically social* situations and aspects. It was therefore natural for them to stick to the older, though less specific, concept and term of "the social"—as the French have also done—and to view culture either as a marginal extension of social activity or as somehow a subdivision or derivative from it.

Logically, the two courses—anthropological and sociological—are equally justified. All culture has human society as its precondition, and conversely all human society is accompanied by culture as its product but also as its own further precondition. To center interest in either aspect is therefore legitimate enough. The real problem is which procedure is the more useful operationally; or rather, to know in what situations it is operationally more productive to give primacy to the cultural aspect of the associated phenomena, in which to the strictly social, and, indeed, in which to the undifferentiated sociocultural. The one thing that cannot fairly be done is to brush the problem aside as immaterial. This is because conceptually cultural and social phenomena are as thoroughly distinct as they regularly coexist in man. Many kinds of insects are at least as intensively socialized in their life-existence as we—some of them perhaps more so—without manifesting more than the barest or most dubious rudiments of culture. This fact of nature lifts the social-cultural distinction out of the range of being only a metaphysical, logical, or verbal distinction and gives it wide phenomenal validation. From this again it follows that there will be certain situations that can be more penetratingly understood through being viewed as primarily social, and others as primarily cultural. Yet such differentiation does not preclude the probability that there will be a third type of situation or problem—perhaps largely concerned with "outside," that is, organic or inorganic, relations—in which an undifferentiated sociocultural approach may be time-saving or even actively the more profitable.

This argument seems to be substantiated by the fact that by and large it is sociologists who have concerned themselves mainly with the social and anthropologists with the cultural aspects of the same or similar phenomena. It would be presumptuous to believe that either study was basically mistaken in its premises and pursuits. Rather is it likely that the division or differential weighting of interests has been legitimate and profitable.

In this differential lineup, the characteristic anthropological attitude proved to develop with a certain simplicity and ease. As a concept, culture emerged much later than society, and when it did emerge it was necessarily a more sharply defined concept than the older, undifferentiated concept of society which included culture. Thus not only Comte but Durkheim (exact contemporary of Boas in birth date!) often speak of social facts or phenomena when the context shows clearly that they mean cultural phenomena. Similarly, Toynbee still often uses "society" and "civilization" interchangeably, though manifesting reluctance at employing the Spengler-contagioned word "culture." At any rate, once they had made culture their own, however come by, most anthropologists found that while the level of the concept might be special, its range was extremely wide, and that it would cover and include phenomena like the family, clan, tribe, or state as readily as phenomena of the type of totem, shaman, fetish, taboo, crisis rite, folkway, myth, tale, proverb, decoration, trade, potlatch, pottery, weaving, or subsistence economy. Indeed, there was social culture, as the anthropologist saw it; but there were also material culture and economy and religion and art and the useful arts and language and fashion. Each of these represented a more or less pragmatically useful segment of culture. But the segments blended and interrelated, and their segregation was incidental and utilitarian on occasion, and what remained significant was their integration into the larger totality of culture.

I think it will be conceded that this was a gratifyingly simple and yet effective attitude.

Equally simple was the attitude of Comte, to whom our social and cultural facts were still all merely social; and, in the main, the position of Durkheim also. But those who came later, after the anthropologists and various German historians and philosophers and Spengler had recognized culture as a special order or level or aspect of phenomena—these later sociologists faced a more troublesome situation. To reject culture, to deny it all conceptual autonomy, became increasingly difficult as the twentieth century progressed. But what was the relation of the social and the cultural to be for them?

One solution was that of Alfred Weber, to which, essentially, MacIver also worked his way: the tripartite assignment of the phenomena in question to social, cultural, and civilization-al-technological-utilitarian "processes" or "orders." But parts of what? MacIver says: of the realm of Conscious Being—which phrase however omits explicit reference not only to society but also to the conscious individual and thus leaves the relation to psychology unaccounted for. Weber's answer is: parts of historical entities, *Geschichts-körper*. But what are these, if not societies, or (anthropologists') cultures, or both? The two answers agree in *de facto* putting social and cultural phenomena on one level, but in then dividing this joint plane into one social and two cultural fields. While this is an arguable view, it flatly contradicts the thinking of anthropologists and others most directly concerned with total culture. There also remains the stubborn

evidence of the cultureless insect societies to cast doubt on such merging of levels. And, finally, are not both answers fairly analogous to a position that physiologists and psychologists might take if they agreed to recognize only an undifferentiated psychosomatic level but then proceeded to divide this into biochemical, cognitive, and affective-conative fields?

Probably the most prevalent view among sociologists is one that with my anthropological pro-cultural bias I find it difficult to formulate justly. It is perhaps being typically expressed by Talcott Parsons. In this view, concern of sociology is with social action and extends as far into culture as strictly social action can be followed. Those aspects of culture which do not "contain" social action—values, symbols, forms, and their histories—are left to anthropologists and others. Even MacIver, who calls the cultural order great and many-sided, says of the sociology of religion that it is "a study of the interdependence of religious experience and social organization—it is not a study of the positive content or substance of religion."[16] That is, whether a denomination is Trinitarian or Unitarian, whether it baptizes infants by sprinkling or adults by immersion, are matters of religion and therefore of culture. Sociology begins to take cognizance of them when they are the basis of schism or union of sects, possess a higher or lower social prestige, or are somehow coupled with congregational, hierarchical, or alternative forms of church organization.

Such a delimitation as that of Parsons and MacIver seems fairly to describe contemporary sociology, and to be consonant both with sociology's own predominant range of actual activity and with claims that might be made on behalf of study fields avowedly concerned with culture. Implicitly the distinctness of the social and cultural levels or aspects is recognized; even though it may be only through context or total approach that a study can be assigned wholly or mainly to one or the other level of operation.

Sorokin has for many years been perhaps most explicit among American sociologists in distinguishing the social and the cultural aspects of sociocultural phenomena, operationally and even in the titles of his books. On the other side, Radcliffe-Brown is most notable among anthropologists for evincing resistance to the concept of culture as such, and, though he has made some concessions of late, he still considers specifically social structure and function the most significant and basic area in the total sociocultural field. As he has also admitted being a sociologist, his view is legitimate enough.

It does remain a fact that as the conceptual distinctness of the social and cultural aspects has become more generally accepted, cultural anthropologists have not felt that they could properly renounce their claim to include the social area in culture [No. 7, Part IV], however inadequately they might yet be cultivating this area; whereas sociologists have shown much more disposition to concentrate on strictly social structure and action and to seek out in culture—or in the remainder of culture, as we anthropologists see it—only its specifically social relations.

To put it another way, the area of human social relationships can apparently be construed equally well in social and in cultural terms.[17] Other segments of culture clearly are amenable to fruitful interpretation chiefly in cultural terms, though, contrariwise, cultural explanations are of course wholly inapplicable to all subhuman social situations. This two-facedly social-or-cultural meaning of social relationships is an anomaly in scientific logic; but empirically it is a fact.

Sorokin, who begins with a sociocultural world in which he distinguishes social and cultural aspects, is nearer the usual theoretical position of anthropologists than are most of his sociological colleagues. They co-ordinate society with culture but deal only with society. Anthropologists tend to agree with Sorokin in distinguishing social and cultural aspects or levels in principle; but in practice they treat societal phenomena on a plane and par with the phenomena of reality culture and value culture, namely, straight-out as culture. Societal phenomena thus have a double aspect: to anthropologists they are part of culture; to sociologists they touch culture but exclude it. Is there logical warrant for such a situation?

Historically, one might say this. As long as social and cultural facts remained an intellectually undifferentiated magma, a single science—whatever its name—sufficed to deal with this realm of phenomena. But once the theoretical distinction was achieved, and it further became evident that cultural facts were the more voluminous, multifarious, and varied as well as inclusive, preoccupation with culture was bound to have an expansive character, but continued concentration on the now reduced field of society tended toward retraction. Cultural anthropology maintains no frontier against those phenomena of culture which happen to have also a social aspect. But sociology must in self-defense set up a barrier against dealing, in focus and systematically, with the nonsocietal aspects of culture.

With this distinction there is undoubtedly connected the further fact that as anthropology in recent decades has tried to establish contacts beyond the cultural level, it has sought them mainly not on the nearest level of the social but beyond that on the individual psychological level of personality.

VI

The trichotomy of social, reality, and value culture is obviously not exhaustive. Language must without doubt be recognized as a fourth primary component, differing from the others in that its special qualities fit it as a mechanism serving these others rather than as an end in itself.

The highly special sphere of fashion is too small to constitute a primary segment, but is difficult to allocate. Fashion is of course dedicated to values, but it is of fashion's nature perversely to keep its values both trivial and unstable while loading them with considerable social significance.

Morality is rooted in values, of course, but is the basic regulator in the social sector, formally so when expressed as law.

As for economic and political activity, we have seen how Weber and MacIver differ in their assignment of these. Since "the state" is one of the conventional captions of sociology, parallel to family, community, and church, its allocation to the technological order by MacIver is surprising. It appears that he is speaking less in terms of static classification—where the state can hardly be other than a social group—than dynamically with reference to political "agencies of control and manipulation." Similarly, for economics, he specifies systems of production and distribution. To Weber, a European and more reactive to Marxism, "economy" apparently suggests political control, and therefore falls along with government into his "social process."

As regards the economic and political spheres, Sorokin characterizes these as being two of the notable mixed or derivative systems of culture. His pure cultural "systems," as he denominates what others call "processes," "orders," or "segments," are six in number:[18] language; science; philosophy; religion; fine arts, that is the nonutilitarian ones, exclusive of technology; and ethics or law-and-morals. In a work three years later,[19] applied technology is cited as

one among the "vast derivative systems," along with economics and politics. Sorokin differs from the other sociologists here considered in recognizing language as a primary system-segment of culture. His remaining five systems fall into the value segment or order of other authors, perhaps because they are "ideological" in level.[20] Sorokin recognizes no social system in culture, since, as we have seen, he consistently makes a prior separation of the social aspect and the cultural aspect of the sociocultural or superorganic world.

However, it is necessary to bear in mind that while Sorokin's "systems" are after all much like the segments or areas or processes or orders of other writers, his chief interest in them is apparently as steps toward his "supersystems"; and that these supersystems in turn represent something quite different from what we have been considering here. These "sensate," "ideational," and "idealistic" supersystems are not segments of cultures at all, nor are they whole cultures, nor aggregations or continuities of culture. They are essentially polar *qualities* that tend to pervade large blocks of higher culture for centuries in a back-and-forth rhythm. They are not substantive culture, in the sense that the reality, value, and social segments of culture are substantive.

VII

In summary, there seems to be a certain importance in the conceptual distinction between those two great segments of human culture which are directed respectively toward reality and values. The distinction is validated by the differential behavior, as it might be called, of the two segments in human history. One is largely diffusional and accumulative, the other ever re-creative. By contrast, a third major segment, the societal, seems to be neither specifically accumulative nor specifically creative.

As we proceed to division into sub-segments however, no new significance of much moment appears. Classification becomes more manifold, preferential, and finally capricious. There are no operational results to aid us in choosing between one and another subdivisional scheme as the more useful. It appears that we have here got to the borders of the realm of mere common knowledge and common sense, without the specific methodology of a science to guide us, where therefore one opinion is presumably as good as another. A step farther and we are back at the rough-and-ready, table-of-contents listing of Wissler's "universal pattern," which neither he nor anyone else has ever been able to do anything with as a tool.

Even the three major segments—or four, with language added—do not exhaust the area of culture. Interstices remain over; and many cultural activities lap over from one to another major segment. Science, for instance, shares qualities with technology, but others with philosophy and religion in the value sphere. The segments must there-fore be viewed not as "areally" delimited and exclusive, like the provinces of a country, but rather as generative foci, or as tracts within each of which certain processes are differentially operative, coupled with a tendency toward clustering of particular activities characteristic of each.

Finally, there exists an anomalous situation under which the primarily social segment can be set off either more or less radically from the others. Anthropologists view societal forms and activities as an outright part of culture and as conditioned by and along with it. Sociologists, on the contrary, see society as primary, to which culture is related by some sort of extension, if not derivation. This unresolved divergence is the more remarkable in that anthropological and sociological theory seem now to be rather close together on other essential points, their differences lying largely in outlook, scope, and weighting of interest—such as the biological, linguistic, and historic proclivities of anthropology and the practical inclinations of sociology.

PART II

KINSHIP AND SOCIAL STRUCTURE

INTRODUCTION

THIS Part II of the book is concerned with a pair of related topics recognized and dealt with by both sociology and anthropology, though in rather surprisingly different ways. Five of the nine selections (Nos. 19, 22, 23, 24, 25) treat kinship, two (Nos. 26, 27) social structuring, and two (Nos. 20, 21) look both ways.

As for kinship, my attitude has been an atypical one that has no doubt seemed extreme to most of my colleagues. The real difference has been one in slant of interest, largely disguised by the fact that superficially they and I were handling the same kind of data and in much the same technical way. However, as we used the data for different purposes, our interpretations came out quite unlike. Each side therefore tended to consider the other in error. It is strange how long it took for us to begin to realize that we might both be right, but wrestling with different problems.

In 1871 Lewis H. Morgan opened the series of "Smithsonian Contributions to Knowledge" with his famous *Systems of Consanguinity*. This massive monograph sprang from an observation by Morgan on the Iroquois—in other words, from personal experience or "field work" with people of a different culture, a procedure that was to become characteristic of anthropological study. Morgan was struck by the fact that certain of the Iroquois terms for kindred had a different range of meaning from our own. For instance, the father's brother was not called by a term corresponding to our "uncle," but was himself a "father"; and analogously the mother's sister was a mother. The nearest Iroquois equivalent to our term "uncle" referred only to the mother's brother. This man's children and one's actual father's sister's children, but only they—whom it is now customary to distinguish as cross-cousins, because the sex "crosses over" between a mother and her brother, between a father and his sister—these children were denominated by a term which is the nearest Iroquois counterpart to our "cousin" but which really designates only cross-cousins. The two other kinds—"parallel cousins"—the Iroquois call simply "brothers" and "sisters." This sort of difference from our own usage is of course semantic, that is, a matter of meaning of words.

Beyond that, there is also a difference in meaning that can be generalized or abstracted into a system. Iroquois distinguishes between cross and parallel relationship for uncles and aunts as well as for cousins; English does not. We follow one principle of classification of kindred, Iroquois another; each is self-consistent and logical. Morgan called the Iroquois logic "classificatory," the English "descriptive"—a bit of ethnocentrism pardonable enough eighty years ago. The ethnocentrism—the mote in our own eye—lies in the fact that English also classifies, as when it includes the father's brother with the mother's brother in the blanket term "uncle," which of course really means "undifferentiated parent's brother."

Morgan went on to connect the Iroquois word usage with an Iroquois institution—their matrilineal clans. It was because of the primacy of the clan and its dominance over the family, he thought, that the mother's sister was so close to the mother that she could be identified terminologically with her; and that therefore her children, one's co-clanmates, were called one's brothers and sisters. Actually, this correlation between terms and institution must have been in Morgan's mind when he coined his designation "classificatory." A system to him was classificatory when its lumping, grouping, or classing together coincided with an institutional grouping. When there was no such correspondence with an institution, as in the case of the meaning of English "uncle," there was to him no particular "significance"—that is, ulterior significance—in the nomenclature, and it was merely denotive or "descriptive."

Morgan went on from here to a grand system of reconstructing the history of human society from promiscuity, through brother-sister and then group marriage, to clans and gentes, and finally our Western type of family. In *Systems of Consanguinity* he developed this speculative evolution and buttressed it with evidence taken from the kinship nomenclatures of peoples all over the world, which he assiduously collected or had compiled for him.

This was of course a procedure characteristic of the "evolutionistic" phase of anthropology as it began in 1861 [see Nos. 16, 17]. Morgan's ideas were also taken up by Engels and incorporated into the orthodox Marxian schema.

By contrast, it is interesting that neither then nor at any time since has sociology been seriously interested in Morgan's analysis of kinship designations or in his theory of social evolution. His views involved primitives, ultimate origins, the comparison of as many different human societies as possible, a ranging through history, and a place accorded our civilization that, though honorably terminal, was one only of first among equals—all of which things sociology was, if not averse to, at least not fundamentally interested in. It was an early example of the diversity in affects and objectives which has kept sociology and anthropology so largely apart in spite of a common framework

of theory and much overlapping of data. In fact, to sociologists accustomed to balance consideration of "the family" against that of the community, state, and church, the anthropologists' preoccupation with kinship term systems, distinctions of cross-cousins and kinds of uncles, and correlation with outlandish customs like exogamy, levirate, and other forms of prescribed or proscribed marriage, must have seemed a rather freakish hobby from which we would not learn how to extricate ourselves.

In line with the views set forth however crudely in selection No. 1, both the Morgan classificatory-descriptive distinction and the evolutionary profile which he deduced from it were anathema to me from the beginning. I disbelieved the whole construct as well as his procedure. I can see now why I disbelieved it. It was because my native and unconscious bents were toward quite different things: toward forms of culture and language as an end of understanding in themselves, not as a mere means of proving an intellectualized proposition. Morgan had reconstructed a history of human marriage and society. From the time I first knew of it, I sensed it as a pseudo-history. To be sure, I was later on to argue with Boas in favor of historical reconstruction, being ready to accept probabilities where he wanted certainties [Nos. 5, 6]. But I was arguing for reconstructed pasts *similar* to known presents—and multiple presents affording cross-perspectives or parallaxes. Morgan's reconstructions, like those of the other social evolutionists, were inferences from known present conditions to something past that was as *dissimilar* as possible. The eventuating schemes were logical enough, but they were insufficiently factual—factual as one gets a feeling, from sufficient reading of history for its own sake, of how human fact has a way of running.

So I got to thinking about kinship terminologies in what seemed to me a proper anthropological manner: that is, viewed in themselves, analytically and comparatively, as against a background ("context"), however shadowy, of total human practice. When a primitive people or the Chinese refuse to lump together the mother's brother and the father's brother into a nondescript "uncle," but differentiate these two relatives who are biologically distinct, logically distinct, and often function quite differently—what is it then, put conceptually, in which their two terms differ from our one? Obviously, in the fact that Iroquois and Chinese recognize the sex of the relative *connecting* one's self with one's parents' brothers—whereas we ignore it. Here, then, is a conceptual category, "sex of connecting relative," which can be wholly or partly present and semantically expressed, or absent and unexpressed, in languages and cultures. From here, a natural thing to do was to go on and see what other variably present and absent categories there might be in human kinship. Such are, for instance, sex of the relative denoted, about which English is consistently concerned, and sex of the speaker, about which it is wholly unconcerned—and therefore unaware of.

It so happens that kinship is a quite limited little universe held within a rigorous biological frame. The ultimate definition of any kinsman is in terms of biological ascent and descent. There is also a psychological limitation inherent in our speech faculty. While normally we all have, actually or potentially, hundreds of nearer and remote kinsfolk whose precise relationship to ourselves is unique at some one or several points, it is characteristic of the way our linguistic minds work, in grouping phenomena and concepts into words, that too many vocables would be difficult to learn, would be overprecise, a strain both in speaking and in listening, and a waste and disadvantage in most situa-

tions of living. It is plain, for instance, that such would be the case if a language had three or four hundred separate terms for kinsmen. If on the other hand it tried to operate with only five or six terms, it is obvious that these would necessarily be so inclusive as to be very inexact. It happens therefore that almost all languages have unconsciously settled on a kinship roster of between twelve or fifteen and fifty or sixty vocables. This range happens to be just about the same per language as that of those basic constituents of speech, the phonemes. There is no specific relation in this correspondence, kinship words and phonemes being quite different classes of linguistic phenomena and having quite different functions; other than that both ranges probably derive from the same set of limiting psychological factors in the underlying faculty for human speech.

Well, one result of this limitation was that the number of "categories" I could find in the languages I examined was also quite limited. In fact, it was only eight, plus one or two supplementary principles like conceptual or verbal reciprocity. It later turned out that there are only these eight that are of any consequence. This restriction appears to be again the result of the simplicity and compactness of the kinship universe: biologically we are always operating only with male, female, and offspring; and logically we remain within the framework of life, mating, generation, seniority within generation, and the necessity of including affinals through the spouse because these affinals are consanguine kin of one's own descendants. I have therefore always thought that the extrication of these kinship categories would have been completed by almost anyone who had begun to think about them at all. I feel that I deserve credit not for having made an "exhaustive" discovery, but for having had the luck of being endowed with an inveterate propensity to compare and classify, and of having applied this propensity to so cleanly delimited a subject as kinship terminology.

A paper I wrote in 1909, the first in the present part, No. 19, set forth the categories and went on to point out briefly that through them the kinship terminologies of peoples could be classified, descriptively as well as quantitatively, into natural types, and that these types seemed to occur areally; of which the unexpressed implication was that the types were historic growths. In modern parlance, kinship terminologies are pattern systems of semantic logic, highly variable in detail and historically derivable, but also classifiable. That was their primary interest to me. Emeneau[1] has recently discussed them as systems whose linguistic and nonlinguistic (sociocultural) classes and subclasses show a partial parallel fit. Greenberg[2] has examined them from the point of view of symbolic logic.

If I were a philosopher, I would probably – and wisely – have stopped here. As an anthropologist, in the face of Morgan, I could not well stop there; both because his primary segregation into classificatory and descriptive types did not hold water, and because it was easy to show that internal conceptual logic, such as of reciprocity, analogy, and consistency, was sufficiently frequent and strong to prevent sets of kinship terms being construed as mere reflections or indices of marriage or other social institutions. Therewith the whole Morgan speculative schema of origin and development of society seemed to me impaired or toppled. I continue to think so until today.

What did cause confusion was my fumbling of terminology. I should have said that kinship systems are linguistic patterns of logic, and that their uncritical or unrestrained use as if they were uncontaminated reflectors of past or present institutions was unsound and dangerous. They certainly possess an interest in themselves, and they do present problems of the relation of language and thought and of both to psychology. Instead of logic, however, I spoke of "psychology," and became intransigent in rebuttal: "Terms of relationship reflect psychology, not sociology." It would have been right to say that, as part of language, kin term systems reflect unconscious logic and conceptual patterning *as well as* social institutions. I fumbled the situation worse when subsequently I began to talk of "general tendencies" or "psychological tendencies"—meaning patterns of logic expressed in systems of word meanings —as contrasted with specific institutions named as specific causes of the particular denotations of terms.

In 1914, W. H. R. Rivers published a little book called *Kinship and Social Organization*, in which he argued against that part of my 1909 article which belittled the institutional origin of kin nomenclatures. Rivers had to write this booklet to clear the road for his larger *History of Melanesian Society*, in which he was to invert some of Morgan's conclusions but relied largely on Morgan's method of reconstructively inferring institutions from terminology. In the following year, Lowie reviewed the Rivers book, very fairly to him and to me.[3] In 1917, I answered Rivers[4]—temperately, I think—but, as the theoretical portion of the monograph in question is also controversial, it is not included here. Moreover, I continued the unfortunate use of "psychological" when it was evident that "logical" or "conceptually patterned" was what was at issue. Otherwise my reasoning and evidence then adduced seem to me sound and still valid.

There usually are deeper personal issues underlying differences of interpretation such as these. Rivers began as a laboratory physiologist who pushed on to psychology and then to ethnology. He was accordingly seeking deterministic proofs as rigorous and definite as in the exact sciences, to use his own words; and he found them in the determination of kinship by social institutions. He wanted to make social science a "true science." I came from humanistic literature, entered anthropology by the gate of linguistics, saw meaning in forms and their relations, but deeply distrusted a determinism that attributed specific, limited, but sufficient causes to cultural phenomena, as set forth in a number of the selections in Part I. Lowie had thought of becoming a chemist before he turned to anthropological problems. He was immensely stimulated by Rivers' *Kinship and Social Organization*, as he recently told me; and, while pointing out accurately where Rivers went too far in his arguments, as well as rejecting my own "universal negative,"[5] he looked forward to the correlation of terminologies and institutional organization as not only a duty but a satisfaction. Apparently I should have found considerably less satisfaction in such correlations, else I would probably have tried to establish some instead of analyzing out the categories. It seems fair to say that my prime interest was in delineating patterns in phenomena; Lowie's, in sound correlations, even if of limited scope; Rivers', in causal determinations supporting a large hypothesis; and Morgan's in a universal scheme at once causal and historical. I include these characterizations of motivation because they do seem to me to have considerably determined the varied conclusions reached.

On behalf of kinship systems, however, it seems to me that it must be conceded that though their analysis may tend to become technically forbidding, it must nevertheless be a precise and rich body of material which can provide stimulation and yield results as varied as the types of interpretation here sketched.

At any rate, I was to return repeated-ly to the subject.

The original "Zuni Kin and Clan" from which No. 20 is extracted contained nearly forty pages on kinship. But they are so full of detail that I have included here only three paragraphs on the use of kin terms within the clan.

No. 21, on kinship in the Philippines, returns to the subject of No. 19, of ten years before, but with more moderation. Correspondences of institutions and kinship are not only admitted but enumerated. The emphasis is now on comparison of *total patterns* of institutions and total patterns of kinship nomenclature. Morgan and Rivers had singled out *particular* terminological features as caused by specific usages. This difference between them and myself I continue to hold to as fundamental in the understanding of cultural manifestations. The causality that is involved in culture has normally accumulated so long and so intricately that on the whole very little of it can be specifically unraveled with authenticity. Boas was big enough to realize this. But the pioneers like Morgan, the men trained in laboratories like Rivers, the ruck of social scientists hoping somehow to imitate physics, kept and keep trying; and yet they achieve either only bits or constructs that are mainly unreal. It is the pattern rather than precise causation that is the meaningful result by and large achievable in the study of culture—as the history of linguistics should long ago have sufficed to teach us.

No. 22, of 1933, turns to China and strikes consciously at pattern. The Chinese kinship system consists of a basic nucleus of terms whose denotations are quite like those of many primitives; but to these have been added a series of metaphorical supplements or qualifiers that render the system as a whole as precisely denotive as most civilized Western and supposedly "descriptive" systems are slovenly.

No. 23 analyzes the kinship systems of five mutually unintelligible tribes sharing very similar, highly specialized institutions in an isolated corner of native California. Their terminologies show a welter of conceptual likenesses and unlikenesses. This chaos resolves into considerable order on the assumption of two quite different kinship patterns—one presumably of northern coastal origin, the other from the interior and south—having met in this area and interinfluenced each other in varying degrees. In this case I distinguished the patterns not only as ends in themselves but as instruments to unravel a complex historical situation. I believe that here lies one of the keys to historical reconstruction. Reconstruction of culture is sound in proportion as it is based on correct recognition of basic pattern, preferably abstracted from causality, since cause is an interest of another order and mainly distracting in this search. We have precedent for this situation in historical linguistics, where proper comparison is not of French and English with Hindi or Sanskrit but of proto-Germanic and proto-Italic with proto-Indo-Iranian—all themselves historically reconstructed patterns which are then compared in order to reach the deeper-level pattern of "super-reconstructed" original Indo-European. Or there is equal example in palaeontology, where the clearer definition of family patterns sharpens recognition of order patterns, and from these one goes on to classes and the interrelations of phyla. Or, more specifically, matured understanding of the tree shrew pattern has led to the transfer of this group from the Insectivores to the Primates, has corrected our comprehension of both these orders, and has probably carried the direct ancestry of man back one step farther.

Selection 24 is a discussion emanating from No. 23 and carried on with Radcliffe-Brown, which I include because it is conciliatory rather than polemical and because it is theoretical.

No. 25 on Athabascan kinship is another pattern reconstruction, or rather, a preliminary essay at such. In this, strictly linguistic considerations are more to the fore. The finding is that no pattern reconstruction, at least in the field of kinship nomenclature, can be complete or fully sound until it has taken account of the resistive conservatism, the brute inertia, of the languages of which such nomenclatures form part, however else they also function.

I hope that these selections will make clear that it is more than an odd addiction that has made so many anthropologists deal with kinship systems: these systems are clean-cut, made-to-order patterns of culture, speech, and conceptualization.

The two or three selections or articles on social structure speak more readily for themselves and need less comment here.

No. 20, retitled "Zuni Clan Functioning," is from my largest monograph on a still natively living culture. It has been included partly because, in contrast with much of my work, it emphasizes function rather than form, and integration more than analytic discrimination.

Nos. 26 and 27, twenty and more years later, are variations on the theme of what may be respectively basic or secondary in pattern of social structure, and what therefore is enduring or transient, essential or superstructural. Beginning so often with an interest in exotica and oddments, the study of culture has managed to catch in its net many conspicuous trivia or striking sports of primitive peoples. Not that these should be ignored; but fundamentals come first. Again it is a question of pattern. In any given case, are such mutations integral to basic social pattern, or manifestions of it, or mere ebullitions?

19. CLASSIFICATORY SYSTEMS OF RELATIONSHIP

1909

THE distinction between classificatory and descriptive systems of relationship has been widely accepted, and has found its way into handbooks and general literature. According to the prevalent belief the systems of certain nations or languages group together distinct relationships and call them by one name, and are therefore classifying. Other systems of consanguinity are said to indicate secondary differences of relationship by descriptive epithets added to their primary terms and to be therefore descriptive.

Nothing can be more fallacious than this common view. A moment's reflection is sufficient to show that every language groups together under single designations many distinct degrees and kinds of relationship. Our word brother includes both the older and the younger brother and the brother of a man and of a woman. It therefore embraces or classifies four relationships. The English word cousin denotes both men and women cousins; cousins on the father's or on the mother's side; cousins descended from the parent's brother or the parent's sister; cousins respectively older or younger than one's self, or whose parents are respectively older or younger than the speaker's parents; and cousins of men or women. Thirty-two different relationships are therefore denoted by this one English word. If the term is not strictly limited to the significance of first cousin, the number of distinct ideas that it is capable of expressing is many times thirty-two. Since then it is not only primitive people that classify or fail to distinguish relationships, the suspicion is justified that the current distinction between the two classes or systems of indicating relationship is subjective, and has its origin in the point of view of investigators, who, on approaching foreign languages, have been impressed with their failure to discriminate certain relationships between which the languages of civilized Europe distinguish, and who, in the enthusiasm of formulating general theories from such facts, have forgotten that their own languages are filled with entirely analogous groupings or classifications which custom has made so familiar and natural that they are not felt as such.

The total number of different relationships which can be distinguished is very large, and reaches at least many hundred. No language possesses different terms for all of these or even for any considerable proportion of them. In one sense it is obvious that a language must be more classificatory as the number of its terms of relationship is smaller. The number of theoretically possible relationships remaining constant, there must be more ideas grouped under one term in proportion as the number of terms is less. Following the accepted understanding of what constitutes classificatory consanguinity, English, with its twenty terms of relationship, must be not less but more classificatory than the languages of all primitive people who happen to possess twenty-five, thirty, or more terms.

It is clear that if the phrase classificatory consanguinity is to have any meaning it must be sought in some more discriminating way. The single fact that another people group together various relationships which our language distinguishes does not make their system classificatory. If there is a general and fundamental difference between the systems of relationship of civilized and uncivilized people, its basis must be looked for in something more exact than the rough-and-ready expressions of subjective point of view that have been customary.

It is apparent that what we should try to deal with is not the hundreds or thousands of slightly varying relationships that are expressed or can be expressed by the various languages of man, but the principles or categories of relationship which underlie these. Eight such categories are discernible.

1. *The difference between persons of the same and of separate generations.*—The distinctions between father and grandfather, between uncle and cousin, and between a person and his father, involve the recognition of this category.

2. *The difference between lineal and collateral relationship.*—When the father and the father's brother are distinguished, this category is operative. When only one term is employed for brother and cousin, it is inoperative.

3. *Difference of age within one generation.*—The frequent distinction between the older and the younger brother is an instance. In English this category is not operative.

4. *The sex of the relative.*—This distinction is carried out so consistently by English, the one exception being the foreign word cousin, that the discrimination is likely to appear self-evident. By many people, however, many relationships are not distinguished for sex. Grandfather and grandmother, brother-in-law and sister-in-law, father-in-law and mother-in-law, and even such close relationships as son and daughter, are expressed respectively by single words.

5. *The sex of the speaker.*—Unrepresented in English and most European languages, this category is well known to be of importance in many other languages. The father, mother, brother, sister, and more distant relatives may receive one designation from a man and another from his sister.

6. *The sex of the person through whom relationship exists.*—English does not express this category. In consequence we frequently find it necessary to explain whether an uncle is a father's or a mother's brother, and whether a grandmother is paternal or maternal.

7. *The distinction of blood relatives from connections by marriage.*—While this distinction is commonly expressed by most languages, there are occasional lapses; just as in familiar English speech the father-in-law is often spoken of as father. Not strictly within the domain of relationship, but analogous to the occasional failure to express this category, is the frequent ignoring on the part of primitive people of the difference between actual relatives and fictitious clan or tribal relatives.

8. *The condition of life of the person through whom relationship exists.*—The relationship may be either of blood or by marriage; the person serving as the bond of relationship may be alive or dead, married or no longer married. Many North American Indians refrain from using such terms as "father-in-law" and "mother-in-law" after the wife's death or separation. Some go so far as to possess terms restricted to such severed relationship. It is natural that the uncle's relation to his orphaned nephew should tend to be somewhat different from his relation to the same boy while his natural protector, his father, was living. Distinct terms are therefore sometimes found for relatives of the uncle and aunt group after the death of a parent.

The adjoined table indicates the representation of the eight categories, and the degree to which they find expression, respectively in English and in several of the Indian languages of North America.

It appears that English gives expression to only four categories. With the exception, however, of the one and foreign word cousin, every term in English involves the recognition of each of these four categories. All the Indian languages express from six to eight categories. Almost all of them recognize seven. But in all the Indian languages the majority of the categories occurring are expressed in only part of the terms of relationship found in the language. There are even Indian languages, such as Pawnee and Mohave, in which not a single one of the seven or eight categories finds expression in every term.

total number of terms of relationship employed by them is approximately the same as in English. The addition of only one category to those found in English normally doubles the number of terms required to give full expression to the system; and the presence of three additional categories multiplies the possible total by about eight. As the number of terms occurring in any of the Indian languages under consideration is not much more than half greater than in English, and sometimes is not greater at all, it is clear that at least some of their

	ENG-LISH	N.A. INDIAN					CALIFORNIA INDIAN						
		Arap-aho	Da-kota	Paw-nee	Skoko-mish	Chi-nook	Yuki	Pomo	Washo	Mi-wok	Yo-kuts	Lui-seño	Mo-have
No. of terms........	21*	20	31	19	18	28	24	27	28	24	28	34	35
Generation.........	21	20	31	11	13	23	24	21	27	24	22	30	26
Blood or marriage...	21	19	31	17	18	26	24	27	28	24	28	32	34
Lineal or collateral...	21	10	20	5	11	25	24	21	28	18	26	34	28
Sex of relative......	20	18	29	17	2	12	16	21	20	20	17	18	22
Sex of connecting relative.............	0	6	6	2	0	20	13	13	14	10	14	19	21
Sex of speaker......	0	3	18	4	0	15	3	3	10	2	12	10	14
Age in generation...	0	3	7	2	2	2	3	4	4	4	4	12	8
Condition of connecting relative.......	0	0	0	0	8	1	0	0	0	0	†	°	1

* All terms are omitted, such as great-grandfather, great-uncle, and second cousin, which are not generally used in ordinary speech and exist principally as a reserve available for specific discrimination on occasion.
† Terms denoting relatives by marriage undergo a vocalic change to indicate the death of the connecting relative.

While in English the degree of recognition which is accorded the represented categories is indicable by a percentage of 100 in all cases but one, when it is 95, in Pawnee corresponding percentages range variously from about 10 to 90, and in Mohave from 5 to 95. All the other Indian languages, as compared with English, closely approach the condition of Pawnee and Mohave.

It is clear that this difference is real and fundamental. English is simple, consistent, and, so far as it goes, complete. The Indian systems of relationship all start from a more elaborate basis but carry out their scheme less completely. This is inevitable from the fact that the

categories must find only very partial expression.

In short, as far as the expression of possible categories is concerned, English is less complete than any of the Indian languages; but as regards the giving of expression to the categories which it recognizes, English is more complete. In potentiality, the English scheme is poorer and simpler; but from its own point of view it is both more complete and more consistent. As English may evidently be taken as representative of European languages, it is in this point that the real difference is to be found between the systems that have been called classificatory and those that have been called descriptive.

The so-called descriptive systems express a small number of categories of relationship completely; the wrongly-named classificatory systems express a larger number of categories with less regularity. Judged from its own point of view, English is the less classificatory; looked at from the Indian point of view it is the more classificatory, inasmuch as in every one of its terms it fails to recognize certain distinctions often made in other languages; regarded from a general and comparative point of view, neither system is more or less classificatory.

In short, the prevalent idea of the classificatory system breaks down entirely under analysis. And in so far as there is a fundamental difference between the languages of European and of less civilized peoples in the method of denoting relationship, the difference can be determined only on the basis of the categories described and can be best expressed in terms of the categories.

A tendency toward reciprocal expression is sometimes of importance and may influence the degree to which categories are given expression. Reciprocal terms are such that all the persons included in the relationship expressed by one term call by one name all the persons who apply this term to them. In the most extreme form of reciprocity the two groups of relatives use the same term. The paternal grandparents call their sons' children, whether boys or girls, by the same term which these children, both boys and girls, apply to their fathers' parents. Nevertheless, the reciprocal relation is just as clear, though less strikingly expressed, when each of the groups uses a different term for the other. Our English words father and child, or brother and sister, are not reciprocal, for the term child is employed also by the mother, and brother is used by the brother as well as by the sister. In fact the only reciprocal term in English is cousin. The tendency toward reciprocal expression is developed in many Indian languages. It is particularly strong in California. In some languages this tendency has brought it

about that different categories are involved in the terms applied to a pair of mutual relationships. The term father's sister indicates the sex of the relative but not of the speaker. The exact reciprocal of father's sister is woman's brother's child. This term, however, does not recognize the sex of the relative indicated, but does imply the sex of the speaker. The two reciprocal terms therefore each involve a category which the other does not express. If the same categories were represented in the two terms, brother's daughter would correspond to father's sister and exact reciprocity would be impossible. When, therefore, the terms found are father's sister and woman's brother's child, it is clear that the tendency toward the establishment of exactly reciprocal terms has been stronger than the feeling favoring the consistent use or neglect of certain categories; in other words, the extent to which certain categories are expressed has been determined by the vigor of the reciprocal tendency.

The categories serve also to indicate the leading characteristics of systems of the same general order. It is obvious, for instance, that the most important difference between Dakota and Arapaho is the strong tendency of the former to recognize the sex of the speaker. Chinook is notable for laying more stress on the sex of the speaker and of the connecting relation than on the sex of the relative—no doubt owing to the fact that the sex of the relative is indicable by purely grammatical means. General differences such as naturally occur between the languages of one region and of another can also be expressed in terms of the categories. All the California systems, for instance, lay much more stress upon the sex of the connecting relative than do any of the Plains languages examined. The Plains systems are conspicuous for their weak development of the distinction between lineal and collateral relationship, this finding expression in two-thirds of all cases in Dakota, half in Arapaho, one-fourth in Pawnee. In seven California languages the corresponding values lie between three-fourths and complete expression. The method can be applied successfully even in the case of smaller and contiguous geographical areas. Of the seven California languages Luiseño and Mohave are spoken in southern California. Their systems show a unity as compared with the systems of the five languages from northern and central California. Both the southern California languages have a greater number of terms; both are stronger in the expression of the categories of the sex of the connecting relative and of age within the same generation; and both are weaker in the category of sex of the relative, than the others. Again, Chinook and Skokomish, both of the North Pacific Coast, are alike in indicating the condition of the connecting relative and in failing, on account of the possession of grammatical sex gender, to distinguish the sex of relatives themselves in many terms of relationship. There is a very deep-going difference between them, however, in the fact that Skokomish is as free as English from recognizing the sex of the speaker and of connecting relatives, while Chinook generally expresses both categories. In short, the categories present a means of comparing systems of terms of relationship along the basic lines of their structure and of expressing their similarities and differences without reference to individual terms or details.

The reason why the vague and unsatisfactory idea of a classificatory system of consanguinity has found such wide acceptance is not to be sought in any primary interest in designations of relationship as such, but in the fact that terms of relationship have usually been regarded principally as material from which conclusions as to the organization of society and conditions of marriage could be inferred. If it had been more clearly recognized that terms of relationship are determined primarily by linguistic factors, and are only occasionally, and then indirectly, affected by social circumstances, it would probably long ago have been generally realized that the difference between descriptive and classificatory systems is subjective and superficial. Nothing is more precarious than the common method of deducing the recent existence of social or marital institutions from a designation of relationship. Even when the social condition agrees perfectly with expressions of relationship, it is unsafe to conclude without corroborative evidence that these expressions are a direct reflection or result of the condition.

In the Dakota language, according to Riggs, there is only one word for grandfather and father-in-law. Following the mode of reasoning sometimes employed, it might be deduced from this that these two relationships were once identical. Worked out to its implications, the absurd conclusion would be that marriage with the mother was once customary among the Sioux.

In the same language the words for woman's male cousin and for woman's brother-in-law have the same radical, differing only in a suffix. Similar reasoning would induce in this case that marriage of cousins was or had been the rule among the Sioux, a social condition utterly opposed to the basic principles of almost all Indian society.

The use of such identical or similar terms for distinct relationships is due to a considerable similarity between the relationships. A woman's male cousin and her brother-in-law are alike in sex, are both of opposite sex from the speaker, are of the same generation as herself, and are both collateral, so that they are similar under four categories. In view of the comparative paucity of terms as compared with possible relationships, it is entirely natural that the same word, or the same stem, should at times be used to denote two relationships having as much in common as these two.

No one would assume that the colloquial habit in modern English of speaking of the brother-in-law as brother implies anything as to form of marriage, for logically the use of the term could only be an indication of sister marriage. It is easily conceivable that in the future development of English the more cumbersome of these two terms might come into complete disuse in daily life and the shorter take its place, without the least change in social or marital conditions.

The causes which determine the formation, choice, and similarities of terms of relationship are primarily linguistic. Whenever it is desired to regard terms of relationship as due to sociological causes and as indicative of social conditions, the burden of proof must be entirely with the propounder of such views.

Even the circumstances that the father's brother is frequently called father is not necessarily due to or connected with the custom of the levirate; nor can group marriage be inferred from the circumstance that there is frequently no other term for mother's sister than mother. A woman and her sister are more alike than a woman and her brother, but the difference is conceptual, in other words linguistic, as well as sociological. It is true that a woman's sister can take her place in innumerable functions and relations in which a brother cannot; and yet a woman and her sister, being of the same sex, agree in one more category of relationship than the same woman and her brother, and are therefore more similar in relationship and more naturally denoted by the same term. There are so many cases where the expression of relationship cannot have been determined by sociological factors and must be purely psychological, as in the instances just discussed, that it is fair to require that the

preference be given to the psychological cause, or that this be admitted as of at least equal probability, even in cases where either explanation is theoretically possible and supporting evidence is absent.

On the whole it is inherently very unlikely in any particular case that the use of identical terms for similar relationships can ever be connected with such special customs as the levirate or group marriage. It is a much more conservative view to hold that such forms of linguistic expression and such conditions are both the outcome of the unalterable fact that certain relationships are more similar to one another than others. On the one hand this fact has led to certain sociological institutions; on the other hand, to psychological recognitions and their expression in language. To connect the institutions and the terms causally can rarely be anything but hazardous. It has been an unfortunate characteristic of the anthropology of recent years to seek in a great measure specific causes for specific events, connection between which can be established only through evidence that is subjectively selected. On wider knowledge and freedom from motive it is becoming increasingly apparent that causal explanations of detached anthropological phenomena can be but rarely found in other detached phenomena, and that it is even difficult to specify the most general tendencies that actuate the forms taken by culture, as the immediate causes of particular phenomena.

The following conclusions may be drawn:

1. The generally accepted distinction between descriptive and classificatory systems of terms of relationship cannot be supported.

2. Systems of terms of relationship can be properly compared through an

examination of the categories of relationship which they involve and of the degree to which they give expression to these categories.

3. The fundamental difference between systems of terms of relationship of Europeans and of American Indians is that the former express a smaller number of categories of relationship than the latter and express them more completely.

4. Terms of relationship reflect psychology, not sociology. They are determined primarily by language and can be utilized for sociological inferences only with extreme caution.

20. ZUNI CLAN FUNCTIONING
1917

KINSHIP TERMS AMONG CLAN MEMBERS

THE Zuni apply kinship terms to all clan mates. But true blood relationship and clan relationship are never confused in the native mind, however confusing the identity of terminology may appear to us. Ministers of religion and of social reform among ourselves have a habit of dealing widely in words like "brother" and "sister" without even making us think of kinship. The Zuni state of mind appears to be very similar. One knows perfectly well who is one's blood relative and who is not. The definiteness of that knowledge in fact is what makes the wider use of the terms possible without inconvenience. A small child knows nothing of clans or his own clan affiliations; but he knows the grandfather who takes him up to play, and the man or men in the house, or constantly visiting in the house, whom he calls kyakkya. Later, he comes to call other men, with whom he is but little in touch, kyakkya also; and in time he learns that the former are his iannikyinnawe or kin and the latter his hamme or members of something called his annota or clan. By the time he is grown, there is no possibility of uncertainty or error. Each individual's personal status with relation to one's self is clear and fixed, and it matters very little what any and all of them are called. The case is very much like that of the occasional American who addresses his wife as "mother" or "sister" or "sis": it is exactly because she is his wife that he can afford to call her sister. That he speaks to her as "sister" and not as "uncle" has undoubtedly a good psychological reason. It is the way the human mind works, or, we might better say, the human mind expressed in its social-channel language; but there is no institutional factor connected with marriage or descent that determines the choice of "mother" or "sister." I cannot see anything else in the Zuni application of kinship terms to clan members.

I realize that this is not the interpretation commonly put on phenomena of this kind in many ethonological quarters. But it seems the only reasonable and unconstrained interpretation of the Zuni facts; and I believe it to be the wisest explanation for facts of a similar nature in general, until something develops, in each particular case, that may demand revision of opinion.

If Zuni kinship terminology had originated in the clans and was only secondarily applied to blood relatives, it would have to be assumed that the religious fraternity was also older than the family: for every member of one's fraternity is a brother, a father, or a son; or, if a woman, a corresponding female "relative." If, on the other hand, kinship terms in the fraternity are secondary, it becomes exceedingly difficult to see why the clan terminology should not also be mere subsequent applications extended from the blood kindred. The only reason for not accepting the alternative would be the demonstrable fact, or the conviction, that the clan was more fundamental, and therefore presumably earlier, than the family. For Zuni this fundamentality appears out of question: family life is too intense and its manifestations too ever present, clan functions too remote and vague, to make even a theory of clan priority tenable. . . .

RELIGIOUS FUNCTIONS OF CLANS

One of the matters of greatest interest concerning the Pueblo clan is its relation to the religious society or fraternity. That such connection exists in some measure, is indubitable. The very resemblance in size, in name or totemic reference, in the fact of organization as part of a scheme, must inevitably cause an approach and partial assimilation that results in certain connections. The clan and the fraternity can be viewed as expressions of two distinct needs or impulses, one social, the other religious; but this fundamental diversity of direction would not prevent one influencing the other, or both taking the same color and similar outlines under the impress of the general culture in which they flourished.

But it is superficial to assume that because the Pueblo clan and fraternity reveal certain associations, they are at bottom one, and that all discrepancies between them are only the distortions due to the meaningless accidents of time. On the ground of theory I could no more believe that the Pueblo fraternities are merely clans ceremonially organized than I can adhere to the view that the clans were once separate local communities.

The question cannot however be settled or even argued with much profit on the basis of opinion, and what is needed for progress toward its solution is facts. We must therefore be grateful to Dr. Fewkes for having presented a valuable body of specific evidence on one aspect of the problem among the Hopi. He gives most of the male and part of the female membership, by clan affiliation, of the fraternities at Walpi. Each of these religious bodies is traditionally linked with a clan or group of clans, which is supposed to have founded or introduced the fraternity and its ceremonies. . . .

It is clear from the statistics that there is a very slender tendency for the traditional founding clan to be more heavily represented in its fraternity, proportionally, than other clans; and that, conversely, the members of a clan incline slightly more to membership in the society traditionally associated with their clan than to membership in others. But the predominant impress of the figures is in the other direction, namely, toward the conviction that membership in all fraternities is shared, and nearly equally, by members of all clans. Thus Horn has only 3 members out of 10 in the Antelope society; Snake, 7 out of 35 in the Snake society; Flute, 3 out of 11 in the Flute society; Rabbit-Tobacco, 6 of 34 in the Tataukyamu; Cloud, 7 of 25 in Kwakwantu; besides which there are three societies associated with a clan group which is extinct. The only exception are the six Cloud people among eight recorded Lalakoñtu members; but there the data are avowedly very imperfect. The results are the same when the figures are read the other way around: 21 of 28 religious memberships of Snake clan people are in fraternities other than the Snake society, 11 out of 12 for Horn, 2 of 11 for Flute, and so on. Even the Cloud clan has 13 memberships in its two associated societies, but 23 in other fraternities.

I cannot therefore agree with Dr. Fewkes in accepting the elaborated native view that the Snake society ceremonies were originally a "zoötotemic" clan ritual of the Snake clan, and that subsequently "the advent of other families . . . changed the social connections of the personnel" of the society and altered the purpose of the ritual, "so that at present it is a prayer for rain and for the growth of corn—a secondary development due mainly to an arid environment." That this interpretation is logically possible is evident enough. But it is precisely something to be demonstrated instead of postulated. . . .

When now we turn to Zuni, there is

a significant statement by Mrs. Stevenson. . . . I am able to confirm Mrs. Stevenson's verdict in the fullest degree. The fraternity affiliations of the 56 members of the Coyote clan are distributed as follows: 17 memberships in 10 fraternities, with 3 fraternities not represented. The largest number of Coyote people in any one society is 3. It is particularly significant that there is only 1 Coyote clan member of the Sanniakyakwe; for the Sanniakyakwe or "Hunters" are often loosely though improperly referred to as Suskikwe, which as "coyote people" can mean either "coyote clan" or "coyote fraternity"; in fact, Suskikwe is probably the more frequent designation of the society in popular usage. A connection of this clan and fraternity would therefore seem specifically indicated; yet is not at all borne out by the facts. . . .

In recording the census of the Tobacco clan, I secured also the fraternity affiliations of men married into the clan. In this case the household solidarity comes out even more clearly. . . . It is clear what happens. A person belongs to a society. One of the family falls sick—a husband, wife, child, sister's child, or a brother or a mother's brother married out. A fraternity is to be called in to cure the patient and receive him or her into its ranks subsequently. Two times out of three, the fraternity is chosen which already has affiliations in that family. An Uhhuhukwe thinks of the Uhhuhukwe to treat his nephew or wife or child rather than the Ne'wekwe or Makkyets'annakwe in which he may happen to have no relatives. In short, it is blood relationship, and beyond this common home life, that most frequently determine choice of fraternity; not clan pertinence. We are confronted by another instance of kinship and the house, in other words, familiar personal association, being the decisive factor at Zuni in affairs which among other clan-

divided peoples have generally been assumed to be ruled by clan laws and clan connections. . . .

GOVERNMENTAL FUNCTIONS OF CLANS

. . . Since the source of all Zuni authority, sacred and profane, lies in certain priests; since these are representative of their priesthoods; and since these priesthoods, in native opinion, receive their origin, venerability, permanence, and even name from the ettowe fetishes with which they are associated, the depth to which these fetishes underlie all Zuni life becomes once more apparent.

Second, the distribution and balancing of civil offices among the clans is characteristic of Zuni procedure. A particular priesthood or ceremonial function may be limited to members of a particular clan; but the total dispositions as to government evince a feeling for an approximately equal representation of each clan in public affairs, or at least a representation roughly proportional to its numerical strength. Once more we gain the conviction that the Zuni view their clans not so much as essential units of consanguinity or locality which are conglomerated into a mass while retaining their separate privileges and activities, but rather as co-ordinated divisions, with special, but parallel and equivalent, functions in a communal entity.

For the choice of the word "equivalent" in the last statement, I am indebted to Dr. A. A. Goldenweiser. It appeals to me strongly that the crux of the whole question of what a clan really is rests in the contained idea. If clans were or had once been separate units, they should possess unequal privileges and different functions, like castes or classes or guilds. Now the overwhelming rule is that they do not exercise distinct kinds of functions, but essentially are equivalent. The only alternative interpretation remaining is that they once were separate bodies but that since their union an equivalating tendency has assimilated them. But, once an equivalating tendency is posited, there is no valid reason, in fact it is gratuitous and arbitrary, to assume that the tendency is only late and secondary; and if it be granted that the tendency is old and primary, there is no logical need for bringing originally distinct clan entities into the argument at all. All that remains to be accounted for is the inclination toward subdivision; and this seems to me to present no difficulty wherever an impulse to systematization, as evinced for instance in secret societies or the Zuni priesthoods, is present in any strength. It is not even necessary to fall back seriously upon local groups, blood groups, or nicknames. A tendency toward systematization might more or less temporarily make use of such accidental or extrinsic groups as a starting point, and the differences of clan organization among various nations may well be due in part to the diversity of such associated phenomena. But, given the systematizing and coordinating impulse, nothing else is required: it would seize upon the most trivial suggestions and break itself a channel of its own. . . .

PLACE OF THE CLAN IN ZUNI SOCIETY

It is impossible to proceed far into the complexities of the social and religious organization of the Zuni without being impressed with the perception that this community is as solidly welded and cross-tied as it is intricately ramified. However far one form of division be followed, it branches off by innumerable contacts into others, without ever absorbing these. Four or five different planes of systematization cross-cut each other and thus preserve for the whole society an integrity that would be speedily lost if the planes merged and thereby inclined to encourage segregation and fission. The clans, the frater-

nities, the priesthoods, the kivas, in a measure the gaming parties, are all dividing agencies. If they coincided, the rifts in the social structure would be deep; by countering each other, they cause segmentations which produce an almost marvelous complexity, but can never break the national entity apart.

Let us take an individual in this society. First to him as to us, in time and probably ultimately in importance, are the ties of blood and of household association. But, basic as these are, they are scarcely organized into a definite pattern: the personal element still outweighs the institutions. But beyond is the clan, into which the Zuni is born. It includes half his kin, indeed, but only half; and it includes a large group of persons outside the lines of blood. The clan, in turn, is more or less associated, directly or through certain fetishes and the houses that hold them, with certain priestly offices. Our Zuni may become a priest of a fetish connected with his clan; or, through kinship running counter to the clan scheme, or through mere personal selection, he can be made a member of a priesthood not connected with his clan. If, as is still more likely, he is not a priest himself, he is almost certain to possess a relation to certain priests through the medium of clan and to others through kinship. His kiva is one of six that perform the outward ritual of which the priests hold the most sacred keys; but there is no connection of personnel between kiva and priests. Our individual is a member of the kiva to which the husband of the woman belonged who first touched him on his entrance into the world. Thus father and son, mother's brother and nephew, the several associates of one priesthood, co-members of a fraternity, are likely to pertain to different and more or less rivalizing kivas. The fraternity is entered occasionally by choice; usually by the affiliation and consequent predilection of the near relatives who summon its medical assistance in case of the individual's sickness. The racing and gaming parties are little known; but everything points to their being in the main independent of every other mode of organization.

Opposed to this actual Zuni condition is a putative type of social organization which has sometimes been ascribed to the Pueblo Indians and more often implicitly assumed for them—and the same is true of primitive nations in other parts of the world. This hypothesis predicates that a group of kinsmen, whom we may call A, originally from a locality A, now constitute clan A of their tribe; and that, essentially if not wholly, they compose the membership of secret society A, of priesthood A, and of club or kiva A. The organization actually found at Zuni, however, differs at every point. There is no evidence that the members of clan A have come from a separate locality A. They comprise the kin groups a, b, c, d; they furnish members to fraternities A, B, C, D; to the priesthoods L, M, N, O; and to the kivas R, S, T, U. Thus a given individual of clan A may be of kin group b, father's clan C, fraternity D, priesthood L, and kiva U; his next clan mate that we encounter will be perhaps of blood group d, father's clan E, fraternity B, priesthood O, kiva S. By the time the tribe has been gone through, every clan, society, priesthood, and kiva is thus likely to be connected, in the person of one or several individuals, with every other, and each with each in about equal degree; but—and this is the significant point—the connections are almost wholly through individuals as individuals, and with reference to the national organization as a solidary scheme. Connection between group and group as such is always faint, often lacking; the plan of the fabric throughout seems calculated to avoid it.

21. KINSHIP IN THE PHILIPPINES
1919

RECONSTRUCTION OF THE ANCIENT SYSTEM

FILIPINO kinship systems appear to reduce to the following former scheme:

1, ama, father.
2, ina, mother.
3, anak or wata, child, nephew, niece, child-in-law.
4, probably a term for older sibling: kaka.
5, probably a term for younger sibling; possibly ari.
6, probably a generic term for sibling, though this, unless it is ari, is scarcely recoverable from the Philippine data alone. The concept, like the words, may be secondary; but its wide prevalence indicates antiquity.
7, apo, possibly nono as alternative, self-reciprocal for grandparents and grandchildren.
8, possibly bapa for paternal and maternal uncle, father-in-law, stepfather, that is, males of the father's generation generically, not excluding the father himself.
9, possibly a corresponding term for females of the mother's generation.
10, 11, one or two terms for brother-in-law and sister-in-law.
12, perhaps a term for parent-in-law.
13, asawa, spouse.

Other relationships are expressed by nonkinship words secondarily given a kinship reference in local usage; by including the more remote relationships in the significance of the above primary terms; or by affix or composite derivatives from the primary terms.

The simplicity and adaptibility of this system are obvious. It operates with its meager resources by merging most collateral with lineal kin; by mostly treating connections by marriage as if they were blood kin, with the implication that spouses are to be considered as being socially like one person; by not distinguishing sex, except in parents, perhaps in uncles and aunts, and possibly in siblings-in-law; and by nowhere bifurcating, that is, discriminating the line of descent, the sex through which relationship exists. The primary consideration is generation; this is slightly elaborated by hesitating and inconsistent introduction of the factors of collaterality, sex, marriage, and absolute age. Reciprocity is of moment. Self-reciprocal terms occur in every Filipino language, and in the Philippines as a whole are found in every class of relationships except the parent-child group.

LINES OF DEVELOPMENT OF THE
ANCIENT SYSTEM

Intertribal divergences, both as regards specific concepts and the words used, are considerable. This fact indicates an active play of etymological and semantic influences. But departures from the general logical scheme are much slighter, so as to suggest that the subconscious pattern of conceptualization has been rather tenaciously adhered to.

This is rather remarkable in view of the fact that pagan, Mohammedan, and Christian peoples, coast and mountain dwellers, literate and illiterate tribes, are involved; and that the degree of exposure of the several Philippine nationalities to Indian, Arab, and Spanish cultural influences has been extremely diverse. It is true that the social fabric as such has probably altered less in the Philippines in the past thousand years than religions and knowledge, and certainly less than material arts and industries. But there have been fairly profound variations of general civilization;

and theoretically these would seem as capable of modifying a scheme of kinship reckoning as are social institutions in their narrower sense. That these variations of general civilization have affected the scheme so little, except in superficial details, shows that a pattern of semantic classification for thinking and speaking of blood relationship may sometimes possess a surprising historical tenacity. It is tempting in the present case to attribute this tenacity in part to the simplicity of the principles on which the system is based and the comparatively strict consistency with which they can consequently be adhered to.

It is true that there are some differences of kinship system corresponding to the differences of level or type of culture: what is interesting is that they are proportionally so small. The pagan systems of northern Luzon are perhaps somewhat nearest to the original scheme, if the attempted reconstruction of this is approximately correct. Among these, however, the extremely simple systems, as represented by Ifugao, may be partly the result of a progressive and extreme process of reduction. The pagans of Mindanao, if the Subanun are typical, perhaps stand nearest to the pagans of Luzon, though the data are too imperfect for any very valid conclusion. The Mohammedans of Mindanao are still rather close to the generic scheme. If the existence of specific terms for uncle, aunt, and older and younger siblings proves to be ancient, the Moro seem not to have departed more than the Luzon pagans from the original system; if otherwise, Malay influence on the Moro is indicated. The Christian peoples, so far as the Tagalog may adequately stand for them, have diverged principally in developing special terms for connections by marriage. This may well be due to the influence of Christian law and European usage.

The Malay system, although indubitably resting on the same foundation, has plainly come to differ more from all the Philippine systems than these differ from one another, not only in actual terminology, but in the introduction of several new methods or points of view. Such a divergence is expectable from the more thorough Mohammedanization of the Malays and their much freer contacts with foreign civilizations.

CORRESPONDENCE OF INSTITUTIONS AND THE KINSHIP SCHEME

The principles characterizing native society in the Philippines are:

1. A lack of political structure or sense, except where foreign influence, chiefly Indian or Mohammedan, is clear.

2. The place of political organization is taken by an organization on the basis of actual kinship, modified secondarily by community of residence or economic interests.

3. The stratification of society into wealthy, poor, and economically deficient is emphasized by the translation of these classes into nobility, free, and slaves.

4. There is no chieftainship other than as based on the combination of personal qualities with pre-eminence among the nobility, that is, precedence in wealth. Exceptions are again due to Mohammedan— or Christian—influence.

5. Property being wholly transmitted by inheritance except for some consumption in sacrifice; and rank inclining to follow wealth, there is a strong tendency for social status to be hereditary.

6. The mechanism of law is economic instead of political. Legal claims are enforced by the threat or exercise of violence, and adjusted by transfers of property.

7. There are no totems, clans, nor any system of exogamy between artificial kin groups.

8. Women are socially the equals of men. This is clear from their position in marriage, descent, and the holding of property. The division of labor between the sexes is on a physiological rather than a social basis.

The distinctive traits thus are the importance of blood kinship and of economic factors, the insignificance of political and exogamous or "arbitrary" aspects of society, and the nondifferentiation of the sexes. These features reveal Filipino society as simple and "natural" in character; that is, close to its biological substratum, and comparatively free from the purely social creations or elaborations that tend to flourish in many other parts of the world [see Nos. 26 and 27].

The kinship term schemes accord well with these institutions. The equality of the sexes is reflected in the paucity of the sex-limited terms of relationship and in the total absence of any terms implying the sex of the ego or person to whom the relationship exists. The failure to separate kindred in the male and female line may be connectible with the same equalizing of the sexes in actual life; or with the want of clans and other artificial exogamic groups which in order to maintain their identity must reckon descent unilaterally; or with both factors. The organization of society on a basis of blood is likely to have something to do with the disinclination to distinguish lineal and collateral relatives. Even the tendency to treat the spouse's kin as blood kin may have some connection with the social balance or nondifferentiation of the sexes. At any rate, where the social status of men and women is markedly and fortifiedly distinct, it seems extremely unlikely that a man could feel his wife's father to be sufficiently identical with his own father for him to call him father: the psychology of the terminology would clash with the psychology of the relation as it does not clash in Filipino life.

THEORETICAL PRINCIPLES INVOLVED

As to the question whether kinship terminologies may be construed as reflecting institutional conditions or rather as expressing patterned systems of concepts, the present material points to the following inferences.

Kinship systems are considerably but superficially modified by linguistic and even dialectic factors. The effect of these factors is great enough to make the prediction of any specific institution from any specific term or set of terms venturesome. Institutions and terminologies unquestionably parallel or reflect each other at least to the degree that a marked discrepance of plan is rare. Institutions probably shape terminologies causally, but in the main by influencing or permitting a logical scheme. In a sense this logical scheme underlies both institution and terminology, so that the correlation between them, although actual, can be conceived as indirect. Development of particular terms or their denotation under the influence of institutions may occur to a greater or less extent, but is constantly liable to distortion by linguistic factors. The influence on kinship terminology of general levels of culture—those other than narrowly social or institutional ones—seems not to have been seriously examined. The present case shows that such influence may be rather less significant than might be expected in a transition from a state of comparative savagery to one of comparative civilization.

IN THE last number of the *American Anthropologist* for 1932, Chen and Shryock contribute an article on Chinese Terms of Relationship which is both valuable for its material and penetrating in its analysis. In one respect their interpretation can be carried further. The Chinese system appears to consist of a "classificatory,"[1] that is nondescriptive, base, which has been made over by additions into a "descriptive" system similar in its working to the English one—in fact, is more precisely and successfully descriptive than this. Relationships through males and through females have not been merged as in western European systems; distinction between elder and younger siblings has been kept; and at the same time the number of describing terms is greater than in Europe. The consequence is that the Chinese distinguish precisely, by terms or phrases of specific denotation, a greater number of relationships than we do, without having recourse to circumlocutory or enumerative phrases; and at the same time they have kept more of their former presumably nondescriptive base. In short, their system shows how a nondescriptive system was made over into a descriptive one by devices different from and independent of our own, yet very similar so far as their effect or functioning goes. The pointing-out of this change is the purpose of the present paper.

The kernel or base of the Chinese system is as follows:

Fu, f.
Mu, m.
Tzu, son (also child)
Nü, d.

Hsiung, o. br.
Ti, y. br.
Tzu, o. sis.
Mei, y. sis.

Tsu, gr. par. (specifically, f.'s f.)
Sun, gr. ch. (specifically, son's son)

Po, f.'s o. br. (also o. br., h.'s o. br.)
Shu, f.'s y. br. (also h.'s y. br.)
Ku, f.'s sis. (also h.'s m.)
Chiu, m.'s br. (also h.'s f., wife's br.)
Yi, m.'s sis. (also wife's sis.)
Chih, sibling's ch. (anciently: wom.'s br.'s d.)
Sheng, sis.'s son, d.'s h.

Fu, husband
Ch'i, wife

Hsü, d.'s h.
Fu, son's w.
Sao, o. br.'s w.

To these can perhaps be added, although they are not separately listed:

Szu, h.'s o. br.'s wife; recipr. betw. wives of brs.
Hsiao, h.'s o. sis.
Ta, h.'s y.? sis.

It is clear that we have here a system still distinguishing the sex of the connecting relative, and giving age as much emphasis as sex in denoting siblings. In fact, age among parents' siblings may once have been consistently expressed; and, in certain cases, the speaker's sex. Ku-chih and tsu-sun suggest that more of the terms may have been reciprocal in denotation. Cross-cousin marriage, as Chen and Shryock point out, was abundantly indicated and accounts for the absence of parent-in-law terms. In short, we have before us, still partly preserved, a system as "primitive" as that of most surviving primitives; closely parallel, in most of its essential features, to those of many American, African, and Oceanic natives.

The present Chinese descriptive system is built up from this kernel partly by combining with one another the original terms of relationship listed, and partly by combining them with non-kinship terms which have acquired a specific—but also classifying—kinship meaning, exactly in principle like our "grand," "great," and "in-law." The chief of these metaphorical extensions are:

Tseng, "added, contiguous," has the force of our "great" before "grand"; it denotes lineal relatives one generation farther removed than grandparents and grandchildren.

Kao, "revered, old, ancestors," and hsüan, "far, distant," go one generation further up and down respectively, corresponding to "great-great" before "grand."

Pao, "placenta," denotes own brothers or sisters, that is, siblings as distinct from cousins. Compare, although the analogy is not exact, our "uterine."

Wai, "outside, foreign," denotes relationship through females.

Nei, "inside, inner," denotes descendants of the wife's brother.

Yo, "high mountain," equals our "in-law" with father and mother, as used by a man.

For different kinds of cousins there are several terms:

T'ang, "hall," denotes first parallel cousins in the male line, that is, the children of brothers.

Yi, the relationship term meaning mother's or wife's sister, also denotes first parallel cousins in the female line, the children of sisters.

Piao, "outside," denotes first cross cousins.

Tsai, "again, repetition," with tsung, "follow, attend," denotes second parallel cousins in the male line.

T'ang piao, "hall outside," denotes second cross cousins.

Tsu, "thrice venerated(?)," denotes third parallel cousins in the male line.

Finally, several true kinship terms, like yi above, are used also with a descriptive or qualifying meaning:

Fu, f., for males of any older generation, whether connected by blood or marriage.

Mu, m., for females ditto.

Fu, h., adult male, for males of one's own or any younger gener., whether connected by blood or marriage.

Fu, son's w., woman, for females ditto.

These last four terms merely denote the sex or age of the person referred to, when they are added to other kinship terms: they are then understood as not carrying their intrinsic significance. Thus ku is f.'s sis.; but ku fu means not f.'s sis.'s f., but f.'s sis.'s husband, that is, the older male associated with the f.'s sis.... This kind of usage is well known as characteristic of the Chinese language as a generic vehicle of expression. The "secondary" or mere sex-age qualifying use of these four terms must be clearly distinguished from their use as primary kinship designations retaining their intrinsic meaning.

Nü, d., and hsü, d.'s h., have analogous secondary use.

A few examples will illustrate how terms are built up from combinations of basic and qualifying elements.

Tsu fu, f.'s f.: lit., "gr.-par. (-par-excellence) old-male."

Tsu mu, f.'s m.: "gr.-par. (-par-excellence) old-female."

Wai tsu fu, m.'s f.: "outside gr.-par. old-male."

Wai tsu mu, m.'s m.: "outside gr.-par. old-female."

These four terms show that even if tsu originally denoted only the specific paternal grandfather, it now functions with the meaning of grand-parent.

Sun, son's son.

Sun nü, son's d. (viz., gr.-ch. who is daughter-like in age and sex; *not* son's son's d.)

Wai sun, d.'s son.

Wai sun fu, his wife.

Wai sun nü, d.'s d.

Tseng tsu mu, f.'s f.'s m.

Wai tseng tsu mu, m.'s f.'s m.

Tseng sun, son's son's son.

Kao tsu fu, f.'s f.'s f.'s f.

Pao hsiung, o. br.

Pao tzu fu, o. sis.'s h.

T'ang ti, f.'s br.'s son, younger than self; i.e., 1st par. cous. through males.

Yi hsiung, m.'s sis.'s son, older than self; i.e., 1st par. cous. through females.

Tsu ti, 3d par. cous. through males, y. than self.

Piao ti, f.'s sis.'s son, y.; also, m.'s br.'s son, y.; hence, any male cross cous. y. than self.

Yo mu, wife's m.

Chih, br.'s son.

Chih nü, br.'s d.

Returning now to a consideration of the pure kinship term basis of the system in the light of the system as a whole, we may infer a reconstruction of this as it presumably was before the descriptive additions had begun to luxuriate. It seems certainly to have been a bifurcate-collateral system, in Lowie's terminology; that is, paternal and maternal uncles and aunts were distinguished from one another as well as from the parents. The same principle perhaps applied to grandparents; that is, four were distinguished, by separate terms, of which one survives, used sometimes in its presumable original specific sense, and sometimes with metaphorical extension to denote grandparental relation of any sort. Nephews-nieces and grandchildren quite likely were similarly distinguished according as their descent was from male or female kin. There is a hint of indication in the preserved old meaning of chih that the terms for nephews-nieces (and perhaps grandchildren) may have been exact correlates or conceptual reciprocals of the uncle-aunt (and grandparent) terms. In full form, this would have involved designation of sex of the older speaker in place of sex of the younger relative, as in some western American systems; but the evidence is insufficient to affirm that the influence of the correlative idea was as strong as this. Seniority was given enforced expression in sibling terms, there

being no word for "brother" or "sibling" in general. Relative seniority may also once have been given wider expression in the uncle-aunt terminology; for which there would again be western American precedent. Words for affinities by marriage were probably restricted in number because cross-cousin marriage, or the habit of thinking in terms of such marriage, suggested blood-kin term designations in their place. There are however some puzzling remnants of sibling-in-law terms. There is no indication of how cousins were called, either parallel or cross, near or remote, since the present designations are all built up on sibling terms, and these would probably not have been employed throughout with normalized cross-cousin marriage.

All in all, the indications are of a former system generically similar to that of many primitive peoples, especially in western America—rather like that of the Cocopa, for instance, as described by Gifford.

The development of the descriptive or qualifying part of the Chinese system probably resulted in some elements of the older system becoming unnecessary and being dropped, and others suffering a change of denotation. The new trends due to the descriptive additions however did not blur at any point the rigorous distinction made between kinship in the male and the female line, either ascending or descending; nor between older and younger siblings. The desire to express these two sets of distinctions is common to the hypothetical old nondescriptive and the historical and present-day descriptive Chinese system. Neither distinction is observed in English or, at least extensively, in most western European systems. The male-female lineage distinction seems to have become lost with us as our systems became descriptive; the elder-younger sibling distinction either was lost or had never been present. To this extent, then, the Chinese system remains the richer and fuller instrument.

The Chinese impulse toward specific denotation has resulted further in the choice of descriptive classifiers which allow of the exact expression of a great many relationships. Chen and Shryock cite 270 terms; and it is evident that the list might be considerably enlarged by applying the cited elements in somewhat altered combinations. To be sure, not all the 270 terms are in customary use; but apparently they would all be readily understood. It would be going too far to say that the Chinese apparatus suffices for the unambiguous designation of every conceivable variation of relationship within the seventh or eighth degree. But it certainly does specify a very much larger portion of the total possibilities than do any European systems.

Take for instance t'ang ti, the father's brother's son younger than one's self. Apart from the seniority which the Chinese term expresses, we cannot possibly, even with expletive auxiliaries, specify this particular relative. "Paternal male cousin" is ambiguous between the father's brother's and father's sister's son; and the phrase would hardly be used ordinarily, and, if it were, might be considered difficult or puzzling. We have just one way to designate this particular relationship precisely: by enumerating the successive steps of kinship first up and then down, or jointly down from a common ancestor. This method of step-enumeration is what we actually fall back upon as soon as the precise denotation of all but the nearest kinship becomes necessary for purposes of science or law or property inheritance. It is a last resource left us after our system, which is built on the fewest possible summarily classificatory principles, is exhausted. We are like people whose number system is so deficient that when

they want to add or multiply above ten they have to fall back on manipulating counters. One interest of the Chinese system is its exemplification that a descriptive kinship system can be at once inclusive and exact. This result is achieved both by the retention of presumably archaic features, such as the categories distinguishing the male from the female line and the older from the younger sibling; and by the formation of descriptive auxiliaries chosen so as to serve fine instead of gross denotation. The Chinese obviously remain interested in kinship, whereas we want to refer to it as sketchily as possible. To use another simile, they are like people who want to know the exact time; we like those who would rather estimate by the sun than be bothered to keep clocks running.

This lumping-by-all-means quality of our kinship thinking is a very real reason why the term "classificatory" as applied to other cultures is misleading in its implications.

In one respect the Chinese and European systems are alike: a man and a woman who stand by birth in the same relation to a third person call him by the same term, in all cases. Put differently, the category of sex of speaker is absent. It is, by the way, an interesting question how often, the world over, the *expression* of this category is a function of the reciprocal principle, as it often is in western North America and Australia.

At another point, Chinese usage parallels a recent English tendency. Chen and Shryock say of the terms used by the wife for her husband's relatives that these "are not common today, for the wife generally uses the same terms as her husband in referring to members of his clan [*sic*, i.e., relatives in the male line]." This is like our habit, especially perhaps among those of pious antecedents, of referring to a brother-in-law as brother, and so on. There is however the difference that our usage is two-way, the Chinese by the wife only.

The actual successive steps in the transformation of the Chinese kinship system from its prehistoric to its historic phase can of course be traced only by the intimate historian of Chinese language and culture. It does however seem reasonably clear that there were such phases and what they were. Starting out apparently with a nondescriptive system similar to those of many genuinely primitive peoples, the Chinese have elaborated this into a supple instrument by the development of descriptive additions strongly reminiscent of the descriptive elements in modern European systems, as regards their general character, but quite different in specific content and function. By judicious selection of these added elements and at the same time retention of a considerable variety of distinctions expressed in earlier times, they have built up a rich system where ours is deliberately impoverished. From the point of view of theory, the interest of these phenomena lies in their presenting a second instance, and with little doubt a historically independent one, of the development of a kinship nomenclature of "descriptive" type—in both cases presumably in association with the transition from a lower or barbaric to a higher or "civilized" stage of culture, and yet with the resultant products very diverse. Presumably this diversity occurred because only the direction of the trends was similar, the historic antecedents as well as the specifically shaping historic influences being different in the two growths.

[*Postscript, 1951:* The definitive treatment of this subject, as it could be done only by a Sinologue or native Chinese, was prepared by Fêng in 1937.[2] His monograph goes far beyond my analysis in exactness, detail, and historic per-

spective; yet it validates the principle of my findings, namely, that the Chinese system operates with one pattern superimposed on another: a set of modifiers attached to a set of "primitive" nuclear terms; and with this double apparatus it attains unusual precision of denotation.

Quite lately, Spencer and Imamura have made a corresponding, though briefer, study on Japanese.[3] The Japanese condition is peculiar, in that there are two terminologies: a native Japanese, preferred in colloquial and familiar situations, and a Sino-Japanese nomenclature using introduced Chinese loan words—both nuclear and modifying—in writing and in situations where politeness is requisite. The native Japanese terms are "generalized" much like English, and in the same direction. Grandparents, grandchildren, uncles, aunts, nephews, nieces, are not distinguished according to whether they are in male or female lineage. In Chinese the corresponding nuclear terms recognize the sex of the connecting relative no less than 13 times out of 23. The one non-European feature of the colloquial Japanese system is seniority among siblings: older brothers and sisters are distinguished from younger. There is even a generalized neuter term for cousin of any kind, as in English. The native or familiar system, by itself, has evidently developed into a close counterpart of our own: it is few in categories, logically slovenly, imprecise, but effective in simple situations. When precision, dignity, or politeness demand it, one falls back on the borrowed Chinese nomenclature: the same written characters can often be pronounced as quite different Japanese or Sino-Japanese words. While the historical development of the native Japanese forms has not been worked out in detail, it is apparent that the logical system of these forms has come to be rather strikingly parallel in pattern to English; but, alongside this, there exists in Japanese the second terminology of terms of Chinese origin adhering to the Chinese double pattern of nuclear words plus modifiers. Japanese has therefore managed simultaneously to conform to the example of the Chinese civilization which dominated it with its prestige, and to work out a native popular terminology surprisingly similar to the systems of civilized European nations. This, though a straddle, constitutes a third solution to the problem of a people's converting its kinship classification from out of a state of largely tribal and nonliterate life into a condition of great national civilization.]

23. YUROK AND NEIGHBORING
KIN TERM SYSTEMS
1934

THE five litle ethnic groups that carry the northwest California culture in its most developed form—the Yurok, Wiyot, Tolowa, Karok, and Hupa—seem to possess almost identical institutions of marriage, society, wealth, and law; yet their kinship systems are of different types. Spier, for instance, in his classification of North American kinship systems into eight types, assigns the tribes as follows:

Yurok: "Salish" type
Wiyot: "Eskimo" type
Tolowa: "Iroquois" type
Karok and Hupa: "Mackenzie Basin" type

These terms are perhaps in certain respects unfortunate, and the classification is to be taken as merely descriptive, without genetic implication. Yet it does suggest a much greater differentiation of plan of kinship designation than of plan of society, and this is borne out by Gifford's full original data. The often discussed general problem is therefore touched, of how far social organizations and kinship terminologies tend to be correlated. Accordingly, the salient features of the systems will be reviewed.

Yurok. — The uncle-aunt-nephew-niece terminology coincides exactly with that of English. That the grandfather and grandmother terms also correspond to ours is less surprising because, out of sixty-eight Indian peoples in California, there are some fourteen others (besides Yurok) whose grandfather-grandmother terminology thus corresponds; but it is probably significant in connection with the last feature. The Yurok further refuse to include collateral relatives of parents-in-law and children-in-law within the range of their four terms for these, covering such affinities by the word ne-kwa, which seems primarily to denote the child-in-law's parent or "co-parent-in-law." This exclusion is unusual in California. Another exclusion is that of uncles' and aunts' spouses. Alone in California the Yurok and Wiyot refuse to recognize these as relatives. For siblings, two quite diverse plans of nomenclature are in use, according as the sibling is spoken of or to. In reference, brother and sister are distinguished without allusion to age, but with different terms according as they are a male's or a female's brother or sister. This gives a set of four terms quite unusual in this part of the world. In address the speaker's sex is ignored, but relative age and sex of the sibling are expressed—as in most of North America—except that in Yurok the younger brother and sister are merged into one. All cousins, cross or parallel, first, second, or third, are brothers and sisters.

This system is clearly of what Spier calls the "Salish" type: terms for uncle, aunt, nephew, niece, grandparent, older sibling, younger sibling, with all cousins named siblings. So far as the actually Salishan systems merge farther than Yurok, it is probably because their dialects, at least on the coast, express sex-gender by affixes, so that a term like "grandparent" automatically appears as either "grandfather" or "grandmother." According to Spier, this system is common to all the Salishan, Wakashan, and Chemakuan tribes; to the Yurok; and

196

possibly to the Alsea of the Oregon coast between the Yurok and Salish. Obviously this distribution is the result of a single historic growth. It seems impossible to avoid the conclusion that the Yurok system is connected in origin with a type of system of which the recent center lies in Washington and British Columbia. In view of Yurok general culture being so prevailingly northern in quality, this finding may not seem so startling; but the situation is not a simple one because the other tribes of Yurok-type culture except the Wiyot do not possess kinship systems fundamentally of "Salish" type; and because the Tolowa and other Athabascans separate the Yurok geographically from the Alsea and Salish.

Another consideration which may be of significance is that according to Sapir both Yurok-Wiyot and Salish-Wakash-Chemakuan speech are derived from a proto-Algonkin base.

Wiyot.—Spier somewhat doubtfully affiliates the Wiyot system with the Eskimo type, in which otherwise he includes only the Algonkins of New Jersey, New England, and New Brunswick. The Eskimo resemblances of Wiyot appear to be secondarily fortuitous. Fundamentally, the system seems allied to Yurok. The grandparent-grandchild, nephew-niece, spouse-of-uncle-and-aunt terminology is the same in plan. That for siblings-in-law is the same, with a reduction from three to two terms. That for cousins is partly the same: all second and fourth cousins are siblings, as among the Yurok; for all first and third cousins there is a special term. Wiyot specializations in major features are two. All full siblings, irrespective of age, sex, or sex of speaker, are denoted by a single term. This is presumably a reduction from a fuller set of terms. For uncles and aunts there are four words: f.'s br., f.'s sis., m.'s br., m.'s sis. This classification may be presumed to be derived from the Athabascans, who,

with the Yurok, completely surround the Wiyot, and who share this plan with the majority of California tribes. The fact that for nephews-nieces the Wiyot follow the logically inconsistent Yurok scheme shows that there has been a blending of two plans.

It seems reasonable therefore to assume that the Wiyot system is at bottom of Yurok-Salish type and has been spottily modified, partly by influencings from quite alien systems and partly by independent internal developments of both growth and reduction.

Tolowa.—The Tolowa system—"Iroquois," according to Spier—is fundamentally different from Yurok and Wiyot. Sex of lineage is expressed instead of ignored. There are four terms for uncles and aunts and four for grandparents, kin through the father being always distinct from those through the mother. The reciprocals, in spite of some irregularities, follow the same plan: there are words for son's child, daughter's child, man's brother's child. Siblings are four: o. br., o. sis., y. br., y. sis.; plus a generic term for brother and a reference word for man's sister—evidently an idea-loan from the Yurok. Cousins are siblings only if parallel; cross cousins are denoted by three terms: male, man's female, woman's female cross cousin. For siblings-in-law there are four terms, on the scheme of man's brother-in-law, plus two special terms for sibling-in-law's spouses of the same sex as one's self. Parent- and children-in-law designations take in siblings of the proper relatives.

A greater contrast than this from the Yurok system would be hard to find. Yurok, except for cousins, carefully distinguishes lineal from collateral relatives, but merges collateral and grandparental ones. Tolowa is most concerned with keeping apart relatives through a male from relatives through a female, whether they be grandparents-grandchildren, uncles-nephews, or cross cousins.

Hupa.—Spier puts Hupa into a California division of his "Mackenzie Basin" class. This class differs from his "Iroquois" chiefly in that cross as well as parallel cousins are called siblings. This is also the chief feature in which Hupa differs from Tolowa, some regrouping of grandchildren, nephew-nieces, and siblings-in-law excepted. This drawing of cross cousins into the group of siblings–parallel cousins is evidently due to Hupa imitation of Yurok, since all other California Athabascans—Lassik, Wailaki, and Kato as well as Tolowa—possess two special terms, unt and tset, for man's male cross cousin and woman's female cross cousin. Hupa seems simply to have discarded these.

Karok.—This is also "Mackenzie Basin" in essentials, according to Spier. More specifically, however, it shows both Tolowa-Hupa and Yurok resemblances. Evidently it was originally a system of one of these types which has been somewhat illogically modified to agree partly with the other. As the Athabascan systems much more than the Yurok tend to agree with those of north and central California generally, and it is there that the Karok have their Hokan speech-relatives, it can be inferred that the Karok changes have been toward the Yurok type, not away from it.

Features of Athabascan or generic Californian type are:

Four uncle-aunt terms: f.'s br., f.'s sis., m.'s br., m.'s sis.; with four reciprocals of type of man's br.'s ch., but including some irregularities. Most of northern and central California has the same four for uncle-aunt.

Three grandparental terms, f.'s f. and m. being merged, m.'s f. and m. distinct. Most of California has four terms, of which the Karok three seem a reduction.

Four siblings: o. br., o. sis., y. br., y. sis. Forty-six of seventy-five California systems follow this plan.

Spouses of uncles-aunts denoted by sibling-in-law terms, as in Tolowa and Hupa. Fairly common in California, especially for f.'s sis.'s husband being called brother-in-law. Yurok and Wiyot treat such spouses as outside the kinship designations.

Yurok features of the Karok system are:

Terms for grandson and granddaughter instead of son's child and daughter's child.

All cousins called siblings.

Siblings of parents-in-law not called parents-in-law; similarly for children-in-law.

It thus appears that there are two basic types of kinship designation in the northwestern California culture: the Yurok-Wiyot and the Tolowa-Hupa-Karok.

The first of these is fundamentally similar in plan to the Salish-Wakash systems. In view of the evident connections in general culture between the two groups of tribes, the not very great distance separating them, and the partial link afforded by the Alsea, the two occurrences of the type of system may be set down as derived from a common source. This source is more likely to have been among the Salish-Wakash than among the Yurok-Wiyot on account of the much greater populousness and extent of the former.

The Tolowa-Hupa-Karok kind of system is widespread in peripheral northern and central California. Spier classes this tract as occupied by Iroquois and Mackenzie Basin systems. As these however are similar, differing chiefly in that the former possesses special terms for cross cousins, they may in the present connection be treated as one. Contrasted with this type of system, inner central and northern California has systems of the "Omaha" class. The range of these corresponds with Gifford's "Central California Valley" area, whereas Spier's Iroquois-Mackenzie distribution in and about California is nearly the same as Gifford's "Mountain" or peripheral area. The ethnic groups in this Mountain or Iroquois-Mackenzie area are: all the California Athabascans; the northeast Hokans, namely, Karok, Shasta, Achomawi, Yana, Washo; Yuki; of Penutians, only the northern Maidu and southern Yokuts, that is, the extreme marginal members of the group; and the bordering Shoshoneans. It seems impossible to say whether the Athabascans were the contributors or the recipients of Iroquois-Mackenzie systems in California. On the one hand, some distant northwestern and southwestern Athabascans fall into this class; but on the other hand the type extends also through Basin, Plateau, and Plains to the Great Lakes region and Atlantic Coast. It is evidently an ancient, fundamental type of kinship system which has come to be widely but irregularly distributed through most of the continent, and in it most Athabascans participated. Its spread in California and the variety of its adherents there argue that it is rather old in this area too.

With this type of system, then, the Yurok-Salish system came into collision around the lower Klamath River at one time or another. Every one of our five tribes shows the result of the collision. Tolowa and Yurok appear the least altered, on the whole, from their original plans; but they too show traces of modification toward each other. Wiyot has taken over the Athabascan uncle-aunt terminology; Hupa, the Yurok plan of calling all cousins siblings. Karok is a "Mountain" or Mackenzie-Iroquois system nearly half-made over on the Yurok plan. There are of course tribal specializations also, and it cannot always be decided whether these are an indirect by-product of system-collision disturbance or mere local luxuriances unconnected with the two basic systems. But the accidental nature of these specializations as compared with the essential features of the two systems involved, is usually fairly clear. "Accidental" in this connection of course means not causeless, but of minor pattern significance; "essential," of major, older, or persistent pattern significance.

So far, then, our unraveling of the history of kinship designation among the five northwestern California tribes. Their actual societal organizations and practices are uniform almost to identity. Their kin terminologies, on the contrary, appear to go back to two quite different fundamental types or patterns. These have traceably influenced each other at a good many points, but are still distinct, Yurok-Wiyot against the others. Whether formerly there were also two systems of social organization, there seems no indication, one way or the other. In the present connection, it does not matter. Whether two organizations blended into one or whether there always was only one, there exists only uniformity now; but in terminology there was and is duality. Evidently practice and the categories of thought and speech do not have to go together. Of these two systems it would be idle to call one cause and the other effect, and certainly misleading to infer from one to the other. The Tolowa and Hupa "Iroquois-Mackenzie" type of terminology evidently coexists as satisfactorily with northwestern marriage and social institutions as does the Yurok-Wiyot type. After all, there is no reason why this should not be. Kinship terminologies are part of language; and that this can and often does go its own way independently of the history of culture is a commonplace. The substantial cultural identity of Athabascan Hupa, Algonkin Yurok, and Hokan Karok is a classic example of the principle. Why anyone should hold that kinship terms necessarily occupy a special and exceptional place in speech, in "reflecting" culture with minimum distortion, is hard to see, except for the wish fathering the notion.

To return from this reasoning about

generalities, we have in the present situation at any rate this that is positive and specific: the probable outline of the history of two kin term systems of somewhat fundamentally different pattern and type, the geographical distribution of which indicates that they originated separately in distinct areas, came into collision in northwestern California, somewhat modified each other there by reciprocal influencing, but still remain essentially different in plan. In short, the patterns have had each a history of its own as a pattern, just as the languages in which they occur have had each a history of its own. The maintenance of the separate patterns is of particular interest because the social organization patterns of the peoples involved have remained or become extremely uniform.

With respect to the history of the ethnic cultures and populations here discussed, some inferences are also possible, although only tentative ones. The "Algonkin"-speaking Yurok-Wiyot need not be derived from the great Algonkin body east of the Rocky Mountains. They may represent a branching-off from the also "Algonkin"-speaking Salish-Wakash,[1] drifting south along the coast. This would go far to explain the strange local focus of northwest coast culture in northwestern California. It would also check with their territorial holdings: nearly a hundred miles of ocean frontage, only about half that distance up the Klamath. Upstream, they came to adjoin the Karok, who are the northwesternmost members of the northern division of Hokans, and the former historic affiliations of the Karok in general would therefore have been toward the south and inland. The Karok could thus hardly have contributed much specific northwest coast culture. The Athabascans of course are admittedly intrusive in California. The Yurok now divide the Tolowa and Oregon Athabascans

from the Hupa and California ones. It would be venturesome to try to decide whether the Yurok had forced a wedge up the Klamath, splitting an originally continuous Athabascan body into two, or whether the Yurok-Wiyot were there first and were then engulfed by incoming Athabascans. There is too much likelihood of local shiftings and readjustments blurring the picture, thus defeating the reconstruction of its original. But there is one partial hint: the Tolowa kin terms seem less influenced by the Yurok system than are the Hupa ones. This looks as if the Tolowa might have come to their specific present habitat the more lately. That in turn suggests their closing in on the coast after the Yurok were established about where they are now, and, with their southern Oregon coast kinsmen, occupying the last stage of the route over which the Yurok had previously come to the mouth of the Klamath. But this inference rests on a slight clue and may not be pressed.

The most significant conclusion of the foregoing discussion seems to be this. Kin term systems, like everything else organized in culture or speech, have essential or basic patterns. Like all other patterns, these are subject to modification from within and from without. There is always a sufficient number of such "accidents" to disguise the basic pattern more or less. The determination of this is indispensable however, if we wish to deal with the relatively more meaningful aspects of our phenomena. Evidently, the essential features of the pattern are also likely to be the ones which have the greatest historic depth. The search for them therefore implies a willingness and ability to view data historically. Without such willingness, it is as good as impossible to separate the significant from the trivial or temporary and local fluctuations; and the work done becomes merely an affair of schemes instead of an approximately true story. In proportion, moreover, as fundamental patterns are uncovered, their relation in space or time or structure to other patterns tends to become clearer. Patterns in different aspects or parts of culture may interinfluence each other heavily, whereupon they tend to aggregate into greater patterns; or they may influence each other relatively little, each essentially going its own way for a long time even within one culture.

Among the five tribes here dealt with, I believe it is reasonably clear that for some time there have been operative two kin term patterns, but only one pattern of social institutions, although this is quite complex, as shown by the adjusted coexistence of "full" and "half" marriage, with patrilocal and matrilocal residence, respectively [No. 32]. It would be extreme to assert that such a dissociation of kinship and institutional patterns was normal or perhaps even frequent. We know of examples to the contrary, even in America and more abundantly in Oceania, where the correspondence of the two kinds of patterns is much greater, even almost neat. But it would be equally unwarranted to argue such occurrences into a universal. Kinship systems are more than imperfect reflections of social organizations, or tools for reconstituting these. They are also thought-systems, and as such have a historic existence and an interest of their own. On account of their compactness and potential self-sufficiency, they lend themselves admirably to historic understanding in their own right. The time for an attack on the problem of their relation to coexistent institutions is, on the whole, after some insight into their history has been attained, not before.

I hope at some future time to return to this subject in a wider geographical frame.

24. KINSHIP AND HISTORY
1936

I HASTEN to admit the contention of Radcliffe-Brown, made in "Kinship Terminologies in California" in a recent number of the *American Anthropologist*,[1] that I claimed too much in stating [in the conclusion of No. 23] that the time for an attack on the problem of the relation of kin terminologies to coexistent institutions was on the whole after some insight into their history had been attained rather than before. Actually, of course, the factual problem of what the correlation is, especially in the norm or average, is not intrinsically affected by historical considerations. Radcliffe-Brown is quite within his rights in attempting to solve the problem as he sees it, which is unhistorically, without reference to complicating antecedents. If one seeks to isolate constants, simplification of the issue and its extrication from the chaos of apparent phenomena are important, and anterior stages may be irrelevant. What I should have expressed was my conviction that the factors at work in the phenomena in question are numerous and variable enough to make it seem highly questionable whether determinations of constants other than of narrow range or vague nature can be made, or at any rate have yet been made, while historical considerations are being omitted. I cheerfully make this correction. That I was not trying to say that probabilities or inferences or hypotheses should be allowed to supersede facts will probably be believed without explicit reaffirmation.

Among "historical considerations" in this connection I reckon language, of which kin terminologies are part. Hupa and Tolowa are Athabascan, and this fact therefore must enter ultimately into the problem of terminological-institutional correlation in northwestern California. One can of course refrain from broad problems and limit the problem to the question of whether or not correlation exists in these particular tribes. This is perfectly legitimate, but it seems rather narrow, and I do not believe Radcliffe-Brown would wish to draw such a limit. In fact I admit without hesitation that there must expectably be some correlation; both because speech is not an independent universe, and because in other cases hitherto we have always found some accord between terminologies and institutions. A much more real problem is how much correlation there is, and what factors have made it stronger at some points and weaker at others. Here I believe language cannot be left out, in the sense that, Hupa being Athabascan, and Yurok being if not Algonkin at least non-Athabascan, the speakers of the two languages must at one time have come into contact and into acquisition of a highly similar culture, not only with differently pronounced words, but —if all precedent holds—with kinship words of somewhat or considerably different meaning. The situation, in short, is characterized by the impingement on each other of a set of social institutions and usages at least highly uniform in the area and of several languages which are thoroughly different—so different that their contained terminologies still remain extremely diverse in plan or system of concepts. I do not doubt that detailed investigation will also reveal a number of differences of social usage corresponding to differences in the terminologies, and that there will be value in knowing all such cases. I shall be happy to assist Radcliffe-Brown, or anyone like-minded, in planning field investigation directed at these very matters. Nevertheless, however many fine points of this sort may have been overlooked by those of us who have studied the tribes in question, enough work has been done to make it clear that the great mass of the social system of the five tribes is similar, so similar as to be fairly designable as one in plan and pattern, whereas their kinship terminologies are of two types or patterns. This fact seems to me of more significance than the expectable one that there has also been a certain amount of adjustment between the impinging institutional and terminological patterns. It seems doubly significant in view of the Hupa and Tolowa being Athabascans, and the Wiyot and Yurok proto-Algonkins, if Sapir is right, and at any rate having a kin system of the type of the Salish and Wakash, irrespective of whether or not the Salish and Wakash are also proto-Algonkin. Perhaps I should say "of greater interest to myself" rather than "of greater significance," for significances change with interests.

The problem has by no means been exhausted even within the frame of the northwestern California area. For instance, I have pointed out that each of the five terminologies shows certain assimilations to the others, contrary to, or on top of, its basic type or pattern. I have assumed that these assimilations were due to interinfluencings of the terminological systems, which are of course also systems of thought or unconscious semantic logic. It is however equally possible, theoretically, that the assimilations are due to the leveling influence of the more uniform institutions. Quite likely both factors have been at work; and it would be interesting to know to what degree and at what points and circumstances. Again, therefore, I renew my invitation to more field work.

As regards the generic problem of term-usage correlation, I am ready to retract some of my intransigence of earlier years, which I now construe as a reaction to the once prevalent abuse of seeing in kinship systems chiefly instruments for reconstructing systems of social structure; and I suggest the following basis for a permanent and productive peace.

The relation of kinship term systems to institutions and practices seems analogous to the relation of dress to the human body. One expects normally a considerable degree of fit; but it would be dogmatic and futile to say that body conformation "determines" dress, or that dress "reflects" the body. Sometimes it does, sometimes it does not. The real problem obviously is when it does and when it does not, and how and why. Styles have a way of traveling their own course, sometimes to the point of requisitioning mechanical inventions to preserve even adhesion to the body. Fit may be loose and cool or snug and warm, comfortable or uncomfortable whether loose or tight. Similarly with the fit of kin terminology to social usage: it may be close or wide. Expectably there will always be some fit, and there may be a great deal, but it may also be remarkably partial. Every kinship system is also a little system of classificatory thought, and unconscious peoples sometimes are as ingenious in their logical productions as are ethnologists in their conscious analyses. There is no reason why such systems should not have a history of their own—not of course wholly cut off and self-determined, but partially so, with their own novelties, growths, diffusions, and contact modifications. They are styles of logic in a limited field of universal occurrence.

But they are also more than this: they are parts of languages which always have a long history and ordinarily change slowly. They therefore tend to contain precipitates of greater or less age: old elements with changed function, also elements with unchanged function inconsistent in a new pattern. The Navaho system, for instance, is almost certainly more than a mirror of Navaho clan system, marriage avoidance, obligations, familiarities, etc., though it will undoubtedly fit these usages in part. It is also still an Athabascan system, presumably not only in its sounds but partially in its concepts. If these concepts have been made over completely to fit the institutions of the Navaho in the Southwest, or Pueblo ideology, it would be a surprising fact. Expectably the Navaho system is an adjustment between functioning Navaho social usages, no longer functioning ones, an ancient northern Athabascan system, and Pueblo ideology, with the two latter in turn the resultant of adjustments between practice systems and thought systems.

A normally large amount of play or give in fit is evident. Portions of a naming system can be indifferent from the point of view of social structure, or vice versa. Grandparents as compared with uncles, siblings with cousins, more often lie in these areas of indifference; but they are no less important, in the conceptual system or in life, except on the premise that fit to social structure is the most important aspect of terminology as a subject. To me it is not: the ideologies as such possess at least equal interest and significance. More, in fact, as long as they continue to be underweighted in pursuit of the social-fit theory. Can we not all meet on the common ground that the determinants are multiple and variable, and then amicably follow the ways of our respective bents as these most profitably lead us, with tolerance also of other approaches? It does seem a symptom of immaturity in anthropology that we should still divide up into militant camps like eighteenth-century Vulcanists and Neptunists. Perhaps I

threw the first stone, but herewith I extend the olive branch.

On the broader question of the relation of sociology and history, Radcliffe-Brown and I have expressed ourselves at greater length in articles in the same and following numbers of the *American Anthropologist*, and a few comments must suffice. In common with most historians, I hold the essential and characteristic thing about history to be neither documentation nor time sequences, but an attitude of mind, a particular approach in trying to understand phenomena. The distinction between the "detailed and documented history of the historian" and "the hypothetical history of the ethnologist" is valid enough but hardly seems to go to the root of things. Neither does the distinction between the "evidence of eyewitnesses" as distinct from inferences "based on circumstantial evidence." The most documented history that limited itself to eyewitness testimony and refused to infer from circumstantial evidence would be only skin deep. Radcliffe-Brown's double characterization sounds like a scientist's conception of history. As I have said before, all historians reconstruct. If they do not reconstruct, they are accomplishing nothing, because historical interpretation *is* reconstruction [see Nos. 6, 8]. And the values of all historiography lie precisely in its being hypothetical, if a categorical paradox may be pardoned. Radcliffe-Brown's distinction of ethnology, which he sees as historical, though apparently condemned to being an inferior kind of history, from social anthropology or comparative sociology, which investigates "the nature of human society," I would accept, with reservation as to the inferiority if that was implied; and with reservation also as to the emphasis on society instead of culture. And I would accept his distinction as referring to two currents within anthropology rather than to two disciplines. We agree that their aims, methods, interests, and I think values, are different. I take it that the investigation of the nature of human society, or culture, has for its end the determination of constants—in other words, of abstractions extricated from phenomena as they occur in space, time, and variety of character. This is a genuinely and wholly scientific objective, evidently very difficult to attain from social or cultural material, but certainly important and significant. Any method which will really bring us there is a good method. Whether the better procedure is to dissociate as much as possible from the historic approach, as Radcliffe-Brown seems to want, or on the other hand to envisage and emphasize the historicity of phenomena, as Lesser advocates, I do not know. Radcliffe-Brown's course seems the purer, more drastic, and to date more sterile. But it may in the end carry us further into new concepts. Good speed on the journey.

25. ATHABASCAN KIN TERM SYSTEMS
1937

IN THE *American Anthropologist*[1] for last year, Morris Opler analyzes the kinship systems of seven Southern Athabascan groups. The data are presented compactly and conveniently for comparison; and a classification is made into two types, called Chiricahua and Jicarilla, of which the first is construed as developmentally earlier. Dr. Opler's paper is executed with genuine workmanship, and his data are a boon; there has not been even one Apache kinship system previously on record, so far as I know. He has however taken no cognizance of Northern or Pacific Athabascan kinship system, long ago recorded by Morgan and then by Gifford; and it seems worth while examining these to see whether, at least on certain points, they do not suffice for a tentative reconstruction of primitive Athabascan kinship, which in turn will illumine the Southern Athabascan situation. . . .

Kinship abbreviations are as introduced by Gifford in *Californian Kinship Terminologies.*

All original Athabascan forms are rough generalizations, not proved or arguable reconstructions such as a philologist would designate by a*. The purpose is recognition of former kinship plans, not of precise linguistic forms.

Grandparents.—Chiricahua and Mescalero have 4 terms: FF nale, FM tc'ine, MF tsoye, MM tco. Western Apache merges the two last, Navaho the two first, Jicarilla and Lipan use MF for both GF, and MM for both GM; Kiowa Apache has again merged and uses MF for all 4 GP. That this is the historical sequence is shown by the California Athabascans having the 4-GP scheme, with close correspondence of forms: FF al (Lassik, Wailaki; others aberrant: Tolowa ame', Hupa maatcwuñ, Sinkyone abak, Kato tcau); FM trene, tcin, tcuñ, tcañ; MF tcugi, tcigi, tchuwe, sagi; MM tco, tcwo, su. Northern Athabascan has only two terms, of type tsian and tsu, or tsun and tsea, for GF and GM; these forms probably correspond to FM and MF. The whole of America east of the Rockies is a region of only two (or one) GP terms, so that the loss of half an original stock of 4 terms in the Northern as also among the Southern Athabascans of the Plains (Jicarilla, Lipan, Kiowa Apache) is infinitely more likely than that the Chiricahua-Mescalero and the California tribes should have independently devised not only 4 concept words but the same stems for them. In short, original Athabascan possessed separate terms for FF, FM, MF, MM. . . .

Siblings.—Original Athabascan had 4 terms, each specifying sex and seniority.

Chiricahua-Mescalero are aberrant with a totally different plan: k'is, parallel Sb, la' cross Sb, without reference to seniority. Both these terms recur among the five other southwestern Athabascan groups, but apparently either with narrower sense or as alternative words. (Opler's tabular data are difficult to interpret on this point because they refer to male egos.) In California,

	Northern	California	Southern
OB	unaga, unda	onung, onaga, on, ungutc	Navaho, Jicarilla, Lipan na'i oB
OSS	ada, ache, yat	at, ati, ade	Western Apache de oSb; Navaho adi oSs; Kiowa Apache dada oSs
YB	acha, chilea, che, chel	tcil, tcel, tcal, kil, tcelc	Navaho tsili yB; Kiowa Apache tcitl'a yB
YSs	adaze, tis, chith	t'eci, te, de, eci, detc	Western Apache dije ySb; Navaho deji ySs; Kiowa Apache detc'a ySs

Tolowa has disle mn Ss, and la'e (mn and wn) B, as evident cognates; in the north, Carrier lthes "Ss" and tetsin "B" may or may not be cognate. There may thus be a second system of original Athabascan Sb terms, based on the parallel-cross principle instead of seniority or absolute sex; as there also is in Algonkin. The Tolowa forms of this type I have previously characterized as "evidently an idea-loan from the Yurok" [No. 23]. If so, Tolowa may have had the supplementary terms ready from its original Athabascan heritage.

In any event, parallel-cross Sb terminology recurs in Kiowa, Tanoan, and especially Keresan. Whether these influenced Southern Athabascan or were influenced by it remains to be seen. The closest linkage in this point appears to be between Chiricahua-Mescalero and Keresan.

Cousins.—While Chiricahua-Mescalero distinguish only parallel Sb and cross Sb, they do not distinguish parallel cousin and cross cousin—in fact, call them all Sb. The equation all cousins = Sb recurs among the Northern Athabascan groups reported on by Morgan. On the other hand, Carrier has zit, "♀ cousin on M side," and unte, "♂ cousin on M side." Of these the first corresponds to Western Apache-Navaho-Jicarilla zede, ♀ cross cousin, and Tolowa, Lassik, Wailaki, Kato seti, tce, tcet, ♀ cross cousin. Carrier unte also corresponds to ontde-si, untu, un'd, unt in the same four California languages, where it always denotes ♂ cross cousin and sometimes ♀ also. Western Apache-Navaho-Jicarilla łna'ac does not seem cognate, but has just the range of meaning of California ontdesi-untu.

It must be concluded that original Athabascan had a pair of terms of a type represented by zede and untu, meaning ♀ and ♂ cross cousin respectively, which have been preserved in Navaho, Jicarilla, Western Apache, but were lost in Chiricahua, Mescalero, Lipan, Kiowa Apache.

Uncles-aunts.—Athabascan designations for P Sb are varied, and the original pattern promises to be difficult to reconstruct. Both in Northern and Southern Athabascan, FB = F and MSs = M sometimes but not always.... If certain cited forms are true cognates, we should have this curious set of Athabascan developments for the concept of FSs:

Chiricahua-Mescalero, FSs ex FB.

Western Apache-Navaho, FSs ex FB-StF.

Jicarilla-Lipan-Kiowa Apache, FSs ex StF, FB different.

California, FSs ex oSs.

Slave Lake, Carrier, FSs ex FB-StF, as in Western Apache-Navaho.

Hare, Yellow Knife, FSs ex GM (but Northern Athabascan also tends to associate StP and GP)....

The original Athabascan kinship system cannot be definitively reconstructed until we shall have records more accurate both phonetically and as to inclusion of meaning from more languages, and until sound shifts have been worked out to allow the determination of true cognates. Even in the present state of knowledge however, thanks to Opler's most welcome new Southern Athabascan data, certain salient features of original Athabascan kinship nomenclature emerge as probable. These are:

1. Four grandparent terms. Where fewer occur, there has been reduction of terms, extension of meaning.

2. More than two children terms, through recognition of parents' sex. On the other hand, son and daughter are sometimes merged for the same parent.

3. Four sibling terms on the widespread American plan of older brother, older sister, younger brother, younger sister.

4. Possibly a second set of two sibling terms, expressing parallel versus cross relationship. (Cross sibling is sibling of opposite sex.)

5. Two cross cousin terms, probably for male cross cousin and female cross cousin, though these meanings have at times been narrowed or altered.

6. An unstable pattern of uncle-aunt designations, with however a strong tendency for the equations step-mother equals mother's sister, and step-father

equals father's brother equals father's sibling equals father's sister.

The various local developments in kinship term pattern were no doubt due both to internal social factors and to external contact influences. America east of the Rockies favors limitation to two grandparents and two uncles-aunts (through merging of parallel uncles-aunts with parents). Some of the Northern Athabascan tribes and the easterly ones of the Southern Athabascan division show these features. California is on the whole an area of four grandparents, four uncles-aunts, four siblings; and the California Athabascans conform, even if they have to use older sister for father's sister and step-mother for mother's sister. Western Apache, Chiricahua, Mescalero, heavily self-reciprocal, are the most western and southern groups of Southern Athabascan, adjacent to Sonoran-Piman-Shoshonean and Yuman tribes, among whom reciprocal expression has its strongest development in America. Contact influences are therefore almost indubitable. Whether it was the logic of nomenclature that was diffused as such, or sets of kinship usages and institutions which were then also reflected in nomenclature, cannot be decided without much fuller knowledge and analysis. Probably both processes were operative; the problem is, at what points and to what degree. What is clear empirically or behavioristically is that *nomenclature logic has diffused;* how far this happened directly, as such, or on the contrary through the medium of social usage or institution diffusion, is something to be ascertained, not assumed. For reciprocal terminology, a corresponding institution is hard to imagine. Reciprocity seems essentially a thought-pattern.

As regards Opler's "guess" that the Chiricahua-Mescalero–Western Apache type of kinship is the older in Southern Athabascan, this is confirmed as probable at some points, rendered highly improbable at others. These three groups, which front Sonora, have certainly had their systems warped away from primitive Southern Athabascan by Uto-Aztecan and Yuman contacts; the Jicarilla, Lipan, Kiowa Apache by Plains (and Eastern) influences; the Navaho, who live essentially between the various Pueblos, by Pueblo influences, I suspect, and perhaps also by Plains influences through the Jicarilla. While guesses are in order, mine is that Navaho, though altered at a great many separate points, has been altered least consistently according to any one systematic pattern or logical plan, and may prove to have preserved a greater number of features of original Southern Athabascan than any one Apache group.

Methodologically, it is clear that, because kinship systems are sets of words, we are neglecting extremely pertinent evidence when we do not use comparative philological findings. Technically rude as Morgan's and Gifford's data from the North and California are philologically, they throw genuine beams of illumination into the Southern Athabascan situation, and show that Opler's excellent typological classification cannot in the main be read historically. Wherever we are dealing with members of a larger indubitable or close-knit speech family—Uto-Aztecan, Siouan, Algonkin, Muskogean, Salish, Eskimo—the same must apply. It seems sterile to grope for understanding of why a particular system is what it is, while philological evidence that contains at least a partial answer is not even examined. Nor is high technical competence of lifelong absorption in the study of a family of languages requisite for preliminary and orienting results. I am certainly not an Athabascanist; and am quite unable to "prove" the cognates which I indicate; I may well have guessed a few false ones. Nevertheless, so much is patent, that, while philologists will correct, they will also no doubt accept the majority of the present findings as self-evident; and I do not see how ethnographers can feel differently.

There has been, for one reason or another, enough discredit cast on historical reconstruction as such, among American and English anthropologists of recent decades, that it seems well to re-emphasize that comparative philology, whether Indo-European, Sinitic, Bantu, Athabascan, or Algonkin, is in its very nature and essence a reconstructive discipline. To be sure, philologists mainly reconstruct the forms or sounds of words, and only secondarily their meanings; and we have in culture relatively little material so sharply formalized as to lend itself to comparison as exact as that of language forms. There is consequently some reason for the difference that in ethnography there is still argument whether one may legitimately reconstruct at all and that in philology the main argument is which reconstructions are the sounder. Nevertheless, it is well to remember that philology in reconstructing follows techniques definitely more rigorous than most of those used in ethnography even when this is not reconstructing. The implications of this fact are too often forgotten.

At any rate, since kinship systems are, first of all, systems of classificatory logic expressed in words which are parts of languages, the analysis and comparison of such systems without reference to their linguistic history, so far as this may be available, is an arbitrary limitation on understanding.

26. BASIC AND SECONDARY PATTERNS OF SOCIAL STRUCTURE
1938

I

IT SO happens that in the cultures of western Europe the male sex has for a long time been given normal precedence over the female in three respects: the exercise of social, legal, political, and religious power or function; the hereditary transmission of name, lineage, and rank; and the residence of husband and wife and place of rearing of children. In current socio-anthropological terminology, Europe has been patriarchal, patrilineal, patrilocal in its institutions. On account of their constant association, the three concepts tended to be identified.

Cases of female precedence over male elsewhere of course became known now and then to Europeans, or some of them, but were evidently regarded as meaningless curiosities until about the middle of the nineteenth century. Then science began to take cognizance of them. At first this was in a naïve way, with theories about origins in promiscuity, deterministic schemes of stages, and the like. But still, there was now a recognition of significance in the phenomena. However, as is inevitable in the beginnings of knowledge, analysis remained deficient; and because European civilization was patriarchal, patrilineal, and patrilocal, primitive culture, or one typical form of primitive culture, was assumed to be matriarchal, matrilineal, and matrilocal.

Before long it became evident that such a simple dichotomy did not obtain in the phenomena. The matriarchate had to be whittled down more and more. At present, very few anthropologists any longer believe that a specific matriarchate exists anywhere; that is, a culture in which the dominant functions and exercises of power are prevailingly in the hands of women. At most would a matriarchate be posited as a hypothetical former condition of which some indicative remnants survived here and there. Next it began to be recognized that lineage and residence did not necessarily go together; that some matrilineal peoples were also matrilocal, but others patrilocal. With this came a slowly growing conviction that residence was not necessarily a humble or secondary factor which was significant only when it coincided with lineage, and an accident or a meaningless deviation when it disagreed with it, but that it was an element of importance in its own right.

I wish now to go a step farther and submit the propositions that a patrilocal matrilineate is in its very nature a quite different thing from a matrilocal matrilineate, normally and perhaps always; and that, so far as it is possible to generalize, residence is at least as important as lineage, if not indeed primary as a factor of influence in the shaping of society and culture.

We need not linger over the classical cases of patrilineal-patrilocal and matrilineal-matrilocal societies, except to bring up one point. We have now a number of established cases—in Australia, among the Californian Miwok and Cahuilla, the northeastern Algonkins, the Ona—in which the patrilineal-patrilocal group is also landowning and autonomous. This means that it is a political as well as a social group: a "tribe," if one will, as legitimately as a "clan."

Radcliffe-Brown's endowment of the resurrected term "horde" with the specific meaning of just such a group refers to Australian conditions, but is as applicable in the other cases. Here is a definite phenomenon with a wide distribution which is also so scattered as to suggest a historical recurrence of the phenomenon; in other words, a recurrent type of social structure. But does the correlate of a matrilineal-matrilocal horde organization occur? There may be cases, but I know of none, and they are almost certainly rare. The presumption then is that such an organization is not a type tending to recur in human history, and if cases of it can be demonstrated, they will be of theoretical interest.

Such matrilineal-matrilocal groups as exist seem to be social units or subdivisions within larger political units: clans or sibs within tribes, as against the clan-tribe nondifferentiation in the patrilineal-patrilocal horde. A Hopi clan is certainly matrilineal and matrilocal, but it is not autonomous: it does not possess exclusive and total ownership of a territory, and it cannot be called a tribe, nation, or state by any legitimate stretch of the meaning of these terms. It is obviously an organ in a tribe, town, or miniature state. It may be that the apparent nonhorde character of the matrilineal-matrilocal group is due to its most frequent occurrence in association with agriculture, which in turn operates toward larger social integration and therefore tends to prevent the horde type of society. On this view the group which, without agriculture, becomes or remains the undifferentiated clan-tribe horde, with agriculture becomes a clan in a tribe; and the fact that normally hordes are patrilineal-patrilocal, but that intra-tribe clans can be matrilineal-matrilocal, would then be due to some influence of agricultural life. At any rate, the two phenomena would be correlated. There is an important problem here,

which Father Schmidt has clearly realized, but unfortunately felt obliged to answer in an envelope of elaborate system. What is needed is an exhaustive review of all possible relevant data without preconceived bias, and such a task cannot be entered upon here.

Let us now examine a matrilineal but patrilocal society, such as exists in the Trobriands. Here the wife goes to live with her husband in his village, but their children are of her lineage, clan, or social group. From the point of view of the children, the society is clearly patrilocal and matrilineal. But, from the point of view of the society as a whole, the scheme is not permanently patrilocal, because a man does not bring up his children in the village in which he was reared, nor is the settlement in which he was born to his father the settlement in which his father was born. A successive stream of male biological descendants living through the generations in one spot or defined territory, such as is found in the Australian horde, is lacking in the Trobriands. A boy grows up in his father's house or village, but when he becomes adult he moves to his mother's brother's settlement. There he lives the rest of his life; there he brings his wife and raises his children, only to lose them again when they are grown and move away to reside with his brother-in-law, his wife's brother. Both men and women therefore live divided lives with regard to locality. A man spends his youth with his father, his maturity with his mother's brother; a woman spends her youth with her father, her maturity with her husband, respectively. Only one thing is constant in the scheme: the succession in any one place or territory of a series of mother's brothers and sister's sons. From the point of view of locality and the permanent structure of society, the scheme is not patrilocal at all, but what might be called "avunculocal."

From what my colleague Olson tells me, this is essentially the plan of organization also of the northerly tribes of the Northwest Coast of America, such as the Tlingit, and Murdock expressly affirms it for the Haida.

There is no doubt that the Trobrianders and Tlingit are as genuinely matrilineal as the Hopi; but they differ from them, and agree with Australian and Californian horde patrilineates, in that a succession of male kinsmen instead of female kinswomen remain attached to a given locality through the generations. This seems as important a point as the fact that with Trobriands and Hopi the successive sib bond exists through females, but in Australia and California through males.

In short, it is evident that we have before us three, and not two, fundamental types of society:

Regions:	Local succession of:	Related through:
Australia, California	Males	Males
Trobriands, Tlingit	Males	Females
Hopi	Females	Females

I would call attention to the fact that the differences not only lie in *where* one lives, which might be considered irrelevant to basic social structure, but are expressible throughout in terms of *persons*. The sex of the persons who succeed each other—often in rank, status, property, and social function as well as in place of residence—is surely at least as important as the sex of the person through whom succession takes place.

It is easy to construe the Trobriand scheme as a compromise formation between tendencies to have males succeed one another in function and to reckon lineage through females. But we do not know that this is what actually happened historically, and other explanations are also possible. Moreover, the Hopi also transmit functions, such as priesthood and office, from male to male, without renouncing their matrilocality. "Matrilocality" here means, fundamentally, the succession of female descendants each one of whom remains her whole life in one spot. The Hopi men shift, spending their childhood in their mothers' houses, their maturity in their wives'. With the Trobrianders everybody shifts. Another way of expressing the difference is that in Hopi everyone lives at all times in a spot (house) "belonging" to a woman; in Trobriand, in a spot (house or settlement) belonging to a male.

In Dobu, among the members of another Massim division, in contact with the Trobrianders, there is no avunculocal system, but an analogous plan of balancing the sexes in spite of the matrilineality of kinship reckoning. A pair of spouses simply lives in alternate years in the husband's and wife's "home" settlement, that is, with the kin groups to which, according to the matrilineate, they "belong." Here we have another way of splitting residence for everyone: the split is an oscillation perpetual through life, instead of a split between childhood and maturity. A child is dragged back and forth between its parents' hamlets; when it matures, it alternately drags its spouse and is dragged by him or her. The purpose may be larger social integration, but the inherent strain on integration is also evident, even without the lurid colors of Fortune's depiction of the Dobu psyche. It may be assumed that this plan is rare or unique in human history because its forced overbalance tends to make it a delicate, transient adjustment. It may have been tried elsewhere, but always with only a short life.

In fact, it is difficult to avoid the impression that Dobu social functioning is motivated by a sort of obsessive conscience in regard to justice and parity between the sexes. The strange balancing which makes everyone uncomfortable by meting out misery to redress misery, if Fortune is correct, may of course be the immediate result of the historic accident of the Dobuans, like the Trobrianders, having been subjected to the influence of two conflicting sets of social institutions, which were nearly equally strong, and working out their particular plans as compromise reactions. But it may just as well be that the influence which affected them was not so much concrete institutions per se as a more generic cultural attitude of suspiciousness, prearranged justice, weighing and paying, and continuing to mistrust while exacting guaranties. Certainly the two cultures, not much over a hundred miles apart, have found related though variant solutions to a problem which they felt in common.

Logically the possibility arises of a fourth plan of society: matrilocal but patrilineal, in the customary terminology; that is,

Occurrence:	Local succession of:	Related through:
X?	Females	Males

I do not know of such a society, and should expect its occurrence to be rare.

The Yuma-Cocopa-Mohave clans show this phenomenon:

Common (group) name of females	related through males

But a name is a very different thing from residence, and Yuman residence is patrilocal; that is, a man and his wife normally live with his father.

II

In favor of priority of the residence factor over the descent factor—pattern priority or historical priority, as one will—is the sum-total of Australian phenomena, as brought together by Radcliffe-Brown. Certainly the vast majority, and perhaps all, of the peoples of Australia were organized primarily on a basis of patrilocal-patrilineal landholding hordes. On top of this organization rested an organization of kinship and marriage which was exceedingly variable, and was therefore secondary, presumably in time and certainly in pattern strength.

In the greater part of the native continent, this secondary organization was dichotomous. It consisted either of simple intermarrying moieties or of dichotomously subdivided moieties, which Radcliffe-Brown calls "sections" if they number four and "subsections" if they are eight. The moieties were patrilineal or matrilineal according as the child belonged to its father's or its mother's moiety. Where there are four sections, the child is of a different section from both father and mother. The sections are always named. If there are also moiety names, the moieties can be classified as patrilineal or matrilineal according as the child's section is in the same moiety as its father's or its mother's section. If, however, there are no moiety names, it is impossible to classify the descent. As Radcliffe-Brown points out, there is a division into patrilineal moieties and also a cross-division into matrilineal moieties. If a man of section A must marry a woman of B and the children must be D, sections A and D obviously constitute a *de facto* patrilineal moiety and B and D a *de facto* matrilineal one. It is only where pairs of sections are grouped into named moieties that one can speak of patrilineal or matrilineal descent. But when descent can be assigned only on the basis of the presence of a name, which often is lacking, it is evidently a literally nominal and superficial phenomenon. While in his text Radcliffe-Brown distinguishes among his four-section tribes those (*a*) with named matrilineal moieties; (*b*) with named patrilineal moieties, and (*c*) without named moieties, on his accompanying map he shows them all in one shading.

Where there are eight subsections, the marriage-descent formula is $A^1+B^1=D^2$, and conversely $A^2+B^2=D^1$; in other words, the section principle is carried one dichotomous step farther. Apparently there are eight-subsection tribes with, and others without, named moieties. So here again we sometimes can, and sometimes cannot, say whether descent is in the male or in the female line, but in neither event does the fact appear to have any deeper functional significance.

In one part of the eight-subsection area, on the Gulf of Carpentaria, there is a system of four named (patrilineal) semimoieties. As Radcliffe-Brown shows, this is really nothing but the eight-subsection system operating with only four names.

How far sex lineage in most of Australia is merely a matter of names is made even clearer by the tribes around Southern Cross in West Australia. These tribes had, by superficial appearance, only moieties, that is, the moieties are their only named divisions; and these moieties were *endogamous*, in contrast to the exogamous moieties of the remainder of Australia. It seems inconceivable that such a fundamental reversal of system could arise in one small area not exposed to foreign influences. Actually, there is no reversal. The Southern Cross system is the widespread four-section system with the divisional names applied differently. In practice, $A+B=D$, as elsewhere; but B has lost its name and taken that of A, so that the nominal formula becomes $A+A=D$; and, conversely, $D+D=A$. The "endogamous" moieties are not descent moieties at all, because the basic four-section feature remains that the child belongs to a different division from both its parents. The natives in fact fully equate the four-section system of their northern neighbors to their own, reckoning the A and B of these tribes as the equivalent of

their own A, and the C and D as the equivalent of their D. Radcliffe-Brown correctly describes this anomalous system not as a moiety one, but as a plan of "named pairs of sections" or "two endogamous alternating divisions." A true endogamous moiety system of course would give $A+A=A$ and $D+D=D$ (or $B+B=B$). With exogamous objectives a culture must of course exact $A+B$; with endogamous, not only $A+A$ but $A+A=A$. The case is illuminating for showing that what counts is the operation of a system, and that both native names and our classifying or generalizing concept terms, such as "endogamy," may be thoroughly misleading if taken at their face value.

We have now reviewed the social organization of all native Australians except half-a-dozen small peripheral groups of exceptional tribes, of whom more in a moment. If we then try to formulate the basic principles or patterns of the social organization of the continent, the following emerge:

1. The local unit, the horde, is autonomous and landowning, and patrilineal or patrilocal, as one may prefer to call it, that is, with sons succeeding fathers in residence and status.

2. As regards marriage, a feeling and specific rules enjoining that certain kin, real or fictitious, must marry are equally strong as the rules decreeing that certain other kin must not marry. As regards kinship, accordingly, the terms "exogamy" and "endogamy" are not properly applicable and are likely to be confusing. Neither can one speak of "forbidden degrees" or "incest taboos," in our sense, without the complement of prescribed kin marriage. The Australian may prohibit marriage with certain kin as we do, and react similarly to the idea; but the idea is not the same, because he balances it, and we do not, with prescriptive kin marriage. One marries only relatives, in Australia. This is an extension of the principle that one has deal-

ings or relations only with kin, close or remote.

3. The basic principle of formal social organization is dichotomy, either simple or repeated.

4. With simple dichotomy, or undivided moieties, the patrilineal-matrilineal distinction obtains, because it must: the child must belong to either the father's or mother's division, if there are only two.

5. But this plan seems to have been uncongenial to the Australians, since in the larger part of the continent they split their moieties into sections or subsections, and then in every case the child belongs to a division different from both its father's and its mother's. Here the concepts "patrilineal" and "matrilineal" become wholly inapplicable, except where moiety names persist in addition to sectional or subsectional names, and in many cases they do not. In brief, where there are four sections or eight subsections the patrilineal or matrilineal moieties appear to be names or historical relics rather than socially functioning units. The local, aberrant plans of apparently endogamous moieties and of four semimoieties prove to be only the normal four-section and eight-subsection systems, respectively, disguised through omission of half the divisional names.

Thus the basic trends of Australian society seem to be toward a simple horde organization with territory held by a succession of males, and secondly toward a species of balanced dichotomy in kinship, marriage, and descent. Formal unilateral lineage reckoning is either secondary or wholly lacking. In other words, patrilocality is real and almost universal, and the dichotomizing tendency is real and almost universal, but unilaterality of lineage is largely nominal and fluctuating.

It may be added that, while various kinds of totemism occur in Australia, such as moiety, sex, individual, and non-localized matrilineal clan totems, the prevailing type appears to be one of totems attached to localities and therefore to the basic patrilineal-local hordes.

Radcliffe-Brown points out that with each normal Australian horde there is "connected" or "associated" a local patrilineal clan. I take it this means that the local clan is another or possible *aspect* of the horde. I agree that the distinction between the two aspects or concepts is important; but I believe its importance to be chiefly logical, so far as Australia is concerned. The aspect which has objective, empirical primacy is the horde, the group of people actually living together, with an indefinite succession of males as its continuum. Even the totemic ritual functions of the group can be construed as pertaining to the horde as easily as to the "clan."

Different from all the foregoing is a type of Australian organization characterized by apparent absence of all moieties or sections. This type occurred in six separate areas, of which the cultures have either broken down or been inadequately studied. We cannot therefore say that the organization of these six groups of tribes was alike, except in the negative feature of lacking the prevalent simple or complex dichotomy. The total area held by the six groups of tribes is small—probably not over a twentieth of the continent. Moreover, they are all coastal groups, and none extends far inland. This peripheral position has led to the interpretation that the nondichotomous organization is a marginal survival. This view receives a certain substantiation from the fact that the unsegmented moiety type has a submarginal distribution, the four-section type the widest one, while the eight-subsection type is central, within the four-section area. I do not, however, wish to argue on behalf of this interpretation, because the distribution of an isolated class of phenomena may yield no more than some presumption of historical inference, the strength of such inferences increasing with the degree to which distributions of other phenomena reinforce one another.

But there is one distributional fact which does seem to have significance. Radcliffe-Brown's map shows seven areas of unsegmented moieties, matrilineal or patrilineal. As the distinction between lineage reckoning is nominal rather than fundamental in Australia, we may ignore it, for present purposes. This reduces the seven areas to four, in my reworking of Radcliffe-Brown's map. Of these four, three are in contact, or virtual contact, with five of the nondichotomizing areas, as shown in the accompanying tabulation.

Moreover, both the noncontact areas are nearly completely cut off by belts from which we have no information and may therefore not be real exceptions.

This can hardly be a meaningless coincidence. In some way the simplest of the dichotomous Australian types of social organization must have been connected with the nondichotomous. Just what the process of connection was is not evident. It may have been loss through reduction; but, without further analysis and probably further data, this would be a mere guess. What the situation illustrates is that a distribution of data properly classified typologically may allow a functional determination to be made—a functional reconstruction, so to speak. Of course, it is a historic reconstruction also, and both historically and functionally it is deficient in that the involved processes have not been ascertained; but the fact of a functional relation does seem established as at least highly probable. A functional determi-

nation within a single culture can of course be made by direct observation and insight alone, for that culture. In full context, however, and for larger masses of phenomena, distribution associations become significant for functional interpretations. That they imply historical interpretations as well is due to the fact that the functional and historical approaches are inherently allied, different chiefly in emphasis, and only selectively contrasted or in conflict.

This matter of association brings up the old point that, the world over, patrilineal and matrilineal exogamic units seem to occur in fairly close geographic associations, as compared with other areas, which are without unilateral exogamic groupings. Much the same appears to hold for the multiple-clan and the moiety types of organization, and again for totemism and exogamic groupings: they associate geographically. It is true that this association has not been proved either cartographically or statistically; but the known facts give a strong impression that the associations are prevalent, and, until exact determinations are available, the impression must serve as a signpost. In short, it seems that in Africa, in Oceania, and again in America patrilineal and matrilineal exogamy, dual and multiple groupings, groupings and totemism, tend to be associated, not only among particular peoples, but massed in large areas, as contrasted with other large areas in which they all tend to be absent. In other words, viewed historically, these social features appear to be at least partially functions of one another.

I am driven to draw the following conclusion from these facts, if the future

	Moiety Areas		Nondich. Areas
N.S.W., Vict., S. Aust.	1	in contact with	2
Southern West Aust.	1	in contact with	2
Northern West Aust.	1	in contact with	1
North Australia	0	in contact with	1
Northern Queensland	1	in contact with	0
	3 of 4	in contact with	5 of 6

continues to establish them as facts. Traits having to do with what we may call formal social organization—clan, moiety, exogamy, unilateral descent reckoning, totemism—which theoretical ethnologists have been so excited about for two or three generations, form part of the secondary patterns of culture—secondary on a broad historical view of culture, and secondary or superstructural even as regards their functional value in many particular societies. They are in a sense epiphenomena to other, underlying phenomena, such as place of residence. This is in one way inevitable, because while one must live somewhere, one can live without artificial exogamic groupings, descent reckoning, or totems; co-residence necessarily brings associations which have social influence; just as one must have kin, but need not have clans.

The phenomena of formal social organization would thus represent a field of experimentation or play on the part of cultures, a fact that accords with their intricacy and variety, which in turn argue relative transience. They would be among the more variable and unstable constituents of culture—among its fashions, so to speak. This would not in the least imply that they were regarded as trivial. In fact, highly impermanent fashions of dress, etiquette, conduct, and belief may be held to with emotional intensity, and the insistence on conformity to them may be very powerful while the fashion is in vigor. A moment's reflection will show that the stable things in culture which everyone takes for granted are less likely to be in conflict or under strain, and will probably have only latent emotional interests connected with them. It is those things which are new and not yet worked out into a stable routine, or with a formerly successful routine which is breaking down, the elements that differ or are beginning to differ from those adhered to by one's father, or by neighboring peoples, or by a class or group in one's own society, about which feeling ordinarily is strong.

At any rate, this view is submitted as a working hypothesis designed to account in a measure both for the variety of forms of what is ordinarily called "social organization," and for their apparent clustering in certain periods and areas. Instead of considering the clan, moiety, totem, or formal unilateral group as primary in social structure and function, the present view conceives them as secondary and often unstable embroideries on the primary patterns of group residence and subsistence associations. They are none the less interesting on that account, both to anthropologists and to the native peoples who have invented them; but if they are mainly secondary elaborations and shifting experiments, it is important to recognize them as such, in contrast to the primary fundamentals.

III

If the present view is correct, an earlier observation of mine needs modification. In an essay on the "Disposal of the Dead," written some years ago, in which I pointed out that both ethnographic distributions and archaeological evidence indicated the choices between burial, cremation, and other alternatives to tend toward impermanence and fluctuation in spite of their emotional involvements, I classified such customs with the "fashion" constituents of culture, as in the case of the traits discussed in the present paper. I went on, however, to suggest a tripartite division of culture into elements concerned with subsistence, institutions, and fashion respectively. Obviously this classification will not hold if institutional features like the reckoning of descent fall into the realm of fashion; or the term "institutional" must be given a restricted definition. I propose therefore to substitute a distinction between patterns and constituents of culture which are relatively primary, stable, and adhered to with unconscious conservatism unless outward circumstances compel their abandonment, on the one hand, and such as are relatively secondary, unstable, within the field of innovation from internal cultural causes, and perhaps more readily invested with conscious group emotions, on the other. What we ordinarily call "institutions" could be of either kind. Even in such basic subsistence domains as food and housing it is evident from our own contemporary civilization that fashion plays a perceptible part. In the fine arts, however, as contrasted with the technological, the "fashion" factor—usually called "style"—is obviously dominant, since no art has ever stood still. The moment it tries to fix its forms, their execution loses its qualitative essence; the history of any art is one of inherent flux.

The innate conservatism of man, as shown by his culture history, his difficulty in making inventions, his blindness to new possibilities while he clings to old routines, has long been proverbial, and, in common with others, I too have chanted this tune. The view is true enough and is necessary to an understanding of culture, especially as a corrective against shallow or subjective evaluations of cultures other than our own. But it is obviously incomplete. When one finds the culture inventories of even neighboring lowly tribes invariably differing in a whole series of features, although their physical environment and external cultural exposure are essentially identical; when one remembers how often a single people or small group of tribes has evolved a really superb art, an intricate and specialized legal, economic, or ritual system, an amazingly novel recombination of ele-

ments of social organization, a successful political fabric, or a system of mythological-symbolical thought, out of much humbler antecedents, one must equally accord our species a very strong latent impulse toward cultural play, innovation, and experiment, a true originality and inventiveness. This may manifest itself in trivialities or in the production of permanent values, and the area of its expression may be small or large and may wander from one to another field of culture. We must particularly guard against underestimating the cultural originality of other civilizations because they have differed from our own in manifesting originality chiefly in domains other than technological invention and scientific discovery. The resistive or repetitive forces may on the whole be dominant in human history; but the innovating or play impulses are no less significant for being more often expressed superficially or transiently.

On the basis of this conception I submit that, in addition to unilateral descent reckoning, much of the formalized social organization of primitive peoples is in the nature of unconscious experiment and play of fashion rather than the core or substance of their culture [No. 27, final paragraphs]. In certain cases, as in Australia, it may well represent the pinnacle of their achievement, just as experiment and play with abstractions, words, and plastic forms resulted in the pinnacles of Greek civilization, while science, technology, and the control or exploitation of nature are those of our own. But pinnacles are end-products, not basic.

27. THE SOCIETIES OF PRIMITIVE MAN
1942

IT IS generally accepted that among primitive peoples society is structured primarily on the basis of kinship and in more civilized nations largely in terms of economic and political factors. The function of kinship is relatively less in higher civilization, and may be absolutely less. But kinship considerations always persist; and they enter integrally or vitally into the total structure or organization. Examples of this are our inheritance, support, and naturalization laws. It may be concluded, consequently, that in broad historical perspective social organization by kinship is early, approximately constant, or that at least some measure of it is inescapable—at any rate it never has been escaped in any society of which we have knowledge—but that developed politicolegal or politicoeconomic institutions have grown later.

One might be tempted to extrapolate or project this finding backward into prehuman conditions, making kinship the sole basis of social structure on that level. But to do so would be an obvious error, contrary to all the facts of subhuman behavior. In animals, whether they be sociable or truly social, it is the association group that counts at any given moment. Whether it is constituted on the basis of kinship or not, is an incident of species or circumstance. The association group is almost certain to contain some blood kindred, and it may be ideally constituted wholly of members of one biological family, parents and siblings, as in all the most highly socialized insects. An ant hive of thousands of individuals consists of one female and her children; a termite colony of a heterosexual pair and their sons and daughters. This kinship grouping is the outflow of inborn biological structure; but it is not recognized by members of the group. Hence the parasitic species of ants perpetuate themselves through fertilized females smuggling themselves into alien hives, and after accustomedness has won them tolerance, supplanting the native queen. Beetles and other insects of different orders in the same way insinuate themselves into ant colonies, to live thereafter in close symbiosis. An individual worker ant separated too long from her natal society and thereby losing her hive identification, be that of smell or otherwise, is refused readmission. It is clear that it is recognition of accustomed and established association which per se is the basis of animal society. Kinship may or may not coincide with this: it is not perceived or realized as such. In fact, in all the most highly socialized Hymenoptera the nuptial flight, which is the initiating act of each society, may indifferently involve brother and sister or wholly unrelated individuals.

In short, animals have consciousness of kind, in the sense that they react to their kind. They also have consciousness of association, of the ingroup and outgroup. They do not have consciousness of kinship, because kinship, while an objective fact, requires abstraction for its recognition. Abstraction involves ability to symbolize, in other words, speech. It is this specifically human faculty that has lifted kinship out of its accidental role in brute societies and constituted it as the basis, or at least one indispensable basis, of human societies.

This mutation, the discovery of kinship, was apparently of profound effect in human development. All human societies not only operate with kinship as such but hold to an incest taboo rule which involves kinship. *De facto* the incest taboo is the complement of kin recognition and kin organization, because so far as knowledge of history and ethnology extends, kin recognition and incest taboo are always coexistent in human groups. Society is structured first of all on the basis of kinship; but marriage alone is excluded either from all or at least from a certain core of kin relationships. Logically it is not clear why this should be so. The explanations given are not satisfactory. They tend to be restatements of the fact, usually in terms of assumed psychological laws; they do not really elucidate the problem of the complementary association. However, the reality of the strong functional relation of kinship and incest taboo cannot be denied, even though we do not know the meaning or reason.

Here, then, we have primitive man, and presumably also early man, started on his career of culture with one feature of social structure to which he has consistently adhered ever since, no matter how complex his civilization became. He has added many other factors to this kinship-incest factor, and he has elaborated and altered it in endless minor variety; but he has stuck to it.

In fact, one thing that many unlettered peoples, and essentially only they, have done is to play or experiment with kinship in the way of elaborating it. This elaboration has taken two principal directions. One is the extension of kinship to all human beings with whom one has personal relations—over the whole structure of society in the largest sense. This brings with it of course the necessity of marrying kin. Kindred of the opposite sex are therefore rigorously divided into those whom one may or must marry and those who are taboo.

It is in the nature of biological relationship, which ramifies widely in a few ascending and descending generations, that to make such a plan operable, certain precise if arbitrary classifications and rules must be worked out. This appears to be the basis of Australian social structure and their regulation of marriage by "sections." A dichotomy, sometimes repeated and not infrequently re-repeated, runs through this structure. The basis of this prevalent formal dichotomy perhaps is the very dichotomy of marriageable and nonmarriageable kindred which is inevitable as soon as the assumption is made that all known persons are or must be treated as specific kindred.

This type of societal structure has been culturally developed most consistently and with relatively little remainder in native Australia. It occurs also in parts of Melanesia; elsewhere it is rare or only partially carried through; though something of its orientation or ideology is likely to crop up wherever society is primarily organized into two complementary classes or groups or "moieties." However, an inclination to address by kinship terms all individuals with whom one comes into closer contact, such as is found in parts of native America and elsewhere, is not necessarily related to the foregoing attitude, because it may represent nothing more than the endeavor to promote particular personal relations by giving to civility a color of warmth.

The other chief primitive elaboration of kinship is its extension not over the whole known universe of persons, but over a segregated part thereof. This inclination results in sibs, clans, and the like, in some cases perhaps, through carrying the process farther, in phratries and moieties. Biological kinship ramifies so as to include a large periphery of highly dilute kinness. Moreover, through marriage it crisscrosses or overlaps endlessly, so that individuals standing in a quite definite and perhaps close kin relationship to each other will at the same time have blood kin relationships to quite different other individuals. (This holds for all relatives except siblings.) Some societies put up with this indefiniteness and its endless ambiguities, and allow contesting groups to pull more or less evenly on an individual equally related to both. Barton has shown this clearly for the Ifugao. In fact, our society is in the same situation. Only, kin bonds form so much smaller a part of the total pulls and pressures in our culture that we are perhaps often not specially aware of this set of strains.

The remedy against such ambiguity obviously is to define groups arbitrarily or artificially, thereby segregating off groups larger and stronger than the so-called biological or household family, and yet small enough, compared with the whole society, to possess a measure of effective cohesiveness. One step in this direction is the extended family or unit lineage. A further one is the sib or clan.

The extended family and the clan are sometimes difficult to distinguish by definition, and such families or lineages have sometimes been designated as "clans." The two principal differentiating criteria seem to be that a clan almost always has a name, whether totemic (i.e., symbolic) or not; and that a clan may be large enough to include persons who are not traceable kin, and perhaps not even actual kin at all in blood, but who are reckoned as such in virtue of their clan membership. A group that includes such individuals, except occasionally through known adoption, is best designated something else than an extended family or lineage. In short, a clan contains, actually or potentially, an artificial extension of true blood kinship. Perhaps this is why it usually has a name: it needs one; whereas the lineage family, consisting of genuine kin—

though one-sidedly—is a patent, indisputable unit even without a name.

Two features are shared by the lineage family and the clan. They are both exogamous, because they are both associations of real or assumed kinfolk. And they are both unilateral in descent, else they would in a generation or two dissolve back into the endless crisscross of bilateral relationship. By the very artificiality of their descent—artificial in the sense that the one-sided reckoning does not exist biologically but is a cultural invention or convention—by this artificiality they establish definition, and therewith a degree of solidarity. Their born members of one sex are forever physically leaving their clan homes by marriage, while in the long run an equal number of members of other clans of the same sex are coming to live in marriage in households of the clan.

True clan membership is usually considered as acquired by birth and retained through life. When a woman marries into a patrilineal clan, she may live and function with it without becoming a member of it. The word "join" sometimes used in such situations is of course ambiguous.

Neither is it any longer believed that all nonmembers of a clan are considered by it as a sort of foreigners or enemies. Specific kinship is invariably recognized; at least half of it would normally be in clans other than one's own. Kindred of one's out-clan parent often have determinate rights or duties, such as caring for corpses. The mother's brother may be specifically influential in patrilineal societies. All such institutions per se are not necessarily the result of clan organization. They reflect an impulse to maintain at least partial balance between the two kinship lines even where the formal reckoning or primary rights reside in one line. They therefore occur also in clanless societies. But, with clans present, they can be extended to other than particular persons, and thus seem doubly striking.

It will be evident that patrilineal differ from matrilineal clans in principle only on the one point of precedence of the sex lineage which determines adhesion. This single point ought not to be unduly weighted as against the several features which matrilineal and patrilineal clans can and mostly do share. The precedence which any society gives to one or the other line is probably in many cases a historical accident, or let us say incident, rather than fundamental to the development of clans. This inference is supported by geographical distribution. Areas of matrilineal clanship mostly lie near areas of patrilineal clanship, or interdigitated with them; and vice versa. It is true that it is difficult to find actual cases of change from one reckoning to another, or to imagine a sure mechanism by which the change could operate. But it is not necessary to go so far as this. The same impulses toward internal segregations might in one society produce male reckoning, and in another, female, according to circumstance of other institutions present. And if there is a change-over, it need not be direct but can take place through crumbling of the existing scheme, and then a new start along the other line, perhaps under the influence of neighboring peoples, or through the invasion of new economic habits.

In fact, it seems doubtful whether sex-lineage reckoning as such is as important a factor as residence—that is, the circumstance of which lineage-group husband and wife go to live with. Normally the two might be expected to coincide. But they need not. And the strange Trobriand and Haida institution of avuncu-local residence, by which a woman goes to live with her husband but he with his mother's brother whose heir he is, seems best explained as an ambivalent attempt to reconcile, or

compromise between, matrilineal and patrilineal proclivities or forces.

In Africa there are a number of instances, both East and West, of coexisting and cofunctioning matrilineal and patrilineal groups. One transmits blood, the other the soul; one land and perhaps the totem, the other personal property or rights. Such cases are further evidence of the strength of lineage-grouping impulses *in toto* as compared with the choice of one sex as the medium of lineage. They also evidence an interest in lineage institutions which is great enough to cause them to luxuriate and penetrate large domains of the culture.

Preoccupation with clan groups may lead to their grouping into phratries and moieties or to splitting into sub-clans, which later may become clans. Moiety organization can thus have two quite different origins. It may be the product of an attempt to superorganize clans; or it may spring from the classification of all kin into marriageable and forbidden. The curious "hexagonal" Melanesian Ambryn and Pentecost situation, which is closely paralleled in districts of Assam, appears to be the result of the coexistence of a dichotomous and a tripartite system of organization. Pentecost descent is asymmetric: bilateral for men, matrilineal for women —hence the triple grouping. Differentiated descent for men and women recurs among the Brazilian Apinayé, mentioned below. These sex asymmetries vividly illustrate the enormous variety of possible organizations, through descent, many of them represented sporadically by actual occurrences.

The many cases of cross cousin marriage pretty clearly have a variety of origins. For one thing, the practice flows almost inevitably from the basic Australian attitude. When this system becomes complicated by re-dichotomization or other consideration, the marriage is likely to be restricted to second cross cousins, or to become one-way, to cousins through one parent only. Whether the system or the marriage is primary is hard to say, and they are better viewed as functions than causally. Avuncu-local residence provides another easy bridge for cross-cousin marriage. The practice also appears in clan-structured societies free from anything dichotomous. Here it may sometimes be connected with the rights and duties specified for kin of the nonclan parent. Old China certainly practiced cross-cousin marriage, without sure evidence of either moieties or matrilineal clans, although the lineage group or extended family undoubtedly was important, as it still is. A mere desire to marry not too far out as well as not too far in, in the interest of more homogeneous family solidarity, may well have sufficed as a determining factor in some cases; or desire for property conservation through the generations. True, such aims would be served equally well by parallel-cousin marriage. The Arabs do follow this practice, and have tended to spread it with Mohammedan influence. This case is highly relevant to the theoretical problem of cousin marriage, which ethnologists have tended to restrict to cross-cousin marriage because of their preoccupation with primitives, clans, totemism, and moieties. The Arabs of course were fairly backward when their institutions were crystallized by Islam.

A neat situation has recently been described for the Brazilian Gê tribes by Nimuendajú and Lowie. Among the one Canella tribe there are no less than four cross-cutting moiety organizations. One of these is matrilineal and matrilocal and regulates marriage exogamously. Another, concerned with racing and hunting during the rainy season, is totemic but nonexogamous; membership is determined by names given by older individuals, theoretically the cross uncle for boys, the cross aunt for girls. The third set of moieties consists of two pairs of age classes, each age class comprising all males jointly initiated within a period. These moieties function in competitive sports in the dry season. The fourth set of moieties has membership also based on bestowed names; but these names are the property not of particular kinsmen but of three groups or subdivisions within each of the moieties, and of two clubs or four societies; the groups have assembly houses localized in the village circle, and they and the clubs function ceremonially in connection with men's initiations. So far the Canella.

Among the Apinayé, there is only one set of moieties, matrilineal and matrilocal, localized in the village circle, not at all concerned with marriage, competitive in sports and concerned with ceremonial, and characterized by possession of a series of personal names bestowed by uncles and aunts. Marriage is separately regulated by four unlocalized kiyé or "sides," where A marries B, B with C, C with D, D with A, for men; but for women, the rule is the reverse (or really complementarily the same), A marrying D, and so on. These "sides" are not clans, because boys belong to the side of their father, girls of their mother. Moreover, the sides group into implicit or unavowed intermarrying moieties, one consisting of A and C, the other of B and D; for A and C both marry with B and D, but never with each other.

Still another Gê tribe, the Sherente, have exogamous moieties which are patrilineal and patrilocal and are divided into six clans, localized in their positions in the village circle, which seem to correspond to the six subdivisions of the Canella ceremonial moieties.

Still another tribe, the Kaingang, associate with their exogamous moieties the totemic division of nature which the Canella associate with their nonexogamous rainy-season moieties.

It is evident that certain cultural forms or concepts have been luxuriantly developed by all these Gê tribes: the moiety, moiety subdivisions, their localization within the circular village, exogamy and unilateral descent, group ownership of names and bestowal of names by individuals of specific kinship relation, competitive sports, ceremonial associations, and grouping of initiates into age classes. Common to all these forms is the principle of grouping of persons, whether dual or multiple grouping. However, the very luxuriance of kinds of groups has led to a variety of ways of combining them, and probably to the devising of new kinds of groups, which made possible still further combinations, or transfer of functions from one set of groups to another. It is difficult to review the structures of these Brazilian tribal societies without a strong impression of their instability: of remodeling, innovation, and experimentation having been active.

Even a caste system may have involvements with the institutions we have been discussing. True primitives rarely progress beyond somewhat indefinite ranked classes, and in many of their societies social evaluation is accorded only to individuals. Their technological and economic capacities seem to be too limited for more. True caste, as in India, of course is logically almost the opposite of the clan. The social cleavages extend horizontally with ranking, instead of being vertical for essentially equivalent units; and marriage must be within the unit instead of outside it. Nevertheless, many of the castes and subcastes of India are subdivided into what appear to be true clans. This is true for civilized castes. As a more primitive example we may cite the Todas, who from the Indian point of view are essentially a caste, and whose "moieties" are subcastes, each of which is subdivided into exoga-

mous clans. The point is that, once the interests of a culture become directed toward social form and structure, it may make the most unexpected combinations of possible social forms.

With all this however it must be remembered that none of these forms need appear simply because a society is backward or nonliterate. The Eskimo, the Great Basin Shoshoneans, and many other societies are instances of extraordinarily simple structures free from any formal organizational features. The factors at work in producing these relatively unstructured societies may be connected with subsistence difficulties; they need not be. Extremely interesting is the discovery by Steward among the same clanless Shoshone of the custom of pseudo-cross-cousin marriage: the mates are stepcousins, no blood kin at all. This was certainly a strange practice to "think up"—how did it come to be? Relatives continue to be avoided, but imitation relatives are sought as mates. Who could deny inventiveness to primitives?

This is the essential moral I am aiming to point: the ingenuity and imaginativeness of the social structure of much of primitive life. Many of these institutions are what I have called them—true luxury products. They serve some function, but it may be a minor one among major possible ends which are left formally unprovided for. A great deal of the total picture suggests the play of earnest children, or the inventive vagaries of fashion. This in turn strongly suggests a high instability of many of these social constructs. This instability cannot ordinarily be proved specifically, because our knowledge of primitives rarely has historical depth; but it is indicated by the totality of the picture.

Political organization, on the contrary, is something which primitives have in general not achieved to any notable degree. When unlettered peoples have done so, as in Africa and Peru, we tend to exclude them from our concept of what is primitive. By complement, high civilizations have throughout history regularly been accompanied by considerable measures of political organization. To what the difference is due is not clear. Weakness of technological and therefore of economic controls among primitives may be suspected as an important factor. If so, a rather vital nexus of political organization through economics with technological development can be inferred. Primitives, being weak in the latter, remained weak in the former. Instead, they threw their cultural interests and energies into the forms of social structure, into the institutions concerned with the nearer interpersonal relations.

In the grand sweep of cultural growth, accordingly, successful technological and political developments, which characterize the more complex civilizations, are secondary and late products reared upon social forms or devices centering immemorially around kinship. Some measure of these kinship forms persists into higher civilization because kinship is biologically inescapable and perhaps equally inescapable psychologically. But the kinship structures of complex civilizations are often reduced, almost always divested of excrescences and luxuriances of pattern; they have become humble, simple, subserving real ends. The experimentation, inventiveness, and instability so evident in the social forms of primitive societies are transferred to the technological and political fields in higher civilization.

PART III

ON AMERICAN INDIANS

INTRODUCTION

MUCH the larger part of my professional work has been given over to the study of the cultures and languages of the American Indians. But the results of such study are descriptive, informational for record, and often voluminous as well as particular. They do not therefore lend themselves readily either to condensation or to excerpting. The selections in this part of the book have accordingly been made not from the angle of giving a representation of the total ground covered but of such special problems, methods, or insights as happened to emerge, often incidentally, in the course of exploratory description and analysis.

My most intensive concentration has been on the Indians of California. This subject I certainly know more about than any other; yet it is represented here only marginally by Nos. 23, 29, 32, and 40. My largest book, *The Handbook of the Indians of California*, issued in 1925, contains blocks of data found only there, as well as many passages of interpretation; but it seemed arbitrary to extract passages at random.

Several of the selections in this Part III deal with the classification of tribal cultures—inquiries about which groups of cultures are more similar or less similar to one another. Such are No. 31 on the Southwest; especially No. 33 on the Eskimo, Northwest Coast, and Plains areas; and, at least in parts, Nos. 31 and 35, dealing, respectively, with the allegedly ultra-primitive and untamable Seri of Sonora and the somewhat puzzling former great nation of the Chibcha in Andean Colombia. No. 33 is from a volume on *Cultural and Natural Areas of Native North America*. It differs from my earlier work and that of most other students of "culture areas" in trying to transcend the static treatment inherent in an areal approach and to reach inferences of growth and development for each culture type. However, certain difficulties and limitations remain in this more dynamic approach, which are touched on in No. 48 in Part V, in connection with the civilizations of Asia, the documented history of some of which is as long as the records for native America tend to be brief.

Before they can be classified, cultures must of course be characterized, by definition of their significant and distinctive features of form and function. Several selections embody or consist of such characterizations: Nos. 31 and 35 already mentioned; No. 32 on Yurok marriage types; and No. 29, which is an attempt to picture the salient quality or ethos of a total culture through the device of a pseudo-fictional dress—about which more in the particular introduction to that selection.

Also really of this group of characterizations is No. 36, which tries to delineate the most notable visual arts of ancient South America in terms of their distinctive aesthetic qualities. Anthropologists have generally hesitated to express themselves freely on matters as overtly qualitative as physiognomies of styles. Students and historians of art expect to make such characterizations, but generally lack the impulse to compare broadly and systematically.

There is one brief archaeological selection, No. 28. The significance of this is not substantive but methodological: the conversion of seriated stylistic traits into temporal sequence, as set forth in the particular introduction to the paper.

No. 34, on "Salt, Dogs, Tobacco," also stands apart. In fact, it is so different in its antecedents and aims from all others in Part III—or in the volume—as to require its own introduction.

28. ZUNI CULTURE SEQUENCES
1916

This is part of my earliest attempt at archaeology, a by-product of the first of three summers spent with the living Zuni people. Slight as the essay is, it carries a certain historical interest as regards method—in two ways, even. It dates from the period when the first stirrings of interest in the relative age of various aboriginal remains in the United States became manifest. Or perhaps, instead of "interest," I should say hope or faith—confidence that time differences could be ascertained. Such backwardness in the second decade of our century seems incredible now. And yet how sporadic in the writings of able men like Holmes and Fewkes and Bandelier are even their hesitant and passing allusions to this being perhaps earlier and that later! The first coherent scheme of relative chronology for any native area north of Mexico was that of Kidder for the Southwest, published in 1924. In 1915, when I made my Zuni observations, only Kidder and Nelson had consciously attacked the problem and begun to get results; and as a result of promises held out by my little flyer, Spier next year made his field study for Chronology of Zuni Ruins— *a model of original and workmanlike method which is still perhaps insufficiently appreciated and imitated.[1]*

Second, my commitment to the study of Zuni kinship and clanship forbade anything concurrent as time-consuming as digging. I was therefore thrown back on observation of stylistic features, however rough and ready, and of their distribution as regards co-occurence or dissociation. As the Southwest with its sparse vegetation and its ceramic richness is a prehistorian's paradise, I was able, with really very little time available, to reach certain outline findings that then were new, by the method of making stylistic seriations, and then, as a working assumption, converting these seriations, especially where they were concurrent, into a temporal sequence. Real verification, or sometimes disproof, comes of course from excavatory stratification. But this is sometimes difficult, costly, and slow, and requires considerable technical skill. Meanwhile, stylistically inferred sequences can serve as provisional constructs, besides pointing up his problems for the spade-and-level archaeologist.

Personally I was much stimulated by my contact with Zuni sherds and ruins, and the experience led me, ten years later, first to a brief sampling in Mexico, and then to two seasons of systematic exploration in the archaeology of Peru.

THE vicinity of the famous Indian pueblo of Zuni in New Mexico has long been known to be rich in ruins. Many of these have been reported and described, some surveyed, and material from various sites has found its way into collections. A large body of specimens was secured through excavations by the Hemenway expedition, but this material and its data remain unpublished.

The region furnishes an unusual opportunity for an attack on the chronology, or at least the sequences of culture, in the prehistory of the Southwest: first, because the restricted area excludes differences due to varying environments and thus renders any observable distinctions directly interpretable in terms of time; second, because of numerous links between the historic and prehistoric periods. Several of the ruins were inhabited in Spanish times. They still bear native names that tally with those mentioned in sixteenth- and seventeenth-century records, and some contain ruins of abandoned Catholic churches.

The tempting opportunity thus offered must of course be followed with the spade for ultimate results. I was in Zuni during the summer of 1915. Pressure of ethnological work forbade digging; but some three thousand potsherds were gathered from the surface of about fifteen once inhabited sites within a few miles' radius of the pueblo. These were supplemented by a thousand fragments from the streets and roofs of Zuni itself.

It was obvious that the pottery was of two well-marked types and that the surface of any one ruin yielded only such ware as plainly belonged to one or the other of the two classes. One set of sites is littered with sherds of which at least half are dull black or dark gray. The other half are as frequently red as white. Three-colored pieces—black and red on a white ground—are found. Corrugated ware is uncommon and about evenly distributed between dark and light.

On the second set of sites, black and red ware are both rare, white or whitish pieces constituting more than nine-tenths of the total. Three-color pottery has not been found. Corrugated sherds are common, but almost always of the light variety.

The first group of sites includes those which are mentioned as inhabited villages in the seventeenth century. Their sherds occur in nearly the same proportion as in modern Zuni. These ruins therefore fall in part into the historic period. The second group of sites is wholly prehistoric. Their ware resembles that familiar as Cliff Dwellers' pottery. The two wares have been designated as type A, the later, and type B, the earlier.

The conditions of the ruins accord with this arrangement in time. Type A ruins normally include standing walls, and loose rock abounds. All type B sites are low or flat, without walls or rock, and show only pebbles in the surface soil. It seems more likely that this condition is due to the decay of age, or to the carrying-away of the broken rock to serve as material in the near-by constructions of later ages, than to any habit of the period B people to build in clay instead of masonry. The latter possibility can be seriously entertained only if excavation reveals no building stone whatever in type B ruins.

Chips of obsidian are usually observable on period A sites, but have not been found on those of period B.

The proportions of different wares are summarized in Table 1.

TABLE 1

Type	Eight Sites of Period A	Nine Sites of Period B
Wholly black	53	5
White or black on white	25	92
Containing any red	22	3
	100	100

Differences between sites of the same period can also be observed. These indicate minor periods of time. Expressed in percentages of the total number of sherds secured at each spot, the frequency of several wares is given in Table 2.

The material as yet at hand is too slight, and too superficial in provenience, to make this classification into subperiods more than tentative for any particular site. The statistics however do allow of three conclusions. First, the two principal periods are almost certainly subdivisible into shorter epochs. Second, these subdivisions shade into one another. Third, there is no gap or marked break between periods A and B. So far as Zuni valley is concerned, the prehistory of Southwestern native civilization has therefore been in the main a continuous development from the earliest known time to the present.

A. V. Kidder's recent "Pottery of the Pajarito Plateau," in Volume II of the

Memoirs of the American Anthropological Association, presents analogous results, obtained by a method differing in some details, for another region of New Mexico; and at San Cristobal, in still another part of the state, N. C. Nelson has excavated a stratified deposit showing four successive layers of different type. It is quite likely that some of the types at these three sites will prove to be similar, or even identical, as soon as the material can be compared. In this event a chronological framework would be established that may prove capable of extension to accommodate a considerable part of the prehistoric data from the Southwest, and to fix distinctive and otherwise undatable local variations of ancient culture. The impression that there were at least two principal periods in the Southwest, the earlier represented by what are currently called Cliff Dweller forms, has of course long been prevalent, but the supporting evidence has been random. The three present sequential determinations promise not only definitely to establish but to elaborate the older general conviction.

TABLE 2

Period	Site	Corrugated	Three Color	Black on Red	Any Red	Black
Present........	Zuni	0*	12	1		
Late A........	Towwayallanna	1	8	3		
	Kolliwa	......	7	2		
	Shunntekya	2	7	2		
	Wimmayawa	2	4	1	22	53
	Mattsakya	3	4	3		
	Kyakkima	4	3	2		
Early A.......	Pinnawa	10	1	8		
	Site W	24	......	1		
Late B........	Hattsinawa	27	......	5	10	19
	Kyakkima West	12†	......	4	8	†
Middle B......	Shoptluwwayala	40	......	2	3	7
	Hawwikku B	49	......	6	12	9
Early B.......	Te'allatashshhanna	66	......	......	......	5
	Site X	71	......	......	3	1
	Tetlnatluwwayala	72	......	......	2	......
Uncertain.....	He'itli'annanna	......				3
	Site Y	......				

* Present, but less than half of 1 per cent.

† Only 25 pieces altogether are available from this site.

29. EARTH-TONGUE, MOHAVE
1922

The composition that follows passes formally as fiction, but in very thin disguise. Actually, it is an example of a special and somewhat heterodox method of picturing a culture. It is as such that it is included here: as a specimen of a technique of presentation possessing both special merits and special limitations.

Even an exceedingly simple culture, when all its practices and beliefs are gathered in, down to their subpatterns and qualifications and items, proves to be a bulky thing to portray. It can hardly be presented in less than several hundred pages. By the time its living personal variations due to individual differences in situation and temperament are included, a thousand pages may have become insufficient. As a matter of adequate record to be ultimately available, this is not a too disconcerting bulk. But even comparative ethnographers, and automatically all nonethnographers, need something far more compact, especially for first orientation. There are a number of ways of condensing or digesting data; but they all have their defects. In proportion as specific detail is omitted, concreteness and reality fade from the picture: it becomes abstractly schematic as a living culture never is, and therefore unconvincing. Leave in the detail, and compaction is impossible. Leave in some only, and that seems irrelevant, its choice arbitrary. Concentration on pattern of culture yields the most coherent picture—but of an increasing bodylessness—until, when all the patterns have been tied together, they subsume into the psychological formula of an ethos or temperament from which all the cultural substance has run out—which indeed might almost equally well fit a culture of quite different content.

Another solution to this problem of compact presentation is the present device of pseudo-fiction—passing an imaginary personage through the culture. One tells what he does, experiences, and feels; one hangs on his lay figure actual incidents that happened to other individuals. The purpose is to portray the culture rather than a psychologically convincing and individuated character. So, if the hero comes out something of a generalized dummy, no harm is done the major end in view, which is descriptive, not creatively literary. In fact, the fewer idiosyncrasies the manikin shows, the more convincingly can he wear significant bits taken from the experiences of quite different actual persons of the right age and sex. This device of the manufactured life-history possesses three virtues. It is the shortest-known cut through a whole culture; it retains a definite coherence not wholly extraneous to the subject matter; and the included segments of culture contained in it are portrayed as concrete phenomena.

The success of such a piece of pseudo-fiction seems to depend on the skill of selection of incidents to fit into an over-all pattern genuinely representative of the culture. Whether the pattern thus sketched corresponds to reality is something the reader is ordinarily not in position to verify. He can only judge empathically whether the pattern is consistent and adds up to something convincing. This is much as we judge of a portrait: not only whether it is good art but whether it impresses as a true likeness, even though we do not know the sitter.

And therewith our pseudo-fictional approach does return us partly into fiction and therewith into the domain of art. For if the reader validates by feeling, the writer has evidently operated with it too. However, a face that is painted, or even a charac-

ter that is delineated in a story, is simple and concrete compared with a culture, which is in its nature a generalization, and whose most aesthetically oriented representation must therefore be heavily sublimated intellectually.

On a larger scale the next step from the made-up biography is of course the historical novel. This aims, avowedly at least, at being literature; though as a genre it is customarily criticized for its inherent hankering after historical and cultural fidelity, a preoccupation that impairs the story's free creative aesthetic flow as fiction. The ample canvas of a novel does allow scope for portrayal of culture, in addition to an array of individuated personages. Yet in general opinion such portrayal of culture reinforces instead of impeding aesthetic success only in those cases where the culture enters incidentally as a background already familiar to the writer and intended reader—as in War and Peace, Vanity Fair, Red Chamber Dream. *A theoretical advantage of the historical novel over the fictional sketch is its multiple characters, which can add to the portrayal of the culture a dimension of depth and body. Of course, the inclusion of these differentiated personalities also calls for additional skill in writing.*

It was by 1922 that Elsie Clews Parsons wangled from twenty-four anthropologists promises to compose a story, incident, or life-history characteristic of a tribe well known to them, and had persuaded Mr. Huebsch to bring them out in a book called American Indian Life. *Some of us complied reluctantly, or even sweat blood in fulfilling our promise; some warmed up to the job; and Lowie took to it with such verve that he threw in three extra tales—one or the other of which was generally regarded by the rest of the co-authors as the best in the volume. Most successful as stories, on the whole, were incidents or sketches: the episode of a ramifying quarrel along the Klamath, the winter of an Eskimo community, days among the Havasupai, a Winnebago's curing, by Waterman, Boas, Spier, Radin; and Lowie's shorter contributions. Such smaller compass allows only glimpses of the culture, but those are vivid and there is less creaking of stiff plot. The full-length pseudo-biography was essayed by Lowie once, by Goddard, Goldenweiser, Swanton, and by myself. Wissler, and apparently Sapir, used actual autobiographies, at least as a base. The entrepreneuse, Mrs. Parsons, remained truest of all of us to professional habits: she proclaims her heroine a lay figure and discusses the probabilities of her participating in this or that cultural alternative.*

It was an interesting experiment, from which no one lost caste; but it was not repeated. Perhaps, all in all, it pays best for scientists to stick to formal presentation and to leave fiction to fictionalists; and yet—there may remain untried possibilities in the method.

EARTH-TONGUE'S earliest recollection was of the dim, cool house, where he picked bits of charcoal out of the soft sand and crumbled it against his hand. Once a cricket appeared on the wattled wall, suddenly went back in when he thrust at it, and only a stream of dry soil sifted out. And then there was the terrifying time when voices burst loudly into his sleep, people crowded in but stood helplessly awkward, while his father's brother shot insults of stolid hate into the ceaseless flood of his wife's vituperation. As the woman turned to beat a girl lurking in the corner and the man interposed and flung her off, Earth-Tongue burst into bawling and clung to his mother. He saw the angry woman stamp on pot after pot, tear open coils of shredded bark and strew them into the fire, and then, suddenly silent, load her own belongings into a carrying-frame and stagger out. The frame caught in the door: as she tore it through, the contents crashed, and a laugh rose in the house; but Earth-Tongue sobbed on a long time.

He was larger when he paddled with other children at the edge of the slough, but still very small as he first remembered himself seeing the great, stretching river that drew by with mysterious, swirling noises in its red eddies. He and his little brother were put into a huge pot which his father and another man pushed before them cross-stream: their hair, as it coiled high on their heads, was just visible over the pot's edge as they swam. And then followed an interminable trudge somewhere through the dust, relieved only by rides on his father's back.

He was older when he shot his first bow; when at dusk he caught a woodpecker in its hole and would not let go, though it hacked desperately at his clasped hands, until a half-grown cousin took it from him to imprison under a turned jar for the night. His father wove a cage the next day, and the captive was installed, but remained wild, and one morning was dead. And then came the time when the boys of Mesquite-Water challenged those of his settlement on a hot summer day after the annual river inundation had half-dried, and they slung lumps of mud at each other from the ends of long willow poles.

There were other events that must have fallen soon after this period, but which he did not remember: when he rolled his hair into long, slim cylinders, began to measure how nearly it reached his hip, and made his first advances to girls.

Even before this he had dreamed of Mastamho, gigantic on the peak Avikwame in the great, dark, round house full of varied peoples; of the two Ravens singing of dust whirls and war and of the far-away clumps of cane waiting to be cut into flutes; and of the river, drawn from its source to wash away the ashes and bones of Matavilya, where the pin-nacles stand in the gorge at House-Post-Water. He knew later that he had dreamed these things as a little boy, even while he was still in his mother; he did not yet think about them, except when the old man his grandfather and his father or uncles sang of them.

One day a runner came up the valley and shouted pantingly that strangers had appeared from the east at dawn and killed a woman and two children at Sand-Back, besides wounding a man and his younger brother. The men leaped for their weapons; the women called in their children, loaded themselves with property, and soon began to track northward in a straggling, excited stream. Earth-Tongue pulled down his bow and raked among the roof thatch for such arrows as he could assemble. Then he joined his kinsmen and male neighbors, who stood in a group in front of one of the shade roofs, exclaiming and pointing at a smoke that rose down the valley. Bundles of crude, blunt arrows projected behind their hips, shoved under cord belts; and many had clubs dangling from their wrists. Earth-Tongue did not own a club: he had never seen battle; and he hung about the outside of the cluster of seasoned men.

Soon, refugees from the nearer downstream settlements began to arrive; and then a body of fighting men from up the valley, bedaubed for war. Earth-Tongue's kinsmen merged with them; and, as they proceeded south, growing in numbers, they met ever more women and children trudging north, and finally those from the point of attack; until, not far away in the cottonwoods, they came upon the men of Sand-Back. The enemy were Halchidhoma from far downstream, they were now informed, not Walapai as at first conjectured. They had avoided the river, traversing the desert to hide in the Walapai mountains and descend at night upon the nearer tip of the Mohave land. They had long since gone off—sixty they were said to number, as they were seen to file over the rocks high above the stream at Pinnacles. They had looted and burned only the group of houses at Sand-Back, had killed not a woman but a man, and had lightly wounded with an arrow one of the men who fought back from a distance: the other reported casualties turned up safe. But the enemy had carried off the slain man's head and would dance about its skin and long hair. Earth-Tongue gazed at the collapsed houses, their charred posts smoking on the sand; and that night he watched the beheaded man's cremation. There was much talk of retaliation, but an immediate attack would have found the Halchidhoma prepared or perhaps removed.

So some months elapsed without a move being made; and meanwhile Earth-Tongue married. In the turmoil of the Halchidhoma invasion, as party after party trooped by, he had been attracted by the sight of a girl, barely but definitely passed out of childhood, and only a little younger than himself, who halted, leaning under her laden carrying-frame, behind her mother, as their group paused for an excited colloquy. He saw that the girl noted his eyes on her and glanced away, and he knew, from the people she was with, that her clan name must be Kata. Not long after, he began to find errands or companions that took him to her settlement. Soon a mutual familiarity of each other's presence was established, the purport of which was manifest even though direct speech between the two young people was infrequent and brief. Both were shy; until one afternoon a blind old man, the girl's father's uncle, who knew of Earth-Tongue's repeated presence from the references of the family, addressed him and her directly. "Why do you not marry?" he said. "Persons do not live long. Soon you will be old like myself, unable to please yourselves. It is good that you sleep and play together. You, young man, should stay here the night." Neither Earth-Tongue nor the

girl answered. But he remained through the evening meal and after; and when the house was dark, went silently to where she lay. The next day, he stayed on; the day after, returned briefly to his home; and from then on, spent increasing time at his new abode, where, without a word having been spoken, he slipped into a more and more recognized status. He did not work, unless special occasion called, such as assisting with a seine-net; and Kata only occasionally helped her relatives farm. Instead, they spent much time together, lolling under the shade, toying or teasing each other, or listening to their elders. Sometimes he sang softly as he lay by her, or she bent over him searching his head or untangling his clustered locks, or tried to draw the occasional hairs from his face with her teeth; and ever she laughed more freely. So the days followed one another.

When at last the Mohave were ready, it was announced that they would once for all destroy the Halchidhoma. The entire nation was to move and appropriate the enemy land. Soon they started, most of the men in advance, weaponed and unburdened save for gourds of maize meal at their hips; water they did not have to carry, since they followed the river. Behind tramped the women, children, and old men, under loads. Foods, blankets of bark and rabbit fur, fish nets, metates, household property, and the most necessary pottery vessels were taken. The remainder of their belongings and stored provisions was buried or hidden away: every house in the valley stood empty.

For five days they walked. Then the men suddenly surrounded a group of settlements. These were the houses of the Kohuana, a far downstream tribe speaking near-Cocopa, wasted by wars with their neighbors, until the pressed remnant had sought refuge half a day's journey above the Halchidhoma to whom they were united less by positive friendship than by common foes and parallel fortunes. For the Halchidhoma, too, remembered having once lived populously among the welter of tribes in the broad bottom lands below the mouth of the Gila. With the Kohuana the Mohave had no direct quarrel; and, though they arrived armed and overpowering, they proclaimed themselves kinsmen and announced that they had come as guests. By night the Kohuana houses overflowed with the mob of Mohave families. Kohuana messengers were dispatched to summon the Halchidhoma to battle at White-Spread-Rock, if they were not afraid. Such a challenge the outnumbered people could not find it in their manhood to evade. So the next day saw them in line at the appointed field, barely a hundred strong, against perhaps four hundred that the Mohave mustered after setting a guard over their families.

Earth-Tongue went into battle with much inward excitement, but little fear, and listened obediently to the admonitions of his seasoned kinsmen. Even before arrows could reach, the shooting began. Before long, arrows flew feebly by, and then it became necessary to twist sharply sidewise to avoid them. At this distance the two lines stood and shot at each other, taunting and leaping, while in the rear half-grown boys and a few old men helped to gather up and replenish bundles of arrows. What the Halchidhoma lacked in frequency of shots, they partly made up in greater openness of target; and, before long, struck men began to withdraw temporarily on each side. The Mohave could have made short work by charging in a body with their clubs; but they had asked for an open stand-up fight, and besides found pleasure in the game, which fell increasingly to their advantage. For hours they sweated in the sun, gradually and irregularly forcing the Halchidhoma line back, and shouting whenever one of the foe was carried off.

At last the leaders called that it was time to cease, and defied the foe to resume in the same spot on the fourth day. Then they trooped victoriously back, without a fatality, though a few, weakened from bleeding or with parts of shafts broken off in them, were carried on the backs of companions. Earth-Tongue had been struck twice. One arrow had grazed the skin of his flank when he became overconfident and failed to bend his body with sudden enough vigor. Then one of three shafts that came toward him almost at once had imbedded itself a finger-joint's depth in the front of his thigh, and hung there until he hastily plucked it out. Neither wound bled profusely, especially after a bit of charcoal was reached him to rub in for stanching; and he returned stiff, tired, and proud. The Halchidhoma losses were severer. None of them appeared to have fallen dead on the field; but at least half had been struck, and a number so vitally or so often that they would die.

For four days the Mohave treated their wounds, talked of the next battle, and ate their Kohuana hosts' provisions. Then they set out. But the Halchidhoma had sent their families downstream and taken up a new stand farther back. Here they joined once more, and the fight went on as before, but with ever more preponderance to the Mohave; until these, wearied by the noon sun, contemptuously drew off to the river to drink. The Halchidhoma seized the occasion to run to their children and women, set these across the river, and strike east over the desert. When the victors reappeared, the fugitives were far on their way. The Mohave thereupon decided to occupy their fields and houses until the dispossessed might come to drive them out; which the latter, by this time safely received among the Maricopa far across the desert on the Gila, had no intention of doing. However, the Mohave lived nearly a year in the land of the Halchidhoma, adjusting themselves as they could. They returned to their own valley only as the next flood and planting time approached, taking the Kohuana along to settle among themselves, where these enforced visitors remained for some years.

Before the stay in the Halchidhoma country was over, Earth-Tongue and Kata had drifted apart. The derangement of accustomed residence, enforced mingling with others, Earth-Tongue's pride as an incipient warrior, the fact that no child was born, all contributed to separate them increasingly. Each formed new interests while vaguely jealous of the other's; and in the end Earth-Tongue brought not Kata but another girl to his parents' house.

Soon after his first child was born— a daughter, called Owich like the sisters of himself, his father, and his father's father—Earth-Tongue grew restless for adventure, and, the time being one of peace, joined himself to those that wished to travel. Ten or twenty in number, they would go out: too few to excite apprehension of treacherous intent to attack, too many to be made away with safely. Each carried maize meal, water in a gourd, his weapons, and whatever he might wish to trade. On shorter journeys they prided themselves on being able to travel at a trot four days without food and with only such drink as the desert might afford, chewing perhaps a bit of black willow wood as a relief for the dryness of their mouths. But these hardships they underwent mostly in emulation of others, or toward the last stretch of a return home with Mohave land close before them. Again and again Earth-Tongue went down the river, through Yuma, Kamia, Halyikwamai, and Cocopa settlements, to the flat shores of the salt sea; or east into the Walapai mountains and down into the chasm of the Havasupai, where he saw strange-speaking and strangely dressed Hopi, heard of their stone

towns, and brought home their belts and, once, a blanket of white cotton.

To the northwest he visited the Chemehuevi and other Paiutes about their scattered springs, and ate their foods of seeds and wild fruits, some familiar, some bitter and strange; and mescal and sometimes deer. Theirs was a strange language too, but he had heard a little of it from the few Chemehuevi who lived at the northern extreme of Mohave valley and beyond it on Cottonwood island; and many of his companions could speak more. They went from Paiute band to band, to where the river no longer flows from the north but from the east, beyond the Muddy, and found each group much like the last in customs, but of new kinds of food. They listened to the stories of the Paiute, who dreamed of the mountain Nüvant as the Mohave do of Avikwame; and to them in return they sang their songs, which the Paiute said they wished to hear.

To the west were many tribes, all different-tongued, but mostly not too hard to understand a little when one knew Chemehuevi. There were the Vanyume on their river that dried into nothing and left them always half-starved; the Hanyuvecha in the range of great pines beyond; northward, about Three-Mountains, the Kuvahye, adjoined by other mountaineers, little tribes, unwarlike, friendly to the visitors, some of whom they hailed as old friends. They offered no smoke, but gave tobacco leaves crushed in a mortar with shells; which Earth-Tongue and his companions ate in courtesy and were nearly all made thereby to sweat and vomit violently. From a crest near here they looked over a vast plain beyond, in which shimmered what one of his companions said were large lakes. He had been there and had seen the people, who lived in long houses of rushes—a hundred fires in line within one house—and ate rush roots, and slept on rushes, and at night worms came up and troubled the sleepers. And beyond in the tumbled range on which they stood, as they looked out, were the Like-Mohave, a very little like themselves in speech, but naked, unkempt, and poor. These Earth-Tongue saw, but not in their own houses.

And, going out again, he traversed the land of the tribes to the southwest, unfriendly, half-sullen, and dangerous to small parties. The Hakwicha dug wells and ate mesquite; beyond them were people in the mountains, about hot springs, who sang to turtle shells instead of gourds; and still farther, stretching down to the ocean that one could see from their peaks, lived the Foreign-Kamia, speaking almost like the real Kamia, but knowing nothing of farmed foods, eating rattlesnakes, and a hostile lot to venture among. They had some grudges to pay off to the Mohave for plundered settlements, but were not a people to travel far from their homes even for revenge.

The Yavapai, too, Earth-Tongue came to know, though theirs was not an attractive country to visit. They dreamed and sang like the Mohave, but of other animals; and some of their stories were the same. Their neighbors and friends were the Roaming-Yavapai, a small-statured, sharp-eyed people, wearing their hair flowing, fierce lance fighters, taciturn, violent, untrustworthy; but inclined favorably to the Mohave in spite of the utter unintelligibility of their speech because they knew them through the Yavapai as traditionally hostile, like themselves, against the Maricopa and that people of innumerable houses, the Pima. These last Earth-Tongue never came to know save on the field of battle.

One early summer, as the river was flooding, its rise suddenly stopped. The inundation being wont to grow in interrupted stages, the people waited quietly for its resumption. But the water fell back and back. Then some began to declare that it might not rise again, and advised planting at once before the moist ground should dry: but others pointed out that high water was yet due, and had often come late, and that present planting in that case would cause the seed to wash out and be lost. So nearly all waited with concern and much discussing; until finally the river was wholly back within its banks and dropping decisively. Then they knew that nothing more was to be hoped for that season, and men and women hastened to save what they might of the crop. But many of the fields had remained wholly untouched by water, and most of the others were already half-dry again. In some, the maize and beans never sprouted; in some they came up indeed, but soon wilted; and though the women carried water in jars, only small patches could be effectively served in this hand fashion.

Soon everyone knew that famine impended, and that so few houses would grow even enough harvest for another seeding that the year after would also be hard to survive. They gathered every wisp of wild seed plants in the uncultivated bottoms; but these wild seeds too had come up thin; and even the crop of mesquite pods was pitiful. The women labored faithfully, and the children watched over the scattered maize to guard it; yet, though the grain ripened, the scattered stalks were too few to keep any house through the winter. Some families did not pick even an ear. A moon after harvest time, the crop was consumed; by winter, the last of the other stores. The men fished daily, but the sloughs and ponds had never filled and were soon seined out, and the river's yield was uncertain and far insufficient. Every one was gaunt; the children lay listlessly about; sickness grew.

Earth-Tongue's wife, and his older brother's, had planted with his mother in his father's ancestral field, which lay low and was long proved rich. So they fared better than many. Nevertheless, before spring the emaciated bodies of two children and an old woman from the house had been burned, and Earth-Tongue had three times sung himself hoarse as they lay dying.

The young men went out with their bows, and now and then returned with a bird or gopher or badger, but oftener empty-handed. People who had new belongings went to the Walapai to trade for mescal and deer meat. Whole families trudged to visit the Chemehuevi, until they brought back word that these hosts too were eaten out. At last not a day passed without columns of smoke from cremation pyres visible somewhere in the valley. It was a terrible year and long remembered before the end of another summer brought partial abatement.

So numerous had been the deaths from bowel flux and cough that shaman after shaman fell a victim to the anger of the kin of those he had attempted to save. Yellow-Thigh, a powerful man and not very old, had lost two patients during the famine, and three more at intervals since. Mutterings were frequent; but no one had found opportunity, or had dared, to work vengeance on him. One morning, Earth-Tongue and a friend, sauntering up-valley on some errand, turned to a house before which Yellow-Thigh lay, for those there were kinsmen of his. No men were about; and as the two visitors stood in the door, his friend on sudden impulse whispered to Earth-Tongue, "Let us kill him." So they sat down for a little and passed the news of the day, then arose, Earth-Tongue reaching for his bow and four cross-pointed arrows, with the remark that they were going to shoot doves. The shaman grunted assent, and the pair passed.

For a time they traversed the brush, planning the deed. At the mesa edge they broke two large cobbles to sharp edges, and then returned. Yellow-Thigh lay under the shade-roof with closed eyes, breathing regularly. The friend went by him to look into the house and, finding it empty, nodded. Earth-Tongue, who had approached, bent suddenly down and struck with all his might at the sleeper's head. The shaman pushed himself to a sitting position as the blood began to pour from the mangled side of his face. The friend started back, then plunged forward to finish the man, and swung; but his excited arm brought the weapon down only on the victim's knee. Then he staggered off, scarcely able in fright and emotion to drag his own legs. Earth-Tongue, seeing the shaman still sitting, strode forward again and with both hands drove the point of the stone through the top of his skull. Two women who had been going through each other's hair in the shadow of the brush fence outside, half-turned at the noise and shrieked, while Earth-Tongue dashed after his companion, seized his hand, and dragged him forward. They ran through the willows and at last lay down to pant in hiding; and here, after they had quieted, Earth-Tongue laughed at his friend's faltering stroke and steps. Then they went on, still keeping to cover, until around the second bend they swam the river.

On the other side, old men were gaming with poles and hoop, and others watched. The two sat down and looked on. Three times, four times, until it was early afternoon, the players bet and threw their poles and one or the other finally took up the stakes. Then Earth-Tongue said, "I have killed a shaman, the large man at Sloping-Gravel."

"Yes, do kill him," answered one of the old men, thinking Earth-Tongue was boasting of an empty intent; and a spectator added, "Indeed, it would be well. Too many persons are dying."

"I have killed him," Earth-Tongue said again, and they began to believe him. So they went to the houses. Soon word came that the shaman was dead;

and then his kinsmen arrived, angry and threatening, and accusations flew back and forth, while Earth-Tongue stood unmoved and silent but wary. The kinsmen finally challenged to a stick fight the next day, and withdrew to burn the dead man.

The people of the settlement commended Earth-Tongue and promised to engage for him; and in the morning they and all his kin, and the kin of those whom the shaman had brought to their deaths, gathered in the center of a large playing field. Each man carried a willow as thick as his forearm and reaching as high as his neck; and in his left hand, a shorter parrying stick. The challengers appeared, somewhat fewer in number and with tear-marked faces, but enraging their opponents by crying out in insult the names of their dead parents and grandparents. Then the two bodies, spreading into irregular lines, rushed at each other. Each man swung at an antagonist's head, now with his staff held in one hand, now in both. Blows beat down on heads through the guard, rained on shoulders, bruised knuckles, and the willows clashed amid the shouts. Now and then a staff broke, and a contestant ran back to seize a new one. The fighters sweated, panted, rubbed blood out of their eyes, and staggered forward and back as the lines swayed in the clamor. Once or twice a maddened fighter, running in under his opponent's strokes, seized his hair to belabor him with his parry-club; whereupon shouts of "Bad, bad! No! No! Release!" arose and a multitude of rescuers' blows drove him back. The shaman's kindred were getting the worst of it but rallied again and again without being driven wholly to their end of the field. Strokes became feebler and feebler. Weary arms could no longer rise. Fighter after fighter leaned on his stick or sat on the ground in the rear. Each side taunted the other to come on again; and at last they drew apart, every man panting, bruised, and

weary, but satisfied at the damage he had inflicted. No heads had been broken and no one died, though some were sick for a few days from maggots that had bred in the scalp under their clotted hair; and then talk died down and the enmity gradually subsided. Earth-Tongue won the praise of all the Mohave who were not the dead man's kinsmen.

Once runners came from the Yuma to invite to an attack on the Cocopa at the mouth of the river. A hundred and twenty Mohave went down. The kohota play-chief of the northern half of the Mohave asked the party to bring back captives, although he already had had several; and Earth-Tongue was one of the men whom he requested to carry food and water for the women prisoners' return journey and to guard against their escape.

The Yuma contingent was even larger than the Mohave one; and the attack was made at daybreak. It was not much of a fight. The first house entered gave the alarm, and the settlement scattered amid yells. Only two Cocopa were killed by the Yuma, and two young women, sisters, called Night-Hawk, were captured by the Mohave. The Mohave stayed with the Yuma four days to watch the scalp dance, but, since none of them had touched the corpses, they were not in need of purification and hence returned home.

The whole tribe came out to escort them to the kohota's house. There the captives were made to sit down, while the kohota stood up and sang the two Pleiades songs over and over. Then men and women, facing each other, danced. When the sun was at its height, they stopped, ate what the kohota's women brought out, then lay in the shade or gambled. In the afternoon the kohota called out a Chutaha singer. Soon the sounding jar began to boom in its trench of sand, the people left off their play, and danced: three rows of young men with feathers tied in their hair, one row of old men, and two women standing off by themselves. Then at last, as the sun was coming low, the chief came with rattles in his hand and at the end of a song shouted: "Let him sing who wishes to! Let any woman sing! I appoint no one!" Women grasped the rattles and carried them, one to a Tumanpa singer, others to those who knew Vinimulya and Vinimulya-hapacha; and one was brought to Earth-Tongue to sing Raven. Soon all four of the dances were in progress at different places, while those women who liked Nyohaiva, having persuaded an old man to sing that, began to revolve about him and his staff, standing shoulder to shoulder. As fast as one song ended, the singers took up another, for the sun had nearly set, and the sweating women clamored for more, while the crowd of people stood about.

With darkness they stopped to bathe and eat and rest, then danced again, singing as before, and new kinds too, while off on the side, by the light of a fire, groups of men played hiding game to the Tudhulva songs through the night. In the morning the kohota had the assemblage bathe, fed them once more, and sent them home to return two days later.

This time they danced again all evening, all next afternoon, and on through the night. As the sun rose, the kohota, still singing, took the two captives one by each hand, and walked toward the river. Behind him came the Tumanpa and Vinimulya singers, each with his crowd, and then the mass of people in procession. The kohota, still holding the two girls, ran out over the bank, splashing into the river, and everyone followed. This made Mohaves of the captives, and people were no longer so much afraid of them. The kohota led them back to his house, where they were to live, and said, "Perhaps these girls will marry and bear children, who, belonging to both tribes, will make peace when they grow up, and there will be no more war." So it came in part. After two years, one of the sisters married, and in time had a child. The other continued without husband. In time, formal peace was made between the Yuma and Cocopa; whereupon the kohota announced, "Since the tribes are friends now, let us not keep Night-Hawk longer." So a party led her to the Yuma, where her kinsmen met and escorted her home. Her sister remained with her Mohave husband.

Earth-Tongue was beginning to grow old. His oldest son and one daughter both had children, and his hair showed the first streaks of gray. He thought more about his youth and commenced to remember what he had dreamed then. He knew he had seen Matavilya sick and gradually dying and then burned, and his ashes washed away by the river which Mastamho made to flow out of the ground with his rod. He remembered, too, Mastamho's house on Avikwame, with the multitudes inside it in rows like little children, and Mastamho instructing them; and how he repeated after him, correctly, until Mastamho said to him, "That is right! You know it! You have it! I give it to you!" Then he had dreamed how Sky-Rattlesnake was at last inveigled from his house far in the south ocean, and his head cut off on Avikwame. Earth-Tongue saw his joints and blood and sweat and juices turn into eggs. From these eggs hatched Rattlesnake, Black-Widow Spider, Scorpion, and Yellow-Ant, who went off to Three-Mountains and remote places, deep in the earth or high in the sky, and from there built four roads to all tribes. When they wish a man for a friend to stay with them, they bite him and take his shadow home with them. "But another road leads from their house to my heart," Earth-Tongue would say, "and I know what they do. And I intercept the shadow before Rattlesnake has led it wholly to Three-Mountains, and sing it back; I break the roads of spittle that Spider has begun to wind four times around the man's heart; and so he lives again."

Then Earth-Tongue commenced to be sent for when people were bitten—first by relatives, then by others. He would stand up at once where he was and sing to bring a cooling wind; and, on reaching the sick person, he would sing over him from the north, west, south, and east—but not a fifth time, lest he die. Then, sending everyone away but a wife or mother, and forbidding all drink, he would sit by the patient the whole night, singing his four songs from time to time. In the morning the sick person used to get up well.

Fighting interrupted these pursuits. It was a summons again from the Yuma, this time against the Maricopa; and nearly two hundred of the Mohave responded. The seventh night they were on Maricopa soil and met eighty Yuma by appointment, as well as Yavapai and their roaming Apache allies; and in the morning they advanced to attack. But the Maricopa had got wind of their presence, and when the fight opened were reinforced by a vast number of the Pima. The horse-mounted Apache and the unstable Yavapai soon fled. The Mohave and Yuma exhorted one another, and though man after man fell, gave ground slowly in a solid mass, fighting back outnumbered.

At last the enemy ran all in a body against them. Part of the Mohave broke before the shock and fled to the north, many of them ultimately escaping. But sixty of them formed with the Yuma on a little knoll near the Gila, where they stood in a dense mass. As the Pima and Maricopa dashed against them, they dragged man after man struggling into their midst, where he was dispatched with fierce club blows on his head or thrusts into his face. Twice Earth-Tongue leaped out to grasp an opponent and fling him over his back, thus protecting his own skull, while his companions beat the struggling foe to death. The fighting grew wilder. The Pima no longer drew back to shoot arrows but swirled incessantly around and into the dwindling cluster at bay. At last the shouts ceased; the dust began to settle; and all but two of the Yuma, and every man of the sixty Mohave, lay with crushed head or mangled body on foreign earth.

30. NATIVE CULTURE OF THE SOUTHWEST
1928

ANTHROPOLOGY has been pursued in the Southwest for a couple of generations. The railroad surveys and early geological explorations brought back descriptions, specimens, and photographs, of both ruins and pueblos, some of which have never been surpassed. Excavations soon followed, and in some cases work was done which will stand for all time: Mindeleff's on architecture, for instance. Meanwhile, Cushing laid the foundation of ethnological study in his residence at Zuni. Materials kept piling up decade by decade.

Fifteen to twenty years ago inquiries took a new turn. The older investigators had been content to describe or, if they explained, felt confident that they could derive origins immediately from their particular data. In time, objectives shifted from origins to development, from ultimate to nearer antecedents, and even these, it was recognized, could ordinarily be determined only through comparative treatment of a wide body of data. In archaeology the tremendous evidential weight of superimposition of remains began to be perceived, and, with the stratigraphic discoveries of Nelson and Kidder,[1] Southwestern archaeology entered the field of the modern sciences. Site after site was explored under the new point of view, until, basing on the long-continued excavations at Pecos, Kidder, in his *Southwestern Archaeology*, was able to weld the prehistory of the most distinctive part of the area into a comprehensive and continuous whole of two Basket Maker and five Pueblo periods. This fundamental work will no doubt be corrected in detail, enriched and intensified, and certainly is in need of areal extension; but its framework promises to be permanent.

Ethnology has not progressed quite so far, but is emerging from the descriptive stage. When Parsons' long-promised monograph appears, we shall have an analytic comparison and partial historic interpretation of at least the important ritual side of Southwestern culture; and studies of its other aspects may be expected to follow. Strong has already made a beginning of an interpretation for the forms of society.

It is opportune, accordingly, to review the problems of cultural anthropology in the native Southwest as they shape themselves at present.

First of all, it must be admitted that we recognize several different Southwests. The archaeologists mean Pueblo and the agricultural antecessors of the Pueblo, when they say "Southwest." Ethnologists mostly have in mind Pueblo and Navaho, with the Pima-Papago as a sort of annex. The Apache are little known; the Havasupai remain undescribed in print; on Walapai, Yavapai, Maricopa there is nothing. Haeberlin long ago did not hesitate to treat the southern Californians as outright Southwestern, but in most discussions they are still left out, as if they were ethnically Californian. Wissler and I, in continental classifications, both extend the Southwest culture south nearly to the Tropic, so that half of it lies in Mexico. No one appears to have challenged this classification, perhaps because data from northern Mexico are so scant. At the same time, it is clear that if this larger Southwest is a true cultural entity, the old Pueblo or even Arizona–New Mexico Southwest is but a fragment, whose functioning is intelligible only in terms of the larger growth....

Maps of botanical distributions show as a well-defined area of desert, characterized by creosote bush and Cactaceae, the territory occupied by almost the whole Yuman family and the Pima,

Papago, and Sonoran tribes, in other words, those Southwestern peoples who might be described as sub-Pueblo. On the other hand, the semidesert in which the Pueblo range falls extends northwestward into the Great Basin. This fact, at first sight seemingly subversive of a correlation between Pueblo culture and environment, nevertheless accords with the extension into Nevada of a form of the Basket Maker culture of which the Pueblo was an outgrowth. . . .

The historic imports of the spatial relations of the various culture types in the Southwest have been little examined except in so far as Kidder has dealt with the southward retraction of the true Pueblo area in its third or Great period, its abandonment of its original focus, the San Juan drainage, at the end of that period, and its gradual northward and eastward shrinkage since. Equally interesting are likely to be inductions based on the space and time distribution of traits transcending the special Pueblo culture: pottery, for instance.

Except perhaps for some of the Athabascans and Yumans, every Southwestern people seems to have been pottery-making. To the west of the trichrome and glazing art of the Pueblos, pottery becomes two-color on the lower Gila and Colorado, monochrome in California. This indicates a relation of marginal dependence on the Pueblo art. But a direct dependence of these peripheral areas on the Pueblo center is not borne out by other considerations. The middle ("Lower") Gila region has to date shown two styles of pottery, recognized but misinterpreted many years ago by Cushing: a red-white-black, and a two-color called variously red on yellow, red on gray, red on red, or, most appropriately, red on buff. This bichrome ware is, as Kidder has pointed out, "so radically unlike . . . all other Southwestern (*read* Pueblo) pottery that it gives rise to the suspicion that it may be the result of an intrusion from some hitherto unlocated culture centre." As to the distinct-

ness of this ware in texture, color, pattern, and probably shape, there can be no question; although the small-element designs figured by Kidder represent only one strain in the style. There can also be no question as to the essential survival of this style in the pottery art of the recent Colorado River tribes, the Yuma and Mohave; and beyond them, in a simplified, usually patternless stage, among the southern California groups. Mohave pottery is almost identical with ancient middle Gila red on buff ware in texture and color; even the designs, although of a somewhat new cast, show indubitable relationship. Modern Pima and Maricopa ware would seem to represent a somewhat more altered making-over of the same tradition, with the substitution of black vegetable paint for the dull red in the designs. From Fresnal, in southern Arizona, Lumholtz has figured two ancient bowls closely similar to the red on buff of the Gila. Seri pottery, according to McGee's description and illustrations, belongs to the same tradition, without more simplification, or more quality of archaic survival, than the ware of southern California. The style thus has a distribution embracing at least northwestern Sonora, southwestern Arizona, southern California, perhaps northern Baja California—an area roughly as large as the Pueblo area at the time of its greatest extension. These two pottery traditions in the main abutted on and excluded each other.

They did however geographically overlap in the middle Gila drainage. Kidder was able to place the Pueblo-like middle Gila trichrome toward the end of the Pueblo Great period (P-3 or early P-4), without having the evidence to place red on buff temporally. Schmidt, who subsequently excavated in the region, showed by stratification and cross-tying of stray sherds that the red on buff is the earlier of the two styles. This brings to the fore the interesting fact that the red on buff, although temporarily displaced by a Pueblo style on the Gila, has maintained itself with relatively little change over most of its area at least since early Pueblo-3 times, whereas during the same period black on white went out, glaze developed and decayed, and modern styles arose in the Pueblo area.

This vitality of the red on buff style reinforces the inferences drawn from its distinctness and extension. It represents a movement no doubt ultimately related but largely independent of Pueblo pottery growth and approximately equal to it in historical and geographical significance. It is merely the fact that we have approached the ancient contact manifestations of this separate growth from the angle of Pueblo development and hesitated to connect it with its natural survivals, which has obscured the picture. We can accordingly no longer with propriety substantially equate Pueblo and Southwestern in speaking of pottery. Southwestern pottery history consists of at least two developments and their interrelations: Pueblo and Gila-Sonora.

This recognition raises the presumption that Southwestern culture in general is to be viewed in the same way. If we could feel sure of doing so legitimately, the anomalous position of the Pima as a sort of irrelevant appendix would at once be done away with. Just as corrugating, black on white, and glazing characterize the pottery of the distinctive Pueblo unit of this larger culture mass, so would storied masonry, community construction, the kiva, cotton, the matrilineate, direction-color symbolism, perhaps priesthood by learning to fill a recognized office, altars, masks, ancestor impersonation, the importance of the ideas of emergence from the underworld and of sex fertilization, characterize Pueblo culture. The Gila-Sonora culture growth is as yet too little known to be equally well definable; but it would seem to lack most or all of the cited Pueblo trends, and to possess, instead, patrilinear institutions, a fighting tradition and war legends, village as opposed to town organization, prevailingly shamanistic control of ritual, probably irrigation. The environmental reflection of the divergence is that the Pueblo area is semidesert, the Gila-Yuman-Sonoran area true desert.

This view would explain the isolated Casa Grande culture as a transient contact phenomenon of the two major culture growths. It might also go far to clear up the puzzling cultural status of the lower Colorado tribes, who on the one hand are specialized away from what it has been customary to regard as "Southwestern" features and on the other hand lack a number of traits common to the Pueblos and the littoral groups of southern California: the kiva-sweat-house, for instance, group fetishes, initiation ceremonies, sand-painting altars, moiety organization. Strong, who recognizes in California older Pueblo and later Colorado River influences, has suggested a migrational irruption of the Yuman tribes to account for the geographical break in recent cultural continuity. It would be less hypothetical to find the explanation in a northward extension of Sonoran culture influences cutting across an earlier westward radiation of Pueblo influences, without commitment as to populational shifts. No doubt the Yuman river tribes specialized considerably the Sonoran culture which reached them. Almost certainly, too, part of the southern culture elements received were passed on by them to the southern Californians—pottery, for example, perhaps the Dying God concept, and the tale of the hero who recovered the bones of his father who had been killed when he lost a game, or whose bones were being played with by his slayers—two myth ideas that it is difficult not to connect with their occurrences in southern Mexico. Such secondary growths and diffusions however enrich rather than break the picture which the history of the larger Southwest is beginning to reveal in outline....

31. CHARACTERISTICS OF THE SERI INDIANS
1931

TECHNOLOGICAL INDIFFERENCE

THE single-bladed paddles seen by McGee and myself were two-piece and hafted with nails. McGee is more interested in balsa propulsion by recumbent women with hands, shells, or unhandled blades. That such crude devices were used along shore or in bays often enough to be mentioned is wholly in line with the conspicuous Seri indifference, slovenliness, and lack of standards; but it is also obvious that, real paddles being known and made, these would be the ones taken on open-sea voyages of a dozen miles in a region of notably variable winds and currents. The Seri are never fools in practical matters within their compass; and they could not have acquired their indubitable navigating skill by letting their women do most of their paddling with bare hands. The one woman I saw aboard was carried as a passenger across the Infiernillo.

What is typical of Seri habits is that the harpoon shaft is also used for poling, and the harpoon cord as anchor rope, towline along shore, sheet rope, and for tying a blanket to a mast and pole to serve as sail; just as the bailer of a leaky skiff is an enamel-ware plate or pot employed at other times for holding food. The whole harpoon, including the rod-iron point, but dismounted, seems regularly to be taken along on a transport voyage....

FACE PAINTING

Face painting seems to be the chief if not only purely aesthetic expression of Seri culture, their mode of life and psychophysiological habits being such as almost to prohibit any other form of visual art. In this face painting, on the other hand, they have achieved a high degree of stylicization and taste. The designs I saw were throughout in the manner illustrated by McGee in his colored plates.

Ethnographically, the interest of this style lies in its similarity to the river Yuman face paintings. The Seri first of all specialize on a horizontal bar across the nose and cheeks, immediately below the eyes; in addition to this, there may be vertical elements dependent over the cheeks. The design deliberately breaks across the natural lines of the face in such a way as to orient itself with reference to the eyes without touching them. Bordering or inclosing of the eyes is avoided; neither are planes like the cheeks, forehead, or chin felt as fields to be filled in with decoration. The fundamental plan attacks the face at once drastically and subtly. That the style has both feeling and rigor is shown by the fact that none of the endless variations of color and design detail depart much from the basic scheme. That this scheme is old is shown by Hardy's description of a century ago. It is a true art of high order within its narrow compass.

The Mohave paintings are somewhat freer and more variable, but also less classical or chaste stylistically. The transverse element below the eyes and the verticals below them are predominant in most cases. Even where the design extends above the eyes, it does not cover the forehead, but terminates in a straight edge paralleling the one below. Where the chin is involved, the Mohave bring solid triangles up from the jaw edge and then leave the chin itself blank, instead of accentuating its contour with color, as a less sophisticated style would do. Like the Seri, the Mohave are a people with deficient material culture and little dress suitable for display. The two tribal styles are unquestionably connected in their history....

SUMMARY AND CONCLUSIONS

Knowledge of the Seri is still in its infancy. McGee's actual observations are excellent but slender in range. He has interwoven them with conjectures, some of which are erroneous and others unproved and doubtful. Intensive study of the Seri will be difficult, chiefly for physical and practical reasons, but, to judge from such explicit data as are in hand, it should prove them to be a tribe unusually interesting indeed, yet fundamentally similar to others in the same region. So many of their known traits are shared with one or another of these tribes that it is practically precluded that complete investigation will leave the Seri as a unique people or even as one set widely apart, except in their historical fortunes.

The most distinctive thing about the Seri is their environment. This is extremely arid and lacking in water supply, but not desert in the ordinary, untechnical sense. Botanists describe it as a succulent-vegetation desert. It is fairly well stocked with food inland and rich in food along shore. This territory is able to support a fair-sized population, but scatters it and keeps it from settling down. The land is also inhospitable and difficult to strangers who are not ready to adopt the Seri mode of life. This fact has helped preserve Seri ethnic integrity and culture to an unusual degree. A considerable fraction of original Serian territory is wholly unoccupied by civilization today, a full three centuries after its frontier was settled. The Indian neighbors of the Seri, all being farmers in fertile valleys, had no more incentive or ability than Caucasians to penetrate Seri territory sustainedly.

Across the Gulf, the peninsula of California presents a very similar environment and was inhabited by tribes of very similar subsistence and residential habits, culture level, and temperament. But the Baja Californians differed from the Seri in being so situated, with reference to the rest of the world, that the length of the peninsula cut them off, except in the northern portion, from nearly all outside relations. Each group in the peninsula thus had contacts and stimuli only from others of similar culture. The Seri, on the contrary, having long been surrounded on the landward side by peoples of higher cultural level, were able to exploit this difference, in part by adopting cultural traits from their neighbors, and perhaps still more largely by preying upon them economically; while their habitat afforded them a refuge from destructive reprisals. Such may have been the condition in pre-Columbian days. At any rate it has been such since the coming of the Spaniards and has made the "history" of the Seri different from that of the Baja Californians.

Three islands—Tiburon, San Esteban, and San Lorenzo—form steppingstones from Seri mainland to the peninsula. The water gaps between them are navigable to native craft and have been navigated by them at times. This raises the question of whether the Seri may not have reached their habitat from the peninsula, or possibly the reverse. The solution of this problem depends on an analysis of full data on physical type, speech, and culture content, and only a partly conclusive answer can as yet be given. In general behavior and temperament, Seri and peninsular Californians seem to have been strikingly alike; but this fact cannot in itself be construed as evidence of common origin, because the similar psychology may be largely determined by similar residence and subsistence habits resting in turn on almost parallel environment—much as pastoral nomads or mariners, in whatever part of the world and with or without historical connections, are likely to exhibit analogous mental attitudes in contrast with rural or urban populations.

In any event, it is wholly unproved that the Seri possess a native endowment which is more animal-like, more dominated by instinctive impulses, and less capable of cultural development than other peoples'. In fact the improbability of such an assumption is indicated by their possession of culture traits, like certain games and their kinship system, which they either share with neighboring tribes or have developed into rather high specialization. The meagernesses of their culture are therefore evidently due to factors in their particular history or geography rather than to congenital deficiencies or abnormalities. This does not mean that it would be easy to convert the Seri to the mode of life of Pima or Mexican. Habits of irresponsibility and unsettlement once established, even through part of childhood only, are notoriously difficult to alter—witness the Gypsies. However, such practical habit difficulties are of course no evidence as to quality of endowment.

The modern Seri are the amalgamated remnants of some three or four of a half-dozen closely related Serian groups formerly recognized. The preponderant one in the fusion of these groups is likely to have been that which held Tiburon and the fronting mainland, on account of better preservation of their numbers and habits in the relatively inaccessible island refuge. . . .

Comparative analysis of the known specific facts of Seri culture . . . shows positive relations in all directions, but outstandingly with three peoples: the Pima, the Arizona desert Yumans, and the Lower Californians. . . .

The Arizona desert Yuman tribes—the Yavapai, Walapai, Havasupai—live farther from the Seri, in fact beyond even the Gila Pima. It is therefore significant that they show almost as many cultural agreements with the Seri as do the Pima-Papago, and fewer disagreements. They are perforce an almost nonfarming population, except in a few spots. It is clear that they and the Seri have jointly preserved many features of an old, nonagricultural, desert-adapted culture. The Yuman tribes of the lower Colorado are much more different, though their geo-

graphical distance from the Seri is no greater. They possess definitely fewer and lack more Seri traits. This is not only because they farm but because they have secondarily specialized their culture away from the old Seri-Walapai substratum.

The Baja Californians must be reckoned as having participated in the same basal, low-level desert culture, though of course like every other people, with certain variants and developments of their own. That we can name fewer Seri traits in their culture than in that of the preceding groups is probably due to the lesser store of our knowledge of them. More significant of relationship is the smallness of the number of Seri traits which they are known to lack. It is entirely possible that if there existed adequate information for both sides of the Gulf, Seri and Cochimí similarity would prove to be the closest of all. But at present this possibility cannot be either conclusively proved or disproved. . . .

The Seri thus relate culturally to other peoples much as might be anticipated from their geographical position and subsistence opportunities. The Seri problem consequently has to be removed from the category of those which hold out a hope or illusion of being particularly significant for the solution of basic questions or broad hypotheses. It is essentially a problem of specific local ethnography, with wider significances revealable only by impartial comparative studies; but of special interest because of the relatively well-preserved status of parts of old Seri culture and the human appeal of three centuries of outlaw history. The thorough study of this culture will involve much grinding physical hardship and possibly some danger. It is to be hoped that when the work is undertaken, it will not be in a spirit of personal adventure, with emphasis on the external difficulties to be overcome, but with a serious desire and competence to secure facts and understanding.

32. YUROK MARRIAGES

With T. T. WATERMAN

1934

IN 1909, one of the authors obtained numerous genealogies among the Yurok of the lower Klamath River in northwestern California, in connection with ethnogeographical studies subsequently published. From the somewhat tangled mass of these genealogies, a list or census of recorded Yurok marriages was then compiled. This census we have analyzed, Philip Drucker giving us competent help, with the following results:

Two forms of marriage exist among the Yurok, full marriage and "half-marriage." In full marriage the man "pays" for his wife and takes her to live in his town and in his house. The children are his: even in divorce he is entitled to keep them if he refuses the refund of the marriage payment. When his daughter is married, or if his son is killed, the payment goes to him. In "half-marriage" the man pays less—normally about half or less of the rated value of his bride—goes to live with his wife in her father's house or adjacent to it in the same town, and is more or less under his father-in-law's direction. The children belong to the wife, that is, to her family, and their bride price or blood money goes to the woman's father or, if he is deceased, to his sons, the woman's brothers. Half-marriage is legitimate and carries no positive disapprobation; but it is presumptive indication of lack of wealth and therefore connotes relatively low social rating in a society which equates wealth and rank.

Incidentally, Yurok half-marriage is of theoretical interest as an example of a mechanism by which a patrilineal culture might become converted to a matrilineal one, or the reverse. There is not the least suggestion that such a shift occurred in northwestern California, or was impending; but the change is conceivable.

The census count shows that 97 of 413 recorded marriages were of the half-type, or 23.4 per cent. If marriages involving a non-Yurok are omitted, the figures are 85 out of 356, or 23.9 per cent. These figures suggest either that the Yurok proletariat, or plebs, was relatively small, or that only part of it half-married, the rest of this social class entering into low-payment full marriage. The latter interpretation seems the more likely, because really wealthy people are so well known, and are so often cited as such, that the frequency of an aristocracy was evidently more restricted than full marriage. Half-marriage, it may therefore be concluded, was in the main a function of factors other than complete poverty.

What these factors were can only be conjectured. Personal inclinations, it is likely, would be influential. If a young man formed an attachment to a girl and his father or paternal uncles objected to the alliance and refused to contribute payment on his behalf, he would normally have no choice but to renounce or half-marry her. That the latter is what would sometimes be done is expectable; particularly, perhaps, if the young man had been clandestinely living with her, and especially if she were pregnant, as in that situation withdrawal would subject him to fine for seduction, plus a second payment if he wished to claim the child. In fact, in such a situation, and more or less in general, a family of moderate means and attached to its possessions must often have been tempted to save the bride price by letting a youth drift into half-marriage. A father with more pride of lineage than avarice would presumably go far to establish his son in the most approved manner. But a father in whom personal greed outweighed other considerations, or one with several sons to provide for and no daughters to bring compensation, or an uncle with a dead brother's sons to sponsor as well as his own—all these might be willing to let some of their grandchildren descend somewhat lower in the scale of rank. It may be conjectured, however, that disagreement between father and son, precipitated by a premature love affair of the son, was often the cause of half-marriage by young men of well-to-do families. The Yurok say that such things happened; and that sometimes, after children were born, the father would make additional payment, so as to render the marriage "full" and his grandchildren of suitable station in life as they grew up. . . .

It seems clear that the concept and practice of fully and highly paid marriage as a thing of worth were deeply rooted in the Yurok system of social ideals and would have operated powerfully to prevent the formation of budding matrilineal foci in their society. Even when circumstances interrupted the continuity of male lineage, the basic point of view was reaffirmed that the desirable and moral course was to pay fully for one's wife and to keep her and one's children at one's natal home. Only thus were the best standards upheld. The matter of residence might be adjusted, and so might the amount; but every compromise reaffirmed the standards. . . .

Our findings may be briefed as follows:

Yurok "half-marriage," that is, legitimate but less esteemed marriage with half-payment, residence in the wife's house, and ownership of the children by her kin, occured in slightly less than one marriage out of four. This type of marriage is of interest as an essentially matrilineal institution in a society definitely committed by its standards to patrilinear descent and control. It was tolerated as an adjustment. It was not frequent enough to have been the regular marriage form of the nonwealthy majority of the population; and it occurred under some circumstances among the wealthy. It was not caused by imitation of aliens, since the Yurok and their neighbors knew of no matrilineal peoples in their world.

There is no indication of a change in frequency of half-marriage between 1800 and 1900. A successful and stable adjustment of the two coexisting types of marriage is therefore indicated.

The Yurok married freely where they chose, except with known blood kin. In their choices, they were influenced by proximity. Relative to the available population, they married most often in their home town, next most often in towns in their home district, then in adjacent districts, and least frequently at a greater distance. Alien speech seems to have been only a slight bar to intermarriage.

There is an unexplained tendency of men to seek their wives downstream. This holds not only as between most of the Yurok districts but for Karok and Hupa in respect to Yurok and for Yurok in respect to Tolowa.

It is clear that the Yurok town was not a relict or incipient clan, as far back as our knowledge carries us. Even though it was sometimes small enough to be composed wholly of a single group of kinsmen and their spouses, this was looked upon as an accident of no institutional significance. The pattern in the terms of which the Yurok thought was one of geography and actual kinship, not clanship.

33. AREAL TYPES OF AMERICAN INDIAN CULTURE AND THEIR GROWTH
1939

A. ARCTIC COAST

SOURCES OF ESKIMO CULTURE

ESKIMO culture is the most specialized of lower-grade cultures in America. It therefore deserves to be considered as constituting a primary division. This conclusion is strengthened by the unchallenged separateness of Eskimo speech from any other American language, and the marked racial differentiation of the Eskimo from other American natives. Over its whole eastern extent the culture has mixed little with that of the Indians, on either side of the boundary. Traits have crossed, but the culture-wholes have remained conspicuously distinct—as have the social temperaments, notoriously. The Eskimo culture has, however, numerous Asiatic relations, especially to the northeastern Palaeo-Asiatics but traceable as far south as the Kamchadal or beyond and west to the Samoyed and perhaps Lapps. Its Magdalenian resemblances, while easily exaggerated and difficult to evaluate, are almost certain to carry some historic significance. This, accordingly, seems the most non-American culture of the continent in its major specific origins. Such a conclusion, however, does not contravene the possibility that the characterization of Eskimo culture as known to us was worked out in America. . . .

ECOLOGICAL PHASES

Steensby's conclusion that Eskimo culture in the Coronation-Melville area developed out of a pre-Eskimo interior culture can hardly be valid; yet his work is of the highest importance as an ethnogeographic study. He has for the first time outlined, for the whole of Eskimo territory, the importance of shore line, seasonal open water, drift and shore ice, driftwood or timber, and other natural features as they determine the presence or accessibility of various animal species and the habitual movements, occupations, and implement types of the Eskimo. What emerges from the total array of his succinctly analyzed data is not the primacy or priority of one particular economic adaptation, but a picture of the totality of Eskimo culture as a unit, modified by emphasis or reduction of its traits in direct response to local exigencies. Here seals are the important food, there whales, or walrus, or caribou, or birds, or salmon, while the others are as good as unavailable. According to ice and water and season, seals are taken by maupok or waiting at the blowhole, utok or creeping, at cracks or the edge of the ice, from the kayak, or by nets. Even this last method, which is so specially developed in Alaska as to look at first as if its spread were determined culturally instead of ecologically, was known in Greenland, Labrador, and the Central regions. Where continuous ice or snow fields are lacking, the sled of course goes out of use, both in southern Greenland and in southern Alaska; but it is employed to the limit of its utility. Caribou are eagerly hunted wherever they can be got. Whether for the most part they are surrounded, driven in fences, intercepted at passes, or kayaked in lakes depends on the opportunities afforded by the country; more often than not, in fact, two or more of these methods are used in support of one another. So with houses.

Where, as on Coronation Gulf and in parts of Baffinland, seals far from shore are the only dependable subsistence available during a considerable part of the year and the Eskimo have therefore to live on the ice, the snow house may wholly displace that of stone or sod. In southern Greenland and on the Mackenzie, on the contrary, driftwood is abundant, good-sized timbered houses are built, and the snow house is lacking except as a travel shelter. On the rocky islets and headlands of Bering Strait, wood is again abundant, and the houses stand on piles against the steep face of a slope. If whale hunting is productive, the umiak is well equipped and paddled; elsewhere it is a freight boat, rowed by women; or where there are no whales and the short season of open sea is spent inland to get caribou, as on the shores of Coronation Gulf and on Boothia Peninsula, the umiak is absent.

These main regional variants of Eskimo economic culture number some twenty-five. These variant ecological adaptations are selections from a basic cultural inventory that is or apparently was substantially uniform over the entire Eskimo range: skin boats, harpoon, bladder or inflated skin floats, spear thrower, three- or four-pronged bird spear, two-winged salmon spear, lamp, stone pot, house platform, type of clothing, ivory carving, kashim or social house, shamanism, type of myth or tale. . . .

CULTURAL CLASSIFICATION AND HISTORY

In contrast to this uniform array of culture elements varied only according to local needs, there is a series of traits, little connected with subsistence, which mark off the western from the central and eastern Eskimo. These include labrets, masks, hats in place of hoods, coiled basketry or other weaving, pottery, grave monuments, mourning feasts or ceremonies, property distribu-

tions, war parties, perhaps clans or moieties. None of these extends beyond the Mackenzie, except for sporadic occurrences, like occasional masks; many of them stop at or before Point Barrow and are therefore wholly Alaskan. In the main these traits seem to reflect the influence of the Northwest Coast tribes, especially the Tlingit, or, in part, of the Athabascans influenced by the Tlingit. Many may be ultimately Asiatic in origin; some, like pottery and coiled basketry, may have drifted in from a long distance away.

The primary division of Eskimo culture, then, is into a Central-Eastern and a Western or Alaska-Siberian form, the former being "pure" Eskimo, the latter Eskimo plus a Northwest American and Northeast Asiatic addition.

It is a fair logical question whether the sequence implied in the word "addition" could not be reversed, and Eskimo culture be construed as having developed in its present richer Alaskan form in Alaska, the region of fullest contacts, and then diffused eastward, the rigor of the Coronation Gulf environment filtering out many of its supersubsistence elements, while necessity, plus paucity of alien contacts, preserved the subsistence devices relatively unaltered, except for a measure of modification among the Coronation-Melville groups. This view involves a further one, namely, that the contact of cultures in and about Alaska which resulted in the formation of Eskimo culture caused not only absorptions from the contributing cultures, such as masks and labrets, but also new productions such as lamps and skin boats, and that on the spread of this culture eastward out of Alaska the absorptions were in general lost and the new specsific products retained. While this seems theoretically improbable, it may well have happened to a considerable extent because of the definite utility of the new productions.

Really, the two views are not incompatible. Influences from several sea-board cultures situated on subarctic or temperate shores may have met in the region of Alaska and produced an Eskimoid type of culture, which then in its eastward spread through the high Arctic became strained out into "pure" Eskimo culture as we know it today, both because of the unusual but necessary concentration in high latitudes on subsistence activities, and because of the specialization of these with reference to sea mammalian life. At the same time, the culture impingements in Alaska continued, leading to further absorptions and a general enrichment of the culture, but also to less homogeneity and uniqueness of cast. On this view, the shores of the vicinity of Alaska would have been both an ancient and a modern meeting ground of various cultural influences, pre-Eskimo, non-Eskimo, and Eskimo; and from the stock of sea-adapted culture there accumulated, the shore peoples eastward selected, not only once but more likely several times or continuously, such elements as they could use, besides of course modifying them. Alaska then would be the point of origin—in the sense of point of crystallization—of Eskimo as contrasted with non-Eskimo culture as a whole, and at the same time the area where this culture remained most "mixed," least set apart by rigorous restriction to its own specializations.

This interpretation of a straining-out of the culture, incidentally, accords well with the situation in racial type and speech, both of which are "purer," more characteristically or undilutedly Eskimo, in the east than in the west, especially if the Aleut are included.

The fundamental difficulty about deriving Eskimo culture from the northern interior of America is that it is hard to conceive of an inland culture originating the many definite and accurate devices relating to the sea and sea life which consitute the most fundamental

and distinctive aspects of Eskimo culture. To take as an example Birket-Smith's "two main props of coastal life" in the far north, the blubber lamp and seal hunting at breathing holes; these both depend on and relate exclusively to sea mammals. The antecedents for the invention or development of these traits are much more nearly given in a subarctic sea-adapted culture than in a ruminant-hunting, wood-burning tundra or forest culture. The case is much like that of a people practicing a specialized agriculture, such as desert irrigation, under rigorously limiting natural conditions. All we have learned of the nature of culture processes in the last generation would lead us to expect such an agricutture to be derived from a more generalized, less conditioned type of agriculture evolved elsewhere, rather than from a tour de force "invention by necessity" by a nonagricultural population finding itself in a habitat with insufficient wild food. . . .

The inland culture of the Chesterfield Inlet—Back River or Caribou Eskimo may probably best be regarded as primarily a specially marked instance of the ecological response variations discussed above. This group seems never wholly to have lost touch with the sea. They have merely gone one step farther than the inland minority of the Point Barrow division. These two groups are of interest as true tundra dwellers; but it is doubtful whether they are very much more specialized away from "normal" Eskimo sea-mammal and shore life than are the Yukon and Kuskokwim salmon-eaters.

SUMMARY

The origin of Eskimo culture is unknown. Its ultimate affiliations seem Asiatic rather than American. The area of specifically Eskimo *characterization* may have been American or Asiatic-American; but it is unlikely to have lain east of Alaska, and it was coastal, with primary dependence on sea mammals and fish. This culture came to extend from Siberia and Alaska to Greenland. After a time it became somewhat modified in the Central area, especially west of Hudson Bay, partly through the lure of caribou hunting, partly through impoverishment due to arctic rigor. Meanwhile, too, perhaps even earlier, the Western Eskimo culture began to alter as a result of the fairly developed cultural contacts to which it continued to be exposed. The most important of these influences were much diminished north of Bering Strait, more so beyond Point Barrow, and practically terminated at the mouth of the Mackenzie, though a few of the older elements may have penetrated sporadically even as far as Greenland. Also, these Northwest Coast and Asiatic influences have continued to recent times, possibly with increased force. Otherwise, Eskimo culture has retained its stock relatively unaltered, except for a modification into about two dozen local phases, which are essentially ecological subsistence adaptations with resultant reduction or emphasis of common culture traits.

B. Northwest Coast

The culture of the Northwest or North Pacific Coast is that one of the more highly developed and differentiated cultures in America which has been least affected by influences from Middle (Nuclear) America. It has been reached to an unusual degree by influences from Asia. Some of these, slat or rod armor and hats, for instance, show distributions as far southwest as the higher civilizational centers of eastern Asia. Many other resemblances are vaguer, or show interrupted distributions, but carry even farther, to Indonesia and Oceania: carving, masks, wealth emphasis. Similarities to the eastern Palaeo-Asiatics, however may be due to cultural currents from America as much as into it.

A third trend of the culture is the unusual degree to which its material, native and imported, has been worked over into its own patterns. The area is evidently one of unusual intensity of cultural activity. This intensity seems to have been still heightening at the time of discovery and to have received a further temporary impetus from the first European contacts. This powerful repatterning has probably disguised the foreign origin of much Northwest Coast culture material. The historic source of material of this kind should prove discernible when intensive knowledge of the area is combined with a willingness to consider the probability of remote origins. The present indications are that perhaps as much of the reworked material derives from Asiatic as from distant American centers.

Recent conditions at the southern end, as well as the slender archaeological evidence available, suggest that the Northwest Coast culture was originally a river or river-mouth culture, later a beach culture, and only finally and in part a seagoing one. This means that the recent hinterland cultures of the Columbia-Fraser drainage (Plateau) and of the Intermountain Athabascans evidently provide approximate illustrations of an early stage of Northwest Coast culture. This situation is implicit in Wissler's basing of both the Northwest Coast and the Plateau culture on a Salmon Area. Of course no mechanical subtraction of hinterland from coast culture suffices for a true estimate of the kind or amount of culture specialized on the coast, even apart from the variant conditioning of subsistence, because the hinterlands have secondarily absorbed culture material and forms from the coast as well as from the east.

The ecological correspondence is remarkably close for the Northwest Coast. The vegetational-climatic area of

the Northwestern Hygrophytic Co-
niferous Forest tallies almost absolutely
with the cultural one. This forest is
generally considered as extending into
northern California. The culture extends to Cape Mendocino and the lower
Eel River, which lie about at the middle
of the Redwood belt. This Redwood
strip may be viewed as a specialized
southern extension of the Northwestern
forest; its denser and more characteristic
part is its northern half, which belongs
clearly to the Northwest culture.

The areal types of the Northwest culture can be formulated only tentatively.
While this is one of the more intensively studied regions of the continent, interest has been away from classificatory
and developmental problems. . . .

The areas are far from equivalent in
cultural intensity and depth. The climax
of the region seems long to have lain in
its northern half, in British Columbia.
The four southern areas are distinctly
subclimactic and culturally peripheral.
During the last half of the nineteenth
century, the climax must be credited to
the Northern Maritime tribes, on account of their aggressiveness and the
vigor of their art. Their culture was
then in an expansive, acquisitive phase.
Previously, the climax was probably
situated in the Kwakiutl-Nutka group,
where the Heiltsuk Kwakiutl worked
out the Hamatsa cannibal ceremonies
which the northerners later borrowed.
Still earlier, the climax may have lain in
the third area, about the mouth of the
Fraser and the opposite shore of Vancouver Island, south of Cape Mudge. If
the theory is correct that the Northwest culture as a whole originated on
rivers and only slowly ventured on the
open sea, this area would be the logical
one for the first stages of its characterization. The Lower Columbia area may
have experienced similar impulses, but
these would have been checked by the
debouching of its river on a straight,
rugged coast, without sheltered salt wa-

ters to encourage the apprenticeship of
transformation. Puget Sound is a back-
wash. It may have been an important
area in early stages of the culture, but
its very shelteredness from the sea
destined it to relative lag as the
oceanward development proceeded.
The Willamette Valley formed even
more of a pocket. It is the only actually
interior culture in the Northwest region
and is probably best construed as an
inland modification of a form of the
primitive river phase. The fact that the
valley contains enough prairie to cause
it to be classified by some authorities as
grassland would have contributed to its
cultural differentiation. It is the only
tract in the Northwest area which is not
continuously forested. The Northwest
California subclimax has clearly been
built up on a basis of river habitat. Its
center lies on the only stream south of
the Columbia to drain from the interior
of the Sierra-Cascades mountain wall,
and nearly at the meeting point of three
forests, namely, the Northwest Coast
Douglas Fir, the Northwest Extension
Redwood, and the California Pine.

It is evident that the descriptive subdivision of the long north-south Northwest area into seven to ten approximately transverse segments resolves itself, as soon as the relations of the segments are viewed with interest in environmental adaptation and historic development, into a classification into
longitudinal belts, nearly but not quite
parallel to the coast and expressive of
degrees of utilization of water, from
river to mouth to still salt water to
ocean, with a subsidiary use of ocean
replacing primary adaptation to inland
salt water where this is not available.
According to ascending degree of water
adaptation, the areas group thus: (1)
Willamette; (2) Klamath, Columbia,
Puget Sound; (3) Gulf of Georgia; (4)
Central Maritime, Northern River,
Northern Mainland; (5) Northern
Archipelago. Within each belt the more

northerly subareas usually have the more intensive culture. Also, except in the most southerly area, the center of intensity within each of these five areas seems to lie in its northern portion. The degree of development of such luxury aspects as art and society rituals is in agreement with this environmental-historical view.

From both the northward centering and recent northward trend of the climax of the whole Northwest Coast, it is expectable that more refined analysis will confirm the conjecture that Asiatic influences perhaps were more potent than Nuclear (Middle) American ones in the specific shaping of Northwest Coast culture. If direct Oceanic influences have ever to be reckoned with, they may complicate the picture.

C. PLAINS AREAS

The view here held is that the Plains culture has been one of the well-developed and characterized cultures of North America only since the taking-over of the horse from Europeans, and that previously there was no important Plains culture, the chief phases in the area being marginal to richer cultures outside. In brief, the historic Plains culture was a late high-pressure center of culture in a region which previously had been rather conspicuously low-pressure. That there is nothing revolutionary in such a view is shown by the fact that as long ago as 1916 Sapir in a sentence analyzed the recent Plains culture into non-Plains origins. The reason why he did not follow the matter further is that his essay was concerned with method rather than with fact.

The Plains tribes, along with the Pueblos, Northwest Coast Indians, Californians, and Eskimo, are among the most intensively investigated in America. The reason has been the incentive to study extended by the saturation of their late culture, plus its preservation well into the nineteenth century. Even today it is possible ot find informants who have experienced the old life and are able to give clear, vivid accounts of it. The returns being richer, more ethnological interest was directed to them. Specialization followed, and on that some inevitable loss of perspective. This relatively rich culture, so much more satisfying to deal with than the remnants of that to the east or the meager

ones of the Plateau and to the far north, began to be intimately dissected in some of its aspects—but mainly with reference to itself, not to its outward relations. Spier on the Sun dance, Lowie on age societies, Wissler on shamanistic and dancing societies, analyzed historic developments within the culture as it was. How the culture as a whole came to be, was less and less asked. Wissler perhaps did most both to extend and to fix the concept of the Plains area and to define its center. He even went so far as to indicate that its culmination lay most probably among the Oglala Teton Dakota, with Arapaho, Cheyenne, and Crow participating next in order.

Another factor contributed to the essentially static conception. Wissler found that when the Plains tribes took up the horse they did not make their culture over radically. Travois transportation, the tepee, the bison hunt under control, had all been there before. The horse was simply put into the old patterns and made these more productive. It was easier for the tribes to do this than to evolve or adjust to a new set of patterns. As an analysis of cultural dynamics or social psychology, this was a valid demonstration. Too largely however it seems to have been tacitly interpreted also as a historical conclusion, that Plains culture after the horse went on much as before. Very little reflection shows that this could not have been so. Could any good-sized group have lived permanently off the bison on the open plains while they and their dogs were dragging their dwellings, furniture, provisions, and children? How large a tepee could have been continuously moved in this way, how much apparatus could it have contained, how close were its inmates huddled, how large the camp circle? How often could several thousand people have congregated in one spot to hold a four or eight days' Sun dance? By the standard of the nineteenth century, the sixteenth-century Plains Indian would have been miserably poor and almost chronically hungry, if he had tried to follow the same life. Showy clothing, embroidered footgear, medicine-bundle purchases, elaborate rituals, gratuitous and time-consuming warfare, all these he could have indulged in but little—not much more than the tribes of the intermountain or southern Texas regions.

In short, ethnologists have gradually become so interested in the specialized manifestations of Plains culture that they have forgotten that largely these are definite luxury developments possible only with the subsistence basis of life adjusted unusually favorably and dependably. That such an adjustment could have been made through the mechanism of dog traction by a migratory people dependent on a migratory animal for their food is highly problematical.

With the horse and all its culturally intensifying consequences taken away from the tribes of the western or true plains, such as the Blackfoot, Crow, Teton, and Arapaho, these have left but a meager stock of culture. The same subtraction from the agricultural Prairie tribes—Mandan, Santee, Pawnee, or Omaha—would leave them far more. In the sixteenth century, then, I believe that culture within the so-called Plains area was richest and centered in the prairies, not the plains, and was not primarily but only incidentally based on bison subsistence. But the Prairie tribes show affiliations to both the Southeast and the Northeast; and the Plains culture is thereby made doubly dependent. In the sixteenth century, instead of being a climax, it was not even subclimax: it was peripheral.

If it seems unlikely that a ritual as elaborate as the Sun dance grew up in a few hundred years, the answer is twofold. First, many of its elements—torture, painting, altar, bundle—occur in other associations and may be ancient, while the complex of elements that constitute the ritual is younger. Secondly, that ceremonial elaborations in this area can be highly unstable is evident from comparison of societies; for instance, the age-graded ones of the Arapaho and Atsina (Gros Ventre). These are alike enough to make it certain that they represent, in the main, deviations from an original common system. The two tribes are closely related in language, and the Arapaho regard the Gros Ventre as the northernmost of their five original divisions. The two groups had separate ranges as early as 1750, but may well has been still a unit in 1600 or even 1650. With the ensuing geographic separation to help, the dialectic divergence between them could easily have been achieved by 1900, it would seem. The differences between the society systems of the two tribes comprise added or dropped societies, transfer of functions from one society to another, and transposition of societies in the age order. What is an elderly, important group in one tribe, is a young group, near the beginning of the sequence, in the other. It is difficult even to imagine a mechanism by which a change like this could have taken place in a system after this had become based on the principle of seniority. It is much as if in some European countries Wednesday came after Thursday. Yet the change is there. If a now closed system could alter as this one has in two to three centuries, a new one could certainly crystallize as quickly, whether it be a society series or a Sun dance.

What it is suggested happened is that not only ritual complexes, but indeed all sorts of cultural patterns, quickly blossomed out in the plains after the introduction of the horse had converted a strugglingly precarious or seasonal mode of subsistence into one normally assured, abundant, and productive of wealth and leisure. This development was strongest where the effect of the horse was greatest, in the true or western short-grass plains. Here, then, there rapidly grew up a new center—an active crater of culture, to use Wissler's figure. This in turn reacted on the agricultural tribes of the prairies, strongly influenced the nearer intermountain tribes as well as several at the edge of the northern forest, and about 1800 sent its influences down the Columbia to the Cascades. The new culture was not only active and intensive, it was still expanding when white settlement killed its roots.

It is scarcely contendable that the western plains were wholly uninhabited before the horse was available. Agricultural groups from east and west probably strayed in now and then and tried to farm. Small groups could make a living by combining bison and river-bottom hunting with berry and root gathering. But the population probably clung in the main to the foot of the Rockies, where wood, water, and shelter were more abundant, fauna and flora more variegated, a less specialized subsistence mechanism sufficient; and from there they made incursions into the plains to hunt their big game, much as the prairie and parkland and even forest tribes ranged in from the east in the historic period. Such habits would account for the dog travois and folding tent. They would give to the plains some human utilization and occupancy. They would not leave room for a specialized culture to center there.

Wissler's views on the Plains have undergone decided changes. In 1907 he advocated substantially the position here maintained. He even spoke of the plains as uninhabited, and the moving out into them as due to the horse. In 1914 he held that the horse "is largely responsible for such modifications and realignments as give us the typical [western, Blackfoot to Comanche] Plains culture of the nineteenth century" and that the "vigor and accentuated association of traits" of this culture could not have been achieved without the horse. On the other hand, "no important Plains traits except those directly associated with the horse [like saddles] seem to have come into existence" after its introduction; "all the essential elements of Plains culture would have gone on, if the horse had been denied them"; and "from a qualitative point of view the culture of the Plains would have been much the same without the horse." While no "important traits, material or otherwise, were either dropped or added," yet "the relative intensities of many traits were changed, giving us a different cultural whole," and leaving to the horse its strongest claim "as an intensifier of original Plains traits." Horse introduction is also held responsible for "reversing cultural values," that is, causing old nomadic (Shoshonean) cultures to "predominate" over the "previously dominant sedentary cultures of the Siouan and Caddoan tribes." In short, a new culture grew up wholly out of old elements through the introduction of the horse. A later paper in 1914, and *The American Indian* in 1917 and 1922, go further, in that they accept this new culture almost as if it were timeless. The purely horse-using tribes are described as forming the "center" of the area, and tribes like the Omaha and Pawnee as culturally less typical and dependent. This is of course a static interpretation of a historic moment. In short, Wissler's first approach was historical; his second, historical and analytic; his third, descriptively analytic.

Returning to the primary consideration, we can summarize by saying that in the main, in the prehistoric period, the cultural emphasis of the conventional "Plains culture area" region lay on its borders; the plains themselves were a cultural margin. . . .

SUMMARY OF TRIBAL HISTORY IN THE PLAINS-PRAIRIES

The outlines of tribal history in the plains and prairies, before the first Caucasian influences made themselves felt, say about three to five centuries ago, may be tentatively reconstructed as follows.

On the west, a series of tribes lived in the foothills and broken country in front of the Rockies, utilizing also the ranges behind and the plains before them, according to season, occupation, and need. Their primary cultural affiliations are likely to have been Intermountain. They consisted in the south largely of Athabascans. The Kiowa may have been among them, or northward. Still farther north, where the lower timber is pine instead of juniper or scrub, were Algonkins representing two drifts, both ancient, but the Arapaho-Atsina older and probably more southerly than the Blackfoot. The Sarsi may not yet have come out of the northern woods to join the Blackfoot. The Crow may already have left the Hidatsa to live at the foot of the western mountains; but this shift may not have taken place until somewhat later. In the sagebrush plains of Wyoming, behind the Laramies and Big Horns, and perhaps in the mountains to the north, were Shoshone.

On the south, Caddoan groups extended up the Red and Canadian rivers far enough, probably, to abut, in the seasonally visited short-grass plains, on the Athabascans. South Texas groups like the Tonkawa were perhaps too predominantly a woodland or scrub-timber people to participate with much importance in these contacts. Of the Caddoans, the Pawnee-Arikara branch had begun to drift northward, perhaps had already passed out of the woodland of Oklahoma-Arkansas-Missouri into the timber-streaked prairies of Nebraska, but maintained successfully the essentials of their rather complex culture.

On the east there were mainly Siouan tribes. The Chiwere group—Iowa, Oto, Missouri—clung most rigorously to the woodland. The Dhegiha, if not already divided, split soon after, with the Quapaw and Omaha-Ponca as extremes: the former hugging the forested Mississippi, facing southward, and reintegrating more closely with the Southeast–Lower Mississippi culture; the latter ascending the Missouri, trending westward into more open country, and beginning to diverge from their old woodland culture. The Mandan and Hidatsa were already in the open, perhaps less far north than later and still cultivating prairie rather than plains soil. Their specific tribal histories were diverse though roughly parallel and later joined and assimilated. The basis of their culture may have been southern—Pawnee-Caddo—in type, more than eastern—Central Siouan. They had perhaps been detached longest from the central body of the Siouan stock. North of the Chiwere were the Dakota: the Teton probably in timber-interspersed prairie, the other divisions mainly in the woods. The Assiniboin perhaps had not yet begun their quarrel with the other Dakota which ultimately led them into a separate history. Somewhere in the vicinity, more or less west of the Dakota and south of the Assiniboin, and presumably in prairie, are likely to have been the Cheyenne, already detached from the main Algonkin body in affiliations and probably in territory, and not yet in serious contact with Arapaho or Blackfoot across the other side of the plains. Cree and Ojibwa were still wholly woodland peoples.

Some of these situations and conditions may of course have fallen earlier than others. It is impossible to assign any precise date for most of them. The intent is only to present the general pre-Caucasian picture.

In the seventeenth century the horse began to come in; at first locally, and with little influence. By 1700 it had definitely affected some tribal cultures. By 1750 it had become in some measure universal, and the historic plains-bison culture was getting into full swing. By 1800 this was flowing vigorously out of the plains and heavily overlaying both the Prairie and the Intermountain cultures, and even the margins of the Southwest. The peak may have been reached only as late as the early or middle nineteenth century.

As soon as the horse made the plains desirable, a drift into them began from all sides. Contributing factors along the eastern front, at least locally, were the pressure of white encroachment, of tribes equipped with firearms, the westward shrinkage of the bison. Thus tribes that had previously met only at long range, perhaps not at all, were thrown into close and often intimate contact: the Teton and Cheyenne with the Arapaho and Blackfoot, for instance. The Arikara moved northwestward until they found a stay with the likewise sedentary Mandan and Hidatsa. Roughly about these village tribes there revolved the greatest turmoil of new contacts, clashes, readaptations, and impartings. To these changes the villagers contributed, and they were not uninfluenced by them. As old settlers, they were not torn from their anchorage of maize fields, pottery, domed houses, palisades, matrilineate. But they became an increasingly smaller factor in the total situation as the new growths flourished around them. Farther south, the Pawnee, a larger unit, perhaps effected a

better adaptation, except for earlier demoralization by white contacts. Still farther south, the prairie narrows, and the culture of the woodland peoples had been too much undermined by French and Spanish contacts and conflicts for them to be able to shape anything notably novel. About 1700 a large part of the Shoshone broke away from their Wyoming sagebrush, followed the front of the Rockies southward, and, as the Comanche, drove the eastern Apache back into the mountains or the Texas scrub, confirming them as marginal Southwesterners instead of the dominant southern Plainsmen which they might otherwise have been. In the far north, Cree and Ojibwa bands were evidently among the last tribes to try to enter upon a plains-prairie type of career.

Of rituals, the Sun dance evidently represents a relatively recent development in the plains proper, which flowed eastward into the prairies with diminished intensity, and crossed the Rockies late and to a still less degree. Whether the Sun dance is an agglomeration around an old Arapaho nucleus, or whether this people merely were the most active syncretists for a century or two, is harder to say. Age-graded societies appear to date back to the older stratum of culture among the village tribes and were taken into the historic Plains culture by only a few groups that had long lived in or at the edge of the plains proper. The history of the ungraded society type of ritual organization is more obscure, but the region of development apparently was the southern prairies.

The bison was exterminated by the Caucasian with Indian aid. Whether the Indian alone, but equipped with horses and guns, could have lived indefinitely off the animal, is an open question. It is entirely conceivable that even then he might have destroyed the species in a century or so. Once the balance turns against an animal, its decline, at first almost imperceptible, is known sometimes to increase with almost incredible rapidity; especially has this been observed of game too large to seek hiding. Before the horse, difficulties of transport, water, and shelter in the plains allowed the Indian merely to nibble at the existence of the bison, so that the perpetuation of the species might have gone on indefinitely. It might easily have been different, however, with a very similar species in a different habitat; say the foothills of the Rockies, which lacked, so far as purely native culture was concerned, the inhospitability of the open plains. A species adapted to such an environment might have met the fate of the historic buffalo of the plains almost as quickly in native times, once certain groups centered their subsistence on it.

34. SALT, DOGS, TOBACCO
1941

This paper is a by-product of a Culture Element Survey of native western North America which I sponsored between 1934 and 1938 and which was carried out by thirteen field investigators, each of whom presented a kind of questionnaire or aide-mémoire list to one or two members of a series of contiguous tribes. The number of different tribes or bands from whom lists of responses were recorded was 254. As each questionnaire dealt with one to several thousand points, the number of ethnographic items, on which a response from at least one supposedly qualified tribal informant was obtained during the Survey, aggregated around half a million. The prime purpose of the Survey was to insure greater comparability of cultural information than existed in the published works of ethnographers. It was not so much a case of previous field ethnographers having been in conflict, as of their not meeting in their work, and not getting around to many smaller groups. They started with diverse interests, went off in different directions, rarely made clear whether traits not mentioned were actually absent from the culture or had not been inquired into, and so on. We originally expected that more evenly comparable data would make possible statistical treatment defining more authoritatively than heretofore the similarity groupings of a long array of tribal cultures, their geographical variation, and inferences as to their historic growth. These hopes were partly realized; but they were also limited by unforeseen factors, such as personal unconformities between the ethnographers who prepared and administered our questionnaire lists; also by time and cost difficulties due to the volume of computations. In the main, the results were in the line of whole-culture classification: the varying degrees of similarity shown by the total cultures of local and tribal groups.

The twenty-five monographs published in the Culture Element Distribution Series of the University of California have had rather little note taken of them by the anthropological profession. The reasons have been several. The Survey was directed at phenomena of native culture at a time when studies of tribal acculturations to our civilization were at the top of their vogue. They were concerned with the clarification of strictly cultural situations in a period when many anthropologists were shifting altogether to culture-and-personality. Of those who retained interest in culture as such, some, like Benedict and Malinowksi, emphasized cultural summarization, integration, or total patterning, and showed little tolerance for any "atomizing" recognition of elements. In general, only the archaeologists were sympathetic on this score. The archaeologists also showed least reluctance toward enumerative and quantitative treatment. Ethnologists and social anthropologists proved, on the whole, averse to quantitative expression, averse to questionnaires in principle, averse to presence and absence data, averse to single informants per tribe or band even when the number of bands ran into the hundreds. The whole procedure was not according to their current folkways; mostly they would have none of it for themselves; and in general they criticized the approach less than they ignored it. While the Survey was planned to develop more systematic methods of recording and interpreting culture-historical data, this very effort probably seemed datedly old-fashioned to most of my colleagues in America. I doubt whether one-

*tenth of them even cursorily read the little review monograph on which the pres-
ent selection is based.*

*I wrote the monograph to show some of the interpretive uses, beyond classifica-
tion of whole cultures, to which our Culture Element Survey data could be put. I
chose salt, dogs, and tobacco because they are limited subjects of concrete content,
necessarily constituting quite small segments in any culture. Data on them are likely to be precise and closely comparable even where they differ drastically. It
seemed therefore that it would prove possible for the systematic information to
build up into histories of the use of this or that aspect of salt or dogs or tobacco in
western native North America—reconstructed inferential histories, of course.
Beyond this, it seemed that as responses varied among two hundred-odd local societies, something could be inferred from them as to the varying intensity of the part
played by dogs or tobacco or salt in the local cultures: how much of the culture
they ramified into, how far they either entered its well-marked patterns or remained outside them undigested. Beyond this there should be characteristic attitudes revealed. Was it salt or meat or tobacco or water that one abstained from at
times of penance or ritual purification? As answers varied, the religious valuation of
the several substances would be indicated. How often, and in what regions, were
such taboo prohibitions followed respectively in all rites of a tribe, or only in some,
or perhaps merely in one? And in which ceremonies or rites of passage? Was it
birth or puberty or menstruation or death or again communal initiations that were
most likely to be emphasized by being studded with taboos on salt or prescription
of tobacco? These were the kinds of problems to which the systematically comparable new data might be expected to furnish answers.*

*On the whole, answers were forthcoming, and often unexpected ones. Farming
tribes proved to smoke mostly wild tobacco in the area considered; whereas most
of the planting of tobacco was done by tribes that never grew food. Tobacco sowing proved related in pattern less to agriculture than to burning-over of ground
cover by hunters and gatherers. Beliefs as to dogs and eclipses, or as to dogs as
speakers of ominous evil, emerged from review of the variations and distributions
of these beliefs as "half-folkways": tribal lore that is held to only waveringly and
intermittently. And so on.*

*Even in social structure, often considered most impervious to a questionnaire
type of approach, intertribal distributions can be significant of attitudes and affects,
as I tried to show in a paper on stepdaughter marriage, based on the same Survey
data. This finding is not included here only because it has already been condensed
in my Anthropology.*

*In short, social and cultural attitudes can be revealed not only by studying indi-
vidual persons within their cultures, but also by extraction from the data of history
or comparative ethnography. This is much as psychological qualities of a style are
revealed—by no means identically, but perhaps to about equal degree—from the
life-histories of its artists and from the anonymous products of the art.*

*After all, the basic culture of all the nonliterate Indians of western America was
fairly similar. From a broad point of view its 254 surveyed exemplars are only local
variants of general themes and patterns. Their variation from community to community over part of a continent, a variation now decisive and now hesitant or conflicting, parallels on a larger scale——macroscopically—and with corresponding significance, the variation from individual to individual personality within a cultural
group.*

As the nature of the data sought emphasized precision of detail, the present con-

Salt, Dogs, Tobacco

densation will do doubt still seem somewhat technical to the nonanthropologist, even though hundreds of listings of occurrences and enumerations of tribal and band names have been omitted, along with footnotes and some passages of less conclusive interpretation. The results of the study thus stand out somewhat more clearly than as it was originally published. If the findings still seem often to refer to minutiae, this is inherent in the method, which aims to build its conclusions cumulatively from sharply definable minimal units: to let patterns emerge from broad collocation of exact items.*

THE field work in the University of California's Culture Element Survey west of the Rocky Mountains was completed in July, 1938. Even though the editing and publishing of data will require time to complete, it seemed desirable to begin interpretive studies. Dr. Driver had indeed already made such a study, and an intensive one, on the Girls' Puberty Rite; but this was begun in 1936, before data were in hand on all areas. I decided to review the materials on several circumscribed topics, as samples of what the list data would yield when treated nonstatistically, by established methods of distributional ethnography. Salt, tobacco, and dogs were chosen as being relatively concrete and specific subjects. The following three discussions present the more important points that emerge from a comparison of the relevant sections of the twenty

blocks of two hundred and seventy-nine questionnaire lists. No attempt has been made to exhaust the materials. Traits that appeared in only part of the lists, or whose occurrence proved local or sporadic, or on which the returns were ambiguous, irregular, nonconcordant, or of little apparent significance, were freely omitted from consideration, except in a few instances where deficiencies in the data seemed to illuminate problems in the technique of list gathering. I have also refrained from making use of the previously published literature, except in special cases. This was deliberate: the paper is designed as a test of how much in the way of significant results old-line ethnologists who distrust questionnaires and coefficients might secure from our Survey data alone. . . .

SALT

The outstanding fact regarding salt in native western North America is that it was used in half of that area and not used in the other half. It is the northern half which was saltless. The line of demarcation is sinuous; but there were virtually no exceptions to the rule that salt was eaten everywhere to the south and not eaten anywhere to the north of this line.

The boundary between the two areas is shown in Figure 2, map 1. . . .

What do the two contrasting areas mean? The following have been or might be suggested as causes of nonuse of salt: prevalence of sea food; of a meat diet; of warmer climate. The first

will not hold: salt-users extend farther north on the coast than inland. As to animal as against plant food, there is no very clear preponderance of either in either part of the region considered. Temperature fits the distribution better, but not exactly: the coast of northern California and Oregon is cool and foggy. A climate causing loss of body salt through sweating might be thought of as causing an increased physiological craving for salt. The strongest attachment to salt, as indicated by the number of deprivation taboos, ritual journeys, and salt ceremonies, evidently exists in southern California and Arizona, an area generally of long hot summers and

Map 1. Salt used.

Map 2. Salt: seaweed.

Map 3. Salt from grass.

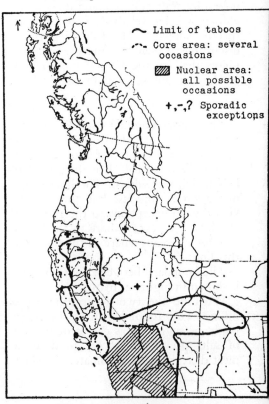

Map 4. Salt taboo in ritual.

FIG. 2.—Salt

heavy evaporation. However, this region constitutes only a small core of the distribution of salt use as shown by the Survey: the peripheral areas are several times as large. It must therefore be concluded that whatever underlying urge there may be in physiology as influenced by diet and climate, the specific determinant of salt use or nonuse in most instances is social custom, in other words, culture.

This conclusion differs from that of M. O. de Mendizabal, "Influencia de la sal en la distribución geográfica de los grupos indígenas de México" (1930). He posits vegetal diet as the primary impulse to the use of salt.

Seaweed.—Along the coast a dark purplish seaweed, determined as Porphyra perforata for the Hupa by Goddard, is dried, matted, or pressed into cakes, and eaten. It undoubtedly has some food value; but the taste is also definitely salty and somewhat bitter. In northwest California, this eating is mainly as seasoning or relish: a piece of the cake is broken off and occasionally nibbled at between spoonfuls of acorn gruel. (This is my personal observation.) Presumably the same holds elsewhere in California and Oregon. On the Northwest Coast, the same purple seaweed, or possibly a related species, is dried into the same cakes, about a foot in diameter, but is then usually cut into morsels. . . .

The distribution of the use of this purple seaweed is peculiar in that there are three areas of use and three of nonuse along the coast (Fig. 2, map 2). . . .

This intermittent distribution must be due to culture, not ecology. As the botanical records show, Porphyra perforata occurs along the whole coast: two of its subspecies range from the Mexican border at least to Washington; another species of Porphyra ranges from there to British Columbia; four species are found from Monterey to Vancouver Island; and two are Alaskan,

including one noted as eaten by Indians. . . .

Salt burned out of grass.—In parts of California and Nevada, a certain grass was roasted or burned in a pit, in the bottom of which "salt" would then collect. The first fuller description is from the Valley Patwin of Colusa; E. Voegelin's notes contain a similar account from the Valley Maidu of Chico. Voegelin is the only one to identify the plant: Distichlis spicata, salt grass according to Jepson, who gives as the habitat "salt marshes and alkaline soil, low altitudes, common along the coast, and in the interior valleys and deserts; extends from southern British America to Mexico." Pending further verification, we can assume that wherever a grass is burned for salt in this part of the world it is Distichlis; except perhaps in eastern Nevada.

Map 3 (Fig. 2) shows that this salt roasting has a much narrower distribution than the plant. Its main area is the Central Valley of California. . . .

It is reasonably clear that what we have here is a practice substituted for the gathering of mineral salt, or sometimes added to it, according to opportunities of local environment. Grass burning never displaces mineral salt gathering over any considerable area: the two habits occur interdigitated, not infrequently among the same group. Thus while most of the Yokuts—prevailingly a people of the valley plains and lower foothills—burned grass, the Choinimni division used a mineral supply, and the Nutunutu, Chukchansi, and San Joaquin Yokuts used both. For 7 Mono groups, the figures are: grass only, 3; mineral only, 2; both, 2; for 6 Maidu: dry mineral, 6; salt spring or marsh, 3; grass burned, 3.

Salt in ritual.—The most general appearance of salt in religion in western North America is as something tabooed on ritual occasions, especially those connected with rites of passage. The distribution of such taboos is, as might be expected, more restricted than that of the use of salt. A thing must be both fairly obtainable and fairly desirable before there would ordinarily be much motivation toward forbidding it. As map 4 (Fig. 2) shows, certain peripheral regions of salt use do not impose salt taboos. These regions are: the coast (including tracts inland to the Sacramento River) from San Francisco Bay to the Columbia River; the Shoshone and Ute territories; those inhabited by the Athabascans of the Southwest except to a minor extent the more northerly and westerly groups; and perhaps the Pueblos also, although no list inquiries on ritual were made among them. This leaves as the heart of the salt-taboo area western Arizona, southern California, and the Central Valley of California, with some extension of the latter on both sides to the central coast region and the nearer of the Northern Paiute groups.

The taboos, endlessly variable, group into classes according to occasion: birth; girls' puberty; menstruation; death and mourning; initiation, boys' puberty, or vision quest. Birth taboos may refer to pregnancy or to postbirth restrictions on the mother, the father, or both. The other classes tend to subdivide analogously. In general, if the salt taboo is rigorous for one occasion, it tends to extend to others which are ritualized. Thus, in the Yuman-Piman area, where war-preparation and enemy-slayer purifications are emphasized, the salt taboo extends to them. Similarly for initiation in southern California and among the Maidu. On the other hand, the Pomo also initiate, but having no salt taboo for crisis rites, do without it on initiation. Of course, the weight of the occasion also counts. If there are frequent but not universal birth taboos in an area, they are likely to be put more frequently on the nursing mother than on the father. Thus of 23 southern

Sierra groups, 16 forbid salt to the mother, only 7 to the father, and these 7 are geographically scattered. The California "semicouvade" is not a classical couvade specializing on the father, but has previously been recognized as a joint parental affair, with all or part of the mother's restrictions extended to the father.

Incidentally, this last example illustrates the manner in which a wealth of comparative data on specific items can illuminate problems of cultural process and cultural direction or emphasis. Driver's data relate to 10 Yokuts tribes. All these taboo salt for the mother, except 2 southerly ones. . . . For the father, the southern exception grows areally by the addition of 2 others, though 2 northern tribes . . . also except him. . . .

The relative "strength" of the several occasions, as shown by the number of tribal participations, is: strongest, mother at birth; next, girl's puberty and death; weakest, menstruation and father at birth. It is evident that the preoccupation of Yokuts culture is greater with birth than with maturity or death, greater with the mother than with the father of a child, greater with the adolescent than with the grown woman. There is indication here of what is primary and more stable in the pattern, and what is secondary and more changeable.

If we consider the scattering cases of salt taboo outside the core area (Maidu to Pima), their reference is as follows: birth (mother, father, both, or pregnancy), 29; girls' puberty, 12; menstruation, 12; death, 1; initiation (really boy's vision quest), 2. Nearly all the lists consider the topics in this order, and it is conceivable that occasional informants or recorders tired under repetition and skimped later cases. But, even with some allowance for this possibility, it is evident that in the marginal areas of salt taboo birth is felt as a definitely important and death as a relatively unimportant occasion for its application. It is also evident that in these marginal areas there is so little difference of emphasis between first menstruation and recurrent menstruation that, contrary to the Yokuts attitude, adolescence in the girl is here scarcely singled out as crucial but rather is considered as already part of her mature functioning.

I have designated the strip from the Maidu to the Pima as the core of the area in which salt taboos are imposed (map 4, Fig. 2). Within this core however a nucleus is evident where taboos are imposed on additional occasions and where there are some positive ritual associations. This nucleus consists of the southernmost part of the core area: southern California, Yuman tribes, Pima and Papago, and a few Southern Paiute bands under Yuman influence.

All southern California groups taboo salt for the boy who is undergoing his puberty initiation. Most of them, especially the Shoshonean ones, extend the menstruant woman's taboo to her husband. Some of the Yuman groups, but not the Shoshonean ones, impose the taboo either on the burier or on the widow of a dead man.

In the Yuman-Piman area, in western Arizona, we find various salt taboos observed by the following numbers of tribes:

Prewar-party fast: 1 tribe.
Purification of enemy slayer: 6 tribes.
Girl's tattooing: 4 tribes.
Boys' puberty: 5 tribes.
Husband of menstruant woman: 5 tribes.
Mourners, or the ritual runners in the death commemoration: 6 tribes.
A salt cycle of songs and myth is sung by 5 tribes.

Finally, the Papago practice an elaborate ritualized journey to the sea to get salt. Both Gifford and Drucker obtained accounts of this in their lists, and it appears to be as sacred an affair as the Zuni expeditions to their salt lake. It may be as old as the Zuni rite or older. The Zuni salt lake was visited by other tribes. Gifford mentions the Hopi, Eastern Navaho, and Warm Springs and Huachuca Chiricahua as taking salt from it with a certain amount of ritual. Apparently the Zuni invested their salt journey with the heaviest elaboration of ceremony, possibly adopting the idea from the Papago journey to the ocean. So far as the other Pueblos and Apache-Navaho ritualized salt expeditions, they seem to have been to the Zuni holy lake.

DOGS

Several of the twenty blocks of lists are defective on dogs, in that they did not specifically inquire whether the animal was kept at all, whether it was bred or obtained from outside, whether it was housed or otherwise cared for. . . .

This gap is the more unfortunate because the Pomo-Miwok region is an area in which dogs were generally not raised or kept. All I can say is that this is a point at which we slipped into the fault that almost every ethnographer sooner or later commits, but which the lists were designed to prevent: to assume a phenomenon, or its absence, instead of specifically inquiring into its occurrence.

Fortunately there are in all lists some references to the use of dogs, as for hunting, and mentions in the notes, which allow at least approximate conclusions on most matters of interest.

Domestication.—Although it is generally assumed that the dog is man's universal companion and dependent, this is of course not quite accurate. There are dogless tribes in South America; and an area half-encircling San Francisco Bay on the north and east has now to be added.

Dogs were not entirely lacking in this region. All the local languages have a word for the animal. But dogs were not kept regularly; they were secured as scattered individuals from outside; they would be bought and would be taken care of as prized pets, somewhat as we keep parrots or monkeys; and they were not used ordinarily for hunting or other useful purpose. The crucial point seems to be that they remained rare enough for a local breed not to develop. The dog therefore was known to these cultures and entered into them as an occasional luxury element, but not as a normal feature or with a standardized function. . . .

Map 5 (Fig. 3) shows the well-defined area in which dogs either were not kept at all or were occasionally imported, kept as pets rather than as hunting aids, and remained so scarce that normally they did not perpetuate themselves by breeding. . . .

It must be emphasized that none of the tribes in question were entirely ignorant of dogs. Scatteringly they even imported them, paid for them, named, pampered, and buried them like persons; but always in small numbers. This affect attitude is evidently the correlate of scarcity. Of the two, the scarcity may be assumed as prior. It is indeed conceivable that an interest and concern in dogs might spring up of itself: Linton has given such a case for the Comanche. But it is hardly conceivable that a people having such an interest should then proceed to get rid of all or nearly all their dogs. The historic Comanche however had another domestic animal: the horse; and Linton's point is that the useful horse was treated as a utilitarian instrument, the useless dog as an object of affect, much as by our Californian tribes. We must rather conclude that the tribes of our Californian area first lost the habit of keeping dogs, and then sporadically began to reimport individual animals as something curious

and interesting. What caused the loss is obscure.

The archaeological evidence corroborates the list survey findings. Heizer and Hewes, in collecting instances of prehistoric ceremonial burial of bears, coyotes, deer, eagles, and other animals in central California, especially in the region of the Sacramento–San Joaquin delta, point out that there is no record of the discovery of dog bones, either in deposits which appear archaeologically late or in those which seem early. This would argue that, at least in the region occupied by the historic Plains and Northern Miwok, Nisenan, and Patwin, the absence of regular keeping or breeding of dogs is an old matter.

Heizer and Hewes's data further suggest that, while certain of the animals may have been caught for use in ritual, at least some were taken young, reared as pets, and then formally buried when they died, or perhaps, in the case of bears, after having to be killed when they became large and dangerous. These ancient indications of pet-keeping, not very frequently but with much fuss when it did happen, fit in exactly with the attitudes of the historic tribes of the region in regard to dogs.

Dogs as food.—In general, dogs were not eaten west of the Rockies. The principal area in which they were regularly used as food centers around the Yokuts of the San Joaquin Valley, with some scattering outliers (map 6, Fig. 3). . . .

Ceremonial eating of live dogs.—The spirit-possessed dancer who devours dogs is known to the Haida; Tsimshian; mainland Kwakiutl; Bella Coola; Wikeno Kwakiutl; the Squamish, Nanaimo, Cowichan, and Sanetch and Klallam Salish. The record is negative for the Tlingit, Vancouver Island Kwakiutl other than Wikeno, Nutka, Makah, Klahuse, Sechelt, Pentlatch, Comox, Skokomish, and, by inference, for all interior tribes. The solid core of the

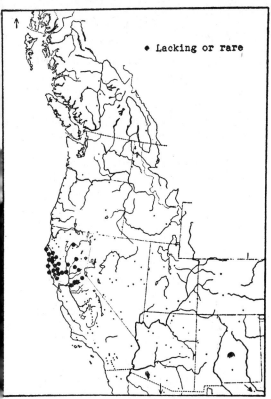

Map 5. Dogs absent or scarce.

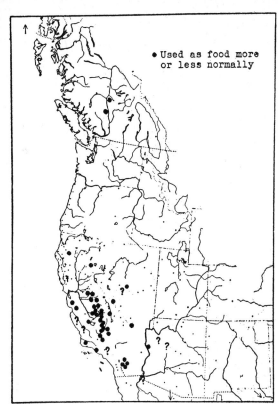

Map 6. Dogs eaten.

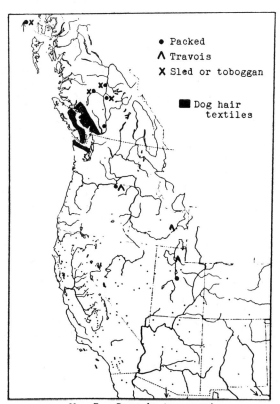

Map 7. Dogs in transport.

Fig. 3.—Dogs

occurrence is evidently Haida-Tsim-shian–mainland Kwakiutl; to the south it is scattering and rather on the inner coast than fronting the ocean.

In the Nothwest again, Barnett records, under Guardian Spirit, "dog-eating power specifically malignant" among Squamish, Nanaimo, and Pentlatch (negatives from Sechelt and Comox). This may be another aspect of the foregoing.

Dogs are occasionally eaten alive by the Zuni Newekwe clowns, but as an incident rather than as a standard performance. There may be other Southwestern occurrences; our list contains no ritual items for the Pueblos.

The Kutenay and Flathead have a Crazy-Dog Society of Plains type.

Dogs believed poisonous.–The Yurok believed dog flesh to be virulently poisonous. Unfortunately this item did not get incorporated in the list for the area, so its extent in northwestern California remains unknown. Barnett encountered the belief only among the Tolowa; the Oregon coast tribes denied it or knew nothing of it. Both Kalapuya informants, the Skokomish, and the Makah are reported +; which however may be an error, since the entries for the Chinook, Klallam, and all Northern interior tribes are —. I suspect a confusion between aversion to dog flesh and fear of it. Inasmuch as to the south the Lassik and Yuki deny poisonousness, and from the Shasta east the item does not appear —the Trinity Wintun upstream from the Hupa and Chimariko even eating dogs—it seems that the belief is confined to a few of the most specialized Northwest California tribes. It is in accord with their puritanical temperament and love of precise fears.

Use in transport.–This is rare and peripheral (map 7, Fig. 3) in the area covered by the element survey. . . .

Dog travois occurs among the Umatilla, Bannock, Promontory Point Shoshone. It was denied by all Southwest-

ern tribes, including Lipan and both Jicarilla divisions. These distributions suggest that the travois is not old in the Columbia region, coming in only with the horse and then being occasionally applied to the dog by poor people; and that on the other hand if the Plains Apache originally used the dog travois, as is generally assumed, they have had horses so long and in such numbers that the dog travois has become forgotten.

Dog wool for textiles.–This is a Coast Salish tract: 10 out of 11 tribes. Gunther adds the Wakashan Makah; but has a denial for the Skokomish of Puget Sound. From the Nutka and Kwakiutl north, Drucker has a universal negative; and Ray does not mention the item either for the interior tribes, Salish or other, or for the Chinook (map 7, Fig. 3).

Mountain-goat wool is used more widely. Dog wool is therefore probably a substitute or supplement.

Hunting.–As might be expected, the use of dogs for hunting was widespread; but it varied in intensity according to the nature of the game and of the country. In general, free-running animals in open country, like the antelope, were not often hunted with dogs. In the Great Plains, whole herds of buffalo might have been stampeded and lost through dogs being turned on them. On the whole, the deer is the animal most often hunted with dogs, especially where it can be driven to water; but in parts of the Basin and the Southwest it is denied that dogs were used for deer. Mountain sheep and mountain goat can often be successfully distracted, held, or driven past an ambush with dogs. For small game the practice varies. . . .

In general, the two most consistently negative areas for hunting with dogs are the Papago-Yuman-Cahuilla tract of low-lying creosote-bush desert, and the Ute–Southern Paiute region of high semidesert. Between were the Apache, Navaho, and Pueblos, who allege that they hunted with dogs. Is it possible that their habit is due to the early introduction of Spanish dogs and Spanish methods?

Training of hunting dogs is mentioned rather regularly north of the Columbia. The specific practices cited include: wild onion in eyes; trained on deer viscera and urine; nose rubbed on meat which is (then) set out for the crows; nose cut, concoction put in; head painted; sung to; heated deer hoofs rubbed on nose; rolled in fresh bear or beaver skin; mountain goat's forefoot warmed and pressed against pup's feet on four successive days. Obviously the training is sometimes practical, often merely magical. No single practice has a wide distribution, but one or more of them occur among most tribes in the north. South of the Columbia they are scarcely mentioned. I do not think this is due to lack of interest on the part of the southern list collectors. Rather did the northern informants volunteer items on training because their cultures were interested in the training of dogs.

Breeds of native dogs.—This is a matter on which reliable information is obviously difficult to get at this date. Several collectors have made the attempt.

Barnett, Gunther, and Ray inquired as to shaggy and short-haired dogs. Ten Salish tribes claim only long-haired dogs. . . . Short-haired dogs, besides shaggy ones, were affirmed by four Salish and two other tribes.

The Santiam Kalapuya specified short erect ears.

"Large" dogs were described by six tribes, all but one more or less in the area of dog transport.

For notheastern California, Voegelin obtained several descriptions, given in her notes. These summarize thus:

One breed only: 3 groups.
Height 12–18 inches, size of fox (or coyote): 4 groups.
Prick ears: 6 groups.
Short hair: 4 groups.

Various colors: 3 groups.
Long hair also: 1 group.
Large dog also: 1 group.

For the Northern Paiute generally, Stewart has the note: "No dogs; only Indian dogs with erect ears."

From the Eastern Navaho Gifford records: "Short-haired type height of fox terrier; long-haired type larger."

It is clear that size as well as coat varied; that some tribes had two or more varieties, whereas others had only one; but that all mentions of ears are to the erect form. . . .

Housing.—Some of the lists omit dog shelters as trivial. Others specify kenneling in a hole in the bank, brush shelters, little domes of willow brush or lean-tos of bark, and the like. The distribution of these several types of shelter usually varies locally within any one list; and it is likely that nowhere was any one form of dog hut standard or constructed for all dogs in the tribe, only proved hunting dogs or special pets being favored. The situation nowhere was like that of the Eskimo, to many of whom the preservation of their dogs is a matter of extreme importance, sometimes even of survival.

Whether dogs were allowed to sleep in the living house no doubt also varied tribally and individually. There is however an area in which it was more or less customary. Driver reports it universally for Northwest California. Here the frame houses were built with an anteroom where firewood was kept dry and the dogs allowed to find shelter. Also, no Northwest California group admitted knowing anything about a dog hut. To the north, in Oregon and Washington, Barnett, Gunther, and Ray report dogs sleeping in the house only here and there. The tribal scattering suggests nonstandardized practice. In Northeast California, however, E. Voegelin reports 8 groups allowing their dogs in the house, only 4 building a dog hut. To the south, the Kato, Lassik, and Yuki also took their few dogs in at night: they were too valuable to be allowed to stray away or to be stolen. The distribution thus radiates out from a Northwest California center.

Dead dogs.—As among ourselves in the country, the carcasses of Indian dogs were variously got rid of without formality or channeled procedure. Only among the Lassik, Kato, and Yuki, who had so few dogs that they bought, sheltered, and pampered them, do we hear of "burial like persons," sometimes with shell money. The Yurok however were likely to throw them into the Klamath, dog flesh being poisonous enough to contaminate springs, air, and land, and the river too polluted anyway to be fit to drink.

On the death of his owner, a dog might be killed or kept. The lists that inquire into the point show much local variation, which no doubt also represents individual variation in many instances. Driver first turned up a specialty: a dog is hanged by the neck from a tree on his owner's death. This he reports for Yurok, Karok, Hupa, Nongatl, and Sinkyone; the other tribes in the area denied the practice. However, so did one of his two Yurok and one of his two Karok informants deny it. Whenever adjacent tribes repeatedly vary in this region of small and sessile groups, we may be reasonably sure that the custom was not too rigorously standardized intra-tribally and that it varied individually or according to occasion. To the south, the Lassik and Kato knew the custom, and to the east the Western and Eastern Shasta, the Trinity Wintu ("because the dog liked it"), and, at a greater distance, the Mountain Maidu. Twelve of Voegelin's Northeast Californian groups answered No to the point. The method is specific, but the irregular distribution shows that the practice is only a hesitant "half-folkway."

Dog-beating at eclipses.—A more or less worldwide custom is to beat pots and pans and make dogs howl in order to scare away eclipses which are under way. This item was not in our original list; but it soon obtruded in field work, with thunder or lightning sometimes being added to eclipses or replacing them. . . .

Data that appear and disappear locally like these obviously cannot bear the usual distributional meaning. They are again "semifolkways." They can carry little compulsive force, except for excitable or suggestible individuals. They may be known to only part of each population. If so, it may be argued that a questionnaire got from one individual as representative of his tribe is inappropriate. I agree. Only, it does make very little difference whether the particular Chilula, whom most ethnologists cannot even place on the map and nearly all nonethnologists have never heard of, do or do not pinch their dogs' ears when the face of the moon begins to be covered up. Any real significance is evidently in a wider distribution. And if in a larger area fifty informants affirm and fifty deny the practice, the distribution of the two answers being randomly scattered, it seems a fair inference that this conflict of opinion means that tribal custom in the area is also conflicting, dubious, ambivalent, or half-hearted. In other words, the culture trait is widely spread but not crystallized culturally; it is perhaps only half-believed in, or not taken very seriously. At any rate, it is in a state of flux, potentially ready either to acquire significant value or to go entirely out of usage; but perhaps, nevertheless, remaining for a long time in indecisive status. It is thus that I would interpret distributional data of this order.

I admit that there are many errors in our lists, and on an item of this sort they are likely to be particularly heavy. Informants are mainly reporting hearsay, and some of it may refer to other groups. However, I doubt whether the most painstaking questioning of ten informants per tribe, with indefinite rechecking, would yield materially different results on this point for the area as a whole. What our questionnaire data do show, and show rapidly, on specific items not easily subject to verbal misunderstanding, is which traits are firmly established in the cultures of a region and are of value to them, and which are not and therefore fluctuate in their appearance. Dog-beating at eclipses and thunder is evidently of the latter character, in northern California: it is culturally unimportant; and this seems perhaps the most important fact about it.

I have gone into this trivial case because it seems worth demonstrating that judgments as to cultural weight, value, function, and affect, which are sometimes thought to be obtainable only by intensive studies on many individuals in still living cultures, can sometimes also be obtained by a more superficial study of cultures existing chiefly in memory, provided that the study is sufficiently extensive—and the investigator of course open-minded to problems.

TOBACCO

Several features emerge from the lists as of interest about tobacco. These are: the use and nonuse of the plant and substitutes for it; its cultivation; its consumption other than by smoking, that is, by chewing or eating; and its ritual functions, especially in connection with offerings and shamanistic practices.

Tobacco substitutes.—Dixon[1] has recently shown the likelihood that the "tobacco" grown and chewed with lime by the Haida and Tlingit was not a Nicotiana at all but some entirely different plant. He also doubts that true tobacco was used anywhere on the coast as far south as Puget Sound. . . .[2]

On the face of the Survey returns there is a large northwestern area extending south to and beyond the Columbia and east to the Rockies, in most of which smoking was affirmed but tobacco was denied. Technically, the British Columbia coast proper is not included in this area; but the Tlingit, Haida, and Tsimshian had a tobacco substitute, though they chewed it; and as for the Kwakiutl and Nutka, Drucker's list inquired only whether tobacco was smoked, not as to the presence of an equivalent for smoking. In the southeastern corner of the area the Flathead and Kutenay were buffalo hunters with tepees and would easily derive tobacco habits from the Plains tribes.

The lists however make nontobacco smoking more universal than do the scattered references in the older literature. The type specimen of Nicotiana multivalvis (the species grown by the Crow but not by the Mandan-Hidatsa) was collected by D. Douglas in 1825 from a Chinook or Kalapuya plantation between Vancouver on the Columbia and Oregon City on the Willamette. Teit has the Thompson and Shuswap not only using but growing a tobacco, seed from which yielded N. attenuata. It therefore seems that we must modify the stark limits of our northwestern nontobacco-smoking area by admitting a southern and eastern fringe of dry country in which true tobacco, locally grown or imported from neighbors, was smoked alongside tobacco equivalents.

Nevertheless, it remains evident that smoking and pipes had an aboriginal range (map 8, Fig. 4) extending considerably farther northwest than the range of the tobacco plant. This fact can hardly be construed other than as meaning that the idea and habit of smoking spread farther from the south than tobacco itself. Historically the function outtraveled the plant, so to speak. Another inference is that the occurrence of pipes in this area may not be inter-

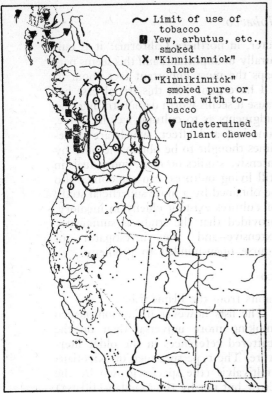

Map 8. Tobacco and substitutes.

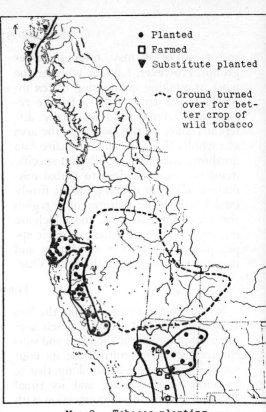

Map 9. Tobacco planting.

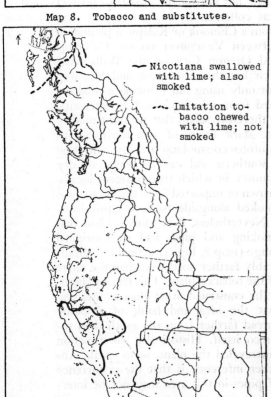

Map 10. Tobacco chewed or eaten with lime.

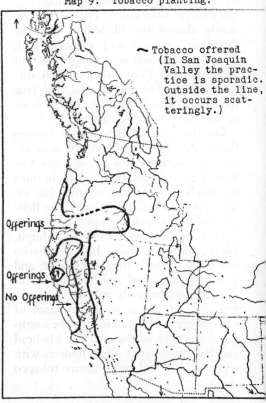

Map 11. Tobacco offerings. (The material, not merely smoke.)

Fig. 4.—Tobacco

preted as evidence of knowledge of tobacco.

The smoking of vegetal substances in place of tobacco is evidently related to the admixture of bark or leaves with tobacco. The one practice employs a surrogate, the other a dilution. Either usage might logically be derived from the other. On the whole, their ranges also adjoin. The Plains and the Great Basin pretty uniformly mix some kind of bark or leaves with their tobacco. In the Southwest and especially California the practice is definitely less common. Some tribes here use their tobacco straight; others mix in curious substances, like pine nuts or angelica-root incense. As regards admixture in general, the original purpose may have been to weaken rank and heady tobacco or to eke out a scant supply; once the latter practice became a habit, the toned-down taste may also have become preferred.

Tobacco cultivation.—It has long been known that tobacco was grown here and there in nonagricultural regions: in northern California, among the Thompson, the Crow in the Plains, not to mention the Haida and Tlingit, who certainly planted something that was used like tobacco. It is however surprising how many tribes prove to have followed the practice. They occupied three or four areas (map 9, Fig. 4), which apparently represent as many more or less separate historic developments.

1. NORTHWEST COAST.—The Haida and Tlingit planted; the product, for chewing, was traded also to the Tsimshian. The Salish, Kwakiutl, and Nootka to the south neither chewed nor had tobacco.

2. NORTHERN INTERIOR.—Inland, according to the lists, only the Kutenay planted. Teit adds the near-by Thompson and Shuswap, though Ray's list informants from these tribes gave denials, possibly because an additional thirty to

forty years have elapsed since the practice was discontinued.

3. OREGON-CALIFORNIA.—A long irregular area of planting stretches southeastward from the Oregon coast to south-central California. . . .

It is notable that all the planting tribes of this area are nonagricultural. Also, there is only rare mention of turning or breaking the ground, though the digging stick was used for bulb-gathering by all tribes in question. The seeds are simply scattered in the ashes. Locally there may be a bit of makeshift fencing, thinning, transplanting, pruning, or "nursing" of plants, or even a little hand-irrigating with a basket. In short, besides deliberate sowing, there is interest and care for the crop, but none of the heavy labor of agriculture.

The Modoc are a borderline case: there is no sowing, but a log is burned to increase next year's volunteer crop of tobacco. The Western Achomawi are one step nearer planting: a brushy place is burned over to improve seed gathering. Next summer, tobacco is likely to have sprung up also. The pods are rubbed between the hands, the seeds sprinkled into the ashes, and these are kicked around. Next year, and for one or two more, tobacco leaves are picked. While this makes the whole process incidental to food-seed gathering, it is also true planting, in that there is deliberate, even though rude, sowing.

On the whole, the process seems most elaborately carried out in northwestern California and perhaps Oregon. Here too the ranks of the planting tribes are unbroken. Eastward and southward there are local defections among the Wintu, the Maidu, and the Miwok; until among the Mono only 2 out of 5 local groups averred that they sowed, among the Yokuts 2 out of 10, among the Panamint 1 out of 3. One cannot be sure, in this marginal and interdigitated area, how far informants' "Yeses" and "Nos" represent individual fluctuations in their recollections or temporary and local variations of usage among small groups, connected perhaps with possession or lack of ample patches of wild tobacco. Nor does it much matter, on a wider view: it is clear that the hold of the planting habit was tenuous in the south, consistent and firm in the north.

Another fact points to this. The Hupa, Yurok, and Karok will smoke only cultivated tobacco; the wild is regarded as poisonous or at least dangerous; it is associated with waste places, graveyards, and death. None of the lists unfortunately deal with this attitude; it is my fault that the specific item was not included. It is inferable that the abstention extends beyond the three "classic" Northwest California tribes to all in that area; because all that sowed denied to Driver that they either gathered or imported tobacco; these practices appear only with the nonplanting Mattole, Kato, and Coast Yuki. To the north, in Oregon, Barnett's list did not inquire as to wild tobacco. In Voegelin's northeastern California lists, the westerly Shasta, adjoining the typically northwestern Karok, plant but do not gather; the easterly do both; which suggests that with them we have passed beyond the range of the poison-ban. The farther northeastern tribes, it is true, all affirmed either planting or wild gathering, never both; but each evidently made its choice according to opportunity, provincial custom, or mode; and the same is true farther south. The taboo on wild tobacco thus appears localized in Northwest California plus possibly the Oregon coast. Therewith the focus of the planting habit is further anchored to the same region, since it is evident that a fear taboo of the wild plant could hardly arise until domestication was pretty firmly established.

This inference leads to another one: the accentuation of planting is most marked at that end of the planting area which is farthest removed from the re-

gion of agriculture to the south. Therewith any direct relation of Californian tobacco planting with Southwestern food farming is weakened. I would not say that all historic connection is ruled out. There may conceivably have been stimulus or idea diffusion; but, beyond that, the California tobacco-planting development evidently followed its own lines independently. Nor would I guess that the place of origin was Northwest California; it is clear only that there the custom had got the heaviest hold on attitudes—was adhered to incisively and with ramifications into other spheres of culture.

In fact, there is another practice, spread through the Great Basin to the east, which may bear on the origin of California planting. This is the custom of burning patches of brush to help the springing-up of wild tobacco next year. This is reported, in the lists, by the Washo; by 12 out of 15 Northern Paiute groups; by 15 Nevada Shoshone, 2 Gosiute, 4 Southern Paiute, without exceptions; by 2 of 4 Northern Shoshone, and 4 of 8 Ute groups; and is denied by the Bannock. The denials are chiefly along the eastern edge of the Shoshonean area. The bulk of the Basin and the part nearer California burn almost solidly. There is no reference to sowing or tending; all the references are specifically to wild tobacco; it is merely recognized that this grows more abundantly after a fire, so fires are set. The practice is obviously part of the widespread one, followed also in most of California, of setting fires to promote the yield of food seeds: brush is destroyed, annuals thrive for a year or two.[3] Here then we have a custom which may have played a part in the development of the California sowing practice. All that was essentially needed to complete the development was the added deliberate sprinkling of seeds, instead of leaving this to the accidents of nature.[4] However, this addition might well have represented a long step, a difficult innovation—not indeed as we look back upon it from farming habits that have become taken for granted, but from the point of view of accustomed attitudes and established motor habits in nonfarming cultures. Therefore, it remains at least possible that the impetus to make the innovating addition did come from some knowledge of food farming elsewhere.

4. SOUTHWEST.—Finally, we have tobacco growing in the area of agriculture. Here we must distinguish three types of practice:

a). Wild tobacco was smoked by all Southwestern tribes. Some used only the wild. . . .

b). Certain tribes "planted" wild tobacco in the open country; that is, they sprinkled its seeds where it volunteered, and nowhere else. . . .

c). True farming, like that of corn, was limited to a few groups: the Mohave, Maricopa, Northeastern Yavapai, Pima, Papago; plus the Yaqui. The Mohave, Pima, and Yaqui planted in wetted-down "basins"; the Papago in "pits" in sand tanks, as for dry-season maize.[5] The Yaqui further transplanted. Here we evidently have a Pima-Papago or Sonoran type which has spread to a few adjacent Yumans: the tobacco is fully integrated into agricultural practices; it is completely farmed. However, all these tribes sometimes used wholly wild tobacco also. The Papago distinguished the two kinds and preferred the domesticated.

Origins of cultivation.—What is most interesting in this Southwestern region of agriculture is that, except in the vicinity of the Gila, tobacco was treated as a nonagricultural plant. It was either left wholly to nature to provide or was given the makeshift assistance provided by some of the California nonfarming groups. As regards tobacco, and tobacco alone, a Zuni had the attitude that we might expect from a Hupa or Karok,

these the attitude expectable in a Zuni. The inevitable question arises, What, if anything, has tobacco to do with native American agriculture, either historically or functionally, in its associations?

To a degree this problem has been recognized heretofore in the tobacco-planting addiction of the buffalo-hunting Crow and in the Haida-Tlingit planting. But the mass of wider data now available through the Element Survey poses the question more sharply and insistently.

If we are to think at all of tobacco growing being historically associated with native food farming, the one patent linkage on United States soil is in the Gila area, among the Pima-Papago. Now these people are nothing but the northern frontiersmen, best preserved through recent historical events such as the Mexican War and Gadsden Purchase, of a large group or nationality that extended far into Sonora or beyond it. Here, in northwestern Mexico, if our American Pima and Papago are fair representatives—and Drucker's Yaqui data suggest it—the association of tobacco with agriculture seems to have been a fact. And from here may have radiated two streams of influence: one to the Pueblos and Apaches, who took over tobacco usage without its farming associations; the other to California, where some idea of sowing penetrated and was retained. We are here entering the possibility of a chain of hypotheses which I explicitly prefer not to develop. It does appear to be sound to believe that if North American tobacco growing is to be derived from general agriculture, the association can be worked out only with reference to the Gila-Sonora region, or Mexico beyond it, as the critical area.

Chewing and eating.—The chewing or eating of tobacco was practiced, as has long been known, in two separate areas: part of the Northwest Coast and central California (map 10, Fig. 4). In both, tobacco or a substitute was mixed for chewing with burned-shell lime. The two areas differ in that for the Northwest Coast it appears that the plant used was not tobacco, the mixture was chewed, and smoking was unknown. In California, true tobacco was employed, it was eaten rather than chewed, and smoking was in vogue alongside of eating. The principal facts follow.

According to Drucker's list and notes, the Northwest Coast plant was probably not tobacco, is said by the Indians not to grow wild, and is therefore no longer determinable. It was chewed, by both men and women, among the Haida, Tlingit, and Tsimshian-Gitskyan. The Tsimshian traded it from the Tlingit and Haida. These two groups grew it; but the Tlingit imported Haida seed. The "tobacco" was ground in a mortar and mixed with burned shell. The Chilkat sometimes substituted ashes; the southern Tlingit, crabapple leaves; the Gitskyan, dried salmon eggs. Among all Kwakiutl, Bella Coola, and Nutka divisions the chewing habit did not obtain. The Skidegate Haida informant affirmed that the cultivated "tobacco" was also smoked; the China Hat Kwakiutl one that yew leaves were smoked in wooden tubes. Drucker doubts both statements; but, in view of yew being smoked by some of the Gulf of Georgia Salish, the Kwakiutl statement may be correct.

In California, eating with lime was practiced by all groups reported on by Harrington and Driver.... J. Steward confirms for Owens Valley and the Shoshone of Death Valley, and adds the Shoshone of near-by Beatty and Lida. Aginsky adds two local groups of Miwok. This makes a solid block of tribes from the Sierra Nevada to the sea and from San Francisco and the Merced River on the northwest to Los Angeles, Tehachapi, and Death Valley on the southeast. Outside this area the practice is consistently denied....

To the rule that the eating tribes also smoked there is no significant exception....

It appears that in the small extension district east of the Sierra Nevada the practice was usual only among women and was weakened from swallowing to chewing; men seem to have smoked in this subarea, except when they specifically wanted an emetic.

Historic relations of chewing.—Are the Northwest and California customs connected historically? The question must be left open. Connection can certainly not be proved at present. The geographical gap is great—half the length of California, all of Oregon and Washington, most of British Columbia. The practices are really far from alike: tobacco as against an unknown plant, swallowing as against chewing, smoking also present as against absent. The common elements are only three: sowing of a plant, mixing with lime, and taking into the mouth.

In this connection, it must be remembered that the California areas of planting and eating overlap but do not coincide. All the northern planting tribes—in a full half of the area—did not chew. Of the chewing tribes, none of the coastal ones planted.

If we knew more about the process of cultural loss, the abandonment of arts and customs—an event that appears to have occurred thousands of times in history, and usually silently—we might formulate an answer to the problem of connection of the Northwest and California. Planting, eating, and smoking are associated in the San Joaquin Valley. If we are ready to assume these as having once been an actual, historical, functioning unit, two of the elements—planting and smoking—carry us to the Columbia, and one—smoking, of yew and arbutus in a tobaccoless region—extends to the northern Salish, leaving only modern Kwakiutl territory to be crossed before the planting-chewing tribes of the north are reached. With a few minor tribal shifts invoked during a thousand years, we have complete connection established. The trouble is that we have made two assumptions: first, of a one-time unit complex; and second, of a series of varying partial losses. As against this, the explanation of separate origins makes only one assumption: that of the abundantly documented strength and variety of the cultural impulses toward experimentation, innovation, and fashion change. In the present case, as in so many others, we are simply left helpless in the choice between the alternatives.

Ritual use of tobacco.—The ceremonial use of tobacco was widespread in North America and of course found expression in many connections. For our western area, two points only will be examined: the use of tobacco as an offering, and shamanistic associations. Offerings and shamanism are universal in the area; particular rituals are likely to be local, so that an association or non-association of tobacco with the former is likely to be more significant than with the latter.

Offerings.—There are two principal forms in which tobacco can be offered: either the material itself or the smoke.

Anyone who has dealt with the Northwest Californians must have been impressed by the frequency with which they offer tobacco to the kihunnai, woge, or ikhareya spirits. A pinch is tossed into the air, or blown off the palm, with appropriate words of gift and request. Harrington has pointed out how with characteristic stinginess the Karok generally give the spirits crumbled tobacco stalks but smoke the leaves themselves.

Driver's lists add to the three classic tribes the Wiyot and Tolowa as blowing or throwing tobacco; also the Kato; and the Chimariko, Nongatl, and Sinkyone as making offerings other than by smoke. Putting of tobacco into the fire

he records for the Tolowa, Yurok, Hupa, and at a distance the Kato; the other tribes denied this.

To the north, on the Oregon coast, Barnett found all tribes making offerings by tossing into the air....

To sum up, the ritual offering of tobacco as a substance crops up sporadically almost anywhere, but is definitely rare except in one area which stretches from the Oregon coast to Los Angeles (map 11, Fig. 4). This is also the area of tobacco planting by nonfarming tribes—or, more exactly, this plus most of the additional territory in which tobacco was eaten. Moreover, the region in which offerings are most abundantly mentioned, and in which the manipulation of blowing or tossing into the air is specified, namely Northwest California and the Oregon coast, is also the region in which all local groups plant and sometimes tend their crop with definite care. Where the planting habit has a more tenuous hold, as shown by varying local practice, as along the flank of the Sierra Nevada, the offering habit has an equally variable occurrence and hold. The immediate Sacramento Valley neither plants nor offers. We are therefore justified in construing the two practices as linked functionally and historically. The patterns for both are either decisive and specific, or informal and unreinforced by much emotional sanction, or limited and rare in their application, or totally absent, in very nearly the same array of societies.

It is not difficult to see the common factor in attitude where the double pattern is strong. Tobacco is obtained in a special and formal way; it is offered in a special and formal way; it is prescribed to be smoked in almost every formalized, elaborate religious activity.

Tobacco in shamanism.—A strong and widespread association of tobacco smoking with shamanism is evident in the lists. It is virtually universal south and east of the Columbia. North of that stream, in the interior, the practice extends as far as the upper Fraser. Among tribes here that had no tobacco, the shamans smoked kinnikinnick; thus the Klikitat, Tenino, Umatilla, Kalispel, Coeur d'Alene.

In general, the list entry is simply: "shaman smokes," the context indicating that he smoked while acting as shaman, not merely that shamans as well as laymen smoked. As no further items are added in any northern list, it can be assumed that the doctor smoked during a cure, or in preparation for it, to strengthen his power. . . .

In southern California the custom of the doctor's blowing smoke specifically over the patient appears. Two Mountain Diegueño groups denied the practice. All other informants in southern California affirmed it. So do the Chemehuevi and Yuma. In Drucker's Arizona list, the item is multiple: "sucking doctor blows smoke on patient"; "curing by exorcising: smokes over patient"; "general doctor smokes to diagnose"; "blows smoke over patient." Every tribe in the area admitted one or several of these items. They are the Mexican Diegueño,

Akwa'ala, Cocopa, Mohave, Walapai, Yavapai, Maricopa, Pima, Papago, Yaqui; also the Shivwits Paiute. What varies is the purpose of the smoke blowing, or the stage of treatment at which it is introduced.

This means that curing by smoke blowing is standard practice among the southern California Shoshoneans, all Yumans, a few Southern Paiute bands adjacent to the Yumans, and the Piman-Sonoran peoples. This is also more or less the area in which blowing of breath or saliva on the patient has previously been reported. The basis of the pattern evidently is blowing as such; tobacco smoke was presumably included secondarily, smoking being already a part of shamanistic performance. . . .

In brief, then, wherever tobacco is smoked, the shaman smokes it as part of his curing treatment; and the practice even extends a little beyond the occurrence of true tobacco, substitute materials being used. The only notable specific variant is the addition of smoke being blown over the patient among southern Californians, Yumans, Pimans, and Sonorans.

35. THE CHIBCHA
1946

THE Chibcha culture is one of the most famous in South America. In fact, it is often spoken of as representing one of the culminations of native civilization in the Americas, equal to, or only just behind, that of the Aztec-Maya and Inca. But the Chibcha left no historic impress, no persisting influence on the modern life in their former area. They have also left surprisingly few physical monuments; their archaeology is meager. Even their speech died out long ago. It is clear that they achieved much less of a cultural construct in their day than did Mexicans or Peruvians. Why then do they stand out in our consciousness?

The primary reason seems to be that they achieved states. They were in a fair way to attaining to political structures of type similar at least to that of the Aztec, if not the Inca. Considerable masses of men had come under the control of individuals, so that they moved, in peace and at war, with direction, and at any rate with the possibility of consecutive development. That there were several such states, and that these were still contending, does not reduce the situation materially below the level of conditions in the Aztec area: not by more than a generation or two. The Chibcha had definitely passed out of the amorphous, endlessly reshifting status of mere tribal life, which seems to us so essentially historyless in its potentialities. It is true that they possessed very little history, as yet, when the Spaniards broke them. But the same might be said, with only relative qualification, of the Peruvians.

To what this political development was due, which in Colombia was so highly localized among the Chibcha, is not wholly clear. The most nearly satisfying explanation, probably, is in terms of a population of superior density, due in turn to a favorable terrain: an altitude sufficient to temper the climate of the tropics, a series of good-sized valleys with much level land, a fertile soil, and a grass savannah interspersed with enough larger vegetation to take it out of the type of mere semiarid plains. Not that these geographical conditions will of themselves produce political organization; but a natural environment more or less favorable to concentration of numbers does seem a necessary requisite for political development to spring up spontaneously, without import. The Chibcha habitat is therefore of significance to an understanding of Chibcha culture.

With all their differentiation from their nearer tribal neighbors on the political side, the Chibcha were however surprisingly on their level in other ways. This is true of success in warfare, trade relations and dependences, religious concepts and practices, and manual industries. They evolved no calendar, no astronomy, no elaborate system of cults comparable to those of southern Mexico and Guatemala. It was organization which they lacked in all these domains, along with their politically unorganized Colombian neighbors. They failed to develop cultural forms which were at once definite and interrelated into something larger. Take away from the Aztec their religious system and all that adhered to it, and the picture would be not so very different.

However, the Mexican religion also rested on a wealth of material symbolic

283

expressions, without which it would appear to us far less choate and effectively organized. These Mexican expressions are largely through art; and the art in turn rests upon a skilled, advanced technology in many media. Technology of this proficiency the Chibcha were very far from having attained; without it, their art remained backward; and without the art, their religion, with which in native America intellectual development was intimately associated, remained on an essential par with that of their tribally cultured neighbors. The Chibcha did not build in stone, were virtually sculptureless, some of their best cloth was painted instead of patterned, and their metalwork and ceramics are recognized as inferior to those of other areas of Colombia whose inhabitants were historically so obscure as to be hardly remembered.

The Peruvians equaled and in some respects surpassed the Mexicans in technology. They were perceptibly behind them in aesthetic and symbolic expression, and still more so in religious and intellectual articulation. They had moved one or more steps beyond them in political integration. It is on these inequalities that the often made comparison rests, of Mexicans to Greeks and of Peruvians to Romans; and in part the other saying, that the Mexicans achieved best with their minds, the Peruvians with their hands. Compared with both, the ancient Colombians were well behind in all aspects; and from the general mass of the Colombians the Chibcha stood out, primarily, in sociopolitical development alone.

It is in the light of these generic characteristics that Chibcha culture will now be examined.

POLITICAL INSTITUTIONS, RULERS, AND NOBILITY

There was little permanence in the larger Chibcha states or "kingdoms"

like those of the Zipa and Zaque. Each district had its lord, who might rebel against his overlord. A powerful or energetic ruler invaded the territories of his neighbors, one at a time, and, if successful, exacted their submission and tribute, after which they were generally left as vassals. No considerable army was brought together by any ruler to oppose the Spaniards. Each awaited his turn. Resistance came more frequently after Spanish occupation than before. How far the overlordship of the Zipa and the Zaque extended is also not clear. To the north of both lived Chibcha who may have paid them prudent deference, but who seem not to have been subdued or even invaded: those of Guane, for instance. The Iraca at Sogamoso was independent of both Zipa and Zaque. In his selection, the neighboring Tundama at times had a voice. But the Tundama's residence was also not far from the Zaque's Hunsa-Tunja. If the Tundama was genuinely independent, the Zaque's proper dominion must have been rather restricted, in spite of his overlordship extending down the Garagoa Valley. One divergent account makes Guatavita supreme in the south, with the Bacatá (Zipa) his "lieutenant and captain general," who had revolted only just before the arrival of the Spaniards. Similarly, Ramiriquí, not Hunsa, is said to have been the original seat of the Zaque.

The political condition was evidently similar to that in the valley of Mexico, or for that matter among the Maya; with this difference, that in Mexico large religious structures provided a nucleus for a physical town which embodied or represented a cultivated district more effectively than among the Chibcha. Otherwise, the rivalries and alliances of Tenochtitlan, Tlatelulco, Texcoco, Tlacopan, Atzcopotzalco, Chalco, Tlaxcala, seem very similar to those of Bacatá, Ubaque, Guatavita, Hunsa, Sugamuxi, etc. We must assume that dominance fluctuated and refluctuated, without the total picture changing much.

What is clear is that in both regions there were noble and powerful families of señores or lords, of whom the greater ruled the lesser, as these ruled their districts. It is specifically said that town chiefs were absolute at home, even though vassals of their overlords. These overlords were shown every respect which native imagination could conceive. Even chiefs never looked them in the face, but turned their "shoulders" away or bent far down in their presence. The Spanish soldiery were thought shameless because they spoke to their own commanders eye to eye. An incorrigible thief was forced to look his ruler in the face, and then was let go as humiliated worse than by death. When the Zipa wished to spit, a dignitary knelt with averted face and held out a cloth. No messenger, and no noble even, was received by him without a gift. The Guatavita exacted his own authorization, in return for gifts, for anyone wishing to wear a cloak of distinctive design in his dominion. Litters were sumptuary furniture, closely restricted; the Zipa's was hung with sheets of gold and was preceded by attendants who cleared the path or strewed it with cloth or flowers. Roads connected the rulers' wooden "palaces" with their wooden temples. The more prominent ones had bath retreats: the Zipa at Tenaguasa, Tabio, and Teusaquillo (the modern Bogotá); the Zaque at Ramiriquí; the Iraca at Iza; the Guatavita at Guasca.

All this ostentation not only re-emphasized rank but demanded economic support, which in turn involved tributes. The Spaniards were disappointed in the amount of gold they were able to seize; by their standards, rulers so absolute and exalted should have had more. But the amount was considerable in view of the fact that the Chibcha imported all their gold; and they certainly used it with conscious ostentation, as in

hanging sheets of it to clank in the breeze in front of their chiefs' doorways, and as in the "el dorado" ceremony of Lake Guatavita. Commoners' tribute appears to have been in cloth, produce, and labor....

Succession to rule, as also to priesthood, was matrilineal. It may well have been so in the population at large also, though the Spaniards seem to be silent on this point. A sister's oldest son succeeded; failing him, a brother. It is specifically said that sons inherited personal property; a nephew, the chief's office (estado). There was a training for succession which resembles that for priesthood. The heir was confined for about six years in a temple, forbidden to see the sun, and allowed out only at night. He abstained from meat, salt, pepper, and sexual indulgence, and was whipped at times. At Guatavita, he went out on the lake in a raft, anointed with gold dust. One version makes this his induction, another a recurring religious rite. The crown prince to the Zipa ruled at Chía, until his accession....

POSITION OF WOMEN

The Chibcha practiced a girl's puberty rite, which is symptomatic of their incomplete emergence from primitiveness. The girl sat for six days in a corner with her face and head covered—as in so much of western North America. Then she was bathed, and there was a feast, with the inevitable chicha beer. Chastity in girls was a matter of indifference, if not distrust; but husbands insisted on their wives' fidelity, with ají pepper ordeals if necessary. Whether this expectation was extended to the feasts, with their general intoxication and the mixing of social ranks, is less clear. The Spaniards certainly construed them as occasions of unlimited sexual indulgence. The significant fact is that women participated in the drinking. Polygyny was widespread and not confined to the nobility, who might have up to a hundred "wives," as against the two or three of commoners. The wives shared one joint room, the husband had another; which tended to make the wives accepting participants rather than competitors. Wives were bought for an agreed price; or a suitor might come and sit at the door with a gift of cloth, a load of maize, and part of a deer.

WAR AND WEAPONS

The Chibcha were no bowmen, at least not in warfare. They occasionally hired archers from their enemies, the Panche and Muzo. In this nonuse of the bow they resembled the Aztec and the Peruvians. Like the Aztec, and the Peruvians of the Early Period, they hurled darts with the spear thrower or atlatl (tiradera). Why this weapon was given the preference over the bow is not clear, but it seems that there must be a functional relation to density of population and the resultant concentration of armed forces, together with need for their more compact organization. It can hardly be an accident that Nahua, Chibcha, and Peruvians sent their armies out without bows, but that more primitive American peoples, of looser political structure, generally employed them. . . .

RELIGION

Priests and shamans.—The office of priest, cheque or jeque, and its acquisition, being somewhat parallel to those of chiefs, suggest that both were filled from the nobility. The priest also acquired his status from his mother's brother. He trained for twelve years in a special building, "fasting," that is, eating only maize once a day, meat rarely, no salt or pepper; and observing continence. Finally, his ears and nose were pierced, like a chief's, and he was "invested" by the ruler with a painted mantle and a calabash container for his coca. Thenceforth, he lived in the temple, or by it; remained chaste, on pain of deposition; received all his food, but was expected to eat little, as well as to wake much of nights and be taciturn. At stated times he fasted and drew his own blood. Perpetual penance seems to have been the first demand of the office. The ruler of Iraca, said to have been the highest priest in the whole land, had wives, so his position may have been an exceptional combination. The observation that there was no hierarchy probably means merely that there was no ecclesiastical organization corresponding to the Catholic Church, but that each district had its own priests, as it had its rulers.

The priests officiated for the public good, as when in time of droughts they threw ashes up from a peak, to turn into clouds. They were also consulted by individuals, on whom they imposed an abstinence similar to their own; after the conclusion of which they received the gold or other offering, gave it to their deity, asked for his answer, and imparted it; their own fee was two mantles and a bit of gold. Both coca and tobacco were taken by the priests; Datura is less certain.

The Spaniards specifically distinguished hechizeros from the jeques—shamans from priests. These "wizards" were generally old men or women, who, not supported by their relatives, wandered about in their poverty, selling cures, poisons, abortions, and aphrodisiacs, diagnosing, finding lost objects, and explaining dreams. In order to see or foretell, they chewed tobacco or drank an infusion of Datura, tyhyquy; or ate two other herbs, yopa and osca; and in this condition they watched for twitching of fingers or movements of joints as omens.

Cults.—Chibcha cults offer none too clear a picture, partly because they were not organized into a clear conceptual system and partly because of the Spaniards' own religious preconceptions. Besides the temples with their "idols," there were shrines to lakes and rivers, caves, and mountains. Lakes in particular were likely to be holy, and had some association with snakes. The Spaniards paid particular attention to offerings because these often included gold and emeralds; and they were naturally interested in human sacrifice. But of course there were innumerable humble and domestic sacrifices; and in many rites penances may have played as important a part as offerings. The temples however were crowded with receptacles of offerings, ranging from gold to cotton cloth; and, as these vessels became full, they were secretly removed and buried. Presumably, most valuables sooner or later were drained off by religion or burial, so that there must have been a steady outflow of Chibcha products to purchase the gold they needed.

Human sacrifices were made primarily to the Sun, who "ate persons." When the Spaniards arrived, they had children thrown or handed to them as being reputed sons of the Sun. There were a number of temples to the Sun; and the town Chía was named after the Moon. Offerings to Bochica and Chibchachum must include some gold, it is said; so that it is natural that they were directly worshiped chiefly by rulers, nobles, traders, and goldsmiths. Bachúe received incense gum; Chubabiba, the rainbow, mainly emeralds and beads from those sick of fever or women about to bear a child. A Nencatacoa, patron of weavers and cloth painters, was given chicha. This constant reference to offerings, if the Spaniards have not unduly exaggerated it, suggests prevalent religious approach for individual benefit, rather than a fixed series of ceremonies for the common good....

The Chibcha thought and grouped mostly in sixes. Priests trained for twelve years, chiefs for six ("five to seven"). Mourning was for six days. Maize was of six colors. At a child's weaning, cotton wet with the mother's milk and wrapped in grass was thrown into the river, and six swimmers tried to retrieve it as a good omen. In races, the chief rewarded the six winners, giving six cloaks to the first victor. The girl's puberty rite lasted six days.

Human sacrifice.—Human victims were variously drawn. Some were war captives, some slaves, some children born into good families. One practice was to buy small children from the Marbachares, 15 days (or "30 leagues") east between the Guape and Guechar rivers. The traders resold them to high chiefs, who might keep as many as three. They were reared in the temples; were sacred and might not touch the ground, so that they were carried about; ate only out of their own dishes; were believed able to converse with the Sun; and when they sang, everyone wept. At early puberty, they were sacrificed, unless they had lost their chastity, which rendered them impure. Amid appropriate songs, they were cut open, the heart and viscera removed, the head severed. This custom presumably obtained at the specific Sun temples.

To appease the angry Sun when there was a drought, priests took a child to a mountain top that looked eastward, and before sunrise killed it with cane knives and anointed the east-facing rocks with its blood. The body was left for the Sun to eat, or disposed of in a cave.

A sacrifice with Mexican reminiscences, but whose occasion is not known, was to bind a slave into a sort of nest on a mast, where he had atlatl darts thrown into him. Priests caught his blood, and later buried the corpse in the mountains.

Captive enemy children, especially of the Panche, were sacrificed at the temple on return, their blood sprinkled on the posts and floor, their bodies exposed on the mountains for the Sun; or they were kept for the same fate before a new war party set out.

Rulers firmed their house posts, and the fortunes of the inmates, by sacrificing girl children, said to have been given from noble families. Each heavy post was pounded up and down on a live child while earth was being poured in. A similar practice is reported for the Suga-muxi-Iraca temple, but with slaves as material.

Rulers were wont to be buried with several wives and slaves, who had been stupefied with chicha containing Datura juice.

Of animals sacrificed, we hear only of guacamayo and papagayo parrots—the latter having first been taught to speak—brought up from the warm country. Their heads were kept. These bird offerings seem like a reduced imitation of human sacrifice.

36. GREAT ART STYLES OF ANCIENT SOUTH AMERICA

1951

THIS essay is an endeavor to characterize the typical values of the principal forms of visual art developed in ancient native South America. Chronological relations are assumed, without citation of their supporting archaeological evidence. The consideration is aesthetic: it is directed at qualities of style.

1. In Peru, the art of the type site of Chavín, at Huántar, is lithic, and is possessed of grandeur in the sense that it is charged with strong feeling, both symbolic and decorative. The lines of this sculpture are at once heavy and flowing, with an effect of massiveness even in small areas; and most objects look larger and heavier than they are. Curves predominate, generally within an implicit rectangular contour. Straight lines are not altogether avoided, especially in relief, but are employed to achieve secondary contrast with the curves, or as part of the frame. The total effect is one of slow motion, often intricate but never flamboyant, without lightness of touch, every detail seemingly significant, and impressive rather than pleasing. In fact, the monstrous is not avoided. Both the type of line and the load of symbolism carry a suggestion of Maya art, though there is no evidence of historical connection.

The freest specimens of Chavín sculpture are heads in the round. Most of these have the faces furrowed, and in some the furrows or the hair are converted into snakes. A second type of stone carving is constituted by columnar monoliths with surface carving. A third type consists of incised or relief carvings on slabs. Feline figures are perhaps most characteristic among these,

the full-spread condor the most readily appreciated on first approach to the art. There are some jaguar representations whose heaviness of line and monstrosity of concept put them among the less attractive Chavín pieces. A dominant trait is the fangs or tusks projecting beyond the lips.

The type site of Chavín has yielded little besides this sculpture, which fortunately is nearly all preserved, either as originals or in casts, at the Museo de Antropología at Magdalena. The entire range of Chavín style art, in metals, cloth, and clay modeling as well as in stone, is recoverable from the remains occurring, more often on the coast than in the highland, from Chiclayo to Paracas. Here there are included: embossed gold from Chongoyape; incised trumpet shells and carved stone jars from Chiclayo; Cupisnique type modeled and incised pottery from Chicama; a modeled monstrous clay idol at Puncurí and a decorative adobe relief at Cerro Blanco, both in Nepeña Valley; in Casma, more clay modeling in pure Chavín type at Mojeque, and at Cerro Sechín incised slabs somewhat deviant from the classic manner but still Chavinoid; at Supe and Ancon, Chavín-like pottery, also bone carvings; at Paracas, in the Cavernas part of the cemetery, pottery modeled, incised, or inlaid under Chavín influence, along with pyrographic designs on gourds. The variety of materials and technologies in which the Chavín manner is expressed evidences the strength of the style.

The Chavín style may be considered the greatest art style evolved in Peru and in South America. Also, it appears

289

to be one of the earliest. Above all, it possesses a line that is unique in its assurance of form, its true dignity, and the inevitability of its curves. Hardly less extraordinary is the slow plastic flow of the surfaces produced by this art. Consistently and consciously symbolic, the art is saturated with feeling equally in its themes and in its forms. At its best it possesses grandeur, at its worst it becomes obsessed with the monstrous.

2. By contrast, on the north coast of Peru, Mochica or Early Chimú art, famous for its sculptural ceramic modeling, was oriented toward representation rather than symbolism, and excelled in painting almost as much as in modeling. This pottery is extraordinarily mature and supple in style. Very few fundamental vessel shapes underlie an endlessly exuberant variety of modeling and painting, executed with high technological competence.

The peak of Mochica art was attained by the so-called "portrait heads." Whether these are individual portraits in our sense is uncertain. The Mochica may have been like the Greeks, Egyptians, and Chinese in being more interested in the type. However, they made the type astonishingly lifelike and often ideal as well. They were equally successful in depicting deformities, mutilations, paralysis and other diseases, the abjectness of prisoners, punishments, ironical as well as macabre caricatures, and erotic scenes. They had the gift of seizing and reproducing salient features and posture. Strict anatomical realism is often violated: many heads are disproportionately large for the body, or eyes for the face; but this becomes evident only on analytic reflection. There is little Mochica representation of the fantastic or chimerically symbolic, as there is in Chavín art. Preference is for a single, free-standing head, body, or animal; less commonly for two or three figures; groups of five or six small figures occur rather rarely, chiefly in scenes of reli-

gious sacrifice, and may represent an influence from Recuay scene-modeling. The Mochica showed themselves thoroughly possessed of true sculptural feeling in preferring permanent form at rest to "story." Certainly their aesthetically best modeling, as well as the bulk of their work, expresses form rather than event.

The Mochica were scarcely less successful as painters, both in monochrome red or brown on the cream slip of their pottery, and in larger flat-color mural frescoes. They preferred depicting couples, groups, or processions. Representation is almost wholly in profile. In sharp contrast with the modeling, it is action, not rest, that is painted; and the action is generally rapid, often vehement. Background is confined to essential indications. Animals, imaginary and fantastic as well as free-realistic, are also represented; and from these there is a transition to merely decorative and geometric figures. The painting stroke was firm, swift, and sure—indicative of a control parallel to that of the modeler. The fresco painter outlined his figures with long, sweeping incisions, then filled in areas with flat-color masses in several hues.

3. Mochica ceramic art was preceded in its own territory not only by the Cupisnique form of Chavín but also by Salinar and then by Negative or Gallinazo. Negative has highland affiliations, especially with Recuay, in vessel shapes and in small-figure modeling, as well as in use of resist or negative painting. But the Salinar white-on-red pottery, a coastal product, seems to be the principal stylistic parent of Mochica. It is a formative, fumbling, experimenting style, attempting many subjects and shapes, but always in a modeler's manner, as distinct from the stone carver's. Like Mochica, it is secular, not stylized symbolically; and it is oriented toward representational likeness, even though crude in achievement. Mochica appears

to have grown out of Salinar by the double process of learning to increase patterned control and to eliminate random efforts. Salinar explored new paths, Mochica channeled and traversed them to a culmination.

4. On the southern coast, the ceramics of Nazca rival Mochica in quality, and are generally considered more or less contemporary, though Nazca metallurgy, brick-molding, and construction are considerably retarded in comparison. Nazca attempts only minimal modeling, but it specializes in polychrome designs, varying from pictorial to symbolic, though never genuinely realistic even to the limited Mochica degree. The ware is fine-grained, thin, metallic, highly polished, and carries many colors in definitely harmonious combinations. An earlier phase has fewer forms, fewer and more somber colors, and a narrower range of designs. The later Nazca phase adds more specialized shapes; more colors, tending toward pastel tints; and a whole series of new designs, such as anthropomorphic deities and rows of women's yellow faces with almond eyes. The designs of this later phase tend toward the flamboyant and exaggerated, as in the multiplication of faces on demons and in providing them with tentacle-like rays. While the earlier Nazca has been found only in the Nazca and Ica valleys, the later phase had a much wider distribution, and in the Sierra it blended into other manners, such as Tello's Huari or Huanca, Chanca, and Rucana.

5. The famous Paracas Necropolis embroidered textiles are obviously allied in theme and line to the painted ceramic designs of Nazca. It is not known which is derivative from the other. The most sumptuous of the embroideries, unsurpassed anywhere in fineness and richness of design and color, are rectangular mantles, bearing alignments of figures of gods, masked impersonators, demons, warriors, or animals. These occur either in a wide border surrounding an empty panel, or in panel and border. The embroideries are in wool, their sheer background is of cotton. Other fabrics have wool weft on cotton warp. The embroidered figures attempt any and every curve, in most untextile-like manner—and successfully. There is known one Paracas mantle which is painted instead of embroidered, but otherwise in the typical style; also a Nazca canvas fragment painted with hummingbirds like those frequent on jars.

Necropolis pottery looks as if it might be a development out of Nazca, though in the direction of having lost former designs. It is a plain ivory-color ware, favoring the double-spout jar, but in a flattened form, with long slender spouts: the effect is one of refined, specialized, weak elegance, a dead end of stylistic development.

6. The Tiahuanaco style is very well defined. It is named after a famous architectural and sculptural ruin with associated pottery, near Lake Titicaca in the Bolivian highlands. The distribution in the Sierra is restricted, except southward into Bolivia. But from Arequipa to Trujillo the Peruvian coast almost everywhere shows a period of specific Tiahuanaco influences, in pottery, textiles, and metals. This Coastal Tiahuanaco manner gathered into itself certain new shapes and traits unknown at Tiahuanaco, such as the flaring double-spout; and the resultant hybrid style then flowed northward along the coast, picking up additional local features on the way. It was this "Tiahuanacoid" art of the northern coast, with only a minor proportion of indubitably Tiahuanaco-derived features left in it, that largely displaced Mochica art. Out of it in turn there subsequently grew, along with considerable resurgence of Mochica forms and manner, the Late Chimú style. Similarly, the ceramics of

Huari seem a blend of late Nazca and Tiahuanaco.

For ceramics, Bennett has worked out stratigraphically a sequence of Early, Classic, and Decadent Tiahuanaco pottery phases at the type site, which is stylistically convincing. The Classic phase has its design elements arranged significantly, and the Decadent meaninglessly, on the whole. Yet a new problem is posed, since Bennett's Early Tiahuanaco examples are far from expressing formative stages, either of representative or of geometric designs, but look like the broken-down complex end-product of some previous style.

Tiahuanaco sculpture rivals that of Chavín. These two are the only South American styles in stone which have achieved thorough control and a degree of grandeur. Tiahuanaco is a severe style, but it avoids the representation of the monstrous and the impression of terror which lurks in Chavín sculpture. With all its condors, cats, serpents, and chimeras composed of them, the Tiahuanaco figures remain decoratively interesting and are never shocking or repulsive, though they may seem barbaric. Allied to the psychological severity of the art is its stiffness, its fondness for straight lines, for chords rather than arcs. It will round its corners, but the implicit design remains rectilinear—in contrast to the flowing curve which still is basic in Chavín even when actual outlines approach the rectangular. This emphasis on the severely straight line in Tiahuanaco may derive from specialties of masonry technique, such as appear in the strangely elaborate stereometric cut stones found at Tiahuanaco itself. The design of most of the relief sculpture, as in the famous monolithic gateway, is so angular as to be easily transferable to tapestry; there is even considerable suggestion of its own derivation from woven tapestry patterns.

Along with the architectural severity of line, Tiahuanaco sculpture has archi-

tectonic organization. This is evident on comparison. In Chavín, the strength is in the form of the detail—the curved lid of an eye, its eccentric pupil, the bend of a fang or claw, the roll of a lip; whereas the total composition may be intricate or bewildering to grasp. The corresponding elements in a Tiahuanaco relief or statue are likely to be insipid in their schematic simplicity. The eye, for instance, is an even square, octagon, or circle; tusks are two opposite-pointing right triangles; a claw is indicated by a square at the end of a rectangular digit or toe. Nevertheless, these vapid geometric units are pulled together in Tiahuanaco art by a strong sense of organization into a composition which is almost always impressive and often interesting. Tiahuanaco sculpture remains attached to the quarry block—even more than that of Chavín, on the whole; but it has made the most of this attachment in developing its peculiar and highly specific stylistic quality of surface treatment.

7. The Pucara style of the northern Titicaca Basin is less impressive, less abundant, more localized, and possibly somewhat earlier than that of Tiahuanaco. Stelae or slabs are carved in relief with representations of fish, occasionally of men, and sometimes geometrically. These last are the best, aesthetically: they handle curves with skill and imagination. Pucara pottery combines modeling, incising, painting, and burnishing even more strikingly than Paracas-Cavernas. There are positive, though not close, Tiahuanaco affinities in modeling, themes, and details. It is a well-controlled, original ceramic not dependent on or imitative of its southern sister.

8. The Recuay style of the Callejón de Huaylas is most fully expressed in high-grade pottery with negatively painted linear designs of highly stylized felines in panels. These cats come in rampant or sitting position, angular, open-mouthed, long-tailed, with ser-

pent-like head appendages, almost re-sembling dragons. The vessels are fre-quently modeled, carrying not only spouts, stirrups, and bridges but figures of men and animals. These modeled figures are smaller, clumsier, and stiffer than Mochica ones, but tend to appear in groups illustrating genre scenes. There are no sure Chavín influences in Recuay, in spite of the close geographical prox-imity of the two type sites.

Callejón and Aija sculpture consists of stone lintels and of statues. The lintels bear relief carving of a squatting or spread-leg human figure flanked by profile felines whose conspicuously eared faces may be turned front. The style of execution is not highly charac-terized. Statues are little more than blocks, slightly shaped from a boulder with a main cut into the stone made be-tween head and trunk. The head con-stitutes about two-fifths of the total length, the nose is long, the eye without expression, the mouth thin and rudi-mentary; the execution is without either skill of line or feeling for planes; it is stylistically meager, almost inept. Ac-cessories in some of the surface relief suggest time connection with Recuay pottery.

9. The highland north of the Callejón is little known. Huamachuco has yielded some sculpture, especially fairly lifelike, full-round, human heads on tenons, pre-sumably for wall insertion; also tenoned, squarish, serpent-horned cats' heads. There are similar pieces from Santiago de Chuco and Cabana, not far south. The handling of the carving is skilful and definite. The human heads come nearer to successful plastic depiction of actual human heads than can be found in any other South American stone sculpture. Chavín is too interested in the monstrous, Tiahuanaco in the schematic, San Agustín in both, ever to be lifelike.

10. The Inca style of Cuzco is the latest of the highland styles. Exemplars occur from Ecuador to Argentina. Most of this wide spread is believed to have occurred within the century preceding the Spanish Conquest. Although little developmental Inca has yet been found, the style is well characterized in a num-ber of media, emphasizes technological control, and possesses a set of firm pat-terns.

The Cuzco people found satisfaction in the fine working of stone, from gi-gantic masonry blocks, as at Sacsahua-mán, and bedrock cuttings of intihua-tana down to utilitarian vessels. All these show a feeling for mass and for planes, for exact fit if they are joined, for sur-face texture, and for functional form.

The best plastic work consists of min-iature figures, mostly of llamas or hu-man beings, carved of fine-grained stone or cast in bronze, silver, or gold. These figures are very simple, not too realistic, but extremely expressive of tactile ef-fect in their curving planes.

Inca pottery is marked by chaste clas-sic form and sobriety of design and color. The number of shapes is limited; so is the range of patterns, which are executed within a channel of good taste but without either strong interest or slovenliness. Painted representation is chiefly of small animals, like flies, or of highly conventionalized birds. Colors tend to the somber; if they are bright, it is without vivid hues. It is the quality of intended and achieved control that the Cuzco ceramics share with Cuzco stonework, rather than an outright transfer to plastic clay of qualities of form—in contrast with the much more direct interrelationship of Chavín lithic and ceramic design. Inca textiles are again different in manner. They favor all-over ornament, with the surface broken into many small panels contain-ing diverse designs, sometimes repeated diagonally. The aim is to fill the frame of the cloth pleasingly, evenly, and with variety, not to organize it.

All in all, Cuzco art is well directed,

steadily controlled, unexuberant, rather deficient in imagination or ambition and in objectives other than technological ones. It keeps a consistent level without falling into weaknesses; but it has none of the smoldering drive of Chavín, the imaginative skill of Mochica, the primitive taste of Nazca, or the compositional ability of Tiahuanaco.

11. In the post-Tiahuanaco period of the last two or three centuries before the Spanish Conquest, a considerable degree of assimilation of culture occurred along the Peruvian coast, even anterior to the Inca conquest. Metal had become fairly abundant, and metallurgical processes were skilful and uniform. Irrespective of material, late designs were stiff even when representative. "Arabesques" of more or less geometrically patterned adobes, or cut into sun-dried stucco, decorated the walls of public buildings. Textile decoration everywhere tended to geometric regularity, and especially to borders and corner fillings of small repetitive elements—geometric cats, birds, or fish. The over-all, large, human-figure or divine-feline designs of Tiahuanaco were on the way out, the over-all paneling of Cuzco not yet well developed. Wood carving was neat, angular, repetitive, and without much feeling for plane surfaces—certainly not for curved ones. Against the relative uniformity of this generalized Late Coast technology, several local variations in ceramic styles stand out: Chimú, Chancáy, Chincha-Ica.

Of these, Chimú pottery is a resurgence of Mochica, with many losses, with the addition of shapes and ornament derived through Coast Tiahuanacoid, and with prevalence of blackware imitative of metal. The portrait heads of Mochica are replaced by stiff, stereotyped faces and figures. The art has the facility of long repetition and some degree of conscious elegance. But it is eclectic, shallow, done without feeling, and superficial in taste. In the mud-brick architecture, geometric relief friezes replace the Mochica naturalistic frescoes.

Chancáy is a black-and-white ceramic, technically poor, hastily made, with embellishments either crude or florid, but showing an original feeling for design disposition in panels, including balanced asymmetry—unlike right and left halves.

Chincha-Ica ceramics have shapes partly influenced by metal vessels; the painting is obviously stimulated by textile patterns; technology and finish are competent.

These variants typify the condition of Peruvian art on the coast in the last pre-Conquest period. This Late art possessed diversity, facility, reasonable skill, occasional taste, but only mild interests and no feeling. In the highlands, Inca art retained a measure of severity, and therewith a certain self-respect; but it evinced little more emotion. The drives were gone which in earlier periods had led to the originality and creativeness of Chavín, Mochica, Nazca, Paracas, and Tiahuanaco.

12. In ancient Ecuador, which had little intimate connection with Peru, art was most developed in the north coast provinces of Manabí and Esmeraldas, with some overlap into adjacent Colombia. In stone, there were chairs and low-relief slabs. The chairs or thrones, without backs, are executed in a single graceful sweep of seat and arms, resting on an Atlantean pedestal of a crouching human figure. The reliefs are partly geometric; in part they represent stylized insects or lizards or human figures of about the naïveté of those in Peruvian sculpture from Pucara or the Callejón.

Most interesting is a secular, informal, lively art of modeling and molding small pottery heads and figurines, sometimes grotesque, more often naturalistic, varied in feature, posture, and expression. Technology and finish are only mediocre, execution is rather careless, but it is marked by verve, dash, and imaginative seizure of characteristic form and attitude. Compared with Mochica, this art is unchanneled, playful, unfinished. It is both more trivial and more humorous. But it is comparable in quality.

13. Colombian goldwork suffers aesthetically from an indecision between three- and two-dimensional treatment, due perhaps to a desire to spread the glitter, even though in flat form. Executed in a baser material, few would linger over this jewelry.

The famous San Agustín sculpture is limited to a small area of occurrence east of the Magdalena headwaters. Compared with Chavín and Tiahuanaco, San Agustín is crude in conception and execution. Everything wavers in this art. Eyes may be circles, semicircles, crescents, almonds, or commas. Mouths may have tusks or be miniature narrow slits. Noses vary from triangles to inverted T's. Proportion of width to height of the total statue ranges from three-tenths to three-fourths. The figures are, if anything, even less extricated from the block than in highland Peruvian sculpture. At any rate they seem less channeled into a coherent style. Each piece begins all over again to express its own idea in its own way. The size of the statues—up to several meters and some tons—results in an effect of monumentality, of stolid weight, of labored feeling, of barbaric strangeness verging on the monstrous, of minimal organization and almost no beauty of line or flow of surface; and yet, an effect of indubitable impressiveness.

14. A remarkable ceramic art once flourished on Marajó Island in the mouth of the Amazon. Decorative devices include modeling, cutting away, incising, painting, often several of these in combination. The art is weakest in figure modeling, strongest when it riots in rich decoration of surface, sometimes suggesting the effects of Shang bronzes. In this pattern ornament, representation is often no longer discerni-

ble: stylization has been carried far; it is intricate and continuous; blank spaces are rare. The fundamental motive varies from a fret or rectangular spiral at its fullest, to an E, L, or H figure at its simplest. Angles are skilfully staggered to oppose or interlock. Design lines are frequently double, or accompanied by shadow counterparts: a heavy line or stripe is paralleled by a fine line or one of lighter value or color. Thin lines may be used as a frame for repetitions of heavier motives and at the same time as a net to draw these heavier masses together. These many devices add up to a rich and imaginative decorative style, varied in its expressions and yet unified in feeling, successful in element detail as well as in over-all effect.

15. Marajó proves to be the local expression of a widespread style which at one time extended along the Atlantic Coast and especially up the Amazon drainage, and of which descendants have survived among backward tropical forest culture tribes at the eastern foot of the Andes. Upstream, ancient pottery from about the mouth of the Madeira, and again from the Napo in Ecuador, skilfully utilizes relief, incision, and polychrome painting with intricacy and control and in the generic manner of Marajó. Wares once made to the south of the Amazon mouth on the Gurupi River, and to the north at Cunany in Brazil and in Surinam, also seem stylistically related to Marajó.

In modern times, pottery painted in a manner allied to that of Marajó has been characteristic of the lower Ucayali and Huallaga affluents of the Amazon in the Peruvian montaña, especially among the Pano-speaking Conibo, Shipibo, and Panobo tribes, but also among the Arawak Piro and Tupian Cocama. In three-color ware, brightened by a resinous coating, a similar design scheme is here maintained, two thousand miles from Marajó and perhaps five hundred years later. There are complete and incomplete spirals; engagement or interlocking of the figures into an over-all pattern; and paralleling or shadowing of lines. At least among the Shipibo, patterns in this style are also painted on human faces and limbs, on the blades of paddles, and are woven into textiles. Inferior qualitatively, but perhaps also related historically, is the pottery painting of the Aguano, Chayamite, and neighboring tribes, who point the corners of their successions of zigzags or diamond figures with tiny black rhomboids. Farther north, the styles of pottery painting of the Baniva and of the Arawak-speaking tribes of the Isana River, and that of the Guianan Carib of Maroni River, show similarities which suggest that they too may be recent local variations of the wide-flung basic Marajó-related tradition.

16. On review of these major art styles of native South America, it is evident that successful naturalism was attained only twice: by the Mochica and in Manabí-Esmeraldas—both times primarily in clay. Far more often the South American Indians achieved aesthetic success by subordinating representation to decoration, to stylized expression of form as such. This holds true equally of their efforts in stone sculpture, in metal casting, in pottery modeling and painting, and in weaving. It holds true equally, also, whether interest was directed primarily to strength of line, to organization of elements, or to over-all continuity of pattern. And finally, wherever the record of sequence is complete enough to allow of judgment, there is evident a general sequential drift from strongly experienced styles of a certain grandeur to manners that are less imaginative and much flatter in meaning and feeling.

PART IV

PSYCHOLOGICALLY SLANTED

INTRODUCTION

A PRIMARY interest in the long-range and world-wide aspects of culture inevitably brings with it preoccupation with the forms which this panhuman phenomenon takes as such, and with the interrelations of these forms. The billions of men, through whom and in whom these same cultural manifestations appear, inevitably shrink and disappear as individuals as the view lengthens. They tend to become taken for granted. They are of course not denied; but they are held constant, abstracted from. The culture historian finds himself in the situation of the palaeontologist who, just because of his telescopic time distances, cannot possibly hope any longer to ascertain the specific causes, the individual mutations, that originated his multitudinous species. How genes work and change is something to be sought in the laboratory and by experiment, here and now; but it is only the palaeontologist who can trace the grand currents of the evolution of life ultimately resulting from what happens to trillions of particular genes, and who can elucidate the directions manifest in these currents. It is through the palaeontologist's and the geneticist's each pressing his particular method to its limit that they finally both advance far enough to effect a junction and establish a synthesis, in which one contributes what actually happened in evolution and the other the precise mechanism by which it is happening and must approximately have happened in the past.

The study of culture is newer and much less systematized than the study of organic life. We do recognize some patchy but exciting outlines of a "palaeontology of culture" through what history, prehistory, and culture comparison have contributed. We have beginnings of understanding of some of the gross mechanisms of culture—a counterpart, say, to a physiology not yet tied to chemistry; but we do not appear to have hold as yet of anything that would correspond to genetics, to knowledge of the ultimate factors that at once keep culture steady and continuous but also cause it to change. It is evident that the mechanisms and basic factors, including such elemental units as may correspond to cell or gene, must in the case of culture reside somewhere on the psychological level.

But psychology is apparently less developed than anthropology. At any rate, very few of its findings are of a nature that can be specifically tied to with profit by students of the emergent outlines and principles of the history of culture. The recent "culture-and-personality" movement represents an effort, or at least a hope, to supply just such a genetic or ultimate explanation of culture in psychic terms. The endeavor is surely warranted; but it has so far been marked by more enthusiasm than clarity, and it seems to have achieved little in the way of either specific method or definite results: psychology just has not yet got enough results to offer. The movement has also attracted some followers who, even if they know in a way what culture is, lack any real or varied acquaintance with its phenomena, which can be obtained only through broad historical knowledge. While hoping to explain culture through personality, they are sometimes really readier to explain it away by dissolving it outright into personality. For my part, while I am convinced that the ultimate "explanations" of cultural manifestations will be found mainly in individual psychic activities, I cannot see that we have as yet discovered anything systematic or coherent as to the psychological causality: such unsystematized understanding as we possess is essentially that of laymen's common sense and common knowledge. That is why the psychological part of this book is its briefest.

I may add that I studied psychology under Cattell before I studied anthropology under Boas. Psychology was my minor subject for an anthropological doctorate. I have undergone at least a brief control psychoanalysis; and from 1920 to 1923 I practiced psychoanalysis in San Francisco, part of the time under medical sponsorship in the neuropsychiatric clinic of a hospital, part of the time independently. At the end of the three years I felt I had acquired many new insights into the human mind, or as we have now renamed it, personality. I did not feel that these insights helped me appreciably to understand culture any better; which was one of the reasons I quit psychoanalysis—fearing the split of trying permanently to carry two professions that seemed irreconcilable. I mention these biographical details in order to substantiate that my negativism toward "culture-and-personality" is the result of disillusionment rather than of prejudgment.

Of the five papers in this Part IV, two (Nos. 37 and 38) are about Freud and his attempt to hew with one stroke of imagination through the Gordian knot of culture. Freud's creative insights make him the greatest single figure that has yet appeared in psychology; and many of the insights stand. But his speculative imagination was little bridled by criticism, and he was avowedly more interested in how far it might carry him than in whether it integrated

little or much with the body of total science. Culture is too tough and intricate a block of facts to be felled and carried off as a trophy by any one-blow claimant. Moreover, to believe in the historically oriented twentieth century in "the origin" of anything is a sort of infantilism [No. 1]. Freud preferred to forage in Frazer rather than to read the intellectually sophisticated works of his own age-mate Boas.

Selection No. 39 does attempt to tackle squarely one aspect of the relation of mind and culture by suggesting that the social rewarding of neurotic or psychotic manifestations might be construed as an index of cultural backwardness or lack of progress. The suggestion has not taken with my anthropological colleagues and students. Perhaps they dislike having the absolutism of their new-found cultural relativism tampered with. At any rate, I am not aware of any professional acquiescence and have met considerable dissent on the point in classes. In a 1951 postscript to the original article of 1940 I have added a modification of the basic proposition.

Nos. 40 and 41 are only mildly or indirectly psychological. The first, on autobiographies, really takes up a methodological question posthumously raised by Boas: Do they better serve psychological or anthropological purposes? The second suggests the existence of a personality type characterized by willing and satisfying adhesion to its stream of cultural tradition—a type perhaps by no means limited to tribal and peasant societies but tending to remain unrecognized while insecurity and frustration are fashionable topics among social and clinical psychologists.

37. TOTEM AND TABOO: AN ETHNOLOGIC PSYCHOANALYSIS

1920

THE recent translation into English of Freud's interpretation of a number of ethnologic phenomena in his *Totem and Taboo* offers an occasion to review the startling series of essays which first appeared in *Imago* a number of years ago. There is the more reason for this because, little as this particular work of Freud has as yet been noticed by anthropologists, the vogue of the psychoanalytic movement founded by him is now so strong that the book is certain to make an impression in many intelligent circles.

Freud's principal thesis emerges formally only toward the end of his book but has evidently controlled his reasoning from the beginning, although perhaps unconsciously. This thesis is (p. 258) "that the beginnings of religion, ethics, society, and art meet in the Oedipus complex." He commences with the inference of Darwin, developed further by Atkinson, that at a very early period man lived in small communities consisting of an adult male and a number of females and immature individuals, the males among the latter being driven off by the head of the group as they became old enough to evoke his jealousy. To this Freud adds the Robertson Smith theory that sacrifice at the altar is the essential element in every ancient cult, and that such sacrifice goes back to a killing and eating by the clan of its totem animal, which was regarded as of kin with the clan and its god, and whose killing at ordinary times was therefore strictly forbidden. The Oedipus complex directed upon these two hypotheses welds them into a mechanism with which it is possible to explain most of the essentials of human civilization, as follows. The expelled sons of the primal horde finally banded together and slew their father, ate him, and appropriated the females. In this they satisfied the same hate impulse that is a normal infantile trait and the basis of most neuroses, but which often leads to unconscious "displacement" of feelings, especially upon animals. At this point, however, the ambivalence of emotions proved decisive. The tender feelings which had always persisted by the side of the brothers' hate for their father, gained the upper hand as soon as this hate was satisfied, and took the form of remorse and sense of guilt. "What the father's presence had formerly prevented they themselves now prohibited in the psychic situation of 'subsequent obedience' which we know so well from psychoanalysis. They undid their deed by declaring that the killing of the father substitute, the totem, was not allowed, and renounced the fruits of their deed by denying themselves the liberated women. Thus they created the two fundamental taboos of totemism." These are "the oldest and most important taboos" of mankind: "namely not to kill the totem animal and to avoid sexual intercourse with totem companions of the other sex," alongside which many if not all other taboos are "secondary, displaced and distorted." The renunciation of the women, or incest prohibition, had also this practical foundation: that any attempt to divide the spoils, when each member of the band really wished to emulate the father and possess all the women, would have disrupted the organization which had made the brothers strong. The totem sacrifice and feast reflected the killing and eating of the father, assuaged "the burning sense of guilt," and brought about "a kind of reconciliation" or agreement by which the father-totem granted all wishes of his sons in return for their pledge to honor his life. "All later religions prove to be . . . reactions aiming at the same great event with which culture began and which ever since has not let mankind come to rest."

This mere extrication and presentation of the framework of the Freudian hypothesis on the origin of socioreligious civilization is probably sufficient to prevent its acceptance; but a formal examination is only just.

First, the Darwin-Atkinson supposition is of course only hypothetical. It is a mere guess that the earliest organization of man resembled that of the gorilla rather than that of trooping monkeys.

Second, Robertson Smith's allegation that blood sacrifice is central in ancient cult holds chiefly or only for the Mediterranoid cultures of a certain period— say the last two thousand years B.C.—and cultures then or subsequently influenced by them. It does not apply to regions outside the sphere of affection by these cultures.

Third, it is at best problematical whether blood sacrifice goes back to a totemic observance. It is not established that totemism is an original possession of Semitic culture.

Fourth, coming to the Freudian theory proper, it is only conjecture that the sons would kill, let alone devour, the father.

Fifth, the fact that a child sometimes displaces its father-hatred upon an animal—we are not told in what percentage of cases—is no proof that the sons did so.

Sixth, if they "displaced," would they retain enough of the original hate impulse to slay the father; and if so, would the slaying not resolve and evaporate the displacements? Psychoanalysts may affirm both questions; others will require more examination before they accept the affirmation.

Seventh, granting the sons' remorse and resolve no longer to kill the father-displacement-totem, it seems exceedingly dubious whether this resolve could be powerful and enduring enough to suppress permanently the gratification of the sexual impulses which was now possible. Again there may be psychoanalytic evidence sufficient to allay the doubt; but it will take a deal of evidence to convince "unanalytic" psychologists, ethnologists, and laymen.

Eighth, if the band of brothers allowed strangers—perhaps expelled by their jealous fathers—to have access to the women whom they had renounced, and matrilinear or matriarchal institutions thus came into existence, what would be left for the brothers (unless they were able to be content with lifelong celibacy or homosexuality), other than individual attachments to other clans; which would mean the disintegration of the very solidarity that they are pictured as so anxious to preserve, even by denying their physiological instincts?

Ninth, it is far from established that exogamy and totem abstinence are the two fundamental prohibitions of totemism. Freud refers to Goldenweiser's study of the subject, which is certainly both analytical and conducted from a psychological point of view, even though not psychoanalytical; but he fails either to accept or to refute this author's carefully substantiated finding that these two features cannot be designated as primary in the totemic complex.

Tenth, that these two totemic taboos are the oldest of all taboos is pure assertion. If all other taboos are derived from them by displacement or distortion, some presentation of the nature and operation and sequence of these displacements is in order. An astronomer who casually said that he believed Sirius to be the center of the stellar universe and then proceeded to weave this opinion into the fabric of a still broader hypothesis would get little hearing from other astronomers.

A final criticism—that the persistence into modern society and religion of this first "great event with which culture began" is an unexplained process—will not be pressed here, because Freud has anticipated it with a *tu quoque:* social psychologists assume a "continuity in the psychic life of succeeding generations" without in general concerning themselves much with the manner in which this continuity is established.[1]

No doubt still other challenges of fact or interpretation will occur to every careful reader of the book. The above enumeration has been compiled only far enough to prove the essential method of the work, which is to evade the painful process of arriving at a large certainty by the positive determination of smaller certainties and their unwavering addition, irrespective of whether each augments or diminishes the sum total of conclusion arrived at. For this method the author substitutes a plan of multiplying into one another, as it were, fractional certainties—that is, more or less remote possibilities—without recognition that the multiplicity of factors must successively decrease the probability of their product. It is the old expedient of pyramiding hypotheses, which, if theories had to be paid for like stocks or gaming cards, would be less frequently indulged in. Lest this criticism be construed as unnecessarily harsh upon a gallant and stimulating adventurer into ethnology, let it be added that it applies with equal stricture upon the majority of ethnologists from whom Freud has drawn on account of the renown or interest of their books: Reinach, Wundt, Spencer and Gillen,

Lang, Robertson Smith, Durkheim and his school, Keane, Spencer, Avebury; and his special vade mecum Frazer.[2]

There is another criticism that can be leveled against the plan of Freud's book: that of insidiousness, though evidently only as the result of the gradual growth of his thesis during its writing. The first chapter or essay, on the "Savage's Dread of Incest," merely makes a case for the applicability of psychoanalysis to certain special social phenomena, such as the mother-in-law taboo. In the second, the psychoanalytic doctrine of the ambivalence of emotions is very neatly—and it seems justly—brought to bear on the dual nature of taboo as at once holy and defiling. Concurrently a foundation is laid, though not revealed, for the push to the ultimate thesis. The third chapter on "Animism, Magic, and the Omnipotence of Thought" refrains from directly advancing the argument, but strengthens its future hold on the reader by emphasizing the parallelism between the thought systems of savages and neurotics. The last chapter is not, in the main, a discussion of the "Infantile Recurrence of Totemism," as it is designated, but an analysis of current ethnological theories as to the origin of totemism in society and the presentation of the theory of the author. This hypothesis, toward which everything has been tending, does not however begin to be divulged until page 233; after which, except for tentative claims to a wide extensibility of the principle arrived at and some distinctly fair admissions of weakness, the book promptly closes without any re-examination or testing of its proposition. The explanation of taboo on pages 52–58 is an essential part of the theory developed on pages 233 ff., without any indication being given that it is so. Then, when the parallelism of savage and neurotic thought has been driven home by material largely irrelevant to the final and quite specific thesis, this is suddenly sprung. Freud cannot be charged with more than a propagandist's zeal and perhaps haste of composition; but the consequence is that this book is keen without orderliness, intricately rather than closely reasoned, and endowed with an unsubstantiated convincingness. The critical reader will ascertain these qualities; but the book will fall into the hands of many who are lacking either in care or in independence of judgment and who, under the influence of a great name and in the presence of a bewilderingly fertile imagination, will be carried into an illusory belief. Again there is palliation—but nothing more—in the fact that the literature of speculative anthropology consists largely of bad precedent.

But, with all the essential failure of its finally avowed purpose, the book is an important and valuable contribution. However much cultural anthropology may come to lean more on the historical than on the psychological method, it can never ultimately free itself, nor should it wish to, from the psychology that underlies it. To this psychology the psychoanalytic movement initiated by Freud has made an indubitably significant contribution, which every ethnologist must sooner or later take into consideration. For instance, the correspondences between taboo customs and compulsion neuroses are unquestionable, as also the parallelism between the two aspects of taboo and the ambivalence of emotions under an accepted prohibition. Again the strange combination of mourning for the dead with the fear of them and taboos against them is certainly illumined if not explained by this theory of ambivalence.

It is even possible to extend Freud's point of view. Where the taboo on the name of the dead is in force, we find not only the fear that utterance will recall the soul to the hurt of the living, but also actual shock at the utterance as constituting a slight or manifestation of hostility to the dead. It is a fair question whether this shock may not be construed as a reaction from the unconscious hate carried toward the dead during their life, as if speaking of them were an admission of satisfaction at their going. The shock is certainly greatest where affection was deepest; persons who were indifferent are mentioned without emotional reluctance if circumstances permit, whereas enemies, that is individuals toward whom hate was avowed instead of repressed, may have the utterance of their names gloated over.

Of very broad interest is the problem raised by Freud's conjecture that the psychic impulses of primitive people possessed more ambivalence than our own, except in the case of neurotics; that their mental life, like that of neurotics, is more sexualized and contains fewer social components than ours.[3] Neurosis would therefore usually represent an atavistic constitution. Whatever its complete significance, there exists no doubt a remarkable similarity between the phenomena of magic, taboo, animism and primitive religion in general, and neurotic manifestations. In both, a creation that has only psychic validity is given greater or less preference over reality. As Freud says, the two are of course not the same, and the ultimate difference lies in the fact that neuroses are asocial creations due to a flight from dissatisfying reality. This is certainly not to be denied on any ethnological grounds; yet the implication that savages are essentially more neurotic than civilized men may well be challenged, although it cannot be dismissed offhand.

The experience of firsthand observers will probably be unanimous that primitive communities, like peasant populations, contain rather few individuals that can be put into a class with the numerous neurotics of our civilization. The reason seems to be that primitive societies have institutionalized such impulses as with us lead to neuroses. The individual of neurotic tendency finds an approved and therefore harmless outlet in taboo, magic, myth, and the like, whereas the nonneurotic, who at heart remains attached to reality, accepts these activities as forms which do not seriously disturb him. In accord with this interpretation is the fact that neurotics appear to become numerous and characteristic in populations among whom religion has become decadent and "enlightenment" active, as in the Hellenistic, Roman Imperial, and recent eras, whereas in the Middle Ages, when "superstition" and taboo were firmly established, there were social aberrations indeed, like the flagellants and children's crusade, but seemingly few individual neurotics. Much the same with homosexuality, which the North American and Siberian natives have often socialized. Its acceptance as an institution may be a departure from pan-human normality, but has certainly saved countless individuals from the heavy strain which definite homosexualists undergo in our civilization. It would be unfitting to go into these matters further here; they are mentioned as an illustration of the importance of the problems which Freud raises. However precipitate his entry into anthropology and however flimsy some of his syntheses, he brings to bear keen insight, a fecund imagination, and above all a point of view which henceforth can never be ignored without stultification.

While the book thus is one that no ethnologist can afford to neglect, one remark may be extended to psychologists of the unconscious who propose to follow in Freud's footsteps: there really is a great deal of ethnology not at all represented by the authors whom Freud discusses. To students of this side of the science the line of work partly initiated by Tylor and carried farthest and most notably represented among the living by Frazer, is not so much ethnology as an attempt to psychologize with ethnological data. The cause of Freud's leaning so heavily on Frazer is clear. The latter knows nothing of psychoanalysis, and with all acumen his efforts are prevailingly a dilettantish playing; but in the last analysis they are psychology, and as history only a pleasing fabrication. If psychoanalysts wish to establish serious contacts with historical ethnology, they must first learn to know that such an ethnology exists. It is easy enough to say, as Freud does, that the nature of totemism and exogamy could be most readily grasped if we could get into closer touch with their origins, but that as we cannot we must depend on hypotheses.[4] Such a remark rings a bit naïve to students who have long since made up their minds that ethnology, like every other branch of science, is work and not a game in which lucky guesses score; and who therefore hold that since we know nothing directly about the origin of totemism or other social phenomena but have information on these phenomena as they exist at present, our business is first to understand as thoroughly as possible the nature of these existing phenomena; in the hope that such understanding may gradually lead to a partial reconstruction of origins—without undue guessing.

38. TOTEM AND TABOO IN RETROSPECT
1939

NEARLY twenty years ago I wrote an analysis of *Totem and Taboo*— that brain child of Freud which was to be the precursor of a long series of psychoanalytic books and articles explaining this or that aspect of culture, or the whole of it. It seems an appropriate time to return to the subject.

I see no reason to waver over my critical analysis of Freud's book. There is no indication that the consensus of anthropologists during these twenty years has moved even an inch nearer acceptance of Freud's central thesis. But I found myself somewhat conscience-stricken when, perhaps a decade later, I listened to a student in Sapir's seminar in Chicago making his report on *Totem and Taboo*, who, like myself, first spread out its gossamer texture and then laboriously tore it to shreds. It is a procedure too suggestive of breaking a butterfly on the wheel. An iridescent fantasy deserves a more delicate touch even in the act of demonstration of its unreality.

Freud himself has said of my review that it characterized his book as a *Just So* story. It is a felicitous phrase, coming from himself. Many a tale by Kipling or Andersen contains a profound psychological truth. One does not need therefore to cite and try it in the stern court of evidential confrontation.

However, the fault is not wholly mine. Freud does speak of the "great event with which culture began." And therewith he enters history. Events are historical, and beginnings are historical, and human culture is appreciable historically. It is difficult to say how far he realized his vacillation between historic truth and abstract truth expressed through intuitive imagination. A historic finding calls for some specification of place and time and order; instead of which, he offers a finding of unique cardinality, such as history feels it cannot deal with.

Freud is reported subsequently to have said that his "event" is to be construed as "typical." Herewith we begin to approach a basis of possible agreement. A typical event, historically speaking, is a recurrent one. This can hardly be admitted for the father-slaying, eating, and guilt sense. At any rate, there is no profit in discussing the recurrence of an event which we do not even know to have occurred once. But there is no need sticking fast on the word "event" because Freud used it. His argument is evidently ambiguous as between historical thinking and psychological thinking. If we omit the fatal concept of event, of an act as it happens in history, we have left over the concept of the psychologically potential. Psychological insight may legitimately hope to attain to the realization and definition of such a potentiality; and to this, Freud should have confined himself. We may accordingly properly disregard any seeming claim, or half-claim, to historic authenticity of the suggested actual happening, as being beside the real point, and consider whether Freud's theory contains any possibility of being a generic, timeless explanation of the psychology that underlies certain recurrent historic phenomena or institutions like totemism and taboo.

Here we obviously are on better ground. It becomes better yet if we discard certain gratuitous and really irrelevant assumptions, such as that the self-imposed taboo following the father-slaying is the original of all taboos, these deriving from it as secondary displacements or distortions. Stripped down in this way, Freud's thesis would reduce to the proposition that certain psychic processes tend always to be operative and to find expression in widespread human institutions. Among these processes would be the incest drive and incest repression, filial ambivalence, and the like; in short, if one like, the kernel of the Oedipus situation. After all, if ten modern anthropologists were asked to designate one universal human institution, nine would be likely to name the incest prohibition; some have expressly named it as the only universal one. Anything so constant as this, at least as regards its nucleus, in the notoriously fluctuating universe of culture, can hardly be the result of a "mere" historical accident devoid of psychological significance. If there is accordingly an underlying factor which keeps reproducing the phenomenon in an unstable world, this factor must be something in the human constitution—in other words, a psychic factor. Therewith the door is open not for an acceptance *in toto* of Freud's explanation but at any rate for its serious consideration as a scientific hypothesis. Moreover, it is an explanation certainly marked by deeper insight and supportable by more parallel evidence from personal psychology than the older views, such as that familiarity breeds sexual indifference, or recourse to a supposed "instinct" which is merely a verbal restatement of the observed behavior.

Totemism, which is a much rarer phenomenon than incest taboo, might then well be the joint product of the incest-drive-and-repression process and of some other less compelling factor. Nonsexual taboo, on the other hand, which rears itself in so many protean forms over the whole field of culture, might be due to a set of still different but analogous psychic factors. Anthropologists and sociologists have certainly long been groping for an underlying something which would help them explain both the repetitions and the variations in culture, provided that the explanation were evidential, extensible by further analysis, and neither too simplistic nor too one-sided. Put in some such form as this, Freud's hypothesis might long before this have proved fertile in the realm of cultural understanding instead of being mainly rejected or ignored as a brilliant fantasy.

What has stood in the way of such a fruitful restatement or transposition? There seem to be at least three factors: one due to Freud himself, another jointly to himself and his followers, the third mainly to the Freudians.

The first of these is Freud's already mentioned ambiguity which leads him to state a timeless psychological explanation as if it were also a historical one. This tendency is evident elsewhere in his thinking. It appears to be the counterpart of an extraordinarily explorative imagination, constantly impelled to penetrate into new intellectual terrain. One consequence is a curious analogy to what he himself has discovered in regard to the manifest and the latent in dreams. The manifest is there, but it is ambiguous; a deeper meaning lies below; from the point of view of this latent lower content, the manifest is accidental and inconsequential. Much like this, it seems to me, is the historical dress which Freud gives his psychological insight. He does not repudiate it; he does not stand by it as integral. It is really irrelevant; but, his insight having manifested itself in the dress, he cannot divest himself of this "manifest" form. His view is overdetermined like a dream.

A second factor is the curious indifference which Freud has always shown as to whether his conclusions do or do not integrate with the totality of science. This led him at one time to accept the inheritance of acquired traits as if it did not clash with standard scientific attitude. Here again we have the complete explorer who forgets in his quest, or represses, knowledge of what he started from or left behind. In Freud himself one is inclined not to quarrel too hard with this tendency; without it, he might have opened fewer and shorter vistas. Of his disciples, however, who have so largely merely followed, more liaison might be expected. I recall Rank, while still a Freudian, after expounding his views to a critically sympathetic audience, being pressed to reconcile certain of them to the findings of science at large and, after an hour, conceding that psychoanalysts held that there might be more than one truth, each on its own level and independent of the other. And he made the admission without appearing to realize its import.

A third element in the situation is the all-or-none attitude of most avowed psychoanalysts. They insist on operating within a closed system. At any rate, if not wholly closed, it grows only from within; it is not open to influence from without. A classical example is Ernest Jones's resistance to Malinowski's finding that among the matrilineal Melanesians the effects directed toward the father in our civilization are largely displaced upon the mother's brother, the relation of father and children being rather one of simple and relatively univalent affection. Therewith Malinowski had really vindicated the mechanism of the Oedipus relation. He showed that the mechanism remained operative even in a changed family situation; a minor modification of it, in its direction, conforming to the change in given condition. Jones, however, could not see this, and resisted tooth and nail. Because Freud in the culture of Vienna had determined that ambivalence was directed toward the father, ambivalence had to remain directed to him universally, even

where primary authority resided in an uncle.

The same tendency appears in Roheim, whose *Psycho-analysis of Primitive Culture Types* of 1932 contains a mass of psychological observations most valuable to cultural anthropologists, but so organized as to unusable by them. None have used it, so far as I know. This is not due to lack of interest on the part of anthropologists in psychological behavior within cultures, for in recent years a whole series of them have begun avowedly to deal with such behavior. Nor is it due to any deficiency of quality in Roheim's data: these are rich, vivid, novel, and valuable. But the data are so presented as to possess organization only from the point of view of orthodox psychoanalytic theory. With reference to the culture in which they occur or to the consecutive life-histories of personalities, they are inchoate. The closing sentence of the memoir—following immediately on some illuminative material—is typical: "We see then, that the sexual practices of a people are indeed prototypical and that from their posture in coitus their whole psychic attitude may be inferred." Can a conclusion be imagined which would appear more arbitrarily dogmatic than this to any psychologist, psychiatrist, anthropologist, or sociologist?

The fundamental concepts which Freud formulated—repression, regression and infantile persistences, dream symbolism and overdetermination, guilt sense, the affects toward members of the family—have gradually seeped into general science and become an integral and important part of it. If one assumes that our science forms some kind of larger unit because its basic orientation and method are uniform, these concepts constitute the permanent contribution of Freud and psychoanalysis to general science; and the contribution is large. Beyond, there is a further set of concepts which in the main have not found their way into science: the censor, the superego, the castration complex, the explanation of specific cultural phenomena. To these concepts the several relevant branches of science—sociology, anthropology, psychology, and medicine alike—remain impervious about as consistently as when the concepts were first developed. It may therefore be inferred that science is likely to remain negative to them. To the psychoanalysts, on the contrary, the two classes of concepts remain on the same level, of much the same value, and inseparably interwoven into one system. In this quality of nondifferentiation between what the scientific world accepts as reality and rejects as fantasy, between what is essential and what is incidental, the orthodox psychoanalytic movement reveals itself as partaking of the nature of a religion—a system of mysticism; even, it might be said, it shows certain of the qualities of a delusional system. It has appropriated to itself such of the data of science—which is the cumulative representative of reality—as were digestible to it but has ignored the larger remainder. It has sought little integration with the totality of science, and only on its own terms. By contrast, science, while also of course a system, has shown itself a relatively open one: it has accepted and already largely absorbed a considerable part of the concepts of psychoanalysis. It is indicative of the largeness of Freud's mind that, although the sole founder of the movement and the originator of most of its ideas, his very ambiguities in the more doubtful areas carry a stamp of tolerance. He may persist in certain interpretations; he does not insist on them; they remain more or less fruitful suggestions. Of this class is his theory of the primary determination of culture. As a construct, neither science nor history can use it; but it would seem that they can both accept and utilize some of the process concepts that are involved in the construct.

I trust that this reformulation may be construed not only as an *amende honorable* but as a tribute to one of the great minds of our day.

NOTE. *Postscript, 1939*—Since the above was written and submitted, Freud has published *Der Mann Moses und die monotheistische Religion*. The thesis of *Totem and Taboo* is reaffirmed: "Ich halte an diesen Aufbau noch heute fest." One concession in the direction of my argument is made: the father-killing was not a unique event but "hat sich in Wirklichkeit über Jahrtausende erstreckt." Of his stimulator, Robertson Smith, Freud says superbly: "Mit seinen Gegnern traf ich nie zusammen." We, on our part, if I may speak for ethnologists, though remaining unconverted, have met Freud, recognize the encounter as memorable, and herewith resalute him.

39. PSYCHOSIS OR SOCIAL SANCTION
1940

PSYCHOTIC FACTORS IN SHAMANISM

ON A chance, I said to an old Lassik Indian woman: "I bet you are a doctor." "Well, I nearly was," she answered. "My baby died. I was sitting around the next afternoon. All at once I heard a baby cry overhead, and fell over unconscious. My sister brought me back; but from time to time I heard the crying again, and became more and more sick. I gave an old doctor twenty dollars to cure me, and he said it was my baby's shadow coming to tell me to become a doctor. But I did not want to; and when the shadow began to talk, urging me, I told him, 'No, I won't,' and urged him to go away. So at last he left off, and I got well, and did not become a doctor."

In our civilization this happening would be diagnosed as a psychosis. It manifests recurrent hallucinations, fits of loss of contact with the sensory world, distress and worry, and a sense of illness. Twenty dollars was a considerable amount for a backwoods Indian woman to pay in a lump sixty years ago.

From the native point of view, one may at once suspect the functioning of a cultural pattern, because all through native northern California the onset of shamanistic power is marked by a seizure in which the candidate experiences a hallucination—always auditory and sometimes visual also—in which objectively he is unconscious, or unaware of his surroundings, and acutely ill. To his family and village mates he seems actually stricken with disease. But the older shaman who is consulted promptly diagnoses the disease as the onset of shamanistic power, predicts cure as soon as the patient adjusts himself to his new

power, and, with other shamans, helps to "train" the novice, that is, to find the adjustment. In most cases, apparently, the novice accepts the power which has come upon him: considerable prestige attaches, in a simple society, to one who can cure or exercise other special faculties.

Usually the spirit in the hallucination appears from nature: he is a spirit of the woods or mountains, of the sky, of a pool, of an animal or monster. In the present instance the spirit was the patient's own child. Here is a superadded pattern: the appearance is that of a dead relative. That this is a genuinely social pattern in the region is shown by a Wailaki episode recorded by Loeb. A dead woman came back one night, grunted outdoors, slid into the house, put her hand on her sister's head, and said: "I love you, I have come back." In the morning the living woman was found lying covered with blood from her mouth and singing. She announced: "My sister came, but I shall not die. I shall be a doctor, I think." She did become one, with her sister as her helping spirit, who talked to her and aided her in curing.

These cases raise several theoretical points. First, in some cultures one of the most respected and rewarded statuses known to the society is acquired only by experience of a condition which in our culture we could not label anything else than psychotic. This is part of a wider situation which I have treated elsewhere, namely: that one consistent criterion of distinction between primitive or folk cultures and advanced or high ones, other than quantity of cultural content, is the fact that the folk cultures in their magic, shamanism, animistic ritual, and the like, recognize as objectively effective certain phenomena which the more sophisticated ones regard as not only subjective but as objectively unreal and therefore as more or less psychotic or deranged. In short, the limits of relation of personality and world are differently drawn. What high cultures stigmatize as purely personal, nonreal and nonsocial, abnormal and pathological, lower cultures treat as objective, socially useful, and conducive to special ability—or at least relatively so. The primary importance of this difference is perhaps for the student of culture, whom it may help to understand somewhat more clearly the "high and low" ratings which he tries to avoid, but never wholly succeeds in avoiding, when he compares cultures.

A side problem is this: If the native recognizes certain psychotic or pathological experiences as partaking of objective reality, the question arises whether we in our civilization do not do the same in certain other areas, being however as blind to the fact as the primitive is. (Logically of course the question could be turned around into an inquiry as to the nature of the limits of objectivity, the individual psychic experience being regarded as primary in reality; but this would of course be scientifically profitless because science assumes that it deals with the objective.) What, in other words, may there be in our own lives that does not participate in reality but which we accept as so participating? Reference is not to group attitudes characteristic of the uneducated or socially disadvantaged, which the sophisticated and detached members of the same population can discern as affectively warped away from reality; but to other attitudes on the part of the sophisticates themselves, of whose nonparticipation in reality they are equally unaware. Obviously, it would be very

hard to give even a tentative answer to this question. But the problem is certainly worth being kept in mind.

Next, there is the old question of deception. Probably most shamans or medicine men, the world over, help along with sleight-of-hand in curing and especially in exhibitions of power. This sleight-of-hand is sometimes deliberate; in many cases awareness is perhaps not deeper than the foreconscious. The attitude, whether there has been repression or not, seems to be as toward a pious fraud. Field ethnographers seem quite generally convinced that even shamans who know that they add fraud nevertheless also believe in their powers, and especially in those of other shamans: they consult them when they themselves or their children are ill. When it comes to the cardinal experience with spirits, on which power is based, this almost always occurs in solitude, or inwardly as in dreams, so that objective demonstration is precluded. While consciously false claims would therefore be easier, there would also be less immediate pressure to make them. The Lassik old woman, at any rate, was genuine: she did not want to be a shaman, and she resisted the urgings of the spirit. There can be no doubt that she really heard her dead child's crying and talking and was troubled by it.

In fact, she felt herself ill in the same sense as among us a psychotic patient generally feels ill. This is the normal description by most Californian tribes of the onset of shamanistic power: The prospective shaman is not only out of his mind and behaving strangely, but also actually sick: he lies down; his relatives are afraid he will die, and call a shaman for treatment; the patient will not eat, wastes away, and remains for weeks or months in this condition. This point seems of some importance: the experience is not a merely subjective one of a moment or a day, but a profound organic disturbance. In this sense it is the more genuinely psychotic.

Two other features are typical. The first is the repetition of the experience. The hallucination, or among other tribes the dream, comes again and again. (Many tribes say definitely that their shamans "dream" their power; but their word for "dream" may include or connote much more than a normal sleep-dream.)

Second, this individual's hallucination was primarily, or perhaps wholly, auditory. Here tribal custom varies somewhat, and no doubt personal experience also; but it is clear from a mass of data gradually accumulated that among all the Indians of California and Nevada the crucial shamanistic experience is normally auditory, whether or not it is also visual or tactile. Almost always there is a song learned, or several. A shaman who did not have an individual spirit-given song would not be a shaman, in prevailing native opinion in this part of the world. Differences exist between tribes who say little about seeing while hearing, and those who give a clear account of seeing, or seeing and feeling, in addition. The Mohave of southern California are in this latter category. But their standard way is to "dream" parts of myths which are already known.[1] And they do this dreaming mostly without seizure or illness. In fact, they profess to begin their dreaming in their mother's womb and to recall these dreams and to continue them later in life. Incidentally, it is also standard with the Mohave to assert that these dreams, or many of them, relate to the creation of the world. They project themselves backward into the beginning of time, where they insist they were really present to hear, see, and feel what was happening. This is a Mohave specialty—a somewhat unusual addition to the usual beliefs entertained. I do not know how often such an affirmed projection into the past is characteristic of our psychotics.

The difference between these primitives and ourselves may be expressed in two different ways. The first is formulated in terms of *reality*. The primitive assumes as actual and real certain phenomena which we hold to have only a mental or subjective existence, and in that sense to be unreal in the sense in which stones and houses and birds are real. Or perhaps it would be more accurate to say that the primitive is also aware of a distinction, but inverts his emphasis. To him a stone or a bird seen or heard in a certain kind of dream is far more important than a physical stone or bird which one can pick up or eat, because it is the potential source of infinitely more power and control. Certain things which we classify as unreal are to him super-real—"surrealistic."

The second difference is formulated in terms of *socialization* or social acceptability. To us a person that hears the dead speak, or proclaims that he sometimes turns into a bear, is socially abnormal, at best useless, and likely to be a burden or menace. To the Indians he is potentially a personality of enhanced powers, which he may indeed abuse malevolently in witchcraft but which primarily result in benefits to the community: enhanced health, food supply, triumph over enemies.

This difference of social attitude or pattern of culture is as important as the difference in attitude toward reality. It is perhaps, in fact, a cause of the latter. At first thought, indeed, one might be inclined to assume the contrary: as enlightenment increases, dreams, visions, and the voices of the dead are more and more recognized as being internal to individuals and unrelated to objective reality as defined by the everyday experience of the mass of mankind. Thereupon society withdraws recognition and prestige value from the visions; they become dubious assets, and finally stigmata and disabilities. This is how we ordinarily assume the change from primitive attitudes to our own to have come about: there is a progressive increase in our understanding of reality. However, it may be doubted whether anything so rational is the efficient cause of the change. Abstractly, it seems at least equally probable that the greater rationality or enlightenment is a by-product of the change in attitudes, and that these attitudes in turn are nonrationally social or cultural.

On this view, certain societies gradually attach fewer approval or premium values to dreams and voices, until they may come, like ourselves, to look upon them as socially useless, if not harmful—abnormal, unfortunate, and to be dreaded. The influences bringing about such a shift of values might be various: increases of the size of the social group, technological or economic factors, the growth of science, a greater sense of security. Enlightenment as such, in the sense of a better discrimination of objective reality, need not be among them. It may be, for all one knows, an effect rather than a cause—a flattering name bestowed on the change after it has occurred.

Obviously, this theoretical interpretation may not be pressed too dogmatically. But it may serve as a counterbalance to the current assumption, which is certainly also dogmatic. And there is one specific point in its favor. The primitive, as has just been pointed out, does not really fail to discriminate the objective from the subjective, the normally natural from the supernatural. He distinguishes them much as we do. He merely weights or favors the supernatural, as we disfavor and try to exclude it. The voice of the dead, the dream, and the magic act stand out for him from the run of commonplace experience of reality much as they do for us; but he endows them with a quality of special super-reality and desirability, we of unreality and undesirability. The values have changed rather than the perception. And values are cultural facts.

To put it in another form, certain of what one calls "psychotic" phenomena are socially channeled by primitives—standardized, recognized, approved, rewarded—but are regarded as wholly outside the approved sociocultural channel by ourselves.

HOMOSEXUALITY

To this there is at least one parallel in the institutional field: the transvestite, in American ethnology often called the *berdache* (French from Arabic *bardaj*, "slave"). In most of primitive northern Asia and North America, men of homosexual trends adopted women's dress, work, and status, and were accepted as nonphysiological but institutionalized women. In Siberia the transformation was generally associated with shamanistic power, control of spirits or possession by them; in America, often not. In both areas, choice of status was left to the individual; if he decided to transform his sex, he was socially accepted as a woman. How far invert erotic practice accompanied the status is not always clear from the data, and it probably varied. It is conceivable that in some cases there occurred a partial sublimation of specific erotic urges into feminine occupation, dress, and association. The berdaches are usually spoken of as willing as well as skilful and strong workers at female tasks. At any rate, the North American Indian attitude toward the berdache stresses not his erotic life but his social status; born a male, he became accepted as a woman socially.

The time is ready for a synthetic work on this subject. The cultural data are numerous. On the involved psychology the information is less satisfactory. While the institution was in full bloom, the Caucasian attitude was one of repugnance and condemnation. This attitude quickly became communicated to the Indians and made subsequent personality inquiry difficult, the later berdaches leading repressed or disguised lives. The fullest account is by Devereux, "Institutionalized Homosexuality of the Mohave," in *Human Biology* (1937). The Mohave are unusually un-inhibited both in sex activity and in speech about it. They even recognized women inverts, active female homosex-uals, who are rare elsewhere. I suspect that many Indian men understood the phenomenon imperfectly, or misunder-stood it. An old Yokuts, born about 1840, who knew the social functions of the transvestites quite well—they were corpse-handlers or "undertakers" among his people—told me that in his opinion they were men who took on female dress and occupation in order to have free association with women and special opportunities for secret heterosexual ac-tivity with them. While this may have occurred now and then, it is obviously in the main a rationalized misconstruc-tion by an unimaginatively normal heterosexual.

That the peoples who accept trans-vestitism are essentially those of north-ern Asia and America, a continuous area, suggests that the institution is a single historic growth. If it were something characteristic of a certain "stage of ad-vancement," it ought to occur much more scatteringly over the world. The ancient Near Eastern development was different: it was associated with specific cults and with mutilation. The pederas-ty which was more or less openly tol-erated in certain advanced civilizations—Greece, later Islam, China in connection with the theater—is also not the same, the emphasis being on sexual practice rather than on transvestite "sublima-tion," and scarcely leading to a lifelong status for many of those involved.

In berdachism accordingly we have another set of psychiatric phenomena, those of sexual inversion, which our cul-ture still regards as abnormal, asocial if not antisocial, and in general views with considerable affect of repugnance, but which certain primitives accept with equanimity and provide a definite social channel for. The case is not wholly par-allel to shamanism but is definitely like it in the point of sociocultural accept-ance instead of rejection. Furthermore, in this matter of transvestitism it cannot be said that the difference between the Indian and ourselves is one of greater enlightenment on our part. It is only since eighteenth-century enlightenment that homosexuality has begun to be re-garded in Occidental civilization as somewhat less than the ultimate abomi-nation and offense. Our tolerance to-ward it has increased in proportion with what we call our enlightenment. And certainly the American Indian system seems to work well from the angle of human happiness: the invert is free to work out his inner satisfactions as he can, without persecution from without; and society does not feel itself injured or endangered. A status of adjustment is achieved instead of one of conflict and tension.

At any rate, we have here a second case in which primitives meet a condi-tion, stigmatized by us as psychologica-ly pathological, with social tolerance and acceptance, if not rewards. Like ourselves, they regard both conditions as not normal, in the sense of not being common, everyday in character, or in line with the majority of experienced events. But their social affects toward these conditions are positive or neutral; ours are negative. This appears to be a better description of the facts than to say that we have come to exceed them in intelligent enlightenment. Undoubt-edly we possess on the whole a far greater body of knowledge, criticism, and understanding than the primitives.[2] But it is doubtful how far this increase is responsible for similarly constituted individuals being accorded respect and influence among many primitives and being classed as dements or social liabili-ties by ourselves. Fundamentally the difference seems rather to lie in institu-tions, which in turn express the emo-tional attitudes of society toward its parts and itself.

ANIMAL IDENTIFICATIONS

An old Kato woman narrated the following as having happened before her birth: A young woman, pregnant, went with her husband and a group of fellow-initiates for a stay in the woods, presumably to cook for the party. There she saw them perform their "tricks" and performances and was made to jump a trench and was pelted with pine cones. All this apparently had some reference to bears. When her child was born, he had a tuft of hair on each shoulder. He grew up apparently stupid and sluggish, not participating much in ordinary activities. Once, when he was being teased, he grew angry, growled, turned into a bear, scattered the coals of the fire, and began to cuff people around. After this incident he was carefully let alone, except when his anger could be directed against the enemy Yuki. He continued generally peaceable but solitary, or at least aloof. He was nearly useless for hunting or ordinary work, but, if a trail was to be broken through the snow, he was sent ahead, and with his bearlike strength performed this task easily and cheerfully.

This tale, which the informant evidently believed to be true as implicitly as her parents had believed it, possesses some of the qualities of a dream among ourselves. However, it is recounted here primarily to introduce the matter of what may be called bear men—a concept similar to the European one of werewolves.

In this case we have a human being with bear nature and shape potential in him, showing only partially most of the time, but under special stimulus temporarily supplanting his human form and character. The stimulus however was everyday and realistic, even though the cause of his latent nature was evidently considered to be something magico-religious or supernatural.

An allied but distinct concept in the area is what the Yuki call the *wa^nshit lamshiimi*, literally, "grizzly bear doctor." (All the concepts seem to relate to the grizzly bear, much the more dangerous of the two local bear species.) The bear doctor might become so by first dreaming of bears. Then young female bears took him into the woods and lived with him; one of them might be reported as having physically carried off the future doctor's person. Other men sought bear power, swimming in forest holes, and dancing toward, clawing, and growling at a tree or stump until hair grew out of their body. The bear doctor cured bear bites and gave demonstrations of strength.

A third type of bear person was what the Yuki called *aumol*, "chewer" or "biter." He was a man trained by older *aumol* to walk about on all fours completely disguised in a bearskin, but carrying a bone dagger with which he stabbed the personal or tribal enemies he encountered, and then disemboweled and scattered their bodies. No doubt his community stood in awe of the *aumol*, but they also considered him valuable for the damage he could singlehanded inflict on their enemies without exposing them to the reprisals of open warfare. It is much to be doubted whether going out to murder from ambush encased in a clumsy bearskin would be physically possible; but the Indians elaborate the tale, speaking of strings of shell beads worn around the body to afford an armor inside the bear hide; of baskets worn in it containing a stone or water to simulate growling or the rumbling of the viscera; and so on. It looks very much as if the whole thing were only an elaborated fantasy never actually acted out. But it was certainly believed in as a reality by the overwhelming majority of the members of a whole series of tribes. Quite likely some men let it be known that they were *aumol*, and perhaps kept a bearskin and some of the accessory paraphernalia. What is of interest is the elaborateness of the physical apparatus insisted on.[3]

A fourth type of person associated

with bears was the initiated dancer, who, wearing a bearhide, performed as a bear at gatherings, just as other dancers impersonated spirits, ghosts of the dead, or eagles. For this office one was trained, and while it had much of the esoteric and dangerous about it, the community knew who the recognized bear dancer or dancers were.[4]

These then are the varieties of men resembling bears. They can be arranged in the following order, according to the degree of their participation in the supernatural: (1) the true bear shaman who, in virtue of power personally received from bears in his manhood, can turn himself into a bear; (2) the man who, as a result of prenatal influencing, occasionally and involuntarily turns into a bear; (3) the man who secretly disguises himself as a bear but manifests preternatural strength, endurance, and ferocity; and (4) the bear dancer, who holds the religious office of impersonating a bear as one part of a cult system magically serving the public welfare. Occurring side by side in a limited area —the southerly part of the northern Coast Ranges of California—there can be no doubt that the four beliefs or practices are historically associated. It is however of interest that the four variations on the one theme differ so much in strength of supernatural participation. In other words, mystic and rational, emotional and objective, expressions coexist in one pattern. Or again, it might be said that suggestion and auto-suggestion ranged from a maximum in type 1 to a minimum in type 4. The Pomo and the Patwin, whose culture was on the whole slightly the most elaborate and systematized in the region, adhered to types 3 and 4; the Yuki, poorer backwoodsmen, to 1 and 3; type 2, along with 3, is recorded from the Kato, who are more or less transitional.

There are similar gradations in regard to the method of curing supernaturally. (There was also curing with household remedies of roots or herbs, for headaches, constipation, bruises, and other minor ills; but these hardly count in the present connection because in any serious or alarming illness only the specialist in the supernatural could help.) The Yuki distinguished three kinds of treatment of disease. Perhaps the most generally effective was by the *lamshiimi*, the shaman or doctor proper, who had in his own person received power from some kind of spiritual being, and after "going into a trance," sucked out the disease (*ha^nchmi*). He used no rattle, sang little, if any, and in modern Indian vernacular is a "sucking doctor." The "singing doctor" was called *moli* by the Yuki, and held a public office: he was caretaker and firetender of the religious assembly house. In addition however, he sang with a rattle, and thereby was able to see and diagnose illness. He "investigated and prophesied." The third type of treatment was named *hilyulit* and used cult ritual. Songs pertaining to the various spirits impersonated by the cult initiates—the Creator and the ghosts— were sung until the patient trembled violently. Thereby it was known which kind of spirit had "frightened" him into illness. Then the cure was arranged by having the corresponding spirit impersonation—singing, dancing, and touching —made for him. This worked homoeopathically.

The Pomo cure in two ways. The *madu* corresponds to the first Yuki type: he has himself dreamed or encountered spirits, and he sucks. However he is, in contrast with the Yuki, considered the less powerful practitioner. Grave illness comes from *k'o'o*, "poison," that is, bewitching, and is handled by the *k'o'o-bakiyahale*, or performer for the poisoned. This type of doctor operated by means of a sack of fetishes, which he used with elaborate rattling, singing, and ritual motions. These paraphernalia and the knowledge associated with them he mostly did not claim to have been given to him by spirits or supernatural beings in a dream or trance, but to have received, with careful teaching, from a previous shaman, ordinarily an older relative. Again the Pomo differ from the Yuki in giving a higher valuation to the more rational (or pseudo-rational), orderly, tangible, formal procedure, whereas the Yuki pin their faith in the person who has had a powerful abnormal experience and more or less repeats it in curing.

Since the general culture of the tribes is closely similar, this variation of predilection toward and away from "psychopathological" manifestations, within the primitive level, is of some interest.[5]

SUGGESTIBILITY

Through all these practices and beliefs there evidently runs a very strong strain of suggestion and autosuggestion. My own conviction is that this factor is decidedly more important than the deliberate deception which undoubtedly also occurs. The audience certainly does not deceive, and it does see miracles. The shamans may know that they deceive, but many of them certainly believe that other shamans do real miracles. Beyond that, we do not know how far, in performing, they use deception consciously or under autosuggestion. When shamans recount how they received their powers, experienced ethnologists pretty unanimously feel that the overwhelming majority of them believe sincerely that they have really had such an experience. Moreover, this experience is of a kind which in our civilization would often be diagnosed as psychotic. I do not wish to rule out the question of "deception," which undoubtedly occurs and is relevant. But of more cardinal importance to an understanding of the shamanism of primitives are the two factors of psychosis-like symptoms and of suggestion. When psychologists as a whole return seriously to the problem of suggestion and suggestibility, striking

at aspects of it that go deeper than conscious propaganda, salesmanship, and advertising, it is likely that anthropologists may be better able to interpret shamanistic performances.

SUMMARY

Among many unsophisticated people, socially sanctioned and distinguished individuals who exercise special powers, especially of curing, acquire their capacity through experiences which in our culture would be stigmatized as psychotic. How far the hallucinations and other symptoms are simulated, autosuggested, or compulsive is not clear; but it is certain that deception will not account for all of them. This means that manifestations which are pathological, or at any rate are so regarded by us, are accepted and socially channeled in many primitive societies. Most of the more backward Siberian and North American natives similarly accept and institutionalize passive homosexuality. At the same time, societies of nearly the same general cultural level may differ considerably in the degree to which they rationalize or ceremonialize their curing or other shamanistic practices away from the psychotic or induced psychotic experience: some put a premium on certain frankly abnormal experiences, others on more nearly normal ones. The situation thus is far from simple; but it evidences the strong bearing which cultural patterns have on the problem of the nature of psychosis.

Postscript, 1951.—In my 1948 *Anthropology* I took the thesis of the present paper, namely, that in primitive cultures certain psychotic symptoms tend to be socially approved or rewarded, and developed it further into one of several touchstones by which culture progress might be objectively validated. This position was of course not a return to the eighteenth- and nineteenth-century assumption of human progress as something spontaneous, inherent, and inevitable. That ethnocentric a priori has been well disposed of by the growing recognition of cultural relativism in which anthropologists took full part. Still, even though we fully accept the modern critical attitude toward the old notion of progress, there can be no doubt that there has occurred, since Palaeolithic times, a great deal of some kind of progress in culture, and a fairly continuous progress at that. The real problem today is to analyze and define the criteria that measure this progress which we cannot avoid admitting. My 1948 suggestion was that one factor in this progress is a long-recognized one, namely, growth of size of societies—which in turn makes possible increased differentiation in the social functioning of individuals. This in its turn tends to lead to development of skills and accumulation of knowledge. Beyond this, advancement is more or less proportional to at least four considerations. The first of these is the total quantity of culture possessed. The second is the point made by the present essay, namely, ability to distinguish subjective experiences from objective phenomena, as against not distinguishing them or even sometimes surrealistically attaching greater value to the objectively unreal. Cultural progress on this score corresponds to atrophy of magic or supernaturalism as reinforced or validated by psychopathology. The third criterion is the diminishing influence, in social situations, of anatomical and physiological considerations, such as blood, menstruation, puberty, death. This corresponds to a loosening of infantile obsessions and shrinkage of dramatizations of physiological events, with replacement by a more mature "humaneness." The fourth touchstone is growth of science and technology—"reality culture," as discussed in selection No. 18.

The second of these four criteria has encountered pretty consistent opposition as I have discussed it with groups of mature students. It seems to them to represent an ethnocentric value preference or judgment. While it might appear such, it seems to me to be saved from being a value-judgment by the fact that the pathology involved is often real pathology. At least it is real in our society, and it may be suspected of being real also among the very primitives and ignorant who socially approve or reward it. When it comes to a matter so basic and subcultural as healthy organic functioning, it would be pedantic to debar value-judgments on the ground that they did not respect cultural relativism.

However, I am now ready to admit a qualification to my previous position, as well as to make an extension of it. The qualification is this: In general the psychopathologies that get rewarded among primitives are only the mild or transient ones. A markedly deteriorative psychosis, even a persistent and pointless delusion, such as a man's acting out the belief that he was a tree, would be rated and deplored by them much as by us. It is the lighter aberrations from objective reality that can win social approval: neurotic symptoms of the hysteric type, involving suggestibility or half-conscious volition. This means that primitives also recognize psychopathology, and that they discriminate the degrees and kinds of it to which they allocate tolerance or esteem. Thus, so far as I know, they do not grant social rewards to compulsion neuroses. The rewards seem to be reserved for individuals who can claim abnormal powers and controls, not for those who are controlled. This qualification is illuminating, but it does limit somewhat my original contention.

The new extension is this. Not only shamans—the professionally possessed or entranced or fraudulent—are involved in psychopathology, but often also the whole lay public of primitive societies.

This is so when suspicion of potential witchcraft becomes widespread or omnipresent and may or may not lead to a constant flow of revenge killings. Here we might well recognize something akin to a specially channeled paranoia, low-grade and diffuse, but persistent and nearly uanimous through the community. It will be noted that the element of suggestibility is again strong.

This additional comparison, plus the preceding limitation, indicates that the problems touched on are understood only imperfectly. However inadequately the argument may have been developed here, I cannot rid myself of the conviction that there does exist a real relation between on the one hand certain symptoms justly reckoned psychopathological when they occur in individuals uninduced by their culture, and on the other hand the degree of cultural advancement or progress of different societies; and that this relation is in need of further clarification.

The proposition might also be turned around to read like this: Cultures that consistently maintain a resistive or regretful attitude toward all manifestations of psychopathology may be rated as having progressed beyond those that tend to induce certain kinds of psychopathology by rewarding them and thereby strengthening a vicious circle of cultural nonreality and individual abnormality.

VERY few autobiographies or biographies have been published from the California Indians, and these only from the eastern and southern edges of the state.[1] The set of the native Californian cultures was not such as to develop striking personalities, and the fortunes of most groups since 1850 have tended toward the humble or squalid rather than toward the picturesque. Nevertheless, with biographies now available from Southwest, Northwest, and Plains, additional comparable material from California would be desirable; and I therefore present a very partial autobiography which I recorded among the Yurok in northwestern California on September 11, 1902. But first a few reflections on the history and function of biography and autobiography in ethnology.

In probably his last paper, printed posthumously in *Science,* Boas challenged the autobiography as being of limited value, and useful chiefly for the study of the perversion of truth by memory.[2] This may seem extreme, yet it should not be lightly discarded as merely the opinion of a man who lived long enough to become outmoded to those for whom recency is the most significant feature of thinking. Of course, Boas did not contend that autobiographies were wholly useless as material in ethnology. The specific problem of method is whether the autobiography will or will not contribute something that cannot be obtained from other approaches to the investigation of culture. As regards the actual content of culture, as well as its patterns, it seems quite possible that Boas was right. No doubt any sufficiently lengthy and detailed autobiography or biography will manage to turn up this and that cultural item or attitude which has managed to escape even a persevering ethnographic questioner. But again, the fullest autobiography or a dozen of them are almost surely bound to happen not to touch on a good many areas or spots of the culture either. There is of course no absolute demarcation between the two approaches. As soon as questioning becomes specific, any informant is likely to supply concrete evidence—whether he names names or not—out of the life-experience of himself, his kinsmen, or other particular members of his society. The problem thus assumes this shape: Is it more advantageous to have a thousand concrete exemplifications all related to the life of one individual, or to be scattered among many individuals? From the point of view of learning what the culture is and how it operates, I think it can fairly be maintained that the latter is likely to give a more random and truer sample. That is probably part of what Boas meant.

Of late it has become fashionable to emphasize that culture is an abstraction—not only culture in general but any culture. This is obviously true, in the sense that life, or a species, or society, or mind, can also be conceived as an abstraction, if one so wishes. What seems to be basically involved in many of the affirmations on the abstractness of culture is a lack of interest in culture as compared with other things. From this point of view, it is not culture which is really to be investigated, but something else, to which, it is true, culture stands in enough relation that it must be considered, even if only to eliminate or control it. This other thing of interest is usually personality, or the interrelations of personalities. From the angle of such an interest in personality, it is evident that a thousand items of culture all having reference to one person are going to have vastly more significance than a thousand items referring to dozens of individuals, especially if these individuals remain anonymous and unidentifiable. However, such a personality interest, while wholly legitimate, is no longer primarily cultural or ethnographic—perhaps not even anthropologic, if the word anthropology is to retain any definiteness of inclusion.

An in-between position was Sapir's, who was interested in culture—as a linguist, first and last, he had inevitably to be keenly concerned in superindividual forms—and who was also interested in personality. He therefore liked to apperceive and interpret cultural data in the humanistic tradition, as seen through the medium of personalities. This procedure presumably raised for him a flat, two-dimensional picture into a three-dimensional, stereoscopic one, with solidity of perspective: it does so for many of us. Sapir, however, was as sensitive aesthetically as he was intellectually. We may cheerfully grant that a culture presented through the medium of personalities is the richer as a work of art, and yet question whether it is rationally sharper or more effective for further inquiry.

We all remember Sapir's passionate plea on "Two-Crows denies this."[3] It is a shrewd suspicion that J. O. Dorsey, inhibited missionary as he presumably was, also preferred his culture saturated with the savor of concrete personality. But he refrained from summarizing the life-history or evaluating the character and proclivities of Two-Crows and the other informants that balance him. Technically, Dorsey was just keeping the record straight as to the sources of his information, where these were dis-crepant—protecting himself in his trusteeship of Omaha culture. He was still a long way from biographies, and much farther from autobiographies.

Many anthropologists perhaps do not realize the extent to which the two differ. A biography—if more than a panegyric—is the intendedly objective story of a life in the setting of its cultural milieu. It can therefore pass, to a certain extent, as an exemplification of a culture by an individual life. An autobiography is necessarily subjective and, if honest, is avowedly so. The culture included may be portrayed truthfully, but it is portrayed subjectively. There are excellent biographies by Plutarch and Ssŭ-ma Chien. Autobiographies—excluding unrounded religious confessions and the meteoric case of Cellini—go back in literature only to Rousseau and Franklin—not quite two centuries. That a genre or method is recent does not condemn it; but it is cause for reflection.

To sum up, it seems we do what we are interested in; which is legitimate enough. All that can be asked is that we know what we are doing and why. The *Son of Old Man Hat* is a concrete document that must have taken hundreds of hours to record. Dyk evidently liked writing down what his informant said, much as the informant liked telling it. If he had liked finding out the forms and functioning of Navaho culture, his patience would have given out before he got a tenth through the endless story, from which, as he drifted peacefully along, he must have seen problem after problem of Navaho culture coming into sight and receding again unanswered.

Perhaps we shall have an answer to the question raised by Boas when someone—if there ever is such—who has done a first-class full-length portrait of a culture, and who has also edited a full-length autobiography from that culture, will pronounce an inside verdict on the relation of the two endeavors.

Now as to my present Yurok document. It was secured, in keeping with anthropological field method at the time, not from psychological interest in individual personalities—even the word "personality" did not then have its present technical sense—but, like J. O. Dorsey's statements from Two-Crows, as a concrete, personal exemplification of the working of a set institution. These were the antecedents.

In 1901 I spent the late winter months among the Gros Ventre of Montana, in a briefer companion study to that which I had made of the Arapaho in 1899 and 1900. The Gros Ventre age-graded ritual organization proved to be more decayed than the Arapaho one; and, to allay some uncertainties as to the sequence of societies, the age of their members, etc., I asked several informants to tell me the order in which they went through the rites. This was elementary enough, and today it might be among the very first requests which a field ethnographer would put; but it seemed to me a new and fruitful device then. So I applied it also to war stories, not with any primary notion of ascertaining how a particular Gros Ventre felt in battle, let alone how raiding parties molded his character, but because a listing of all a man's fights, and better yet all the fights of several men, would give a truer sample of the nature of the average Gros Ventre war exploit, of the average war participation, and the like, than giving informants their head to select those episodes which best satisfied them. Then, hearing of a woman who had gone on a war party, been captured, and escaped, I secured her story.[4] That I should record this cluster of incidents but nothing of her previous or subsequent life, will seem strange to the generation that is young now; but that is the way investigations were being made forty-four years ago. We were trying to find out about whole cultures then because we were interested in them; we were not using cultures as stepping stones to analyze out personalities or techniques of social climbing or class conflicts or ways of bettering the world.

Later in the same year of 1901, I returned to California, and to the Yurok, whom I had briefly visited in 1900; and in 1902, I spent a long summer with them and neighboring tribes. Hearing of Sregon Jim as the Yurok who had fought most and lived to tell about it, I wanted his story for much the same reasons that I had got the Gros Ventre ones eighteen months before. I was merely following a pattern through in a somewhat new situation. That is why I secured a reminiscence instead of an autobiography. . . .

41. A SOUTHWESTERN PERSONALITY TYPE
1947

RECENTLY Kluckhohn presented an autobiographic sketch by a Navaho[1] which at once reminded me of a corresponding narrative which Gordon MacGregor obtained from a Walapai.[2] The two personalities evidently had much in common or at least saw themselves in a similar light. It is proposed to discuss this resemblance.

The two cultures are alike in possessing no town life and few fixed statuses or offices, and in that they have never been construed as favoring the development of a restrained, classic, Apollinian type of personality. Both farmed—the Navaho somewhat more—but depended also on gathering. They differed in that Walapai culture was far less patterned, more slovenly and amorphous, than Navaho. Its ritual ways were of minimum development. There was no wealth: no solid, heavy hogans, no flocks, no woven blankets, no accumulation of silver and turquoise; existence was eked out with few reserves, formerly as today.

Like Mr Moustache of the Ramah Navaho, the Walapai Kuni or Cooney was a respected leader, a "chief." They were both born not far from 1869. Kuni's age was not recorded, but he was not much above sixty when our Laboratory party knew him in 1929. He was then mainly looking back upon his life: a year earlier, his personal spirit had told him in a dream that he would be sick once more, recover, and then live to be very old. This sickness overtook him soon after: he was therefore facing the beginning of his last chapter when we knew him. Mr Moustache was about sixty-eight when he told Kluckhohn "about his life, right from the beginning," in 1936. Kluckhohn had then known him personally for fourteen years; though the recording of this life-story represented Kluckhohn's first day of professional ethnologizing and Mr Moustache's second. Our group of six at Kingman had known and studied with Kuni and several other Walapai for a month to six weeks before life-histories were asked for.

Both biographies are brief. The Navaho one runs to less than three thousand words in English, the Walapai barely two thousand. (Of three other Walapai life-histories secured, one is about as long as Kuni's, two others definitely longer.) In both accounts there is emphasis on making a living, much preoccupation with subsistence. In both, the father's influence is dominant and explicit. In both, there is a strong sense of teaching and following, of receiving basic wisdom and passing it on. Both narrators are obviously well-integrated characters with a strong social responsibility sense manifested in similar channels.

In editing our Walapai autobiographies in 1935, I said:

> The Walapai scarcely think in terms of a career. Kuni is a partial exception, in that he defines standards and evinces a certain pride in having lived up to them and having been successful. The same attitude is evident in his dreams. But a career to him is a normal one, a getting through life properly. There are only traces of a sense of individual differentiation and achievement, while the idea of carrying on from generation to generation is stronger.

These remarks, I suspect, would apply almost equally well to Mr Moustache.

My collaborators also secured dreams from three of our four biographees, as well as from two other informants. I had the impression that the dreams revealed more personality than the life-histories. Not that the Walapai dreams obtained are in any sense extraordinary. But a dream is bound to be personal, while a life-history can be heavily de-personalized; and that evidently was Kuni's idea of a biography. In view of the fact that autobiographies—other than religious or moral confessions—are not quite two hundred years old as a recognized literary genre in our civilization (Cellini's being a sport, if not a romance), Kuni's and Mr Moustache's attitude is not surprising. Evidently the few full-length life-stories that have been secured from American Indians represent personalities of unusual orientation or were elicited through special coaxing or training. The latter is admitted for the Hopi Sun Chief, though he clearly was also an apt pupil. The Navaho Son of Old Man Hat evidently had faithful and total recall—a trait we encounter every so often in our own society. The Kwakiutl Charley Nowell really tells more about his people's customs than about himself: he is frank enough, but tends to be an auto-ethnographer rather than an autobiographer. This inclination is evident also in our two present subjects. Kuni has hardly begun to tell of his father's first lesson to him when he lapses into telling how the yucca leaves are split and braided into a belt to tuck the dead rabbits' heads under. Every third paragraph of Mr Moustache begins: "My father said" or "My father told me." The instructions cited are the explicit behavioral standards and aims of Navaho culture. As Kluckhohn says, his account is "much more a kind of philosophic homily than a proper life history." The same is only slightly less true of Kuni. After Kuni's father dies, what Serum and

Spencer said becomes important in his story.

However, the three other Walapai life-narratives differ from Kuni's in containing less ethnography, less homily and torch-carrying, and more events—jobs held, marriages, happenings of good and bad luck, and such, though avowed feelings are little if any more in evidence. In short, the Walapai stories do not all run to one type; but one Walapai and one Navaho story resemble each other in content, selective attitude, and tone. This is what justifies the hypothesis that they express a personality type which goes deeper than tribal conditioning.

We may thus suspect that among nonliterate tribal folk some normal elderly persons are likely to feel their life not as something interesting in its individuation and distinctiveness, but as an exemplification of socialization. Such a person is conscious of himself first of all as a preserver and transmitter of his culture.

Michelson's records of Cheyenne and Arapaho women's lives bear out this finding.[3] The Arapaho woman in particular is careful to suppress every spark of personal feeling, except the desire to please her relatives by obedience and to conform to accepted standards. The one time she shows independence is when her third husband proposes an improper plural marriage. Even then she merely "prefers to sever the relationship entirely," so as to have "no hard feelings toward my cousins and this woman." Her mother played the same dominant part in her early life that Moustache's and Kuni's fathers did in theirs.

The Cheyenne life-story is generally similar in its mother-role, amount of ethnography, and correct conformity; but it loosens up occasionally. She was "instructed in all the ways of courtship" by her father's older sister. Twice she even reports feelings. On being taken hold of the first time in an act of sexual aggression, she experiences fright, strangeness, and bewilderment. And as to her husband: "I surely loved him. His death made me very lonely. It was a terrible event in my life." This might be partly conformity with expectation or really felt individually; but the next statement is surely emotionally personal (as well as surprising in a Plains woman): "Apparently I missed him more than I did my four children who died afterward." Yet, apart from these few flashes, this Cheyenne narrative is as impersonal and as ethical-social as its Arapaho companion. Michelson had both these accounts recorded for him by younger native tribesmen (and no doubt kinsmen). Some of the ethnography of a past generation may have been introduced by the narrator for the benefit of these ex-schoolboys; it was not, at any rate, due to the story's being directed at a white and presumably ignorant stranger.

To return for a moment to the book-length autobiographies, it is to be assumed that these represent different moods, intentions, and perhaps personalities from the one-day life-stories. Crashing Thunder, the earliest, also comes the nearest, in its predominant orientation toward religion and conversion, to the early autobiographies of our own civilization—St. Augustine's, for instance. However, Part II, which is non-narrative but which Radin says the "informant regarded as part of his biography," is labeled "My Father's Teachings." Sun Chief was trained for several years to write out everything: the printed work is a small selection of his total. The Son of Old Man Hat we know little about objectively, subsequent to his first twenty years, except that he was urged to omit nothing from the telling, even if unimportant. This instruction he certainly obeyed faithfully. Most of the incidents are trivial; their value lies in that fact; they give intimacies, nuances, minutiae of highly personal relations that one would despair to get by any system of questioning: they must come out incidental to something else if they are to be secured at all. Avowedly personalized reminiscence is perhaps the one medium in which these allusive and delicate implications will grow; and an informant who will reminisce in full detail and endlessly—and as honestly about his feelings as Son of Old Man Hat—is ideal if the purpose is the assemblage of nuances. What has not been generally observed is that even a thousand nuances will not by themselves make a personality: they seize its ever changing surface at the expense of its fundamental structure. Son of Old Man Hat is the perfect mirror; but, no doubt for that very reason, I can formulate less conception, less picture even, of his personality, than of Mr Moustache from his brief, bald little account. If this is a personal obtuseness or blind spot on my part, I shall stand corrected when someone succeeds in sketching in a few strokes a definite, incisive characterization of Left-Hand, Son of Old Man Hat.

In other words, we are collocating qualitative noncomparables in the two Navaho narratives: their tellers aimed to do different things. On the contrary, Mr Moustache and Kuni aimed to do much the same thing, and did much the same; so did the Cheyenne and Arapaho women. On the other hand, Walapai informant B, Blind Tom, though started off alongside Kuni with the same previous tutelage, came visibly nearer to Son of Old Man Hat. He is the less skilful of the two, less sensitive, too brief where we would like more; but there is the same adding of further beads of incident on one string, the same maintenance of level through episode after episode. Blind Tom went on four times as long as Kuni; and this without urging to "leave out nothing, no matter how trivial."

To come back to personality as shown by dreams, I quote what I said of Kuni's:

He is a settled character with sound principles instead of imagination, docile to the teachings of his elders or accepted religion, reliant on himself and his luck. When a spirit instructs him, it is directly, with meager incident and imagery. Mostly Kuni appears to have dreamed when it was time to. When it is evident that something is about to come to an issue, Kuni dreams the outcome; and so it comes out. He is like an ancient Roman, pious, sober, dependable, practical, acceptive of established forms. When he naps while herding, he is a little anxious about the horses escaping, but reassures himself that he can find them again. During the night, he dreams the dreams of the just: his horses will never get away from him. His dream life has the simplicity of a child's; but the combination of self-reliance, determination, and fatalism of his waking character carries over into his sleep.

There is no need to analyze the twenty dreams. They are all to the point, pithy, and mostly reassuring. It would make an interesting comparison if Kluckhohn had happened to secure a series from Mr Moustache. One would venture to predict that his dreams would reinforce one's impression of him as an unimaginative, practical, responsible, conservative conformist, careful but courageous, self-reliant through his sense of being in accord with the accepted rules of his world.

This is a type likely to crop up in nearly all societies. However, its formal self-expression at Hopi and Zuni might be considerably different; though probably no more individuated. On the Plains, some men could perhaps be expected to deviate further from the type than almost all women, through the individually competitive war-honors pressure. Alice Marriott's *The Ten Grandmothers*, probably far more authentic than its semifictional dress suggests, portrays consciously individuated Kiowa personalities (Sitting Bear, Eagle Plume) as well as the present type of average-successful-conformist (Young Sitting Bear). It would be interesting to know to what extent the personality type under discussion may be encountered among the Eskimo. Almost undoubtedly it occurs; but the Eskimo habit of swinging from boasting to self-depreciation, or of boasting through understatement, might alter the form of expression of the personality type.

At any rate, the rather striking similarity of the untutored, unguided self-depiction of a particular Navaho and a particular Walapai raises the question whether the likeness is a coincidence (which I do not believe); or mainly due to a regional though supertribal resemblance of culture; or whether perhaps it is generally expectable in folk cultures, as a recurrent type definable in social-psychological terms, although varying somewhat in its outer cultural dress. In the latter case the essential recurring element would probably lie in the attitude of thorough acceptance of one's parents, kin, society, and their cultural values and standards.

Put differently, the problem is: How common is such a personality orientation in other or all cultures?

At any rate, it is evident that anthropological studies in personality do not have to be directed primarily toward deviations, traumas, aberrations, frustrations, and peculiarities, nor toward uncovering deeply buried childhood experiences. There are also successful parent-child adjustments and successful careers, as there are successful cultures.

PART V

HISTORY AND PROCESS OF CIVILIZATION

INTRODUCTION

THE theory of culture developed in Part I of this book is in considerable part methodological: it discusses how culture may be investigated and understood. The present final Part V is also oriented theoretically, but with exemplifications of method rather than discussion of it.

About half the selections deal with problems of process in civilization [Nos. 42, 44, 45, 48], half with the results of process as manifest in history [Nos. 43, 46, 47, 49, 50]. The two approaches are partly interwoven.

In all the selections in this part, the materials discussed refer mainly or wholly to our own culture or to other literate and historical cultures. The term "civilization" in the title of this part is therefore deliberate. The word is here used in its general and popular sense.

The first essay in the group, No. 42, was published in 1919 and is therefore of the era of thinking that produced "The Superorganic" [No. 3, 1917]. All the others are from between 1939 and 1951. This latter was the period in which I was either working on *Configurations of Culture Growth* or trying to follow farther the problems raised therein.

While Nos. 42 and 45, on fashion changes, were separated by twenty-one years and while both the scope and the compass of the later monograph are much larger, it nevertheless is a continuation as well as an extension of the previous one. To save space, I have therefore made the reprinted portion of the earlier essay serve also as an explanation of the technique of measurement used in both. The purpose of both studies is to find pattern in so fluidly capricious a thing as dress fashion, and to express quantitatively and objectively something of the qualitative behavior of change in the pattern. In 1919, having established long-term trends of direction of pattern, which left little room for random caprice, I spoke blithely of law or at least of order and regularity in civilization. At that time demonstration of the mere fact of pattern in culture seemed a triumph. However, it is plain that even then I was not seeking to establish recurrent uniformities between different cultures. The regularities announced exist within one small domain of a single civilization: they are a piece of a history. They show merely that, within this story, a degree of organization and order rules in what superficially seems only a limitless sea of fluctuating wills or accidents.

On the second try, with Jane Richardson [No. 45], we went farther, and inquired statistically also into the incidence of very short-term and individual fluctuations of fashion. Such fluctuations proved to vary greatly in strength according to period. The decades of strong fluctuations were also on the whole times of sociopolitical unrest. Further analysis showed that the immediate correlation of the fashion fluctuations need not be construed as being with these rather remote sociopolitical conditions, but more likely was with an unconscious basic pattern of ideal dress characteristic of the civilization over a period of some length. According as the fashion of the moment conformed to this basic pattern or conflicted with it, its fluctuations were mild or violent. Whether this hypothesis be correct or not, it at least applies wholly within the cultural level; and the interesting variation in variability is beyond doubt.

No. 44, on "Stimulus Diffusion," suggests a process of intercultural influencing which tends to efface its own record, because the diffusion or transference is not outright but is limited to a stimulating idea which then leads to a reinvention, or to a new, allied invention, in the influenced culture. The process is applicable in problems of culture history. While stimulus diffusion is conceptually isolable as an abstraction, its recognition necessarily must often involve widely ranging intercultural relations. Thus by its factual content this paper might be classed also with those dealing with the history of civilization. Indeed, it has some overlaps with No. 47.

"Culture Groupings in Asia," No. 48, while formally a classificatory commentary, touches on several problems that involve either process or theory. One is the problem of relating the static concept of a regionally limited type of culture, the "culture area" of anthropologists, to the flow of culture in history—a relation already touched on in No. 33 and again in No. 43. Another problem concerns the nature of the complementary or symbiotic relation between sedentary and pastoral cultures within one region: between "part cultures"—segment or organ cultures, they might also be called. It is clear that this concept needs further elaboration; but it is already clear that cultures which are essentially non-self-sufficient cannot profitably be treated as of the same kind or order as autonomous ones. Similarly with a third problem, that of the "footnote cultures" of little backward peoples, especially when situated among large advanced nations. Their regressiveness and "historic parasitism" forbid these minuscule cultures being construed as if they were really on a level with great civilizations. Nevertheless, in their very aberrance they may have some of the taxonomic interest of isolated survivals in organic evolution, such as the king crab, lancelet, lamprey, or monotremes.

Of the selections concerned with the history of civilization, the one on "Cultural Intensity and Climax," No. 43, is the earliest. It is actually taken out of my book on *Cultural and Natural Areas*, but partly anticipates the one on *Configurations*. It was written toward the end of the long task of composing the former, shortly before the latter was actually undertaken. The name at least of "climax" is taken over from ecological botany. The concept really examined is one of Flinders Petrie's (whom alone, besides Spengler, I had then read of those who have written on the typical course of whole civilizations—Toynbee, Sorokin, Danilevsky were to come later). The qualitative rating of intensities, though related, is of course really a third issue dealt with in this selection; whose transitional nature thus is clear.

With the belated review of Toynbee in No. 46 in 1943, there is the first formal expansion beyond the somewhat special approach of my own *Configurations*. While I have since read much and written somewhat in this field, I have published little, and of this there is included only one example, No. 49. To many, the chief interest of this selection (No. 49) will lie in the "disintegrating or reconstituting" alternative, with special reference to our Western civilization of today. There is however a purely intellectual problem involved, beyond the practical concern. How are civilizations to be delimited from one another other than by Danilevskian common usage or Spenglerian monadal insight? Historians, falling back on the undoubtedly actual continuity of events, institutions, and cultural content between civilizations, have on the whole refused to face the problem of the qualitative separateness of cultures. Toynbee, coming out of history, has faced it. But his answer, it seems to me, is not in outrightly qualitative terms, just as it is not wholeheartedly cultural. Instead, he advocates a group of formulae of *events* (such as the transformation chrysalis of religion) as the mechanisms of civilizational individuation. Some of these formulae are novel and valuable. But they appear largely to deprive the civilizations of the cultural substance which they possess and which one even senses Toynbee to be keenly aware of their having. What is qualitative in the civilization tends, similarly, to be too often excised or repressed by him, except for ethical qualities. My own preliminary answer is in terms of over-all pattern limitation, reconstitution, or atrophy and disintegration. This hypothesis will need much fuller examination, especially by its extension to other cases than our own civilization. Back of that lies

a more fundamental question: How far is it legitimate to infer from particular style patterns to an over-all whole culture pattern? These are problems for the future to answer; but their bulks are beginning to loom in sight.

In the "Oikoumenê" [No. 47], focus is shifted from the diversity or parallelism of civilizations to the history of all civilization seen as an intricately interconnected single whole, gradually coming to cover the main land mass of our planet. How far, in short, can the history of higher civilization be seen as a unitary process, as a single, large-scale, long-term *event?* And No. 50, on the novel, is an attempt to build out from this conception. It inquires how far the Oikoumenê concept can in turn be used for understanding secondary, parallel growth developments that have arisen separately on it as a basis.

1919

TWENTY years ago the project of inquiring into the principles that guide fashion arose in my mind, and I went so far as to turn the leaves of volume after volume of a Parisian journal devoted to dress. But the difficulties were discouraging. Pivotal points seemed hard to find in the eternal flux. One might measure collars or sleeves or ruffles for some years, and then collars and sleeves and ruffles disappeared. One lady in a plate was seated, another erect, a third in profile, the fourth elevated her arms. If one took as a base the total length of the figure, coiffures fell and rose by inches from time to time, or were entirely concealed by hats or nets. I abandoned the plan as infeasible.

In 1918 I renewed the endeavor, this time with less ambitious scope and greater readiness to seize on any opening. I decided to attempt only eight measurements, four of length and four of width, all referring to the figure or dress as a whole, and to disregard all superficial parts or trimmings. Strict comparability of data being essential, it was necessary to confine observations to clothing of a single type. Women's full evening toilette was selected. This has served the same definite occasions for more than a century; does not therefore vary in purpose as does day dress, nor seasonally like street clothing. The material remains silk, and there have been no totally new fundamental concepts introduced, such as the shirtwaist and tailored suit. The variations are therefore purely stylistic. And while this range promised to be perhaps somewhat narrower than those of certain other types of women's wear, this was of little moment. If any principle could

be determined, it would apply also to the more changeable kinds of clothing.

MEASUREMENTS

The measurements made were the following:

1. Total length of figure from the center of the mouth to the tip of the toe. If the shoe was covered, the lowest point of the skirt edge was chosen. The selection of the mouth obviated all difficulties arising from alteration of hairdress. (This measure serves as a base against which other measurements were percentaged.)

2. Distance from the mouth to the bottom of the skirt. This equals the last measurement less the height of the skirt from the ground.

3. Distance from the mouth to the minimum diameter across the waist. This serves as some sort of indication of the length of the "waist" or corsage, that is, of the upper part of the figure. The true waist line of the dress has been disregarded. It would have been much more significant stylistically and probably shown more decided variations; but there are periods when it vanishes. . . .

4. Depth or length of decolletage, measured from the mouth to the middle of the corsage edge in front.

5. Diameter of the skirt at its hem or base. . . .

6. [Discarded.]

7. Minimum diameter in the region of the waist.

8. Width of shoulders, or more accurately, width of the decolletage across the shoulders. . . .

Ten figures were measured for each calendar year, the first ten suitable for measurement being taken from each volume, so as to insure random instead of subjective selection. . . .

It must be admitted that ten measures are not a very large maximum from which to derive reasonably true averages in so variable a thing as fashionable dress, where each design strives almost as keenly after distinctiveness as after conformity to the prevailing style. . . .

The absolute dimensions in millimeters were throughout converted into percentage ratios to the length of the entire figure as it has been defined (1). The percentages for each measure were then averaged for each year. It is these year percentage averages that are brought together in the summary tabulation, are plotted in the charts, and are

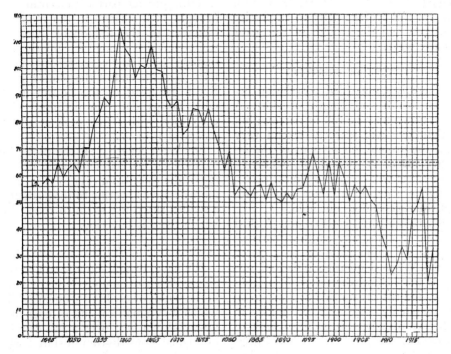

Fig. 5.—5, width of skirt

But . . . for a preliminary investigation it seemed wiser to obtain a comparatively long series of small groups of measurements than to operate with measurement groups of a size more reliable for averages but covering fewer years. . . .

I may here express my conviction that any farther quantitative investigations that may be undertaken as to the course of stylistic changes should be planned to cover if possible a period of from one to two centuries, whether they concern fashions of dress or of jewelry, silverware, or furniture.

throughout referred to in the discussion that follows. . . .

WIDTH OF SKIRT (5)

Of all the elements of dress examined, that of diameter of skirt yields the most impressive results, especially in graphic plotting (Fig. 5). The irregularities of the rhythm of change are also more quickly understood in this point of fashion than for most others. Nevertheless, the superiority which skirt width enjoys over other factors as an index of demonstration is more apparent than actual. It is even exceeded by some of them in the wave length of their periodicity. . . .

The average width of skirt for the 76 years from 1844 to 1919 is 65.3. It will be seen that from 1852 to 1878 inclusive this figure is exceeded each year, whereas before and after that period it is never attained, except in 1880 (68) and again in the spasmodic flares of 1896 (68) and 1899 (65). On the plot the horizontol line for this average helps to emphasize the crest and the trough of the great secular wave.

LENGTH OF SKIRT (2)

There is a one-sided correlation between width and length of skirt. A short gown may be full or narrow; but a tight one will scarcely extend very near the ground, on account of the inconvenience. A period of decisively close skirts will therefore almost necessarily be a period of short skirts also; but the reverse does not hold.

There is a further difference. A skirt may be of almost any width or narrowness in a fashion plate or on a posed model. When slenderness is desired, one leg is put behind the other, in a front view, and the dress made to cling to an exaggeratedly slim calf or ankle. In other words, there is no fixed limit of extremity. The possible length of a dress is however automatically cut off when it reaches the ground, or when, in an illustration, it descends far enough in front to conceal the feet. Yet a gown can shorten almost indefinitely. This brings it about that when skirt length attains its maximum, it remains apparently stationary for a time, whereas at its minimum it reaches a climax and quickly descends again. It might be said that fashion clearly tries, and is prevented only by physical impossibility, to draw the bottom of the dress several inches into the ground. In the chart (Fig. 6), this discrepancy has been indicated by two lines: a level horizontal one at the maximum of 100 per cent;

and a dotted one suggesting the ideal curve which the data indicate that style would follow if it could.

The rhythmic period for skirt length is only a third that for width: about thirty-five years as against a century. . . .

DIAMETER AND LENGTH OF WAIST (7, 3)

A first glance at Figure 7 suggests that the greater part of a century has brought little change in the minimum diameter of the fashionable woman's waist—and that change irregularly fluctuating. The only very striking movement is at the end of the plot (Fig. 7). But a grouping of the figures in the table brings out two definite swings each way, with a first peak at 1872, a second at 1914. . . .

For waist length (3), the plot (Fig. 6) shows a marked shortening or raising of the waist from 1851 to 1867, a still more decisive lowering to 1903, and then a sudden sharp rise again to 1909, after which there is hovering. . . .

COMPARISON OF THE SEVERAL RHYTHMS

We have, I think, now found reasonable evidence of an underlying pulsation in the width of civilized women's skirts, which is symmetrical and extends in its up-and-down beat over a full century; of an analogous rhythm in skirt length, but with a period of only about a third the duration; some indication that the position of the waist line may completely alter, also following a "normal" curve, in a seventy-year period; and a possibility that the width of shoulder exposure varies in the same manner, but with the longest rhythm of all, since the continuity of tendency in one direction for seventy years establishes a periodicity of about a century and a half, if the change in this feature of dress follows a symmetrically recurrent plan.

There is something impressive in the largeness of these lapses of time. We are all in the habit of talking glibly of how

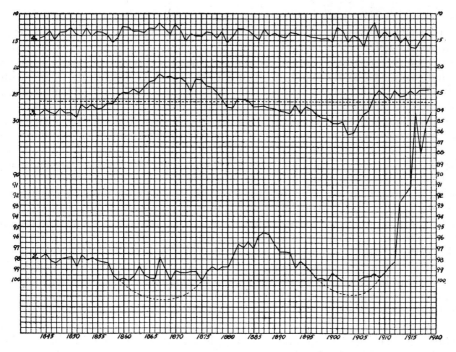

FIG. 6.—2, length of skirt; 3, length of waist; 4, decolletage

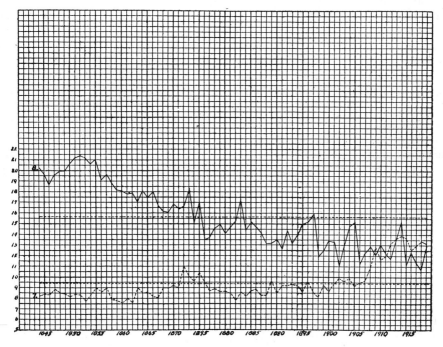

FIG. 7.—7, width of waist; 8, width of decolletage

this year's fashion upsets that of last year. Details, trimmings, pleats, and ruffles, perhaps colors and materials—all the conspicuous externalities of dress—do undoubtedly alter fairly rapidly; and it is in the very nature of fashion to bring these to the fore. They are driven into our attention, and soon leave a blurred but overwhelming impression of incalculably chaotic fluctuations, of reversals that are at once bewildering and meaningless, of a sort of lightning-like prestidigitation to which we bow in dumb recognition of its uncontrollability. But underneath this glittering maze, the major proportions of dress change rather with a slow majesty, in periods often exceeding the duration of human life. . . .

It is not to be expected that the development and decline of every trait of dress or civilization should follow a normal curve, that is, a symmetrical course. For an element of civilization wholly unrelated to all others, such symmetry could perhaps be anticipated. But completely autonomic elements are an idea rather than a fact. There must always be some interaction with other factors in the same and cognate phases of culture, and occasional interferences from more remote domains. A certain proportion of features should therefore follow irregular courses, or asymmetrical curves; and in this class it seems that diameter of the waist and depth of decolletage should be placed.

Secondary tremors ruffling the even-ness of the great pulsations are at first sight disturbing to the concept of orderliness, but on analysis are confirmatory, in that they reveal an increase of the intricacy of the operative forces without diminishing their prevalent regularity. In this manner the long-range curves for width of skirt and shoulders, each bearing about three superimposed but symmetrical minor crests, add substance to the generic conclusions reached.

Finally, while it would make for the greater simplicity of historical causality if it were found that acmes of fashion came in recurrences of equal periodicity, such regularity can hardly be expected. There is no conceivable reason why there should be anything inherent in the nature of dress tending toward a change from full to narrow and back to full skirts in a century. All historical phenomena are unique in some degree, in the field of nature as well as of human activity; and a similar rhythm of fashion might well extend over a thousand, a hundred, or ten years in different eras or among separate nations. Again, therefore, there is if not support for the idea of "law," at least no disconcertion in the fact that the past quarter-century on the whole evinces distinctly more rapid and extreme variations of fashion than the half-century preceding. This is the case for every feature examined except shoulder width.

[*This inquiry is continued in No. 45.*]

43. CULTURAL INTENSITY AND CLIMAX
1939

THE eighty-four areas into which North America has been divided are cultural in the sense that, within each, culture is relatively uniform. Many of them also approximate natural areas; that is, they often possess one or more features, such as drainage, elevation, land form, climate, or plant cover, which also are relatively uniform over the tract, or alter at its borders. They are, further, historical areas, in that their relations with one another reflect currents or growths of culture, as soon as the areas are viewed not as equivalents but as differing in intensity or level. The ten or so larger culture areas hitherto customarily recognized differ from one another essentially in culture material or content; consideration of differences in level has usually been avoided as subjective or unscientific. The more numerous areas of native North America dealt with in the present work are in part based avowedly on culture intensity as well as content.

In practice, these two aspects of intensity and content cannot be rigorously separated. A precise calendar system, a complex interrelation of rituals or social units, invariably embodies special culture material as well as intensity of its development and organization. Simple culture material cannot well be highly systematized; refined and specialized material seems to demand organization if it is to survive. What we call intensity of culture therefore means both special content and special system. A more intensive as compared with a less intensive culture normally contains not only more material—more elements or traits— but also more material peculiar to itself, as well as more precisely and articulate-

ly established interrelations between the materials. An accurate time reckoning, a religious hierarchy, a set of social classes, a detailed property law, are illustrations of this.

Granted this interdependence of richness of content and richness of systematization, it should be possible to determine an approximately objective measure of cultural intensity by measuring culture content—by counting distinguishable elements, for instance. This is a task which no one is yet ready to perform for the continent; but theoretically it is feasible; and it might be worth while. Wider historical conclusions can hardly be formulated without consideration of intensity factors. Permanent neglect of these will tend to limit investigations to narrowly circumscribed regions and periods, or to abstract consideration of processes as such.

Each of the six major areas here dealt with, except that of the Eskimo, shows at least one climax or focus of cultural intensity—even the Intermediate tract possesses a low-grade one in California. These climaxes, though not indicated in the general maps, have been discussed in the text. The accompanying map (Fig. 8) is a provisional attempt to go farther by representing various degrees of culture intensity. Primarily, the grades indicated are intended to show differences between unit areas lying within the same major area; but in an approximate way they also suggest relative differences of culture intensity between units lying in distinct major areas. The map pretends to no more than a personal estimate. Yet by the method of counting culture elements that have index value for systematization, it should prove pos-

337

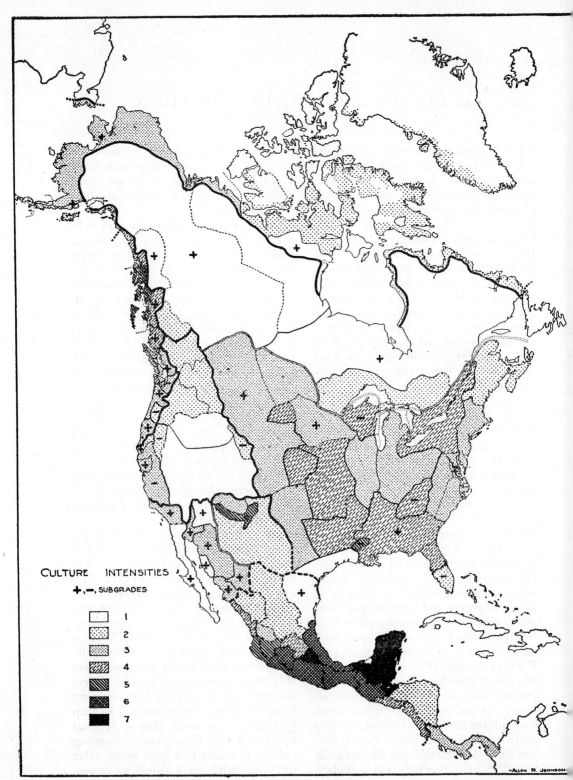

CULTURE INTENSITIES

+, −, SUBGRADES

1
2
3
4
5
6
7

—ALLEN R. JOHNSON—

FIG. 8.—Map of intensities or "levels" of native cultures, by areas. Subgrades are indicated by plus and min
signs. There are as yet no generally recognized objective criteria for judgments of the kind expressed in th
map, yet they are often rendered by ethnologists either approximately or implicitly.

sible, after sufficient analysis, to prepare a more objectively founded table or map of the same purport.

In general, a culture climax or culmination may be regarded as the point from which the greatest radiation of culture material has taken place in the area. But it is always necessary to remember that as a culture becomes richer, it also tends to become more highly organized, and in proportion as its organization grows, so does its capacity to assimilate and place new material, whether this be produced within or imported from without. In the long run, accordingly, high-intensity cultures are the most absorptive as well as the most productive. It is by the interaction of both processes that culture culminations seem to be built up. Consequently, an unusually successful degree of absorption tends to lead to further "inventive" productiveness and outward influencing, and so on, until the process fails somewhere and a condition of stability is reached or a decline sets in; or a newer center begins to dominate the old.

On the whole, accordingly, it can be assumed that culture climaxes are not mushroom growths; though their finest flowerings are evidently brief, and the introduction of a radically new subsistence mechanism, such as agriculture or the horse, may occasionally cause a rapid growth. Where there is no evidence of such fundamental economic introduction, it may be taken for granted with a reasonable degree of assurance that a climax in the historic period was also a climax, or at least a subclimax, in the later prehistoric period, and probably at least of fairly high level of intensity before that. Maya, Aztec-Toltec, Southwestern archaeology—in general that of the continent as a whole—confirms this assumption.

Archaeology does indicate some minor shifts of climax area: of the Maya from the base to the tip of the Yucatán Peninsula, of the Pueblo center from San Juan to Little Colorado and upper Rio Grande drainage. Analogous to these is the hypothetical northward movement of the Northwest Coast culmination. On the whole, however, these shifts are of small range. The only region of the continent in which there is evidence of a large-scale culture recession is the Ohio Valley. Even here the lowering of culture intensity from the prehistoric to the historic period seems not very great; and the whole eastern major area of which the Ohio Valley forms part is the one whose historic climax is the least.

Of all the greater currents in American prehistory, that which brought stimuli of Mexican origin to the region of the Mississippi and Ohio is the most obscure, on account of the unusually low-level cultures intervening in Tamaulipas and Texas. The Southwest is more evenly linked to central Mexico by tribes like the Opata, Tarahumar and Cáhita, Sinaloans and Cora. At any rate, agriculture is continuous from the Southwest to central Mexico; discontinuous from the Southeast. The Northwest Coast seems so free, relatively, of specific Mexican influences that its culture, beyond many general American elements, is readily construable as a reworking primarily of Asiatic and possibly Oceanic stimuli. It therefore presents quite different problems. The most satisfactory hypothesis to explain the more intensive eastern culture is that this was due to the same influences which introduced maize agriculture, presumably from Mexico; and that with the introduction of this fundamental subsistence factor all cultural values shifted, and there ensued a period of unsettlement and activity, during which now this and now that local center forged ahead. Gradually, however, cultural productivity or "creativeness" diminished in these minor climaxes and became more evenly diffused, owing presumably to the fact that Mexican relations

never became established as something
direct and continuous. Since no region
in the area thus had a first monopoly of
culture import nor continued to have its
intensity reinforced by maintenance of
contacts with the high center, the result
was a gradual leveling, along with sporadic retention here and there of this or
that introduced element. Some slight
precedence still remained, until early
Caucasian times, in the region where it
seems inherently most likely that the introduction of maize first occurred—
about the lower Mississippi; but even
this was waning.

The opinion of the early French observers that the Natchez represented but
the remnant of something greater is,
then, perhaps not wholly unfounded.
With reference to what has just been
said about culture content and organization, the Natchez make the impression
of having possessed a type of organization more developed than the simple
content of their culture as a whole
called for. The material of this culture—
its arts, war customs, ritual elements—
was only barely distinguishable from
that of Muskogi culture; the conscious
emphasis put on the system of social
values appears to have been perceptibly
greater. It has always seemed a problem
how such a system could develop from
the inside, spontaneously as it were,
among a small ethnic group. It is much
easier to see it as a survival from a time
when the content of the culture was also
richer.

In a measure, the same type of situation appears to be true of the Pueblo
climax. Pueblo culture material of the
historic and late prehistoric period, to
be sure, remained relatively rich as compared with earlier prehistoric times—
perhaps even continued to increase; but
one has an impression that its organization was still more preponderant.

On the Northwest Coast the reverse
seems to hold. The patterns of the culture are definite enough, and the im-

pulses toward organization obvious. But
no single consistent scheme appears to
have been evolved. Everything is elaborated and rated, and yet there is no real
system. Active production of culture
material was evidently going on, but the
attempts toward its organization were
still vigorous rather than successful.

Northwestern climax culture then
was in the ascendant phase and near-
ing its culmination; Southwestern and
Southeastern were declining—the former
slowly, owing to long intrenchment of
its system and perhaps partial maintenance of exposure to Mexico; the latter, never firmly established nor well
connected with its fountainhead, already almost at the bottom of the descent. Reference is to culminations: the
general level of the culture of an area
may well rise while that of its climax
sinks.

In Mexico, Aztec and Maya civilizations in A.D. 1500 evidently contrasted in
a parallel manner: the one probably in
the ascendant, the other surely declining.

If it ever proves possible to find some
objective measure of culture intensity
other than indicators chosen from
among its contents as suggested above,
the relative strength of the two factors
of cultural evolution and devolution
would be computable, and the history
of nonhistoric peoples and cultures
could be better projected than now
when feeling or intuition is our chief
guidance.

Parallels with historic civilizations
suggest themselves. Wherever one of
these attained a clearly recognizable culmination, this seems to have corre-
sponded essentially with a period of successful organization of culture content—
organization in part into a conscious
system of ideas, but especially into an
integrated nexus of styles, standards,
and values. Before the culmination, the
absorption or development of culture
material was apparently outstripping its

organization into new values, as in Greece from 800 to 500 B.C. At the culmination, organization overtook and mastered content: the value-system of the culture was set. After the culmination, there followed a period at first usually of continued production or assimilation of material, but this soon slackened, while organization, though more and more limited to revision or perpetuation of the value-system, continued to be maintained: as in Greece after 200 B.C.

Ancient Egypt is now well enough known to show the same cycle in outline. The specific developmental process must have been under way by 4000 B.C. The culmination was reached soon after 3000, perhaps around 2600. After that, consolidation prevailed. This brought its benefits, and the greatest realm extension, wealth, and perhaps population were not attained until 1500. New culture material also continued to be taken in and assimilated: bronze, iron, the horse, and so on. But the standards and values had been essentially settled on by about 2600, and altered relatively little after that. Art, writing, architecture, religion, remained cast in the familiar molds. These molds largely survived the political breakup after 1100, and the first foreign conquests. Even Greek domination did not more than partly obliterate the old patterns, and it required several additional centuries of strong Roman and Christian influence, in part even the Arab shock, to reduce the obsolescent survivals to extinction.

Flinders Petrie has gone so far with the concept of cultural cycle as to try to determine the respective moments of culmination of the several aspects of a number of civilizations, and to derive from these a recurrent pattern. Climax attainment in sculpture precedes that in painting, for instance; literature also comes early; science and wealth reach their peaks late in each cycle, he argues, specifying both achievements and dates

for each civilization. He is at times so peremptorily immediate in his judgments, and so individualistic in his chronology, that his essay has won little following. Even in those who might be interested in his idea, distrust has probably been aroused by the drastic handling of facts. Nevertheless, art or literature or both do seem to culminate earlier than mechanical science, wealth, and population in the Egyptian, classic Mediterranean, and Occidental civilizations, probably in Chinese, Indian, and Mesopotamian also, and there is no clear example of a reversal of order. The indication thus is that Petrie may have got some hold on a general principle of culture growth.

In native America both literature and science were relatively undeveloped and are imperfectly known. Art, however, attained to some high developments, and its recovered specimens have generally been sedulously preserved. It is possible, therefore, to take this part of Petrie's scheme—that the culmination of art tends to come early in the history of a culture—and to test it against the inferences on developmental phases reached on other grounds in the foregoing pages. In short, the hypothesis, based on precedent in the Old World, is that a culture with a flourishing art would still be in the ascendant phase; one with a decaying or dead art, at its peak or in the descendant.

The Maya culture fits perfectly. All the known great sculpture of highest fine-art value comes in the Old period, before A.D. 900 by the usual reckoning. The semigeometric architectural decoration, the Toltec-influenced reliefs and frescoes of Chichen, and the codex illustrations of the Late period cannot begin to compare in quality with the Old Maya art. And yet calendar, script, religion, architecture, kept their essential forms more than half a thousand years longer.

In the valley of Mexico and environs,

decision upon what is earlier and later among many pieces of art is more difficult. There may have been successive and more or less discrete pulses of Toltecan and of Aztecan period. Still, one would be inclined to doubt the essential separateness of these on the same spot: Old World precedent is too uniformly to the contrary. With the two periods reckoned as parts of one culture growth, we have left, in sculpture, a number of specimens that can be pretty positively assigned to each. Among these, precedence in aesthetic merit almost certainly goes to the "Aztec" examples. This culture, then, by hypothesis, would still have been in or near the ascending phase at its discovery.

The lesser Mexican cultures like the Zapotec and Totonac are too little known, so far as time development is concerned, to make their discussion in this connection profitable. To pass to South America, however, we have in Peru a partial fit to theory. The Late or Inca culture was evidently the richest attained there, in totality of content as expressed by number of inventions or known devices. Quipu, balance, roads, suspension bridges, bronze, for instance, are either Late only or not known to be Early. Easily the best sculpture, however, is that of Tiahuanaco, the finer and still earlier sculpture of Chavín, and, if clay modeling be included, the pre-Tiahuanaco Early Chimú pottery. All these date long before the Incas. This is not a wholly comparable illustration, because the Early cultures in which the arts culminated were markedly local or provincial, Inca culture essentially pan-Peruvian. It is conceivable that this Late civilization marked the beginning of a new era on a wider areal basis, and that this was still so new that its pure art had not begun to develop. This suggestion, however, leads to a number of counterconsiderations, which are too complicated to follow up here. It does remain a fact that Inca sculpture is inferior to the best Early Peruvian sculpture, and that where a local art, like that of Chimú pottery, can be traced consecutively, the summit of aesthetic quality is Early (Mochica), whereas variety, elegance, and geographical spread culminate in Late Chimú times.

In the Southwest, plastic and pictorial art never reached even moderate achievements, but the history of pottery is well known. The finest types are generally considered to be the Mimbres and the Sikyatki wares, with which some would rank certain of the San Juan black-on-white styles. These all fall in Pueblo period 3 or early 4. Post-Spanish wares are generally deteriorated, except for very recent Caucasian-stimulated renaissances. This accords with the general recognition of period 3 as the Great Pueblo period—great with reference to its values. In quantitative richness of total culture content, periods 4 and 5 perhaps equal or surpass it: for instance, there are no positive indications of masks in the prehistoric periods; and it is hard to believe that any ancient town maintained rituals so elaborately organized as those of modern Zuni. The content and system of the culture have been well maintained; its best art has been dead several centuries. Here, then, is another illustration of fit to hypothesis.

In eastern North America art was at a low level at the time of discovery. The finest specimens all seem prehistoric; pottery trophy heads in Arkansas, incised shell gorgets from about Tennessee, Hopewell culture ornaments of copper, mica, and bone in Ohio. None of these productions rises to the level of a great art; but a number evince both skill and feeling in a definite, rather unique style. This agrees with the interpretation, advanced above, of Mississippi Valley culture—as a growth that reached its modest peak some centuries before Caucasian advent, and had then spread and shallowed, with fragmentary persistences like those among the Natchez. These, however, were essentially organizational and unaccompanied by aesthetic productivity. The somewhat scattered and diverse art achievements point to provincial and transient flowerings.

Northwest Coast art, on the other hand, was fairly flourishing when discovered, and was evidently stimulated to higher quality by its first Caucasian contacts. The archaeological remains in the area are cruder, and none of them shows the full style of the historic period. To be sure, they are rather scant; but in view of the unanimously simple quality of such specimens as there are, their fewness itself argues a lack of aesthetic vigor. Here, then, an active and successful art exists in a culture which on other grounds has been construed as still in its growth phase.

The tantalizing and fundamental subject of cultural phase can hardly be pursued farther here, for a variety of reasons, among them the outstanding one that the exactest determinations of period can obviously be made best on datable and therefore documentary materials. What I have tried to show is that both in art and in degree of systematization the more outstanding American cultures seem to conform to a general pattern of culture growth, the outlines of which gleam through the known historic civilizations. Further, the very concept of climax, or, if one will, culture center, involves not only the focus of an area but also a culmination in time. Through the climax, accordingly, geography and history are brought into relation; or, at any rate, the areal and temporal aspects of culture cannot be really related unless consideartion is accorded to climax. This view has guided me in the present work—which in turn, I trust, validates the view by its concrete exemplifications.

44. STIMULUS DIFFUSION
1940

I PROPOSE to discuss a particular form of the widely occurring process of diffusion or spread of cultural material. Diffused culture material often contains concrete or specific elements by which the fact of diffusion can be subsequently recognized even in the absence of a record of the event. In some cases it happens that the diffusion is definitely piecemeal; only fragments of a larger complex or system reach the affected culture or are accepted by it. In this event the fragments or isolated items may be put into an entirely new context in the culture which they enter. Such partial bits may diffuse more widely than the patterns or systems or complexes of which they form a part. In the interinfluencing of cultures, it must frequently happen that a new item or specific trait fills some need or is of obvious advantage in a culture which has not previously possessed it; or at any rate that there is nothing already established with which it would have to compete for acceptance. On the other hand, a system or pattern, being a larger thing, is more likely to encounter a corresponding system already in operation. Even if much of a system is of such a nature that the receiving culture might be hospitable or neutral toward it, there may be items within the system which the receiving culture will resist with sufficient vigor to preclude acceptance of the system as a whole.

The type of diffusion which I am now about to examine is in some ways of an opposite kind. It occurs in situations where a system or pattern as such encounters no resistance to its spread but where there are difficulties in regard to the transmission of the concrete content of the system. In this case it is the idea of the complex or system which is accepted, but it remains for the receiving culture to develop a new content. This somewhat special process might therefore be called "idea diffusion" or "stimulus diffusion."

Obviously this process is one which will ordinarily leave a minimum of historical evidence. In a great many cases in history, as just pointed out, evidence as to the process of diffusion is much more scant than of the effects. In other words, much diffusion takes place below the surface of historical record. The evidence for it is therefore indirect or inferred, although the conclusions may be none the less indubitable. With idea diffusion the situation is different, because while systems or complexes in two or more cultures may correspond in functional effect, the specific items of cultural content, upon which historians ordinarily rely in proving connection, are likely to be few or even wholly absent. Positive proofs of the operation of idea diffusion are therefore, in the nature of the case, difficult to secure long after the act, or wherever the historical record is not quite full. Theoretically they would be best observed in contemporary culture, were it not that the culture historian necessarily lacks perspective in interpreting the contemporary; he cannot discriminate, in the flux that surrounds him, which features will develop and lead to further effects, and which will prove to have been only transient fluctuations or abortive starts.

Fortunately, however, we possess a few cases that are at least near-contemporary and supported by a fair degree of factual evidence.

1. One of these instances concerns

344

the invention of porcelain in Europe in the early eighteenth century. Chinese porcelain had been coming to Europe for nearly two hundred years and naturally excited admiration. A definite goal was accordingly set: to produce porcelain without the heavy expense of import from China. The problem was to find the necessary materials at home and to develop the required technical skills. After a considerable period of conscious experimentation the necessary kaolin deposits were discovered, first in Germany and then elsewhere in Europe, and the specific technologies needed were developed.[1] The consequence is that we have here what from one angle is nothing else than an invention. Superficially it is a "parallel," in the technical language of ethnology. However, it is equally significant that the invention, although original so far as Europeans were concerned, was not really independent. A goal or objective was set by something previously existing in another culture; the originality was limited to achieving the mechanisms by which this goal could be attained. If it were not for the pre-existence of Chinese porcelain, and the fact of its having reached Europe, there is no reason to believe that Europeans would have invented porcelain in the eighteenth century, and perhaps not until much later, if at all.

2. Another historic example is furnished by the invention of the so-called "alphabet," really a syllabary, for the Cherokee language by Sequoya, or John Gist or Guest or Guess, about 1821.[2] Although part white in blood, he grew up without knowledge of English and without schooling. He did become impressed with the advantages which writing gave to the whites and resolved to provide the Indians with a corresponding instrument. The result was his singlehanded creation of a new system of writing. In this he discarded the alphabetic character of English writing and substituted a syllabic one. It is not

clear why he made the substitution. It is true that a syllabary more easily represents the Cherokee language than a syllabary would represent English, because Cherokee lacks the heavy consonant accumulations so characteristic of English. However, the fact that syllabic writing did readily represent Cherokee satisfactorily is in itself no reason which enforced the choice of the syllabic system, for modern linguists have no difficulty whatever in writing Cherokee with a suitable alphabet. It is therefore possible that Sequoya's choice of a syllabic system, which involved a change from his model, rests upon a psychological fact, namely, that nonliterate peoples have again and again been found able to syllabify their words on request, that is, to break them up without difficulty into their constituent syllables, but are in general unable to break up the syllables further into the constituent elemental sounds or phonemes. They can of course be taught to do the latter, but rarely if ever make the analysis spontaneously.

Sequoya's choice also constitutes rather strong internal evidence that, while he had picked up some facts about the system of English letters—he is said to have had a spelling-book in his house —his knowledge remained so deficient that he had not grasped the alphabetic principle. If he had, he would almost certainly have applied this principle with such minor modifications as seemed to him desirable to make it fit the sounds of Cherokee. At any rate the degree to which culture conditions the individual makes it possible, if not probable, that this is what would have happened if Sequoya had started with adequate control of English writing. He would in that case have been no more than an adapter or applier—a sort of supplementary inventor. That he altered the basic principle of writing stamps him as a person of originality capable of a primary invention.

However, it is clear that if it had not been for the presence of writing in the Caucasian civilization with which he was in contact, Sequoya would certainly never have had the objective or goal of a system of writing arise in his mind. In this sense his original invention was dependent upon culture contact and is an example of diffusion as well as of invention. It seems that this case exemplifies very well the appropriateness of the terms "stimulus diffusion" and "idea diffusion."

Moreover, we have tangible evidence that diffusion was operative, in the fact that Sequoya included among the symbols of his syllabary many characters of the English alphabet. He did not draw upon the whole of the alphabet, and those letters which he adopted are sometimes turned upside down, or sometimes lower-case instead of capitals. Of course he needed more characters to represent the syllables of his language than twenty-six. His system contains eighty-six symbols. Some of these, besides those taken over from English, appear to be modifications of English letters; others are devised outright, without visible relation to English characters.[3] In no case does a character borrowed from English retain its English phonetic value. Thus A is written for the sound cluster "go," B for "ya," C for "tli," D for "a," and so on.

It is thus clear what happened. Sequoya took over from Caucasian civilization not only the goal or objective of his invention but certain of its specific items or content like the shapes of particular letters; but, operating on a new principle, he "misapplied" these borrowed items, so that their value or function in the new system was quite different—wholly arbitrary, or we might say erroneous from the point of view of the system which induced them.

For this reason if we had no information whatsoever about Sequoya and his life-history, but had subsequently discovered the Cherokee writing as a system of whose history we knew nothing, it would be difficult to decide whether or not the Cherokee system was a derivative from the English (or Roman) one. Culture historians would almost inevitably seize upon the identical symbols like A, B, C, as possible evidence of connection; but then would be baffled by the fact that these symbols both have a nonconcordant value in Cherokee, and form part of a system constructed on a fundamentally different principle. The chances are that historians might therefore in such a case harbor suspicions of influence, but, being unable to account for much the larger part of the Cherokee system by transmission, would consider the case for connection unprovable.

3. It is an interesting fact that there is a fairly close parallel to Sequoya's diffusion-invention in Africa, only a little later, before 1849, among the Vei or Vai of the Liberian coast. Here, too, writing and its utility were observed by a native, Doalu Bukere, who, having in his youth experienced a few months of missionary schooling in English, set himself the task of devising a system for his countrymen suited to their native language. As the result of a divine dream, or during it, he devised a syllabic system of more than two hundred characters, which for a time found enthusiastic acceptance.[4] It is not necessary to go into this parallel case except to remark that if we did not know its specific history and if by any chance of history the Vai had been cut off from continuance of European influence but had happened to preserve their writing, its origin when discovered at some later time would also undoubtedly have been a puzzle, and perhaps an insoluble one, for historians.[5]

4. It is a natural step for inference to pass from these historic examples of the origin of systems of writing to those

whose origin is still veiled in obscurity. Not that we can use the principle of idea diffusion to assign a specific origin to Egyptian or Mesopotamian or Chinese writing, but the principle does at least come into consideration as a possibility. Particularly is this true when we find writing appearing on the cultural scene at more or less the same time in countries as close together as Egypt and Mesopotamia. The time-space relation is such as inevitably to suggest a connection. On the other hand, the Egyptian and Mesopotamian characters, their sound values where they represent sounds, and in part the principles employed are so different that all attempts to derive cuneiform from hieroglyphic or vice versa have been rejected as insufficient and forced. It is, however, entirely possible that after writing had developed in one of the two areas, knowledge of the possibility and advantages of writing was carried to the other area; and that because of this stimulus someone in the second area devised a system to fit his native language, customary thought-processes, and available technological materials; with the result that the specific system evolved was totally or preponderantly diverse from the one which had stimulated its invention. As between Mesopotamia and China, the geographical gap is considerably greater, and the lapse of time between first appearances is probably also greater. However, the system of strokes composing the characters is undeniably somewhat alike. That Terrien de Lacouperie's old attempt to show a connection through specific similarities of form and meaning of characters is a failure may be unhesitatingly accepted along with the majority of scholars. Nevertheless, there does remain the possibility of a real connection through the transmission of the idea of writing and of this acting as a stimulus toward an original but induced local invention, presumably in China.

5. Even our own, the so-called Phoenician alphabet, may well have been the product of this same process. It is well known that alphabetic symbols for the complete consonantal scheme occur in Egyptian as a minor factor within a system of several hundred characters, most of which denote syllables, whole words, or ideas without reference to sound. This mixed system had been in use for two thousand years before someone hit upon the idea that ninety-five per cent of the apparatus of the Egyptian system could be discarded and any or all words could be written, at least in their essential consonantal outline, with twenty to twenty-five phonemic characters or letters representing sound elements. In this case the essence of the invention was the discarding of what was unnecessary. Once this idea entered the mind of some Phoenician or other East Asiatic, he might conceivably have taken over the Egyptian consonantal letters, or characters from cuneiform or some other system of writing already in use, and started with these; their form however changing, during the early development of the alphabet, sufficiently that when we encounter the first preserved inscriptions some centuries later, the letters are so altered that they cannot with certainty be referred to Egyptian, cuneiform, or any other original models. An alternative possibility is that the inventor started fresh: that he invented his symbols as well as his scheme; or, like Sequoya, only partially borrowed the already existing letter symbols. If this is what happened, it would of course be impossible to derive the Phoenician alphabet from Egyptian or any other writing by the usual method of tracing specific links of evidence, because in that case the links of evidence never existed. This second alternative must be recognized as a possibility; and if continued efforts to derive the Phoenician alphabet from other writings yield only negative results, the possibil-

ity of its origin being due to stimulus diffusion will be correspondingly enhanced.

6. The history of Japan furnishes several cases of possible stimulus diffusion from China. There are of course many known cases of Japanese derivation of cultural items and systems from China. The time required for the transmissions varied heavily, ranging from about a century to a millennium or more.[6] This variability must be held in mind. It is not necessarily an argument against a stimulus diffusion having occurred because a Japanese institution appears later by a short interval or by a long interval than the corresponding institution in China. In other words, decision as to the authenticity of a possible connection must be made, in the main, on grounds other than the lapse of time.

Three forms of dramatic art are recognized in Japan; the No or religious drama, the puppet play, and the secular drama with human actors. The last two, however, are best treated as one in the present connection because they grew up and culminated simultaneously and in part had plays written for them by the same authors. As a literary form, therefore, they are essentially identical even though the stage performance is different. On the other hand the No and the secular drama are separate growths. The No has religious associations, is built up very considerably out of citations from extant poetry, and was aristocratic in its sponsorship. The secular drama does not attach to shrines or religious legend, creates its own poetry, and appealed to the bourgeois or plebeian classes. The No originated toward the end of the fourteenth century, reached its culmination early in the fifteenth, and has been preserved ever since as a conscious and cultivated archaism. The secular drama began to develop about 1600, reached its peak about 1700 with Chikamatsu, and then slowly declined in quality although continuing to prosper in appeal. More or less is known about its origins. It grew up locally out of at least two ingredients: public recitals accompanied by music, or romances chanted in a sort of free verse; and dances for entertainment.

The origin of Chinese drama appears to be very little known. Certain literary legends may be discounted. It is, however, clear that this drama suddenly appears in rather full-blown form and with wide appeal under the Mongol Dynasty. However rapid its rise, the first development therefore probably occurred before any literary recognition at all was accorded it. Even subsequently the drama was never admitted to classic Chinese literature. The earliest extant play, but one only, is ascribed to Sung times. The florescence is put under the Mongol Dynasty, with some prolongation into earlier Ming. We can safely say, therefore, that the origin falls into the thirteenth century, or at least not later than the thirteenth century, and the culmination by or before 1400.

This allows an interval of a century between the Chinese drama and the Japanese No, and of more than three centuries to the secular Japanese drama. Of the two, the latter is more similar to the possible Chinese prototype. The No is very thoroughly different in form, subject, manner, and status. Nevertheless it is conceivable, especially in view of the constant drift of features of Chinese culture to Japan, that the No represented an original Japanese creation in response to the stimulus of knowledge of dramatic performances in China. This is the more likely because the No was to a considerable extent developed by two individuals, Kwen-ami and Se-ami Motokiyu, father and son, who also brought its narrow and specialized form to highest perfection. They would, in short, more or less correspond to Sequoya as individual inventors. With the No it is not a question of broad currents affecting a considerable segment of the Japanese population.

It is also possible that Chinese stimulus acted upon the later secular drama rather than upon the No; or that it twice affected Japan.

7. There is, however, another possibility for the secular Japanese drama: European influence. The first origins of this drama are dated about sixty years after the arrival of the Portuguese in Japan. By the time the drama had developed well-characterized forms, the policy of isolation was in force. However, there remained one permanent Dutch trading colony, and there were imports and exports, naturally mainly of specialties, curiosities, and luxury articles. There was at any rate enough intercourse for the possibility that knowledge of lay dramatic performances was introduced to Japanese consciousness. Certain resemblances between the plays of Chikamatsu and of Shakespeare have been noted. He has been called the Japanese Shakespeare, not only because of his pre-eminence but because of nameable qualities of resemblance, such as in vigor, strength of dramatic conception, and looseness of construction.[7] These resemblances are too vague to count for much as evidence of connection. It is extremely unlikely that any translations of plays of Shakespeare reached Chikamatsu or his associates, although they wrote a full century later. It is however conceivable that with the knowledge which the Dutch continued to impart to at least sections of the Japanese population, there may have been included some knowledge, not necessarily wholly in the abstract, of dramatic performances. The Dutch themselves possessed a school of drama which culminated about the middle of the seventeenth century. It is clear that the evidence is too tenuous to allow of the case being pressed; but the possibility of a connection by diffusion is sufficient to warrant further investigation. I would not go so far as to suggest that the Japanese secular drama in its entirety was due to European stimuli. Certainly the use of puppets was not derived from Europe but from Asia. In the same way the plays with living actors were gradually crystallizing out of dances and recitals, as a native development, a century before Chikamatsu. I am suggesting nothing more than that after the formation of dramatic patterns on a purely Japanese basis was under way, the development may have been furthered and precipitated by added European stimulus example.

8. This case would accordingly be somewhat parallel to that on which we have some evidence in the history of native pottery in what is now the American Southwest. We possess a rather full archaeological record of pottery in Pre-Pueblo and incipient Pueblo times in the San Juan drainage in the Southwest. Unfired clay or mud with fiber temper was first used in housebuilding, then for lining baskets, then in shapes of its own and with sand replacing the vegetable tempering; only after this does fired pottery appear, and then painting.[8] If we had only this single piece of archaeological history, we should inevitably conclude that pottery developed independently and on the spot in the American Southwest. Nevertheless, the consensus of American archaeologists has been to give greater weight to the fact that Pueblo culture shows innumerable resemblances to that of Mexico. Maize and probably most of the other cultivated plants are Mexican in origin. Masonry buildings, ball courts, religious ritual, and the like have Mexican parallels and almost certainly antecedents. The mass of such evidence is so great that it cannot be left out of account. It is therefore entirely possible that both explanations are true: that the ancient Pueblos or Pre-Pueblos were groping toward pottery when they received the reinforcement of more developed skills

reaching them from Mexico.[9] Or it is conceivable that the first gropings took place in an endeavor to reproduce pottery which was known from the South but without precise knowledge of the involved skills—something as Europeans groped for a time to imitate Chinese porcelain.

9. Let us, however, return to Japan and the possible effect of European, especially Dutch, influences. The Japanese seem to have remained unconscious of their grammar until the latter half of the eighteenth century, when Motoori in 1779 started its development. His grammatical works appear not to have been translated, and it is therefore impossible for me to adduce internal evidence which might be decisive. The Japanese at any rate believe that Motoori originated the conscious analysis of the structure of his native language. Derivation or stimulus from China is out of the question because there is no Chinese grammar. Native Chinese linguistic efforts were in the nature of the case directed to description of the phonetic aspects of writing and to discovery of the tones. These were accomplished in the third and fifth centuries after Christ.

There was, however, during the eighteenth and early nineteenth centuries, a small group of Japanese scholars who specialized in Western learning for the national benefit. They worked under tremendous handicaps, from lack both of materials and of instructors. It does seem probable, however, that at least one copy of a Latin or vernacular grammar or philological work would have been among the number of books that reached this class of "western scholars." In fact it would be highly improbable that this had not happened. And through this source a stimulus, a realization of the idea that such a study as grammar was possible, perhaps even an actual model, however imperfectly translated or understood,

may have set Motoori's mind in operation to make its original creation.

In this instance it is probable that proof or disproof can be brought. A comparison of Motoori's grammatical works with Latin and Dutch grammars of the preceding century might show decisively whether in his concepts and categories he did or did not draw upon them—like Sequoya with his English-shape characters.

10. The following is an instance of direct, not stimulus diffusion, but it has a certain pertinence. In the thirteenth century, as the Sung Dynasty was tottering toward its end, there developed in China a quite unique form of algebra. This operates on principles pretty thoroughly different from those of Greek, Arabic, and European algebra, and its antecedents are completely obscure. When it emerges into the historic record, it is already functioning in a well-characterized pattern. Its development continued for about two generations, reaching its climax just after 1300; after this time no further additions seem to have been made. The entire duration of the activity, so far as is known, therefore, falls into the period 1245 to 1305. After this it tended to go out of use. Sixteenth-century scholars in commenting on it showed that they no longer understood it; and still later, it dropped out of scholarly mention. It was not until after 1800 that the Chinese were able to recover the works of their greatest master in this field, Chu Shih-chieh, partly from Korean sources.

At some time between 1300 and 1600, this algebraic art was carried to Japan. Shortly after 1600 we find the Japanese beginning to take it up and develop it further. The principles are those of thirteenth-century China, but the Japanese quickly raised the art to a higher pitch. The greatest master was Seki Kowa, 1642–1708, who has been compared to Newton, and at any rate was a contemporary of Newton. This algebra continued through the eighteenth century, in fact until 1868;[10] but it seems to have exhausted the fundamental possibilities of its pattern after 1750 and to have gone off into specialties and refinements. The Japanese had apparently completed the activity by the time they decided to Westernize.

In this instance there is no doubt that the Japanese began where the Chinese left off. There is continuity of specific activity and performance in spite of the gap of three hundred years. But it is entirely obscure why this algebra stopped developing in China before it had been pushed to its limits, and why three centuries later, after they had presumably long had access to the Chinese works on the subject, the Japanese suddenly took the activity up and carried it farther. It may be added that in both cases the art was of the people. That is to say, it did not emanate from the scholarly class in China or the corresponding aristocracy in Japan. It did not enter into the official educational system of either country. The participants were private individuals and largely of the middle classes. In both countries too the art was essentially an end in itself. It seems to have been used in relation neither with scientific inquiry nor with technological development. This concentration of the activity upon itself very likely helped its intermittent flaring up and dying away.

As already said, this is not a case of stimulus diffusion; the connection is proved. The specific stimuli that led first to the Chinese and then to the Japanese growth are obscure. But the idea of such an algebra lay dormant in Japan for some time, then suddenly became influential, and further development resulted. It is the awakening of the idea or method, its revivification, one might almost say its reinvention, that furnish a partial parallel to the preceding cases.

11. A number of tantalizingly vague parallels between Greece and India have long troubled culture historians. There may be other connections which have not even been suspected. If, for instance, fifty years ago anyone had ventured to assert specific Greek influences in Indian and Far East Asiatic art, he would have received little attention. The discovery of actual remains of Gandhara art in northwestern India completely changed the situation. Here were abundant remains of sculpture from the earlier Christian centuries, ranging by all conceivable intergradations from almost pure Hellenic or Graeco-Roman statuary to pure Buddhistic in the native Indian manner. Discoveries in central Asia uncovered corresponding links between Greek and Gandhara art and that of China and Japan. It is still difficult for the layman to see any but the most vague resemblances between a Chinese Kwan-yin and a European Madonna. The specific stylistic qualities of European and Far Eastern art remain very fundamentally different in two such pieces of statuary. Nevertheless the archaeologist and historian of art can trace specific connections which cannot be denied. This is not saying that a Kwan-yin is a Chinese attempt at a replica of the Madonna. It does mean that specific influences within the field of sculpture, and probably painting, did get across from the Far West to the Far East. How far the Western influences are responsible for the beginnings of plastic art in India and China, and how far they merely shaped and colored native developments that were already under way, is another question, and one that is harder to answer; partly because historians take up most of their time either in proving the specific connections, or in having to speculate about the scanty evidence that remains from the period previous to Western influences.

At any rate, one inference may be drawn from this example: that contacts did occur and that they did have influence far beyond what we could directly infer from the preserved documentary literature. In other words, the absence of direct historical records as to connections between Greece and India is no proof that there was no connection.

Whether the Hindu drama was derived from or stimulated by the Greek drama has long been a matter of debate. The dates permit of such a derivation. The earliest Indian references are to the first century after Christ, the earliest preserved specimens from the second, and the culmination occurred under Kalidasa soon after the beginning of the fifth. The time interval is therefore ample for connections to have been operative. The internal evidence is inconclusive. Direct historical testimony is completely lacking. Western recorders would not have been much interested whether the classic Greek plays performed in the Greek Bactrian kingdom about 200 B.C. were or were not followed by Sanskrit imitations in India three or four centuries later. Nor would the Hindus, with their culturally self-centered attitude, be interested in the fact that the beginnings of their drama had been stimulated from abroad. The question has been reviewed at length by Winternitz[11] on the basis of previous monographic studies.[12] His conclusion is ambiguous. There does seem to be agreement that if there was influence it was not from the great classic drama of Sophocles and Aristophanes or Menander but more likely from the later Greek mimus. We can leave the matter there.

12. At an earlier period we find the Pythagorean theorem appearing in the Hindu Sulva-sutras. As usual in India, the date of the Sulva-sutras is highly problematical: the range of estimates is from the eighth century before to the second after Christ.[13] The theorem appears in quite different context, in connection with the construction of altars, and in a number of numerical appli-

cations instead of as an abstract geometric theorem. On the other side there are elements in the Pythagorean cult which have generally been construed as non-Greek: the reputed transmigration of souls, for instance, the taboos on certain foods, the whole cult or school-like character of the movement. The question accordingly is in this case a two-way one: Did some knowledge of incipient Greek geometry reach India to be embodied in the Sulva-sutras; or did Indian philosophy affect Pythagorean mathematics, doctrine, and cult?

13. Soon after Buddha's death monastic orders seem to have been in full operation in India. It is ascetics in retirement from profane affairs that seem at all times to have directed the historic fortunes of Buddhism. In the West there were monastic communities in Palestine at the time of Christ: the Jewish Essenes since about 150 B.C.; and definite monastic organizations became prominent fairly early in the history of Christianity, especially in fourth-century Egypt. The principle got a firm hold in Latin Christianity only some centuries later and did not reach its full development there until the high Middle Ages. So far as I know there is no proved historic link between Buddhistic monasticism and Near Eastern–Christian monasticism; but the relation of space and time, as well as of intrinsic concept, is such as to make one inevitably think of a connection. After all, the fundamental idea of the institution is a simple one, and it need not have impressed more than one or two individuals of unusual intensity of conviction and persuasiveness, for them to apply it in the setting of an entirely different religion, and, when the "time became ripe," for the institution to take root and flourish.

14. I might mention one other possibility of Greek-Indian connections of the type which we are discussing: the development of quantitative meter in India. As is well known, all Greek poet-

ry, as far back as we have record of it, is quantitative. Latin poetry made itself quantitative in direct imitation. Classic Sanskrit poetry is also quantitative. The two great Sanskrit epics, on the other hand, count syllables, but they do not arrange long and short syllables into rhythmic patterns. The basic plan of verse structure is much as in the Romance languages, where form is also determined by the number of syllables but without consideration of whether the syllables are long or short. Roughly, it may be said that Sanskrit poetry of the pre-Christian centuries counted syllables, that of the post-Christian centuries measured them.

Now the question arises whether this development in India represents an internal growth or may also possibly have been stimulated from Greece. The former is usually assumed. However, if on fuller analysis of data it should prove more positively probable that Hindu drama or early Hindu mathematics, or both, were influenced from Greece, the presumption of a connection in the matter of verse form would obviously also be strengthened. Not that a case can ever be proved by parallel ones; but the prospect that an additional connection is provable is necessarily enhanced by previous cases. I admit that origination from mere stimulus is more difficult to conceive in the case of the fundamental form of poetry than for most of the matters so far considered. One would imagine that before a new and strange verse form could appeal sufficiently to anyone for him to wish to apply it in his native language whose poetry was based on other forms, he would have to be subjected to considerable exposure to the alien type. Strictly, therefore, in such an instance we would have stimulus plus exposure. It seems doubtful whether the idea alone and as such could take root in a new special medium. In the case of Latin quantitative meter we know that this was introduced by Greeks or by southern Italians who had been under Greek influence; and it seems almost inescapable that there were non-Greek Italians and even some Romans who knew Greek and had been exposed to the swing of Greek poetry in the first half of the third century when the innovation began to be introduced. But from what we know of the general historic setting it can hardly be imagined that the few Greeks in India or the fewer Greek-speaking Hindus set themselves to introduce quantitative meter in India. The mechanism therefore remains obscure even if we entertain the possibility of the fact.

Classic Persian poetry of the Middle Ages is also quantitative. This makes four great Indo-European literatures whose poetry is built up on the quantitative principle. It has therefore sometimes been supposed, and was natural to suppose, that quantity as a poetical instrument was an original Indo-European inheritance which spontaneously came to the surface as soon as literature reached sufficient development. However, quantity in Persian literature was quite evidently taken over directly from Arabic, just as were rhyme and strophic forms and many themes. What happened here, accordingly, is a parallel of what happened in Latin; with only this reversal, that the influenced Romans were the conquering people and the influenced Persians the conquered nationality. Nevertheless, with two of our four cases eliminated, it is clear that the interpretation of the spontaneous growth of quantitative verse out of something inherent in the nature of Indo-European speech must be abandoned. If we add the fact that early Sanskrit poetry is not quantitative and that the first appearance of quantity in India is centuries later than in Greece, it does look as if the situation called for an examination of the problem whether all Indo-European quantitative verse may not go back to a single origin among the Greeks.

15. However, the problem is not yet finished. Arabic poetry, as far back as we know it, is also quantitative. We have the works of a number of Arab poets preserved from the century before Mohammed. These works show a very definite form indicative of a previous development; but all record of earlier stages has been lost. Through the accidents of the fortunes of historical preservation we therefore have quantitative Arab verse appearing suddenly about A.D. 500. Now how did such a special form-pattern grow up in backward Arabia? Earlier Semitic and Hamitic poetry does not seem to rest on quantity. Its forms are both less strict and quite different. In A.D. 500, however, the Arabs had been just beyond the frontier of the Hellenic civilized world for eight centuries. It does seem at least possible that in some manner, of which all record has been lost, the quantitative pattern of poetry managed in these eight centuries to get itself transferred from one language to an entirely different and unrelated one, and from highly civilized to definitely backward peoples. I admit that on first impression such a hypothesis seems fantastic. It violates all our preconceptions as to the imbedding of poetic form in speech medium. Further, it must be granted that in this case the mechanism of transfer to a non-Indo-European language is more difficult to imagine than between the common Indo-European languages of Greece and India; though as the quantitative pattern passed from Arabic to Persian, it might also have passed from Greek to Arabic. Moreover, there is in this case no geographical gap as between Greece and India: the Arabs and the Greeks of Syria and the Roman Empire were in actual permanent contact and communication. I therefore submit the possibility for what it may be worth. Further knowledge may strengthen or eliminate it.

16. While we are on the subject of poetical form, a few words may be said about rhyme. The origin of this is a vexed problem. It appears, apparently independently, in Arabic and in early Latin church poetry. It appears gradually, and considerably later, in the vernaculars of Europe, often after passing through the stage of half-rhyme or assonance. I do not wish to enter into the difficult problem of interrelationships between these literatures. There is intricate evidence that bears on these problems, and I am incompetent to handle it. We do know, however, that Persian poetry, beginning about 900, grew up in imitation of Arabic poetry and took rhyme over from it along with other features. Somewhat later, toward the twelfth century, rhyme begins to appear in India, and the later poetry of India, especially in the vernacular, is both rhymed and quantitative. In fact, the Hindus characteristically pushed the device toward its logical limit, demanding double-syllable rhyme and often using triple. In the works which I have consulted I do not recall a direct statement to the effect that Indian rhyme was taken over from Persia. But in view of both the geography and of what we know of relations after 1000, all the probabilities would be against the Hindus having developed their rhyme independently. Presumably the principal historical problem would be whether they derived it from Persian poetry alone or from both Persian and Arabic.

So that I may not be interpreted as advocating a single origin for every set of similar phenomena in history, I wish to add that there is one other development of rhyme which I consider unquestionably independent of those so far mentioned. In China rhyme is well marked in the earliest preserved examples of literature. This antedates by a millennium and a half the first known examples in Arabic or Latin. Moreover, the nature of the Chinese language is such, with its phonetically limited number of syllables, which are also words, that both rhyme and syllable-counting were devices that were bound to be obtrusive. A third factor which is ready to hand in Chinese, and available to serve poetic form, is tone. However, the Chinese did not become formally conscious of their tones until the late fifth century,[14] and soon thereafter, by or during early T'ang times, did add them to their repertory of poetic devices.

It is accordingly impossible for rhyme in China to be derived from rhyme in the West; and while the reverse is theoretically possible, I am not even suggesting it. The gap in time and in space is too great. Moreover, it would be unfortunate to adopt a negativistic attitude toward independent origins. All I am arguing in this essay is that independent origins are not necessarily proved because we are unable to prove specific connection by specific historical documents. There is bound to be a category of cases which are indeterminate, or indeterminate at present; and what I am propounding is that in at least part of these indeterminate situations the principle of stimulus diffusion may have been operative.

17. As Chinese tones have just been mentioned, it may be worth dwelling upon them a few moments longer. It is really rather remarkable in the abstract that the Chinese should not have been aware of their tones until the fifth century after Christ. It is of course theoretically conceivable that older Chinese was nontonal and that the recognition of tones came late because the tones developed late. However, I do not know that any authority has suggested this, and it seems unlikely for as late as post-Christian times. I will therefore venture another suggestion. That the Chinese did not develop a grammar or linguistic analysis of their spoken language is natural enough in view of the extreme paucity of strictly grammatical features in Chinese. They did, however, possess an intricate system of writing their language, and from a fairly early time devoted considerable effort, as well as ingenuity, to organizing their knowledge of the written system. After about the beginning of the Christian era Buddhist influences became strong in China. The Buddhist texts were in Sanskrit, and along with the texts, or following them, there was introduced some knowledge of grammar as worked out in Sanskrit. This form of grammar would have been both difficult and sterile to apply outright to Chinese. But I suggest that what may be called philological curiosity and interest were stimulated by it; that the Chinese for the first time became speech-conscious as well as writing-conscious; and that the result was the discovery of the tone system which is so characteristic of their speech. Theoretically this case is of some interest because if my suggestion is valid, Panini, who lived in northern India probably between the sixth and fourth centuries B.C., is brought into historic connection with Shen Yo, who "discovered" tones in China toward A.D. 500. The results of their activities are necessarily so different, on account of the divergence of the languages, that ordinary inferential historical evidence would prove nothing as to the connection if the connection did exist. Historic documentation could give us evidence upon this problem only if it happened to be so precise as to give us details as to the training and educational influences to which Shen Yo and his predecessors were exposed.

It is, of course, on the whole easier for a foreigner than for a native to become conscious of the structure of a language. In principle, therefore, it is entirely conceivable that the first recognition of tones in Chinese was not made by Shen Yo, to whom the discovery is attributed, but by Indian or other non-Chinese Buddhist monks who learned Chinese in order to translate their scriptures into it, and that Shen Yo is simply that Chinese scholar who first became aware of what the foreign missionaries had recognized and thought it worth while or profitable to announce to his countrymen.

According to the usual accounts, the addition of the new or tonal poetry to the older verse forms came in with the T'angs. This would be roughly a century after Shen Yo's so-called discovery. T'ang literature was tonal poetry written by men trained in scholarship. It is therefore entirely possible that the addition represented a conscious experiment: a transfer from formal philology to formal poetry. On the other hand, it may be believed that in China as elsewhere changes did not always originate at the top; that there may have been developments which went on below the surface and were given official and literary recognition only after they had become an accomplished fact. It might therefore be that both the philological recognition of tone and the use of tone in poetry are only common functions of such a subofficial growth. Which alternative is the truer one could perhaps be readily determined by an competent Sinologist interested in bringing together all the relevant data.

18. The whole history, the world over, of the growth of linguistic self-consciousness to the point of the development of an analysis of structure, or what is ordinarily called "grammar," seems to go back to a small number of origins. Arabic grammar is derived from the Greek, probably via Syrian; and Hebrew grammar is patterned after Arabic and follows it in time. The various European vernaculars one after the other had their grammars determined after the analogy of Latin and Greek, or of one another. Modern comparative linguistics is little more than a century and a half old and essentially represents the extension of analysis of languages first examined individually. If we tentatively accept the suggestion just advanced that Chinese philology is derived by stimulation from Indian sources, and Japanese from European, there remain not over two wholly separate first origins of grammatical study: one in Greece, the other in India. This immediately brings up the question whether these two cannot be connected.

Priority in time certainly goes to India. The date of Panini has been variously estimated from the eighth to the fourth century B.C.[15] Whatever his absolute time, Panini represents a refined development, not a first beginning. His grammar is very thoroughly worked out, skilful, and technically competent. It must have had predecessors; and he refers to predecessors. In Greece we find the first timid grammatical conceptualizations appearing toward the end of the fifth century. By the time of Aristotle the system has developed somewhat but is still far from complete. It is not until the second century before Christ that Greek grammar in its full classic form was worked out by Crates and Dionysios. It is probably significant that this completion was the work of a Cilician and a Thracian: that is, of men to whom Greek presumably was an acquired rather than a mother-tongue, or who at any rate were probably bilingual. It is psychologically less difficult to analyze a system in whose use one has not become automatic.

However, I hesitate to draw the inference that Greek grammar owes its development even partly to stimulation from the earlier Sanskrit example. The case would be much stronger if we had positive knowledge of other diffusions in the same direction, either direct or idea diffusions. Internal evidence, in the shape of apparently borrowed categories, seems also to be lacking. Perhaps it has not been looked for; at any rate it has not been adduced. And finally we have the hesitant developmental steps within Greek itself. Per se, this argument need not be conclusive. I have refused to accept it as decisive in the case of Southwestern pottery. But as a reinforcement of lack of other evidence, it must have some weight. It would perhaps be going too far to make a positive pronouncement in favor of complete independence of the Greek and Indian growths of grammar. It is always impossible to predict what new evidence, or the analysis of old evidence from a new point of view, may bring forth. Still, the situation appears to resolve itself preponderantly in favor of no connection.

I am fully aware that the principle of stimulus or idea diffusion can be abused. It could easily be invoked for wildly speculative leaps of historic fantasy. However, this cannot be helped. Those who will speculate on minimal evidence will no doubt continue to do so whether they use the principle of stimulus diffusion or some other principle as a pole with which to vault. If stimulus diffusion does take place, it is a process which it is necessary to recognize. Some focusing of attention on it as a principle will no doubt help to delimit its nature and its scope. Any overestimations of the principle may be expected to show themselves as such, and ultimately to help in the delimiting. After all, in the last analysis it is a matter in each case of how much evidence there is, and whether the evidence is construed with ordinary reasonableness.

It is also well to remember that while diffusion in space, like transmission in time, is an exceedingly common process, it is not something that operates automatically. There are selective factors making for and against diffusion, of which we are beginning to have some comprehension. There are also a number of mechanisms involved in the process; and these it is obviously desirable to distinguish, as far as possible. Idea diffusion is only one of these mechanisms,

and probably a rather special one. After all, diffusion happens so frequently and so continuously that we know more about its results than about its operation. We can often be sure that diffusion has been effective, as evidenced by internal part-for-part similarities, when we can only guess its route or carriers or reasons. More understanding of the types of mechanism through which the generic diffusion process operates will certainly be worth having; even though in the case of the particular mechanism here discussed we may mostly be on difficult ground. Stimulus diffusion may be provable in only a minority of the cases in which we can suspect it. But we do have some indubitable instances of its operation. I suggest nothing further than the desirability of open-mindedness toward other possible instances. With more awareness of the mechanism and more experience in dealing with it, we should gradually become better able to distinguish the probable and the improbable instances of its operation.

Finally, the process is of interest because it combines development within a culture with influence from outside. It contains the element of invention in the wider sense, as well as that of diffusion of a special kind. What is really involved in every true example of stimulus diffusion is the birth of a pattern new to the culture in which it develops, though not completely new in human culture. There is historical connection and dependence, but there is also originality. Analogically, ordinary diffusion is like adoption, stimulus diffusion like procreation, with the influencing culture in the role of the father; though by strict rules of historical evidence paternity is sometimes clouded. In essence, stimulus diffusion might be defined as new pattern growth initiated by precedent in a foreign culture.[16]

[Further examples are touched on in No. 47.]

45. THREE CENTURIES OF WOMEN'S DRESS FASHIONS: A QUANTITATIVE ANALYSIS

[*By* JANE RICHARDSON and A. L. KROEBER]

1940

This selection is an extract from a monograph that carries on and expands the inquiry begun in No. 42, twenty-one years earlier. In that article the basic dress dimensions are described on which both studies are based; and it should therefore be read as an introduction to the present one.

In this later study Dr. Jane Richardson and I were associated. We were able to find reasonably adequate series of measurable data continuously back to 1787 and forward to 1936—for 150 years, as compared with the 76 years (1844–1919) of the earlier investigation. In addition, we secured intermittent data for about 150 years earlier, affording some sketchy glimpses of the profile of fashion events then, and bringing our total range to three centuries. We extended the former computations on periodicity; but the main emphasis was now on variability and stability and the problem of their causes. The finding is that in matters of fashion, and perhaps in other domains of cultural flow as well, causality is less of a one-to-one, stimulus-reaction, reflex-arc type as between specific elements, and more a matter of adjustive relations between basic patterns of different segments of culture.

I. PERIODICITY

IT SEEMS worth inquiring in how far there may be any more or less constant duration to the swings of the fashion pendulum; whether there is any period of years within or near which such swings tend to accomplish themselves. There is, of course, no necessary reason why even in one feature or dimension the time for change from one extreme to the opposite and back again should be constant over several centuries, nor why the rate of change should be the same in separate features within a given century. At the same time there might be a cause or causes tending to operate toward uniformity; and in so far as there might be, the first step toward its recognition would be determination of the degree of uniformity which exists, and of the time value expressing the uniformity.

On the whole, the style changes are so long in their range, and so progressive, that there is no great difficulty, as soon as data are sufficiently ample, in determining recurrent maxima and minima. We call a full wave length the time interval from one crest to the next, or from trough to trough. For instance, skirts were clearly at minimum width in 1811 and again in 1926; at their fullest, not far from 1749 and about 1860. This gives wave lengths of 115 and 111 years respectively; or half wave lengths —one-way swings—of 62, 49, and 66 years. For waist width, correspondingly alternating maxima and minima fall at about 1780, 1807, 1860, and 1923, giving wave lengths of 72 and 116 years, and one-way swings of 27, 45, and 71 years.

COMPARISON

If we bring our six sets of periodicity findings together, we have the data given in Table 1.

We are not wholly clear how much weight should be attached to this clustering of the wave lengths of change in our six dress dimensions around a value approximating a century. The question is in how far the significance lies in the intrinsic fact of a century-value, or, on the other hand, in the nearly synchronous clustering of peaks in certain periods, which might be due to a common cause. This problem is discussed further in Section III.

One thing, however, is certain—whether or not the six mean wave lengths do or do not bear relation to one another—namely, that women's dress fashions change slowly, as regards the fundamental proportions of the silhou-

TABLE I

COMPARISON OF SIX PERIODICITIES

Dimensions	Mean Wave Lengths (Years)
No. 2, Skirt length	100
No. 5, Skirt width	100
No. 3, Waist length	71
No. 7, Waist width	93
No. 4, Decolletage length	71
No. 8, Decolletage width	154
Mean of six...............	98

ette or contour. On the average, any one proportion is a half-century swinging from its extreme of length or fulness to extreme of brevity or narrowness, and another half-century swinging back. This is more than would usually be supposed, in view of the civilized world's general assumption that women's dress fashions are in their nature not only unstable but capriciously and rapidly unstable.

II. OSCILLATIONS

It also seems worth while to try to estimate the average duration of minor fluctuations or transient oscillations over and above the major swings or trends so far considered. This would require first of all the reliable determination of the long-time trends. The deviations from this of the actual averages for each of a series of years would then give the peri-

ods for which the actual style, with respect to any one trait, remained above or below its underlying trend. . . .

The average length of oscillation, between 3.5 and 4 years, is not far from the average duration generally assumed for the business cycle. This is probably a coincidence. The value will scarcely be very significant until there are more individual measurements available for each year and until more technical statistical consideration is given the moving-average "trend" which forms one of the two variables whose relation expresses the oscillations.

The *size* of deviation of the actual average for each year from the [five-year] moving-average trend is however almost certainly significant for stability of style, and is discussed below.

III. VARIABILITY AND STABILITY OF STYLE

The question of when, under what circumstances, and why traits of fashion are relatively stable and unstable is approached by us in two ways.

One is a year-by-year comparison of the standard deviations of the means for each trait; that is, the variability *inter se* of the actual measurements which go into the annual average. This is probably the most satisfactory expression of stability and instability.

The second method is to compare each annual average with the "trend" or moving average for the same year. If the latter is held constant at 100, how many per cent above or below 100 is the actual average for the year? Thus for skirt width, the moving average for 1801 is 45.2, the year's mean 42.1, or 6.9 per cent less. For 1802, on the other hand, the moving average has gone up only to 45.6, but the year's mean is 59.6, or 31 per cent higher. For 1803 the deviation is 10.3 per cent under. Obviously this is a period in which the style for skirt width was highly variable from year to year, even though the trend is pretty consistently in one direction for two decades. By contrast, the years 1854–58, which also show a strong one-way trend in this dimension, run 101.1, 101.7, 101.8, 90.8, 100.3; and 1839–43, with the trend change mild, show 97.8, 99.1, 103.5, 98.2, 99.8. It is plain that the year-to-year fluctuation was much more marked in 1801–3 than in 1839–43 or 1854–58. In other words, the fashion, with respect to this trait at least, was much less stable in its trend in the earlier period than in the two later.

The objection which can be made against this second measure is that it expresses the relation of an actual year average to a short moving average to which it contributes; also that the moving average, our base, possesses properties, in relation to the actual sequence of events, which vary according to the nature of the sequence of events. It behaves somewhat differently when it is steadily progressing in one direction and when it is turning a corner; and again, in different parts of its curve around the turn. It is for this reason that the series of simple percentaged standard deviations, or variability coefficients, is probably sounder. However, these coefficients directly express only the variability or instability within one year: how much the several fashion plates for 1801 differ from one another, for example; instability over several years must be inferred by comparison. The annual deviations from the moving average directly express variability within a span of years. We therefore use this measure also. On the whole, the two measures give results fairly in agreement. Those by the method of deviation from the trend will be presented first.

YEAR-TO-YEAR VARIABILITY

(Percentage Deviations of Annual Mean from Moving Average)

The percentages by which each annual mean deviates from the five-year

moving average for the same year—the basic data for this section—are given in full in a table [here omitted]. More convenient is Table 2, which expresses the same values averaged for five-year periods. . . .

TABLE 2

FIVE-YEAR AVERAGES OF ANNUAL DEVIATIONS FROM TREND, 1788–1934

Period	2	3	4	5	7	8
1788–91.....	.8	7.3	16.8	3.0	21.5	14.0
1792–96.....	.8	6.2	19.3	8.5	13.8	15.0
1797–1801...	.7	2.8	11.2	4.8	14.6	4.8
1802–06.....	1.5	2.6	11.5	11.7	5.5	10.1
1807–11.....	.6	5.2	6.1	8.8	4.0	5.5
1812–16.....	2.1	5.4	7.3	9.6	3.4	7.2
1817–21.....	2.2	10.8	14.2	3.5	7.3	10.5
1822–26.....	1.8	4.5	9.6	6.8	8.1	9.9
1827–31.....	1.4	4.8	2.0	6.9	6.8	6.4
1832–36.....	1.8	1.5	4.0	2.4	1.6	9.7
1837–41.....	.2	1.8	1.7	4.2	2.4	2.8
1842–46.....	.3	.9	1.8	1.9	2.5	4.1
1847–51.....	.3	1.9	4.1	3.6	1.7	.8
1852–56.....	.1	1.8	4.1	2.0	3.3	2.0
1857–61.....	.3	1.2	6.3	5.1	1.7	.5
1862–66.....	.4	1.5	1.6	2.9	4.1	2.1
1867–71.....	.6	1.4	6.3	4.7	3.9	5.3
1872–76.....	.2	3.5	3.5	4.9	5.7	7.1
1877–81.....	.2	2.2	5.1	6.6	2.0	4.5
1882–86.....	.4	1.9	5.2	2.9	3.8	4.6
1887–91.....	.4	.5	3.0	5.1	5.0	2.8
1892–96.....	.3	2.6	1.4	5.0	3.6	4.2
1897–1901...	.3	.7	4.4	9.2	4.3	9.1
1902–6.......	.1	2.8	7.3	4.7	2.9	12.6
1907–11.....	.4	3.2	6.1	8.2	5.6	3.9
1912–16.....	2.1	2.2	5.8	12.4	3.2	9.9
1917–21.....	1.5	2.5	4.0	25.1	1.7	5.1
1922–26.....	3.6	7.6	6.0	10.1	3.8	3.1
1927–31.....	5.9	5.1	7.9	5.9	6.9	4.9
1932–34.....	1.1	2.3	8.7	7.6	14.6	9.8

First of all, it is clear that the proportionate amount of deviation varies among the six dimensions dealt with. On the whole, the large diameters have low variabilities. Thus skirt length, the absolutely largest dimension, has 5.9 as its highest five-year mean percentage deviation (Table 2), while 19 out of 30 values are under 1.0. Waist length rises to a maximum of 10.8, and only thrice falls below 1.0. Decolletage depth, on the other hand, rises as high as 19.3, and never goes below 1.4. The transverse diameters, which of course average lower than the longitudinal, run about like decolletage depth.

Next, it is clear that while 1835–1910 is a time of small deviations or high year-to-year stability for all six traits, these traits vary considerably among themselves as to whether their greatest instability falls in the period before or after the long quiet span, and whether early or late in 1788–1835. . . .

Figure 9 shows graphically all deviations of the year from the trend, above a certain magnitude. This magnitude has been chosen so that the number of large deviations represented would be about the same for each of the six dimensions. Convenient values are 3 per cent for No. 2, skirt length; 6 per cent for No. 3, waist length; and 12 per cent for the others. These are designated in the figure as "fluctuation units." For instance, for trait No. 4, decolletage depth, the year-from-trend percentage deviations beginning in 1788 are 3.5, 12.0, 19.4, 32.2, 8.9, 47.0. In terms of 12 per cent units, these equal 0, 1, 1, 2, ·0, 3; and they are entered by as many crosses on the vertical line denoting dimension No. 4 in the figure.

The number of crosses in this figure is approximately the same for the six traits, as shown in the accompanying tabulation.

Dimension	No. of Fluctuation Units	No. of Years in Which These Occur.
2..........	16	13
3..........	28	23
4..........	24	19
5..........	29	22
7..........	21	18
8..........	23	22

That there is a relation between large year-to-year fluctuations and wave crests or troughs is clear from Figure 9, as compared with [detailed Table 8 of original monograph, omitted here, but approximately summarized in] Figures 10–12. It is however also clear that the relation is by no means simple or complete. Sometimes the fluctuations pile up in the years immediately surrounding a peak; thus, for dimension 2, around peak of 1927. In other cases, the fluctuations are most extreme some years before or after: dimension 3, peak in 1817 (see Fig. 11); 4, 1803; 5, 1926 (Fig. 10); 7, 1807, 1923 (Fig. 11). Several times the fluctuations cluster continuously (Fig. 9) between a near-by crest and trough (Figs. 10, 12): dimension 4, 1788–1803; 5, 1915–26; 8, 1795–1832. On the other hand, there are crests without any accompanying marked annual fluctuations: dimension 2, 1860, 1903; 3, 1903, 1917; 4, 1841, 1868; 7, 1860; and smaller clusters of fluctuations remote from any peak: dimension 8, 1897–1903 (Figs. 9, 12).

Essentially, each larger fluctuation represents a one-year reversal of the current five-year trend. Periods of many accentuated fluctuations therefore are periods in which style is, as it were, two-minded or under strain; even though it may be moving rapidly in a certain direction, the movement is meeting with resistance. Periods of only minor fluctuation, on the contrary, may be construed as times in which style is progressing harmoniously and wholemindedly, whether the change be rapid or slow. It is clear that 1840–1900 was such a period of harmony, although it attained maxima in fulness of skirt and slenderness of waist and near-maxima in length of skirt and both long and high waistedness. Table 3 summarizes these differences by both five- and fifteen-year intervals.

It will be seen that the pre-1836 period of unsettlement is really double. The fluctuations are most marked and most numerous before 1800, then di-

Fɪɢ. 9.—Frequency of deviations from five-year moving-average trend, by fluctuation units per year, 1788–1934.

minish, to resume again after 1815 and straggle along until about 1835 (Table 3 and Fig. 9). In historical terms, the Revolution-Directoire epoch was highly unstable, the Empire fairly settled, the twenty years after Moscow and Waterloo unsettled again. By 1830 quiet was impending, and 1848 was well within a long calm.

Unsettlement began again, in one feature, about 1900; became acute in another in 1911; in still others about 1920, 1923, 1930. By 1933 it had definitely diminished, except possibly in one feature: waist width. It is evident that the beginning of the era is pre-World War [I], its peak post-World War [I]. Only in one trait, skirt diameter, do the greatest fluctuations occur during the war itself. The specific cause of this exception seems to be a sharp reversal about 1915 in a narrowing trend which had come to a preliminary peak in 1912, but did not reach its extreme until 1926. This extreme was reached and passed with much less wobbling.

If we compare the two eras of frequent annual reversals, it is apparent that the earlier, 1788–1837, is more accentuated and may prove to have been longer—at any rate if the quieting-down since 1932 [proves to] continue after 1936. Fluctuations in all waist and decolletage dimensions are definitely more marked during the earlier unsettled era; in skirt proportions, during the later. This difference is of interest because the Napoleonic period also attained sharp climaxes in shortness and narrowness of skirt—but rather peacefully, so to speak, as compared with the 1926–27 climaxes. It would seem as if 1811–14 manipulated the skirt as far as it could without basically questioning its nature, whereas 1926–27 was calling its very existence into question—temporarily trying to rupture the basic pattern of skirt, so to speak. The earlier era was somewhat similarly, though on the whole less acutely, disturbed about waist and de-

TABLE 3

FREQUENCY OF FLUCTUATION UNITS, 1788–1934

(As per Fig. 9)

Period	In 5-Year Periods	In 15-Year Periods
1788–91	14	37 (14 years)*
1792–96	17	
1797–1801	6	
1802–6	8	19
1807–11	6	
1812–16	5	
1817–21	13	25
1822–26	6	
1827–31	6	
1832–36	3	3
1837–41	0	
1842–46	0	
1847–51	0	1
1852–56	0	
1857–61	1	
1862–66	0	2
1867–71	0	
1872–76	2	
1877–81	0	1
1882–86	1	
1887–91	0	
1892–96	1	8
1897–1901	2	
1902–6	5	
1907–11	4	16
1912–16	4	
1917–21	8	
1922–26	12	29 (13 years)†
1927–31	12	
1932–34	5	

* At rate of 40 in 15 years.
† At rate of 33 in 15 years.

colletage proportions. In brief, its revolutionizing attempts concerned the bust; the recent ones, the legs. . . .

However, the long nineteenth-century or Victorian calm of small fluctuations is clearly beyond doubt.

VARIABILITY WITHIN THE YEAR

This is the standard deviation or sigma of the individual measures around their mean for the year. For uniformity among the six dimensions, these sigmas are expressed in percentages of their means; that is, they have been converted into coefficients of variability, $V = 100\ \sigma/M$.

The full list of V's is given in a table [omitted here]; their ten-year averages in Table 4.

TABLE 4

TEN-YEAR AVERAGES OF PERCENTAGE SIGMAS
1787–1936
$(V = 100\ \sigma/M)$

Period	2	3	4	5	7	8
1787–96	1.3	7.0	30.4*	8.9	9.3	17.9†
1797–1806	1.2	8.4	14.7	20.7	9.5	13.7
1807–16	3.6†	12.0†	13.9	34.4†	9.4	16.5
1817–26	2.4	10.0	6.6	8.3	3.6	6.0
1827–36	2.5	7.5	9.4	8.3	7.5	10.6
1837–46	1.3	5.0	12.0	8.7	10.1†	12.0
1847–56	.8	4.2	10.2	6.5	6.5	7.6
1857–66	.6	4.5	11.1	4.6	8.6	9.6
1867–76	.9	6.2	10.7	12.5	7.4	14.2
1877–86	1.5	5.0	9.5	25.8	7.9	12.2
1887–96	1.1	6.3	10.6	21.9	10.2	14.6
1897–1906	.3	5.8	14.6	9.9	8.2	18.7
1907–16	2.5	7.4	17.7	27.8	12.2	14.6
1917–26	4.1*	12.6*	20.7	42.2*	10.6	15.4
1927–36	3.3	10.9	24.3†	28.2	19.8*	23.2*

* Highest value in column.
† Second highest (other than in adjacent decennia).

It is at once evident that the variability is markedly different among the six dimensions. Dress length, dimension 2, again shows much the lowest variability, and waist length next least. The four other dimensions run about alike; though the two decolletage measures show a strong preponderance of V's between 10 and 20. The little subjoined summary (Table 5) shows the distribution of size of five-year averaged V's.

It can be concluded from this that dress length, and next to it waist length, can be varied least from the ideal norm of a given moment if a dress is to be within fashion. With respect to decolletage and all transverse dimensions, the style is much less strict, and much more variability is exercised, within the year and within a five-year period. What our

aesthetic taste assumes as primary in the style norm, and inhibits too great departures therefrom, is the length of the dress as a whole; next, the position of the waist constriction. Skirt fulness, waist diameter, and length and breadth of decolletage are allowed much more individual variation from dress to dress.

The first thing that is evident from Table 4 is that there are once more an early period of high variability, a middle one of low, and a recent one that is high again. A table could be constructed that would be similar to Table 3. Instead, in Table 6 we give the maxima of V in five-year means.

As before, high variability tends to be associated with extreme of dimension, but not consistently so. The reason for the inconsistency is in this case clear, and will be the next point discussed.

It occurred to us to plot together the dimension means and their variability coefficients on scales calculated to bring

TABLE 5

DISTRIBUTION OF SIZE OF VARIABILITY COEFFICIENTS (FIVE-YEAR AVERAGES) AMONG THE SIX MEASURES

Variability Coefficients	2	3	4	5	7	8
1.9 or less	19					
2.0– 4.9	11		1	2	3	2
5.0– 9.9		17	7	8	14	5
10.0–19.9		6	18	10	12	22
20.0–50.0			4	10	1	1

out such similarity of course as they might or might not possess. Five-year averages were used to plot skirt and waist, ten-year for decolletage. Figures 10 to 12 show the results.

It is clear that in four cases out of six, and mainly in a fifth, there is a definite and surprising relation between *large* dimension and *low* variability; conversely, when the dimension shrinks, the variability goes up. This is very conspicuous for both skirt and both decolletage diameters (Nos. 2, 5, 4, 8; Figs. 10, 12). It holds also fairly well for waist length (No. 3; Fig. 11), except before 1821 and after 1921, when it reverses. Waist width (No. 7; Fig. 11) must be read reversed (low variability accompanying low mean values) throughout, to achieve the best fit.

Now what is the meaning of this relation of dimension magnitude and variability? Evidently that when fashion brings a given trait to a certain magnitude, the style is harmonious and well-knit on that point, and individual productions, or designs, are in close concord. Conversely, when this magnitude is departed from, the style is under strain as regards that feature, and efforts are made simultaneously to recede from the magnitude attained and to advance beyond it. In other words, from the angle of underlying pattern of style, there seems to be an optimum magnitude or proportion for each feature, when variability is low, and the style is concurred in because it is felt to be satisfying.

There appears no reason why this explanation should not be applicable to the minority of cases in which low variability accompanies low mean values. That is to say, in most of our traits the basic style is felt as satisfying, and remains stable, when the silhouette dimension is ample; but in other traits, when it is small or medium.

On this interpretation we can construct a basic or ideal pattern of Occidental women's evening or formal dress during the past 150 years. It has a long skirt, ample at the bottom; an expanse of bare breast and shoulders, as deep and wide as possible, although for mechanical reasons only one diameter can well be at maximum at the same time; as slender a waist as possible; and a middle or natural waist-line position, between 22 and 30 by our scale; when the waist gets beyond these limits, and crowds either the breasts or the hips, the basic

pattern is violated, resistance and extravagance are developed, and the variability rises.

To put it differently, a confining corset may be uncomfortable to the wearer, but it is felt as aesthetically satisfying by Europeans of the last century and a half,

TABLE 6

MAXIMA OF FIVE-YEAR AVERAGES OF COEFFICIENTS OF VARIABILITY

Period	2	3	4	5	7	8
1787–91			34			40
1792–96						
1797–1801					11	
1802–6						
1807–11		12		37		
1812–16	4					
1817–21						
1822–26						
1827–31					11	
1832–36						
1837–41					11	
1842–46						
1847–51						
1852–56						
1857–61						
1862–66						
1867–71						
1872–76						
1877–81						
1882–86						
1887–91						
1892–96						
1897–1901						
1902–6						
1907–11						
1912–16						
1917–21	5			44		
1922–26		16				
1927–31						
1932–36			32		20	29

even if it constricts unnaturally, provided it comes at or near the natural waist. Skirts on the other hand cannot be too full or too long, and breast and shoulder exposure too ample in evening dresses, to satisfy the ideal of the style.

However, we have not only this basic pattern or ideal style, which is aesthetic with a tinging of the erotic, but also a concept of temporary mode or fashion as such, which demands change, and, when it has exhausted the possibilities of material, color, and accessories, goes on to alter the fundamental proportions, in other words, the basic aesthetic pattern. With such alteration there comes strain, simultaneous pulling forward and back; violent jumps in opposite directions within one or two or three years, and heightened statistical variability.

The several proportions are successfully attacked and distorted by fashion at somewhat different times, and hence the picture is complicated. Nevertheless, there emerge periods of a generation or so when fashion is particularly active in its attempts to break up or pervert the basic pattern. Such are the decades 1785

to 1835, and 1910 to the present [1936]. Between them, there lies a longer period of essential agreement and stability and low variability, in which fashion accepted, or fulfilled, the pattern while modifying it in superficial detail.

We have too few data to compute variabilities before 1787. This is unfortunate because most of the eighteenth century evidently resembled the middle and late nineteenth in holding fairly close to what we have determined as the basic pattern: the skirt full and rather long, at least not markedly short; the waist, if not narrow, at least accen-

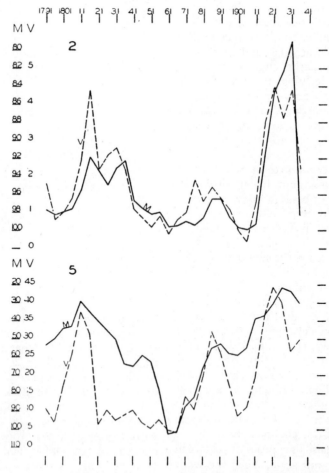

Fig. 10.—Relation of variability (V) and amplitude of dimension (M) in skirt length (2) and width (5), 1787–1936.

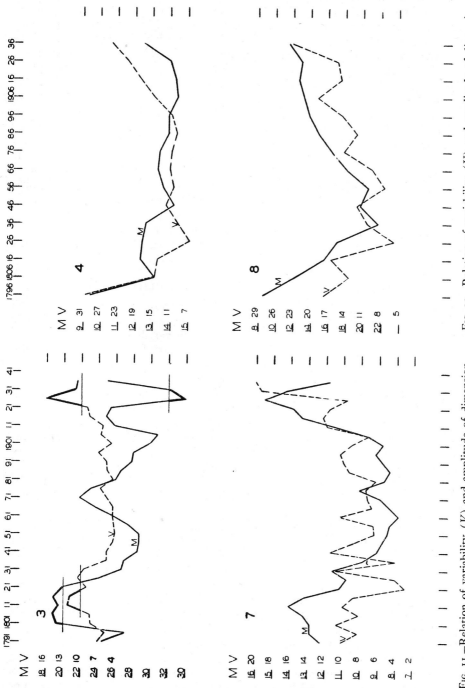

FIG. 11.—Relation of variability (V) and amplitude of dimension (M) in waist length (3) and width (7), 1787–1936.

FIG. 12.—Relation of variability (V) and amplitude of dimension (M) in décolletage depth (4) and width (8), 1787–1936.

tuated, and in median position; decolletage considerable. If our hypothesis holds, the bulk of the eighteenth century should accordingly prove to be a period of low variability, on assembly of sufficient data.

However, we can make the trial assumption that the specific associations of variabilities with crests which we have found to hold since 1787 also held before that date, and see how the results plot out. That is to say, while we have no reliably computable variabilities for most of the seventeenth and eighteenth centuries, we do have fair approximations to the points in time at which the maxima and minima of dimensions fall; and by plotting the maxima and minima for the whole three-hundred-odd years, we may hope to discover whether the pre-1787 period shows a tendency toward clustering of crests comparable to that after 1787. The result of the experiment is shown in Table 7.

TABLE 7

EXTREMES OF DIMENSION AND VARIABILITY
BY PERIOD

PERIOD (ROUNDED)	YEARS	DIMENSION EXTREMES			
		Low Var.	High Var.	Total	Per Decade
1630–80....	50	(6)	(4)	10	2.0
1681–1777..	97	(1)	(1)	2	0.2
1778–1817..	40	4	7	11*	2.7
1818–1902..	105	7	2	9	0.9
1903–34....	32	4	6	10	3.1

* The variability type of three crests before 1787 is not known.

It is clear from this table that there occur in European women's dress alternating longer periods in which a basic pattern of style is rather stably adhered to, relatively few extremes of proportion or dimension are sought, and those all in a direction accompanied by only low variability from year to year and dress to dress; and shorter periods in

which basic pattern is disrupted or transformed, extremes of proportion are numerous, and high variability prevails.

This differentiation of periods is positive in all respects for the era since 1787. It holds as regards stability of basic pattern and infrequency of extremes for most of the hundred and eighty years preceding. Whether it also holds for the association of variability with those extremes which conflict with enduring stable patterns, we have not the evidence to prove or disprove; but at least there is nothing in the imperfect pre-1787 picture to argue against such variability association [and there is some suggestion that there may have occurred a third high-variability period between 1630 and 1680].

CAUSALITY OF CHANGE

We are now in position better to weigh the several possible causes of changes in variability.

The primary factor would seem to be adherence to or departure from an ideal though unconscious pattern for formal clothing of women. The consistent conformity of variability to certain magnitudes of proportion—mostly a conformity of low variabilities to high magnitudes—leaves little room for any other conclusion.

A second possible explanation, that high variability is a function of extremes of proportion, falls as such. It is true for a full waist and a narrow or short skirt, untrue for slender waist or full or long skirt. The explanation holds only so far as it is subsumed in that of the basic pattern.

A third possible explanation, that generic or nonstylistic factors unsettle fashion at certain times, is not eliminated, but is pushed into the background of further investigation. After all, such a cause would be an ultimate, not an immediate one. It may well be that unsettled times make for unsettled styles. Revolution, Napoleonic and world wars, struggles over the rights of man, communism and fascism, the motor and jazz, may contribute to fashion's trying to stretch and disrupt its fundamental stylistic pattern. But while such an influence is easily conjectured, it is difficult to prove. In any event, there seems no clear reason for the specific fashion extremes which such a set of causes might be thought to produce. Social and political unsettlement as such might produce stylistic unsettlement and variability as such; but there is nothing to show that it would per se produce thick waists, ultra-high or low ones, short and tight skirts. If there is a connection here, it seems that it must be through alteration of the basic semiunconscious pattern, through an urge to unsettle or disrupt this; and that when increased fashion variability occurs, it is as a direct function of pattern stress, and only indirectly, and less certainly, of sociopolitical instability. In short, generic historic causes tending toward social and cultural instability may produce instability in dress styles also; but their effect on style is expressed in stress upon the existent long-range basic pattern of dress, and the changes effected have meaning only in terms of the pattern.

Concretely, it would be absurd to say that the Napoleonic wars, or the complex set of historic forces underlying them, specifically produced high-waisted dresses, and World War [I] low-waisted ones. They both probably did produce an unsettlement of style, which, however, resulted in extremity of high- and low-waistedness respectively.

Herewith arises another question: whether the crests and troughs of waves of fashion, its periodicities discussed in Section I, are perhaps also to be sought not in anything inherent in fashion, but rather in more general historic causes. In favor of such a view is the heavier clustering of trait extremes in Revolutionary-Napoleonic and in World War

and immediately subsequent decades. But again there are crests also in the intervening period. What is specifically characteristic of the agitated periods is not so much extremes of dimension or proportion, as extremes of high variability; and these in turn correlate with certain minima and maxima of proportion, but not with their opposites. The significant fact remains that high variability is not associated with *any* dimensional crest, but always with only one of a pair of opposing extremes. This throws us back on the basic pattern as something that must be recognized.

Now one can indeed accept this basic pattern, but accept it as something intrinsically tending to remain more or less static over a long period, or the whole of a civilization; and then attribute the more marked variations from it to broader historic disturbing causes, rather than to anything stylistically inherent and tending from within toward swings away from and back toward the pattern. On this view the century-long cycle which we have found to hold for most of our fashion traits would not be a property of style per se, but a by-product of the fact that Europe happened to be generically disturbed in the decades around 1800 and 1920.

IV. CONCLUSIONS

Our first finding is that the basic dimensions of modern European feminine dress alternate with fair regularity between maxima and minima which in most cases average about fifty years apart, so that the full wave length of their periodicity is around a century.

By comparison, annual changes, and even those of moderately long periods, generally are markedly less in degree or amplitude. This conclusion applies to the major proportions of the total silhouette. Superstructural features have not been examined quantitatively, but appear to develop and pass away completely in briefer cycles. The present study is concerned with the variations in persistent features.

There appear accordingly to be two components in dress fashions. One is mode in the proper sense: that factor which makes this year's clothes different from last year's or from those of five years ago. The other is a much more stable and slowly changing factor, which each year's mode takes for granted and builds upon. It cannot be pretended that these two factors are definably distinguishable throughout. Behavioristically, however, they can mostly be separated by the length and regularity of the changes due to the more underlying component.

It is evident that the basic features of style as distinct from more rapidly fluctuating mode, being taken for granted at any given moment, are largely unconscious in the sense that they are felt as axiomatic and derivations are made from them, but they are not tampered with, except again unconsciously.

This in turn seems to imply that the role of particular individuals in molding basic dress style is slight. The influence of creative or important individuals is perhaps largely exerted on the accessories of transient mode. How great it is there, has never been objectively examined, and would be difficult to investigate. Historians of fashion may be partly right or mainly fictitious in the influence they assign to Marie Antoinette, Récamier, Eugénie, and the various Princes of Wales. The reverse is much more likely, that individuals conform to the style which they find in existence, operate in minor ways within its configuration, and at times of coincidence receive false credit for "causing" one or more of its features.

The long swings of proportion which we have determined seem comparable to what economists call "secular trends," which also carry oscillations or lesser cyclic movements on their surface. No one attributes either these larger economic trends or the fluctuations to individual initiative. It is of course conceivable that economic determinants are social in their nature and stylistic ones individual. In fact, this is often assumed. However, such an assumption is naïve in the sense of being critically untested. It is rather more likely that what holds in one domain of human culture will more or less hold also in another. At any rate, the burden of proof must rest on the contrary view. And this burden has certainly doubled since we have shown that dress-style changes behave historically somewhat like economic ones—in the stateliness of their march, or trend, for instance, and in their superimposed cycles or oscillations.

The evidence to date shows that when a proportion has swung one way to its extreme and gone halfway the other, it may oscillate for a decade or two part way back toward the first extreme, but normally it resumes its swing toward the opposite. But this is a behavioristic finding, and a priori may just as well be due to cultural as to personal causes. So far as individuals are concerned, the total situation seems overwhelmingly to indicate that the actions of any one person are determined by the style far more than he can ordinarily hope to determine it.

No generic significance can be claimed for the value of a century found for the average periodicity or wave length of dress proportions. It is only a mean, though it is rather closely adhered to in three of our six features. Obviously, other features, or styles other than modern European ones, may possess quite different periodicities. In fact, there is no reason why style in general, or even dress style, should necessarily swing rhythmically back and forth. Our findings apply only to the material analyzed.

Definitely significant is the fact that there are periods of high and of low variability of style. These come out much alike whether it is a matter of variations of yearly averages from the five-year moving mean, or of variations of individual dresses from the year's mean. Within the last century and a half, 1787–1835 (especially before 1820) and 1910–36 are periods of high variability. The intervening seventy-five or more years show low variability. The available measures scarcely allow of variability computations for most of the eighteenth century, but the general pattern apparently underwent no very marked alterations in that century until after 1775.

The two high-variability periods also contain more crests or extremes of proportion than the intervening seventy-five years or than the stable bulk of the eighteenth century. There is therefore a relation between extremes and variability.

However, this relation is one-sided. For four of the six proportions examined, variability rises as the proportion or diameter shrinks, becomes low as this reaches ampleness. For a fifth proportion, waist width, the relation is the opposite. For the sixth, variability becomes acute when the measure is either very high or very low.

High variability thus is more completely limited to certain periods than are extremes of the proportions or diameters themselves. Those of the diameter extremes which are accompanied by low variability fall in some cases into the long stable interval.

The best explanation that we are able to suggest for these phenomena is that of a basic pattern of women's dress style, toward which European culture of recent centuries has been tending as an ideal. This pattern comprises amplitude in most dimensions, scantness or medium value in others. As these proportions are achieved, there are equilibrium, relative stability, and low variability. The pattern may be said to be saturated. At other times, most or all of the proportions are at the opposite extreme, which may be contrued as one of strain, and variability rises high. This basic or ideal pattern, for Europe of the last two or three centuries, requires a skirt that is both full and long, a waist that is abnormally constricted but in nearly proper anatomical position, and decolletage that is ample both vertically and horizontally.

The periods of computed high variability and therefore of "strain" or perversion of pattern coincide fairly closely with the Revolutionary-Napoleonic and World War–post World War [I] eras. Generic cultural or historic influences can therefore probably be assumed to affect dress-style changes. Sociocultural stress and unsettlement seem to produce fashion strain and instability. However, they exert their influence upon an existing stylistic pattern, which they dislocate or invert. Without reference to this pattern, their effect would not be understood.

While we have no reliable variability measures before 1787, it is clear that in the decades surrounding 1650–60 there was an accumulation of proportion extremes similar to those of 1787–1835 and 1910–36. The mid-seventeenth century may thus have been a third period of pattern strain, rapid change, and variability.

The explanation propounded is not that revolution, war, and sociocultural unsettlement in themselves produce scant skirts and thick and high or low waists, but that they disrupt the established dress style and tend to its overthrow or inversion. The directions taken in this process depend on the style pattern: they are subversive or centrifugal to it. By contrary, in "normal" periods dress is relatively stable in basic proportions and features: its variations tend to be slight and transient—fluctuations of mode rather than changes of style. In another civilization, with a different basic pattern of dress style, generic sociocultural unsettlement might also produce unsettlement of dress style but with quite different specific expressions —slender waists and flaring skirts, for instance, or the introduction or abolition of decolletage.

It is conceivable that the method pursued in this study may be of utility as a generic measure of sociocultural unsettlement. Also, it provides an objective description of one of the basic patterns characteristic of a given civilization for several centuries, and may serve as a precedent for the more exact definition of other stylistic patterns in the same or other civilizations.

It also seems possible that the correlation with general conditions explains the near-regularity in the periodicities of dress. If these largely express pattern disturbances due to disturbances more general in the culture, there is no need to fall back on assumptions of an un-

known factor inherent in dress itself and making for rhythmic change.

We have deliberately avoided explanation of our phenomena in terms of psychological factors such as imitation, emulation, or competition, which are a stock explanation: the leaders want to surpass the mass, so they keep going one step farther, until a physical or psychological limit is reached, when they turn about and head the procession back. We do not deny that such psychological motivations may be operative. We do believe that as explanations they are conjectural and scientifically useless, because, to date at least, they depend on factors which are unmeasurable and undefinable. On the contrary, we think we have shown that through behavioristic and inductive procedures operating wholly within the sociocultural level, functional correlations can be established for such supposedly refractory cultural manifestations as style and fashion changes.

46. TOYNBEE'S *A STUDY OF HISTORY*
1943

TOYNBEE'S *A Study of History* is just that. It is a careful, voluminous, intelligent endeavor to find a recurrent pattern enabling a better understanding of the whole range of human history. Its focus of interest lies in civilizations, of which events and personalities are regarded as expressions or indices. Six volumes have appeared; about nine more are projected.

The work has elicited interest interprofessionally and among laymen. Historians, while sometimes benevolent of its piecemeal merits, have on the whole left it alone because it is too sociologic. Orthodox history still regards the comparative beyond its proper jurisdiction. Sociologists mostly appear still too unhistorical-minded, and sometimes too blithely ignorant of history, to be able to assimilate the staggering mass of Toynbee's varied and subtle historical material. The autodidact engineer-philosophy of Pareto, with its formulation of rediscovered old concepts in a terminology that seems new because of its arbitrariness, has made a greater splash in sociology. In its avowed preoccupation with culture as such, anthropology should theoretically be most concerned with Toynbee's attempt. That it has not been is presumably due to the timidity which many anthropologists still feel toward material which happens to come documented instead of self-recorded, and which thus inhibits them from cultivating the fertile domain of comparison which history shows little inclination to occupy—a domain, in fact, which Eduard Meyer formally ceded to anthropology in the preliminary volume of his last edition. Toynbee may fairly be described as a historian who has consciously entered this domain with the intent of developing it.

Another characterization of his work would be as an endeavor to grapple empirically with the problem which was intuited but not set by Spengler because Spengler's dogmatic genius was able only to give answers. By contrast, Toynbee insists that his procedure is empirical; and in the main it is. A dominating pattern of thought has inevitably led him to considerable selection of material. Nevertheless, he tests his hypotheses step by step against evidence, and the evidence is given at enormous length—whence the six volumes without completion. Spengler he is highly critical of—in spite of a latent admiration—and in IV, 12, he acutely analyzes out a characteristic Spenglerian lapse of logic.

Toynbee's basic theme or hypothesis is that civilizations follow a pattern of origin, growth, breakdown, and disintegration; that in this pattern there are certain parallel processes at work; that these lead to certain characterizable stages; and that as civilizations disintegrate, much of their content may enter into new civilizations whose relation to their predecessors is definable.

The least tangible of this set of concepts are the effective processes of growth, such as challenge-and-response, withdrawal-and-return, and etherealization. These are all quasi-psychological. Challenge may lie in an environment, in a social survival situation, in a cultural problem. Withdrawal-and-return is abundantly illustrated by significant individual careers—Mohammed, for instance—but its social parallel is more difficult to document with enough unequivocal cases. Etherealization, an unfortunate word, means simplification with increased efficiency (III, 174–92); like the reduction of mixed-system writing to alphabetic writing by omissions according to a principle. There is an important concept here in spite of the term.

With these fluid psychoid concepts Toynbee has not progressed far beyond many another philosopher of history or sociologist. The historian in him begins to come out when he characterizes the historical stages in his pattern: such as the time of troubles, the universal state, the successor states, the Völkerwanderung; or when he distinguishes between the functioning of the internal and external proletariat of a civilization.

Some few societies or civilizations are wholly unrelated; the majority have some external relation. Some are "infra-affiliated" with others, through having for a time constituted the external proletariat of these; thus Hellenic of Minoan, Indic of Sumeric (through the Indus Valley having presumably once been a province of Sumeric culture, though outside its society). Others are "affiliated" through their internal proletariats. In this case the relation is through a "universal church," which functions as a "chrysalis" between the parent and child civilizations. The "creative germs" that pass through this chrysalis—the metaphor mixing is not mine—may be indigenous or alien. They are indigenous when the universal church which serves as chrysalis originated among the ancestors of the society which carries the filial civilization: like Hindu civilization succeeding Indic, Arabic succeeding Syriac. When the germs are alien, the universal church which forms or launches the filial civilization has originated in another society —like Buddhism of the later Far East in the Indic culture, the Christianity of Europe in the Syriac. Or again there may be filial societies related to their parental ones through dominant minori-

ties, like the Babylonic. Finally, there are "abortive" societies which miscarried, like Scandinavian Viking; and "arrested" ones, which lived but were stunted, like Eskimo and Ottoman.

It is evident that some of these concepts have a value that is wide even if it does not prove universal, but that they are old. Such are the political formulations of time of troubles, universal state, successor states, and coup de grâce of invading Völkerwanderung. The socio-religious concepts of the two kinds of proletariat and of the intended universal church which serves at once as the encapsulation of a moribund culture and the opportunity of birth of a new one, appear to be new, or at any rate are applied extensively and intensively for the first time.

The proof of the value, and even of the validity, of concepts such as these is in the degree of regularity of their fit in specific cases, one after the other. Specific cases, in this instance, mean different civilizations. According to how these are delimited and segregated, we have more or fewer instances, and the fit of the conceptual pattern becomes reasonably satisfactory, ambiguous, or forced and poor. We are touching here on an old problem: What constitutes "a civilization"? How do we define its beginning and end? Since every culture constantly changes qualitatively, how much change must take place to constitute a "new" civilization?—areally or temporally? This is perhaps an insoluble problem, and some no doubt consider it an unprofitable one. But it is a problem that fundamentally touches the whole understanding of culture. Toynbee definitely commits himself, recognizing about thirty civilizational entities. These are (I, 131, 186; IV, 1):

Abortive: Far Western Christian (Irish), Far Eastern Christian (Nestorian, etc.), Scandinavian (Viking), Syriac (but cf. below).

Arrested: Polynesian, Eskimo, Nomadic (of central Asia), Ottoman, Spartan.

Wholly unrelated: Egyptiac, Andean; and *Wholly unrelated to earlier:* Sinic (old China), Minoan, Sumeric, Mayan.

Infra-affiliated: Indic (to Sumeric), Hittite, Syriac (also under "Abortive"), Hellenic (to Minoan).

Affiliated I, through alien church: Western, Orthodox Christian in the Near East, its Russian offshoot, Far Eastern in China, Far Eastern in Japan.

Affiliated II, through indigenous church: Islamic Arabic; Islamic Iranic, which swallowed the last; Hindu (as distinct from Indic).

Supra-affiliated (i.e., almost a continuation): Babylonic (to Sumeric), Yucatec (to Mayan), Mexic (to Mayan; swallowed Yucatec).

Some exemplifications will clothe this skeleton list with more meaningful flesh.

Egyptiac society reached its zenith in Dynasties 4 and 5. Dynasties 6–10 were its time of troubles; 11 and 12, the universal state, corresponding to the Roman Age of the Antonines. The Hyksos constitute the Völkerwanderung debacle. But Dynasty 18 restored and resumed, much as if Justinian had fully and enduringly restored the Roman empire.

Sumeric civilization, established early, and with Mohenjo-daro as a colonial daughter- or sister-culture, reached its time of troubles under Urukagina, Lugalzagisi, Sargon, and Naramsin, *ca.* 2677–2517. Its universal state, consisting of Sumer and Akkad, was established *ca.* 2298 by the Sumerian Ur-Engur and restored *ca.* 1947 by the Amorite Hammurabi. The successor state was the Aryan Hyksos, who dominated Syria after Hammurabi—with its last convulsions marked by the sacking of Babylon by the Hittite Mursil *ca.* 1750, and its conquest by the Kassites immediately after.

Babylonic civilization embraced three states—Babylon, Assyria, Elam—and ended in 538 with the fall of the former. There is question whether the Babylonic civilization should be regarded as merely the "dead trunk" of the Sumeric. If so, Toynbee recognizes that parallel construals might bring down the number of true cultural entities from thirty to about twenty.

Minoan society had its time of troubles culminating with the first destruction of the palaces at the end of Middle Minoan II, *ca.* 1800–1700. Then followed the thalassocracy of Minos as the universal state, until *ca.* 1425 the Achaeans overthrew this and destroyed the palaces again to mark the end of L.M. II. From 1425 to 1125 is the interregnum between Minoan and Hellenic. Traces of the universal church which links societies standing in filial relation to Minoan are the mother-goddess worship, the death of Zeus, the double ax; and the Greek Mysteries and Orphism as a "ghost" of such a church. But Minoan civilization was "apparented" to Syriac as well as to Hellenic.

It will be noted that Toynbee does not recognize any Roman society or civilization. He apportions this to the Hellenic and Western Christian ones. On the other hand, he carves out of the Hellenic course a separate Spartan entity, a pure conquest-society parallel to the central Asiatic Nomadic and Ottoman societies, which also were arrested. Both his data and his interpretations on this group are extremely interesting.

His construal of Indian developments summarizes as follows. Mohenjo-daro being part of Sumeric, Indic culture was not autonomous or "unrelated" but "infra-affiliated." Its universal state was the Gupta empire, 375–475, its successor states and Völkerwanderung the Huns and their successors, 475–775. Its universal religion was Hinduism. About 800, Hindu civilization emerges with Sankara's Vedanta, the extinction of Buddhism and Vedic sacrifice, the replacement of Prakrits by modern vernaculars, the beginnings of Rajput genealogies. If the "dead trunk" interpretation is admitted, Hindu civilization would of course be only the ossified prolongation of Indic. This is nearer the usual view; though the customary if vague recognition of "mediaeval India" from about 800 on foreshadows Toynbee's more decisive segregation.

In China, a split in her history around the end of Han has been previously recognized, as by Spengler. For Sinic, the time of troubles is of course the Chan Hwo or period of Contending States, 479–221. The universal state is Ts'in and Han, 221 B.C.–A.D. 172; the Völkerwanderung or interregnum between Sinic and Far Eastern falls during 172–280. The universal church through which the new Far Eastern civilization emerged is Mahayana Buddhism. All this is equivalent to recognizing pre-Buddhistic and Buddhistic China as two cultural entities in parent-child relation.

Toynbee's Syriac-Islamic picture is somewhat ambiguous. The Syriac society begins in the time of Solomon and Hiram, just after 1000. It includes the Hebrew contribution to religion. Its rise is marked by the dominance of Aramaic and the alphabet over Akkadian and cuneiform. It is really Syro-Iranian with Syria dominant. Its universal state was the Achaemenian empire. However, the Achaemenian-Mazdaist-Magian religion is hardly given due place as a universal church by our author. His whole concept of Syriac civilization smacks strongly of Spengler's Syro-Magian, and is almost as ill-defined. Interspersed are acute observations such as that Islam subsequently developed in a Syriac environment from which Hellenism had been expelled, and that Nestorianism represents an abortive Syriac reaction against Hellenism (I, 83; II, 286)—that is, Hellenism as filially expressed in Orthodox Christianity. Syriac civilization finally developed Islam as its universal church; the Abbasid caliphate—a "reintegration" of the Achaemenian empire —was its universal state; and the Turk, Mongol, Berber, and Carmathian Arab invasions of 975–1275 were its Völkerwanderung. This means that the civilization was suspended for a full thousand years between Achaemenians and Abbasids—a startlingly unique historical concept, which is illustrated but not in the least proved by the analogy with the hedgehog which becomes a rigid ball when a dog approaches but afterward resumes its course unchanged.

Islamic society since 1275 is twofold: Iranic and Arabic. The latter ended when the Turks took Cairo in 1517.

The major American civilizations are treated passably on the basis of secondary sources. Andean society originated with the coastal Chimu and Nazca about 1–500, in the sixth century stimulated Tiahuanaco, underwent its time of troubles from 900–1000 to 1430 (though about 1100 there was a revival of culture on the coast, which was never lost again), and became the Inca universal state about 1430 under Pachacutec. The Maya First Empire is accepted as a genuine universal state with all cities under a central government on the authority of Gann and Thompson. The Yucatec and Mexic are derived from it. Toynbee is not altogether blamable for unawareness of the uncertainty of the historical record which he construes here. Our technical works on ancient Mexico and Peru are unintelligible to any but specialists. The general books, in spite of *pro forma* warnings, try to make themselves readable by effacing instead of demarcating the line between knowledge and guesses. Toynbee being an extraordinarily skilful historian, his deficiencies in this field chiefly mirror the deficiencies of Americanistic historical efforts.

The Eskimo and the Polynesian are, with the Andean, the only wholly nonliterate societies dealt with by Toynbee.

He seems to have selected them because both met with an environmental challenge—the Arctic and great overseas distances—which they successfully overcame; but then had nothing left over with which to go on, so became "arrested." Physical environment, in certain connections, bulks large in Toynbee's scheme of thought. Sometimes he goes far in accepting Pumpelly-Yale environmental determinism—his is a catholic mind. Sometimes he writes acutely and in detail as a historian eager to understand thoroughly the geographical frames in which his stories unfolded. However, even with a bias toward the geographical coloration of his nonliterary societies he might have included the Pueblos, the American Northwest Coast, the Congo–West African culture —which surely has an entity beyond Islamic reflexes. Here too there were challenges amazingly responded to, and at least efforts toward universal states and religions. Evidently the Eskimo and Polynesians are part of the semiromantic equipment which we acquire in childhood and which remains with us as common-stock knowledge; but the other peoples are merely part of the endless chaos of ethnography. We do not expect a mediaevalist to know about Benin, or an Islamist about Hopi; but it would be a happy day if a comparative historian knew of both. How far the fault of not seeing significances in these cultures is Toynbee's or the anthropologists', might be harder to judge. Some fault is undoubtedly ours.

I have reviewed Toynbee's culture entities in some detail, rather than his pattern formula; but one is implicit in the other. There is just so much organized cultural manifestation extant in the world, or known to us, and a universal scheme must account for substantially all of it. If this mass of manifestation segregated into fifteen cases of historical entities, their recurrent and explicative pattern would obviously be different than if there are thirty. But we all control at least one or more specific cultures, and can estimate from an author's treatment of these how satisfactorily he is likely to have treated the rest. On the contrary, discussion of any generic explanation pattern or formula tends quickly to resolve itself into a dealing with definitions or logic of concepts like universal church, Völkerwanderung, response to challenge, withdrawal, or etherealization, and then the words fly thick and interminably. The first business of the historian is to deal with concrete phenomena; and Toynbee is first of all a historian, and an excellent one, though he also tries to be more: the interpreter of human history.

As a solution of an endlessly intricate Gordian knot, his formula, like any other, is foredoomed to formal failure, or at least to be inadequate. The value of his book lies in the significance of its parts, and in their illumination of specific masses of phenomena. Universal churches, for instance, vary so much that they coincide in only a relatively small common denominator. What is significant in them is their pattern of aiming at the universal, of detaching themselves from local cult or tribal custom, of formulating a general philosophy and trying to harden this into a creed, of seeking an adjustment on some basis with a universal social and political fabric, and a conscious expression in a universal language which is thereby elevated also into the supernational medium, potential or actual, of a great culture. This is as true, in pattern if not in success, of Nestorianism, Manichaeism, Mithraism, and Jainism as of Christianity, Buddhism, or Islam, and separates them immeasurably, as historical forces, from the infinite array of merely ethnic religions. That there are arguably transitional cases, like Judaism, Shinto, the Church of England, later Hellenism, Gnosticism, enriches the problem without detracting from the significance of the patterning in the phenomena—inherent patterning, here, and not a formula. It is in the imaginative, often unconventional, recognition of such patternings, which express themselves recurrently in variety, that Toynbee shows himself to be not only a penetrating historian, but, what is rarer, a fruitfully comparative one. His formal scheme presumably will mostly go the way of sociologic fit-alls. Actually, however he himself may regard it, this scheme has served him well as a scaffold from which to rear a most stimulating structure of fertile comparative interpretation of a large part of human history.

The three thousand or so pages that have already appeared are too long. But it is easy to see why the work could not have been condensed without verging toward sterility. The author's mind is associational; if it were not, he would have chosen narrower tasks. Some of his best is in excursuses and subappendixes, or in long quotations from illuminating sources which lie off the standard highways; or of philosophers ranging from Plato to General Smuts. Citations are, if possible, in the original: it is a difficult book for the unilingualist to attempt. Nor can the style be called easy to read. It is a mixture of felicities, richness, dilatation through encapsulation of subsidiaries and qualifications, and slow dilatation in an effort to be clear in spite of the winding path followed. It is at any rate a style adequate to its purpose. And this purpose is large; its execution, marked by illuminating insight.

47. THE ANCIENT OIKOUMENÊ AS A HISTORIC CULTURE AGGREGATE

The Huxley Memorial Lecture for 1945
1946

THE one proper foundation of all broader studies in ethnology as in history is the precise, intimate, long-continued examination of the culture of an area or a period. It is only upon such detailed examinations that sound comparisons and wide inferences may legitimately be based. My own lifework having been concerned primarily and often rather minutely with the indigenes of California, Zuni, and ancient Peru, I take that fact as justification for considering, on this occasion commemorative of Huxley, some general aspects of the long-term development of culture in the antipodal hemisphere.

The Greeks gave the name *Oikoumenê*, "the inhabited," to their supposed total habitable world stretching from the Pillars of Hercules to the Indians and the Seres. Since centuries, of course, this term has proved no longer to correspond to its original extent of meaning. But the tract referred to by the Greeks does still correspond to a great historic unit, to a frame within which a particular combination of processes happened to achieve certain unique results. Especially, the forces at work there managed to achieve the most important forms of civilization as yet produced by mankind. The old name Oikoumenê, with a partial shift of meaning from the "range of mankind" to "range of man's most developed cultures," thus remains a convenient designation for an interwoven set of happenings and products which are significant equally for the culture historian and for the theoretical anthropologist.

Cultural anthropology is a contextual study, at any rate so far as its orientation is historical. Obviously it is the placement of items, complexes, or constellations of culture in relation to the totality of known culture that gives them the fullest significance. It is only this sort of relating that can bring out the uniqueness, the individuality, or, respectively, the genericness or universality, of any one parcel or piece of culture. It is only by comparison—often, no doubt, an implicit process, and yet even then one of relating—that cultural values can be described, weighed, and defined. While any national or tribal culture may and must for certain purposes be viewed and analyzed by itself, I agree with my colleague Lowie that any such culture is necessarily in some degree an artificial unit segregated off for expediency and that the ultimate natural unit for ethnologists is "the culture of all humanity at all periods and in all places."[1] Let this be my apology, if one is needed, for envisaging, not, indeed, the totality, but as large a sector of it as the millennially interrelated higher civilizations in the connected main land masses of the Eastern Hemisphere.

I

Some years ago, in a comparative examination of the growth profiles of some principal aesthetic and intellectual activities, I arrived at the following summary of the histories of high-level sculptures.[2] There was first an early and intermittent activity, but prolonged for over two millennia, narrowly confined to the eastern end of the Mediterranean—Egypt to Mesopotamia. Around

379

600 B.C. this growth definitively collapsed, and Greek sculpture replaced it to the west and Persian to the east. This latter in turn was followed within a very few centuries by still more easterly developments arising in India and China. Just so, Greek sculpture, having about exhausted itself by late pre-Christian times, was succeeded in the earliest Christian era by Roman, centering one step or peninsula farther west. True, Roman sculpture is not generally rated among the very great arts. But it did contribute one innovation which has persisted: individual portrait realism; and it may therefore be reckoned into the company of its betters. Indian sculpture culminated by about A.D. 500, Chinese probably somewhat later, during the first half of T'ang. India had a series of more easterly colonial offshoots in Champa, Cambodia, Siam, and Java, whose zeniths fall variously between 700 and 1200. Chinese sculpture had its daughter—again farther east—in Japanese, which flourished a first time almost concurrently with the T'ang peak in the mother-country, and once more— this time probably in apogee—in the twelve hundreds. By then, however, mediaeval ecclesiastic architectural sculpture was fully under way, centering in France, farther west and north in Europe than successful sculpture had ever before been developed; and this Gothic movement maintained itself until surpassed by the rising European Renaissance.

It is evident that throughout this sequence each new important focus or climax of sculptural high productivity tended to lie more marginally, farther out from the original center. Eastward, we have successively Fertile Crescent, Persia, India, China, colonial India, Japan; westward, Fertile Crescent, Crete, Greece, Rome, Atlantic Europe. The simile inevitably rises to mind of a spark somehow falling on a textile, slowly smoldering, and finally beginning to eat its enlarging way through the fabric, the greater intensity of combustion being always where the flame has reached only just lately, until the spatial frame of the cultural web is reached with, so to speak, the oceans.

In presenting this picture of the spread of high-value sculpture, I observed that it was also the outline of the history of higher civilization;[3] and in an accentuated form—because sculpture as a single, limited activity ought to epitomize more sharply than the multiple composite of total culture. However, the same profile of events with its centrifugal trend recurs in other cultural productivities that are conveniently isolable—painting, for instance, and drama,[4] and science, and probably technology—though in some cases the story begins later than for sculpture, and in others the early record is preserved only fragmentarily. Thus it is only lately beginning to be realized concretely to what extent Greek science rested on antecedents in the Fertile Crescent; and the successive culminations are, eastward: India, 500 or 600; China, 1300; Japan, 1700; while in the Occident our contemporary growth of science has only just completed its fourth centenary.

This consistent expansion of spatial range in the successive moments of greatest creativeness of civilization removes the Oikoumenê from the class of merely outworn or outmoded concepts —in fact, seems to validate it as having a modern significance of historic depth. What happened in eighteenth-century Japan was not irrelevant to what was happening in eighteenth-century Britain, secluded as the one society tried to be and self-centeredly unconcerned as was the other. Their developments were mutually relevant because both these advancedly individuated civilizations, even more different in outlook than remote in their spatial placement, spring ultimately from the same root-stock of all higher civilization—or, let us say, root-stock of heightening civilization. In fact, the Pacific part of the World War which has just concluded may well be construable, in larger sweep, as a social disturbance due to the translation of the Occidental productive flame-front of civilization—or cutting edge, one might call it—its translation from Europe across America into the Pacific; to impinge there on the most actively intense Oriental periphery, which simultaneously is also trying to move beyond its previous confinement to the land mass of Asia, off the continent and into the Pacific. Because our planet is a globe, these two civilizational fronts, sometimes stationary, sometimes creeping, sometimes leaping, have at last met; and some clash between them was probably inevitable.

II

Such reflections lead to another consideration. However we may define or reckon the larger civilizations or cultures, the Islamic growth is certainly one of their number. It manifests unusual cohesiveness and uniformity in spite of its vast spread; and it possesses not only a "universal" idea system or church, to speak with Toynbee, but a universal language and writing in Arabic. Yet Islam lacks some of the most significant features of other great civilizations. It had no infancy and no real growth, but sprang up Minerva-like full-blown with the life of one man, something as German world dominance would have sprung with the will of Hitler if it had become realized. The formally basic law of Islamic civilization is still colored by the idiosyncrasies of the person Mohammed—his greeds, his astuteness, his amorousness, his practical wisdom and fervor, his intellectual illiteracy. The religion which is the patent spring and reason of Islamic civilization is not an enlargement of monotheistic Judaism and Christianity, but a

reduction of them. There is nothing new, nothing specific to it, other than the accidents of the man Mohammed and his home town and the meteorite that once fell there. Ideologically, the peculiarities of Islam are restrictions. There are to be no idols, no other gods, no room for any Holy Ghost, Virgin, or future Messiah; no wine, no gambling, no usury, no industry but by hand and for caches of coins or consumable luxury goods. Now, how could a church whose only distinctive features were negations give rise to a civilization which has for a millennium and a third competed with the intrinsically so much richer ones of the West, of India, and of China—often successfully, as shown by its having gained territory from all three; and which is still maintaining itself? There is no parallel in history.

The explanation, or let us say part of it, seems to lie in the fact that Islam arose in the very region of that first hearth of all higher civilization—in the Near Eastern area of the Neolithic Revolution, of the first farming and towns and kings and letters. But it arose at a time when constructive cultural impulses had long since moved out from that hearth, had begun to move beyond Greece and Persia even; yet at a time when the Near East still lay covered with a detritus of forcibly imposed and presumably uncongenial Hellenic and Iranian civilization—a detritus that had long since become heavier and deader with each generation. There was apparently no longer any hope, in our seventh century, for a really creative new great civilization—creative by the standard of total human culture—to spring up in this Nearer East, among the palimpsested, tired, worn societies of Egypt, Syria, or Mesopotamia. For that to happen would have been, so to speak, to burn over again the ashes of the past. But there was a chance for a reduced, retractile civilization, an anti-Hellenic,

anti-Sassanian, anti-Christian civilization, to throw off the foreign cultural
yoke and to establish its own free society—without art, without much intellectual curiosity or profundity, without many of the aspirations customary
in civilizations—but fervid over its new
autonomy and well satisfied at being at
last able to impose its culture on others
once more—no matter at what level—
instead of having their culture and influence imposed upon it.

Also it is probably no mere meaningless accident that the founder of this
church and state was no member of the
age-old Egyptian or Syrian or Mesopotamian societies, but, to use a Toynbee concept once more, a member of
the "external proletariat"—external to
those nationalities as well as to the
Graeco-Roman imperium and the revived Iranian monarchy. Mohammed
was of the Arab nation: that people
which had then for three or four thousand years lived in a back alley around
the corner from civilization. They were
in touch with higher cultures, but not
partaking of them; until at last they had
come to prefer to avoid the responsibilities of being civilized. With that they
had remained ignorant, renegade, illiterate, poverty-stricken in possessions as
in ideas; but proud and covetous and
untamed and tumultuous. They were a
proletariat—not, indeed, dulled with op-
pressive toil in metropolises, but of the
waste places, and passionate of an empty
freedom and spiritual beggary.

Mohammed appeared and gave them
a society and civilization of novel cast.
The civilization was new precisely in
its proletarianism: its appeal to the common denominators and therefore to the
commonnesses of men; its discarding of
much of the heritage of the past; its
simplification of ideas; its leveling and
denunciations; its long list of prohibitions. The new society asked little else
of its members than adherence; but for

that it offered unity, success, power,
and wealth.

In consequence the old Iranian civilization of Mesopotamia and Persia was
overthrown as it were overnight, and
soon destroyed. Christian society,
though larger, lost Syria and Egypt to
the Arabs just as quickly and permanently. Subsequently, impetus carried
Islamic culture to Spain and India, to
Anatolia, to the Balkans and the East
Indies. But its permanent homeland, the
area within which it made such constructive contributions to total human
civilization as it did make, remained the
Near East, the stretch from Egypt to
Persia. Elsewhere it influenced, here,
some oppressed strata of India; there,
certain neglected frontier populations
of China; and backward and limited
peoples like Malayans, Turks, Sudanese,
and Negroes.

For a world civilization extending
across a hemisphere, the cultural contributions of Islam are signalized by the
meagerness already remarked upon.
Reference is to innovations, additions,
advances: it is obvious that so far as
concerns its own survival Islamic society and civilization were definitely successful for a thousand years—they probably still are gaining ground among retarded and disadvantaged populations.
Islamic architecture was Roman. Representative art was banned. Purely decorative patterning—the name "Ara-
besque" is characteristic—provided only
a lower-level substitute. Islamic philosophy and science were basically those of
the Greeks. It seems likely that we over-
estimate their achievements through
contrast with the still lower level of
European philosophy and science between, say, 700 and 1100. This Occidental Christian retardation was presumably due to the geographical factor
of distance: France is more remote than
Arabia from the centers of origins at
Ur and Memphis, as well as from the
later outposts of Edessa, Alexandria, and

Byzantium. Our insistent habit of seeing all science as a one-line development from the Greeks to ourselves makes the Arabic bridge across the edge of the Western Slough of Despond loom more impressive than it actually was. Politically, also, Islam evolved nothing new, nor economically; nor, it seems, technologically much of first consequence. At any rate, it is difficult to name important devices or machines indubitably invented by Muslims.[5] Even the acceptance of certain utilities, like printing and playing cards, was definitely blocked there by taboos meant to hedge in the Koran. This is an atmosphere hardly favorable to invention.

The cultural activity in which the Mohammedan society may claim genuinely high rank on its own initiative and merit is literature. Poetry was a pre-Mohammedan Arab achievement, with forms of its own, such as rhyme and quantity, and with a stylized content and even a standard, pan-Arabic dialect of its own. This poetry must have possessed a quite extraordinary vigor and appeal; for it succeeded in transmitting much of its form and style across the barrier of speech diversity to the Persian language, and ultimately to Turkish. This is the more remarkable in that the Iranian peoples, producers and possessors of an empire and a religious philosophy for twelve hundred years, had all this time remained without the faculty of expressing themselves in a successful national literature; but finally did achieve it under the stimulus or prod of the Arabic example. They perhaps even surpassed their model in quality, and at any rate in range.

This unparalleled Persian event seems intelligible only in terms of Arab poetry being the one vigorously creative activity of culture which Near Eastern society possessed at the moment of its Islamization. All the other activities that went into it were either crude through stripping down, or old and fossilized, or

were incorporated like foreign bodies. For instance, as just said, Greek science and philosophy were given their mediaeval interpretation later in Latin Europe than in Arabic countries. Yet this interpretation served in the Christian West as the stimulus for an independent reworking of both science and philosophy on thoroughly original lines and more productively in the centuries since the Renaissance; whereas contemporaneously a long intellectual night settled on Islam.

The argument, in fine, is that Islamic society was effective and successful because it reduced and simplified culture, and that this contraction was necessary for any civilization which was to succeed, within the long-worked and worn "heart area" of higher civilization, at a time when the crucial front, the firing line, of innovating and progressing civilization had long since moved out beyond the Near East. This inference in turn validates the concept of a historically interconnected totality of culture throughout the main mass of the Eastern Hemisphere—the old range of the Oikoumenê: not only as a fancy in which we may indulge if inclination so leads us, but as a tool which should be included in intellectual operations if our aim is the completest possible understanding of the highly complex history of civilization.

III

In all cultural comparisons—and increasingly so as the area or duration is greater—three aspects of phenomena are involved. These are, first, the cultural content, which may remain identical, or nearly the same, wherever it is carried. Second, there is the form of culture, or its style, which varies both regionally and temporally. This is the pervasive factor which gives to the culture of, say, China a different total quality from that of India or Western Europe; which endows it with a distinctive color or cast that may be maintained for thousands of years, even though it is of the essence of such national styles that they cannot be arrested, but must change. Third is the consideration of the values of the contents and styles achieved. These values vary not only between different content-assemblages each held together by a style—in other words, different civilizations—but between successive periods or phases of the same civilization. It is such values, essentially, that are being dealt with in the consideration of the wanderings of high-level sculpture, or productive science, as just referred to.

What a world like the Oikoumenê can share in common, to a large extent, is cultural content; though its regions can never share identical content so long as they are regionally diverse in style or form. This is because a style or manner must always be partly dependent on its content, and at the same time must select and determine its characteristic content, so far as selectivity is open to it. Styles or civilizations may accordingly run partly parallel and may present analogies, but they tend to remain individuated; whereas their total contents tend to assimilate, through the inclination of cultural items to interchange and spread when not prevented. Values, finally, seem quite particularly limited and transient. The higher the values, the more rarely are they being produced, and, we may infer, the more rarely do they stimulate further value production. But the already cited slow wanderings of the foci of value productivity do also seem to have a definite reference to the Oikoumenê as a unit totality. Since, however, the highest-level value productivities have a very specific relation to the growth of styles in civilizations, which we may in turn regard as particularly individuated pattern constructs of selected culture content, it is evident that all three aspects—content, style, and value—are involved

in understanding what happened and is happening in the Oikoumenê. Empirically and inductively the first approach to such understanding, or at least the simplest, would seem to be through an examination of the degree to which the content of culture in the Oikoumenê tends to spread and uniformize.

IV

Let us therefore review some of the cultural material which became shared across the breadth of our Oikoumenê, how it became shared, and what happened to it in the process.

We may pass over as familiar the group of basic subsistence and survival techniques which were devised in the time just before and after the invention of writing and of history. Such are the artificial growing of the fundamental large-field food crops such as barley, wheat, and millet; the domesticated breeding of cattle, sheep, pigs, and other animals; metallurgical processes connected first with copper-bronze, and then with iron-steel. The origin of most of these techniques is in current opinion placed somewhere in or near southwestern Asia, with a spread thence into China, India, nearer Africa, and Europe. For China, the comparative tardiness of arrival of these fundamental contributions is attested negatively rather than positively. Our earliest knowledge of them there is later—usually considerably later—than in western Asia; but archaeological search began more recently, and our recovered story is shorter, in China. And there have probably been gratuitous exaggerations of the shortness, like Bishop's claim of the absence of the cattle-drawn plow from China before the fourth century B.C.[6] This is a question which only Sinologists are competent to settle. Witness the repeated mentions of plowing in the translations of the Shih Ching well anterior to that century:[7] philological experts must say what the words translated there as "plow" really mean. An anthropologist may only hazard the general estimate that the fourth century seems unduly late for a people finally to accept the ox-drawn plow who had long had its customary associations of broadcast-sown grains and cattle and vehicles and a dense population and cities and organized government.

In addition to the basic plants and animals which have been longest shared by East and West, there are those like rice and sugar cane which are limited to southern ranges, or like buckwheat to northerly or elevated ones, and which spread intercontinentally later or more slowly or perhaps sporadically. Among animals, the hen, though first attached to man in the Far Eastern tropics, proved to be little limited by climate; but the reindeer was definitely so limited. In fact, this sole member of the Cervidae to be usefully domesticated, though its range is intercontinental also, has always been kept only beyond the pale of higher civilization, as a surrogate among the backward, and among the less fortunately situated, for the more valuable cow or horse. The totality of reindeer culture thus gives a strong impression of being an adaptive marginal reflection. The theory that all pastoral life commenced with the reindeer seems to be a turn of fancy more interested in discovering the unexpected than the likely.

The bred horse, though its precise origins remain as indefinite in time and place as those of most domesticated animals and plants, is of interest as one of a small group of culture acquisitions which may well have been made in inner Asia.

An institution shared by East and West, with the record as usual earlier in the West, is divinity of kingship, with its appanages on the one hand of retainer burial and on the other of corvées or mass labor conscription for construction of dykes, canals, walls, palaces,

temples, and tombs. Abandonment of retainer burial seems to have occurred relatively late in China and later in Japan.[8] It is even possible that the practice had been given up in Mesopotamia and Egypt before it became established in the Far East.

Of particular interest is eunuchism, which can be traced back about four millenia in Mesopotamia as a ritual mutilation. This practice, however, seems not to have spread widely beyond its western Asiatic origin. Harem eunuchism apparently is a later institution; it is found well established in China of Chou times, and may be older than that. There is room and need for a scholarly comparative study of eunuchism, with emphasis on its functions and associations rather than on its mere fact, and with reference also to the documentable history of animal castration.

Eunuchism became established in Byzantine Christian Constantinople and in Mohammedan Osmanli Constantinople, but never got a real foothold in Occidental civilization. This means, almost certainly, that it struck a definite resistance. It also never crossed the Strait of Tsushima from Korea to Japan. Here, then, we have an institution which was able to traverse the main breadth of Eurasia at a fairly early time, but did not succeed in penetrating the two extreme peripheries. The cause of the double check is perhaps that the peripheries began to participate in higher civilization late enough for human mutilation to be on the decline or defensive, if not yet wholly outmoded; much like other mutilations, human sacrifice, taboos of parturitional, menstrual, and mortuary defilement, and other social recognitions or emphases of the human body and its physiology. In China, India, western Asia, eunuchism had long been intertwined with the pomp and prestige of royalty, and maintained itself—in China until 1911; but taste, let us call it, had advanced too far in the

Oikoumenê generally for it to gain any new ground in Europe and Japan at relatively late dates.

There is a group of systems of magico-ritual practice which are now generally accepted as being the results each of a single, interconnected growth in the Eastern Hemisphere, especially since they have no strict counterparts in the Western Hemisphere, or only much slighter ones. These systems include the blood sacrifice complex; divination from parts of animals; astrology; and alchemy. The sacrifice complex involves not only the taking of animal life in religious offering, but also the shedding of blood; the consumption of the flesh largely by the worshipers, until sacrifice to the gods and meat-feast become near-equivalents; and the associated dedication, and again consumption, of fermented drink. Fifty years ago we were still unaware of the full potentialities of the method of "probability history" as it operates with the indirect evidence of occurrences in supplement to the direct testimony of historic statements. The resemblances of the sacrifices of pagan tribes in Borneo and Luzon, of Lolos in Yünnan, of backward groups in British India, of West African Negroes, to the hecatombs of Homer and the burnt offerings of Aaron in Leviticus, at that time seemed due rather to something emerging from men's makeup spontaneously, without reference to time and place and circumstances, and hence outside the specific concatenations of history. Now, in 1946, few if any would doubt the high probability of all these cases being interderived, at least through the whole breadth of the Eastern Hemisphere; and if the Americas are provisionally excluded, it is because corresponding occurrences there are fewer, more spotty, and less closely parallel in detail.

Divination follows a variety of techniques; but at least those which specif-ically operate with parts of animals seem again to form a true system. These include examination of entrails, especially of the liver or bile sac of victims; interpretation of heat-produced cracks in shoulder blades of deer or sheep, carapaces of tortoises, and the like; or of the pattern of bristles slid into the fora-mina of thigh bones. The very arbitrariness of these techniques, coupled with the frequency of the association with sacrifice, practically precludes any random or spontaneous causality; as does their absence from native America, except for an extension of scapulimancy alone across its subarctic north.[9] Divination from the behavior of tame or wild birds may be a related branch technique. But the throwing or drawing of lots, scrying, and such, rest on different principles, follow separate techniques, and presumably have only a logical or psychological connection, not a historical one.

The basic origins of astrology must be ascribed to western Asia, especially to Mesopotamia. It was developed further in Alexandria, as by the addition of the week; and, having entered the later Helleno-Roman culture, was transmitted to both Occidental and Islamic civilizations. Similarly, the system spread eastward to India and its derivative cultures, where, for instance, our weekdays figure conspicuously, not with reference to a day of rest or ritual service, but for horoscopes and determination of the fortune of individuals. This diffusion spread with little diminution as far as Bali, that easternmost remnant-refuge of directly mediaeval Hinduism. Into the Chinese sphere, on the other hand, our week, like our zodiac, did not seriously penetrate. Geomancy, the interpretation of the supernatural influences of heaven and earth, or wind and water, fêng shui, took its place. Geomancy had a different ideology and different techniques from astrology. Fêng shui, incidentally, was carried to

Annam and Korea;[10] but its hold in Japan seems to have been transient and rather light.[11]

Alchemy, that "immature chemistry of the Middle Ages," with its Graeco-Arabic name, also received its first Western formulation at Alexandria, shortly after astrology, but may be Far Eastern in origin, as Seligman has already, though somewhat diffidently, suggested.[12] The gap in space between East and West is greater than the interval between the times of appearance there. But the basic ideas of alchemy as a system of magic or false science—the making of gold from base metals, the use of an elixir not only to do this, but to prolong life into immortality, the claim to association with a profound but hidden philosophy—all these are already well developed in China in Early Han times.[13] This is earlier than any specific record which I have been able to find for the West. If the leap from Ch'ang-an to Alexandria seems long for it to have been made in a century or two, I can only plead that so much other cultural freight was evidently, first and last, carried over this route, and some of it at almost express speeds, that absence of knowledge of the intermediate stations, of the rate of transmittal, or of the associations or manner of the spread —such ignorance is not too serious a deterrent of acceptance of the connection as more probably indicated than not, in view of the high incompleteness of the total record in the premises anyhow.

It has often been remarked that the period of the sixth century B.C.—or possibly a two- to three-hundred-year block inclosing some point in that century—produced Lao Tze and Confucius, Buddha and probably Zoroaster, as well as Thales and his nearer successors in Greek philosophy to Plato. Also it is clear that by 200 B.C. creativeness was either definitely past or rapidly ending

in all these growths. The reason for the coincidence might be, first, "accidental"; that is, diverse causes happening to produce similar effects contemporaneously. Second, it might be some as yet undefined, underlying major current or immanence, which would be akin to a telic destiny. Third, it might be a specific antecedent which had not long before managed to become realized in all the areas—say, something on the order of the establishment of letters, though the chronology of that example does not too well fit the case. Fourth, there might have been a direct spread, by contagion, of a spirit of inquiry, of an attitude demanding a reasoned system of thinking instead of the medley which traditionalism has a way of accumulating. It is perhaps not yet possible to choose with positiveness between these several alternatives. A few years ago I examined the first three of them.[14] I now add diffusion as a fourth possible explanation because of what seem the undoubted intercontinental spreads of blood sacrifice and organ divination which preceded and those of astrology and alchemy which immediately succeeded. At any rate the sequence of ideologies quite clearly was: (1) a cult of magical ritual directed toward the sensory appeasement and favor of anthropomorphic powers; followed in reaction by (2) a depersonalized, largely deanimized, pragmatic, investigatory way of thinking; but this again soon followed in counterreaction by (3) a pair of parallel systems of reanimized imitations of science. All three steps had a distribution from the Mediterranean to the Pacific. If the first and third were due to diffusion, as perhaps will be generally accepted, there would be some presumption of diffusion having been operative also for the in-between phase. It must be admitted that the spread of an attitude of mind is not quite the same as the spread of a congeries of specific ritual practices or magical beliefs. But it seems warranted to submit the tentative suggestion.

V

Let us review some more specific or tangible items of culture content.

Cavalry.—We have seen that it is modern convention—or inference from absence of evidence—to attribute the taming of the horse to central Asiatics. Both to the West and to the East, the animal was first driven, then ridden. War chariots precede cavalry. The latter comes on the historic scene in the West toward 700 in Assyria, in China not until nearly 300 B.C. The Persians retained obsolescent chariots, in addition to cavalry, until Alexander. In India, though Poros and Chandragupta already had horsemen, chariots lingered on, at least for officers, until Harsha of the seventh century.[15]

Stirrups.—The stirrup saddle comes to the surface of history about simultaneously in Constantinople around 580 and in China possibly in a mention of 477 and indubitably at Ch'ang-an in T'ai Tsung's grave reliefs in 649.[16] The second-century reliefs from Shantung show saddles, but no stirrups. An invention of the stirrup neither in the East nor the West, but in central Asia, is possible, but present data are too few to permit even a probable designation of the locus of origin.

Money.—Disk coinage spread rapidly from seventh-century Lydia. It had become established in both India and China before 300 B.C., other shapes being superseded in China during the following century. As for the peripheries, Celtic Gaul was coining distorted imitations of Macedonian staters in the second century B.C. and Britain in the first; but Japan did not mint until A.D. 708. This disparity seems to reflect a general precocity of economic and technical aspects of culture in the marginal west, a retardation in Japan, as compared with the development of letters, arts, religion, and refinement generally.

Water mills.—Water wheels used as power for mills have their Western origin attributed to the first century B.C., probably in Hellenic Asia, with a spread to Italy in the next century.[17] The Chinese credit the same invention to their Tu Yü about A.D. 260, with an improvement by Ts'ui Liang under the Wei dynasty, 386–532.[18] India is said to have got its water-driven mills from a Persian sent by Constantine the Great. Legendary as some of these accounts may be, they all point to a period of a few hundred years within which the discovery might well have been transmitted.

Felt.—Felt was thought by Laufer to have originated in inner Asia.[19] This is unproved; but it is evident that both in material and in process the manufacture of felt would be more consonant with pastoral life than is loom-weaving. In any event, the occurrence of felt on both sides of central Asia is old. The earliest Western record is Homeric; for both China and India there are mentions from the fourth century B.C.; reports and finds from central Asia are, naturally enough, later.

Cotton.—The basic textile fibers have changed surprisingly little and slowly in their areas, on the whole, except for the spread of cotton from India. Cotton, in the end, largely displaced wool in Mesopotamia, linen in Egypt and Europe, hemp in China and Japan. Cotton is also the most important plant cultivated both in the Old World and in the pre-Columbian New. Its abundant growth and use in Peru precedes that in either China or the West.

Chess.—The game of chess originated in India, according to Middle and Near Eastern tradition, which is corroborated by the derivation of its Persian and Arabic names from Sanskrit *chaturanga*. The earliest datable Indian reference is from just after A.D. 600, by which time however chess is generally believed to have been already established in Persia. The Arabs took over the Persian game; played it almost unchanged for many centuries; developed champions, problems, and a literature; and passed it on to Western Christendom probably by 900. This date is indicated by the phonetic forms of the terms employed in the West; the earliest discovered documentary mention is from about 1010. The enlargement of range of the queen's and bishop's moves, the final major improvement, rendering the game more concentrated, occurred in Italy or possibly France or Spain about 1485. After this there were no further changes, except for finding a consensus among the fluctuating rules about castling and the taking of passing pawns. Byzantium knew chess by 800, under a name derived from the Persian, not Arabic, pronunciation. Russia perhaps got the game via the Khazars rather than from Constantinople. Chinese, Korean, and Japanese chess are increasingly differentiated from the Indian and Western forms. The game was known in China by 762; it appears to have been not yet known in Japan in the tenth century. Since chess is pre-European also among the Turkish, Mongol, Tibetan, Farther Indian, and western Indonesian peoples, it serves as an excellent criterion to define the range of the Oikoumenê as here dealt with. The most remote Asiatic tribes and the most backward interior ones, Oceanians beyond direct Indian and Islamic influences and non-Islamic Negroes, do not play chess. Two other board games, backgammon or nard and merels, seem to have had a similarly penetrative distribution.[20]

The further items which might be cited as having long since spread across Eurasia are numerous. Falconry, the crossbow,[21] gunpowder and firearms, the compass, the concept of the dragon,

will all serve in illustration. Let us however pass on to some larger and more elusive complexes.

VI

Printing.—Seals, which in the Near East and India are immemorially ancient—almost as old as writing itself—are said not to have reached China until the third century B.C. Within a comparatively short time—A.D. 105 is the conventional date—paper was invented in China, and therewith multiplication was made possible in place of authentication as the goal of all copy-producing devices—with the sequel that block printing began to be operative within about six centuries, and movable-type printing within another four. Playing cards and paper money were accompaniments.[22] The course of paper manufacture, and less continuously of single-sheet block printing, has been traced from China through central Asia into Muslim Irak, Egypt, and Morocco, and from there into Catholic Europe. Cards appeared suddenly in western Europe four centuries after their mention in China.[23] There is almost certainly a connection. Possibly Islam, though it forbade avowed acceptance of the gaming apparatus, managed to transmit it. Type printing also began in Europe four centuries later than in China.[24] In this case direct derivation is extremely uncertain, for a variety of reasons: mechanical difference in the problem to be met, due to the deep difference of systems of writing; difference of material of the types, of kind of ink, of the manner of impressing; and, above all, the complete nonparticipation of the intervening Islamic world. For this nonparticipation, the negative evidence is in this case overwhelmingly compelling. In fact, Islamic nonparticipation in printing soon became a hostility which continued—with the exception of one history issued in 1729—until 1825.[25]

Royal tombs.—Quite recently Gordon Childe has enunciated as an empirical archaeological finding that "with progress in civilization a dwindling proportion of society's growing wealth has been devoted to the preparation of tombs and their furnishing."[26] Apparent exceptions are "royal tombs" since the Bronze Age on or in which was lavished "a quite substantial proportion of their occupants' wealth." These occur in Egypt of the first four dynasties; in Kish and Ur; and they include Mycenaean shaft graves and tholoi, Kuban, Kerma in Nubia, German barrows, Celtic chariot-burials and Viking ship-burials, and Shang tombs at Anyang. In all cases, Childe finds, such tombs reflect recent and rapid accumulation of wealth and transition to a new sociopolitical structure, due to foreign commerce and contact with higher civilization; and by contrast the tombs of later kings and chiefs are more modest, even though the wealth of the living community had become greater. This conclusion seems equivalent to the definition of a general or near-universal "stage" of development such as indeed Childe devoted his Huxley Lecture of 1944 to expounding.[27] Nevertheless, it is also the affirmation of a single historical continuity, the spread of a specific practice which we may call "first-flush display-wealth burial"—an irregular, spasmodic, but persistent spread-out from the Fertile Crescent to northwestern Europe on one side and China on the other. And, again, it is a phenomenon of the same order as the development of fully liberated and self-sufficient sculpture or drama, or the birth of formal philosophies, which have already been discussed.

Christianity and Buddhism.—The mechanisms and apparatus shared by Christianity and Buddhism are familiar. With Buddhism originating in northern India and spreading into eastern Asia, these resemblances involve a continuity of distribution from Atlantic to Pacific, only partly interrupted by a subsequent Mohammedan wedge. The common elements include the following. Above all there is organized monasticism, including nunneries, with similar seclusion, conduct of life, and vows, extending even to details like begging and tonsure; and in earlier periods hermits or anchorites. Then there is the use of bells, candles, and rosaries in worship; the nimbus or halo in art; and relics and pilgrimages. Next, the notion of paradise and of hell—technically perhaps only purgatories, but filled with flames and devils. To this last dualistic concept an Iranian origin is generally ascribed, and it reached the Mediterranean barely in time for absorption into Christianity; but it entered Buddhism secondarily and late, as something really contradictory of the original ideology. Also, the strains of Buddhism chiefly affected were the northwestern and landward-traveling Mahayana and Lamaism varieties, with their greater exposure to both Iranian and Christian contacts. A derivative item is the saying of "masses" for the souls of the dead. In the areas of both religions, the first block prints were the product of an effort to furnish the multitude of the pious with a cheap means of permanent edification through picture or legend or both.[28]

Some of these similarities may be superficial or even verbal rather than intrinsic, and others may be the results of independent convergence. It seems unlikely that all of them are such, because too few crop up in other religions, except for Taoist imitations of Buddhism. Islam, for instance, consciously rejected most of the elements in question. Few of them seem to have got a lodgment in national religions like Shinto, Judaism, Parseeism. Again, few appear in the older Mediterranean national cults, which at least in their later history overlapped in time with Buddhism.

Grammar.–The first discovery of grammar may be attributed to India [No. 44, § 18]. A seeming rediscovery was made on the Greek language a little later. We know something of the stages of this rediscovery. It was three centuries in the making, and therefore looks like an autochthonous evolution. But the total record shows that grammars are likely to be formulated in imitation of existing grammars, and by bilingual speakers. This is clear for Latin, Syriac, Arabic, Hebrew, and all European vernaculars. Without exception the grammars of these languages are, historically, only adaptations of Greek grammar to a new body of speech–or of a derivative from Greek. Similarly, Chinese phonetics, including tone recognition, was worked out in the last three pre-T'ang centuries, the period of greatest Buddhist and Indian influence in China. Similarly, too, Motoori's traditional invention of Japanese grammar in 1779 followed on two centuries of possible exposure to Latin grammar through Jesuits or Hollanders [No. 44, §9]. It may therefore be that the final Greek formulation was also made under some degree of stimulation from India–especially as it was made as late as the second century B.C. by non-Greeks in Anatolia and Egypt. If there was such stimulation, there must have existed threads of connection running below the surface evidence of recorded history.[29] To reknit such putative threads is obviously a difficult and risky undertaking, calling for the most sensitive tact. If nevertheless I maintain the suggestion, it is because of the group of recurrences which obtrude analogous suggestions: the sixth-century philosophies, alchemy and astrology, monasticism–for that matter blood sacrifice and organ divination, perhaps even writing as such.

Nineteenth-century anthropologists could still fall back on a sort of spontaneous generation to explain cultural likenesses remote in space or time. Today we hesitate to invoke autogenesis: we shrink from it almost as fervently as do biologists. Partly this is because absences of potentials have acquired for us almost the same evidential weight as occurrences of actuals. The result is that specific universals in human culture have shrunk to be vanishingly few. There is thus as much evidence needed for an assumption of independent origins as of a connection: the burden of proof is equal. In practice, we make decisions first on the degree of part-for-part homologous resemblance of the seeming parallels; and perhaps even more largely on the size of the space and time interval, with a heavy sidelong look at the number and firmness of other threads spun across it. Yet these procedures often leave us facing a dilemma, even when the total context of a situation leaves little moral doubt of there having been a connection of some sort. Was the connection due to a conscious and specific imitation of something foreign, though perhaps also with deliberate adaptation to a different environment? Or was it an ideational germ which was transported and which slumbered, perhaps for centuries, until its environment awoke it–possibly through the environment's having been mellowed by enough other consciously imitative imports or enough sprouting of other germs? There evidently exists a twilight zone of historic parallels in which there is no available evidence whatever of imitative adoption, but in which the total precedent of experience makes independent repetition of origin uncertain. The temporary verdict may often have to be: "Nothing provable." But the problem remains to vex and intrigue us. And the situations suggest that if we knew more about indirect or delayed transmissions between cultures, and about the effect of cumulative impact of previous transmissions on later ones, many of these twilight cases might resolve themselves into reasonable clarity.

VII

On the basis of the foregoing illustrations and analyses, the Oikoumenê may perhaps be redefined as a great web of culture growth, areally extensive and rich in content. Within this web or historic nexus, first of all, inventions or new cultural materials have tended to be transmitted, sooner or later, from end to end. This is true even though the major styles of civilization in the Oikoumenê have long persisted in their individuations: culture in China, for instance, was already characteristically Chinese three thousand years ago.

Second, new ways of thinking, or sets of specific practices rooting in an idea-complex or attitude, have shown a tendency to propagate themselves across the long stretch of the area, sometimes rapidly, almost like a wave or pulsation.

Finally, the primitives in the area, or adjoining it, derive their cultures mainly from the civilization characteristic of the Oikoumenê as a whole, through reductive selection. They preserve old elements largely discarded elsewhere, and they do without elements which their retardation makes them unable or unwilling to accept. Basically, however, these retarded or primitive cultures in or adjacent to the Oikoumenê are fully intelligible only in terms of "Oecumenical" civilization. They usually add to what they share some lesser measure of their own proper peculiarities and originations, and they have often developed a distinctive style of their own. But in the main these backward cultures depend and derive from the greater ones whose nexus we have been considering. Perhaps that is why it does not seem to matter unduly whether they are geographically interior or marginal: the relation remains equally one of dependence.

For example, a people like the Lolo of Yünnan and Szechwan illustrate by the very diversity of relation of the content of their culture how completely this is enmeshed in the greater web. Lolo speech is composed of monosyllabic tonal elements as the result of being either cognate with Sino-Tibetan or influenced by it. Lolo writing seems built on a Chinese model, but with reduction to fewer strokes in characters, progress from left to right, and genuinely phonetic syllabic character.[30] The Lolo themselves derive it traditionally from Confucius' "left-hand script." It is used only by the p'i-mo priests to help them remember prayers and spells; but the ritual includes some Taoist deities and texts. There are obvious relations with Farther India and the East Indies in the Lolo iron-pointed lance and machete, in the manner of blacksmithing these and farm tools, in the bamboo houses laid and lashed together, in palm-fiber raincoats, in divination with cock femora. Ties with inner and northern Asia appear in the growing of buckwheat and oats, the use of wool, the presence of a "black-boned" aristocracy, and inspirational shamans who are often women and beat the drum left-handedly. American staples, both maize and potatoes, have been introduced via undetermined Asiatic neighbors. Also Lolo, but indeterminate as regards origin, because of their wide spread, are blood sacrifice of cocks and pigs, eating of the victims' flesh, libations of alcoholic drink to the four directions, shoulder-blade divination. Here and there in the inventory a local, possibly indigenous, trait crops up, positive or negative: say, pulverization of dried meat or absence of pottery.[31] The number of such peculiar or original elements appears to be quite small in the total. Such poverty of unique traits usually proves to hold when we have wide enough comparative knowledge, whatever the people in question. But it is the geographical range and the multiplicity of relations and derivations of Lolo culture which are specially impressive and which illustrate not only the nature but the functioning of the large growth of civilization with which we are dealing.

A similar case could be made out for the Todas, that small caste with its highly specialized culture; except that the Toda position near the tip of the Indian subcontinent has made all relations with the world first pass through a specific Indian filter.

As we pass "upward" to peoples like, say, Naga, Shan, Fulah, Ashanti, Kurds, Lapps, it is evident that there exists a transition from societies having only their "folk culture" to others possessing also additional and increasing measures of sophistication or literary culture or participation in a universal church; until, when one of these latter constituents is well marked, the adhesion of the people in question to some great civilization, and through it to the international oecumenical culture, is evident. The difference between the many tribes and nations within the geographical range of the Oikoumenê is not that the backward populations among them have been exempt from the influences of this mass of culture, but that they have failed to be reached strongly by its later, more advanced, or more effort-demanding layers and waves, or have managed to resist them.

Among the very "lowest" units, such as Vedda, Bushman, Sakai, Aeta, it would seem that their status of cultural poverty is mainly the result of a negative selectivity due to a psychological attitude, circularly reinforced by habits of a mode of living. To infer, as is frequently done implicitly, that these peoples still are basal "primitives" through having somehow remained such automatically for the last ten thousand years, completely insulated or in a geographical vacuum, seems contrary to the probability of our total experience of history. Whatever may have been their motivation, or the fortunes to which they were subject, these tribes have escaped the brunt of impact of the main mass of world culture; and either by their own endeavors or by fate they have largely managed to keep their culture at maximal meagerness. Comparative analysis of such content as it has, however, would regularly show, I believe, that this content is widely shared and is therefore to be construed as derivatively secondary, not primarily original.[32]

VIII

How far is it reasonable and profitable to draw the limits of our Oikoumenê?

Australia may fairly be omitted from it, in the main. There are some evidences of percolations; but the significant fact seems to be the degree to which percolations have failed. Warner's analysis of the long-term ineffectiveness of known Malaysian relations with the Murngin[33] seems highly typical in this connection. I would be inclined to project it as a fair sample, typical of Australian indigenous history in general.

New Guinea is more transitional; there are Australian features, but also Melanesian and probably Indonesian ones. Melanesia, in turn, has certainly had some impact of historical forces from the Oikoumenê, as indicated by its pigs and shell-money transactions and pottery. But it appears also to have rioted in local specializations and luxuriances of plans of social structure whose bases perhaps reach back to pre- or proto-oecumenical days [No. 26, 27]. Polynesia stands in an unusual position. Distance and environment, especially that of low and small islands, have deprived it of rice, metals, the loom, usually pottery, and other technologies and economies. But the culture was not seeking retraction, and therefore it

managed to keep, and sometimes to develop further, its attitudes and ideologies, especially its philosophic, mytho-
logic, literary, and hierarchical ones.

South Africa, like Australia, points
spatially away from the main land mass.
But it lies widely open to it, though
separated by a tropical belt and with its
extreme at considerable distance. Perhaps it would be reasonable to construe
that southern Africa was considerably
more a part of the Oikoumenê than was
Australia, but that its relations were irregular, intermittent, and retarded, especially until rather recently.

Native America, like every other
area, has undoubtedly experienced some
connections with Eurasia, both early
and late. All in all, however, its culture
has evidently both developed and crystallized independently of that of the
Oikoumenê. The New World possesses
its own heartland of higher civilization,
stretching from central Mexico to
somewhat beyond Peru. The axis of
this cultural Nuclear America is oriented
without reference to that of the ancient
Oikoumenê. It is both well separated
from it and pointed in a different direction. We are beginning to be able to
trace a few of the pulsations within this
American heartland as well as some of
those emanating from it; and they do
not correspond with those of the Oikoumenê—neither in specific content
nor in time nor with spatial continuity.
Characteristic diffusions within Nuclear
America are metallurgy, many cultivated plants, pyramids, masonry, a calendar; out of it, into the peripheries,
probably pottery, loom-weaving, maize,
head trophies, directional and other ritual symbolism. Since Boas, we have been
in the habit of citing the absence of
plow, wheel, iron, stringed instruments,
and proverbs from pre-Columbian New
World cultures. We might now add, as
theoretically achievable in the relatively
advanced Nuclear civilization, but actu-

ally lacking from it: philosophy, alchemy, writing, money, monasticism,
organ divination, eunuchism, games of
mental skill. And while blood sacrifice
and a sort of astrology occur, it is with
quite diverse concrete expression.

Northern North America has obviously received by import from Asia a
series of items, such as the composite
bow, slat armor, conical tents, scapulimancy, bear rituals, the shamanistic
tambourine drum, the magic flight
story, and perhaps all told some dozens
more. But these are disparates. They
are not held in any one nexus or woven
into an ideology or style. Therefore,
their very presence, with the concurrent absence of systematically organized culture of Old World origin, mili-
tates against construal of northerly
America as a passageway for historic
continuity between the Oikoumenê and
Nuclear America. At any rate there
clearly was no corridor of transmission
corresponding in kind, or even seriously
in degree, to the way in which, say,
Turkestan has functioned as a conduit
between the developed West and developed China. I would not deny that
first and last a great many seeds of culture passed, by land or by sea, from
Asia to this or that part of the Americas,
and that some proportion of them germinated, or at least stimulated new
growths on the soil. This would be in
addition to such stock of basic knowledge as the first populators of the New
World, or perhaps the several waves of
such, brought with them. Yet the story
of major civilizational growth in America, as we are beginning to adumbrate
its totality in outline, gives no indication of integrating with the corresponding story in Eurasia. The two are not,
so far as we can yet see, parts of a single
plot. Resemblances are either analogies
instead of homologies; or, where they
are the latter, they are also *disjecta
membra*.[34]

We have perhaps seemed to travel a

long way. And yet the speed of diffusibility of culture content is so great under optimum conditions that the period of half-a-dozen millennia which we have been considering would have sufficed for particular items—say, like smoking or coffee—to have spread around the planet again and again and again. What counts for total comprehension of the story of man's doings, however, is not these flashing meteoric bits, but the concatenated masses of culture and the interrelations of these—interrelations of transmittal and absorption of content, along with regrouping and refashioning according to national and supernational style of civilization. It is in connection with the understanding of major drifts such as these that the concept is here submitted of an Oikoumenê consisting of a specific, preponderant, interwoven, definable mass of culture charged with a modern significance additional to its original sociogeographical designation in which culture reference was at best only implicit.

48. CULTURE GROUPINGS IN ASIA
1947

IN VOLUME II of the *Southwestern Journal of Anthropology*, Elizabeth Bacon has made a valiant and valuable first effort to classify the cultures of Asia in areal terms. Wherever "culture areas" have been developed as useful conceptual tools, it has been essentially by gradual concord of opinion, even though there was also a definitive formulation, as by Wissler. It is in this spirit that I submit herewith a series of comments on Miss Bacon's findings, hoping that these may stimulate the reactions of others as she has stimulated me.

The comments are ordered in the sequence of her areas....

AREAL CONSIDERATIONS

2. *Southwest Asian Sedentary.*—This area is characterized about as expectable, with considerable continuity (mudbrick, barley) from 4000 B.C. to the present. Islam fits in as regards origin; but many more Mohammedans are now in Africa, India, and Indonesia than in the Near East. That is one trouble with ideas and religions in these areal classifications: they wander; while subsistence mechanisms mostly have difficulty traveling out of their environment. In "The Ancient Oikumenê" [No. 47], I have tried to interpret Mohammedanism as a phenomenon of the class which Toynbee calls "etherealization," but for which a term like "reduction by segregation" would be more appropriate—at any rate less spiritually poetic. (The extrication of the alphabet out of the earlier system of mixed writing by segregation and reduction is an example.) Such a simplified ideology and set of values was perhaps the only effective reformulation that could be evolved in

the area of the original hearth of higher civilization after four thousand years. At any rate, the Mohammedan reduction-formulation was successful not only in the hearth but on three continents wherever it entered feeble, arid, or undeveloped cultures. Therewith, to a certain degree, it carried Near Eastern culture as far as to Malaysia and to West African Negroes. All this is not a criticism of Miss Bacon, but an illustration of the difficulties inherent in areal classifications dealing with cultures that possess a known history and are on markedly different levels. My "reduction" explanation tries to salvage something for the "culture-area" approach when this floats onto the biggest rocks, as in the Near East.

3. *Pastoral Nomadic.*—In a mapped classification of Asiatic cultures, there is no recourse but to recognize the pastoral belt. Yet the farming and part-farming communities within the belt render the pastoral designation highly inexact. It is even doubtful whether the nomads outnumber the farmers. Evidently their specialized and unstable life impresses our mind as so distinctive that we fail to consider the settled people in the same area. What we really have is a dichotomized culture, one pole of which is much like that dominant in adjacent areas; the other, pastoral. The purely pastoral part of the society does make the total culture distinctive as compared with more usual cultures which contain no such nomadic-pastoral element. Nevertheless, a mere nomadic segment of a society is not the same as a wholly nomadic society. The difference is of import both conceptually and in historic actuality. For instance, there

is Lattimore's view that eastern nomadism is a secondary extension from mixed farming when this got into territory so near the environmental limit that it became more secure or profitable to abandon the double-barreled approach, move out into the steppe, and plump on animal-breeding with mobility. Whether this was actually "the" origin of East Asiatic pastoral nomadism, or of all pastoral nomadism, I do not know; and I suspect it cannot be either proved or disproved, at least not at present. But the mere fact that the view can be reasonably entertained shows that nomadism can theoretically be construed as a special derivative form of other cultures, and is not necessarily a basic form of culture in its own right. Seen in this way, pastoralism would be a part-culture. It would be a well-marked profession within cultures, something like smithing or doctoring, say, except for being raised to include a higher fraction of the total population and being more nearly self-sufficient. As a matter of fact, I doubt whether any pastoral nomad group is wholly pastoral even as regards its subsistence. No doubt some of them might be, if necessary; but it is certainly not usual, and the exclusively herding life would certainly be narrow and meager, except so far as it might be enriched by plunder.

In short, I submit that there is considerable reason for regarding pastoral nomadism not as a complete culture but as a culture facies; much like the river-boat-dwelling sector of the southern Chinese population or like the Orang Laut among the Malay, to whom no one has yet given a separate color on a culture-area map. Incidentally, if one proceeded to actual, accurate mapping of the area of pastoral nomadism, difficulties of representation would at once appear. These difficulties ought to suggest that this culture is not conceptually coordinate or equivalent with others. The Arab Ruwala in Arabia would be "Pas-

toral Nomadic," but Arab Mecca and Yemen in Arabia would be "Near Eastern Sedentary." And the Nomadic area would have to be stretched beyond Asia to Morocco, if the concept were valid....

5. *Southeast Asia and Indonesia.*—The definition of this area is hazier than need be. Southern China is more or less included by implication, and then there seems to be a theory of origin in central China. The latter theory seems highly speculative. No evidence is outlined. The view is perhaps a reflection of Heine-Geldern's.

Actually there is enough solid and clear-cut basis for a Farther Indian–East Indian culture area to render complicating speculations unnecessary. From Assam to the Philippines and Lesser Sundas the surviving pagan cultures have long been recognized as presenting many marked resemblances. There is plenty of local diversity, but it seems not so much intrinsic variation as due to the survival of the old general culture only in spots between the invasion and spread of literate cultures, which took up all the larger and fertile plains and coasts. Considering the scattered localization of the pagan, prehistoric culture today, and the length of time since disruption of its continuity, the variability is not at all excessive.

The overlays and intrusions are as follows. In southern China (central China does not belong and probably never did), in Tongking, and, since some centuries, in Annam and Cochin China: Chinese culture. In the remainder of Farther India and Indonesia: Indian culture; followed later, in Indonesia and Malaya, by Islam. In Farther India, the limits of prevalent Chinese and Indian influence are quite sharp. So far as Annamese is today the dominant language, we have Mahayana, ideographs, mandarins, chopsticks, etc. Laos, Cambodia, ancient Champa go with Siam and Burma in being overwhelmingly determined from India, primarily by overseas influences. This is one of the few Asiatic frontiers of the oil-and-water type.

All three of the languages of the politically dominant nationalities of Farther India have gained territory southward within the historic period, as Miss Bacon observes, and may have done so previously. An early, wide, and perhaps continuous distribution of Mon-Khmer dialects over the southern half or more of the Farther Indian peninsula is thus indicated. This would be analogous to the persisting continuity of Indonesian dialects in the archipelago.

The remnant populations different in culture and physical type appear to be the "Primitive Nomadic" peoples of Miss Bacon's "6." These were certainly of much less import toward later cultures than the far more numerous early Mon-Khmer and early Indonesians that were established in most of the area—almost certainly with agriculture—when the only slightly more civilized Burmese, Thai, and Tongkinese infiltrated or conquered southward on the mainland, and when the Hindus arrived on both the mainland and island coasts. I would construe the large and relatively uniform Mon-Khmer and Indonesian bodies, with their indubitably similar cultures, as the effective social substratum on which the immigrant populations with their more efficient political organization deployed to constitute what we call the "history" of the area.

6. *Primitive Nomadic.*—It seems of doubtful value to reckon the Australoid Sakai, Negrito Semang, and similar fragments as having a type of culture taxonomically co-ordinate with, say, the Chinese. Least of all can this be done in terms of *areas* of culture: these scraps of tribes occupy only spots which are so small as to be difficult to enter on a map of the continent.

I should like to propose the view that the culture-historical significance of these primitives, as influences or ingredients, has always, in the past as in the present, been negligible. Their significance to us resides in an attitude to which they hold, namely, to get along with all possible *minimum* of culture. This is a most interesting experiment for them to have performed for the benefit of those of us who are concerned with the processes and nature of culture. But it virtually eliminates them from having been of any real influence on the development of the culture of a continent or the world.

Blend 1. Korean.—I agree entirely with Miss Bacon that it is remarkable how little we know about Korea. There can be no doubt that when the heavy Chinese influences are subtracted there is a solid native remainder. This presumably shares many features with adjacent Tungusic culture. But it would seem most profitable to determine first the "native," i.e., non-Chinese, constituents of Korean culture, and subsequently to compare them with Tungusic for their degree of commonalty. There seems to be much that is distinctive of Korea: position of women, their "seclusion," curfew for men, men's topknot and adulthood only by marriage, near-outlawing of Buddhism, the general irreligiousness, the strange political "parties," the alphabet, the female *mutang* exorcists who both are possessed by spirits and evict spirits that cause illness in others, the blind male *pansu* shamans or diviners who are *taught* to control spirits, the special kinds and uses of Broussetonia paper, the shapes of the horsehair hats, the packing on bulls.

The Chinese constituent in Korea can be appraised in two ways. First, by an enumeration of Chinese items and patterns found in Korea. Any return flow would presumably be negligible. Second, by a comparison of the histories of the two countries. The total profiles of these histories run parallel at so many points as to indicate common currents of causation; which presumably amounts to consistent Chinese influence on events in Korea. Strong coincidence of pulse could hardly exist without an enormous amount of the plasma of culture being common. The parallelism is most evident in the segmentation of Korean history into natural or accepted periods; of which I therefore subjoin an outline.

I*a*. (Legendary) 1122 B.C., or Chou accession, Shang refugees establish a kingdom at Phyong An.

I*b*. In 193 B.C., about a generation after the conquest of the northeasterly Chinese kingdom of Yen by Ts'in, following the end of Chou, refugees from Yen seize Phyong An.

II. In 108 B.C. the great Han warrior emperor Wu-ti temporarily annexed what is now northern Korea. The reaction to this, beginning in about a half-century, was the formation of three native Korean states (there had been only tribes before), whose interrelations constitute the political history of the peninsula for the next seven centuries. This is the "Period of the Three Kingdoms," Silla, Korai, Pakche. Silla, the most remote from China, was organized first, in 57 B.C.; Pakche last, in 16 B.C. About halfway through the period, writing, Buddhism, sculpture, etc., were introduced from China and soon transmitted to Japan (generally within one to two centuries more). Silla seems gradually to have become the most advanced culturally as well as the strongest of the three Korean states, and finally took the Japanese "colony" or outpost of Nimana in southern Korea. The three-kingdom period corresponds closely in time to the Chinese later Han, Three Kingdoms, and Six Dynasties periods; in both countries it was an era of political though fairly stable division.

III. In 589 China was reunited under the Sui dynasty, soon succeeded in 618 by the T'ang. At this time Silla had encroached on and was threatening its two neighbors. Soon after the T'angs were well established, around 650, there was an alliance between them and Silla, and another between Pakche and Korai, who soon called in Japan after Pakche had been conquered. In 663 the Japanese invaded Silla but were beaten by the Chinese; and by 668 Korai and Pakche had been "annexed" to China and Silla was a vassal. Actually, before long, the peninsula was ruled by Silla under nominal suzerainty to T'ang China. This condition continued until 935.

IV. In China, this date of 935 comes twenty-eight years after the final end of T'ang, and about halfway through the succeeding time of national political breakdown and rival states preceding Sung. In Korea, 935 stands for the overthrow of Silla by Wang Kien of Korai, who founded his own dynasty, independent of China, which was to last for all of 457 years, until 1392. The later rulers became vassals to the Mongols, but kept the dynasty going, which endured longer than any post-Chou dynasty in China. Wang Kien's line corresponds closely in time to Sung, Southern Sung, and Yuan, which covered 960–1368.

V*a*. In 1368 the Mings expelled the Mongols in a burst of Chinese nationalistic patriotism. Twenty-four years later, the Koreans founded a new dynasty, to rule Korea as Cho-sen from Seoul. On the one hand, there was now strong Chinese imitation: literary examinations and Confucianism were introduced or reestablished. On the other, Koreanism was emphasized. A state printing office was set up, with the famous great font of bronze types, rumors of which may have served to stimulate Gutenberg: the types were of Chinese characters, but were movable. A few decades later a true alphabet was devised which rendered the sounds of Korean efficiently. These were early developments; but in the sixteenth century manifestations of independence continued: Buddhism was heavily repressed; Fusan was taken and relations with Japan broken for sixty years; and, about 1575, the peculiar and unfortunate system of Korean political parties or factions took shape. This dynasty also had an extraordinarily long life, namely, of 518 years, until 1910. But this lapse was broken a bit before its middle by the Japanese invasion and conquest of 1592–98.

V*b*. By 1598, the Mings were running

out; the Manchus were soon to replace them. Korea was "loyal" to the Mings, who had come to its rescue against Japan, though only with failure. As the Manchus rose in power, they had to conquer the Koreans twice, in 1627 and 1636. After the second time, Korea went into seclusion, becoming the famous "hermit nation." Even with China its relations were now cut to a minimum, on account of the hated Manchu rulers: the embassy to Peking was limited to a month, trade took place only under it. It is interesting that the seclusion was broken by the Japanese, who in 1876 forced a Perry-like treaty on the reluctant Koreans; also that the dynasty ended in 1910 by annexation, a year before the Manchus in China ended by revolution.

This analysis evidences the degree to which the national and cultural history of Korea is a reflex of that of China in its major profiles, in spite of quite conscious and considerable ethnic and cultural particularism. No such parallelism of events can be designated for Japan; nor, for that matter, does it hold for Tongking-Annam in spite of the contiguity of the latter to China.

Blend 2. Japanese.—Miss Bacon is not wholly clear here between southern China coast and Indonesia as the main source of the nonclassic-Chinese constituent of Japanese culture. The southern China coast is Sansom's suggestion, and the most reasonable one, with the Japanese-speaking Ryukyus serving as the presumptive link. In fact, it is difficult to see why Indonesia should ever have been dragged into the problem, except that more speculative views are sometimes the more interesting. Scattered items like tooth-blackening will prove nothing for a large, rich culture like Japan's. I should doubt whether wet rice would have to be posited as the nucleus of the southern ingredient; for, in that case, how about Korean rice-growing—is that also derived from Indonesia? After all, there is no need to assume porous loess and a dryish continental climate as the sole environment of

"north" or standard Chinese civilization. Miss Bacon's "may have reached Japan indirectly by way of Indonesia" I do not understand. Is this perhaps a slip for "ultimately from Indonesia but indirectly so" (viz., via southern China or Formosa-Ryukyu)? On the other hand, I agree with her implication that the Ainu have not seriously affected Japanese civilization.

Blend 3. Indian.—All cultures are composite in the origin of their content and multiply so. What a term like "blend" really can mean definitely is that most of the content of a given culture has entered it so recently or massively from other cultures that it can be explicitly referred to these with assurance. In short, blended cultures are essentially derivative cultures. That is something which Indian civilization is not. It has given much more than it has borrowed (except perhaps for its last thousand years of conquest-subjection to Islam). The three outstanding centers in Asia of creativeness of great systems of values and ideas are the Near East, India, and China. Miss Bacon would, I am sure, agree with this. Why then the Near East and China should stand on their own feet as originating areas, but India be a blend and derivative, is hard to see. Is it the wheat and cattle versus rice and buffalo dichotomy of subsistence in India? Or Vedic Indo-Aryan culture uniting with a hypothetical and undefinable Dravidian one? The essential event in India was the forging of the characteristic idea system (plus the influence of this on other parts of the world), not the contact or mingling of one or another subsistence or ethnic element. . . .

GENERAL CONSIDERATIONS

"Culture areas" are of course primarily not areas at all but kinds of culture which are areally limited. They are usually more simply and briefly labeled by their region than by their distinctive content or qualities. That they can be mapped implies that they are either static formations or represent moments in a time flow. The concept was first developed systematically for native North America north of the Rio Grande, and has proved most convenient and usable there. This is because the total area was large enough to contain conspicuous diversities, yet the cultures were rather close together in level; and they also were all virtually historyless. They could therefore be treated as co-ordinate. Around 1910–15, the archaeology of the areas was less systematically known than the ethnology. It did not extend back very far from the period of discovery. Hence it mostly revealed no very marked differences from the historic or recent culture of the same area. So the static classification worked pretty well. The same sort of classification applied south of the Tropic of Cancer did not work out nearly so consistently or usefully—there was too complicated a history, too varied an archaeological past.

This situation can be generalized. The more history is known, the more difficult is it to evolve an acceptable "culture-area" classification. Simon-pure historians have never used the concept. They have not refuted it; often they would admit the areas; but they take them for granted, and then operate with changes within or across them. Miss Bacon's difficulties are due to proceeding basically as if one could divide Asia into static areas, while yet remaining aware of the historic changes across the areas. The result is a varying degree of inconsistency of scheme.

I have tried not only to point out the inconsistencies but to suggest an approach that may remove them. Where we possess reasonably adequate historic or archaeological knowledge, this should be given the primacy. The cultures should be viewed first as developments or growths; their areas, as sec-

ondary attributes. On this view, areas are often seen to expand, contract, or overlap—much as cultures change or blend. But in general the cultures will prove areally definable for any given moment. The ultimate outcome might be a series of culture-area mappings. But this would be a very different thing from a mapping or assignment that tried to reconcile areal differences, or ignored them, or was ambiguous in face of them.

It will be seen that mostly I have not attempted areal definitions. That means that my effort also is incomplete, and serves only as a take-off for future formulations.

Primary reliance on subsistence mechanisms has made almost as many difficulties for Miss Bacon as has primary formulation in terms of present conditions when there is a long past. I suggest it be admitted that political-religious-lettered culture can alter drastically and independently of subsistence culture. The fact complicates the total picture but must simply be accepted.

Another recognition that ultimately will have to be made is that pastoral societies normally are symbiotic complements of sedentary ones. Conceptually their cultures contrast with the sedentary ones, but functionally they are not independent. This becomes specially evident on an endeavor to map them in detail.

Finally, groups like the Semang and Vedda maintain their place in our consciousness for the same reason as Platypus and Amphioxus—they are types of evolutionary stage. Also like these biological forms, they are insignificant in an ecological consideration, whether static or historical; and ecological is what a culture-area classification essentially is. These insignificant survivals should therefore be ignored, or relegated to footnote rank, rather than allowed to blur the salient outlines of large historical and areal conclusions.

49. IS WESTERN CIVILIZATION DISINTEGRATING OR RECONSTITUTING?

1951

IT IS possible to conceive civilizations as being each constituted to a considerable extent of an assemblage of styles and as being specifically characterized as to their particularities by these styles. A style, in turn, is a self-consistent way of behaving or of doing things. It is selected out from among alternatively possible ways of doing. And it is selective with reference to values; that is, the things the style does and the way it does them are felt by the doers as intrinsically valuable—they are good, right, beautiful, pleasing, or desirable in themselves.

This most characteristic part of civilizations, which we may call value culture, is not their only component. There is also what may be called reality culture [compare No. 18], concerned with finding out, mastering, and directing nature—and sometimes mastering and directing fellow-men as well. Technology, the useful arts, ways of successful practical living, are the avenues by which reality culture is expressed. There is a third component, social structure and relations, which in principle might be thought to be independent of the rest of civilization or culture, because it also occurs well developed among cultureless, nonsymbolizing animals, especially the social insects. But since human societies always operate with symbols and thus possess culture, their social structure and relations are channeled into variable cultural forms instead of being constant, autonomous, and mainly hereditary. Social culture is therefore, in man, always interwoven with value culture and reality culture. Anthropologists generally see it as such. Sociologists tend to see the same set of phenomena, namely, social culture, as "society," something abstracted from culture and underlying it—as divorced from the remainder of culture, most anthropologists would say.

Within any one civilization, the various styles constituting its value component not only coexist in the same society, region, and period; they also tend toward a certain consistency among themselves. If they were not interconsistent at first—as might well be the case, owing to some of them having been introduced from outside in the frequent hybridizing to which cultures are subject—the styles would nevertheless tend to become more consistent as they remained associated. This assumption seems validated by the simple consideration that consistent and coherent civilizations would on the average work out better and get farther, and presumably survive better, than inconsistent ones dragging on under malfunction and strain.

It is in their reality ingredients that civilizations chiefly show the quality of accumulativeness which has been noted as one of the properties that distinguish human cultural development from subhuman organic evolution. Technological activities, while not unmitigatedly accumulative, are more accumulative, on the whole, than other parts of culture. By contrast, a value activity, such as a fine art, a philosophy, or a science, contains a creative ingredient. As long as it retains this, it is prevented from repetitiousness. It tends first to develop and progress, even though it later degenerate and die. An art or a philosophy moves on; it cannot continue to spin on a pivot. Those more trivial

402

styles which we call fashions, as in dress, change with particular rapidity. Not expressing or achieving much of intrinsic value significance, they lack the full rise and fall, the consistent growth curve, of greater styles; but they are even more restless in the profile of their movement.

The more creative activities of civilizations thus are imbued with change in their very nature. To each such activity there corresponds, at any given time, a style, a bundle of manners and qualities all its own. The style successively forms, develops, matures, decays, and either dissolves or atrophies into a dead petrification—unless it has previously budded into a new style. The one thing a style does not do is to stand still. Styles are the very incarnation of the dynamic forms taken by the history of civilization. They are the most sensitive expression extant of cultural change—its most delicate galvanometer.

As to the causes of styles, we know very little. Obviously, the causes of qualities and values are going to be difficult to find. At best, we can do little more than describe the circumstances amid which a style forms. From there on, however, the story of the career of a style has unity. Its history usually possesses an internal self-consistency proportional to the discriminateness of the style itself. A style definite in its themes, its manners, its affects, can be expected to run a definite course. Its successive stages we tend to describe in terms like groping, growth of control, full power, slackening, dissolution; or, again, as formative, developing, climactic, overripe, decadent.

When we possess enough examples of an art, and adequate information as to the time sequence of its individual products, a newly discovered specimen within the style—say, an anonymous or hitherto unassigned example—can normally be dated within a half-century, and often within a decade or two. This is possible on the basis of two things. First, the specific quality of the piece in question, and second, the recognized flow of successive qualities within the style. This ability of experts to agree in assigning its place in the style to any object holds for Mediaeval sculpture, for Renaissance and modern painting, for five or six centuries of European music, for Greek vases and poetry, for Chinese painting. Such dating is in a sense prediction: we predict what the date will turn out to be when all the facts are in. The whole procedure certainly implies that a style has a one-way course.

Equally convincing, as to the compulsive strength of style viewed as a course, is the long-recognized clustering of great men in time-limited constellations within each civilization or national subcivilization. This clustering certainly is as conspicuously true for intellectual as for aesthetic creativeness. Looking for cause, one can here argue indefinitely in a circle. Is it the greatness of geniuses that causes a style to come into being, such as the geniuses need to express themselves? Or does the growth of the style evoke successively greater geniuses until the culmination is reached—after which there is increasingly less left for talented individuals to do within the confines of the style? Yet as soon as we leave off the vain effort of tracking down the original or ultimate cause of the phenomenon of clustering, and concentrate on its recurrent generalized form or pattern, it is an indubitable fact that genius *occurs* preponderantly in conjunction with the developmental courses of outstanding styles within successful civilizations.

As for one-wayness, a true style does not travel so and so far and then retrace its steps; nor does it suddenly go off in a random new direction. The tendency is very strong for its direction not only to persevere up to a culmination, but to be irreversible. At its culmination, a style is utilizing its potentialities to their utmost. A bit of reflection shows that this quality of irreversibility is really implicit in most of our formulations of what style is, provided only that we let ourselves conceive it as flowing in time, as it normally does flow.

It is because of this one-wayness of growth that we often speak of the history of a style as if it were a life-history. It is also why a concrete exemplification taken from one style, such as Greek sculpture, of what is meant by terms like "archaic severity" or "primitive stiffness," or by "increasing freedom of control" or "full liberation"—why such an illustration often suffices for us to recognize a corresponding stage of development in a wholly different art. Qualities such as flamboyant, overornate, Churrigueresque, Rococo, which were first defined as characteristic of particular developmental phases of Gothic and Renaissance architecture, can at times be applied with aptness to analogous phases in literatures, or in decorative and applied arts, or in music. Again and again we find in diverse arts a similar course beginning with restraint, attaining balanced mastery, and ending in luxuriance, conscious emotionality, extremity, and disintegration.

Let us now proceed to examine how far the special stylistic quality of irreversibility attaches also to civilizations, which we are construing as consisting at least partly of more or less coherent associations of styles. Or again, conceivably, whole civilizations, being so much larger phenomena than styles, may possess special properties leaving room if not for outright reversibility, at least for divertibility into new directions.

The idea of "direction" is fundamental in this inquiry because we are examining civilizations not as static objects but as limited processes of flow in time.

Greek civilization probably tends to serve as our archetype when we think generically about civilizations and their direction. The Greek civilization was sharply characterized, high in creative power, brief in duration. To an unusual degree, almost all the activities of Greek civilization culminated nearly simultaneously, and at least overlappingly, within a mere three centuries. The course of this civilization is therefore particularly like that of a style. It unrolls like the consistent plot of a drama. Consequently it suggests strongly the quality of irreversibility. And irreversibility, whether of entropy in physics or of human destiny, carries implications of fate and doom.

It is evident that Spengler's system of declines and extinctions—his *Untergang* means literally a "sinking" or "setting" —was derived basically from a contrastive comparison of Greek civilization with European or Western civilization. And as this latter is still a going concern, his idea of the pessimistic fate and extinction awaiting it was evidently taken over from what had happened to Graeco-Roman civilization.

Spengler assumes as something that does not need to be argued—and so does Toynbee—that Greek culture and Roman culture were only the two halves of a larger Graeco-Roman civilization. Spengler calls this larger unit "Classical Antiquity"; and Toynbee calls it simply "Hellenic civilization." Historians also often group the two together as "Ancient History," as against Mediaeval-Modern History which deals largely with other peoples in another part of Europe in a subsequent period.

A next step brings us to the period often called the Dark Ages, the interval between Ancient and Mediaeval times. This is the period of Goths, Lombards, Saxons, and Franks; of decay of government, arts, letters, and wealth —a time when our Western civilization had not yet begun to crystallize out but the Imperial Roman days and ways were irretrievably over. It was a time definitely of cultural retreat, of sag and decay, both quantitative and qualitative; not a distinctive civilization as such, but a chaotic, amorphous interregnum between civilizations. It was a time of disintegration of the patterns of one civilization that had ceased functioning—a very decomposition of its substance and form. And at the same time there must have been dim stirrings, blind gropings, the germinating seeds from which Western civilization would begin to grow within a few centuries.

In short, our Dark Ages are not really a reversal, a retracing, of a current of flow. They mark the cessation of flow of one civilization; a consequent slack water and hesitation of confused fluctuating drift; and then the gradual and slowly increasing flow of a new Western civilization—new precisely because the set of its current is in a new direction.

Our slump, the Dark Ages, accordingly is the falling-apart and the dissolution of most of an old civilization, because of which dissolution a new civilization was able to arise—and move in a new direction.

With the Graeco-Roman civilization essentially dead in the West around A.D. 500, its still surviving patterns disintegrated still more for some centuries thereafter. Christianity, though established, was still too raw, too nearly illiterate and undisciplined, to have evolved many new patterns of creativity outside its own immediate functioning, in contrast with the way it did evolve them later. The Dark Ages following 500 were dark not only because of ignorance but because people had lost the old patterns and had not yet evolved new ones of any definiteness or moment. This absence of specific Dark Age patterns, due to previous ones having dissolved away and new ones having not yet formed, is the symptom

that most marks off Ancient from Western civilization. The nexus of patterns and values in Europe after the Dark Age interregnum was, all in all, more different from the nexus existing before, during Graeco-Roman Antiquity, than it was similar. We have here, incidentally, a tentative, empirical definition of what a particular civilization is, what sets one off from another: it is an excess of distinctive patterns, values, or directions over shared ones.

Some time after Charlemagne, around 900 or 950, the new Western civilization at last emerged. Compared with the vague stirrings of germination in the preceding dark centuries, it now emerged with definite form, however rude and in need of further development. It manifested several patterns that were to continue in its structure thereafter. First of all, the new civilization was unmitigatedly committed to being Christian. There was no room in it for anything else religious; and its Christianity was still unified. Second, the European nationalities had pretty definitely crystallized out by 950, much as they were to endure for a thousand years. There were now Frenchmen, Germans, Italians, Englishmen, Danes, Poles, instead of tribal agglomerations or the loose Frankish empire of Charlemagne. These nationalities found political expression in feudalistic monarchies. Fortified castles were rising, and in their lee, or within their own walls, towns grew up—still puny but a beginning toward urban life. Romanesque-Gothic building got under way, and then the associated sculpture and glass-staining. A revival of learning had commenced— still very modest but to bear fruit within a century in the first pulse of Scholastic philosophy. Much in the same way, the writing of vernacular tongues —French instead of Latin—also emerged in the nine hundreds, proceeded to poetical compositions in the ten hundreds, and culminated in the vernacular

Mediaeval literatures—French, Proven-çal, Castilian, and German—in the eleven and twelve hundreds.

This civilization here arising was Western civilization; but it was Western civilization in its High Mediaeval phase or stage. It came to a conspicuous peak—its Christianity and church, its monarchies, its Christian architecture and sculpture, its Christian philosophy —in the mid-thirteenth century: let us say in the decades around 1250. In fact, the *Summa* of St. Thomas Aquinas in 1265 may be construed as the literal summation, formal and inward, of the High Middle Ages.

This High Mediaeval civilization did not wither away. Instead, its patterns loosened and partly dissolved, during the two centuries or so following 1300. But as they broke down they were also *reconstituting* themselves, and on an ampler scope. This went on until, at some time between 1500 and 1600, the filling-in of these newly enlarged patterns, the actualization of their new and greater potential, had got under way: and therewith "Modern History" began—the history of the second or Modern phase of Western civilization.

What had confronted western Europeans around 1300 or 1325, though they could not of course see it in the perspective of subsequent history, was an alternative. They might either adhere to their cherished patterns of High Mediaeval civilization as they had first begun to rough them out four centuries before, and had since filled them in and realized them so successfully. In that case, the saturation of the patterns having been essentially achieved, life under the continuing culture would have become increasingly repetitive, creativity would have been checked, atrophy ensued, and an irrevocable withering of the Mediaeval civilization would have got under way. The other choice was for the Europeans of 1300 to stretch their cultural patterns to accommodate a civilization of larger scope: to stretch them if necessary until some of them burst; to stretch them by stuffing into them a content of far greater knowledge of fact, more experimentation and curiosity, new undertakings, wider horizons, greater wealth, a higher standard of living.

Unconsciously, they took the risk of this second course. They did stretch their patterns of living a civilized life, they ruptured many of them, they developed more new ones in their place; until, after two to three centuries, the set of patterns, the over-all design for living, had been reconstituted, and a new stage of Western civilization, the Modern stage, was entered upon.

High Mediaeval civilization was like its cathedrals of high-reared arches but narrow base. What it lacked seems almost incredible today: at least it seems incredible that Mediaeval men—our ancestors and the founders of our civilization of today—could have been complacent about it. As against the contented parochialism of High Mediaevalism, the thirteen, fourteen, and fifteen hundreds brought first a wider knowledge of Asia, next of the African peripheries, then of America. Trade followed, industry grew, wealth expanded. A true civilian architecture arose in Italy; painting blossomed beside sculpture. The hold of the Church—that Church from which so many of the High Mediaeval patterns had ramified— this hold was loosened or broken. The papacy was dragged to Avignon, then split in the Great Schism; Councils were held to heal the breach and—unsuccessfully—to combat the worldliness and profligacy of churchmen, a worldliness that in turn was building up sentiments of anticlericalism, and the dissidency of Wycliffe and Hus. Not long afterward, the Reformation tore away from the hitherto unified Church nearly half of Europe.

All this was certainly a process of disintegration of what had been firmly fitted around the Church in the true Middle Ages. In philosophy, the Scholastic system was similarly disrupted by the skeptical negativism of Occam or dissolved into mysticism by the Germans—after which its field lay fallow. Science, after a thousand years' sleep, was slow in reconstituting itself. It finally got into motion toward the end of our period of readjustment with Copernicus' 1543 revolution of astronomy, and with contemporary Italian discoveries in mathematics and medicine. Printing was invented to meet the demands for more knowledge and ideas on the part of a greatly enlarged civilian and urban clientele of sharpening curiosity.

In many ways this era of Reconstitution and Rebirth between the Mediaeval and Modern periods of Western civilization must have felt to the people of Europe much as the twentieth century feels to us. It was a period of strains and unsettlement. The timorous must often have wondered if the world were not coming wholly out of joint.

True, such sentiment must also have been felt in some degree in the Dark Ages. The difference is that the Dark Ages were an actual recession: more civilization was abandoned than was originated in them.

By contrast, there was more knowledge in 1400 and 1500 than in the High Middle Ages, increased understanding and cultivation, and more urbane living and wealth and graciousness. Growth, not recession, continued through the interval, even while the reconstitution of set and structure was taking place. That, incidentally, is why no one has yet proposed separating the Middle Ages off from the Modern period as being two wholly distinct civilizations. Their respective sets or directions, though altered and enlarged in the period of Reconstitution, were not wholly torn apart, nor was there loss or destruction of most of what had existed in Western Civilization I—the Middle Ages—during the Reconstitution into Western Civilization II—Modern Europe.

Our Western period of Reconstitution evidently corresponds fairly to A.D. 200–600 in China, which was also a time of unsettlement and reorientation, after which Chinese civilization resumed its course on a reorganized and broadened base. Therefore the prevalent usage seems justified of recognizing the two phases as China I and II, or as Ancient China and Mediaeval-Modern China, rather than as two disparate civilizations separated even by their names, Sinic and Far Eastern, as Toynbee proposes.

There is one interesting difference from Europe, however: China acquired a new organized religion, Buddhism, in its era of Reconstitution; Europe loosened the hold of Christianity on its nonreligious activities.

When now we match the present condition of our civilization comparatively against these two analogues, it seems that the correspondence is greater with the previous European stage of Reconstitution than with the Graeco-Roman final stage of Dissolution. This is because now, as in 1300–1550, population, wealth, curiosity, knowledge, enterprise, and invention are definitely still in an expanding phase. It appears somewhat likely, accordingly, or at any rate possible, that we are now in the throes of a second stage of Reconstitution of our civilization. In that case, Period II of Western Civilization would already be mainly past, whether we in it so recognize or not; and Period III of Western Civilization would lie ahead of us whenever we shall have finished reorganizing our former cultural style patterns into a resultant new over-all pattern or set.

Civilizations are like life-histories in that they are normally marked by a developmental flow, and by the fact that they are not reversible into a series of beats and back-and-forth swings. But cultural processes and organic processes are so distinct in their factors that it would be unwise to expect their manifestations to run parallel, except in occasional features. There does seem to be this difference, that, while a civilization cannot retrace its past course rearward any more than can an organism, a civilization can regather or regroup itself and start off in an altered or partially new direction, with expanded and reconstituted value patterns. After all, the organic parallel or analogy must not be pressed too hard. Birth, maturation, senility, and death characterize the individual organisms whose repetitions constitute a species; and what civilizations in their size and compositeness evidently more nearly resemble than they resemble individual organisms is

species—and especially the groupings of species into families or orders of common properties and qualities.

The foregoing has turned out to be an endeavor in applied anthropology— a somewhat new kind of applied anthropology, of a long-range variety. It leans little on economics or sociology or psychology or personality study, but a great deal on history. Only it asks that history be viewed now and then with maximum of elbow room and freedom of perspective; with emphasis, for the time being, not on the mere events of history, which are as unending as the waves of the sea, but on the qualities of its secular trends; and that these trends be construed, so far as possible, in terms of the style-like patterns which so largely characterize civilization, and in terms of the developmental flow, interactions, and integration of these patterns.

I

IN A recent essay in the *Journal of the Royal Anthropological Institute* [No. 47, above], I re-emphasized the holistic concept of the Oikoumenê as a genuine historical unit of interconnected development of higher civilization in Asia, Europe, and North Africa. For a typical illustration I selected sculpture as a fine art of high achievement. . . .

In summary, the story of the great achievements in sculpture as there outlined is: an origin in the Near East, a slow spread to the farthest east of Asia and to the farthest west of Europe. Diagrammatically, it may be visualized as a great Y. I have suggested another image: a spark falling on a fabric, smoldering, enlarging, with maximum intensity of flame flaring here and there as combustion slowly eats its expanding way. The only repetitions have been at the geographical peripheries of the Oikoumenê. The whole interior area has remained "burned out."

Viewed in isolation, this condensation of the story of high sculpture is an oddity or curiosity. But when the plot is repeated, as it is in the world-wide history of drama, and in that of science and technology, it evidently expresses a trend. For the drama, it is true, the usual first chapter is lacking and we have to begin with the Greeks. And the connections are more tenuous or dubious. But the course is the same: India fifth century, China thirteenth to fourteenth, Japan seventeenth to eighteenth, Europe seventeenth—the Near East never manifesting anything of note. In science, though it is also customary to begin with the Greeks, the very considerable achievements of their Near Eastern antecedents, especially in astronomy, are becoming well established.

In fact, culminant civilization as a whole can be seen as having followed the same general course. This indeed we might expect as a consequence of the foregoing findings; and equally so whether total culture be looked upon as a summation of discrete activities such as sculpture, or these as its products and parts. And it is even possible to fit Islamic civilization into the story by construing it as a reaction formation against domination from Alexander to Justinian of the old, burned-out Near Eastern hearth by the high culture developed outside by the Greeks—but resisted within the Near East [No. 47, § II]. A repeat civilization of first rank erected in the Near East on the slag and ashes of two or more millennia was presumably impossible. But a reduced, simplified, contractile civilization, with emphasis on its autonomy and self-sufficiency instead of an intensive cultural creativity, might well be conceived as arising anew there; and to call forth such a form of civilization was Mohammed's historic function. This train of thought on the relation of Islamic culture to the total history of culture cannot be pursued here. It has been developed in the Oikoumenê essay, and is mentioned here only as part of the general system or background of ideas from which I proceed in considering the historical place of the novel in human civilization.

II

The thesis in brief is this. Spatiotemporally, the course of the novel as a literary phenomenon—as it will be defined in a moment—is obviously roughly parallel to the course of sculpture, of drama, of science. There is, however, this difference. For sculpture, drama, and science the connections between manifestations occurring at different places and times can often be traced—such as between Hellenistic, Gandhara, Indian, and Chinese art. Or at least connections may reasonably be suspected. The several manifestations of the novel, on the contrary, show a minimum of historic connection by diffusionary influence—perhaps none whatever. They seem rather like secondarily parallel products of long independent cultural developments, whenever and wherever these developments happened to reach a certain concatenation of phase or stage. In other words, the novel seems to me more than merely another example of the principle that is operative in sculpture, drama, and science. I suggest that the novel has been the product of a somewhat different though related principle.

I classify as novels fictional, narrative prose works of considerable length and complexity, observing almost no formal requirements; consciously natural or realistic in their representation of life, and thus omitting supernatural elements;[1] interested in individuated characters and not in types; using plot and suspense freely but using them as contributive to the development of character; and normally concerned with a series of personages rather than with one only. A full-length novel has many resemblances to an epic, but avoids poetry and everything grandiose, heroic, exaggerated, impossible, unspecified, generalized, or repetitively formal. It must be factually sharp in incident and wholly unstilted in dialogue; and it admits humor.

This statement aims to define the most developed and distinctive form of novel. Other and more inclusive definitions could be given; but the present one will be adhered to in this essay.

Wholly successful full-type novels have been developed only three times: in Japan, in China, in Western civilization, in that order; though there have been some partial approaches or adumbrations elsewhere. The Graeco-Roman, Islamic, Indian, and derivative and earlier civilizations produced no true novels.

I shall sketch first the positive occurrences; then review the subnovelistic attempts in the same or other civilizations; and conclude with some general considerations.

III

It is remarkable how closely Lady Murasaki's *Genji*, written in Kyoto about 1004, conforms to our definition of the fully developed novel. Being concerned with peaceful court life and written by a woman, it emphasizes feeling more than action, and love more than public affairs. But it is real, unpartisan, subtle in its psychology, civilian, and unheroic, though also refinedly aristocratic. It deals wtih a multiplicity of personages, runs on through a lifetime, and definitely mutes plot for incident and character. The sophistication of *Genji* recurs in some contemporary collections of tales, and especially in frankly subjective diaries and "pillow" sketches. Even as a novel *Genji* does not stand alone, but occurs in the historic company of a cluster of other wholly natural, nonfantastic fictional narratives. The Ochikubo and Hamamatsu Chiunagon precede it, the Sagoromo and Torikaebaya follow it within a half-century. Together they evidence a patterned stylistic growth, of which *Genji* constitutes merely the culmination.

This ancient Japanese novel genre developed earlier than systematic literary writing of avowed history. It was preceded by several centuries of cultivation of poetry, especially tanka. These poems, strictly native in form, long tended to be purely native in language too, that is, free from Chinese words. The novels of the *Genji* group also were written in women's speech, that is, in un-Sinified Yamato, refined but unpedantic.

Novels were again successfully written in Japan eight centuries later, especially in the first pre-Perry decades of the nineteenth century, during the Tokugawa decline. This group of works has been little translated, and I have to rely chiefly on secondary descriptions of them. The principal writers are Kioden, Ikku, Bakin, Samba, Tanehiko, and Shunsui.[2] The birth dates of these, at any rate of the first five, all fall between 1761 and 1783. There is therefore no doubt that they constitute a significant constellation and represent a definite current in Japanese literature. On the other hand, their works are variably described as realistic, romantic, sentimental, and humorous. Also, besides novels in our stricter sense, they wrote collections of short stories, tales of wonder, fantasy, and the supernatural; translations from the Chinese; imitations of *Genji;* picaresque wanderings; and humorous sketches. What the group had in common was that they were professionals writing for a living, and that however they might drift also into other genres, they all at times attempted to portray actual life, including low life, naturally and as it is. Like Hokusai and other contemporary print artists, they were interested in the *ukiyo,* the actual world of life; and they catered to a wide instead of a select public. This orientation, in fact, goes back to the seventeenth-century early Tokugawa period, when Saikwaku or Saikaku, 1642–93, was perhaps the outstanding exponent of naturalistic erotic narrative in Osaka and Kyoto.

Bakin, 1767–1848, is usually considered by Japanese the greatest of his group. It seems dubious whether any of his writings can really be classed as naturalistic novels within the scope of our definition. The characterization is somewhat schematic and external. Emphasis is on plot, in which Bakin shows inventiveness: he has the storytelling gift. But from adventure he mostly runs on sooner or later to the marvelous, fantastic, impossible, and miraculous. He is Chinese-influenced, outrightly moralizing, fond of showing learning. Much of his prose is a rhythmic alternation of five- and seven-syllable lines—which in Japanese makes it unacknowledged poetry. All in all, he seems far from Thackeray, Balzac, or Tolstoy—much farther than Murasaki, whose *Genji,* however pallid, one feels to belong to their category.

It might be added that in the centuries between their two novel-producing periods the Japanese developed a manner of prose narrative that might be called either romantic history or historical romance. It was historical in subject but emotional in interest, and neither outrightly critical nor overtly fictional in treatment. It was from prose of this undifferentiated sort, and from poetic-heroic and dramatic treatments of the same materials, that the later Japanese novel as a form or genre had to extricate itself by increased emphasis on the mundane, contemporary, and undignified. Its limitations would seem partly to have been due to the extrication having remained more or less incomplete.

IV

In China, genuine historical writing is far older than in Japan, but possibly for that reason the novel emerged later. The first novels, dating from about the Mongol period, are historical or pretend to be so: the famous *Three Kingdoms* and *River Margins*—the latter being Pearl Buck's gratuitously retitled *All Men Are Brothers.* The trend seems to have been from embroidered history to imagined history or historical romance. About the fifteenth century a novel of civil or family life and manners, with love plot, began to develop, culminating in the late-seventeenth-century *Red Chamber Dream*.[3] Others of the type are the *Yüh Kiao Li, P'ing Shan Lêng Yen, Kin P'ing Mei, Hao K'in Chuan, Erh Tou Mei, Yeh-sao Pao-yen*. These are written largely by scholars, but in style varying from near-classical through semicolloquial to colloquial vernacular. They deal mostly with young scholars, their love affairs, and the fortunes of their gentry families. The pace of events is leisurely, the personages numerous, their characterization varied and consistent, the psychological insight extraordinary. Though written in English, Lin Yu-tang's *Moment in Peking* and *Leaf in the Storm* are in the same tradition of successfully informal narrative portrayal of life and times, manners and personalities.[4]

V

The nations principally contributing to the novel of modern Western civilization were first the Spaniards; next the British; then almost contemporaneously the French and the Russians; and, after 1860, Scandinavians, Poles, and others, including a second group of Spaniards. Italians and Germans participated with surprisingly little major success. The peak of German literature indeed fell in the period of the novel, but the German preference, or gift, was for near-novels rather than for standard ones. A few distinguishing national traits will perhaps be worth citing even in a field so well known.

The career of the great Spanish novel ended just a century before that of the English began. Obviously, the products of the two nations were different. The *Celestina* of about 1500 is a nondifferentium of novel and play, really extraordinary for its time. It foreshadows the Spanish preoccupation with roguery and low life; which resulted, within a half-century or less, in the first outright picaresque novel, *Lazarillo de Tormes*. At the culmination, between 1600 and 1620, *Guzmán de Alfarache, Viage entretenido*, and *Obregón* cluster around *Don Quijote* and evidence a definitely patterned movement. Yet the picaresque form is retained in *Don Quijote*, though also transcended.

Robinson Crusoe and *Moll Flanders* preceded Richardson's *Pamela* by twenty years, but Defoe, despite his inventive power, essentially never went beyond the fictionalized biography. Richardson is also still limited basically to a one-person story, even though psychological dissection replaces plot; but he did antagonize and stimulate Fielding into the first full-bodied many-charactered novels in English. The roster from then on illustrates the variety of subject, treatment, and manner of which a national school of the novel is capable: Sterne, Walpole, Smollett, Goldsmith, Burney, Radcliffe, Edgeworth, Scott, Lewis, Austen, Lytton, Eliot, Thackeray, Dickens, Trollope, the Brontës, and their successors.

The French slid into doing full-dress novels much more gradually than the English. Le Sage's *Gil Blas* is a revival of the Spanish picaresque manner of a century before. Voltaire's *Candide* and Rousseau's *Nouvelle Héloïse* are obviously novels in name only. Prévost's *Manon Lescaut* is moving, Bernadin de Saint-Pierre's *Paul et Virginie* emotional, but both remain tales rather than novels. In De Staël, purpose still dominates the telling of the story. The full novel as a form flowers in France only with Stendhal when he was almost fifty. and immediately thereafter with Balzac, Hugo, Dumas, Mérimée, and Sand, who were all born in the quinquennium 1799 to 1804. This is not much earlier than the first and greatest Russian crop, Gogol, Goncharov, Turgenev, Dostoevsky, Tolstoy, with births from 1809 to

1828. Just so, the French second flight—Flaubert, the Goncourts, Daudet, Zola, France, Loti, born between 1821 and 1850—precede only slightly the later Russians centered around Gorky.

VI

This adds up to only three or possibly four relatively brief periods in which true novel-writing was achieved in human history. The regions of productivity were the Eurasiatic Far East and Far West. And, except for early Japan, all nonhistorical novels have been produced within the past four centuries—in fact, mostly within parts of these centuries. Except possibly for China, no one nationality has maintained its novel at peak quality for much longer than about a hundred years. This spottiness, or rarity, is really a remarkable phenomenon. I shall try to validate briefly that it is a fact, by inquiry into the negative cases.

The whole of Greek and Roman civilization never came even near to producing a novel. Where the term has been used, it is a sorry misapplication. Xenophon's *Cyropaedia* is a moralizing daydream in pseudo-historical dress. Its dulness of plot and narrative is striking in the face of Xenophon's ability to write extremely interesting actual history. Toward A.D. 400 the Greeks produced a type of fictional narrative that outwardly seems to be a novel—such as *Leucippe and Cleitophon*—but it consists of cliché adventure plot, childish coincidences, and manikin personages. *Daphnis and Chloë* contains an idyllic tale or sketch—a genre which the Greeks did develop, as they did the biographic *vita* at the hands of Plutarch. The *Golden Ass* of Apuleius is not without realism, but even more frankly does it revel in the fantastic and magical. The *Trimalchio* has genuine novelistic, even picaresque, quality; but the quality was never strained clear of its satiric origin. Perhaps the hand of the epic lay

too heavily on the Greeks and Romans to allow a nonheroic prose counterpart in the shape of the novel to originate among them; as possibly, in England, Milton had to be digested and superseded before Richardson and Fielding could come along. Fielding in fact is conscious of the epic foil in his passages of mock heroics which to modern seasoned novel readers seem such inopportune misfirings. Yet they evidently still carried point in his day of the incipiency of the genre.

In India also the novel may have been inhibited partly by the epic. But a larger factor is likely to have been the Hindu penchant for extravagant exaggeration, which alone would be fatal to the novel as here defined.

Arabic literature did make a seeming start toward a novel in the *maqāma*, a sort of predecessor of the picaresque tale. But the episodic atomism of the *maqāma*, and its being strung on a one-personage thread, as well as its emphasis on purely stylistic form, would have had to be overcome before a true novel could have emerged.

Persian literature, partly derivative from Arabic and partly specialized away from it toward the epic and toward the long semiepic tale poetical in sentiment as well as in form, was obviously no breeding ground for a novel.

The late Middle Ages of western Europe developed a genuine gift for effective telling of a tale in unvarnished prose—witness the *Jongleur* and Boccaccio. But it remained what we should call a short story. Its quality was in its directness and simplicity, qualities which the novel must in its nature transcend in some measure to be a novel. Longer and more complex High Mediaeval narratives were usually treated in verse, in near-epics on romantic themes developed from Arthurian and other legend.

With the breakup of the Middle Ages, rambling, stilted prose romances of love and chivalry took the place of the narrative near-epics. The *Amadis of Gaul* in Iberia, Malory in England, serve as examples. These in turn were developed in Italy by Pulci, Boiardo, and Ariosto into a worldly court poetry, playfully romantic and akin to the idyl. Allegory also invaded narrative, continuing on as late as *Pilgrim's Progress;* and Utopias had their rise. On the opposite side, Rabelais plunged into humor, grossness, exaggeration, and riot of fantasy through the medium of narrative. These are mentioned merely to illustrate the variety of forms that prose narrative can take without ever reaching the novel and which it did take in Europe for six hundred years.

The mid-seventeenth century, after the Spanish burst of great proto-novels was over, did bring, in France, the long-winded Scudéry historical romance—*Grand Cyrus, Clélie*—formally a novel except for being heroic and lacking flesh-and-blood reality, especially of persons.[5] With Fénelon, Voltaire, and Rousseau we are back again in the didactic narrative, contemporaneously with the genuine novelists Richardson, Fielding, and Sterne across the Channel.

It is notorious that Germans have consistently failed, by comparison, in our genre, even though their greatest writer, and the greatest in Europe of his century, wrote three "novels" of enormous fame: *Werther, Wahlverwandschaften,* and *Wilhelm Meister.* These simply are of a different category, in intent and execution, from what has come to be standard in the world's novels. Goethe could produce incisive realism, but he saved it for spots in his dramas. In his novels he aimed instead, with a strange stubbornness, at generalized form, with a minimum of individualized events, persons, dialogue, and characterization. Others of the greater figures in German literature also departed from the European pattern, if they attempted the novel at all; and those who conformed were usually the lesser epigones. The qualities of casualness, unstrained normality, and spontaneous humor seem to have had little appeal to German authors—down to Thomas Mann of our own day. It may be no accident that perhaps the most marked exception is Reuter, who wrote not in German but in Plattdeutsch dialect. The German language itself, its stylization and pitch, very likely had some effect in this particular deficiency.

In Italy the sense of form that Goethe sought after was established early. It may be thought to have operated against the growth of the novel, much as it hindered the development of a vigorous, effective, natural drama such as Spain, France, and England produced. The idyl, the improvised *commedia dell'arte,* the masque and the opera illustrate the Italian leaning toward typical stock characters. The tale as a genre can operate with type characters; but, for a valid novel, sharp individuation of personalities is requisite. Except in passionate moments, Italian literature tended toward a light touch expressed decoratively. This means, as it were, pleasing forms in pastel shades, whereas the novel aims at characteristic and therefore unflowing line, with strong color and chiaroscuro.

VII

What do our several occurrences of fully developed novel-writing mean historically?

Connection, influences, diffusion are out of the question in accounting for the similarities. The differences of speech medium alone tend to set at least temporary barriers in the field of the novel such as have no counterpart in the spread of science or sculpture. The resemblances between our several historic growths of true novels are independently arrived at. They must in the main be the result of the secondary concurrence of certain circumstances. Sometimes these are present and a novel grows up. Sometimes one or more of the antecedents is lacking.

Nevertheless, parallelism of the Japanese, Chinese, and European preconditions is less plain than similarity of the products.

For instance, it is evident that, logically considered, the full-scale novel is in some ways the equivalent of the epic. Both have size, variety, sustention, but incline to lack climax. They are orchestral, not melodic. Yet Europe had epics and near-epics in its tradition, China and Japan did not. Possibly that is why the Far Eastern novel came earlier: the psychological need for a novel was the greater because there was no poetic equivalent. But we are on precarious ground with such arguments: they cannot be proved or disproved.

The negative cases are as illuminating as the occurrences. The factors that can inhibit the rise of the novel are probably more numerous than those that work toward its formation. With the Greeks, the persistent dominance of the epic may have stood in the way. But the Arabs, like the Far Easterners, never had an epic. Evidently a liking for sharp individual characterization, for the savor of particular events and persons, is a requisite. In fact, where this hankering is present, the novel is intrinsically a more satisfying medium than the epic, because it comes in wholly free prose and is unlimited in range. It is our cultivation of this taste through addiction to novel-reading that has undoubtedly contributed to the prevalent inability of moderns to appreciate epics. Yet an adequate prose style is on the whole a harder thing for a literature to acquire than an adequate poetic style. Just because there is less form, there are more choices, and more sophistication is involved.

A step beyond naturalistic characterization is a propensity for the gross or raw or macabre as such. This was a Roman trait as compared with the Greeks, and cropped out in the terminal Middle Ages: Villon, for instance, and again Rabelais. On the whole, this is a streak more likely to kill off development of a novel than to further it, unless the dosage is mild. In Japan, the novel of the early 1900's was preceded, a century earlier, by the vogue of an unrestrainedly lewd and low-life type of story, which had to run its course and die before the more balanced novel of Bakin's group replaced it.

The precise courses of development are thus sufficiently varied. In Japan it would seem that both the Heian and the Tokugawa novel evolved as a reaction against the overthinness and high formalism of metrical literature. In China the novel appears rather to have grown out of the long-established and skilful prose writing of history, which began to be fictionally embroidered with psychological weighting, and finally went over to civilian and domestic life and manners, along with a loosening from the condensed classic style to colloquial vernacular. The European sequence is complex because it was multinational and the nations differed enormously. The reason for Spanish precedence is unclear. But the Spaniards scarcely attempted the many-strand or symphonic form of novel. The English stood alone in their eighteenth-century novel, which was still somewhat indeterminate in type—witness the contrast of Richardson, Fielding, Sterne, Walpole. But the nineteenth-century British, French, and Russian schools of the novel were almost concurrent and fairly parallel, though each was tinged with national quality; whereas Germany and Italy remained aberrant or undeveloped.

From every angle, then, the parallelism of the several achieved growths of novel-writing is only partial. More accurately, the similarities may be described as convergent. And they seem to be autonomous. In this they differ from the several occurrences in different civilizations of sculpture, and probably of poetic drama—which show derivations, traceable historic connections. Yet the three activities have this in common, that during the past thousand years, and especially in the last five hundred, all of them have flourished outstandingly only in the Eurasiatic Far East and Far West. This coincidence most likely roots in the fact that during the late period it was only on these two peripheries that there existed forms of civilization which were at once mature and yet still vigorously productive in creativity.

NOTES

NOTES

2. BELIEF IN USE INHERITANCE

1. "Social" in the wider sense: that is, "cultural" today.

2. "Mutationists" in the original.

3. This last paragraph has been edited in the direction of less harsh and condemnatory wording.

4. THE POSSIBILITY OF A SOCIAL PSYCHOLOGY

1. *Psychological Review*, XXIII (1916), 279–302.

2. *Principles of Sociology*, § 12. The statements by Spencer discussed in the two following paragraphs are in his §§ 6 and 3.

*8. HISTORICAL CONTEXT, RECONSTRUCTION, AND INTERPOLATION

1. *The Life of Reason*, V (1906), 50.

10. HISTORY AND EVOLUTION

1. *Southwestern Journal of Anthropology*, I (1945), 221–48.

2. "Processes in culture" (*ibid.*, p. 221) presumably means processes in phenomena, and it seems doubtful whether separate temporal, formal, functional, etc., *processes* may properly be recognized as *residing* in the phenomena. They appear rather to be separate aspects from which we can view, approach, and analyze the same phenomena; in which case White has dragged in an unnecessary assumption that might be hard to defend.

3. Windelband, Simmel, Rickert; among contemporary Americans, Mortimer Adler and Hugh Miller.

4. *Op. cit.*, pp. 225–28: Boas, Kroeber, Lowie, Radin, Mead, Chapple and Coon, Radcliffe-Brown, Tax, Redfield, Gumplowicz, Park.

5. The stages are discussed in *Anthropology* (New York, 1923), §§ 130–33, pp. 263–68, and in § 105, pp. 223–25; the historical part of the chapter, on the alphabet, covers §§ 134–49, pp. 269–92. In the 1948 edition, stages of writing in §§ 202–5, pp. 509–14; the history of the alphabet in §§ 203–21, pp. 514–37.

6. Probably four or more could actually be distinguished.

7. W. Milke, "Ueber einige Kategorien der funktionellen Ethnologie," *Zeitschrift für Ethnologie*, LXX (1938), 481–98: "eine Typologie möglicher Entwickelungen ... deren ursächliche Bedingungen weitgehend unbekannt bleiben" (p. 492).

8. *Op. cit.*, p. 243. This table is a reworking, with minor additions and eliminations, of the table on p. 385 of White's "Science Is *Sciencing*," *Philosophy of Science*, V (1938), 369–89. This earlier article develops many of the views of the 1945 one.

9. The other illustrations in the table are "evolution of universe, stars, galaxies, molecules, etc.," "of life, of species," and "of traits, institutions, philosophic systems, of culture as a whole."

10. The key to growth is obviously in heredity, and White does not place genetics in his classification of "processes."

11. The paper "*Sciencing*," p. 375, is a bit more explicit: the spatial relationships of events or objects constitute a *structure* when regarded as constant, a *function* when regarded as variable.

12. That is, different at points beyond the just discussed nonmeeting of the space and form rafters in the roof joint of White's scheme.

13. "Generalizing," "theoretical," "nomothetic," "exact" science.

14. Recognition of these levels seems to stem empirically from the development of knowledge; their number also is empirically determined by considerations of utility of subdivision. Psychic and social levels can be intercalated between the organic and cultural, when it is convenient—a biochemical level between the physical (chemical) and the organic (physiologic). The organic level is generally most usefully taken as a unit; but a splitting of organic phenomena, into those seemingly unaccompanied and those accompanied by psychic manifestations, corresponds close-

ly to the subject matters of botany and zoölogy, respectively.

15. Lever, pulley, fall of bodies, etc.; equal areas of orbit in equal periods.

13. WHITE'S VIEW OF CULTURE

1. To wit, that I have considered "culture a mystic entity that exists outside the society of its individual carriers and that moves by its own force" (Boas, *Anthropology and Modern Life* [1928], p. 235). "Mystical phraseology.... Like Kroeber they have called in a force he calls the superorganic to account for the cultural process" (Benedict, *Patterns of Culture* [1934], p. 231). "The culturalistic fallacy" is shown in the tendency "to hypostasize culture and to conceive it as a transcendental, superorganic, or superpsychic force which alone determines human, historical destiny," and by "the assumption that culture is a force that may make and develop itself" (Bidney, *American Anthropologist,* XLVI [1944], 42).

2. White's resting of physiology on anatomy introduces a different principle, that of structure-function. It seems doubtful whether this has much to do with level. Likewise, astronomy is not subjacent to physics and chemistry but is the application of physics and chemistry to remote spatial areas—and with *historical* reference to the unique events in these remotenesses. *Position* in the cosmos can in any event scarcely be a criterion of level.

3. Much as on p. 181, White introduces social psychology into his diagram between psychology and sociology, but on p. 189 omits it again.

4. P. 209: "Scientific interpretation will appear first and grow faster in those areas where the determinants of human behavior are the weakest and least significant."

5. Apart from the difficulties caused for many Germans by their use of the ambiguous "spiritual" (*Geist, geistig*) which sometimes means merely "psychological" but sometimes "outside the realm of nature and science."

6. Bidney in *Journal of Philosophy,* XXXIX (1942), 449–57; *American Anthropologist,* XLVI (1944), 30–44.

7. In the case of a house the "material cause" would be its wood; the "formal," the plan or design of the building; the "efficient," the carpenter; the "final," the goal of shelter.

8. As shown by the fact that we now have in America a dozen or two of systematic books on social psychology which all deal with psychosocial mechanism and nearly all carefully refrain from dealing with the cultures "produced" by the mechanism.

9. Bidney (in the two passages cited in n. 6) has suggested that "material" and "final" causes also enter into culture; but forms and form relations seem to me most characteristic.

10. How far values are included in culture patterns is a separate problem.

11. Which of course is itself a phase of a pattern.

12. And I was still so crude as to call them "social" half the time, when I obviously meant cultural!

*18. REALITY CULTURE AND VALUE CULTURE

1. *Anthropology* (1948), §§ 127–28, pp. 296–304; also in chap. i, § 5, pp. 5–6.

2. The most notable exception among anthropologists seems to be Richard Thurnwald, long noted as sociologically inclined—and as the editor of *Sociologus.* In *Der Mensch geringer Naturbeherrschung: Sein Aufstieg zwischen Vernunft und Wahn* (1950), he says: "Civilization is to be reckoned as the equipment of dexterities and skills through which the accumulation of technology and knowledge takes place. Culture operates with civilization as a means" (p. 107). "Civilization thus refers to an essentially temporal chain of variable and accumulative progress—an irreversible process" (Pl. 11). "The sequence of civilizational horizons represents progress" (p. 38). Culture, on the contrary, is defined (p. 104) as "the totality of usages and adjustments which relate to family, political formation, economy, labor, morality, custom, law, and ways of thought. These are bound to the life of the societies in which they are practiced, and perish with these; whereas civilizational horizons are not lost." "Culture" thus is not associated specifically with values, but its "civilizational" part or means is technological and cumulative.—V. Gor-

don Childe realizes something similar in *Progress and Archaeology* (1944): "The progress that archaeology can confidently detect is progress in material culture.... The effects of the advances ... are clearly cumulative.... Regressions are generally only temporary" (p. 109). But the relation of this line of cumulative technological progress to the totality of culture is not explicitly considered by Childe, much as I, beginning with the larger totality, failed until recently to get the relation clearly into focus.

3. "Disposal of the Dead," *American Anthropologist*, XXIX (1927), 308–15.

4. Alfred Weber, "Prinzipielles zur Kultursoziologie," *Archiv für Sozialwissenschaft und Sozialpolitik*, XLVII (1920), 1–49.

5. R. K. Merton, "Civilization and Culture," *Sociology and Social Research*, XXI (1936), 103–13.

6. R. M. MacIver, *Society: Its Structure and Changes* (1931), pp. 225–36; *Social Causation* (1942), pp. 272–88.

7. See above, n. 6.

8. *Social Causation*, p. 286.

9. *Ibid.*, p. 273.

10. *Ibid.*, p. 278.

11. *Op. cit.*, p. 109.

12. *Social Causation*, pp. 278–79.

13. *Ibid.*, p. 281.

14. Chap. iii, esp. § 13, p. 97.

15. *Social Causation*, pp. 275–76.

16. *Ibid.*, p. 274.

17. Any human social structuring must necessarily be a cultural phenomenon also, because it is conscious and has come to be established by symbolism, tradition, and speech. It is only subhuman social structure-and-functionings (subhuman systems of "social action") that are noncultural and therefore *purely* social.

18. *Society, Culture, and Personality: Their Structure and Dynamics* (1947), pp. 317, 318.

19. *Social Philosophies of an Age of Crisis* (1950), p. 197.

20. "Total empirical culture ... is made up of these three levels of culture: ideological, behavioral, and material." Ideological culture consists of "meanings, values, and norms." Behavioral culture is the actions through which the meanings, values, and norms of ideological culture are objectified and socialized. Material culture is "the other vehicles" through which the ideological culture is "manifested, externalized, socialized, and solidified" (*Society, Culture, and Personality*, p. 313).

INTRODUCTION TO PART II

1. M. B. Emeneau, "Language and Non-linguistic Patterns," *Language*, XXVI (1950), 199–209.

2. J. H. Greenberg, "The Logical Analysis of Kinship," *Philosophy of Science*, XVI (1949), 58–64.

3. In *American Anthropologist*, XVII (1915), 329–40.

4. *California Kinship Systems* ("University of California Publications in American Archaeology and Ethnology," IX [1919], 339–96), theoretical considerations from p. 387 on.

5. Or near-negative: the last paragraph of No. 19 is somewhat conflicting: "reflect psychology, *not sociology*"; but: "determined *primarily* by language and can be utilized for sociological inferences only with *extreme caution*."

22. PROCESS IN CHINESE KINSHIP

1. The term "classificatory" continues to be used, although all the discussion about it does not meet the objection long ago raised that fundamentally the common criterion of classificatory systems is that they are different from European ones. Until the term is purged of this culturally egocentric connotation, it is as unfortunate as "agglutinative" in linguistics, "Turanian" in ethnology, and "irrational" as a means of distinguishing the other animals from man. Important, too, is Lowie's point (*American Anthropologist*, XXX [1928], 264) that classificatory and descriptive are logically not complementary.

2. Han Yi Fêng, "The Chinese Kinship System," *Harvard Journal of Asiatic Studies*, II (1937), 139–275.

3. R. F. Spencer and K. Imamura, "Notes on the Japanese Kinship System," *Journal of the American Oriental Society*, LXX (1950), 165–73.

23. YUROK AND NEIGHBORING KIN SYSTEMS

1. Fellow-members with the Salish and Wakash of the putative Macro-Algonkin family, in modern terminology.

24. KINSHIP AND HISTORY

1. XXXVII (1935), 530–35.

25. ATHABASCAN KIN TERM SYSTEMS

1. Morris E. Opler, "The Kinship Systems of the Southern Athabascan-speaking Tribes," *American Anthropologist*, XXXVIII (1936), 620–33.

28. ZUNI CULTURE SEQUENCES

1. For Kidder's and Nelson's work around 1915, see n. 1 to No. 30.—Spier's *An Outline for a Chronology of Zuni Ruins* is in the series "American Museum of Natural History Anthropological Papers" (XVIII, Part III [1917] 207–331).—Kidder's 1924 systematization is of course *An Introduction to the Study of Southwestern Archaeology*.—I published a more discursive and biographical version of the present selection (which was compacted for the austerely impersonal *Proceedings of the National Academy*) under the title "Zuni Potsherds" (also as of 1916 in "American Museum of Natural History Anthropological Papers," Vol. XVIII (pp. 1–37).

30. NATIVE CULTURE OF THE SOUTHWEST

1. N. C. Nelson, "Chronology of the Tano Ruins," *American Anthropologist*, XVIII (1916), 159–80; A. V. Kidder and S. J. Guernsey, *Archaeological Explorations in Northeast Arizona* (Bureau of American Ethnology Bull. 65 [1919]). A nonstratigraphic attack on the sequential problem was made by Kidder in "Pottery of the Pajarito Plateau," *Memoirs of the American Anthropological Association*, II (1915), 407–62.

34. SALT, DOGS, TOBACCO

1. "Tobacco Chewing on the Northwest Coast," *American Anthropologist*, XXXV (1933), 146–50.
2. But Heizer ("The Botanical Identification of N.W. Coast Tobacco," *American* *Anthropologist*, XLII [1940], 704–6) cites Eastwood ("Leaflets of Western Botany," Vol. II, No. 6) to the contrary: the Haida plant was a tobacco.

3. For the Northern Paiute, O. Stewart directly associates burning for food seeds with burning for tobacco, but has burning for seeds affirmed by 4 fewer groups. The 50 Basin Shoshonean groups all smoked tobacco, by the way.

4. That in timbered northern California and Oregon the burning usually centered around a log or stump instead of extending over a field is natural enough.

5. The Yavapai, who are the only non-farming or scantily farming tribe of the six, sowed broadcast "in ashes," which suggests type *b* rather than true farm-planting.

37. TOTEM AND TABOO
(Footnotes of 1951)

1. That *specificities* in this continuity of the psychic life of successive generations were due to "tradition," that is, to transmission of culture by learning, was clear to most anthropologists, sociologists and psychologists by the time Freud wrote *Totem and Taboo*. They had pretty well got over trying to derive specific features of culture from the amorphous, indeterminate "human nature" that biological heredity provides. It was Freud who had not hesitated to fall back on Lamarckian heredity as a basis for culture, without much concerning himself whether this mechanism was actual or not.

2. Freud, in short, drew on the "evolutionists," who bet that they could guess origins and he ignored all other anthropological work.

3. Reflecting over a lifetime of direct and indirect experience, I find nothing to substantiate this view that nonliterate peoples are more sexualized and less socialized than others. It just fits Freud's thesis.

4. With all his imagination, Freud is methodologically mid-Victorian here. To the contrary, understanding of the nature of a phenomenon is *not* dependent on knowledge of its origin. Granted that it has "an" origin (which is usually a simplistic assumption), explanation from this origin is almost inevitably an explanation of the partly understood from an unknown.

39. PSYCHOSIS OR SOCIAL SANCTION

1. See No. 29, "Earth-Tongue, Mohave," above.

2. See No. 18, "Reality Culture and Value Culture," above.

3. In the *Handbook of the Indians of California* I have described these customs for the Yuki, Pomo, Maidu, and Yokuts. The Yuki account there given however runs the *waⁿshit lamshiimi* and the *aumol* into one: the inconsistency is noted, but attributed to Yuki mentality. Additional information, secured in 1938 in co-operation with F. Essene, makes it clear that the Yuki distinguished the two types by name, as set forth above.

4. The Patwin distinguish the cult bear dancer, *sika*, from the bear-disguised murderer, *napa*. The latter has become the name of a California county and city.

5. Margaret Mead (in *Psyche*, VIII [1928], 72–77) has pointed out a similar difference between Samoans and other Polynesians. "Contacts with the supernatural were accidental, trivial, uninstitutionalized" in Samoa. Religious and unstable individuals were "given no accepted place in a pattern."

40. THE USE OF AUTOBIOGRAPHICAL EVIDENCE

1. Julian H. Steward, *Two Paiute Autobiographies* ("University of California Publications in American Archaeology and Ethnology," XXXIII, 423–38 (1934). See also Gertrude Toffelmier and Katherine Luomala, "Dreams and Dream Interpretation of the Diegueño Indians," *Psychoanalytic Quarterly*, V (1936), 195–225, in which is imbedded a shamanistic autobiography. Julian H. Steward, *Panatübiji': An Owens Valley Paiute* ("Anthropological Papers," No. 6; Bureau of American Ethnology Bull., 119 [1938], pp. 183–95; this biography was obtained posthumously from the subject's grandson.

2. Franz Boas, "Recent Anthropology," *Science*, XCVIII (1943), 311–14, 334–37.

3. The actual title is: "Why Cultural Anthropology Needs the Psychiatrist," *Psychiatry*, I (1938), 7–12. Republished in D. G. Mandelbaum, *Selected Writings of Edward Sapir* (1949), pp. 569–77.

4. *Ethnology of the Gros Ventre* ("American Museum of Natural History Anthropological Papers," Vol. I, Part 4 [1908]). On succession of rituals, pp. 233–34; war records, none wholly complete, pp. 196–216; woman's narrative, pp. 216–21.

41. A SOUTHWESTERN PERSONALITY TYPE

1. Clyde Kluckhohn, "A Navaho Personal Document with a Brief Paretian Analysis," *Southwestern Journal of Anthropology*, I (1945), 260–83.

2. F. Kniffen *et al.*, *Walapai Ethnography*, ed. A. L. Kroeber ("Memoirs of the American Anthropological Association," No. 42 [1935]): Kuni's life-history, pp. 205–8; dreams, pp. 231–36; origin myth, pp. 12–26; other data *passim*, designated "K."

3. Truman Michelson, *The Narrative of a Southern Cheyenne Woman* ("Smithsonian Miscellaneous Collections," Vol. LXXXVII, No. 5 [1932]), and "Narrative of an Arapaho Woman," *American Anthropologist*, XXXV (1933), 595–610.

44. STIMULUS DIFFUSION

1. First by Böttger and Tschirnhaus in Dresden, 1708–9.

2. Grant Foreman, *Sequoyah* (a biography) (University of Oklahoma Press, 1938). J. C. Pilling, "Guess," in *Bibliography of the Iroquoian Languages* (Bureau of American Ethnology Bull. 6 [1888]). "Sequoya," in *Handbook of American Indians* (Bureau of American Ethnology Bull. 30, Part 2 [1910]).

3. Eighteen characters are English capitals, two are numeral signs (4, 6), three are inverted capitals (J, V, Y), seven are minuscule or lower-case English letters, the remaining fifty-four are about evenly divided between modifications of English capitals (usually by the addition of one or more strokes) and free inventions. Most of the latter consist of curve combinations somewhat in the manner of rounded and heavily shaded English handwriting, but without being reducible to specific letters of the alphabet.

4. S. W. Koelle, *Grammar of the Vei Language* (1854); G. W. Ellis, *Negro Culture in West Africa* (1914).

5. In this case, only ten or a dozen char-

acters bear resemblances to European letters or numerals, and in practically no case
is there complete identity of shape. Koelle's
specimen of the syllabary appears to be
lithographed from his own hand-written
copy from native text. The strokes are
heavy, and straight, angular, or in simple
curves. Ellis' specimen is much more cursive
in quality. Whether it, or the original form,
has been influenced by Arabic writing, I
am incompetent to say. Certainly Koelle's
sample does not look so. But he makes clear
that the Vei were in contact with Mohammedans and that the inventor recited Arabic
prayers.

6. Thus, in approximate centuries, the lag
is: block printing, 1; Sung-style painting,
2–3; end of retainer burial, 3; official recognition of Buddhism, 5; movable-type printing, 5; neo-Confucian philosophy, 5; money
minting, 10; bronze, at least 11; writing, at
least 15; abolition of feudalism, 20.

7. W. G. Aston, *Japanese Literature*
(1899–1933), p. 278.

8. E. H. Morris ("American Museum of
Natural History Anthropological Papers,"
Vol. XXVIII [1927]), pp. 125–98.

9. Or, according to excavations at Snake-
town, from the Hohokam of southern Arizona, on the route from Mexico.

10. The last great name is Aida, 1747–
1817; the last of the line, Hagiwara, 1828–
1909.

11. *Geschichte der indischen Literatur*,
III (1920), 174 ff.

12. Such as H. Reich, *Der Mimus*.

13. Further, the older and younger portions may differ in age by as much as three
centuries.

14. Discovery attributed to Shen Yo, 441–
513.

15. 350 B.C. is the most usual estimate, the
fifth century has some support, and the
seventh and even eighth centuries have been
suggested. His predecessor, Yaska, is mostly
set somewhere between 700 and 400.

16. Two other possible instances might
be mentioned. One, which I owe to the suggestion of Paul Benedict, is the historically
wholly isolated script, or rather scripts, of
the Lolos in China. The other is the rise of
Christian iconoclasm in Byzantium about a
century after this empire came into contact with image-condemning and puritan
Mohammedanism.

47. THE ANCIENT OIKOUMENÊ

1. R. H. Lowie, *The History of Ethnological Theory* (1937), pp. 235–36.

2. *Configurations of Culture Growth*
(1944), pp. 239–316, esp. pp. 310 ff.

3. *Ibid.*, p. 311.

4. *Ibid.*, p. 447.

5. Windmills are a probable exception.
The Arab geographer al Mas'udi saw them
in Persia, 915–43, and they are also referred
to by al Farsi al Istakri later in the same
century. See G. Sarton, *Introduction to the
History of Science* (1927), I, 638, 674; A. P.
Usher, *A History of Mechanical Inventions*
(1929), p. 128.

6. C. W. Bishop, *Origin of Far Eastern
Civilizations: A Brief Handbook* ("Smithsonian Institution War Background Studies," No. 1 [1942]), p. 15; also in *Smithsonian Report for 1943* (1944), pp. 463–512.
Laufer's "Some Fundamental Ideas of Chinese Culture," *Journal of Race Development*, V (1914), 160–74, is cited by Bishop,
but Laufer's tenor is contrary: he sets up
a cattle-plow-wheel complex as *shared* by
China and the West. In "Origin and Early
Diffusion of the Traction Plough," *Antiquity*, 1936, republished in *Smithsonian Report for 1937* (1938), pp. 531–47, Bishop
develops his argument for lateness, which,
however, rests pivotally on an undocu-
mented statement by A. W. Hummell
"cited" in his n. 65.

7. For instance, A. Waley, *The Book of
Songs* (1937), pp. 161, 162, 163, 164, 171. It
is barely conceivable that these "plows"
were drawn by gangs of men while cattle
are constantly mentioned in the same group
of songs.

8. The Shih Ching song 131 attests it for
Chou China of 621 B.C. It was perhaps last
practiced in China for Shih Huang-Ti, died
210 B.C. The Nihongi has the custom abolished for Japan in A.D. 2, which date may
have been set back by legendary chronology several centuries before the fact; especially since a Chinese notice for A.D. 247 records the burial of many of her attendants
with Queen Himeko (W. G. Aston, *Shinto:
The Way of the Gods* [1905], pp. 56–58).

9. J. M. Cooper, "Scapulimancy," in
*Essays in Anthropology Presented to A. L.
Kroeber* (1936), pp. 29–43.

10. A. H. Broderick, *Little China: The*

Annamese Lands (1942), pp. 87, 191, 204, 235, 238, 239. John Ross, *Korea* (1879), p. 358.

11. The one specific instance of geomantic practice mentioned in G. B. Sansom, *Japan: A Short Cultural History* (1943) is for 793 (p. 190). Cf. Aston, *op. cit.*, p. 344: "practised to some extent."

12. C. G. Seligman, "The Roman Orient and the Far East," *Antiquity*, Vol. XI (1937); republished in *Smithsonian Report for 1938* (1939), pp. 547–68.

13. See, e.g., the remarks about Wu Ti, 140–87 B.C., in K. S. Latourette, *The Chinese: Their History and Culture* (1942), I, 119.

14. *Configurations of Culture Growth*, pp. 83–88, 789–90. The writing of this work was completed six years before publication in 1944; hence the "few years ago."

15. V. A. Smith, *The Oxford History of India* (1923), p. 81. The classical organization of Indian armies was into infantry, elephants, cavalry, and chariots. Chess derived its name from this fourfold division. The Hindus may have kept talking, characteristically, in terms of the scheme for some centuries after chariots were no longer used in actual combat.

16. The Byzantine reference is in the *Strategikon* of Maurice, who reigned 582–602. The Chinese literary reference of 477 is mentioned by Toynbee, *A Study of History* (1934), III, 164, citing O. Münsterberg, *Chinesische Kunstgeschichte* (1910), p. 162.

17. Usher, *op. cit.*, pp. 120, 124, 135. The basic data are assembled in R. Bennett and J. Elton, *History of Corn Milling*, Vol. II: *Watermills and Windmills* (1899).

18. B. Laufer, *Chinese Pottery of the Han Dynasty* (1909), p. 33.

19. B. Laufer, "The Early History of Felt," *American Anthropologist*, XXX (1932), 1–18.

20. All statements are based on H. J. R. Murray, *A History of Chess* (1913), which has largely replaced A. van der Linde, *Geschichte und Litteratur des Schachspieles* (1874). Some interesting statuses of the game are reported. It flourished in Islam, although its permissibility was long under debate (like that of coffee after 1500). According to one accepted tra-

dition, Mohammed held that a believer should restrict his amusements to his horse, his bow, and his wife (p. 189)—an almost crass exemplification of the contractile bent of Islam discussed above. In mediaeval Latin Christendom chess was an upper-class pastime; among the Greeks, it encountered intrenched church opposition and languished; in Russia, at any rate after the fifteenth century, it was more widely played than in western Europe. In China and Japan chess has always been less esteemed, that is, has had lower social class associations, than the "inclosing game."

21. C. M. Wilbur, "The History of the Crossbow, Illustrated from Specimens in the U.S. National Museum," *Smithsonian Report for 1936* (1937), pp. 427–38, summarizes the principal comparative data, which give priority to China: probable mention fourth century B.C.; certain mention, third century, and again Former Han; preserved trigger blocks of bronze, Han; Rome, first mention *ca.* A.D. 386; representations, perhaps fifth century. The European crossbow of steel, necessitating a windlass or goat's-foot lever to draw, dates only from the fourteenth century. Wilbur sees "nothing but negative evidence for the whole region of Central Asia and the Near East" until the sixteenth century.

22. All the data are of course from T. F. Carter, *The Invention of Printing in China and Its Spread Westward* (1925).

23. Playing cards, probable reference to, in China: 969; European first references: Germany, 1377; Spain, 1377; Luxembourg, 1379; Italy, 1379; France, 1392.

24. *Ca.* 1450 as against 1041–49.

25. Since this paragraph was written, I have come across G. F. Hudson's *Europe and China* (1931), in which he argues (pp. 164–68), with an engaging reasonableness, for the probablity of transmission of the *idea of* movable-type printing from China to Europe. The route he suggests is novel and plausible: Korea, the Mongol Khanates, Muscovy, Hansa.

26. V. Gordon Childe, "Directional Changes in Funerary Practices during 50,-000 Years," *Man*, XLV, No. 4 (1945), 18.

27. *Archaeological Ages as Technological Stages* (Huxley Memorial Lecture for 1944), pp. 1–19.

28. Laufer in "Origin of Our Dances of Death," *Open Court*, XXII (1908), 597–604, tries to connect death-dance representations in Lamaism and Catholicism, not altogether convincingly.

29. This problem has been discussed—somewhat more negativistically—in my *Configurations*, already cited. See especially pp. 217, 221–23, 225, 234.

30. Ching-chi Young, *L'Écriture et les manuscrits Lolos* (Geneva, 1935).

31. A. F. Legendre, "Les Lolos de Kientchang," *Revue de l'École d'Anthropologie*, XX (1910), 185–205; translated in *Smithsonian Report for 1911* (1912), pp. 569–86.

32. This interpretation of Negrito culture was first advanced in my *Peoples of the Philippines* (1919; rev. ed., 1928), pp. 42–47.

33. W. L. Warner, *A Black Civilization* (1937), Appendix I, "Social Change in North Australia," esp. pp. 453–68.

34. This is clearly the upshot of that notable piece of documented proof, Erland Nordenskiöld's *Origin of the Indian Civilizations in South America* ("Comparative Ethnographical Studies," Vol. IX [1931]).

50. THE NOVEL IN ASIA AND EUROPE

1. Or at least, any supernatural elements must be extrinsic, so that they could be subtracted without damaging the self-sufficiency of the naturalistic remainder (cf. n. 3).

2. I have had access to Bakin's *Moon Shining through a Cloud Rift*, translated by Edward Greey as *A Captive of Love* (1886, 1904, 1912); to Bakin's *Okoma*, illustrated and translated or abbreviated (?) into French by Felix Regamey in 1883; and summaries and extracts in Revon, Florenz, Aston, etc.

3. The *Red Chamber Dream* contains a supernatural element in the divine rock with which the narrative opens and of which skilful symbolic use is made here and there in its course. But on the whole this ingredient seems to serve as a decorative and dignifying frame rather than as an intrinsic component. The motivation and causation remain human.

4. Other contemporary novels available in English though written in Chinese, and in continuation of native tradition, are Lin's *Nun of Taishan* and Shaw's *Rickshaw Boy*.

5. Pallid stiltedness does not apply to Mme de La Fayette's delicate, limpid, and tragic *La Princesse de Clèves* (1678). But it is not yet a novel in that it lacks full-bodiedness in range of characters, mood, and events. Its quality is rather that of a theme from Corneille narrated in prose by Racine.

SOURCES AND PERMISSIONS

SOURCES AND PERMISSIONS

PART I
THEORY OF CULTURE

1. "Explanations of Cause and Origin." Part of "Decorative Symbolism of the Arapaho," *American Anthropologist*, III (1901), 308–36. About half or less of the original is presented here.
2. "Cause of the Belief in Use Inheritance," *American Naturalist*, L (1916), 367–70. By permission.
3. "The Superorganic." Originally in *American Anthropologist*, XIX (1917), 163–213. Republished, with stylistic revisions, by Sociological Press of Hanover, New Hampshire, in 1929.
4. "The Possibility of a Social Psychology." Extracted from the *American Journal of Sociology*, XXIII (1918), 633–50. Parts of pp. 633, 634–38, 639–44 have been used.
5. "Historical Reconstruction of Culture Growths and Organic Evolution," *American Anthropologist*, XXXII (1931), 149–56.
6. "History and Science in Anthropology," *American Anthropologist*, XXXVII (1935), 539–69. About one-seventh of the original article is included here.
7. "So-called Social Science," *Journal of Social Philosophy*, I (1936), 317–40. Two pages of Addenda have been omitted.
*8. "Historical Context, Reconstruction, and Interpretation." Not previously published. From lectures given at the University of Chicago, April 7–28, 1938.
9. "Structure, Function, and Pattern in Biology and Anthropology," *Scientific Monthly*, LVI (February, 1943), 105–13. By permission.
10. "History and Evolution," *Southwestern Journal of Anthropology*, II (1946), 1–15.
*11. "Culture, Events, and Individuals." From abstract of a talk at Viking Fund, October 25, 1946.

*12. "Causes in Culture." Expanded from mimeographed outline of a talk at Viking Fund, December 12, 1947.
13. "White's View of Culture," *American Anthropologist*, L (1948), 405–14.
14. "The Concept of Culture in Science." From a lecture delivered November 1, 1948, at the University of Chicago in a symposium on "The Landmarks of Scientific Integration." Republished by permission from *Journal of General Education*, III (1949), 182–96.
15. "Values as a Subject of Natural Science Inquiry." Read before the National Academy of Sciences, April 25, 1949, and published in its *Proceedings*, XXXV (1949), 261–64.
16. "A Half-century of Anthropology," *Scientific American*, CLXXXIII, No. 3 (September, 1950), 87–94. By permission. The original, titled simply "Anthropology," was one of a symposium on the development of science during the half-century.
*17. "The History and Present Orientation of Cultural Anthropology." Prepared for the Berkeley meeting of the American Anthropological Association, December 28, 1950, but not previously published.
*18. "Reality Culture and Value Culture." Expanded in 1951 from a paper read before the National Academy of Sciences, April 24, 1950. Not previously published.

PART II
KINSHIP AND SOCIAL STRUCTURE

19. "Classificatory Systems of Relationship," *Journal of the Royal Anthropological Institute*, XXXIX (1909), 77–84.
20. "Zuni Kin and Clan." From *Zuni Kin and Clan* ("American Museum of Natural History Anthropological Papers," XVIII, Part 2 [1917], 39–205), pp. 72–73, 150–54, 182–83, 183–86.
21. "Kinship in the Philippines." Pages 81–84 of article of same name in "Ameri-

can Museum of Natural History Anthropological Papers," XIX (1919), 69–84.

22. "Process in the Chinese Kinship System," *American Anthropologist,* XXXV (1933), 151–57. Somewhat condensed.

23. "Yurok and Neighboring Kin Term Systems." ("University of California Publications in American Archaeology and Ethnology," XXXV, No. 2 [1934], 15–22.)

24. "Kinship and History," *American Anthropologist,* XXXVIII (1936), 338–41.

25. "Athabascan Kin Term Systems," *American Anthropologist,* XXXIX (1937), 602–8.

26. "Basic and Secondary Patterns of Social Structure," *Journal of the Royal Anthropological Institute,* LXVIII ("1938"), 299–309 (actually 1939).

27. "The Societies of Primitive Man." From REDFIELD, ROBERT (ed.), *Levels of Integration in Biological and Social Systems* ("Biological Symposia," Vol. VIII [New York: Ronald Press Co., 1942]), pp. 205–16. By permission.

PART III

ON AMERICAN INDIANS

28. "Zuni Culture Sequences," *Proceedings of the National Academy of Sciences,* II (1915), 42–45.

29. "Earth-Tongue, Mohave." Republished from PARSONS, ELSIE CLEWS (ed.), *American Indian Life, by Several of Its Students* (New York: B. W. Huebsch, 1922), pp. 189–202. By permission.

30. "Native Culture of the Southwest." Extract of pp. 375–80 from same title, in "University of California Publications in American Archaeology and Ethnology," XXIII (1928), 375–98.

31. "Characteristics of the Seri Indians." Extracts from *The Seri* ("Southwest Museum Papers," No. 6 [1931]), pp. 21, 27–28, 52–55.

32. "Yurok Marriages" (with T. T. Waterman). ("University of California Publications in American Archaeology and Ethnology," XXXV, No. 1 [1934], 1–14.)

33. "Areal Types of American Indian Culture and Their Growth." Selections from *Cultural and Natural Areas of Native North America* ("University of California Publications in American Archaeology and Ethnology," Vol. XXXVIII [1939]), pp. 20, 22–28, 30–31, 76–79, 86–88.

34. "Salt, Dogs, Tobacco." From *Salt, Dogs, Tobacco: Culture Element Distributions XV* ("University of California Anthropological Records," Vol. VI, No. 1 [1941]), pp. 1–20. Reduced by omission of pages and of many tribal names.

35. "The Chibcha." Selected from pp. 887–88, 902–3, 904, 905–6 of article of same name in *Handbook of South American Indians* (Smithsonian Institution, Bureau of American Ethnology, Bull. 143 [1946]), II, 887–909.

36. "Great Art Styles of Ancient South America." From TAX, SOL (ed.), *The Civilizations of Ancient America: Selected Papers of the XXIXth International Congress of Americanists* (1951), pp. 207–15.

PART IV

PSYCHOLOGICALLY SLANTED

37. "Totem and Taboo: An Ethnologic Psychoanalysis," *American Anthropologist,* XXII (1920), 48–55.

38. "Totem and Taboo in Retrospect," *American Journal of Sociology,* XLV (1939), 446–51. By permission.

39. "Psychosis or Social Sanction," *Character and Personality,* VIII (1940), 204–15.

40. "The Use of Autobiographical Evidence," pp. 318–22 of "A Yurok War Reminiscence," *Southwestern Journal of Anthropology,* I (1945), 318–32.

41. "A Southwestern Personality Type," *Southwestern Journal of Anthropology,* III (1947), 108–13.

PART V

HISTORY AND PROCESS OF CIVILIZATION

42. "[On the Principle of] Order in [Civilization as Exemplified by] Changes of

Fashion," *American Anthropologist,* XXI (1919), 235–63. About a quarter of the original is included here.

43. "Cultural Intensity and Climax." From *Cultural and Natural Areas of Native North America* ("University of California Publications in American Archaeology and Ethnology," Vol. XXXVIII [1939]), pp. 222–28.

44. "Stimulus Diffusion," *American Anthropologist,* XLII (1940), 1–20.

45. "Three Centuries of Women's Dress Fashions: A Quantitative Analysis" (with Jane Richardson). ("University of California Anthropological Records," V, No. 2 [1940], 111–54). About a sixth of the original is included here.

46. "Toynbee's *A Study of History,*" *American Anthropologist,* XLV (1943), 294–99.

47. "The Ancient Oikoumenê as a Historic Culture Aggregate: The Huxley Memorial Lecture for 1945," *Journal of the Royal Anthropological Institute,* LXXV ("1945"), 9–20. Article preprinted in 1946; volume issued 1949.

48. "Culture Groupings in Asia," *Southwestern Journal of Anthropology,* III (1947), 322–30.

49. "Is Western Civilization Disintegrating or Reconstituting?" *Proceedings of the American Philosophical Society,* XCV (1951), 100–104.

50. "The Novel in Asia and Europe," *University of California Publications in Semitic Philology,* XI (1951), 233–41.

INDEXES

Index of Names

INDEX OF PRINCIPAL TOPICAL CROSS-REFERENCES

[References are to selections and numbered parts.]